JOAN BEAUMONT is Professor Emerita at the Strategic and Defence Studies Centre, Australian National University. She is the author of the critically acclaimed account of Australia's experience of World War I, *Broken Nation*, joint winner of the Prime Minister's Award for Australian History, and winner of the NSW Premier's Prize for Australian History and the Queensland Literary Award for History.

'Vividly illustrates the clashes and complexities of the crisis.'
GEOFFREY BLAINEY, *The Australian*

'By restoring the prominence of the Great Depression in public memory, Beaumont has produced an exceptional work that powerfully demonstrates we forget this at our peril.'
JOY DAMOUSI, *The Sydney Morning Herald*

'What distinguishes this book is an immersion in the Depression moment . . . outstanding history.'
BENJAMIN HUF, *Australian Book Review*

AUSTRALIA'S GREAT DEPRESSION

How a nation shattered by the Great War survived
the worst economic crisis it has ever faced

JOAN BEAUMONT

ALLEN&UNWIN
SYDNEY·MELBOURNE·AUCKLAND·LONDON

Allen & Unwin
Cammeraygal Country
83 Alexander Street
Crows Nest NSW 2065
Australia
Phone: (61 2) 8425 0100
Email: info@allenandunwin.com
Web: www.allenandunwin.com

*Allen & Unwin acknowledges the Traditional Owners of the Country on which we
live and work. We pay our respects to all Aboriginal and Torres Strait Islander
Elders, past and present.*

A catalogue record for this
book is available from the
National Library of Australia

ISBN 978 1 76106 887 4

Index by Garry Cousins
Maps and figures produced by CartoGIS, Scholarly Information Services,
The Australian National University
Set in 11/15.5 pt Minion LT by Midland Typesetters, Australia
Printed by C&C Offset Printing Co. Ltd, China

10 9 8 7 6 5 4 3 2 1

For my grandchildren,
the coming generation of Australians,
so full of promise

CONTENTS

LIST OF MAPS, TABLES AND FIGURES

INTRODUCTION

Australia's Great Depression

Some generations are born unlucky. Australians born in 1895 might have served in World War I. If they survived, they might then have fought once more in a second global conflict in 1939–45. Even worse, they might have sent their children to that war. In the intervening years, they endured the worst economic crisis that Australia and the world have ever confronted, the Great Depression. In 1932, perhaps a third, or even more, of the Australian workforce was unemployed, dependent for their survival on charity, community support, limited government aid and their own resources. Many thousands lost their businesses, farms, savings and homes. Government budgets were slashed and the nation itself faced insolvency.

Remarkably, however, most Australians survived. Although the year 1930 saw the highest rate of male suicide in the twentieth century, most men and women somehow found the will and resources to cope. Moreover, Australia's political and social institutions survived the ordeal. The Great Depression, like World War I, generated bitter and often violent disputes about the inequality of sacrifice across different social and economic sectors. But despite a high level of political and civil unrest, the legitimacy of the democratic political system was never seriously threatened. There was no revolution such as World War I triggered in Russia and central Europe, and no fascist authoritarianism such as that which sprang out of the Great Depression in Germany. Instead, like many individuals, the Australian political and social fabric proved resilient enough to adapt and accommodate the economic crisis.

Why was this so? What were the sources of resilience, individually and collectively, that sustained Australians through yet another shock to afflict this one generation? These are the questions that inspired this book. It a story of survival. To be sure, there was great hardship, anger, anxiety and despair, but there was also extraordinary endurance, self-reliance, mutual support, adaptation and resilience.

Most Australians can tell you something about the Great Depression. They recall their parents or grandparents being risk-averse, hoarding their savings in the bank rather than spending them on luxuries, and being timid about financial exposure. They remember, too, tales of shanty towns on Australia's riverbanks or town outskirts, long queues of desperate men waiting for work or the dole, and single men hawking pathetically small bags of low-value items from door to door. This was the human face of economic disaster. Understandably it has featured prominently in past histories, especially those that have tapped the rich, if subjective, oral histories of people who lived through the Depression.

There was, however, more to this national crisis than the masses of unemployed, central though they were. The Depression was self-evidently a crisis of the Australian economy. Heavily dependent on exports of primary commodities, such as wool and wheat, Australia was acutely vulnerable to the collapse of global prices in the late 1920s. In the previous fifteen years, its governments had accumulated huge debts, from fighting World War I and then funding repatriation and visionary projects of national development. Many of these debts could not be serviced when investors in London took flight in 1929. The threat of national insolvency and the nightmare of default on external borrowings has none of the drama and human interest of stories of human suffering. Loan conversions, interest rates, Treasury bills, sterling reserves, exchange rates and that pillar of the 1920s banking world, the gold standard, do not make easy reading. But the servicing of Australia's external borrowings was *the* issue that dominated the Depression years, affecting in some way or another the lives of almost everyone in the country.

Debt servicing was an issue that became profoundly politicised. Economics is never value-neutral, and the problem of managing Australia's overseas debts polarised the political debate. Rarely have Australians been so politically engaged and the Australian political system under such strain. The Australian Labor Party (ALP) government of James (Jim) Scullin (1929–32) had the profound misfortune to come to power just in time to preside over the worst years of the Depression. Just as the ALP had split when it inherited the responsibility for leading Australia in wartime in 1914, so it now foundered on the intractable issue of how to keep the nation solvent while mitigating the acute social distress of many Australians. The Commonwealth (federal) government had few of the policy settings with which to manage a crisis of this unprecedented scale. Responsibility for aiding the poor had traditionally resided at the local level, with charities, churches, voluntary organisations and municipal authorities. The state governments soon accepted, in many cases for the first time, that they had to do more to intervene by offering the dole (or 'sustenance') and part-time relief works. But with default on Australia's loans ruled out as a policy option, and the Bank of England demanding deflationary policies as the price of continuing national solvency, these programs always fell short of the mounting need.

As unemployment soared in 1931–32, the debate about policy responses descended into a bitterly contested 'battle of the plans'. Ultimately the Scullin government lacked the power, the institutional apparatus and perhaps the courage to introduce radical policy options, be they the expansion of the monetary supply to stimulate the economy or the adjustment of, or even default on, Australia's external debts. A formidable array of forces—a Nationalist (conservative) Opposition majority in the Senate, the bankers in London, the Commonwealth Bank at home and even some of the emerging cohort of professional economists—all tended to favour financial orthodoxy and 'sound finance'. A form of deflation ultimately prevailed. Federal and state governments committed themselves to balancing budgets while wages, pensions and interest rates were all cut in an effort to ensure 'equality of sacrifice' across the population. The ALP split for the second time in a generation, and the non-Labor forces reorganised in a way that enabled them to win and hold power at the federal level for the rest of the decade.

Through all this political turmoil, Australians erupted in protest. The unemployed and radical activists on the left took to the streets, clashing with police and officials over sustenance, the restrictions on relief works, the right to free speech and the eviction of tenants who could not pay their rent. Disillusioned conservatives formed grassroots populist movements that demanded structural reform in the political party system. Paramilitary movements emerged from their clandestine pasts to oppose communism and the radical New South Wales Premier Jack Lang, by armed force if need be. Across the nation, regions and states demanded greater autonomy through the redrawing of state boundaries and even secession from the federation.

This political ferment has long attracted the interest of historians, especially historians of the industrial and political labour movements. This book does not replace this literature, nor the authoritative analyses of past economic historians.[1] Rather, it offers an integrated history of the multiple dimensions of Australia's Depression. Historians in their silo fashion have often separated them, but in reality they were intertwined and inseparable. External economic forces placed implacable constraints on political flexibility, while ideological preferences and political values infused the debates and choices about policy options for economic recovery.

This book seeks, too, to widen and complicate our understanding of the impact of the Depression. Yes, it was a profound disaster for many Australians, but its impact was variable across Australia's vast continent. Some sectors of the economy, such as manufacturing and construction, were savagely hit; others, such as sugar, remained relatively unscarred. No state was left unaffected, but some states, such as South Australia, were particularly disadvantaged. Inevitably, too, class mattered. The professional middle classes tended to be insulated from the worst of the Depression, given their jobs were more secure and they often had assets and capital to draw on. Those Australians who were already vulnerable—Aboriginal Australians, the homeless, the itinerant and casual worker and the recent immigrant—were at far greater risk of abject poverty.

There was, then, no single 'Australian' experience of the Depression. It is this that accounts for the bewildering range of memories captured in the oral history projects of the latter half of the twentieth century. For some

Australians, the Depression remained an unmitigated personal and social catastrophe; for others, a time of family cohesion, community solidarity and even positive personal development. This book tries to mirror this diversity, while arguing that, on balance, the more cataclysmic view of the Depression's impact on Australians' wellbeing is unwarranted. We will never be able to quantify the extent of the mental illness triggered by the humiliation of unemployment and the struggle for survival, but it seems clear that few Australians died of starvation.

The time frame of this study is 1919 to 1937. World War I did not cause the Depression, but this conflict bequeathed some structural weaknesses in the international economic system on which Australian prosperity depended. One was a distorting round robin of payments, first for debts that many belligerents had incurred while waging the war, and second for reparations imposed on the defeated Central Powers by the victors. Another was the increase in global production of primary commodities, such as wheat, that were central to Australia's terms of trade. A further legacy of the war, no less powerful for being subjective, was the memory of the deaths of more than 60,000 Australian men and women. Their loss infused the political culture of the 1920s and 1930s. The pursuit of 'men, money and markets' under the Nationalist government of Stanley Melbourne Bruce (1923–29) was driven by a vision of a better future for a society traumatised by war. Likewise, the enthusiasm of some Australian states for imperial immigration—programs that contributed to their indebtedness—resonated with the need to replace the generation of young men 'lost' to World War I. Then, when the Depression finally hit, the memory of the war served to constrain policy responses: options that would have compromised the privileged position of the returned soldiers were excluded or mitigated.

Our narrative also begins well before October 1929 and the New York stock market crash that is commonly assumed to have triggered the Depression, because Australia was experiencing serious economic difficulties well before this date. Events in the United States after October 1929 indisputably sent seismic shock waves around the globe for years, delaying the international recovery on which Australia's economic recovery largely depended. But Australia was in recession before 1929. Some disadvantaged suburbs and regions were suffering significant distress in 1927, and the flow of capital from the City of London was drying up as 1929 opened. Given the enmeshment of the Australian economy with the British Empire, London mattered more than New York, at least when it came to debt servicing and trade preference.

The year 1937 provides an appropriate end date, because the financial consensus hammered out in the Premiers' Plan of mid-1931 framed the agenda of the first two terms (1932–34 and 1934–37) of the United Australia Party (UAP) government under Prime Minister Joseph (Joe) Lyons. Furthermore, Australia's economic recovery had begun some years earlier. To be sure, unemployment, that most visible and politically sensitive of the economic indicators, remained high throughout the 1930s. Full employment was achieved only as a result of wartime mobilisation in 1941. But by many other economic indicators the worst of the Depression was over by 1937. Most importantly, around that time the priorities of the Australian government changed. While avoiding slipping back into recession remained a dominant concern, the focus of the Lyons government was increasingly on the threat of war in Europe and the expansionism of Japan. Appeasement, defence policy and rearmament were played out in the shadow of the Depression, but they are another story.

The focus of this book is on the worst years of the Depression, 1929 to 1932. We follow the narrative of the political and policy turmoil at the federal and state levels: the almost intractable problem of avoiding default on Australia's debts, the contestation over which policy responses to the Depression were feasible and legitimate, and the fractious battles of planning that would ultimately prove the undoing of the Scullin government. At times we pause the narrative, to focus on the key policy responses by the state, such as sustenance and relief works, and the mobilisation of communities, the voluntary sector, families and individuals to fill the gap left by these state responses. Later, we turn to those Australians who for various reasons were on the margins of this mobilisation, including those whose ethnicity made them the target of prejudice and the xenophobia that economic crises so often generate.

Through all this diversity, the issue of resilience—institutional, community and personal—is woven. How did Australians survive?

The research for this book began in 2016, with the support of the Australian Research Council, but many chapters were written in Melbourne during the lockdowns necessitated by the Covid-19 pandemic in 2020–21. It was a time when earlier national crises, such as the Great Depression and the 'Spanish' flu epidemic of 1919, were commonly alluded to. Comparisons between 1919, 1929 and 2020 might be perilous, given that the earlier crises occurred at a time when the powers of the federal government were relatively limited, the policy tools available to governments were undeveloped and the value systems of Australians were very different to today's. Moreover, it is premature to make judgements about the impact of the as yet unfinished Covid-19 pandemic. Still, at the risk of some ahistorical speculation, some similarities and contrasts at the time of writing might be noted.

All three crises confronted Australians—and, indeed, populations across the globe—with an almost existential threat from external forces that neither they nor their governments could control. All were crises that involved the stress of having no predictable end date. All required constant adaptation and resilience on the part of the state, communities and individuals. Perhaps most strikingly, all three crises had the effect of affirming the importance of local and state identities. Any nation formed as a federation has always to compete with the states for the loyalty of its citizens. During World War I, pride blossomed in Australia's national character, as manifested in the mythologised Anzac, but local communities also revelled in the exploits of locally sourced military units and locally born heroes. In the Depression, likewise, local loyalties were paramount, given that state and municipal governments coordinated the delivery of such systems of social welfare as were provided. In 1929 few Australians had travelled widely beyond their state and former colonial identities were still in living memory. The outsider was obvious, and unwelcome, when competing for local jobs.

The power of local identification during the Covid-19 pandemic came, however, as something of a shock. The closure of state borders was an effective means of containing the spread of the virus. Public authorities in 1919 had resorted to this measure, as well as to what we would now call 'social distancing', such as the wearing of masks, the cancellation of public events and the restriction of the use of public transport. But the invocation of state/local identity in the Covid-19 crisis went far beyond the pragmatic. Premiers spoke of 'my' people as if their state was a sovereign nation. Borders that were the creation of the nineteenth century became the boundaries of 21st-century quarantine enforcement. Organic social and economic communities that spanned these boundaries were sliced in two, even though there was no difference in the infection rates across these lines. Such attitudes resonated with the public, to judge by the results of elections in late 2020 and early 2021 in Queensland and Western Australia respectively, two of the most fortress-like states. Fear made communities look inwards. They expected their political leaders to protect them, *and only them.*

From some perspectives, this retreat within state boundaries can be seen as regressive, and the impact on the Australian federal structure remains to be seen. Still, if communities can be exclusive, they can also be inclusive. One of the 'lessons' of all three national crises is that many of their victims drew resilience from local communities and families. The ability to access aid at the local level and to lobby local councils, as we shall see, underpinned societal and personal resilience during the Great Depression. Family support, too, was of inestimable value when many thousands of Australians lost their income and accommodation. Ninety years later, the sense of community went some way towards mitigating the corrosive social isolation of Covid-19 lockdowns. Communities in 2020 might have been virtual, mediated by Zoom and other digital technologies, but they were communities nonetheless. At times they even had an intimacy that face-to-face exchanges lacked. In enforced confinement in their own homes and protected by the 'distance' of a technological interface, people found a willingness to concede to others their emotional frailty and psychological battles.

Yet if there were similarities between the Covid-19 and the Depression crises, there was at least one major difference: that is, the response of governments to Australians' need. In 1929 the social welfare state was rudimentary. While certain cohorts of Australians, such as returned soldiers, the elderly and the ill, could access pensions and medical assistance from the state, the safety net for the unemployed was minimal. When Australian governments accepted that this must change, their responses were faltering, hesitant and incomplete. Their inadequacy was evident in that most poignant of images from the Depression: families being evicted from their homes, their furniture unceremoniously dumped with them in the streets, regardless of the weather.

The Covid-19 pandemic saw no such scenes of destitution, at least in its first eighteen months. This was partly because in the nine decades after the Depression the social welfare state had become an integral, if often contested, part of the political landscape. But the response of national and state governments went well beyond this acceptance of the state's role in mitigating social distress. With a speed and generosity that contrasted dramatically with the Great Depression, Australian governments in 2020 devised a far larger safety net. Through the so-called JobKeeper payment, the federal government ensured that Australians continued to receive income while the businesses that employed them lost their revenue stream. Through JobSeeker it increased the payments to those already on unemployment and sickness benefits. Businesses were allowed to trade when insolvent, while banks provided many borrowers with mortgage 'holidays' and deferral of loan repayments. All of these schemes had their limitations. JobKeeper and the increase in payments under JobSeeker lasted only until March 2021. Minimal provision was made for casual workers, those on temporary working visas and international students (often one and the same). In early 2021, the banks started to require homeowners to repay their loans, and tenants became vulnerable to eviction as rental moratoriums ended.[2] However, as lockdowns continued during 2021 in the face of the more infectious Delta variant, the federal government renewed its financial support to individuals and industries that faced significant loss of income and revenue.

The responses of governments to the Covid-19 pandemic, incomplete and politicised though they might have been, attested to a radically different understanding of the role of the state from that of 1929. Today's politicians, of course, have the benefits of more sophisticated policy tools, computerised modelling systems and decades of macroeconomic debate, including Keynesian economics and Friedmanite monetarism. Governments also have

the capacity to service national indebtedness at levels beyond the imagination of the Scullin and Lyons governments. Within two months of the first
national lockdown, some $105 billion was raised by the Australian Office
of Financial Management by issuing government bonds to the market.[3] But
Australian governments in 2020–21 also had the will to prevent social disaster
on the scale of 1929–32. In parliamentary debates the Covid-19 pandemic
was universally described as 'the worst recession since the Great Depression'.
Queues outside Centrelink, the office responsible for social security payments,
led some commentators to invoke the spectre of the 1930s. Such comparisons
threw the severity of the pandemic into stark relief. But they also attested to
a universal conviction that, however severe the economic implications of the
pandemic might be, Australians should be protected from the extreme social
distress of the 1930s. As Prime Minister Scott Morrison told Parliament,
invoking not just the memory of the Depression but of wartime:

> We know who we are as people, and the legacy and inspiration that has
> been given to us from those who have come before us and shown us
> the way through challenges and tests just like this. So we summon the
> spirit of the Anzacs, of our Great Depression generation, of those who
> built the Snowy. Of those who won the great peace of World War II and
> defended Australia. That is our legacy that we draw on at this time.[4]

Yet if the memory of the Great Depression infused the response to the
Covid-19 pandemic, it was a memory that lacked any specificity. Unlike
the two world wars, the details of the crisis of 1929 to 1932 seem to have been
lost in popular memory. Economic hardship seems unable to compete in
national imagination with the mass slaughter, destruction and genocide of the
wars that preceded and followed it. The centenary of World War I produced a
torrent of publications and an orgy of commemorative activities. Memorials
to the wars of the twentieth century populate virtually every town in Australia.
The names of those who died in war are enshrined in stone and now made
readily available to family genealogists via accessible websites. But anyone
looking to find memorials to the Great Depression will be disappointed, and
few of the public works erected during the 1930s boast plaques acknowledging the role of Depression relief workers in their construction. No one has

proposed that we invest the same amount of taxpayers' money in recording the names of the countless thousands thrown into unemployment, bankruptcy and poverty during the 1920s and the 1930s. None of the anniversaries of key events of 1929 to 1932 appear on the national commemorative calendar.

This relatively low profile of the Great Depression is partly a function of the way that historians, both in Australia and globally, have viewed the past. The classic periodisation of the twentieth century has deemed the 1920s and 1930s to be the 'inter-war period'. These decades are relegated to being an intermission between the great global conflicts that preceded and followed them. This is not to say that the Great Depression has been eclipsed, but its bookending by war has somehow sucked attention away from it. It is a trend that has been reinforced by the changing intellectual concerns of academic historians in the past three decades, as issues of race, gender and memory have displaced the interest in class, labour relations and the economy that inspired much of the earlier research about the Depression. It is the purpose of this book to again give the Great Depression the prominence that it merits in Australian public memory. As the worst economic crisis of the twentieth century, it tested to the limit Australia's political institutions, the capacity of its communities to mobilise in support of each other, and the adaptability of individuals. Their endurance and survival provide one of the most impressive narratives of resilience in the nation's history.

Part I

LEGACIES OF WAR

CHAPTER 1

The soldiers come home

World War I and the Great Depression were separated by little more than a decade. In every sense, then, the experience of the war framed the way that Australians understood and endured the later economic crisis. This is not to say that Australians remained frozen in the moment of 1918, with all the fractures of a 'broken nation' unresolved and immutable.[1] The war, to paraphrase Emily Brontë's *Wuthering Heights*, stayed with Australians 'ever after', going through and through them 'like wine through water', altering the colour of their minds. Any study of the Great Depression must therefore start with the shadow of war.

The most visible legacy was the returned soldier. Nearly 300,000 men and women embarked for war service during World War I. More than 60,000 were killed or died of wounds or illness. At least 150,000 were wounded in body and mind: the French graphically called them *les mutilés*. With the coming of peace, this cohort of damaged men and women had to be cared for, placed in employment and provided with medical treatment. Moreover, they had to be 'culturally demobilised'.[2] Men who had been inured to 'the habit of killing' and whose minds were 'agog with war motion' had somehow to shed the mindset of war.[3]

The signs were not especially promising. The Australian Imperial Force (AIF) had gained notoriety for its lack of discipline, especially in Egypt and on the Western Front. The British commander-in-chief, Field Marshal Sir Douglas Haig, considered the Australian troops to be the most refractory element in his armies. Indeed, in 1917, absence and desertion rates in the five AIF divisions were four times greater than those of other divisions. In August 1918, the percentage of Australian soldiers in prison was seventeen times greater than for the whole of the British Expeditionary Force.[4] Those Australians who returned home during the war also behaved as if they were 'beyond the reach of law and order'.[5] Drunk and disorderly, they roamed the streets of Australia's cities, begging, damaging property and occasionally assaulting civilians. Returned soldiers also led much of the physical violence at public meetings during the conscription debates in 1916 and 1917.

As for their behaviour on their voyages back home in 1919, this again verged on the lawless. According to the semi-fictional account of Angela Thirkell, when one troopship stopped at Colombo (Sri Lanka, then Ceylon), the soldiers tore the town apart:

> The hotel people were putting up shutters and closing the front door. The rickshaw men mostly took to their heels. The diggers were turning the passengers out, not too gently either . . . fat old Cingalese birds [were] being turned out of those rickshaws like a pudding out of a bowl, but it was getting beyond a laughing matter.[6]

Several other returning troopships witnessed mutinous incidents when soldiers became frustrated with delays caused by quarantine restrictions introduced to contain the 'Spanish' influenza epidemic.[7] This final bitter episode of war-related loss raged through Australia in 1919, killing between 12,000 and 15,000 people. Many of them were men of military age who might have been expected to help rebuild Australia in the war's aftermath.[8]

Officials and families alike, then, feared that the mass return of soldiers in 1919 would raise the levels of violence in a society already polarised by the debates about conscription and inequalities of sacrifice in the war effort. Initially these anxieties seemed well founded. By one count, around twenty major returned-soldier riots erupted in Australia in 1919 and 1920, occurring in almost all the capital cities, bar Perth, and in major regional centres including Townsville, Broken Hill and Kalgoorlie.[9] These disturbances could involve hundreds, even thousands, of men, and sometimes lasted a number of days, with significant damage to property. The rioters no doubt had a mix of motivations: sheer vandalism, emotional release, the hope of increasing their repatriation entitlements, and anger at the working and personal conditions to which they returned. The soldiers, it must be remembered, were not a political monolith. The AIF had been drawn from all regions and socioeconomic backgrounds. Many were labourers and returned to the trade unions to which they had belonged before the war (though the trade union membership lists do not tell us how many). For these returned soldiers it was galling to see jobs taken by the 'shirkers', 'scabs', 'volunteers' or 'Nationalists'— choose the term according to your political persuasion—who had stayed at home and been recruited by loyalist governments to break the general strike of 1917. Some veterans would soon join the industrial unrest that exploded in 1919 and continued throughout the next decade.

More conservative returned soldiers took to the streets to counter disloyalty to the British Empire, and the menace, as they saw it, posed by communism after the Russian Revolution of 1917. Most famously, in central Brisbane, in the 'Red Flag' riots a mob of returned soldiers attacked a group of demonstrators, which included some of the local population of 3000–4000 Russian–Australians.[10] In two hours of fighting on 23 March 1919, perhaps nineteen police officers and probably even more of the assailants were injured. Police horses were brought down by stones and gunfire, and the Russian Hall was virtually demolished.

Four months later, this time in Melbourne, soldiers took to the streets during the celebrations in July 1919 to mark the signing of the Treaty of Versailles on 28 June. After an initially festive march, through streets festooned with 'a perfect blaze of flags' listing the major battles of the war, with aircraft flying overhead, and crowds cheering and weeping, the returned soldiers seized trams, smashed shop windows, forced restaurants to close and clashed with the police, who 'used their batons freely'.[11] A soldier was shot dead. The next day, after the chief commissioner of police refused to meet a delegation of the rioters who were demanding the release of those who had been gaoled the previous day, a crowd of 8000–10,000 stormed the state parliament. There they shredded documents, rifled desks and tore pictures from the wall. One protester struck the premier, Sir Harry Lawson, on the back of the head with an ink stand.[12]

Yet for all this spectacular disorder, the violence on the part of the returning soldiers was ultimately contained. In contrast to the chaos in Germany, Russia and other European countries, Australia did not face revolution, nor anything approaching it. This might have been for the simple reason that the men who took to rioting did not represent the larger body of returned soldiers. The disruptive veterans attracted considerable media attention, but they numbered only in their thousands. Many more stayed at home. They might well have been embittered and alienated, but there is every reason to think that, for a highly individualistic mix of personal and socioeconomic reasons, many men found the resilience they needed to construct their post-war lives. For all their trauma, they reverted to relatively stable, healthy levels of psychological and physical functioning. Sometimes the stresses of war did not retard their development but rather operated as 'catalytic agents of resistance, or of more constructive responses'.[13] The South Australian Charles Hawker, for example, was grievously wounded in the war but refused to accept the limitations of his disability. He established such a successful public career in the 1920s and 1930s that he was considered a possible prime minister before he died in a plane crash in 1938.[14] It is possible, too, that many returned soldiers did not view themselves as victims—the dominant trope used today to describe World War I soldiers—but returned home believing that, on balance, the war had been a positive experience, and not only because their side had won. J.J. (Digger) Carroll, for one, claimed in his later life that the war was 'an invaluable source of education' that broadened his view on life, and 'the world and its people'.[15]

Still, we need to look beyond the individual to the deeper structural reasons for Australia's relatively smooth transition to peace. Critically, the Australian state—that is, the combination of the Parliament, the executive, and the judiciary and the justice system that together institutionalise political power—survived the war intact.[16] Yes, there had been significant public violence during the debates about conscription and the general strike of 1917, and the war had seen a major increase in the emergency powers of the executive branch of government, including censorship. But the structures of the democratic system remained. Elections continued to be held and their results were respected. Parliament met as usual, and the state retained a monopoly of force. Furthermore, Australia did not experience the collapse of monarchical authority, a key pre-war anchor of states such as Austria–Hungary, Germany and Russia. Finally, Australia had the inestimable advantage of having won the war. As part of a victorious coalition of Allied Powers, its government was not burdened with the 'culture of defeat' that proved particularly destructive in post-war Germany.[17]

Remote from the war and ethnically homogeneous, then, Australia did not confront the toxic mix of defeat, a weak state, ethnic rivalries, pogroms, invasion and counter-invasion that spawned widespread transitional violence in what has been called the 'shatterzone' of central and eastern Europe.[18] The potential for violence on the part of Australian soldiers was dissipated. It would not entirely disappear, of course. Rather, it was deflected publicly into strike action for those on the left, or into paramilitary movements for those on the right. Privately, it could erupt in domestic violence. But the secret armies of the inter-war years in Australia were scarcely aggressive 'vanguards of terror' like the German *Freikorps*.[19] As we shall see, they served more as adjuncts to the state, and were generally concerned with preventing rather than fomenting revolution.

A further reason for the neutralisation of veteran violence in Australia was the policy innovation on the part of the Australian state. Recent scholarship suggests that war-induced brutalisation of post-war societies was not a foregone conclusion. Rather, the brutalising moment for veterans 'was not the war itself, but the experience of the transition to peace'.[20] If veterans were given material and spiritual compensation, the violence of battle was less likely to spill over into and corrupt post-war life. Australia's returned soldiers got both kinds of compensation. Here, their status as volunteer soldiers was critical.[21] From late 1914, in an effort to entice men to enlist, the federal government promised them or, if they died in service, their families a cornucopia of benefits. These included medical care; war pensions, graduated according to the individual soldier's level of disability; preferential access to employment; education and vocational training opportunities; and financial and other inducements to settle as farmers on the land. 'Repatriation', as it became known, was an adroit and rapid policy response suggesting that the Australian state, like individuals, could prove resilient, maintaining its effectiveness and the 'robustness and buffering capacity to adapt to changing circumstances'.[22]

Admittedly, in practice there was often a yawning gap between the policy promises and the delivery of veterans' benefits. The soldier-settlement scheme, notably, was monumentally flawed and misconceived.[23] At least half the settlers would fail by the late 1930s. While some soldiers had experience of rural life, many others had lived only in cities. They lacked the skills, capital or equipment needed for successful farming, while their land was often uneconomic in size and unproductive, sometimes lacking even adequate water supplies. The capricious Australian climate—the 'droughts and flooding rains' of Dorothea Mackellar's 1908 'My Country'—and environmental degradation added to the soldier-settlers' woes.

Many soldier-settlers were also simply too damaged to farm. While many made heroic efforts—compensating for lost limbs or energy with technology, or calling on wives, family or friends for assistance—official files are full of the stories of desperate men who found life impossible. One settler explained that he was disabled by an ulcerated war wound on his leg. His bones would break through the surface of his skin and become infected. In 1932, the trouble with his leg was 'so serious that the amputation of my leg has been suggested, therefore I am thus precluded from performing the ordinary duties of a farmer'. Faced with debt repayments, estranged from his wife, and with no children, he could only turn to hired labour for help.[24] Men such as these would be desperately disadvantaged during the Great Depression, when prices for primary commodities collapsed. While thousands somehow clung on to their holdings, some even consolidating them into more viable blocks when others failed, many fell into further debt. By 1943, the accumulated losses of the soldier-settler scheme across Australia were a staggering £45 million.[25]

The Repatriation scheme also failed to live up to the expectations of many returned soldiers. For them it was an entitlement, a reward for their service from a grateful nation. Politicians and the public agreed, but many officials administering the scheme were keen to discourage idleness and dependency. Infused with the values of self-reliance, independence and the dignity of work, they saw Repatriation not as a war bonus or charity, but rather as an effort to re-establish the soldier in civilian life. Some (though not all) medical bureaucrats saw their role as being custodians of the public purse, policing fraudulent claims, and resorting to surveillance and control in order to ensure 'economy' in the use of public funds.[26] Many pensions were set at levels below 100 per cent. Some did not cover the cost of living for a man with a family. The press, meanwhile (both in 1919 and later), was prone to suspect that the system was being rorted by 'unworthy applicants'.[27]

Furthermore, the aetiology of some the veterans' illnesses was poorly understood. While there could be no querying an amputation—for which there were fixed rates of compensation—it was far more difficult to prove that illnesses such as malaria, asthma, gastroenteritis and the ignoble venereal disease were 'war-related'. Even though the medical profession's understanding of mental illness grew in the 1920s, some doctors and officials continued to view shell shock as malingering, cowardice or perhaps the consequence of a hereditary disposition. It was the man with 'nerves', not the war, that was to blame for his condition.

Yet for all this, the privileges of the returned soldiers were significant and unassailable, thanks to the advocacy of the formidable Returned Sailors' and Soldiers' Imperial League of Australia (RSSILA, later the Returned and Services League, RSL). From 1919, this was led by a canny Gallipoli veteran, Gilbert Dyett, who managed in 1919 to persuade Prime Minister W.M. (Billy) Hughes to add a war gratuity to already approved benefits.[28] Although the RSSILA officially discouraged digger violence, it did not hesitate to imply that the government might face a violent reaction if it failed to accede to veterans' demands.[29] Meanwhile, the populist newspaper *Smith's Weekly*, financed by the Sydney entrepreneur Sir James Joynton Smith, relentlessly championed the cause of the digger, who was 'always right, bless him', against the 'cyanide gang' of the Repatriation Commissioners. Famously, in July 1923, *Smith's* published a story of one Trooper Rolph, a victim of mustard gas. With his skin unable to grow back after the gas attack, Rolph was forced to lie constantly in a tepid bath in Randwick Military Hospital because he could not bear the pain of lying on a bed. The water supported his weight.[30]

With advocates such as these and a high level of public support, the 'Repat' became one of the most generous schemes of material support provided by the nations that fought World War I.[31] Twenty years after the war, some 257,000 Australians (both incapacitated soldiers and dependants) were being assisted by war pensions, 1600 were still in hostels and homes for the permanently incapacitated, and around 23,000 outpatients were being treated in repatriation hospitals each year. More than 4000 artificial limbs had been supplied,

21,000 homes had been built, and 133,000 jobs had been found through Repatriation bureaus.[32] This was material compensation on a level that Australia could scarcely afford during prosperous times, let alone during the Great Depression. But such was the status of the returned soldier in national memory that in 1931 war pensions were among the items that would be partially protected from deflationary budgetary cuts.

Perhaps even more significant than this ongoing material compensation was the symbolic compensation accorded Australian soldiers. The story of the origins and promotion of the Anzac legend in the aftermath of World War I has been told often elsewhere.[33] Suffice to say here that the mythic narrative of the Anzac legend, which the 1915 landing at Gallipoli spawned, served the function, so critical to societal and personal resilience, of investing the huge losses of World War I, and hence the veterans' life histories, with meaning.[34] Not only did it assure the many thousands of families who had lost sons, brothers, fathers and husbands during the war that their grief had a purpose, but the returned soldiers, too, knew that their service was valued. Each Anzac Day they heard the state and their communities acknowledge their sacred obligation and debt of gratitude. The war memorials erected in virtually every town and suburb also attested to the returned soldiers' status. Most memorials were made possible by community donations and voluntary planning, and, notably, more than half of them listed every man who chose to serve, not just those who died in battle. This practice, which was virtually unknown in France and Italy and unusual in the United States, Britain, Canada and New Zealand, affirmed a cult of the Australian volunteer as the superior citizen.[35]

When the Great Depression came, then, returned soldiers were poised to claim some protection by invoking once more the gratitude of the nation. Individually, many veterans slipped into unemployment and desperate poverty, and would give voice to bitter disillusionment and a sense of betrayal. But as a collective, the Anzacs would be constructed as the model that the nation should again emulate. They were the very acme of patriotism, who had already shown the willingness to sacrifice their own interests for the collective good. As the *Canberra Times* would write on Anzac Day 1930, 'The spirit of Anzac was its unselfish sacrifice for country. This is the spirit which is needed in Australia to-day more than all else.'[36]

CHAPTER 2

Politics reshaped

The Australian state might have survived World War I, but the pre-war political landscape did not. In what has been called an 'adaptive cycle' of systems resilience, actors and institutions jockeyed for position at a time of great instability 'to determine winners, losers and the nature of new regimes and relationships'.[1] The new political alignments that emerged after 1917 reflected the competing values, attitudes and, at times, ideological positions that would shape the responses of Australians to the mass unemployment and deep social distress of the years to come.

From 1917 to 1929, federal politics was dominated by the Nationalist Party, a coalition formed in early 1917 when the leader of the Australian Labor Party (ALP), Billy Hughes, and other Labor pro-conscriptionists joined forces with the Opposition Liberals in the aftermath of the first conscription referendum. At the state level, similar hybrid arrangements emerged in 1916–17, although these tended to be more makeshift and temporary. By 1925, the ALP was back governing in five of the six states.

At the time of its formation, the Nationalist Party had little unifying purpose other than winning the war and through that victory ensuring the survival of the British Empire. With the coming of peace the party struggled to find any ideological coherence. While Hughes remained true to much of his Labor tradition, his Nationalist colleagues were bound more by a consensus on values and moral positions than by any specific policies.[2] 'Loyalty' to Britain remained a core value, although it was rarely pursued by Hughes or his successor, Stanley Bruce, at the expense of Australia's distinctive interests. As heirs to much of Britain's nineteenth-century liberal and Protestant traditions, Nationalists also gave primacy to the freedom of the individual. Unlike the ALP, which emphasised class conflict and economically determined social stratification, the Nationalists stressed the need for individual citizens to be virtuous, enterprising and capable of independent moral judgements. Collective action—be it the closed shop of the trade union, or the formulation of Labor policies by industrial and political organisations outside Parliament—was anathema. Socialism and, even worse, communism, were to be resisted at all costs.

Still, Nationalists accepted that the state had some limited role in the economy. Not only should it provide major infrastructure, such as rail, telecommunications and water, but it should also ameliorate the worst social injustices and protect the most disadvantaged of society. The policy debate at the time of federation about the respective merits of free trade versus protection had been resolved in favour of a 'new protection'. Under what became later known as the 'Australian settlement', the government provided tariff protection for fledgling Australian industries while workers were guaranteed a minimum standard of living and a needs-based wage, set by an independent system of arbitration and conciliation. The wages of Australian workers were also shielded from the competition of cheap foreign labour through the restrictive White Australia policy, an article of faith not just for the Nationalists but all political parties. Finally, in the 1920s Nationalists became great champions of the state driving Australia's economic development through ambitious programs of public works and capital investment.

The ALP shared many of these commitments but was historically a party for the Australian worker. Originating with the trade union movement in the 1890s, it was a broad church ideologically, incorporating progressive liberalism, socialism and some elements of anarchism and syndicalism. The potential for doctrinal dispute was endemic and, as the split of 1916 showed, the ALP struggled, when it came to hold office federally, to reconcile class objectives with the need to govern on behalf of the nation. While the more radical elements of the movement saw the compromises of power as a betrayal of core Labor values, many parliamentarians chafed at the limits on their flexibility as a result of their pledge to adhere to the policies determined by local ALP branches and conferences. Such were these centrifugal tendencies that Hughes blamed them, rather than conscription, for the 1916 split.[3]

Officially the ALP was committed to socialism. But the 'socialization objective' adopted in 1921 was an uneasy compromise, allowing for private ownership where it functioned 'in a socially useful manner and without exploitation'.[4] In reality, moderation and pragmatism were 'the watchwords' of the early Federal Parliamentary Labor Party.[5] The ALP had little choice in the inter-war period but to 'effectively put [socialisation] into cold storage', given that many upper houses in state legislatures were dominated by conservative interests, and the electorate refused in several referendums to increase the Commonwealth powers to deal with monopolies, combines and trusts.[6] The most, then, that Labor governments of the 1920s aspired to achieve were reformist policies, with a preference for 'big' government.

The ideological disputes within the ALP about the use and limits of power reflected the often internecine feuding within the party's industrial base. At this time Australia, like New Zealand, was one of the most highly unionised countries in the world. By 1920, the trade unions represented more than 50 per cent of all employees.[7] (In contrast, in 2020 the figure was 15 per cent of the workforce.)[8] But the industrial movement was far from monolithic, and debates raged throughout the 1920s as to the optimal mix of tactics: electing Labor governments that could legislate in the workers' interests; direct action, in the form of the strike; reliance on the systems of wage determination through arbitration courts and wage tribunals: and even amalgamation into One Big Union that could speak with one voice for multiple unions and be capable of taking sustained and united action.[9]

Some critics have claimed that Australian trade unions became too dependent on a system that not only determined wages but also bestowed registration, and thus official status vis-à-vis other rival unions or employer-funded organisations, on the organisations that they controlled.[10] But even unions such as the Australian Workers' Union (AWU), the 'largest, the most bureaucratically controlled, and the most conservative of the large unions', saw arbitration and wage tribunals as only one of a mix of methods through which to pursue their goals.[11] Affiliation with the political arm of the movement, the ALP, was always critically important. Hence when elected Labor governments proved unable to protect workers' interests during the Depression, the sense of betrayal was visceral. In their wrath and impotence the wider labour movement, in the deeply factionalised New South Wales especially, would trigger a second split in the ALP, almost as disastrous as the one over conscription.

The search for consensus on the left was complicated further by the success of communism in Russia. Before 1917, Marxism had only been one among many of the doctrinal positions embraced on the left, but the victory of the Bolsheviks in late 1917 inspired working classes across the globe to consider the option of revolution. After some manoeuvring, the Communist Party of Australia (CPA) came into existence in 1920, although it would take two years before rival groups resolved their competing claims and the party gained formal recognition and direction from Moscow. The party never gained large numbers before World War II. According to its own, almost certainly optimistic, figures, it had only 500 members in early 1928. It thus hardly posed a threat to the state.[12] But when not proselytising—delivering public lectures, running educational classes, holding open-air meetings and printing newspapers—the party sought to infiltrate and capture control of other labour organisations. Moderate and pragmatic union leaders and Labor politicians would have none of this. As they saw it, class-based violence was not only repugnant in itself, but would alienate Australian voters who prided themselves on their evolutionary traditions of social welfare and democratic innovation. Hence throughout the 1920s—and indeed into the Depression— many in the labour movement spent considerable energies attempting to rid the labour movement of communism and neutralise its appeal to their worker base.

The Nationalist government, meanwhile, exploited the bogey of communism for all the electoral advantage it offered. Anti-communism would become one of the leitmotifs of inter-war politics. Employing the highly resonant language of pandemic, the Australian Intelligence Branch described the CPA as being controlled by 'the most silent, militant and dangerous' of malign infestations, which planted 'germs cells' that then multiplied in fission fashion, 'ever extending the sphere of [their] cankerous inoculation'.[13] Such rhetoric ignored the improvisation and amateurishness of much of the CPA's early operations, but it legitimised a growing use of the state powers of censorship and repression. Only when the crisis of capitalism that communists so routinely predicted finally came in 1929, did they have the chance to widen their appeal, offering some alternative leadership to unemployed Australians who felt that the established political parties had failed to protect them.

A further political player thrust on the national stage by World War I was the Country Party.[14] Agrarian movements were not new in Australian politics. For many decades rural communities had seen themselves as separate from the cities, both physically and in terms of their interests. They resented big government, urban elites, banks, and the tariffs that raised the costs of primary production. World War I persuaded them that it was time to form their own political movements. With the closure of enemy markets and the shortage of shipping, Australian primary producers were forced to rely on the federal government. Hughes not only persuaded the British government to make bulk purchases of key commodities, such as wool, but he also created central commodity pools to manage exports. Primary producers predictably found fault with some of these arrangements, but they came to accept that the government could play some useful role in regulating the scale of production, fixing prices and coordinating marketing.

Moreover, the experience that primary producers gained in World War I convinced them of the value of parliamentary representation. After some success in Victorian and Western Australian elections, the country movements persuaded Hughes to introduce preferential voting for the House of Representatives in 1918. This change, whereby electors ranked candidates in order of their choice, was a global innovation that lasts to this day. In December 1918, then, a candidate from the Victorian Farmers' Union was elected to federal parliament in a by-election at Corangamite, to be followed a year later by twelve country representatives elected in December 1919. A few weeks later, on 22 January 1920, some of these new parliamentarians formed the Australian Country Party. Initially under the leadership of a Tasmanian journalist, William McWilliams, from April 1921 the party was led by one of the more remarkable politicians of the inter-war years, the frenetic but 'inventive political strategist' Earle Christmas Page, a Grafton surgeon.[15]

The Country Party claimed to be the third force in politics. It had an anti-political populism that would erupt in citizens' movements in 1931 and continue throughout the decades to come. But if supposedly independent from the Nationalists, the various farmers' organisations were generally opposed to organised labour and the socialisation of property. With the exception of the more radical Victorian Farmers' Union, they progressively identified with the Nationalists, that identification being most complete in New South Wales (where they called themselves Progressives for some years). In the inter-war period, the relationship between the two non-Labor parties would not always take the form of a coalition, but on critically important occasions they would present a united front against Labor.

Infusing all Australian politics at this time was a poisonous hostility between Protestants and Catholics. Sectarianism was as old as white settlement (12 per cent of the convicts were Irish), but it had become an especially powerful fault line during the conscription debates of World War I, when Hughes and other conservatives equated being Irish and Catholic with disloyalty. This toxin continued to infect public life in the years after the war. A few examples must serve to paint the picture. In 1920, Catholic Archbishop of Melbourne Daniel Mannix marked St Patrick's Day by parading with fourteen Catholic winners of the Victoria Cross as a guard of honour—the point being that not only Protestants had risked their lives in defence of the nation.[16] A huge crowd of about 30,000 watched from verandas, balconies and even the top of lampposts and telegraph poles.[17] The Protestants countered with their own rallies, which culminated in fervent renditions of 'Rule Britannia' and 'God Save the Queen'. In the first post-war federal election, held on 13 December 1919, conservatives urged Australians to 'Vote Protestant'. The Catholic Church purportedly wanted to make Ireland a republic and Australia a colony of Ireland.[18] Nearly a year later, a Labor federal parliamentarian, Hugh Mahon, accused the British government, after the death of an Irish hunger striker, of being 'a gang of false-hearted hypocrites', ruling over 'a bloody and accursed Empire'. For his pains he was expelled from Parliament, the only case in the history of the Commonwealth parliament of such disciplinary action. Mahon failed to win the by-election that followed.[19]

Intriguingly, however, we will find that, although Protestants and Catholics continued to live in largely separate spheres in the aftermath of war, the political significance of sectarianism abated during the Great Depression. Why this is so remains unclear. Perhaps after Irish independence in 1922, the question of Irish home rule no longer infused Australian domestic politics with the toxicity of earlier years. Perhaps, too, economic crisis, no matter how disastrous for individual Australians, did not pose an existential threat to national security that could be readily projected onto local 'enemies'. Irish Catholics, for all their irredeemable theological apostasy from a Protestant perspective, could not be held accountable for the behaviour of the bankers of London and the amorphous global trading system that brought the Australian economy to its knees. Instead, much of the energy that anti-Catholicism had engendered in the war years seems to have been rechannelled into those other great crusades of the right, anti-Communism and opposition to Australia's defaulting on the debts it owed to creditors in London.[20]

CHAPTER 3

War and the economy

World War I inevitably forced significant changes on the Australian economy, as well as on people and political parties. In the early twentieth century, this economy was still in many ways a colonial one. Australia supplied raw materials, foodstuffs and mineral resources, predominantly to Great Britain, but also to other industrialised countries. In return, Australia imported much of its manufacturing and technological needs. Since the domestic savings of the small population could not fund the development of the continent and its growing cities, government capital and borrowings rather than private investment funded transport systems, communications and other infrastructure. The shattering of the globalised economic and financial system by war thus had a major effect on the Australian economy. Not all of the changes were negative, but in economic terms World War I was on balance 'a bad one' for Australia.[1] In particular, the war left Australia with significant debts. The way these were managed would have serious implications for Australia's policy options during the Depression a decade or so later.

As soon as war was declared, it was clear that Australia's export trade was in serious jeopardy. With former trading partners such as Germany becoming enemies, significant markets were closed. This impacted on wool, Australia's primary export—as the popular saying went, Australia rode on the sheep's back—and also the base metals produced by the mines of Broken Hill, western Tasmania and Queensland. This disruption of Australia's exports continued throughout the war, as Britain maintained a harsh blockade on Europe and restricted the trade of neutral powers. Some relief was provided by the commodity agreements Hughes negotiated with Britain whereby it purchased Australian wool, lead and copper, even though much of these commodities could not be delivered given the acute shipping shortage. These agreements were generous—Britain needed Australia to remain solvent if it were to keep feeding troops into the maw of war—and Australia was able to improve its terms of trade and maintain parity of the Australian pound with sterling (a status that was considered sacrosanct by bankers).[2]

The dislocation of Australia's imports trade by the war was also accommodated, to some degree, by the growth of certain sectors of the domestic economy. The textile, clothing and footwear industries benefited from supplying the burgeoning AIF with uniforms, footwear and blankets; they would continue to be major employers into the 1920s and beyond. Two long-standing saddlery and coach-building businesses in Adelaide, Holden's Motor Body Builders and T.J. Richards and Sons, transformed themselves into modern motor-building enterprises. By 1926, Holden produced more than half of the national output of motor bodies and was fulfilling orders for its major customer, the US company, General Motors.[3]

The war also contributed to the growth of an independent base-metals industry in Australia. In 1914 almost all of Australia's output was sold to a German cartel, but Hughes seized the opportunity 'to smite [German companies] hip and thigh'. He shepherded through the federal parliament legislation that rendered null and void all contracts with companies that were deemed to be 'enemy'.[4] The Broken Hill Proprietary (BHP) steelworks at Newcastle, which had been under construction when the war began, expanded rapidly. Whereas Australia produced just 14,000 tons of steel in 1913, by 1929 its output was 400,000 tons.[5] Concurrently, copper refining at Port Kembla expanded, the Port Pirie lead smelter became the world's largest, and a large zinc refinery was opened in Tasmania by the Electrolytic Zinc Company, formed by four Broken Hill companies. The metals-based group of industries (iron and steel, machinery and engineering) were thus positioned to become 'in a very real sense the leader in Australian industrial development' in the years after World War I.[6]

Yet, if there were some positive outcomes of the war, the development of new manufacturing industries from 1914 to 1918 was 'erratic and desultory'.[7] While there was the opportunity for import substitution, domestic demand was depressed while so many men were absent, serving overseas with the AIF. They had been higher wage earners than the women they left behind and now they spent their disposable income in the shops, cafes, bars and brothels of the United Kingdom, France and Egypt, not in Australia. The building industry, especially, suffered an acute depression with the disruption of marriage patterns during the war. Notably, too, Australia did not develop a significant munitions industry, as Britain and other belligerents did. Some companies (for example at Lithgow, New South Wales, and Maribyrnong, Victoria) produced simple weaponry, but Australia's attempt to help address the critical shortage of British shells in 1915 resulted in only 15,000 18-pounder shell cases being made in Australia.[8] To put this into perspective, 1.7 million shells were fired by British artillery in one week alone before the Battle of the Somme began on 1 July 1916.[9]

Thus, despite some positive adjustments, real aggregate gross domestic product in Australia declined by 9.5 per cent between 1914 and 1920, and per capita income declined by more than 16 per cent. As one economic historian has put it, 'Had this occurred in peacetime it would be classified as a depression.'[10] The 1920s would bring some recovery, as we shall see, but that growth was not sustained and the economy remained as vulnerable as ever to the external shocks that caused such mayhem in 1914.

Perhaps the most negative impact of the war was Australia's war debt. In the heat of the patriotic moment of August 1914, when the caretaker Liberal government of Joseph Cook promised Britain an expeditionary force of 20,000 men and the use of the Royal Australian Navy, it also committed Australia to covering the costs of maintaining these forces. No one, of course, anticipated that the war would last for more than four years, but it seems that the nation's capacity to service this debt was never seriously reviewed or challenged.

By June 1920, the direct cost of the war to the Australian government was £377 million. In 1913–14 the government had raised revenue of £21.7 million and spent only £15.5 million.[11]

Like many other belligerents, Australia did not cover the full costs of war by raising revenue. Taxation, as always, was electorally risky, and the federal government had limited taxation powers: mostly tariffs and excises, with a small amount being raised from land tax. Ultimately, the federal government did increase tax revenue, but still only about 20 per cent of Commonwealth war expenditure was covered by revenue.[12] The federal government financed the war effort, first, by increasing the quantity of Australian notes in circulation, from £9.6 million in June 1914 to £52.5 million in June 1918.[13] The resulting inflation not only angered the labour movement, fuelling the opposition to conscription, but it also generated in the thrift-minded middle classes a deep distrust of monetary expansion. This would be intensified by the nightmarish hyperinflation of central European countries in the early 1920s and, as we shall see, would seriously constrain the policy options of the Scullin government during the Depression years.

Second, Australian governments borrowed. Ordinary Australians were cajoled by highly inventive publicity campaigns to subscribe to seven war loans and three peace loans. About £258 million were raised by war loans and war certificates. This was 'a stupendous achievement for Australian patriotism'—to quote the governor of the Commonwealth Bank—but at various times in the 1920s these borrowings, together with the gratuity that Hughes agreed to pay returned soldiers, had to be converted (that is, rolled over into a different loan structure) or repaid to Australians.[14]

The other source of borrowing was London. During the war, the British government provided a number of imperial loans, while the War Office, Admiralty and Ministry for Shipping provided services that were estimated in June 1919 to amount to £38.4 million.[15] High levels of debt were inevitable in such a long, industrialised war. Britain, itself, which had served for the previous half-century as a major creditor nation, was forced to seek vast amounts of finance from private US investors in order to sustain its hugely expensive war effort.[16] During the course of the Battle of the Somme from mid- to late 1916, for example, the dominant Wall Street house of J.P. Morgan spent more than a billion dollars in the United States on behalf of the British government—and this was only 45 per cent of the British war spending in those months.[17] Britain, while owing much to the United States, also acted as a creditor to its European allies, including Russia, and to the rest of the empire.

Yet, if debt was the price of victory for all but the United States, Australian governments compounded the problem by continuing to borrow on the London money market, even during wartime, to fund domestic public works. These were popular with the electorate since they provided employment opportunities and social benefits. The British Treasury argued with reasonable logic that if millions of pounds were spent upon public works that generated local employment, many men might not feel inclined to volunteer for the AIF, but Australian governments continued to raise loans on the London money market.[18] The war ended with the states, and for the first time the Common-wealth, having a substantial level of indebtedness.

Hughes hoped that Australia's war-related debts would be covered by reparations from the defeated powers. But, for all his grandstanding at the Paris Peace Conference, he was to be deeply disappointed. By 1931, Australia had received only £5.571 million against its original claim of £464 million. Moreover, this was largely made up of ships seized in Australian ports and the value of expropriated property in the former German colony of New Guinea.[19]

How then was Australia's war debt to be funded?[20] The British government suggested at the end of the war that Australia might discharge some of its debt by using part of the £175 million surplus it had accumulated in Britain as a result of the wartime commodity agreements. Hughes blocked this. Concerned with Australia's balance of trade and the expectations of wool growers at home who were now being wooed by the new Country Party, he insisted that the money be repatriated.

After further negotiations, Australia finally agreed in May 1921 to discharge nearly £92.5 million of its war debt over a period of 36 years. With an interest rate of 5 per cent and a 1 per cent contribution to a sinking fund (money set aside for the gradual repayment of a debt), the cost to Australia was estimated to be more than £5.5 million per annum. But Hughes, a terrier-like politician if ever there was one, would not let the issue go. When in December 1921 wool prices slumped and the terms of trade moved against commodity prices, he tried to extend the time frame to 48 years by cutting sinking-fund payments.

British Treasury officials were unimpressed. They believed that Australia had already gained significant concessions when the amount to be repaid had been agreed upon. Britain was repaying its own war debt to the United States, and other Dominions were discharging their obligations without Australia's equivocation. Canada had repaid its debt and was a net creditor to Britain. South Africa had already paid £8–9 million of the £21 million it owed. India had liquidated £80 million of its £100 million debt, while New Zealand had not only met its interest payments but also agreed to repay its debts in full by 1927–28. An irritated Treasury official, Otto Niemeyer, commented: 'Australia gives us more trouble than all the Dominions put together. Mr Hughes is always excessively unbusiness like and never keeps any kind of bargain.'[21]

Some two years later, Prime Minister Bruce made another attempt to renegotiate the 1921 agreement, this time on the grounds that the British were supposedly paying a lower rate of interest on their war debt to the United States, and Australia had a current account deficit of more than £43 million. Of this, nearly £30 million came from invisibles including the war debts payments, which made up one-sixth of this figure. But the British refused to make any changes to the agreed debt repayment schedule. When, in 1926, the issue was raised by Bruce once more, Treasury officials in London maintained, with a growing testiness, that Australia had actually done well out of the 1921 agreement and 'has in fact paid us less than the money she borrowed cost us'.[22] Bruce might claim that Britain's European allies were receiving more generous debt-funding terms than Australia, but the British argued that these allies had ended the war with an immense weight of debt and had suffered from the considerable destruction of physical capital and infrastructure. Had their British and American creditors not treated these countries generously, they would have had no option but to repudiate their war debts.

These negotiations might now seem arcane, but the war debt had a significance well beyond financial diplomacy. For many Australians it was seen as a 'blood debt', an unwarranted imposition that should be repudiated by the Australian government. Had not Australia already given enough with its 60,000 dead? In London, meanwhile, Australia's haggling over the war debt, particularly as it continued to borrow even more heedlessly on the London money market (see Chapter 5), convinced some officials that Australian politicians were unwilling to face the implications of their own borrowing practices. The British Treasury, it must be said, was a bastion of economic orthodoxy, and some imperial visionaries in London were far more sympathetic to Australia's grandiose visions of post-war national development. But in 1930, when the foreign-capital flows ceased and Australia was in danger of defaulting on its manifold debts, it was the Treasury, the Bank of England and none other than Niemeyer himself, who joined the bank in 1927, who had the power to dictate a bitter deflationary medicine. As they saw it, Australians, through their own financial mismanagement, had sown the wind and were reaping the whirlwind. To quote Niemeyer when on his mission to Australia in September 1930:

> As Australia has borrowed abroad something like £200,000,000 since the date of the war loans, and has always represented her prospects and conditions in glowing terms on those occasions, it is quite ridiculous of her to suggest there is any reason why she not pay a pittance for her prior war debts. This is an odd country full of odd people and even odder theories.[23]

Part II

RECOVERY, VISIONS AND RECESSION, 1919–29

CHAPTER 4

Recovery and development

It is tempting, in retrospect, to see the 1920s as little more than an intermission between two catastrophes. But these were years of considerable economic change, political turmoil and policy innovation. In the aftermath of World War I, the modern consumer society was born. As the national economy recovered and state governments invested in infrastructure, new suburbs mushroomed in the capital cities. Many of these new households had the discretionary income to purchase household durables and cars, and to enjoy new leisure activities such as the cinema. Manufacturing began to account for a greater share of domestic output and employment, and the Australian economy began to shift away from its traditional reliance on resource-based industries. The 1920s also ushered in new visionary schemes of national development: programs that aimed to replace the men lost in battle and the Spanish influenza pandemic, to attract new foreign capital for public works and to develop new markets for Australian exports. This pursuit of 'men, money and markets' would not achieve its more ambitious targets, and the search for capital would bring Australia to the brink of insolvency, but these policies set the scene for the Depression to come.

The first four years of peace were, as far as federal policymaking was concerned, the tail end of war. Billy Hughes remained prime minister, relying on his prestige as the wartime leader and the reputation he had gained through his performance at the Paris Peace Conference. When he came back to Australia in mid-1919, returned soldiers draped him in flags and carried him shoulder high through the streets. Seeking to capitalise on this popularity, Hughes went to the electorate in late 1919. The campaign was rowdy and boisterous. In one notable incident, a group of mostly returned soldiers, many from suburban Essendon, descended on Ararat, Victoria, and then tarred and feathered a former Labor parliamentarian, J.K. McDougall. He was targeted because the Nationalists had used in their campaign a reworded version of an anti-war poem McDougall had written in 1900, which was now taken as evidence of Labor's contempt for the digger.[1]

The 1919 election confirmed the transformation of federal politics by the realignments of World War I. The Nationalists lost sixteen seats in the lower house, but the beneficiaries were not the ALP, which gained three seats, but rather the Country Party representatives, who won eleven seats. In the following months, Hughes' base of support within the Nationalists and the wider business community eroded. Many Nationalists resented his erratic methods of managing government business and his unbridled rudeness. Others suspected him of being at heart 'socialistic' and in policy terms, extravagant. In 1920, his deputy and treasurer, William Watt (a former Victorian premier), resigned while undertaking financial negotiations on behalf of the government in London. His frustration with Hughes had been mounting since at least 1918, and became too much when Hughes pursued negotiations about wool without informing him.[2]

Hughes then made some attempts to court the Country Party, but Page would not cooperate. As the champion of country voters, he opposed the new labyrinth of tariffs the Hughes government introduced, after a major revision of the schedule conducted in 1920 by the Minister for Trade and Customs, Walter Massy-Greene. Moreover, Page was a good hater and detested Hughes. For his part, Hughes thought Page 'a bumbling amateur', and was yet to realise that behind this country-town doctor's 'fixed smile, shambling gait and torrential and rambling speech [lay] a keen political brain and ruthlessness equal to Hughes' own'.[3]

In an effort to shore up his position with the Nationalists, in December 1921 Hughes appointed Bruce as his treasurer. It proved a momentous decision. Bruce had entered Parliament in 1918 with the support of the National Union, a behind-the-scenes group of Melbourne businessmen that provided much of the finance for the Nationalist Party and was critical of Hughes for his financial policies and extravagance.[4] Bruce could boast impeccable business credentials and was categorically 'loyal'. Though born in St Kilda, Victoria, he had lived in England as a child, studied at Cambridge University (where he rowed), managed the family business in London before World War I, and served with British units at Gallipoli, where he was twice wounded. Often lampooned for wearing spats, a quintessentially English shoe-covering for outdoor wear, and for driving a Rolls-Royce, he was typical of many wealthy Anglo-Australians of that time. He believed the country should remain firmly anchored within the British world of which Australia would be an integral part. But Bruce was also conscious of the need to engage with a wider world: he represented Australia at the League of Nations in Geneva in September 1921. Most importantly, Bruce believed that Australia should be governed 'in the ways of common sense and good sound business principles'.[5] This was a conservative mantra that would become familiar in the 1920s and throughout the Great Depression.

Hughes continued to cut an impressive, if often infuriating, figure on the international stage. Though he remained a fervent imperialist, he passionately defended Australian interests at the 1921 Imperial Conference, and objected powerfully when in September 1922 he learned through the press rather than from London that Britain expected Australia to contribute to a contingent to the Dardanelles should war break out with Turkey over its rejection of the 1920 Treaty of Sèvres.[6] But international profile was no longer enough, and when Hughes went to the electorate again in December 1922, he met his nemesis. After a campaign that was considered by contemporaries to be one of the dullest on record, Nationalist parliamentarians were reduced to 26 seats in a house of 75. Of the ex-ALP group only Hughes and one other parliamentarian survived. The ALP itself gained another three seats, but the Country Party was again the biggest winner. Now with a block of fourteen seats, it held the balance of power.

Hughes hoped to survive by forming a coalition or a minority government, but Page vetoed this option. Thus, in February 1923, Hughes resigned, and Bruce formed a coalition between the Country Party and the Nationalists. Hughes' survival skills had been astonishing during the war years, and Bruce consoled him with the thought that he had been only 'temporarily removed from the arena'.[7] Yet Hughes was never again prime minister. He would remain in Parliament throughout the inter-war period, proving a thorn in the flesh for Bruce and trying unsuccessfully in 1929 to create a new party, the Australian Party. He would hold ministerial roles in the Lyons governments of the 1930s and would even lead the United Australia Party (the successor to the Nationalists) in opposition during World War II. But much to Hughes' irritation, the coalition that Page and Bruce stitched together with considerable reservations in 1923 would prove to be one of the great structural adjustments of the Australian political system. With Hughes' demise, too, the Labor influence on the Nationalist party was further diminished. The Bruce–Page government that led Australia into the Great Depression, then, was one that embraced a conservative form of liberalism, more sympathetic to business and increasingly hostile to the trade unions.

By the time Hughes lost power, the Australian economy seemed to be on the path to recovering from the war. Despite a short sharp global recession in 1921, for many Australians it seemed that an era of new prosperity lay ahead of them.[8] The return of the soldiers, increased immigration, and the drift of population to the cities combined to fuel a housing boom in the early 1920s. The suburbs sported row after row of new brick or timber villas and Californian bungalows, complete with clipped front hedges or grid-wire fences and backyards capable of housing 'chooks' and vegetable gardens. Many homes were connected to electricity by 1930 and, as discretionary income and hire purchase arrangements increased, previously unaffordable luxuries became necessities. Sales of motor cars, radios, washing machines, refrigerators, gas cookers, vacuum cleaners and the like grew. Specialist and department stores fed this new consumerism, while cinemas and other recreational activities grew at an astonishing rate. In 1927 there were 1250 theatres selling 110 million tickets. All this stimulated the growth of imports but also encouraged significant growth in local manufacturing, construction and services. Whether this growth was possible only because of the tariff protection that the federal governments provided for local industry is debatable, but thanks to a range of stimuluses—the relative ease of accessing capital, new avenues of hire-purchase credit, the rise of new consumer durables, and the growth of population and income—manufacturing came to increase its share of employment and output.[9] Ultimately this sector would play a significant role in Australia's recovery from the Depression.

This, of course, was at the macroeconomic level. Each of the Australian states and regions had a distinctive economic profile which, in turn, shaped the experience of their citizens in the 1920s and the Depression. New South Wales was, in many respects, the giant. In the 1921 census, the last before the Depression years, it housed 38.6 per cent of Australia's population of 5.4 million.[10] Sydney, with 43 per cent of the state's population, was heavily dependent on manufacturing, services and shipping. Mining and the associated smelting and refining of metals were to be found across New South Wales: in the coalfields of the Hunter Valley and nearby Newcastle; in Broken Hill in the far west; and in Mount Kembla (and from 1927, Port Kembla) to Sydney's south. In 1927 the state produced 82 per cent of Australia's black coal, but only 3.5 per cent of the nation's gold. Sheep, beef, dairying and wheat were the life blood of many rural regions, including New England, the Riverina and the Illawarra, stretching along the southern coast from Wollongong to Bega. In 1927, New South Wales produced 29 per cent of the nation's wheat, had 23.5 per cent of its beef and dairy cattle and a remarkable 53.4 per cent of the nation's total sheep (see maps 4.1, 4.2 and 4.3 for the distribution of major primary industries across states in the mid-1920s).[11] In some ways, rather than Australia riding on the sheep's back, it was New South Wales that did so.

Just over half of Victoria's 1.53 million population lived in Melbourne, where manufacturing industries were strong, especially in textiles and clothing. Victoria's rural areas were major producers of dairy products, wheat (29 per cent of national production in 1927) and, to a lesser extent, wool (14.3 per cent of Australia's sheep in 1927). Thanks to the soldier-settlement scheme in the 1920s, the production of wheat and wool was pushed out into the more marginal lands of the Mallee, in the state's north-west. Gold was no

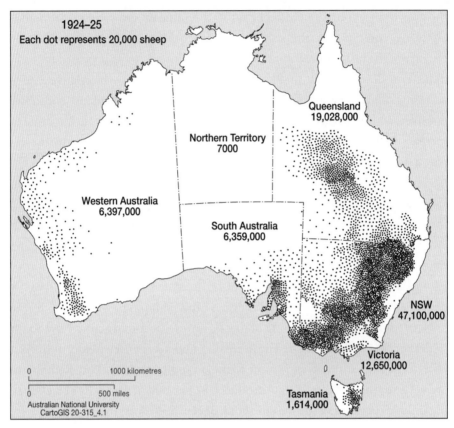

Map 4.1: Distribution of sheep, 1924–25
Source: Year Book Australia, 1929, p. 659.

longer the engine of growth it had been in the nineteenth century—Victoria supplied only 7.6 per cent of national production in 1927. The mining of brown coal and the generation of electricity were, however, being established during the 1920s in the Latrobe Valley, Gippsland, and in 1924 the model town of Yallourn was created to house workers.

None of the other states could match New South Wales and Victoria in population or manufacturing capacity. Queensland, where more than 70 per cent of the population of about 750,000 lived outside the capital city, had a unique dependence on the sugar industry, which stretched along the coastal belt. Producing 95 per cent of the nation's sugar, this industry was protected from international competition by embargoes and tariffs. A national government

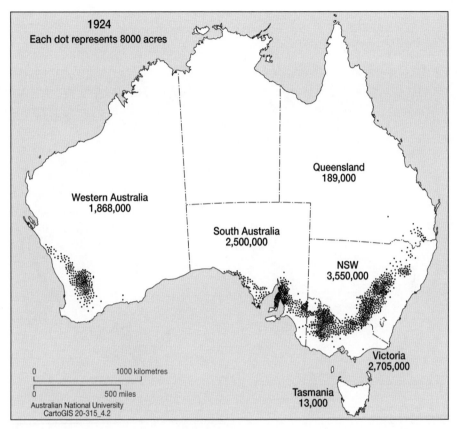

Map 4.2: Distribution of wheat acreage, 1924
Source: Year Book Australia, 1929, pp. 695–6.

agreement dating from 1923 also regulated prices. Bruce was convinced that a viable sugar industry in Australia's north was necessary not only to limit imports but also to defend Australia and 'to preserve our cherished White Australia policy'. In return for abandoning the use of low-paid Melanesian labourers, the sugar industry had a guaranteed home market.[12] From 1920 to 1925, when a coastal railway was extended from Brisbane to Cairns, cane acreage in the state jumped by 65 per cent.[13] Beyond this, the Queensland economy was dependent for its exports on cattle (46 per cent of the nation's total), sheep, horses and mining. The more important minerals were copper in Chillagoe and Cloncurry (the birthplace, incidentally, of the Royal Flying Doctor Service and destination of the first Qantas flight); tin mining in

45

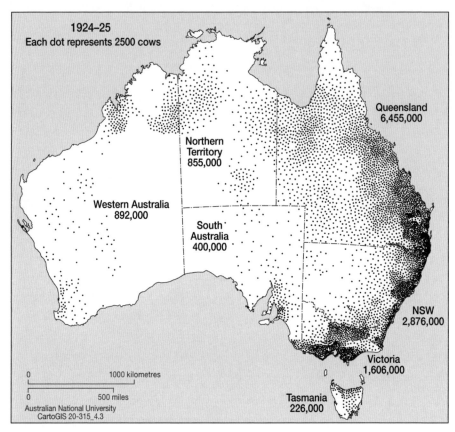

Map 4.3: Distribution of cattle, 1924–25
Source: Year Book Australia, 1929, p. 660.

Irvinebank; and lead, zinc, copper and silver ore at Mount Isa, though Mount Isa mining did not realise its full potential until after World War II.

Most of South Australia is semi-desert—the 'driest state in the driest continent', as South Australian schoolchildren have learned over the generations. In 1927 more than half its European population of nearly 500,000 lived in the capital, Adelaide. The economy relied heavily on agricultural and pastoral production—it produced 22 per cent of Australia's wheat in 1927—with some pockets of industrial production, such as motor bodies. The manufacturing sector struggled to overcome its distance from large markets and its lack of access to coal for power generation.[14] The copper mines, which had made the state the third-largest copper producer in the world by 1850, were in decline

46

after rising prices during the war, but iron ore had been discovered in the Middleback Ranges, inland from Whyalla on Eyre Peninsula. This was shipped to Port Pirie and elsewhere for smelting. The state also possessed some of the oldest wine-growing districts in the country, in the Barossa Valley, Clare and Coonawarra regions. Wine was also grown along the Murray River, especially near Loxton, Barmera and Renmark, where irrigation from the 1890s on had enabled fruit and dried-fruit production along the river's course into Victoria. Like dried fruit, the wine industry was heavily export-dependent, with large quantities of sweet wine being exported to Great Britain in the 1920s under a bounty scheme and tariffs that gave preference to produce from members of the British Empire. This bounty would shrink dramatically in the late 1920s, as oversupply caused both a build-up of stock and a drop in prices.[15]

Like South Australia, Western Australia, with its population in 1921 of 327,000, was largely bypassed by the industrialisation processes that had occurred in the eastern states. Distance and poor transportation posed huge logistical problems for pastoral developments beyond the south-west corner.[16] The state's vast expanses were being progressively developed, however, for wheat production (19.2 per cent of the national production in 1927), market gardening, orchards, sheep and cattle. Soldier settlement stimulated the wine-growing industry. The area of land under lease to pastoralists grew from 59 million hectares in 1905 to 105 million hectares in 1921.[17] This, as so often across the continent, was at the expense of the Aboriginal people, who lost their traditional lands and were recruited, sometimes against their will, to provide the pastoral workforce. A distinctive feature of Western Australia's economy was its gold production, especially in the 'Golden Mile' near the towns of Kalgoorlie and Boulder nearly 600 miles east of Perth. In 1927 the state produced some 80 per cent of Australian gold, and this industry would actually enjoy a revival in the 1930s.

Tasmania was the state that struggled most economically. With a population of only 214,000 in 1921, the state's economy was dominated by mining and rural activity. Tasmania played little role in manufacturing or the staple export industries of sheep and wheat. Attempts at encouraging closer settlement in the 1920s floundered, and the profitability of the state's mining enterprises on the west coast was undermined by falling metal prices. The Tasmanian population actually declined in the 1920s, as people moved to the mainland, reducing the state's tax base to a level that limited government options.[18]

As for the two territories, the Federal Capital Territory (FCT, now the Australian Capital Territory or ACT) and the Northern Territory, the FCT was tiny, with only 2572 residents in 1921. The federal parliament did not move to Canberra until 1927, and important government departments, such as Defence, remained in Melbourne until the 1950s. To cynics, Canberra was the most brightly lit paddock in the world. The Northern Territory, too, had a very small non-Aboriginal population: only 3867 in 1921. No one knew precisely how many Aboriginal Australians lived in the Territory's hinterland, since to use the racialised language of the day, 'full blood' Aboriginal Australians were not counted in any census. In 1911, however, it was thought there might be 50,000 Aboriginal people in the Northern Territory.[19] In the period after World War I, large areas of the Territory were classified as reserves for these peoples, who were wrongly assumed to be dying out. Their traditional lands were again leased to vast pastoral enterprises that would employ Aboriginal men and women, often on exploitative and abusive terms.

These snapshots of the state economies mask many complexities within the primary, manufacturing and mining sectors. Much of primary production was not confined within states but rather spilled over borders. Still, it is clear that the diversity of economic life across Australia was so great that terms such as 'Australians' and 'Australia' obscure important local variations. Like the other variables that we will meet in this narrative—age, marital status, gender, ethnicity and former military service—they shaped the ways Australians recovered from war and faced economic crisis.

With the election of Bruce, Australia's economic development was defined by the aspiration to attract what the prime minister memorably called at the 1923 Imperial Conference 'men, money and markets'.[20] The war had intensified the longstanding belief that the potential of the continent needed to be further exploited. A larger population would mitigate the risk of invasion, while closer settlement of the land would tap the energy and masculinity seemingly so manifest in the heroic Anzacs. As a contemporary exponent of national development, journalist and poet Edwin J. Brady said in his aptly named 1918 book, *Australia Unlimited*:

> The European War has taught Australia many lessons. The nation realizes at last the necessity for developing its own trade and industry . . . We intend to utilize within the boundaries of our Commonwealth opportunities which we have hitherto wasted or left undeveloped . . . It is the policy which is going to make Australia the richest and most powerful, as she is now the freest and most prosperous nation, of the world . . . The breed that stormed and held the heights of Anzac will grow stronger and more self-reliant as their generations follow.[21]

Critics pointed out that 'a desert by any other name is just as dry', and that from the population point of view, Australia was 'like a very large but empty frame, rich gilt surrounding comparative blankness'.[22] Notions that the continent, being roughly the same size as the United States, should be capable of carrying a comparable population of 100 or even 200 million were simply fanciful. But, as the soldier-settlement scheme showed, the popular and political faith in further closer settlement of the land was unshakeable. It was Australia's version of the British aspiration for 'homes fit for heroes'.

In many ways this was what inspired the search for new immigrants, the 'men' of Bruce's trifecta. It was a search that was largely confined to Britain, although the 1920s did see significant numbers of Italians arrive. With over 97 per cent of Australian residents in 1928 being born in Australia, New Zealand or the British Isles, regular immigration from the 'home country' was not just a demographic strategy but a means of reinforcing the deep imperial and familial ties.[23] As it happened, in London a number of imperially minded politicians, though not the Treasury, thought likewise, seeing immigration to the Dominions also as a way of alleviating the problems of British post-war unemployment.[24] In 1921, then, the Imperial Conference agreed on a program of overseas settlement and, under the *Empire Settlement Act 1922*, Britain and the Dominions committed themselves to jointly funding schemes of assisted migration. In 1925 Australia and Britain also signed the so-called £34 million agreement, which had the lofty ambition of settling in Australia some 450,000 new British settlers over the next ten years.

This government-funded immigration was complemented by a bevy of other schemes. Some of these were state-initiated, as was the South Australian Barwell scheme, named after the fervent imperialist and Liberal premier of 1920–24, Henry Barwell. Others were managed by non-government or Protestant organisations, often driven by the social engineering goal of rescuing disadvantaged British children from the corrosive effects of slum life in England. Among these organisations were not just the well-connected Big Brother (Generals Sir John Monash and Thomas Blamey were Big Brothers in Victoria) but the Young Men's Christian Association (YMCA), the Boy Scouts, Barnardo's (a British-based charity that cared for vulnerable children), the Fairbridge Farm School in Western Australia, and the Sydney Millions Club (later Millions Club of New South Wales, an organisation that aimed at building the population of that state to 1 million people). The Salvation Army, for its part, hired a ship in each of the years 1925, 1927, 1928 and 1929 to bring young immigrants and some married couples to Australia.[25]

In much of this voluntary activity a further legacy of the war is evident. The loyalist elites who had invested prodigiously in patriotic fundraising in 1914–18 now found a new outlet for their energies in immigration. In Queensland, for example, Canon D.J. Garland, who had been one of the architects of early commemorations of Anzac Day, managed Anglican schemes for adults and farm boys. In Sydney, Dr Mary Booth became the founding president of the Women's Migration Council of New South Wales and an office holder in the New Settlers' League of Australia. In wartime she had raised funds for war widows and 'Allied Babies'; established a teetotal soldiers' club in Sydney; and then, in 1921, formed an Anzac Fellowship of Women to foster the commemorative spirit of Anzac Day. She now converted the Empire Service Club, originally a club for returned servicemen, into a centre for young immigrants, while taking a personal interest in the welfare of young people arriving under the Dreadnought Scheme, named after the formidable battleships of the era. (Developed before 1914, this organisation sponsored young men from British rural districts who were on the cusp of military age.) For nearly twenty years, too, Booth published a monthly magazine, *The Boy Settler*, the purpose of which was to help young immigrants keep in touch with each other and access practical advice about farming and country life.[26]

By these various means, then, around 300,000 people were settled permanently in Australia between 1921 and 1929. Some 18,000 of these immigrants were teenagers, even children.[27] In some ways, it seemed, the 'lost generation' of the war years was being replaced—at least demographically. Not only had the 'racial stock', which many feared had been diluted by the wartime voluntary system of recruitment, been renewed but the immigrants also went some way to counter the decline in the marriage rates in the 1920s after the short spike of post-war reunions. The fertility rate also declined as more couples used birth control to limit family size. The average number of babies a woman could be expected to produce in her reproductive lifetime was 3.1 in the early 1920s.[28]

Yet if the immigration schemes of the 1920s had an emotive power, they did not fulfil the most aspirational targets of their advocates. By the end of 1928, only £8.84 million worth of projects had been approved under the £34 million scheme, mostly in Western Australia, some in Victoria. The cost, too, was disproportionate. In total, it has been estimated that land-settlement schemes settled 478 families at an outlay of £15 million: that is, £31,400 per family.[29]

For the immigrants themselves, the experience of migration was mixed. Many settled in the cities but most of the young men brought out under assisted programs were destined to undertake manual labour on farming properties; the girls were employed as domestic help. Some had benevolent employers, who included them as part of their family. Many found marriage partners or progressed to further education. A few even inherited the properties on which they worked.[30] One immigrant interviewed in later years recalled that 'it was the best thing I ever did. I wouldn't have swapped my life for anything with anybody.'[31] Yet, less positively, some immigrant farmers and labourers found that remote and arid regions of Australia bore little resemblance to the 'newer England' they had been promised. The shortage of capital meant that few could move from being labourers to landowners, as some of the immigration schemes assumed. Moreover, as the soldier-settlement scheme was showing, small-scale settlement was often unproductive.

Young immigrants were at greatest risk. They could be housed in crude accommodation, work long hours and be denied minimum wages. The trade unions suspected that child labour was a means of undercutting wages.

A higher incidence of suicide among young immigrants between 1923 and 1925 also suggested that the loneliness and hardship proved intolerable for some. Most vulnerable of all were the thousands of unaccompanied minors under the age of fourteen who migrated in the inter-war years.[32] Some were illegitimate, abandoned or simply removed from their homes. Some came with their parents' consent, though how 'informed' this consent was remains debatable. The connections between the children and their families were often severed, since the orthodoxy of the day was that child immigrants had the best chance of 'a fresh start' in a new country if all ties with their families were broken. The trauma that might follow a complete rupture from parents—however dysfunctional their relationship might have been—was not appreciated fully. Beyond this, many children were vulnerable to exploitative work demands and emotional abuse. The degree of sexual abuse is hard to determine given the absence of data for the pre-1945 period.[33]

Of one thing we can be certain: many thousands of immigrants who arrived in the 1920s were plunged within a few years into the maelstrom of the Great Depression. Many, such as the Italians employed in the north Queensland sugar industry, would stay in work but find themselves the object of xenophobic protest. Others, like those who had support from middle-class 'Big Brothers', found help in their search for work. Yet others stayed in rural employment with minimal if any pay, but at least with food and accommodation provided. But many presumably swelled the ranks of the urban unemployed. A vocal minority claimed that they were victims of 'a confidence trick' and demanded that they be repatriated to the United Kingdom. As we shall see, the Australian governments that had brought immigrants halfway across the world had little interest in helping them to reverse that journey.

What of the 'markets'? As Bruce saw it, these meant not just global markets for Australia's primary industries but imperial preference: that is, a system of mutually agreed duties and tariffs whereby Australian and British goods would gain privileged access to the other's markets.[34] Some such tariffs and duties were already in place, but Bruce aimed for a more extensive system. At the 1923 Imperial Conference, he proposed a model of graduated tariffs that would make the British Empire a self-sufficient food and agricultural community. His case was a measured one, backed by copious statistics prepared by the effective Australian and dried-fruit industry lobbyist Frank Lidgett McDougall. Born into a family whose name was 'literally a household word in Britain'—McDougall's grandfather had made a fortune in flour milling and agricultural chemicals—McDougall had migrated to South Australia in 1909 where he grew fruit on a Renmark property he tellingly named 'Purgatory'! From 1923, he became a key adviser to Bruce. With complementary personalities and skills, they formed a 'long and productive association', not only while Bruce was prime minister but when, as high commissioner in London (1933–45), he represented Australia at the League of Nations and was chair of the Food and Agricultural Organization in Geneva.[35]

For a time it seemed that the British might make the desired tariff concessions to Australia, but domestic politics intervened. Tariffs on primary imports were political dynamite, in that they would raise the price of food for domestic consumers. The British Treasury, too, feared losing revenue if existing tariffs on imports were reduced. Thus, in the election campaign of December 1923 the Conservative prime minister Stanley Baldwin promised not to tax foodstuffs. The minority Labour government that then came to power also refused to support imperial preference. When Baldwin returned to power later in 1924, he renounced protectionism and 'acquiesced in five years of free-trade orthodoxy'.[36]

In compensation the Baldwin government offered to support imperial trade through a system of so-called 'voluntary preference'.[37] Aggressive marketing and promotional campaigns would encourage the British public to *choose* to purchase goods produced by Australia and other parts of the British Empire. A specially constituted Empire Marketing Board launched a wondrously inventive campaign from 1926 on. It produced advertisements in national and local newspapers, created posters to be displayed on more than 1700 hoardings in 450 British cities and towns, organised 60 empire 'shopping weeks', filled British windows with display material, made radio broadcasts, sent educational materials to schools, and produced documentaries (the board can claim to have founded the British documentary film movement). These various media promoted not only specific commodities—Australian wheat,

New Zealand lamb, Irish bacon, Singaporean pineapples and so on. They also sold 'the idea of Empire', a family of 'kith and kin', a system of complementary economies and 'a cooperative venture' stretching across the globe.[38] Maps that made cartography 'the servant of ideology' positioned Britain at the centre of the 'highways of Empire'. Australia was helpfully relocated in the middle of the Pacific, while New Zealand was stretched to the equator.[39] One map of Australia did not feature the state capitals, preferring to populate 'a pleasantly, if optimistically, green Australia with wheat, sheep, cattle and a few desultory kangaroos'.[40] Giant kiwis promoted New Zealand lamb. The non-white colonies, meanwhile, were depicted as exotic outposts of empire in racialised terms. Half-naked Africans bore pineapples and shields, 'natives' toiled while white officers lounged, and scantily dressed Asian women cultivated rice. It was a construction of empire that resonated well with that of Bruce and other loyalists, and Australia participated enthusiastically in the work of the Empire Marketing Board (McDougall was on its executive and provided much of the voluminous data it generated). Posters were displayed widely in public places in Australian railway stations and shop windows, while major stores held their own empire shopping weeks.

Yet it all seemed to make little difference. The proportion of British imports from Australia did not improve markedly.[41] Australia, which continued to increase British preferential tariffs in the mid- to late 1920s, sustained a persistent trade imbalance with the United Kingdom. Patterns of trade were changing, with Australia turning from the empire towards Western Europe, Japan and the United States. In essence, then, imperial rhetoric, however ingeniously promulgated, could not compete with pragmatism and the 'realities of supply and price'.[42] But while the Empire Marketing Board, which had been chronically underfunded by Treasury, was abolished in 1933, the imagination that infused its various campaigns—of an interdependent imperial trading system—survived, and would soon have its day. When many nations turned to autarky and economic nationalism in the early 1930s, Australia continued to see imperial preference as its salvation. In 1932, Britain, having adopted its own general tariff, would at last be willing to respond to the appeals of Australia and other Dominions.

CHAPTER 5

The voracious borrower

No aspect of Bruce's 'men, money and markets' agenda had greater implications for Australia's future than 'money'. In the 1920s, the federal and state governments borrowed huge amounts on the London money market and to a lesser extent in New York. This funding helped create lasting and useful social assets for the suburban population and the growing manufacturing sector: water and sewerage facilities, electricity, sealed roads, and telephones. Public works also generated many employment opportunities for Australian workers. But external loans became increasingly difficult to service, especially in the later years of the decade as Australia's balance of trade deteriorated. Well before the New York stock market crash of October 1929, Australia was sinking into recession and struggling to service its debts. The threat of default on public borrowings would come to dominate politics at all levels of government, and place immense constraints on the policy options for dealing with the social distress that many Australians faced.

Like the desire for immigration and the search for markets, Australia's pursuit of external capital was not new. Nor, for that matter, was it exceptional. All countries in the early stages of industrialisation required significant investments of capital. In the nineteenth century, Australia had borrowed heavily. In the 1880s, by most estimates at least 45 per cent of investment was financed externally. The figure in the 1920s was, by comparison, relatively modest: 20 per cent, rising to average about 25 per cent in the last quarter. But Australia's reliance on external capital sources in the 1920s posed at least two problems: first, perhaps 70 per cent of the capital inflow in the 1920s took the form of borrowing by public authorities, and was added to the already existing war debt; and, second, these borrowings were often used to fund infrastructure to support closer settlement, suburban expansion and other projects that did not increase Australian productivity in the short term. Nor did they generate the export revenue that could, in turn, service Australia's overseas borrowings.[1]

Most of the capital Australia borrowed in the 1920s was raised through the floating of bonds issues, whereby investors agreed to lend the government money for a specific period in exchange for periodic interest payments. London was the traditional source of capital, not just because of imperial sentiment but because the British *Colonial Stock Act 1900* had given the Dominions a privileged borrowing position vis-à-vis domestic borrowers by conferring trustee status on Dominion stocks.[2] Thus, when the City of London sought to re-establish itself as the centre of international trade and payments after the chaos of World War I, Australia had little difficulty in having its flotations in London underwritten at low rates of interest and without much prelim-inary scrutiny.[3] On occasion, however, Britain suspended overseas lending: notably in the immediate post-war years and just before it returned, in 1925, to the gold standard (that is, the valuing of sterling by a direct link to gold).[4] Access to the London loan market was also disrupted by frequent movements of speculative balances within Europe, by the British government's own funding needs, and, in 1928–29, by the flow of capital to feed the frenetic New York stock-market boom. All this made it difficult to regulate Australian borrowings in a way that kept the inflow of funds and levels of expen-diture within Australia relatively stable.[5] Beyond this, London money could come with political strings attached, given the conservatism of the City brokers and their connections with British landed society.

In 1920 Edward (Ted) Theodore, as premier of Queensland, confronted 'a storm of opposition' in London financial circles when he passed legislation aimed at substantially, and retrospectively, raising Crown rents on pastoral properties. Although these rents were artificially low, conservative landed interests viewed this change as 'repudiation, pure and simple'.[6] Their outrage, it should be noted, was fuelled by Sir Robert Philp, a former premier and founding member of Burns Philp, a shipping company that had a history of blackbirding—that is, enslaving Pacific Island labourers to work on sugar plantations—and now operated as merchants, shipping agents and plantation owners in the region. In 1920 Philp led a delegation to London to galvanise opposition to Theodore and deter loans to his government—all the while denying that he was engaged in any conspiracy.[7] Ultimately, Theodore would manage to get some assistance from the Bank of England, but in the interim in 1921 he had to turn to New York for funds. Only after reaching a deal with the Queensland pastoralists was Theodore able to return to the London market for the conversion of a £13 million loan that matured in 1924.[8] More generally, the radical ambitions of his government were accordingly tempered.

The Commonwealth and New South Wales governments, too, turned to the New York market in 1925, when they could not access enough funds from London. Although there were some regrets about drifting from the British fold, the emerging financial power of the United States gave an air of inevitability to this adjustment. As the *Newcastle Morning Herald* suggested, the world order in the Asia–Pacific region was changing in the aftermath of World War I:

> the greater the American stake in Australia the more certain we shall be of a Big Brother, when we need him—if ever we do. For assuredly at the same time as the flag follows finance, the sword, if wanted, follows the flag. And though we rejoice in our British connection it is not without some satisfaction that we shall be able to contemplate two arrows to our bow where formerly there was only one . . . America is a Pacific Power in real earnest, and so is Japan, and possibly China will become one . . . The United States allows no liberties to be taken where the dollar shines.[9]

By 1927, then, New York had emerged as an alternative source of finance to London. Australia took advantage of the competition between the two markets and the issuing houses in London and New York. But it was on the London money market that Australia became notorious as a voracious borrower.

Between 1923 and 1929 Australian governments absorbed more than a quarter of total overseas government issues in London and about a seventh of new overseas capital raisings of any kind.[10] In the period 1925–28, it borrowed more than double the combined total for Africa and the Far and Middle East. In the thirteen months between July 1927 and July 1928 alone, Australia raised ten separate cash loans, for a total capital sum of £63.5 million.[11]

It was extravagant and dangerous. The greatest risk for a debtor is not the amount borrowed but the costs of servicing the debt. This became an increasing burden for Australian governments as the 1920s progressed. The cost of interest and dividends remittances overseas rose sharply from 16 per cent of exports in 1919–20 to 28 per cent in 1928–29.[12] In order to pay interest, Australian governments rolled over their debts by taking out new loans to repay the existing ones—somewhat akin, in family terms, to using a credit card to pay the mortgage. When long-term funds were not available, they borrowed on overdraft, which then became the first charge on the next cash loan.[13]

The risks associated with high levels of borrowing were clear at the time. Yet Australia's capacity for formulating and managing national economic policy was rudimentary in the early to mid-1920s.[14] The Commonwealth Treasury, a pre-eminent policy adviser today, had little influence over the federal government. Staffed at the senior level by accountants, its role was confined to supervising the collection of government revenue and expenditure, and managing loans issues (together with the Commonwealth Bank). Professional economists were only just emerging as an external source of policy research and advice. Political economy had been part of university curriculums for many years, but the Faculty of Commerce at the University of Melbourne was established only in 1925. Under the leadership of the New Zealand–born Douglas Copland—of whom we shall hear more—the Economic Society of Australia and New Zealand was created, together with its journal *Economic Record*. Copland had earlier revived economics at the University of Tasmania, a state that in 1919 appointed perhaps the first official statistician to advise on financial and economic matters, the Cambridge-educated former state Labor parliamentarian L.F. Giblin.[15]

In the early 1920s, central banking, too, was in its infancy. The Commonwealth Bank, created in 1911, was primarily a savings and trading bank, although it had been heavily involved in managing the federal debt during World War I, when the Commonwealth began borrowing overseas for the first time.[16] In 1924 Page, an energetic and proactive treasurer, tried to re-create the bank as a central bank, a bank of deposit, issue, discount, exchange and reserve. But little changed. The only central banking function the bank performed was controlling the note issue. Its board of directors consisted of men drawn from commerce and industry but with little or no banking experience. Even its chairman, the Scottish-Australian Sir Robert Gibson, was a man of limited financial and economic knowledge. Although he had a record of administrative competence and business acumen, he was suspicious of 'expert' advice and would become excessively rigid and inflexible in the years to come. The Commonwealth Bank, as he saw it, was the custodian of 'sound finance', not an institution that might work with government to implement such policies as the political leaders thought socially and politically desirable.

The private trading banks, the major ones of which were in Melbourne and Sydney, likewise insisted throughout the 1920s on their right to determine their own policies, guiding the economy as they saw fit. They successfully resisted Page's attempts in 1924 to make it mandatory for them to lodge 5 per cent of their deposits with the Commonwealth Bank. In the years before the Depression, these banks also controlled Australia's international reserves, mainly as sterling balances in London banks, with the result that the Commonwealth lacked both accurate knowledge and control of these reserves.

The first efforts at national coordination of financial policy came in 1923, when federal and state politicians created the Loan Council.[17] The impetus for this change was the need to coordinate borrowings within Australia, since governments were competing for these as well as for external funds. The federal government faced the repayment of part of a 1918 public war loan and wanted to persuade as many of the public to manifest—yet again—an appropriate patriotic sentiment by not taking cash but converting their holdings into the new issue.[18] Within a few years, the council moved from being an advisory body to a statutory body. In 1927 the federal and state governments negotiated a new agreement amending federal–state financial relations, later ratified overwhelmingly by the Australian public in a referendum. A major development in the history of the federation, this ensured a central role for the Loan Council in national economic policy while making it the central authority for approving international borrowing. It determined the amounts to be borrowed each year and the conditions attached to loans, including interest rates. The states, however, retained control over their public works expenditure and could claim any political advantage that these projects won with their electorate.

In a portent of the disputes that lay ahead, New South Wales was absent from the Loan Council between June 1925 and October 1927. Its Labor premier at that time was the pugnacious Jack Lang, who insisted on his state's right to determine its rate of development and to borrow freely. Individual state loans, Lang argued, would be smaller and cheaper than larger loans raised by the Commonwealth. Moreover, since New South Wales was 'one of the strongest States in the Empire', he could not 'abrogate or weaken the right of the State Treasurer to approach the money market in any way and at any time he thinks fit'. Lang's leaving the Loan Council has been judged 'a typical Lang gesture combining his ingrained contrariness and lack of vision with his populist need to project himself as the strong man who could defy any force that seemed likely to oppress the masses'.[19] That said, state rights were dear to all premiers; and the Labor premier of Western Australia, Philip Collier, a much more moderate figure, was inclined to agree with Lang.[20]

One driver for the strengthening of the Loan Council was the mounting criticism of Australia's borrowings in London. As early as 1923, Joseph Cook, the former Liberal prime minister and now the high commissioner in London, had warned about anxieties within the City of London.[21] These were not entirely because of Australia's behaviour. Certain elements within the British Liberal Party, and economists such as John Maynard Keynes, were concerned about the levels of foreign investment generally. They argued that it was not necessarily in Britain's interests to allow such large capital outflows for development overseas. Should not these domestic savings be channelled towards local investment and the creation of employment at home?[22] To this concern was added an increasing scepticism about Australia's economic and financial policies. Advocates of free trade, such as Winston Churchill, Chancellor of the Exchequer from 1924 until 1929, looked askance at Australia's tariff walls, its use of bounties to support primary industry, and the maintenance of what outsiders believed to be an unduly high standard of living and an over-regulated labour market. Other officials were wearying of what they saw as Australia's unreasonable expectations of British largesse. During a 'long and unedifying wrangle' about the funding of assisted immigration, the Overseas Settlement Office in London complained that 'there is not quite the right spirit in Australia in regard to Empire Settlement . . . they think they can squeeze so much out of us'. Otto Niemeyer, too, continued to find reasons to judge Australia harshly. In 1926 he queried:

> How is [Australia] going to pay her way, if this process continues? She can only do it by increasing her exports and restricting, if she can, her imports. But owing to increased wages, etc., in Australia, resulting from lavish public works, it is becoming increasingly difficult for Australia to sell some of her main exports in world markets even with subsidies . . . Australia in fact already shows many signs of a country where public works out of loan moneys have been developed too rapidly for economic health.[23]

Even more damaging, as far as wider confidence in the City was concerned, was a survey of Australian finance by two London stockbrokers that was published to coincide with the 1926 Imperial Conference. This concluded that:

> In the whole British Empire there is no more voracious borrower than the Australian Commonwealth. Loan follows loan with disconcerting frequency. It may be a loan to pay off maturing loans, or a loan to pay the interest on existing loans, or a loan to repay temporary loans from the bankers . . . is the system safe? . . . It is, in fact, high time to ask the question—Is Australian finance sound?[24]

The authors of the report took particular issue with the rapid growth in Australian debt relative to national income; the rate of increase in government expenditure from consolidated revenue; and the competition between state-controlled concerns and private commercial interests. Objectively, some of this criticism was well founded. Sinking funds set aside for the gradual redemption of debt were 'totally inadequate in most states', and the prospectuses detailing share offers were 'written in the vaguest possible terms'. Australian governments seemed to accept their London borrowing status as an entitlement rather than a privilege.[25]

The 1926 survey, though widely circulated, did not have an immediate impact on the price of Australian stocks. But Bruce and Cook felt compelled to reassure the City of London. Bruce suggested at the 1926 Imperial Conference that a delegation of British businessmen come to Australia to investigate the economic situation. To British bankers he explained that Australia, as a new country with a limited population, needed governments to assume roles that in large countries might be left to private enterprise. The use of the money was 'productive', in the sense that new rural industries and more intensive production would greatly increase Australia's wealth, assets and its capacity to absorb new immigrants.[26] Some months later, in a well-advertised public lecture in Adelaide in July 1927, Bruce noted that a large part of Australia's public debt was the war debt—a 'dead-weight debt' that was being paid off systematically. Furthermore, a relatively small part of the war debt (less than a third) was owed to the British government, as opposed to the Australian public. (Rolling over debt was less difficult when the creditors were Australian.) Rehearsing the familiar trope of imperial loyalty, Bruce said: 'None would desire to challenge [this war debt] . . . it was incurred in order to enable Australia to play the great and wonderful part that was hers in support of the mother country and the Allied cause.'[27] As for the rest of Australia's debt, this was essential for the development of infrastructure, such as the Murray River irrigation scheme, that was beyond the capacity of the private sector to finance. No Australian government had ever defaulted on its debts and Australia was making adequate provision for repayment of all its obligations.

Still, the doubts persisted. In February 1928, an insurance company chairman in London warned Frank McDougall that his co-directors were keen to realise Australian securities because of their doubts as to Australia's immediate economic future. A few months later, the chairman of Barclays Bank conveyed to Richard Casey, Australia's liaison officer in Whitehall, his anxieties about 'a lack of soundness' in the way Australia was conducting itself. He claimed that 'Rightly or wrongly, [that criticism] was voiced daily by countless men in the

City in the interminable discussions and conversations that go on with regard to the securities that are on offer in the City'.[28] This might have been a farrago of rumour but confidence is everything on stock markets. From the mid-1920s on, Australian loans floated in London were chronically undersubscribed, leaving the underwriters to take up large amounts. At times, the prices of Australian securities on the London capital market even fell to the point where sinking fund money, accumulated each year to service the national debt, was used to buy up bonds and so increase the price.[29]

In late 1928, the British economic mission that Bruce had proposed in 1926 finally arrived, with broad terms of reference to review the state of the economy. It was also asked to advise on ways of developing resources in Australia and on matters of 'mutual economic interest' that might promote trade and increase settlement in Australia. All the delegation's members were nominated by the British government, and, after travelling some 20,000 kilometres and speaking to diverse groups of Australians, their conclusions were generally negative.[30] The development projects funded by external borrowings were judged to be inadequately planned. Insufficient consideration had been given to the markets for the commodities resulting from these projects; collaboration between states had been inadequate; and some schemes had been promoted by sectional interests without due regard to their financial or economic justification. Rather than pushing roads and railways into undeveloped territory, Australia should use land more intensively, exploiting the expertise of the newly established Council for Scientific and Industrial Research that Bruce had established in 1926. Moreover, the Australian government should restrict its borrowing in the future and ensure that the projects it funded were capable of becoming self-supporting within a reasonable amount of time. To be sure, the government had to play a role in major development projects such as the Murrumbidgee Irrigation Scheme, the Murray River scheme including the Hume Reservoir, and soldier settlement—the latter was 'a debt to honour to the returned soldiers'—but the levels of government activity should preferably be reduced to allow a greater role for private enterprise.

Beyond this, the report of the economic mission took issue with the three semi-sacred pillars of Australian economic policy: the tariff, the arbitration system and the basic wage. As 'the settled policy of Australia', the report said, protection possibly had benefits beyond the economic, but it risked giving inefficient industries too much assistance, for too long. Together with the arbitration acts, it had raised costs to a level that put 'an excessive and possibly even dangerous load upon the unsheltered primary industries' that had to compete in the world markets. Meanwhile, the practice of fixing wages by reference to a basic wage determined against an index of the cost of living was 'open to the gravest criticism as giving to the workers no interest in the reduction of the cost of living'. The arbitration system, too, needed reform that would eliminate the overlap and conflict between the Commonwealth and state jurisdictions.

It is hard not to hear the voice of Bruce in these strictures. He had already launched an assault on the arbitration system and the industrial power of the labour movement, an assault that would prove in 1929 to be his undoing politically (see chapters 6 and 7). Bruce must also have taken heart from the mission's conclusions that Australia's financial position was sound, in the sense that its national income and public revenue could cover the costs of government and service the public debt. Yes, Australia's frequent recourse to the loan market in recent years had to some extent damaged Australian credit, but the magnitude of the debt was not in itself 'evidence of an unwise policy'.

[Australia's] creditors have no cause whatever for present anxiety, because she is still borrowing well within her actual and potential resources, but . . . she has not in past years always borrowed wisely, and . . . she has pledged to too great an extent those future resources, and mortgaged too deeply that future prosperity upon which she can reasonably reckon, thus throwing the burden of her borrowings upon future generations who will have their own needs to meet.

The burden was actually about to fall on the current, not the future, generation. Although the price of Australian securities held up after the failure of the January 1929 issue, by August 1929 the price of Commonwealth stock was falling. The external interest bill was rising, while the prices for wheat and wool exports were collapsing. Investors started to sell Australian stocks and the orgy of borrowing was over. Australia soon faced the unthinkable: national insolvency and default on her debts. As Copland wrote in 1934, 'Australia had worshipped false economic gods for many years. 1930 was her nemesis.'[31]

CHAPTER 6

Recession

By many indicators the expansion of the Australian economy in the early to mid-1920s had stalled by 1927. Competition from cheaper imports increased sharply, and investment in manufacturing and industry declined. Tariffs kept rising but domestic manufacturers found their profits squeezed as local costs rose. In retrospect, it is possible to identify significant structural problems as labour and capital shifted from the previously productive agricultural sector to the less productive manufacturing and tertiary services. Even more troublingly, towards the end of the decade, Australia's terms of trade deteriorated alarmingly as prices for its staple exports collapsed. The full implications of this downturn started to be felt well before the New York stock exchange crash of 1929, and had early political consequences. From 1925 to 1929, Prime Minister Bruce, convinced that Australia had to become more competitive, embarked on an increasingly confrontational crusade to reduce wages. His assault on the arbitration system would ultimately force him out of office in October 1929, leaving the hapless leader of the ALP, James Scullin, to gain office just as the world slid into depression.

◆

For many Australians the poverty that was so visible in the Depression years began much earlier—or had always been their lot. As early as 1921 to 1923, thousands of families in Newcastle, New South Wales, came 'close to starvation' when the iron and steel plants of BHP and Lysaght closed, albeit temporarily, in the face of competition from overseas suppliers.[1] An out-of-work returned soldier published a 'Digger's Lament' in the *Newcastle Sun* in April 1922:

> Still on in search of work I plod,
> Rebuffs give me the blues; . . .
> Now like a hungry, beaten whelp,
> I throw away my pride,
> And ask you one and all to help
> The men you've cast aside . . .
> They starved in trenches over there,
> And now they're starving here.

Newcastle's industries recovered somewhat in the mid-1920s, but the town continued to have a floating workforce of unskilled and casual labourers. It soon developed one of those quintessential markers of economic depression across the world, 'grim jerry-built shantytowns'.[2] Constructing 'humpies' from whatever they could scrounge—canvas, corn bags, kerosene tins, old timber, freshly cut logs, abandoned tramcars, large pipes and tanks—the homeless would camp on Crown or public land, where local councils charged nominal, if any, rent.

The working-class suburbs of the capital cities were also struggling with poverty well before 1929. In the early 1920s, Footscray, in the west of Melbourne, had scores of families 'so destitute that parents could do little more than put the barest of fare before their children'. Unemployment grew to the point where the Footscray Council was 'at its wit's end' by early 1928. Labour activists demanded that the council provide 'work not charity' and threatened to march on Parliament; but the council was caught in its own poverty trap: its revenue from rates was shrinking as impoverished property holders defaulted on payments. By late 1929, the immigrant had become the scapegoat. In the face of public protests against Italian workers and stall-holders at the Footscray market, the council confined its aid to locals, as opposed to 'foreign residents'. It also decided, in late 1929, that all tenders and contracts for road and buildings works would be granted only to 'ratepayers of Australian and British birth'.[3]

In another Melbourne suburb, Richmond, unemployment was so high by 1928 that the resources of the council and charitable organisations were stretched to the limit: this was despite their giving support only to needy and 'deserving' families, as the charitable norms of the day dictated.[4] The one local non-government organisation that received any financial support from the state government, the Richmond Ladies' Benevolent Society, ran out of funds by October 1928.[5] Other voluntary organisations, such as the Catholic St Vincent de Paul and the Salvation Army, had to rely on parishioners, the council and other local generosity.[6] In the face of growing need, the council, which became the hub of charitable efforts, created the Mayor of Richmond's Unemployed Relief Fund. Its official organiser, the president of the football club, J.H. Archer, placed collection boxes at 34 hotels across Richmond. Dances were held at the cricket ground pavilion, donations collected at football matches and fundraising concerts staged in local theatres.[7] The town clerk solicited support from local businesses: 'We are all apt to become selfishly indifferent to the misery and anguish of our fellow beings,' he wrote in July 1928, 'but the amount of distress at present existing calls for a united effort to at least see that they are not deprived of the necessities of life.'[8] Ominously, some companies replied that they could not make a contribution since they were already struggling to keep their employees in work: 'truthfully speaking', wrote one businessman making malt for brewing, we 'have paid away in wages more than the industry should rightly have been called upon to bear'.[9] Hearing of Richmond's need, farmers beyond the municipality donated tons of potatoes.[10] The Salvation Army issued free soup and bread to some 450 people every day, and provided 100 children, many of whom 'would have been sent to bed hungry', with a tea of cocoa, bread and jam, biscuits and sometimes cake.[11] All this was in 1928!

Similar scenes were being played out in South Australia, a state that would be savagely hit by the Great Depression proper. In December 1927, the local Catholic Church newspaper noted that, with cuts in public programs, 'retrenchment is the order of the day'. 'The year which is just closing has not been a good one for South Australia and its people.'[12] By 1929, unemployment had reached 17.8 per cent, compared with the national average of 13.1 per cent.[13] On 18 February 1929, a procession of unemployed made its way to Government House, claiming that some 7000 men and 2000 'girls' were without work in the state, and only twenty jobs were being offered daily at the government's labour bureau.[14] In response, the Adelaide City Council, with the newspaper proprietor and philanthropist Sir John Langdon Bonython as mayor, launched an appeal for funds to assist married men and their families, while forming unemployment relief committees in various districts.[15] By May 1929, the council was also considering whether it could employ men to work on footpath construction and the levelling of the banks of the River Torrens between the weir and Hindmarsh Island Bridge.[16] Again the unemployed resorted to erecting tin and bag humpies, in this case on the riverbanks. Here some men contemplated 'the strange ways of a world that was eager for [their services] in 1914', but now denied them a job.[17] Such was their need that the South Australian Soldiers' Fund distributed between March 1929 and March 1930 the highest amount of any year since the war ended.[18]

Port Adelaide became a destination for many seeking work. But, even in better years, unemployment in this suburb had never fallen below 10 per cent. As early as 1926, the local council introduced a ration scheme and worked with the (Methodist) Central Mission to give aid to 'the genuinely homeless and hungry fellows to procure the necessities of life, if only for a few days until they get work'. A camp for unemployed men sprang up in nearby Rosewater, and the state government supplied 100 lamb carcasses in the winter of 1928.[19] The council itself launched a number of public works programs such as road building, while that standard philanthropic response to social need, a committee chaired by the lady mayoress, raised money to provide boots, blankets and clothing for the unemployed.[20] Still, the Labor member for Hindmarsh, a compassionate Methodist and campaigner for workers' rights, Norman Makin, told federal parliament in February 1929 that men, women and children were 'starving', while in many homes all the furniture had been sold to buy food.[21] Further north in the state, at Port Augusta, a town dependent on the railway that crossed Australia from east to west, the mayor reported in August 1928 that some 60 single men, who were without rations, were 'absolutely destitute and sick'.[22]

Similar distress was evident in Perth, where the unemployment problem was so severe by July 1928 that the city council convened a meeting of all religious denominations, and representatives of business and industry, to discuss how to stimulate employment and provide relief.[23] According to the president of the Western Australia Winegrowers Association, the local wine export trade was 'dead', throwing many soldier-settlers into financial difficulties.[24] Queensland, too, was suffering a severe recession from 1926, in this case largely because of that scourge of Australian farmers, drought, which lasted from 1926 to 1929. Sheep and cattle numbers dropped alarmingly, as did the value of wool exports. At least those out of work in Queensland had access to an unemployment relief scheme, introduced by Theodore's Labor government in 1922, with the aim of alleviating the short-term seasonal unemployment among shearers and sugar workers.

Finally, in Tasmania, the 'desperate' situation in early 1929 was captured in a letter to the premier from a father of two. The Benevolent Society gave his family a weekly allowance of 1 pound (450 grams) sugar, 6 ounces (170 grams) tea, a small tin of jam, 1 pound (450 grams) rice or oatmeal, 3 pounds (1.4 kilograms) meat, and bread. He did not want charity—he wanted work— but the 'business people of Hobart are quite indifferent as to whether we starve or not . . . Surely we have the right to live, & not live in a continual state of semi-starvation?'[25]

Beyond the cities thousands of small farms were collapsing. The stories of these personal tragedies are legion, but Bill Ince was typical of many. He took up a soldier-settlement block on the Atherton Tableland, Queensland, but after three years 'walked off, carrying our suitcases'. According to his son, Ken, 'He was absolutely shattered at his failure and just bloody well crawled away. He shot through and left his debts.' Bill did ultimately manage to find work in Castle Creek, where his family was housed in a tent measuring ten by twelve feet (3 by 3.7 metres), with a fly in front as a dining room. The kitchen was in the open air. But Bill fell out with his employer, and the family was evicted. Ken recalled:

Mother had us, two tiny children, and we were both down with sandy blight [trachoma], blind with it. The tent was pulled down over their heads! It was late in the day and they got everything on the dray and went as far as they could in the fading light. The old man just lit a little cow dung fire and, in the morning, we were still there, huddling in the smoke, afraid to move because of the sand flies.

Remembering this incident Bill's daughter, Margaret, later said:

Before mother died she cracked up . . . She'd cry. She'd say, 'They pulled the tent down and we had nowhere to go!' Crying on my shoulder, as an old lady, fifty years later, 'But Margaret, we had nowhere to go!' Mother came from Kent: a lovely, green, civilised area.[26]

Human tragedies such as these were common in marginal farming lands such as the Mallee, in the north-west of Victoria and the hinterland of the Murray in South Australia. The south of the Victorian Mallee had first been settled, with some success, in the 1880s, but from 1924 to 1928, agriculture was pushed out into the region around Millewa. The unreliable rainfall and water supplies combined with the excessive clearing of the land for wheat production to create an undulating landscape of drifting sandhills. Then came the dust and sandstorms and collapsing wheat prices. It was Australia's own Dust Bowl, years before the environmental catastrophe of America's Great Plains. One returned soldier near Loxton, South Australia, lamented: 'I often wonder why when I blew up [at Ypres] I ever came down again. True, I did fairly well up to 1926, but since then it's been war to make a living.'[27] A British immigrant settled near Mildura said in February 1929 that 'even a bumper harvest will not put things right for us. Many of us are literally anxious to know where our next meal is coming from.'[28] Some families gave up and moved to camps dotted along the River Murray. Others hung on, without 'even elementary comforts'. As a journalist visiting the 'New Mallee' in September 1929 wrote:

The dwellings—huts of bark, hessian or iron—were intended originally to serve only as temporary shelters until the profits from the first crop had made it possible to build suitable homes. As there have been no crops, the temporary shelters have become permanent homes. It is not uncommon to find families of 8, 10, and 12 persons living in hessian humpies of two or three rooms. The women strive bravely to make them as comfortable as their meagre resources will permit.

A mother of six children wept as, with a sweep of her hand, she gestured at the surrounding bare sandy landscape: 'I come from beautiful Devon where everything is green.' Still, she declared that she would battle on with her husband until 'they had good seasons and achieved success'. Her immediate wish was to give her children some respite from the dust and sand.[29] Such resilience almost defies understanding, but it attests to a stoicism and endurance that countless thousands of Australians would display as the economic disaster deepened.

Prime Minister Bruce was separated from these Australians by an almost unbridgeable class divide, but he was well aware that the country was slipping into recession. From 1925 to 1929, he launched an assault on the arbitration system and the trade union movement in an effort to address what he saw as the root cause of Australia's economic problems: the costs of production and the level of wages. The escalating confrontation between government and unions was evident in the frequency and scale of strikes. In the year that Bruce came to power, 1923, the number of working days lost to strikes was 1.15 million; in 1929 it peaked at 4.47 million.[30] In mid-1925, the ever-volatile waterfront erupted when the Arbitration Court deregistered the Federated Seamen's Union. Under the leadership of the radical Tom Walsh, the union had been employing disruptive tactics, such as delaying a ship's sailing until workers' demands for better conditions had been met.[31] When negotiations between the owners and workers failed to reach any resolution, the union called a general stoppage. Over a period of six weeks, some 46 vessels were laid up at Sydney and 24 in Melbourne, throwing out of work several thousand seamen, and many others in industries that depended on shipping.

For Bruce, reliable shipping was a vital national interest.[32] There was no air cargo at this time; and, with his family business in importing, Bruce had developed something of a 'special relationship' with the chairman of the shipping company P&O, Lord Inchcape. More ideologically, radical unionism threatened 'the kind of peaceful, prosperous, scientific and rational domestic and international order' to which Bruce aspired.[33] The maritime strike also seemed to testify to the penetration of communism into the body politic that conservatives so feared. Walsh, and his wife Adela, a member of the famous Pankhurst family of reformers in Britain, had been foundation members of the Communist Party of Australia, although they had left by 1925. Bruce thus rushed through Parliament in July 1925 two pieces of legislation: the *Navigation Act*, which threatened to undercut Australian wages by opening coastal trade to British and foreign ships; and the *Immigration Act*, which allowed foreign-born agitators to be deported during any 'serious industrial disturbance prejudicing or threatening the peace, order or good government of the Commonwealth'.

Armed with this legislation, Bruce declared an industrial emergency when the maritime strike continued in solidarity with British seamen whose wages had been reduced in the United Kingdom. A Deportation Board was established to deal with the Irish-born Walsh and the Dutch-born Assistant Secretary of the Seamen's Union, Jacob Johnson. Premier Lang, however, refused to make any of his New South Wales Supreme Court judges available to serve, or to instruct his state police to enforce the Commonwealth law. So, after rushing through further legislation to establish a new federal police force—called, in a classic oxymoron, 'peace officers'—Bruce decided to put the matter to the Australian electorate in November 1925.

In the election campaign, Bruce played the 'law and order' card for all it was worth. The great issue, he said, was 'whether this country is to be governed by the Parliament duly elected by the people, under our democratic and constitutional form of government, or whether their authority is to be flouted and the destinies of the people determined by irresponsible extremists, who are attempting to arrogate to themselves an autocratic dictatorship over this nation'.[34] Nationalist posters spread a similar message, depicting the ALP as a donkey ridden by a Bolshevik, or as revolutionaries shooting citizens in front of a burning church. It could almost have been the Germans rampaging through Belgium in 1914 again. But the message seems to have resonated with voters. When 90.4 per cent of the electorate voted—it was the first election in which voting was compulsory—Bruce's Nationalists and the Country Party gained 51 seats in the House of Representatives. The ALP, now under the leadership of the innocuous Matthew Charlton, won only 24. In the Senate, the coalition won all 22 seats on offer, leaving it with a control of 28 to eight.

Bruce now had a strong mandate for his anti-union platform. Charlton, too, blamed the seamen's strike for his electoral loss.[35] But the High Court then ruled the deportation of Walsh and Johnson invalid, on the grounds that the unionists were British subjects and had lived so long in Australia that they could not be classified as immigrants. Mortified, Bruce sacked his attorney-general, Littleton Groom, who had drafted the legislation, replacing him with the brilliant, if somewhat desiccated Melbourne barrister John Latham. The *Crimes Act* was quickly amended to declare unlawful any association that advocated or encouraged revolutionary and seditious activities, or the destruction of property owned by the Commonwealth or used in international and interstate trade.

Bruce's next target was the arbitration system, which, he claimed, fuelled industrial disputation and high wages, not least because of the overlapping jurisdictions between state and Commonwealth courts. Although the jurisdiction of the federal court was confined generally to disputes that transcended state boundaries, unions often moved between state and federal courts, picking out the eyes of the respective awards. In September 1926, then, Bruce sought public approval, via a referendum, for an extension of the powers of the federal parliament to legislate with respect to corporations, trusts, unions and employer associations, and to protect the public from any actual or probable interruption to essential services. But Australians voted no—just as they had in 1911, 1913 and 1919, when previous governments had sought to increase federal powers over the economy.

Thwarted again, Bruce turned to one of his favourite devices, a royal commission, to inquire into the efficiency of the Australian Constitution, including its provisions on industrial relations. In the event, this recommended by a majority that the Commonwealth should cease to have powers over industrial relations, but it did not report until November 1929. In the meantime, in December 1927, Bruce introduced new legislation that empowered the Commonwealth Court of Conciliation and Arbitration to conduct secret ballots of trade unionists, impose penal regulations against strikes, and indict anyone who tried to stop others from working in accordance with the terms of a valid award. The legislation also stated that courts determining industrial awards should take into account the 'probable economic effect' upon the industries concerned. This was a radical departure from the established principle that wages should be set, not by the industry's profitability, but by the needs of a worker and his family. Scullin, who replaced Charlton as ALP leader in April 1928, called the legislation 'a declaration of war against the organized workers of Australia'.[36]

The stakes continued to rise when, in September 1928, Justice George Beeby, one of Bruce's appointees to the Commonwealth Court of Conciliation and Arbitration, adjusted the waterside workers' award in a way that removed several concessions the union had won over the past few years. Even though the union leadership was inclined to accept the Beeby award, a number of port branches, from Fremantle to north Queensland, refused to work. With shipping immobilised, Bruce blasted through Parliament yet another piece of restrictive legislation, the *Transport Workers Act*. Soon to become notorious as the 'Dog Collar Act', this required that all waterfront employees, unionists or not, obtain a licence to work, which the government could cancel if the worker refused to work under a valid award. The effect was to open the wharves formally to non-union labour.

The waterfront erupted in violence as non-union labourers made their way to the docks under police protection. In early November 1928, a group of unionists in Melbourne stormed Princes Pier and showered police with metal that happened to be piled on the wharf. As a press report recorded:

The police then drew their revolvers, and fired more than 50 shots into the air. This caused a lull for a few moments, and then the strikers broke up into two parties, one of which jumped down on to the beach and tried to clamber back on to the pier to the rear of the police, but as fast as they reached the decking they were thrown back, between 30 and 40 of them falling into the sea . . . a large party of strikers, who had previously been little more than onlookers, dashed along the pier. The position of the police was now a desperate one, and after a final warning had been given and more shots fired into the air, the sub-inspector ordered his men to fire into the crowd. Four of the unionists fell, and that stopped the advance as if by magic.[37]

One of the injured strikers, Allan Whittaker, later died of agonising complications from a bullet wound in the jaw. He happened to be a Gallipoli veteran, permanently incapacitated by a wound to the ankle suffered on the day of landing in April 1915. A coronial inquest in April 1929, however, judged Whittaker's death to be 'necessary' and justified, not, as the unions saw it, 'murder' at the hands of 'capitalism's assassins'.[38]

In Adelaide, the atmosphere on the docks became so tense in early October that the police called on citizens to support them in protecting the non-union workers. Some 2000 business leaders, members of the professions, students and returned soldiers flocked to join the Citizens' Defence Brigade.[39] Their role, the authorities stressed, was purely defensive, and the 'wartime memories' they evoked as they took up rifles and bayonets and established their camp at Fort Largs, near the docks of Port Adelaide, seemed to invest them with a moral legitimacy.[40] They were not, as the Adelaide *News* saw it, strikebreakers but rather 'excellent types of citizens', who once again were 'answering the call'.[41] With the forces of the state so solidly behind the use of non-union labour, the waterside workers had no choice but to capitulate. When they did so, there were often few jobs left for them, and many joined the burgeoning unemployed.

Caught up in this conflict, the Bruce–Page government was losing its hold on power. When it faced the electorate once more in November 1928, it found a more formidable opponent in Scullin. Originating from Ballarat and now holding the seat of Yarra in Melbourne's inner east, he had been a grocer, an organiser for the AWU and the editor of a labour newspaper. By the 1920s, Scullin's earlier firebrand, pro-Irish and socialist convictions had mellowed, but he retained a strong commitment to social justice, the White Australia policy and high protection for manufacturing industries. An effective orator in the 1928 campaign, he also articulated a powerful case against the federal government's mismanagement of the economy, especially its increased budget deficits, and the 'appalling number of unemployed'.[42] Travelling some 16,000 kilometres and giving scores of speeches, Scullin promised—to cite only the most important policy proposals—a review of Australia's borrowing practices and public works programs, further protection for manufacturing, reform of the Commonwealth Bank to make it a 'People's Bank' as originally conceived, unemployment insurance, a review of old age and invalid pensions, and some modification of the arbitration system that was currently inimical to industrial peace.

All this was not enough to win power, but the Nationalist–Country Party coalition was reduced by nine seats, to 42. The ALP increased its members of the House of Representatives from 23 to 29—although significantly for the future, it held only seven of 36 seats in the Senate. Among the new parliamentarians were men who would dominate the ALP's future: John Curtin, a journalist who won Fremantle; Ben Chifley, a former train driver who won Macquarie in New South Wales; and J.A. Beasley, 'the darling of Sydney Trades Hall', who won West Sydney.[43] Theodore was already in federal parliament, after relinquishing the Queensland premiership and winning a by-election for the Sydney seat of Dalley in January 1927. It was not the victory the ALP wanted, but national government was almost within its grasp.

CHAPTER 7

Over the cliff

During 1929, Australia slipped from recession into depression. As it did so, Bruce continued his crusade against organised labour and the arbitration system, but the problems of the Australian economy remained intractable. All that the prime minister achieved was his own political demise and the further polarisation of Australian politics. The legacy that the incoming Labor government under Scullin inherited in October 1929 was a toxic mix of an aggrieved union movement, soaring unemployment and national debts of such a scale that the policy options for dealing with the emerging social and economic crisis were excruciatingly limited.

The year began with another major industrial dispute, this time within the timber industry.[1] In January 1929, Justice Lionel Lukin, another of Bruce's recent appointments to the Commonwealth Court of Conciliation and Arbitration, reduced the wages of timber workers and set their working week at 48 hours, rather than the 44-hour week many of them already enjoyed. When the workers insisted on continuing under the old award, Lukin deemed them to be on strike. Bruce ignored the advice of Latham and invoked penal sanctions against the union. The court itself ordered a secret ballot of union members. It seemed, Theodore told a Sydney audience of over 3000, that the court no longer had the character of 'a fair, reasonable, unbiased tribunal'. Australia enjoyed 'less freedom than it had had for ten years past. Liberty was slowly being filched from the public, and especially from the organised workers.'[2] A conference of federal unions, convened by the recently formed Australasian Council of Trade Unions (ACTU), decided to boycott the Arbitration Court.[3]

The Arbitration Court could order a secret ballot, but it could not command compliance. Only 40 per cent of the possible votes in the ballot were cast, and the vast majority of the recorded votes opposed a return to work.[4] The ballot, meanwhile, provided the strikers with an energising agency. In Sydney, where the strike was longest and most tenacious, a mass rally ceremonially burned unused ballot papers, so-called 'love letters for Lukin'. The crowd flew the red flag, and sang 'The Internationale' and 'Solidarity Forever' while burning an effigy of the bearded Lukin.[5] The strikers also picketed the timber mills. As one later recalled: 'We used to . . . try and keep the scabs out [and] jeer at them as the loads left the yards. Every load of timber that left the yards with a scab driver had to have three or four policemen with them to protect the timber. We had some effect . . . but we never managed to stop them entirely.'[6] The wives of strikers joined the pickets, spitting in the scabs' faces, throwing dirty dishwashing water over them, and allegedly attacking one man with a cork impregnated with needles.[7] In the tightly knit working-class suburb of Balmain, women collected donations from factories and workshops, vegetables and meat were supplied from the market, the local butcher cut up the meat, and food was distributed to families in proportion to their size. Beyond local relief committees, the strikers also drew support from the New South Wales Labor Council and the ACTU.[8]

It was a demonstration of a powerful community solidarity, of a kind that would sustain many working-class suburbs through the coming years. But the conservative press spied further evidence of 'the extent to which the Communist forces were directing the industrial and political Labour movement'.[9] In fact, the Communist Party did organise the demonstration at which Lukin's effigy was burned, and communist leaders Jock Garden and Jack Kavanagh were prominent in the strikers' cause, as were the communist auxiliaries the Militant Minority Movement and the Militant Women's Group.[10] Garden and Kavanagh were eventually arrested and fined, under state anti-picketing legislation, while the federal government moved to prosecute the secretary of the Melbourne Trades Hall Council, E.J. (Jack) Holloway, for inciting workers to strike against a valid award.

In this environment, the industrial peace conference that Bruce had promised during the 1928 election campaign collapsed when convened in February 1929. The timber workers' mass picketing continued throughout the year, and some timber companies were broken by the strike. But as the union ran out of funds and it seemed that the ALP might win the next federal election, the strikers reluctantly agreed to go back to work—although again not of all of them would regain their jobs.

The industrial unrest had now spread to the coalfields. The coal industry in New South Wales, with many small pits, had become increasingly unprofitable in the 1920s. Domestically, black coal was being displaced by brown coal and hydroelectricity. International markets were also shrinking as cheaper coal was being produced in greater volume in countries such as South Africa, India and China. By one estimate, New South Wales coal, which had been the cheapest in the world in 1913, was the among the most expensive in 1929.[11] Bruce thought the solution was yet another royal commission, while the New South Wales government offered in 1928 to reduce the price and subsidise coal if the coalmine owners and workers were willing to absorb some of the costs. In early March 1929, however, a group of mine owners in the northern coal district of Maitland–Newcastle locked out some employees from most of the biggest mines in an effort to force the unions to accept lower wages.[12] Nearly 10,000 miners (though not the 'safety men' who kept the mines free of water and fire, and maintained the ventilation equipment) were told that they would be dismissed if they did not accept the companies' terms.

The legality of this lockout was questionable, and Latham, under pressure from the ALP, announced on 21 March that a prosecution had been started against one of the most powerful and stubborn mine owners, John Brown. Three weeks later, however, Bruce announced at a conference of mine owners and miners that the prosecution had been withdrawn. The Opposition predictably trumpeted that there was one law for the rich, and another for the poor. As the representative for Hunter, New South Wales, told federal parliament during an acrimonious debate:

The Prime Minister has never shown the same action against the coal owners who have broken the law as he and the Attorney-General have shown against workers who have committed similar breaches. When you leave here to go to your various places you go to fulness [sic] and plenty. I am going into the midst of starvation, want, and degradation.[13]

Bruce's parliamentary majority was now fearfully thin. The 1928 election result had left the government exposed in the House to what Page called 'an irregular Opposition' of dissident Nationalists and rural independents.[14] Among them was the restless Hughes, who had not been offered a place in the Bruce–Page ministry when he lost the Nationalist leadership in 1923. Nor had he been placated with a prestigious exile in the high commission in London, as had prime ministers George Reid, Andrew Fisher and Joseph Cook before him. That said, Hughes had been relatively supportive of Bruce during his first term. Such bitterness as Hughes felt at his dethronement tended to be directed against Page and the Country Party, both of whom attracted the full blast of the man's incomparable invective.

By 1929, however, Hughes had become disaffected with many of Bruce's policies. These included the sale of the Commonwealth Shipping Line that Hughes had created during World War I, the 1927 financial agreement with the states, and, of course, Bruce's assault on the arbitration system and the trade union movement, Hughes' original power base. The Nationalists, Hughes concluded, had become 'the servile tool of great vested interests'.[15] By March 1929, he was 'in open mutiny and shouting to the crew to arise and make him captain right off', as *The Bulletin* put it. Never one for discreet diplomacy, Hughes openly colluded with Labor politicians and was approached by businessmen outside the Parliament with a view to forming a new political party. (When in late 1929 he finally launched his new Australian Party, it withered for lack of support and never contested an election, being incorporated in 1931 into the United Australia Party.)[16]

All the economic indicators were now looking alarming. In April–May, there had been an ominous decline in wool and wheat prices, while unemployment rose across the year to 13 per cent of the workforce.[17] The finances of all but two state governments were in deficit, and those that were in surplus were receiving financial assistance from the Commonwealth. One option was to reduce government expenditure, but Bruce continued to believe, as he told a premiers' conference in May, that the 'basic cause of all the economic problems of Australia to-day is the high cost of production'.[18] In a desperate last throw of the dice, the prime minister announced his intention to eliminate duplication between the state and Commonwealth arbitration courts. Objectively, this change was hardly likely to lower wages or reduce the level of industrial disputes, which were as much a symptom as a cause of Australia's economic fragility. But, as Bruce told Casey in London:

> I am . . . going 'over the top' and saying quite definitely that the present system of dual control of industrial matters is impossible, and that either the Commonwealth or the States must be the sole authority . . . This will unquestionably cause the biggest political turmoil we have ever had in Australia. It is, however, essential to face the position unless disaster is to come to us.[19]

The reference to 'going over the top' is telling. It was as if Bruce were once more in the trenches of Gallipoli, serving with the British Royal Fusiliers.

Bruce indeed found himself under siege when Parliament met in August. Theodore, leading the Opposition in the absence of a sick Scullin, moved to censure the ministry for withdrawing the prosecution of John Brown. After an all-night sitting on 21–22 August, the government survived by only four votes. A few hours later, Hughes, who had poured ridicule on the government and voted against Bruce, was told that he and another dissident, E.A. Mann, would no longer be regarded as members of the Nationalist Party. The same afternoon, Bruce introduced the bill that would allow the Commonwealth to relinquish its arbitration power, with the exception of the federal public service and shipping.

It did not help Bruce's cause that Page introduced, at the same time, a deficit budget, the third in as many years. Moreover, the government proposed an increase in income tax and a new tax on the gross takings of all places of entertainment, including cinemas and non-British films. The entertainment tax was a response to yet another royal commission that Bruce had set up in 1927 to investigate the movie industry—its importation, production and employment implications—but the proposed tax aroused the formidable opposition of cinema owners and fuelled popular prejudices about Bruce's patrician foibles. As patrons of the traditional theatre, Bruce and his wife Ethel had little time for the American movies that had become so popular with the Australian population. Nor did Bruce welcome the new cinema 'temples' built in Melbourne in the late 1920s: the Moorish fantasy of the State Theatre (later the Forum and Rapallo theatres) and the architectural exuberance of the Regent and Plaza theatres. 'If these damn fools are going to spend all their damn money in building their wedding-cake palaces,' Bruce said, 'do they think I'm going to be such a damn fool as to leave them alone?' A more pragmatic concern was that 14 per cent of the annual receipts of Australian cinemas were being remitted to the United States, since American companies controlled the distribution of films.[20]

After heated parliamentary debate, lasting a fortnight from 23 August, the second reading of the Maritime Industries Bill was carried by only four votes. But a few days later Hughes struck. He moved an amendment that the bill should not be proclaimed until Australians had voted on it, either in a referendum or an election. By repealing the *Commonwealth Conciliation and Arbitration Act* and leaving industrial relations largely to the states, the bill purportedly divested the national parliament of the powers conferred on it by the Constitution. Some furious lobbying for votes followed until the amendment was carried by one. Groom, now speaker of the House, got his revenge for being dumped from the ministry in 1925 by refusing to vote.[21] Bruce could have put aside Hughes' amendment, but he later told his biographer: 'We couldn't have wriggled out of it this way. We would have taken our time to sort out the industrial problem if we had not been so obsessed by this impending financial and economic cataclysm that we believed it was imperative to put our own industrial house in order, and at once.'[22] So the prime minister decided yet again to go to the electorate. Perhaps he did so because he did not want to be in office when Australia would be hit by the economic disaster that he sensed was imminent—although Bruce denied this, saying that this would make him out to be more Machiavellian than he ever was.[23]

As the parliamentarians streamed out of the chamber after the amendment vote, Hughes was seen 'to pause, with a Sphinx-like smile, in the King's Hall, to light a cigarette in a slow deliberate manner which told the discerning that he was very well pleased with himself, and that a certain young gentlemen from Victoria had good and sufficient reason to regret having taken him so cheaply'.[24] Hughes seems to have hoped that the governor-general would call on him to form a government, possibly heading a new centre party; or, that Scullin might be commissioned to form a Labor government and would bargain for the support of Hughes and other rebel Nationalists. Newspapers speculated on these possibilities, or perhaps a Nationalist government led by Latham. But it was no longer 1916, and there was no Governor-General Sir Ronald Crauford Munro Ferguson, who had allowed Hughes to cobble together a new government after he had lost the referendum on conscription. Instead, Governor-General Lord Stonehaven granted Bruce a dissolution of Parliament.

The election campaign that followed lasted only three weeks and was largely fought on the issue of arbitration. As Scullin put it at one public meeting:

> The proposal you are being asked to vote for is nothing less than the abolition in one fell swoop of our Federal arbitration system, the system which has grown out of the misery and oppression of the workers, the system which our fathers won for us, and the humanitarian statesmen have given us, building it up, Act upon Act ... Because the system is not perfect, because it still needs mending, [the prime minister] would end it, and cast hundreds of thousands of workers into the 'open economic ring,' where for years wage earners fought so many unequal fights. Was there ever a greater betrayal of principle?[25]

Scullin also spoke eloquently about the Bruce government's financial misman-agement, as evident in its budget deficits and the worsening terms of trade.[26] Even Bruce's Minister for Trade and Customs, Henry Gullett, conceded in late September that Australia was in 'a state of industrial depression', the depths of which it had probably not plumbed.[27]

Bruce tried, as ever, to tar Labor as disloyal. Of Theodore he said: 'He is one of the most lusty individuals you could imagine, yet what did he do in the war? He almost preached disloyalty . . . he conducted a peace by negoti-ation campaign, which did a great deal to hearten our enemies.'[28] For many

Australians, however, arbitration was one of the nation's foundational achievements. Almost 150 unions, with about 700,000 members (including public servants, bank officers and insurance workers) were bound by the awards of the Commonwealth Court of Conciliation and Arbitration and would have been left in a limbo if there were only state courts.[29] Bruce also suffered political damage on the issue of the entertainment tax. Although he quickly made some concessions in the face of the public outcry, a specially convened 'Amusement Protection Association' ran an effective campaign during the election. With control over the cinemas, they promoted negative advertisements, exhorted moviegoers to sign petitions, and sent all parliamentarians telegrams of protest.

When Australians voted on 12 October, they humiliated Bruce. In the House of Representatives (the Senate was not being contested), the ALP won 46 of the 75 seats. Bruce himself lost Flinders, the first time an Australian prime minister lost his seat in a federal election. Even more gallingly, Bruce lost Flinders to Holloway, the unionist who had been prosecuted during the timber workers' strike. It would be 78 years before another Australian prime minister, John Howard, lost both the federal election and his own seat. In both cases, the defeats owed much to the government's overreach on industrial relations.

This election, and the bitter struggles over industrial relations that preceded it, were a testament to the resilience of Australian democratic political institutions. The Australian electorate seized the opportunity to reject the Bruce–Page government's assault on the established rights of the labour movement. For Labor leaders, the return to federal government after thirteen years in the wilderness was 'a glorious victory' that represented success beyond Theodore's 'wildest dreams'.[30] A crowd of 5000 excited people armed with confetti gathered at Spencer Street railway station, Melbourne, to send Scullin off to Canberra. His train was greeted with enthusiastic demonstrations along the route, and on his arrival in the capital, he was greeted by a band playing 'See the Conquering Hero Comes'.[31]

Yet if the election was, as Scullin put it, 'exhilarating', federal Labor came to the task of governing the nation with major limitations on its power.[32] First, the election of October 1929 was for the lower house only. The conservative coalition continued to have a majority in the Senate, where it could block any legislation to which it was opposed for ideological or other reasons. Second, the federal government presided over a federation in which its role was relatively weak vis-à-vis the states. It would have to rely on state governments, and beneath them municipalities and local communities, to provide the sustenance programs needed to assist the growing army of unemployed Australians. Third, any solution to the crippling problem of Australia's international indebtedness that Scullin inherited again involved the states. The state leaders will thus play a more prominent role in the narrative that follows. In late 1929, only two of these leaders were Labor: Collier in Western Australia, and a farmer-turned politician, Edmond (Ned) Hogan in Victoria. But there would be regular changes of government as voters turned on leaders, Labor and non-Labor, who were unable to alleviate the economic crisis. Ironically, it was a Labor-led state, New South Wales, that from late 1930 on inflicted irreparable damage on the aspirations of the new federal Labor government. Finally, the most intractable problem that Scullin confronted was the terrible timing of his government coming to power only days before the New York stock market crash. He inherited a situation in which he had virtually no chance of success.

A classic image of Australia's Great Depression: a family in their makeshift tin hut, c. 1932. (*The Sydney Morning Herald, SMH*)

Men waiting for the dole, Coffs Harbour, 1930. One of the dominant memories of the unemployed was the humiliation, and sheer tedium, of claiming support from the state. (State Library of New South Wales, SLNSW)

In the 1920s a number of immigration schemes were introduced, inspired by the social engineering goal of 'rescuing' disadvantaged British children from slum life in England, and the need to replace the 'lost generation' from World War I. (Barnardo's/TopFoto)

A PREFERENCE FOR STRONG FOOD.

THE LION. "NOW, MY BOYS, I'M SURE YOU'LL LIKE THESE NICE DRIED FRUITS."
CHORUS OF CUBS (led by Australia). "MEAT, PLEASE!"

The search for greater access to the British market for Australian meat was a constant theme of inter-war trade negotiations. In this 1923 cartoon, the Australian cub is depicted as particularly obstreperous, insisting on its share at the expense of other Dominions. (Punch Cartoon Library/TopFoto)

The kangaroo was considered an effective marketing device for anything Australian, as this 1928–29 Empire Marketing Board poster shows. (National Library of Australia, NLA)

British/imperial identity was also commonly invoked for marketing purposes: not a trace of Australia's semi-desert interior here! (NLA)

A fine exemplar of one of Australia's key exports in the inter-war years, wool. (SLNSW)

The conservative (Nationalist) Prime Minister Stanley Bruce (right) and his (Country Party) Treasurer Earle Page miscalculated the mood of the electorate and the power of the cinema lobby when they proposed an entertainment tax in 1929. (4 September 1929, *Australian Worker*, AW)

BRUCE: How disgusting to see people so anxious to enjoy themselves! Put a tax on them, Page!"

Prime Minister Jim Scullin (right) and Treasurer 'Ted' Theodore (left), in December 1929, soon after the ALP came to power nationally. Commonly seen as one of Australia's most competent treasurers, Theodore would be dogged by scandal and stymied by relentless opposition from conservative advocates of 'sound finance'. (*SMH*)

Australia's war debt was an enduring grievance for many Australians, who thought the huge loss of life in the war was contribution enough. Here the British bondholder is depicted as a modern-day Shylock, demanding his 'living pound of flesh'. (27 August 1930, *AW*)

"Dead men pay no interest. Give me my living pound of flesh!"

The crowds in Sydney on Anzac Day, 1930, testified to the power of the returned soldier in Depression politics. They were one of the few groups whose benefits were protected from the worst cuts of the Depression years. (*SMH*)

An increase in tariffs was an early policy response of the Scullin government, intended partly to create work in Australia through import substitution. In this cartoon, 'Santa' Scullin places 'Work for Australian Workers' into the stocking of 'Tariff' before hanging it on the bed of 'Unemployment'. (4 December 1929, *AW*)

"The increased hosiery duties will mean the employment of many more Australian workers."—Daily paper.

SOME XMAS CHEER IN THE STOCKING.

Many of the unemployed sought to earn at least something by hawking low-value items in the streets. Here a man tries to raise funds by selling pencils in Brisbane, c. 1932. (State Library of Queensland)

Champions of deflationary economics: the Bank of England emissary Sir Otto Niemeyer (left) and chairman of the Commonwealth Bank Sir Robert Gibson (centre) in Sydney, 1930. (*SMH*)

GLAD: "Australia's O.K. now!"

GLOOM: "But Niemeyer says Australia's in a terrible hole."

GLAD: Blow Niemeyer! We've won the ASHES!"

Cricket provided a welcome distraction for Australians and a means of scoring points against Britain. This cartoon dates from the time of the visit of Otto Neimeyer, whose dire analysis of the Australian economy was intended 'to discourage shallow optimism' among Australians.
(27 August 1930, *AW*)

The conservative fear that any increase in the money supply, as some in the ALP advocated, would be inflationary is parodied in this *Australian Worker* cartoon. (12 November 1930, *AW*)

"See that bloke, Bill. He eats a seven-course meal three times a day and then waddles off to his club to argue about the dangers of inflation."

Fundraising for the Lord Mayor Relief Fund in South Australia, c. 1934. Like the patriotic movements in World War I, local communities, organisations and councils invested extraordinary efforts in raising money, this time for the relief of the unemployed. (State Library of South Australia, SLSA)

Part III

━━◆━━

DEPRESSION, 1929

CHAPTER 8

What caused the
Great Depression?

Australia was not alone in facing profound economic difficulties in 1929. Over the next three years, all countries relying on the exports of primary production and virtually every manufacturing economy would be drawn into the vortex of the greatest economic catastrophe of modern history. The struggle of Australian governments to manage this crisis and the misery it inflicted needs to be positioned within this wider global context. So what caused the Great Depression?

Despite reams of scholarship by economists and historians, there is no explanation that commands universal support. This is not just because the economic crisis itself was so complex—it was a series of crises within crises, generating an ever more disastrous cumulative effect—but because the Depression played out differently in various countries. It was, for instance, more savage in the United States, Germany and Australia than in Britain or France. The debate about the Depression also continues to this day because economic theories are products of their times. Their explanatory power changes with their ability to illuminate the present as much as the past.

For all the differences of interpretation and emphasis by those who have studied the Great Depression over the decades, there is consensus on one point: it was not *caused* by the Wall Street crash of October 1929. Disastrous though the bursting of the speculative bubble was for millions of investors—by one estimate, one in ten households in the United States had money invested in the stock market—by late 1929, the New York market seemed to have stabilised close to the level it had reached in early 1928.[1] By April 1930, it had recovered its July 1929 level.[2] So why did a routine, if spectacular, business-cycle downturn spiral into a depression of unprecedented proportions? How did it spread beyond the United States to infect the rest of the globe? And why did it last so long?

Structural explanations begin with the fragility of the international system, politically and economically, in the aftermath of World War I. Opinions differ as to whether the war brought about a lasting disjuncture in the global economic order, or whether the open—some might say globalised—system that had characterised the pre-1914 period was largely restored by the early 1920s.[3] Whatever the preferred position, most scholars agree that the post-war economic system suffered from a number of weaknesses.

The first was the instability that was generated by the victorious Allies' demand for Germany and the other defeated powers to pay reparations and the reluctance of the United States to reduce, or even wipe off, the debt that the European Allies had incurred in fighting the war. Much of this debt had been raised on the New York money market, and the pressure in the US Congress to introduce tax cuts and avoid European entanglements ruled out any write-down of US loans to Europe.[4] War debts thus spawned in the 1920s a round robin of transfers of capital, involving some 28 countries, that was unproductive and contributed to the profoundly destabilising hyperinflation in Germany. Second, the increase in primary production across the globe after World War I led ultimately to surpluses that caused commodity prices to collapse, eroding the terms of trade of economies such as Australia's. Wheat, in particular, was in chronic oversupply in international markets from 1925 on.[5]

Finally, there is a consensus that the powers that won World War I failed to provide the united leadership that might have mitigated these post-war problems and, when the Depression threatened, have contained its worst effects. Throughout the 1920s, economic issues were entangled with political and security disputes, especially about how to enforce the Treaty of Versailles.

WHAT CAUSED THE GREAT DEPRESSION?

The United States refused to join the League of Nations, while Britain and France were often at loggerheads, with policy disputes made toxic, it has been suggested, through deeply racialised suspicions of the French on the part of the British.[6] When the Great Depression came, many governments looked not to international cooperation but to economic nationalism and protectionism.

At the epicentre of the post-war economy was the United States, *the* winner of World War I. Between 1914 and 1918 most European economies contracted, as millions of men were siphoned off to die in battle and industrial production was focused on producing the tools of war. But the United States, to the chagrin of many people, including Australia's Hughes, entered the war only in 1917, and ended the conflict with its competitive economic position enormously enhanced. In the 1920s, the United States would become the world's largest exporter, and the world's second-largest importer, after the United Kingdom. Even more significantly, since the United States had acquired much of the world's gold reserves during the war, it became the major source of capital. Although Australia borrowed mostly from London, it was the United States that, between 1924 and 1931, was responsible for around 60 per cent of total international lending. About a third of this went to Germany, to enable it to pay reparations and to improve its population's standard of living. Other countries that attracted US investors were Austria, Hungary, Greece, Italy, Poland—nations that were seeking to rebuild their war-ravaged economies— and several Latin American countries, trying to respond to the slump in commodity prices.[7]

For some time, this transactional system worked smoothly, especially while low domestic interest rates in the United States encouraged investors to seek better returns overseas. In 1928, however, the banks of the US Federal Reserve System began to tighten monetary policy, seeking to dampen the orgy of speculation on the stock market. Interest rates rose steadily and US overseas lending, much of which was short-term 'hot money', was sucked in from Europe. With the stock market crash, the flow of US capital overseas was disrupted even more disastrously. There was a brief revival in early 1930, but then US foreign investment into Europe dried to a trickle, and countries that had relied on these capital imports were thrown into the chaos of savage deflation, unemployment and even financial collapse.

It has been classically argued that, in this and other respects, the United States failed to provide the leadership of the international order that its economic dominance required.[8] In the pre-1914 period, London had often played a stabilising role in times of crisis: providing counter-cyclical lending, maintaining a relatively open market for distress goods (that is, goods sold at reduced prices to clear debts) and discounting (that is, reducing interest rates for short-term loans). But Britain's global dominance had been dealt a terminal blow by World War I—even if this was not yet fully apparent to many in Whitehall—and the City of London could not fully recover its pre-war role as the world's clearing house for overseas investment, finance, shipping and insurance.

The United States refused to take up the role of an economic 'hegemon' for a mix of reasons, including the preference of many among US political elites for detachment from Europe's internecine intrigues. The Federal Reserve System, it must be said, was scarcely functioning as a central bank in the sense we would understand it today. Established only in 1913, it consisted of twelve regional Federal Reserve Banks theoretically under the supervision of a Federal Reserve Board in Washington DC. Consisting of political appointees, this was, as J.K. Galbraith memorably said, 'a body of startling incompetence' in 1929.[9] For all this, during the 1920s, the Federal Reserve of New York, the largest of the twelve banks, emerged as the driving force of the Federal Reserve System, with its governor, Benjamin Strong, serving as the 'chief pilot of the whole system'. It helped international economic relations that Strong established a close personal and professional relationship with the governor of the Bank of England, the redoubtable Montagu Norman. But then, at a critical moment in the unravelling of the global economy, in late 1928, Strong died, leaving 'a political vacuum within the system as a whole'.[10]

Even more seriously, in the relative absence of international leadership from the United States, there were no formal transnational regulatory regimes. Early in the 1920s, Norman floated the idea of a league of central bankers who would take responsibility for stabilising European finances and promoting world economic recovery. But the Americans feared that this might became a conclave in which the European debtors colluded and ambushed the United States.[11] In 1930 the Bank for International Settlements was created in an effort to institutionalise economic cooperation, but although it became something of a club for central bankers and would try to intervene in the financial crises that hit Europe, it failed to provide an effective mechanism for international monetary cooperation. Meanwhile, in the 1920s there was nothing comparable to the Bretton Woods system and International Monetary Fund that were established in response to the disasters of the 1930s and the even greater catastrophe of World War II.

A further feature of the international economic system that, in retrospect, seems to have been deeply problematic was the gold standard. This was the monetary system whereby the value of a country's currency was linked directly to a specific quantity of gold. Each national treasury bought and sold gold at a specified price, which in turn set the value, or exchange rate, of its currency. With all currencies fixed against gold, they were all fixed against one another. Each central bank was required by law to maintain a certain quantity of bullion as backing for its paper money, but this money was freely convertible into its gold equivalent. Thus, banks were obliged to exchange gold bullion for any amount of their own currencies, and even individual citizens could convert their notes into their value in gold. The amount of gold held by a country determined the supply of money and credit within its country. As Liaquat Ahamed put it in his Pulitzer Prize–winning study of central bankers:

> In order to control the flow of currency into the economy, the central bank varied interest rates. It was like turning the dials up or down a notch on a giant monetary thermostat. When gold accumulated in its vaults, it would reduce the cost of credit, encouraging consumers and businessmen to borrow and thus pump more money into the system. By contrast, when gold was scarce, interest rates were raised, consumers and businesses cut back, and the amount of money in circulation contracted.[12]

When adopted in the nineteenth century, the gold standard was assumed to provide the trust necessary for global trade, since it linked paper currencies to something that had tangible or 'real' value. Indeed, the gold system was a stable one before 1914. According to a leading scholar on the gold standard, Barry Eichengreen, this stability was attributable to the system's credibility and to cooperation between the central banks and monetary officials of different countries. Paradoxically, this credibility was possible because of the lack of well-articulated theories as to how money supply and credit could be managed to stabilise production or deal with unemployment. Few authorities understood how central bank policy affected domestic economies, and since unemployment and other social issues did not have the prominence in domestic politics that they later acquired, monetary officials could give primacy to maintaining exchange rates through the gold system. The confidence that they would do this, regardless of the domestic economic implications, was what invested the gold standard with credibility. When the global credit conditions were overly restrictive and some loosening was required, adjustments would be made by several central banks, with the Bank of England—depending on your interpretation—either leading or signalling to banks in Paris and Berlin the need for such transactions.[13]

World War I, inevitably, shattered this cooperation. Countries progressively went off the gold standard, prohibiting the export of gold, and resorting to borrowing and printing money, with no backing by gold, to fund their war effort. Australia was not alone in funding only a small proportion of war expenditure by taxation. Germany raised barely 10 per cent of the $47 billion it spent on the war from taxes.[14] When the war ended, however, a return to the gold standard was thought desirable. Not only would it restore the monetary stability needed for economic recovery, but gold would control the inflation that reached truly terrifying proportions in central European countries in the early 1920s. It was also believed that gold would impose discipline on politicians who were prone to excessive public spending, since a lack of fiscal restraint would lead to a loss of bullion. Norman has been described as thinking about gold in existential terms: 'It was one of the pillars of a free society, like property rights or habeas corpus, which had evolved in the Western liberal world to limit the power of government—in this case its power to debase money.'[15]

For the British, too, the restoration of the pound to gold had a profound symbolic importance, in that it might help to reclaim some of London's former financial dominance. In April 1925, Britain returned to the gold standard, as did, with some eagerness, Australia, whose currency was tied to sterling.[16] Most of the central and eastern European currencies returned to gold between 1924 and 1928, while the French franc was restored to gold convertibility after it was officially devalued in June 1928. The United States had remained on gold since 1879.

Traditionally, it has been argued that Britain's return to the gold standard and the setting of sterling at its pre-1914 value overvalued the currency and thereby made British exports uncompetitive.[17] British manufacturing and staple export industries of coal, steel and shipbuilding were hobbled in world markets by a high exchange rate, and had chronically high levels of unemployment throughout the 1920s. France, in contrast, by devaluing its franc in 1927 had a competitive edge over Britain and other trading partners. More generally, the return to the gold standard by many countries is thought to have exacerbated the global slide into recession, and then depression, in the late 1920s and early 1930s. The gold standard was inherently deflationary, in that nations were obliged to redeem their currency in gold, and when they imported more than they exported, or massively invested abroad, they would typically be forced to pay for these goods or investments by using gold, or reserves of sterling and US dollars that were backed by gold. As their reserves shrank, they would have to reduce imports, generally through deflationary monetary and fiscal policies, such as restricting domestic credit and reducing public spending. Their economies were thus pushed into recession with rising levels of unemployment.

The gold-standard system is thought to have fostered divisions among central banks and favoured those banks that held significant gold stocks over those that did not. During the 1920s, the United States, which had accumulated vast amounts of gold during World War I, and France, which began to sell its foreign exchange to gain gold, accumulated 60 per cent of the world's stock.[18] There was no obligation for these countries holding gold reserves to increase their money supply or to do anything to counter the deflationary effects that their control of so much gold generated in other countries. It has been said that with France, 'the gold flowed in, but never flowed out, because the Paris money market remained insufficiently developed to lend on the necessary scale'.[19] The Bank of England, meanwhile, operated with stocks of gold that were too slender to support its reserve currency role. At times it had to increase interest rates in order to attract foreign funds to boost its inadequate reserves of gold, but this had the deflationary effect of raising the cost of money locally.

Beyond this, the linking of all currencies to gold, and the fixed exchange rates that this involved, denied national governments flexibility in monetary policy. The option of devaluation of a currency, in an effort to make exports more attractive, was not available to policymakers. This rigidity of the gold standard, of course, was more obvious in retrospect than in the 1920s. At that time, the governors of the major central banks saw the gold standard as, in effect, a managed-currency regime of which they were the managers.

The final problem with the gold standard in the 1920s was that the commitment and cooperation that had stabilised the system before 1914 was now weakened. With the enfranchisement of working classes, monetary policymakers and politicians could no longer so easily ignore the domestic political and social ramifications of maintaining the gold standard. If forced to choose between the defence of exchange rates and the pursuit of domestic policy goals, such as low unemployment, it was no longer certain that they would, or even could, choose the former. Nor was there any consensus among various national policymakers, and their central bankers, as to how they should analyse—let alone resolve—the problems resulting from war debts, reparations and economic instability in the countries defeated during the war. Many seemingly economic decisions were deeply politicised. Should everything be done to protect the international economy or should the main objective be to contain the resurgence of German power? Historians remain divided as to whether the British, the French or the Americans were more culpable in the failure to resolve these tensions, but manifestly the lack of unity on these core questions among the victors of World War I had profoundly destabilising effects.

Despite all these problems confronting the international economic system, there was no inevitability about the Great Depression. The descent of the globe into economic catastrophe after 1929 was ultimately the result of the decisions made by governments and politicians. Predictably, historians and economists have continued to debate the wisdom or otherwise of these policy choices, but there is a consensus that some had the effect of causing the deflation and financial crisis to spread across the globe.

Again, the role of the United States was critical, since its dominant position in international trade and global finance meant that its own domestic depression spread like a contagion. For some months after the stock market crash, it appeared that the US economy would recover. The Federal Reserve reduced interest rates and embarked on vigorous open-market operations (that is, the buying and selling of government securities in the open market in order to expand or contract the amount of money in the banking system). US overseas lending revived for a time. From the end of 1930, however, the US economy dropped precipitously, and although there were signs of recovery at various points in the next two years, the Depression reached a nadir in early 1933. From then on—to take the story to its conclusion—the US economy was on a roller-coaster. There was some recovery from the second quarter of 1933 on, but another serious downturn occurred in 1937. Ultimately, recovery was secured by the rapid expansion of the monetary supply in the mid- and late 1930s with a huge inflow of gold to the United States, due mainly to political developments in Europe. It was a trend that continued dramatically during World War II when the flight of capital from Europe continued.[20] War, too, brought the Depression to an end by massively increasing the demand for US defence production, revitalising industry and creating new employment.

The scale of the American economic disaster at the worst of the Depression was breathtaking. Between August 1929 and March 1933, output fell by 52 per cent, wholesale prices by 38 per cent and real income by 35 per cent. Gross private domestic investment, measured in constant prices, which had totalled US$16.2 billion in 1929, slumped to only $0.3 billion in 1933. Gross expenditure on new private residential construction—one of the booming industries in the 1920s—plummeted from $4920 million in 1926 to $290 million in 1933. Consumer expenditure, at constant prices, fell from $79 billion in 1929 to $64.6 billion in 1933. The number of wage-earners in manufacturing dropped by 40 per cent. In the automobile industry, another of the core industries of the 1920s, half the workforce was laid off. Reliable unemployment statistics are always difficult to agree upon, but, by one estimate, the number of wage-earners in manufacturing fell by 40 per cent. Many workers supposedly 'employed' were working on reduced hours and lower wages.[21]

One of most savagely hit sectors was agriculture, where there was a fall of 65 per cent in farm income. With prices collapsing, desperate farmers produced more, only for this to deflate prices further. Rural indebtedness exploded, and banks foreclosed on mortgages, calling in loans and curtailing lending: in effect, gaining liquidity by bankrupting their customers. The US financial system was poorly regulated, undercapitalised and based on unit, rather than branch, banking: in the 1920s there were some 25,000 banks, many of which were single small banks, providing financial services to their local communities, and not connected to other larger banks. Only half of the banks had joined the Federal Reserve System, although they accounted for about three-quarters of all deposits.[22] Between 1930 and 1933, some 9000 banks failed in successive waves. As they did so, their customers, robbed of their savings and with no access to credit, reined in their spending and investment, generating further downward pressures on business activity, manufacturing and employment.

We do not need here to engage with the more technical and quantitative analyses of this economic catastrophe. The consensus is that a mix of monetary and non-monetary factors, together with ill-conceived policy interventions, contributed to the downward spiral. A dominant, though by no means uncontested, explanation, popularised in Milton Friedman and Anna Schwartz's 1963 work *A Monetary History of the United States, 1867–1960*, is that the Federal Reserve contributed to the Depression, by tightening credit in 1928–29 in an effort to stem stock-market speculation and then failing to expand the money supply from 1930 on. The Federal Reserve also refused to stabilise the banking system by acting as a lender of last resort (that is, a bank that lends to banks or other eligible institutions when they are experiencing financial difficulties or are close to collapse).

In contrast, John Maynard Keynes, who wrote his seminal works *A Treatise on Money* (1930), *The Means to Prosperity* (1933) and *The General Theory of Employment, Interest and Money* (1936) in response to the inter-war economic crisis, argued that the Depression was prolonged by the failure of governments to regulate money and debt, and manage aggregate demand—that is, the total demand for goods and services within their markets. Rather than relying on the free market to correct itself, governments needed to intervene and compensate for the decline in private investment, by running budget deficits and providing fiscal stimulus. Increased demand would then tend to have a positive 'multiplier' effect, creating employment in industries that depended on consumer spending.

The politicians facing the crisis of the early 1930s, of course, had only limited exposure to Keynesian and monetarist theories, both of which were in their infancy. Even the New Deal introduced by Franklin Delano Roosevelt after his election as US president in late 1932 was arguably not Keynesian, in that it used neither fiscal nor monetary policy as a tool for economic revival. Roosevelt was a fiscal conservative, and budget deficits were small and unplanned.[23] Only in retrospect, as they reflected on the disaster of the 1930s, did economists, policymakers and government officials begin to learn the lessons that would inform political and economic planning after 1945.

In 1930, then, policymakers floundered between improvised and unco-ordinated policy choices. One of the most disastrous of these was the resort to protectionism. As commodity prices collapsed in the United States, the powerful farming lobby persuaded a Republican-controlled Congress to pass, first, the *Agricultural Marketing Act 1929*, under which a Federal Farm Board purchased agricultural surpluses and farmers were given financial support. Then, in July 1930, Congress passed the Smoot–Hawley tariff. This notorious piece of legislation increased duties on imports of agricul-tural products, including sugar, wheat, cotton, meat and dairy products. The legislation was contrary to the recommendation of a World Economic Conference of 1927 that the nations of the world should adopt a tariff truce; more than a thousand economists publicly warned President Herbert Hoover that other countries would retaliate by raising tariffs themselves. Restricting trade, they said in an article in the *New York Times*, was no way to increase employment. Nor did tariff walls 'furnish good soil for the growth of world peace'.[24] Indeed, Hoover received protests from 33 foreign govern-ments, and many businesses with foreign markets. The president's priority was, however, to protect companies that paid high wages from competition from cheap imported goods, and he approved the legislation.[25]

Economists still debate the importance of tariffs, relative to other factors such as decline in national income, in distorting international trade, but the Smoot–Hawley tariff was perhaps the quintessential example of the failure of the United States to provide international leadership.[26] As Charles Kindleberger wrote in 1973, 'The action was important less for its impact on the United States balance of payments, or as conduct unbecoming a creditor nation, than for its irresponsibility.'[27] It was a 'beggar thy neighbour' response—it sought to improve US conditions at other countries' expense— that did nothing to improve the circumstances of US farmers. As predicted, the majority of European countries increased their tariffs, while the British Empire turned, at the Ottawa Imperial Conference of mid-1932, to its own system of imperial preference (see Chapter 33).

In sum, then, whatever existed of the liberal internationalist order after World War I gave way to autarky and the narrow economic nationalism of tariffs and competitive devaluations. In this context, those countries that were dependent on agricultural exports, and already facing significant balance-of-payment and debt-repayment problems—Australia among them—found it profoundly difficult to improve their terms of trade. They had either to deflate savagely or, as did some Latin American countries, default on their international obligations—or do both.

In Europe, 1931 was the *'annus terribilis* of international financial relations', when major banks started to fail, taking the gold standard with them.[28] The domino-like crisis began in Austria when, in May 1931, the country's largest bank, the Creditanstalt, announced that it was facing bankruptcy. Part of the Rothschild financial empire, it was the country's major creditor: an 'Austrian colossus' on which, by one estimate, some 60 per cent of Austrian industry depended.[29] Like other central European banks, the Creditanstalt was heavily reliant on foreign loans, many of them short-term, and had a weak capital base after the hyperinflation of the war and post-war years. In 1929 it had been forced by the Austrian government to merge with another large industrial and agricultural bank, the Bodencreditanstalt, on terms that represented a severe loss to shareholders. When news of the Creditanstalt's losses emerged in May 1931, domestic and international investors lost confidence, withdrawing their deposits and, in many cases, converting them to other currencies. As the flight from the Austrian schilling gathered pace, the government appealed for international help.

Initially some help came, since other central banks had much at risk in their own central European investments. They were well aware of the disastrous implications not just for Austria but for the wider political and financial system, should the Austrian economy unravel. Thus the major central banks—in Britain, France, Italy, Germany and the United States, together with the Bank for International Settlements—provided Austria with some funds to stabilise the situation. But the loans were only temporary and more substantive help failed to materialise in time. The Bank of England was so weak that it could offer no more than token assistance, a situation that so distressed Norman that he collapsed under the nervous strain in August 1931. Loans from the French, with their larger gold reserves, came with impossible political strings attached. In March 1931, the Austrians and Germans, the axis of the alliance that opposed France in 1914–18, had announced that they were forming a customs union. This initiative, which had been negotiated in secret, was a bombshell that, as historian Adam Tooze has put it, 'unleashed the first true landslide of the Great Depression'.[30] The French saw the customs union as both a violation of the Treaty of Versailles and the first step towards an *Anschluss* or a political union between Austria and Germany. Paris thus made financial support for Austria conditional on its agreeing to an inquiry by the League of Nations into its economic and financial situation, and its renouncing the proposed customs union and any future *Anschluss*. The Austrian government, given only a few hours to respond, refused to accept the terms. It kept the Creditanstalt afloat but also imposed exchange controls, ended the convertibility of the schilling, and in effect moved off the gold standard.

The importance of these events lay not simply in their impact on an already traumatised country—Austria had been defeated in World War I, lost most of its imperial territory in the post-war dismantling of the Austro-Hungarian

Empire and had experienced catastrophic hyperinflation and currency depreciation—but in its knock-on effect throughout the European financial systems. As a League of Nations survey in 1932 concluded, with the Austrian crisis it became evident that 'neighbouring debtor states, and particularly Germany, would be at once exposed to the danger of panic withdrawals of capital. A crack had developed in the carefully constructed and patched facade of international finance and, through that crack, already timid investors and depositors caught glimpses of a weak and overburdened structure.'[31]

Indeed, no sooner had Austria started to suffer significant drain on its reserves, than Hungary followed and then—far more importantly for the future of European peace—Germany. Many German banks had already failed in 1929, and by 1931 the harsh deflationary policies that were being imposed as a result of the loss of overseas loans were generating political and economic chaos. German unemployment rose to 4 million over the winter of 1930–31, and the National Socialist (Nazi) Party, which had won only twelve seats in the Reichstag elections of 1928, won 107 seats in June 1930.[32] Trying to manage popular discontent and neutralise some of the Nazi appeal, the (Catholic) Centre Party Chancellor, Heinrich Brüning, called for an end to the payment of reparations. His Finance Ministry professionals told him that it was more important to maintain the confidence of American private investors—who had $2 billion tied up in Germany—than to gain some modest savings on reparations, but Brüning replied that he could not afford to be seen as less nationalist than Hitler.[33] Investors and creditors, however, did take fright, thinking that Germany would default not just on reparations but on other foreign debts. The reserves of the Reichsbank (Germany's central bank) plunged rapidly towards the minimum level required to maintain gold exchange for the currency. At last, under pressure from an increasingly desperate London, Hoover announced on 20 June 1931 a moratorium on payments of German and inter-Allied war debt. This, however, was for one year only and applied only to inter-government debt, not private debt. Moreover, the French had not been consulted! Already deeply aggrieved at the American refusal to create an international security system to replace that planned at Versailles, the French resented the Americans acting unilaterally and, as they saw it, putting the interests of long-term creditors ahead of reparations.

They delayed their approval of the moratorium for two weeks. It may not seem long, but in these weeks the German financial system haemorrhaged hundreds of millions of Reichsmarks in foreign exchange and collapsed.

On 13 July 1931, the second-largest German bank, the Darmstädter und National (or Danat) bank, closed its doors and a run on many banks ensued. The government and Reichsbank had no choice but to introduce stringent exchange controls, nationalise all private holdings of gold and foreign currency, set exorbitant interest rates and, like Austria before it, effectively leave the gold standard. Since the memory of hyperinflation was still raw, the Germans did not devalue the mark but continued with draconian deflationary policies at a time when unemployment was rising, reaching more than 30 per cent in 1932.

The crisis of 1931 has been seen as the 'defining moment' of the Depression, and it is one of those junctures that in retrospect generates a sense of profound anguish at lost opportunity.[34] Less than twelve months after the banking crisis, in July 1932, the Nazis gained 230 seats at an election. This made them the largest party in the Reichstag and they would form government in January 1933. It is too simplistic to say that the Depression—or the 1931 banking crisis—created Nazism, but it certainly spawned the climate of despair in which many conservative Germans—battered, like the Austrians, by defeat and hyperinflation—were willing to turn to radical politics.

The final episode of the 1931 drama was the crisis of the British currency, sterling. The British banking system was more stable than those of the central European powers, and across the Depression years, no British bank or building society would fail. By 1931, however, Britain was suffering serious problems with its balance of payments. Since about 40 per cent of British overseas trade was with primary-producing countries, which had to restrict spending when investment dried up, the demand for British exports declined in the late 1920s. Moreover, the important balance of earnings from so-called 'invisibles'—shipping, tourism, financial services, and interest and dividends from abroad—was significantly weakened. In better times, the Bank of England would have covered a current account deficit (that is, a situation where the value of the goods and services being imported exceeds the value of exports) by raising interest rates and thereby attracting 'hot money'. But as the European banking crisis unfolded, the banks of the City of London were themselves dangerously overexposed.[35] Wealth holders looked for safer places for their money, in New York, Geneva or Paris.

In the latter half of July, the Bank of England lost more than £33 million in gold and £21 million in foreign exchange.[36] This flight of capital drove reserves of gold far below the minimum deemed necessary and could not be staunched, even when, in August 1931, the minority Labour government of Ramsay MacDonald was replaced by a National government committed to reducing the budget deficit through public-sector pay cuts and tax increases. On 19 September, then, Britain was forced off gold and abandoned convertibility. Sterling was devalued, falling 25 per cent against the US dollar.[37]

The world's second experiment with the gold standard thus came to 'its inglorious end'.[38] Whereas in 1931, 47 countries had been members of the gold-standard club, by the end of 1932 the only significant members were Belgium, France, Poland, Switzerland and the United States. Within a matter of weeks of the British leaving gold, all the Dominions, except South Africa, and the rest of the British Empire followed 'mother'. Australia, as we shall see, effectively left the gold standard in late 1929 (see Chapter 9). The US dollar, meanwhile, also came under speculative attack, but was successfully defended by the Federal Reserve, although at the cost of intensifying an already serious depression. The United States would finally leave gold in 1933 and devalue its dollar. France, too, abandoned gold in 1936.

It must have seemed as if tectonic plates were grinding, but it is now clear that the end of the gold standard was not all loss. Keynesians and Friedman-ites agree that fixed exchange rates threw the burden of adjustment unduly on the debtor countries and served as 'a transmission belt for deflation'.[39] The departure from gold, in fact, was 'a prerequisite for recovery'.[40] But that journey to recovery was slow, full of policy stumbles, and marred by the impoverishment of countless men, women and children around the globe. Many Australians were among them.

CHAPTER 9

Scullin's poisoned chalice

The Irish playwright George Bernard Shaw once quipped: 'Life contains but two tragedies. One is not to get your heart's desire; the other is to get it.' So it was with the Scullin government. Not only did it inherit an unserviceable debt and an economy that was already in deep recession, but it also came to power at the very time the speculative bubble in the United States finally burst. On 24 October 1929, the New York stock exchange lost 11 per cent of its value at the opening bell. Five days later, about 16 million shares traded as the panic selling reached its peak. 'Black Tuesday', 29 October, remains one of the largest one-day drops in stock-market history. The Wall Street collapse did not, as we have seen, make the Great Depression inevitable, but it presaged the implosion of the international economic order on which Australian recovery depended. Many in the labour movement had predicted a crisis of capitalism, but when it happened, to their fury they found that the government they elected had little capacity to mitigate its disastrous effects.

The Scullin ministry confronting this crisis lacked experience in national government after thirteen years in Opposition. Scullin himself was a distinguished parliamentary and public speaker, and was admired for his idealism, honesty and directness, but he had no formal training in economics. Not that

Bruce thought that mattered. In a 'farewell' speech given to the Canberra Golf Club in late October 1929, he said:

> Some people are under the delusion that you have to have brains to be a Prime Minister, but only one qualification is necessary, an amazing amount of physical strength. The only way to maintain that is to play golf. I could not have remained Prime Minister for nearly seven years and retired as fit as when I started but for the fact that I played golf the whole time.[1]

Scullin did not play golf, only the occasional game of bowls—and the violin. In retrospect, the sympathetic journalist Warren Denning concluded that, had Scullin 'permitted himself a little more healthy amusement', he might have survived the trying years ahead of him'.[2]

It was to his advantage that Scullin could draw on the expertise of two former state premiers. The first, Lyons, though a newcomer to federal parliament, had been premier of Tasmania from 1923 to 1928. He gave the cabinet a necessary representation from that state and became postmaster-general and Minister for Works and Railways. The second former premier was Ted Theodore, who became treasurer. It was a role in which he would excel. In Boris Schedvin's 1970 opinion, he was probably 'the most able holder of the Treasury portfolio in Commonwealth history'.

> This view is based more on his outstanding intellect, his imagination and grasp of the wider issues than on any assessment of his legislative record. His imprint is everywhere evident in Treasury policy papers. Whereas most inter-war Treasurers were content to 'approve' a recommendation or otherwise, Theodore examined every clause in detail and commented extensively . . . he found himself in the unique position of having a firmer theoretical and practical grasp of the situation than his senior Treasury officials.[3]

Denning even judged Theodore to be better equipped than Scullin for the national leadership role:

> [he was] readier to face the realities of a difficult situation; more ruthless, more determined, more constructive, more tenacious, more

instinctively a fighter and less of an apologist . . . he would have repressed with a remorseless hand the factional spirit which grew up so quickly within the [Labor] party.[4]

It was one of many disasters to afflict Scullin that Theodore would soon be undone by a scandal that stemmed from his time in power in Queensland.

Notably, John Curtin was not included in the ministry. It has been said of him that 'few members have entered parliament with more extensive grassroots experience or better intellectual preparation'. He had been reading the works of the English economists Keynes, Arthur Pigou and others, and talking to academic economists.[5] He would ultimately become one of Labor's most celebrated prime ministers, presiding over an even greater national crisis during World War II. His exclusion from the 1929 cabinet owed something to the fact that Western Australia had only two members in the Federal Parliamentary Labor Party (or caucus), and the other, Albert Green, was older and had been a parliamentarian since 1922. Possibly, too, Curtin's reputation as a heavy drinker and ex-Catholic who had turned freethinker might have troubled the upright Scullin.[6]

In many ways the new ministry represented one side of the post-war divide of Australian politics. Many of the cabinet, like the wider caucus, were members of at least one trade union. Four, including Scullin himself, were members of the AWU. But, if solid in union matters, the government lacked military experience. Perhaps only seven of the 54 in the caucus were ex-servicemen.[7] None of the cabinet had enlisted in World War I, and all had opposed conscription in 1916–17. Their opponents were thus quick to depict them as 'cold-footers' whose only work during the war had been 'to stump the country with the object of preventing us getting recruits to relieve those at the front'.[8]

Strikingly, eight of the thirteen men in Scullin's initial ministry were Catholics. This number would increase to nine in March 1931 and ten in June 1931.[9] Scullin was of Irish-Catholic parentage, a regular churchgoer, a teetotaller and non-smoker with a frugal lifestyle.[10] Theodore, of mixed Romanian and Anglo-Irish extraction, was 'privately ambivalent' about Catholicism, but he had managed to retain 'an ambience of faith' during his period in

Queensland politics.[11] Lyons, too, was of Irish-Catholic descent. His younger wife, Enid, with whom he had twelve children (one born while he was prime minister), converted to Catholicism on their marriage; she would become his closest adviser and later a politician in her own right.

Yet if the cabinet was disproportionately Catholic, this does not seem to have been the liability that might have been anticipated. For one thing, many non-Catholics must have voted for the ALP in 1929. Scullin maintained, when interviewed in Rome in late 1930, that it was proof of the 'broadmindedness' of non-Catholics that he had been elected to office.[12] Melbourne archbishop Mannix, who was a close friend of Scullin, also declared in April 1930 that 'There were those who thought that Mr. Scullin and himself had daily and especially nightly consultations [but] . . . the Church leaves politics to the politicians.'[13] For his part, Scullin asserted that his cabinet adopted a non-sectarian approach to political problems.[14] Indeed, submerged in intractable economic problems, the Scullin government did little that might be considered specifically Catholic. The historian Patrick O'Farrell claimed that Scullin 'did as much for Catholic policies as the non-Labor government led by the Catholic Joseph Lyons . . . that is, nothing'.[15]

Far more significant for Scullin than any Catholic–Protestant enmities were the ideological disputes within the ALP that the economic crisis fuelled— and here some of his most severe critics would be Catholic. Like politicians around the world, Labor simply did not know how best to respond to the Depression. Although Scullin had been a prominent advocate of the sociali-sation objective at the 1921 ALP interstate conference, he had also supported the compromise formulation, and his early radicalism had moderated with time and experience.[16] When attacking the record of the Bruce government in 1927–28, he had promoted the need for 'sound' financial and economic policies. Theodore, too, was torn between his in-principle commitment to socialism and the pragmatic requirements of gaining and holding power. He had been a leading opponent of the socialisation objective and strongly opposed to the presence of communists within the ALP.[17] When invited in 1925 by a New York magazine, *Current History*, to reflect on his time as Queensland premier, he wrote:

[Australia] suffered no Czarism that must be the father of Nihilism; no thousand years of vested interests that bred Communism . . . Australians will have only the Australian way—the reasoned and gradual progress to the objective as the only progress that can be permanent; the education of our political opponents to the wisdom of preventing the exploitation of one citizen by another, and of giving all citizens a fair deal; the security of every man's honestly acquired possessions; the care that toil shall not be but half requited; the holding of the balance truly between effort and result; and the constant motion to the betterment of the citizen by the removal of the fear of poverty from all men; until at last we shall banish poverty by eliminating waste from a world that produces more than enough for all.[18]

As premier of Queensland, Theodore had supported state enterprises but adopted an orthodox approach to state budgets, seeking to cover mounting expenditure by taxation based on the principle of 'ability to pay'.

Lyons, too, professed to be a socialist, but this commitment was tokenistic by 1929. As Tasmanian premier he had been respectful of conventional economics and orthodox finance, relying on the advice of economists Giblin and Copland. He had pruned state expenses and reduced loan expenditure, while encouraging new industries, such as wooden pulp and mining. Moreover, he had refused to legislate for the cherished goals of the labour movement, the 44-hour week and preference for unionists. Tellingly, Lyons cancelled his subscription to the AWU paper, the *Australian Worker*.[19]

If Scullin, Theodore and Lyons were pragmatists, many in the Labor caucus remained passionately committed to the more radical traditions of labour. Among them was Frank Anstey, the new Minister for Health and Repatriation. Described as 'the influential stormy petrel of Labor politics and its most experienced parliamentarian', Anstey had been a passionate critic of the 'enslavement of labour' by 'rival capitalists' during World War I.[20] He had split with Hughes, believing that the prime minister had betrayed his party and principles to the 'Trusts, Combines and Monopolies, the Profiteers, Exploiters and the great vested interests of capital'.[21] An effective publicist, Anstey had welcomed the Russian Revolution, and had warned in his 1919 book *Red Europe* that 'Capitalism listens with quaking soul to the drumbeats of the Armies of Revolution. Those beats grow louder and louder—they draw nearer and nearer.'[22] A second important radical was Jack Beasley, appointed honorary minister assisting Scullin in the industry portfolio. Although only 33 years old, he had been president of the New South Wales Trades and Labour Council for seven years and was well blooded in 'the cockpit of [that state's] Labor factionalism'. By the time he entered federal parliament in 1928, Beasley had moved into the camp of Jack Lang, whose policies he would soon promote at the federal level.[23]

Few incoming prime ministers have had their agenda set so implacably by factors beyond their control as did Scullin. In his first days, he made no comment on the Wall Street crash. Like many other observers he perhaps thought that this was the inevitable and necessary correction to an extremely overheated market. The *Canberra Times* quoted the President of Chase National Bank as saying that the crash was 'the natural fruit of the orgy of speculation in which millions of people have indulged'.[24] The Adelaide *Advertiser* was also sanguine, noting on 30 October that 'Stock Exchanges are liable to periods of uneasiness as the condition amounting almost to panic in New York within the last few days illustrates. The restoration to normality so far as Australian securities in London are concerned is sufficient evidence that it is realised in financial circles that our bonds are gilt edged.'[25]

But Scullin was quickly made aware of how dire Australia's position actually was. Almost immediately after the election he was given a briefing by Gibson of the Commonwealth Bank on Australia's financial position and external borrowings. It was the first of many uncomfortable meetings to come. 'I was staggered,' Scullin later recalled. 'Those obligations had to be met at a time when prices had tumbled and the volume of exports had fallen.'[26] Theodore, too, found that Page's budget estimates of August had been overoptimistic. Instead of the projected surplus of £360,000, Theodore estimated a deficit of £1.2 million.[27] The accumulated deficit was £5 million, at a time when the government's total revenue from taxation in 1928–29 was £56.3 million, of which £15 million was dispersed in payments to the states.[28]

These troubling discoveries notwithstanding, Scullin at first projected an image of confidence. Exploiting the novelty of a Fox Movietone News broadcast from the gardens of Parliament House, he told Australians on 25 October that he 'had no doubt that the problems would be solved . . . He and his colleagues would strive earnestly, zealously, and fervently towards the ideal which they had set themselves.'[29] Conscious that the labour movement would expect immediate action on some of its deepest grievances, Scullin suspended the licences mandated for waterside workers under the 'Dog Collar Act'—an action that prompted a leading Nationalist to speak of Scullin being compelled to act by 'the Communistic malcontents which haunt constitutional Labor like a bad dream'.[30] The government also addressed seamen's concerns by overturning the Nationalist government's policy of throwing open the Tasmanian passenger shipping run to British vessels.[31]

In addition, Scullin moved rapidly to halt another signature policy of the Bruce government, the ambitious assisted-immigration programs. The labour movement believed that newcomers competed with Australians for ever-scarcer jobs, and, as Holloway said in his maiden speech to Parliament:

> The policy of bringing to Australia shiploads of people to look for work with an already overstocked labour market, is a crime not only against the unemployed in our midst, but also against the people who are enticed to come here under such conditions . . . There could be no greater paradox than occurs when overseas ships arrive here with their holds filled with manufactured goods which help to diminish production, and employment in our own factories, and the cabins of the same ships are crammed with immigrants seeking employment.[32]

In fact, in 1929 the excess of British arrivals over departures was only eighteen, as opposed to 9309 in the first seven months of 1928; and 16,898 for the corresponding period of 1927.[33]

In its first heady flush, the Scullin government also abolished the system of compulsory military service. National service for home defence, when first introduced in 1909, had the support of the ALP, but in the aftermath of the wartime conscription debates the party had committed itself to abolishing national service of all kinds. As Attorney-General Frank Brennan said in

111

November 1929, Australia needed 'to envisage a higher conception of defence than teaching childhood the way to kill'.[34] In Parliament, the policy change provoked the usual accusations of Labor disloyalty. The Nationalist Thomas White, who had been a prisoner in Turkey during World War I and was now commander of the 6th Battalion, declaimed:

> The real motive behind the government's action . . . must be to give effect to some of its international ideals, when it is recalled that Mr. Scullin made very unsavoury references to returned soldiers some years ago at Wangaratta, and Mr. Brennan made a most poisonous attack on the A.I.F. during the War. The move is too un-Australian and unpatriotic to be above suspicion.[35]

It should be noted that the abolition of national service in 1929 had minimal impact on Australia's immediate national security. Certainly the voluntary militia that remained in place after the abolition of compulsory service was starved of funds, manpower and equipment in the 1930s.[36] But in 1929, when military service was abolished, there was no serious threat to regional and global security. Indeed, the British government, whose thinking shaped imperial—and in turn, Australian—defence planning, was operating on the premise that the empire would not be engaged in any great war during the next ten years. This notorious 'ten-year rule', which set the clock anew each year, was only jettisoned in 1932, and it would be several more years before British rearmament—and with it, Australia's war preparations—seriously began. Even then, priority was given not to the army but to naval power, which would complement imperial defence strategies centred on the British base at Singapore. For all the Nationalist polemics, the conservative United Australia Party that came to power in January 1932 did not make any effort to restore compulsory military training.

Scullin further outraged patriots when he decided to delay work on the construction of the Australian War Memorial in Canberra. The rationale was financial stringency, but, as the federal Opposition saw it, the government was betraying the 'sacred pledge' given to soldiers during the war—while also forgoing an opportunity to provide local employment.[37] In the event, the memorial would not be finished until 1941.

A further policy response of the Scullin government in its first days in office was to increase tariffs. The additional customs revenue helped the federal government's budget problems and it was imperative to reduce imports, given the dire state of Australia's sterling reserves. Furthermore, the Labor government believed that the protection of Australian manufacturing was one of the few ways it might stimulate local employment as the capacity of state governments to fund public works collapsed. For Scullin's power base, unemployment was *the* policy priority for the government. The Labor member for Adelaide, George Yates, launched a sensational attack in Parliament on 22 November, 'shouting loudly, thumping his desk' and glaring at Theodore, because there was little relief, if any, in the budget for those who had brought the government to power.[38] Latham, now Opposition leader, meanwhile, taunted Scullin that 'almost every week [of the past seven years] the Labour party twitted the Government on the subject of unemployment. I had believed in my innocence that somewhere or other concealed in the brains of that party was a remedy for unemployment.'[39] To which Scullin replied:

> Finance is, of course, the key to an immediate solution of unemployment, but there is great stringency in the money market. Even if the Labour Ministry were able to raise large sums for public works, that would provide only a temporary alleviation of the unemployment difficulty. A more lasting alleviation will be found in the revised tariff schedule and already there have been announcements that manufacturers are adding considerably to their staffs to cope with the increased home demand that will be created under the protective tariff.[40]

The early days of the new administration thus witnessed something of a tariff orgy. More than a thousand applications for protection were received in the first two months, and deputations of employers and union officials besieged the government.[41] Importers and primary producers disadvantaged by the 'crushing' duties protested.[42] But Scullin defended giving priority to local manufacturing, telling the children of the nation in a Christmas message: 'I hope that Santa Claus will not forget any of you, and that when you hang up your stockings you will see that they are Australian-made'! Exploiting a technicality in parliamentary procedure, he managed to delay the potentially controversial debate about tariff schedules until October 1931.[43]

These initial policy responses by the Scullin government now seem a finger in the dyke before the bursting of the dam wall. With the savings from defence and immigration, increased tariffs and some proposed new individual and company taxes, Theodore's first financial estimates, delivered in late November 1929, managed to project a small budget surplus in 1929–30. This was unduly optimistic in that it assumed no further fall in export income and loan expenditure, but Theodore assured Parliament that he did not 'view the future with alarm or pessimism': 'Australia has wonderful recuperative powers, and a stout-hearted and industrious community. If we are blessed with good seasons, our troubles will soon disappear, and we shall commence a new era of progress and prosperity.'[44]

It was already an illusion. In the September quarter of 1929, there was a sharp decline in the balances of sterling held by Australian banks in London. It was quite common to have an adverse balance of trade at this time of the year, given the seasonal drop in wool sales and wheat exports. But the September deficit was greater than normal because commodity prices were crashing. Moreover, all Australian governments were experiencing problems in convincing London bankers that their overdrafts should be allowed to increase. With their holdings of sterling stretched, governments had to draw on those held by the trading banks. It was an unsustainable position in anything but the short term, given the banks were under no obligation to supply governments with London cover.[45]

In August, the Loan Council had attempted to address the sterling problem by issuing tenders in London for some £5 million of sterling Treasury bills (whereby London investors lent the Australian government money in sterling) with a currency of twelve months. Scullin soon found that the procedure had to be repeated. Seeking to reassure London investors, he claimed that his government had no plans for financial experimentation and would pursue policies of economy and prudence. Already he was being forced by the logic of the money market into policies of what would be called 'sound finance'. Still overdrafts in London were not reduced, and at the end of 1929, Australia's total short-term debts (that is, government overdrafts and Treasury bills) amounted to more than £23 million.[46] Australia's foreign exchange and gold reserves, with which it might service this debt, had fallen to £60 million; in contrast, throughout 1928–29 they had been £100 million.

The government concluded that it had no option but to pass legislation that allowed the Commonwealth Bank to control all the gold holdings in the country. At that time, banks and others seeking to obtain credit in London could present notes of Australian currency to the Commonwealth Bank and demand they be converted into gold, which they could then ship to London and thereby gain credit. The new legislation prohibited the unapproved export of gold and required the trading banks to exchange any gold they held in Australia for Australian currency. In effect—though this was not stated publicly—Australia was abandoning the gold-standard principle of convertibility.[47] Predictably, business circles and the conservative press claimed that the change would damage public confidence.[48] Page, too, made political capital of the issue, calling for a full inquiry by a Senate Committee before the legislation was passed. He told Parliament in early December:

> Our problem is that imports already exceed the exports to such a degree that we are bringing down this measure [of exporting gold] to deal with the problem. But this will not help us much if we do nothing else. We would simply lose our gold, and find ourselves at the end in the same position as at present but the poorer for our gold.[49]

He was right. By 30 June 1930, some £27.7 million in gold had been exported and surplus gold reserves were nearly exhausted.[50] Yet the threat of national insolvency and default on borrowings was even more immediate.

Meanwhile, the Scullin government's credibility with its domestic political base was being damaged by its inability to resolve the New South Wales coal strike. This had continued throughout 1929, punctured by conferences between employers and unions, and tactical disputes between the union leadership, the rank-and-file membership and the communist-led Militant

Minority Movement. During the election campaign of October, Theodore had promised rashly that a Labor government would reopen the coalmines within fourteen days of being elected: 'The John Browns of Australia must not be permitted to hold up the country to ransom,' he said. 'The coal-owners must open the mines, or the Labour Government will open them in the name of the people.'[51] The Scullin government soon found, however, that it had little power to intervene in what was essentially a state matter. A conference Scullin called between unionists and owners on 23 November failed to produce agreement.

In late November, the Nationalist premier of New South Wales, the reserved and aloof T.R. Bavin, finally decided to open the mines, if necessary without union labour. The first mine to be opened was the Rothbury colliery, near Branxton. On the night of 16 December, miners from across the district streamed in to prevent the hated 'scabs' from starting work. Somehow—the details have been disputed—clashes broke out between the strikers and the police. As the miners stormed the colliery, shots were fired, presumably by the police, though some blamed the miners. A 29-year-old worker, Norman Brown, was mortally wounded by a ricocheting bullet. At least ten other miners and six police were wounded.

The actual events at Rothbury were soon buried under 'thick layers of mythology'.[52] Brown became a labour martyr, commemorated in songs and poems, one of which included a chorus damning the 'murderous coppers' that shot him down. Scullin was pressured by outraged representatives of the miners to use the defence forces to protect them from the police. Some even called for the miners to arm themselves, an appeal that triggered the creation of a Labor Defence Corps staffed and trained by miners who had military service. In the years to come, this would become something of 'a trade union counterpart to the New Guard', though its numbers were perhaps only around a thousand in January 1930.[53]

The tragedy at Rothbury inflicted serious political damage on Scullin, within the federal caucus and the powerful New South Wales labour movement. Failing to visit the coalfields, Scullin blamed the continuation of the strike on 'the small irresponsible group [who favoured] lawless or unconstitutional action'.[54] He seemed troublingly immune to the suffering of the strikers. When Labor member of parliament for the coalmining electorate of Hunter, Rowley James, attacked Scullin in Parliament, he responded that this was not the only district in which 'misery stalks the land'. Many other electorates, his own included, were suffering the effects of long-term unemployment.[55]

Throughout the dispute, Scullin refused to act unconstitutionally. Instead, after the Rothbury fatality, he referred the dispute to the Commonwealth Court of Conciliation and Arbitration, where the notorious Beeby actually recommended in December the reopening of the mines at the old coal-hewing rates desired by the miners. The award, however, was ruled invalid, on the grounds that the dispute was not an interstate one. As dismay at the resumption of work at Rothbury mounted, a constellation of federal and New South Wales parliamentarians and union leaders virtually summoned Scullin to Sydney on 21 December. Subjected to a barrage of criticism, Scullin rejected most of the demands of the meeting, including the use of the army. As he said, a future non-Labor government might find it convenient if Labor set a precedent of using the military in industrial disputes. His only concession, made to pacify Beasley especially, was to consider legal action against the New South Wales Minister for Mines.[56] (It was a promise upon which his government never delivered.) The union officials, in turn, gave Scullin the authority to conduct whatever negotiations he thought appropriate. After ten hours, the meeting was limping to a halt when Lang made a dramatic entrance—at 10 p.m.! With all the luxury of being in Opposition, he declaimed:

> I am not surrounded by legal people . . . I know the right thing to do— it is the lawyer's job to tell me how to do it . . . If I were the Prime Minister fresh from the elections with a mandate to open the mines in a fortnight I would seize them, and work them under the conditions of a lawful award . . . Seize your mines, and if necessary pass your law later on.[57]

Such political theatre achieved little at this point and nothing came of the conference. But it was an ominous signal of Lang's intention to challenge Scullin's authority, no matter how impracticable or illegal his proposals were. It was clear, too, how little weight Scullin, as a longstanding member of

117

the AWU, carried in the jungle of New South Wales Labor politics, where that union was a minority faction.

The coal strike dragged on into 1930, with strike action spreading to other mines in New South Wales, Victoria and Queensland. In November 1929, the New South Wales government passed an *Intimidation and Molestation Act* outlawing a wide range of actions aimed at intimidating strikebreakers. The police formed what were called 'flying squads' or, more pejoratively, 'basher gangs', roaming the coalfields region, breaking up demonstrations, raiding the homes of unionists, searching for bombs and ammunition, crushing mass pickets with batons, and arresting unionists for alleged intimidation of colliery staff. The first months of 1930 have been described as 'a reign of terror' by 'an army of occupation'.[58] As miner George Teerman later remembered:

> There was the Woolloomooloo Wreckers. They were a lot of scum they picked up in Sydney and brought to Cessnock to act as special security men. They'd parade up and down the streets in trucks, sitting back to back down the centre. They'd give them a mug of rum before the truck left and where there was a demonstration . . . they drove through the demonstration. And where they had mounted police they drove the bloody horses through the marchers.

George's wife, Freda, claimed that 'Not more than two people were allowed to assemble. If there were two or three kids, teenagers, standing on a street corner, the police would just belt them down where they stood.'[59] The local population responded by boycotting any hotel that served beer to the police or non-unionists, and denying police access to shops and services. Sporting events, evangelical meetings and concert parties were formed to maintain the morale of the strikers.

Eventually, the strike petered out. In March, the Bavin government stopped payments of unemployment relief to any miners who refused to work at the pits on the current rates.[60] By mid-1930, the miners were forced to accept terms that were only slightly better than those demanded by the employers at the start of the strike. Many never worked in the mines again. One historian of the town of Cessnock wrote, some fifteen years after the strike,

Across the community and the minds of the people is a dark shadow; it is that which comes from the economic collapse of 1929 and the incidents which followed in subsequent years . . . Mental attitudes have become so warped by suffering and disappointment that suspicion and bitterness are uppermost. It has estranged many from the Australian society as a whole and engendered a permanent spirit of antagonism toward their fellows. It has bred a deep pessimism which hangs like a thick fog over the whole town. No one believes that the future can equal the past.[61]

CHAPTER 10

The unemployed

For most Australians the most visible and intractable problem as the economic crisis deepened was unemployment. In 1930, the percentage of trade union members who registered as unemployed rose from 14.6 per cent in the first quarter to 23.5 per cent in the last quarter. This figure would climb relentlessly through the next two years, peaking at perhaps 30 per cent of trade union members unemployed in the third quarter of 1932.[1] Even at the end of 1936, the unemployment rate would be 10.7 per cent. The resulting human drama—long dole queues, home evictions, shanty towns and destitute men and families roaming the country in search of work—has dominated many histories of the Depression. But this is not the complete story. The impact of the economic crisis varied significantly across different cohorts of Australians.

It is difficult to know the exact number of Australians who became unemployed. The figures quoted in Table 10.1 were compiled by trade unions, and were almost certainly an underestimation. They recorded the status of the skilled and semi-skilled workers who were union members, but they did not capture the situation of those who let their union membership lapse as an economy measure, or that multitude of casual workers who so often form the underclass in times of economic crisis. Furthermore, union data did not measure the underemployment that was endemic during the Great Depression. As many workers and employers concluded that part-time employment was better than none, the 'rationing' of work, or going 'short time', would become widespread, if never condoned by some unionists.[2]

Table 10.1: Percentage unemployment among trade unionists in each state and Australia, 1923–38

	NSW	Victoria	Queensland	South Australia	Western Australia	Tasmania	Australia
1923	9.2	5.4	7.1	4.6	5.7	3.8	7.1
1924	12.6	7.1	6.4	4.6	5.5	3.8	8.9
1925	11.0	8.6	6.6	4.3	6.1	7.8	8.8
1926	7.4	6.4	8.4	5.2	7.1	13.9	7.1
1927	7.0	7.4	5.9	7.2	5.4	11.1	7.0
1928	11.3	10.9	7.0	15.0	8.2	10.6	10.8
1929	11.5	11.1	7.1	15.7	9.9	13.4	11.1
1930	21.7	18.3	10.7	23.3	19.2	19.1	19.3
1931	30.8	25.8	16.2	32.5	27.3	27.4	27.4
1932	32.5	26.5	18.8	34.0	29.5	26.4	29.0
1933	28.9	22.3	15.3	29.9	24.8	19.1	25.1
1934	24.7	17.4	11.7	25.6	17.8	17.9	20.5
1935	20.6	14.0	8.7	17.6	13.4	15.9	16.5
1936	15.4	10.7	7.8	10.8	8.1	12.7	12.2
1937	10.9	9.0	7.3	8.2	5.6	7.3	9.3
1938	9.9	8.6	6.4	8.3	5.7	7.9	8.7

Source: Broomhill, *Unemployed Workers*, p. 13, citing Australia, *Labour Report, 1923–38*.

Despite their limitations, trade union data were accepted at the time by economists such as Giblin as a rough indicator of the level of unemployment in Australia. Moreover, a later 1957 international comparison of unemployment during the Great Depression concluded that Australian trade union data were relatively robust. Because of the high degree of union organisation, the data covered a large percentage of the Australian labour market: the sample on which they were based was substantial, and the range of industries they covered was wide. Moreover, the data had a 'fairly close correspondence' with the other major source of information about employment at the time, the national census conducted in 1933. Hence, trade union data 'mirrored with considerable accuracy the prevailing level of unemployment'.[3] Some historians continue to dispute this, arguing that possibly more like 50 per cent of Australians were unemployed.[4] The consensus, however, is that unemployment ranged between 25 and 30 per cent, being worst in 1932. This positions Australia as being one of the hardest hit of the more developed countries, exceeded perhaps only by Germany.[5]

These are aggregate figures, however, and unemployment was not uniform across the country. As Table 10.1 shows, South Australia and New South Wales were particularly hard hit, though no state was left unscarred. Nor were all sectors of the economy equally affected by the economic crisis. The bulk of the recorded rise in unemployment between 1928–29 and 1930–31 was concentrated in the building and construction industries and manufacturing. The former was devastated by the massive reduction of government funding for public works, as overseas lending dried up in the late 1920s, and by the collapse of new investment in residential and commercial structures.[6] Take Adelaide: only 51 houses were built in 1931, *less than 2 per cent* of the number erected in 1926. Some 63.6 per cent of workers normally employed in the industry were without a job in 1933. The brick and tile manufacturing industries that had employed more than nine hundred people in 1926–27 employed about a tenth of that number in 1931–32.[7] The knock-on effect for trades associated with building was dire. Thirty employees of the Adelaide Electric Supply Company were laid off in one week of April 1929 because of the reduction in connections.[8] Across the state, even in 1933, unemployment among plasterers was 72.1 per cent; bricklayers, 69.5 per cent; painters, 67.9 per cent. Moreover, many people 'employed' in the brick and tiles industry were possibly working, on average, about half time.[9] A carpenter in Adelaide later recalled:

I remember I used to look around for a job for carpenters . . . and watch the papers: I used to get up very early in the morning and I'd see: 'Wanted, Carpenter', so right, I'd get on my bike, and I'd pedal for miles . . . I used to be out at a job there about half past six in the morning, waiting on the job, to find dozens of other blokes there waiting too, to get the job.[10]

It was little better elsewhere. In March 1930, the Bricklayers' Union in Victoria claimed that around 75 per cent of its members were out of work. In Sydney, building activity in 1932 is estimated to have reached only 6 per cent of that recorded in 1929. In Melbourne, in contrast, it was 20 per cent.[11]

In the manufacturing sector, the levels of unemployment varied across industries. In the Sydney metropolitan area, where 45,256 fewer people were employed in factories in 1930–31 than in 1928–29, there was a 20 per cent decline in employment in industrial metals; a 16 per cent decline in food, drink and tobacco; a 19 per cent decline in printing and paper; and a 29 per cent reduction in textiles and clothing (although textiles was one of the first industries to show signs of recovery between 1931 and 1932, thanks to the government's strict control of imports).[12] In South Australia, according to employers' returns, the worst-affected industries again included clothing, but there were dramatic declines in employment in the agricultural-implements industry, furniture and footwear. Boots, unlike food, were a discretionary item on which many people chose to economise, even if it meant that their boots ultimately fell apart.[13]

Demand also collapsed for heavy industry—metals, motor vehicles and engineering—especially because of the loss of government contracts.[14] One motor-body builder who finished his apprenticeship just as the Depression began later recalled:

> I was 4 years out of a regular steady job. There was many jobs of short duration, and I took on what I could get. I did mechanical and body repairs in the back yard etc. Most of this was from people who knew me but money was short all round. I used to take off once a week. I lived in Northcote [more than 6 kilometres from central Melbourne]. I would walk to the city, see my old firm in North Melbourne, visit all [the] shops I knew of in the City, South Melbourne, then walk through Richmond, Collingwood to Kew. Then home again . . . But it was always the same answer. They had plenty of their own 'Old Hands' off work.[15]

In Adelaide, the newly developed motor industry shrank catastrophically. Holden had produced more than 50,000 car bodies in 1926–27; by 1931–32, this had dropped to 3245. According to employers' returns, only 17 per cent of those employed in this industry in 1926–27 were still employed by 1931–32.[16] Not without cause were the workers of Adelaide reported as saying: 'The definition of an optimist is someone who takes their lunch to Holden's.'[17] The pressure was such that in 1931 Holden merged with the American company General Motors to become General Motors-Holden.

The high levels of unemployment in manufacturing, building and construction meant that the Great Depression bore most heavily on manual workers and their families. Working-class precincts that had long battled poverty became the epicentre of unemployment. By one estimate, the inner Sydney suburbs of Alexandria and Redfern had unemployment figures of 44 and 48 per cent respectively.[18] The impact of the Depression on other sectors of the economy, however, was less severe. Most of the service industries, with the exception of transport, were relatively unaffected (the 'relatively' is important, nonetheless). Thanks to the issue of ration tickets under the systems of sustenance that governments introduced in 1930 (see Chapter 14), food production, too, was sustained, if at lower levels than before. Men and women working in the retail sector were also relatively secure, assuming they worked in major stores. For example, while employment in typical 'corner' shops in South Australia decreased by almost 50 per cent between 1928 and 1931, the department store John Martin's reduced its staff numbers, which totalled some 1128 in 1929, by only seven in 1931. Myer actually increased employees by 8 per cent.[19] In November 1933, John Martin's even scheduled the first of its Christmas pageants, which are beloved by South Australians to this day. In its first year, the pageant had only about twelve floats and four bands, but it included the rocking horses, Nipper and Nimble, that every girl in the crowd ached to ride, wearing fairy dresses and wings. It culminated naturally with a silver-bearded Father Christmas, soon to be installed in his Magic Cave. He had been joy-riding in a plane earlier that day, reindeers, it seems, not being readily available in the semi-desert state. Some 200,000 spectators witnessed the parade, the largest crowd since the Australia Day processions of the war years.[20] Yet the spectacle of the Christmas pageant aside, it was common practice in the retail sector for workers to be employed on reduced hours.

For other non-manual workers, the impact of the crisis was again variable. It seems that many clerical staff in struggling factories were made redundant: male clerks are thought to have suffered an unemployment rate of at least 50 per cent in 1932.[21] Those working in the public sector had a greater degree of security, but numbers were still reduced by early retirements, severe restrictions on new recruitment and the dismissal of individuals whose performance was deemed unsatisfactory.[22] As in retail, 'short time' was extensive, and public-sector salaries were reduced under the Premiers' Plan in 1931 (see Chapter 24). Yet, to offset this, the number of teachers in New South Wales increased until 1931, after which there was a slight decline.[23] In Victoria, according to the 1933 census, education had an unemployment rate of only 2 per cent. This presumably did not take into account those many recent teaching graduates who were unable to enter the profession.[24]

The health sector, meanwhile, experienced relatively low unemployment rates. In Victoria, this was recorded as 7 per cent in 1933 (even though the funding situation of the hospitals was precarious as early as 1930). In New South Wales, a small but steady increase occurred in hospital staff from June 1928 to June 1934.[25] Nursing, a traditional field of employment for women, continued to offer some girls opportunities. As one nurse later recalled, 'Girls, who had lost their jobs in offices and banks, swamped the hospitals to train as nurses . . . Training as a nurse . . . has its compensations as I had a job and the hospital was my home for four years.'[26]

The professional classes, meanwhile, had varied fortunes. Architects, surveyors and civil engineers, whose fortunes were linked to those of the construction industry and government contracts, lost considerable income. Some accountants slipped into unemployment:

> my boyfriend [one oral interviewee later recalled] was a qualified accountant and the only work he could get after the depression hit . . . was delivering ice [presumably for domestic non-mechanical refrigerators] in the summer-time and wood and coal in the winter. For delivering ice for 'Annabels' Ice Works he was paid £3 per week, starting

work at 5.30 a.m. and finishing around 2 p.m. The wood and coal job was much harder as he had to go each night and chop the wood and bag it, and the coal and deliver it next day.[27]

But while some professionals slipped into 'tragic genteel poverty', many lawyers, ministers of religion, bankers and doctors seem to have weathered the economic storm without significant difficulty, especially as the cost of living declined in real terms. In Adelaide, about 90 per cent of doctors in private practice earned more than double the basic wage in 1932–33, as did about half of all lawyers and dentists.[28] Yet, to counter this, anecdotal evidence records doctors and dentists forfeiting income by not charging destitute patients for their consultations.[29]

Those in business had a range of experiences that again make generalisations difficult. Large companies, such as BHP and CSR (Colonial Sugar Refining) were relatively quarantined from disaster. Their profits declined but BHP paid dividends to its shareholders in all but one year of the Depression. So, too, did the agricultural business Elder, Smith & Co.[30] Other companies, such as the Adelaide *Advertiser* (which absorbed another local paper, *The Register*, in 1931) grew through mergers and takeovers.[31] The situation of small business, however, was more precarious. The number of business insolvencies jumped sharply in 1930–31 (some 4645 as opposed to 2145 in 1928–29) before declining in the following year.[32] Probably many other family or one-man businesses closed their doors without record. Some may have masked their unemployment. Close to 26,000 of the men who said they were self-employed in the 1933 census earned less than the basic wage in the previous year.[33] As one taxidriver later recalled, 'I've sat all night in Rundle Street, Adelaide . . . and didn't get anything at all. Driving a cab in the depression was just a flash way of being unemployed.'[34] Yet it is important to note that even at its worst, the number of bankruptcies represented less than 1 per cent of those defined as employers or self-employed.[35]

In many ways, the impact of the Depression was mediated through class. Life in many middle-class suburbs continued, it seems, with relatively little hardship. Those who retained capital could even purchase assets at prices well below their previous value. The stock market also recovered in 1931 and 1932, while throughout the Depression years dividends continued to be paid. Of course, lifestyles were often more modest than in the 1920s, and many white-collar workers were deeply anxious that they, too, might join the unemployed. But their experience was more one of cost cutting and 'tightening of belts' than destitution. The 'Situations Vacant' column in the *Sydney Morning Herald* thus recorded a decline in the demand for domestic servants after 1928. But some demand still existed.[36] In 1933, the unemployment rate among female domestic servants was 13.7 per cent.[37] The wages of domestic servants, after all, were more like pocket money, their main remuneration being of a pre-industrial kind, in the form of a subsistence income of free board and food, for which any amount of work might be demanded in return. With a tinge perhaps of retrospective bitterness, women employed in domestic service in Woollahra, one of Sydney's prosperous eastern suburbs, would later say of their employers: 'Oh the Depression didn't affect them. It was another world. No, I don't think they even knew it was going on.' 'Life went on just the same for them, they denied themselves nothing. They had no need to . . . They had all the parties they wanted to.'[38] Yet if life went on, many of these more prosperous women, as we shall see, felt compelled by a sense of *noblesse oblige* to devote many hours to voluntary relief work (see Chapter 11).

The differential impact of the Depression can be mapped onto geography as well as class. Self-evidently, the collapse of wool and wheat prices from 1929–30 on had a ruinous impact on rural communities. The 1930–31 season was 'one of the leanest in the history of the wool industry' as prices declined by 48 per cent from 1928–29 levels. The following year was little better; and only in 1936–37 did wool exports reach the value of their 1920s peak.[39] That great swathe of wheat farming, stretching from the north and north-west of Adelaide, through Victoria and the Riverina, across central New South Wales to the Queensland border, was also devastated as average wheat export prices halved between 1927–28 and 1930–31.[40] By one estimate, a quarter of wheat farmers devoted between one-third and one-quarter of their income in 1931 to interest obligations.[41] As we shall see later, the federal and state governments would attempt, not always very effectively, to address the question of farmers' debts, a matter of the highest priority for the Country Party, but the anger and distress of country Australians was so great that it would also fuel political demands for new states and even secession (see Chapter 21).

Wheat and wool producers were particularly vulnerable because they were export-oriented and had to compete in global markets. Wheat was in chronic oversupply globally, as Australia and the other major producers, such as Canada, Argentina and the United States, increased production while importers increased protection for domestic growers.[42] The sugar industry in Queensland, in contrast, was quarantined from disaster by its almost complete monopoly of the domestic market. In 1930 the sugar industry in Queensland was able to keep employing 28,000 men in the field and 7000 in the mills, while the domestic price of sugar was sustained at three times the global level.[43] The sugar embargo was a particular grievance of housewives' associations in other states. The South Australian Housewives' Association protested in October 1930 that the 'sugar interests' were taking £600,000 per year from their pockets: 'Think what that could do towards developing South Australian industries.'[44] For the workers on the Queensland cane fields, however, the threat was not price inflation but an outbreak of Weil's disease, or leptospirosis, a haemorrhagic disease spread by rats (see Chapter 31).[45]

To geography and class, we need to add other variables: age and gender. It seems that during the Great Depression it was a liability to be under 21 or over 55. Young men stayed at school beyond the official leaving age of fourteen because of the lack of work and shortage of apprenticeships. In New South Wales in 1932, only 404 indentures of apprenticeships were registered, a decrease of 72 per cent on the 1929 figures. Even in 1935 there were 33 per cent fewer than in 1929.[46] As a Sydney child R. Andrews later recalled, when his brother was chosen from 300 boys for an apprenticeship at the Sydney County Council, his mother wept. It was the only time he could remember her doing so in his childhood.[47] Yet for all their vulnerability, the young unemployed tended not to be classified as unemployed, possibly because, as the Bureau of Census and Statistics later estimated, they might have added an extra 2.4 per cent to the total unemployed.[48] The young unemployed fell into a limbo: as one nineteen- to twenty-year-old said in 1934: 'I am now too old for some jobs and have no experience or qualifications for others. My outlook is one of blank despair. I was born either 10 years too soon or ten or twenty years too late.'[49]

At the other end of the age spectrum, older men were at risk because of their loss of the physical strength that manual labour demanded. Many slipped into long-term unemployment. Moreover, contemporary social mores and wage structures gave preference to younger married men with family responsibilities. As one fitter and turner later recalled:

> The boss came down and said to the foreman. What's this? It isn't an old man's home. You'd better get rid of him! . . . The sort they [employers] liked was a young married man, young enough to be active, and old enough to be experienced. And a married man stays put, they've got him tied down. He'll work overtime if they want him to.[50]

As for gender, the data suggest that women's employment was less adversely affected than men's. The 1933 census, for example, shows the national level of unemployment for women was 14.9 per cent, with the percentage being a little lower for rural divisions.[51] This was possibly because the workplace was segmented along gendered lines and women were concentrated in sectors that were less damaged by the economic crisis. As Table 10.2 shows, the vast majority of women in manufacturing were to be found in textiles and clothing production, an industry that was protected to some degree by the high tariffs on imports. A further significant cohort of women worked in food production, for which there continued to be demand. Women, too, were often employed as teachers, nurses, shop assistants, telephonists and typists—again sectors that had relatively low rates of unemployment.[52]

Beyond this, the female unemployment rate might have been lower because many women simply did not actively seek paid work. The prevailing social attitude, especially among the middle classes, was that a woman's primary role was in the home, caring for her husband and family. Certain kinds of work were thought to be beyond a woman's biological capacity. The Commonwealth Public Service Board, for example, stated in 1923–24 that:

The general experience throughout the world, as indicated by statistics published in many countries, is that the effective service of women is considerably below that of men, even in the same occupations, and that this is due principally to (1) loss of services through marriage, (2) greater absences on account of sickness, and (3) sapping vitality of unmarried women at an earlier age of life.[53]

Table 10.2: Employment in manufacturing by industrial subdivision, 1927, 1932, 1937

Gender	Males '000			Females '000		
Year	1927	1932	1937	1927	1932	1937
Non-metal mining	21.1	8.7	22.2	0.5	0.4	0.8
Chemical	9.6	8.5	12.5	3.3	3.5	5.2
Metals	132.2	79.1	153.1	4.0	3.6	8.4
Textiles/clothing	34.1	29.4	39.2	79.2	63.0	86.4
Leather	5.6	6.4	8.5	1.3	1.5	2.4
Food	53.4	48.5	57.3	14.6	14.0	20.1
Wood	47.5	20.0	40.7	2.5	1.6	3.4
Other	33.6	29.5	39.2	12.1	10.9	15.8
Total	**337.2**	**230.0**	**372.7**	**117.5**	**98.5**	**142.3**

Source: Vamplew (ed.), *Australians: Historical Statistics*, pp. 291–2.

A distinguished Macquarie Street specialist, meanwhile, writing for the *Women's Weekly* in June 1933, said:

there are many posts and positions held by men in the Commonwealth and State Civil Service, that common humanity, let alone the considerations of the biological make-up of woman herself, would not approve of woman undertaking. I doubt very much if the most enthusiastic women's rights advocate would suggest that sewer work, ploughing, or even many less objectionable forms of manual labor are physiologically suitable for women. Only the Soviet authorities have carried [the idea of equal rights of sexes] to its logical conclusion.[54]

Paid work for women, then, was often seen as 'an episode' before marriage, or a necessary safeguard if a women was left unsupported.[55] Middle-class women usually gave up work after marrying. In New South Wales, meanwhile, married women were banned from teaching in 1932, a policy that lasted until 1947, despite opposition from women's groups such as the United Associations of Women. The rationale was that the dismissal of married women would allow the employment of young teacher graduates.[56] The Commonwealth Public Service also required women to resign on marriage (the so-called marriage ban was not lifted until 1966). Married women might return to work, usually as typists, a job regarded as unsuitable for men, but their status was temporary, with few entitlements or superannuation rights. As non-permanent officers, women were barred from holding supervisory positions. They were thus always clustered at the bottom of the public-sector hierarchy.

The Depression probably reinforced this trend more widely, forcing many single working women back into the traditional role of supporting their mothers at home. Those who remained in employment, especially when they were married, could be accused of competing for scarce jobs with married men who had family responsibilities. As a correspondent to the Adelaide *Advertiser* put it, employers should take a 'firm stand' against hiring women who have husbands earning good salaries. It might save many homes from 'wreckage' by making 'married women stay at home and do their duty to their husbands and children'.[57] 'You didn't wear a wedding ring to work,' one married female worker later recalled.[58]

All this did not mean that women were spared the worst of the Depression. As we shall see in Chapter 26, their security was often at risk. Those who remained in employment were frequently reduced to part-time work. Their rates of pay were already lower than men's, given that the Australian arbitration system, at federal and state levels, had long differentiated between women's and men's labour, and the payment each should receive. Beyond this, if female workers became unemployed, their needs were not adequately met in the relief systems that prioritised males, and married men at that. Single women, often in their teens, and without family support, could slip into destitution. Perhaps most importantly, mothers and wives worked to the point of exhaustion in the home, economising, improvising and denying their own needs, to keep their families fed and clothed. It was simply that, as ever, much of women's work was unpaid.

In summary, unemployment rates were so variable across Australia that it is difficult to generalise about the social impact of the Great Depression. Many of the efforts of governments, charities, churches and community organisations that we shall now explore were focused on the urban unemployed, whose plight and distress was visible, desperate and acute. But the experiences of those who were less affected by the Depression should not be forgotten. Their stories have often been lost, in part because they lacked the public profile that came with violent protest, and in part because their stories do not make such engrossing reading as do trauma and suffering. But they need to be remembered in the 'Australian' narrative of the Great Depression nonetheless.

CHAPTER 11

The voluntary sector to the rescue

Australians thrown into unemployment in the late 1920s faced possible destitution as there was nothing resembling a modern social welfare safety net. The federal and state governments, with the exception of Queensland, had few systems for dealing with the social distress caused by unemployment. Traditionally, the care of the poor and destitute had been the responsibility of charitable and voluntary organisations. It would soon become clear that these largely voluntary groups could not cope with the massive unemployment of the Depression, but even then governments continued to rely on benevolent societies, church organisations and proactive individuals to deliver relief. They also looked to these organisations to increase the volume of aid provided by the state through countless fundraising activities. This community engagement formed a critical part of the response to the Depression and an integral part of social resilience—even though many volunteers had deeply moralistic understandings of the causes of poverty that were anachronistic, given the structural economic crisis now afflicting Australia.

The scale of charitable relief activities was remarkable. To quote only some statistics: in 1927 the New South Wales Benevolent Society assisted more than 23,000 unemployed. In 1931, this number had multiplied seven times and the society distributed 1.3 million loaves of bread, 1.54 million pounds (nearly 700,000 kilograms) of meat, 1.3 million pounds (over 500,000 kilograms) of sugar, more than 1.1 million tins of jam and nearly 900,000 tins of condensed milk.[1] By September 1931, its counterpart in Victoria, the Melbourne Ladies Benevolent Society, had supported some 6000 families.[2]

Such services depended upon voluntary labour provided largely by middle-class women and professional men. We know little of these people apart from their names, but it has been said of the women who staffed the Melbourne Charity Organisation Society, a coordinating agency for some 25 loosely affiliated societies: 'They were Protestants. They were not rich, but comfortable; their gentility was based on good schooling rather than wealth. They lived in respectable rather than grand suburbs. Most remained unmarried. They spent years even decades in welfare work.'[3] For many such women, voluntary work was a means of filling the hours left empty by the lack of occupational opportunities for women of their class; or it gave expression to their religious convictions, humanitarianism and sense of social obligation. Many were 'joiners', serving in other reforming organisations like the Woman's Christian Temperance Union, an association long dedicated to eradicating the scourge of alcohol but now also engaged with issues of peace, social justice and Aboriginal welfare. Many volunteers were almost certainly the same 'patriotic feminists' who had filled the void left by absent sons and husbands during World War I by throwing themselves into fundraising for comfort parcels for the troops.[4] As one woman said when proposing a plan for the relief of unemployed women and girls in 1931, the project 'can be splendidly done by real co-operative and enthusiasm among women of all classes such as the world witnessed during the war'.[5] These women were also, in some cases, supporting the very same men who filled the trenches of Gallipoli and the Western Front a few years earlier.

Many of these volunteers had values and attitudes more appropriate to the Victorian era than the crisis now confronting them. They saw poverty not so much as the result of global or national economics but as a matter of individual character. Yes, some of the poor were 'deserving'—being the victims of sickness, low earnings or the death of the breadwinner—but many were guilty of drunkenness, gambling, crime or being needlessly out of work. As the Secretary of the Victorian Charities Board, a government body responsible for coordinating the distribution of relief funds, said in mid-1930: 'As case after case is brought before you, the conclusion is at length inescapable that some weak point in character is at the bottom of almost every case of distress and to strengthen character . . . is the only remedy worth applying.'[6] From this perspective, the role of charity was not just to provide relief but also to intervene as a moral saviour, discouraging the 'loafer and the professional beggar' and instilling the family breadwinner with a sense of responsibility and a work ethic of thrift, independence and sobriety that could then be passed on to his children and benefit the community.[7]

Given these attitudes, the various benevolent societies established their own value-infused hierarchies of merit and need. Mothers and children were almost automatically entitled to support. So, too, were women who had been widowed or deserted. Sympathy was readily accorded to the 'good type of man', the 'very superior class of man', families with an 'honest' husband or father, and those afflicted by illness or bereavement.[8] The Melbourne Ladies Benevolent Society in January 1930 deemed as 'very pathetic', the case of a man who 'in desperation decided to leave his wife and children, as he felt that . . . he was unable to obtain work and was only adding one more mouth to be fed, whereas help might be more willingly and easily arranged for his wife and children. The wife had no reason at all to doubt her husband's affection for her and the children, and was very broken-hearted over the position.'[9] Another case deemed 'worthy' was a returned soldier with neurasthenia, a nervous complaint, who received no pension because he was an 'imperial soldier'.[10] In contrast, the man who was alcoholic or sported a criminal record could be deemed unworthy. The Brisbane Charity Organisation Society rejected a family that liked horseracing and whose neighbours accused them of being unscrupulous in their dealings.[11]

It was obviously necessary for the charities to establish priorities, given that demand always outstripped supply. But their methods sometimes verged on the inquisitorial. Charity workers compiled in-depth case files: checking the bona fides of applicants through official records; interrogating shopkeepers; interviewing neighbours; and visiting the homes of the unemployed. The New South Wales Benevolent Society made nearly 85,000 home visits in 1930.[12]

These calls served to assess a family's need, but the poor might be damned if their houses were untidy or their dress and attitude inappropriate.[13] The claim of a well-dressed applicant to the Charity Organisation Society in Melbourne was dismissed, in part, because her fingers were much stained with nicotine.[14] The condition of the Brisbane shanty house of one family excluded them from relief: 'a more disgusting place it would be impossible to imagine', the Charity Organisation Society case file read. 'The careless habits of the father and mother naturally had a demoralising effect upon the children. The Society cannot encourage families of this sort.'[15]

One of the obsessions of charities and government officials alike was to winkle out fraud by 'the clever cadger and the plausible imposter'.[16] The potential for duplication was rife, given the large number of charitable and official relief schemes. The lack of central records meant that some people were able to move from one system of relief to another, with repeat applications. The Bavin government in New South Wales responded by setting up a central register in mid-1930, which required charities to provide monthly lists of the names and addresses of their clients and limit the assistance they gave to those receiving government relief. If charities failed to comply, they risked losing such government funding as they had. Many took the risk, in order to protect their clients' privacy, but throughout the 1930s they had to furnish the government with details of their clients when applying for annual grants.[17] For all this, two detailed studies of charity organisations suggest that the cases of 'professional mendacity', as the Charity Organisation Society called it, were few.[18]

In this climate, the efforts of the charities to assist the unemployed were often disparaged. One man interviewed decades later said, 'The churches, the social workers, all the charities . . . Where would they get their lovely feelings from, if they didn't have the poor to operate on? Where would they get their worthiness from?'[19] Such tensions were fuelled by the loss of self-respect that many of the unemployed experienced. Another man recalled in 1994: 'The very fact you were out of work was a humiliation, because in the end the heels of your shoes went down and you wouldn't be human if you didn't say, "Oh, I've had this".'[20] Later historians, too, have depicted the charities as agents of social control. Arguably, they were concerned not just with humanitarianism but with establishing a physical and moral hegemony over 'the dangerous classes', thereby safeguarding middle-class morale and property, and the moral and social order.[21]

Yet such criticisms of the charity workers should be qualified. While some were certainly judgemental, patronising and moralistic, not all were so. The Melbourne Ladies Benevolent Society housed a range of opinions, with some women espousing a more scientific, professional approach to unemployment relief.[22] Attitudes within charities also softened as the scale of the social catastrophe grew. Some charity workers embraced new ways of thinking about class, dependency and social disadvantage. They came to recognise the role of structure, accident and injustice in impoverishment and, facing their own financial struggles as the Depression deepened, gained a heightened sensitivity to explanations of penury that went beyond flawed character and moral weakness. Destitute people were taken more at their word. Often, charity workers developed friendships with the poor and became their advocates.[23] Moreover, even in their distress, the recipients of aid retained a strong sense of pride and agency. They were 'a great deal more than puppets on the end of *bourgeois* strings'.[24]

Many charity workers also worked tirelessly to the point of burnout. As early as November 1930, the Unemployment Relief Committee in the Perth suburb of Bassendean, which was severely affected by the Depression, noted that 'the ladies' carrying out fortnightly collections were 'practically worn out with the work' and found it 'impossible to continue with their voluntary work on account of the strain imposed, which caused them to suffer ill-health'.[25] The finances of these organisations were often so stretched that they had no option but to cease operations. Still, they had an unfailing commitment and a dedication that succeeded in mitigating the direst effects of poverty on many Australians. Like the local councils that we will meet later, by being 'there' they contributed to the sense of community that was one of Australians' sources of resilience.

The same can be said of another major player in the charitable landscape, the Christian churches. Like many in the benevolent societies, with whom they often overlapped, church leaders tended to approach the Depression as a moral and spiritual issue. Just as they had seen World War I as a calamity visited upon the human race to chastise it for its lack of righteousness, now Protestant clergy saw the Depression as the 'divine dispensation' of God upon a wayward people. As the official statement of the dour Lutheran leaders put it in May 1931, Australians had slipped into 'decadence' with 'a general lowering of moral standards in public and private life'. Divorce, adultery, murder, suicide, birth control, slander, defamation, disrespect for authority, dishonesty in public life and the 'thoughtless, selfish and sinful waste of money on superfluous things and often worse than useless pleasures': these and 'a thousand other sins' were the 'real causes' of Australia's Depression.[26] The Queensland Congregational Union, too, argued that the Depression was due to the economic waste caused by man's drinking and his excessive pursuit of pleasure.[27] In a similar, if less puritanical vein, Anglican leaders argued that the cause of the Depression lay in the unchristian attitude of 'putting ourselves first, whether as a nation, a community or as individuals'.[28] Australians had been extravagant, wasteful and had lived beyond their means, spending money that they had not earned. This, it might be noted, did not stop Anglicans in Western Australia, at least, from maintaining an ambitious program of building church educational and hospital facilities during the Depression years.

There were, of course, more nuanced interpretations. Many clergymen appreciated the role of easy national borrowings, unwise spending and fiscal barriers in Australia's economic problems.[29] The Dean of Brisbane in 1931 blamed advances in science that allowed machines to replace workers.[30] Catholic thinking, meanwhile, was shaped by the encyclical issued by Pope Pius XI in May 1931, *Quadragesimo Anno* (Reconstructing the Social Order), which addressed the ethical challenges facing workers, employers, the church and the state as a result of the Depression, and the need for a more just distribution of wealth and wages than that being provided by the capitalist economic regime. Lay Catholics were inspired by its agenda to establish Catholic Action groups to work for a reconstruction of society inspired by Catholic principles.[31]

Generally, however, the leaders of the Christian churches failed to articulate a coherent or radical vision as to how to alleviate unemployment. In contrast to Britain and the United States, where liberals enjoyed considerable influence in Protestant circles, 'advocates of social reforms, disciples of J.M. Keynes and critics of capitalism were not prominent in the [Australian] "churches of the Reformation"'.[32] Instead, given their values of thrift, sobriety and self-denial, the churches were inclined to embrace the economic orthodoxy of 1930–31, that Australians must accept a reduced standard of living and that the unemployed should work for the dole. To quote a manifesto released by the Protestant churches in 1931, 'all public measures of relief for the unemployed should aim at providing some kind of work, so that those receiving aid may preserve their self-respect, and guard against the weakening of character'.[33] Since many Protestants were also fervent imperialists, they refused to entertain the radical option of repudiation of the debts owed to the mother country—a policy that would, in any case, have transgressed the moral code of honesty.

Still, if they were bereft of policy innovation, many churches across the denominational spectrum recognised the urgency of providing relief for the unemployed. As the Dean of Newcastle, the Very Reverend William Johnson, said, unemployment was 'an affront and corrosive poison' and the churches should 'hear [Christ's] voice saying: "Inasmuch as ye did it unto one of the least of these my brethren, ye did it unto me"'.[34] Across the country, then, the churches offered practical aid in huge quantities. The detail can be overwhelming, but is worth citing to demonstrate the impressive range and reach of the support provided by non-profit agencies. It also attests to the role that highly motivated individuals played in creating what we might now call a social economy.

The Catholic efforts were spearheaded by the St Vincent de Paul Society. In 1930 it provided relief to more than 50,000 people in New South Wales alone.[35] In Brisbane, it operated a hostel that supplied hundreds of meals and beds daily to the unemployed, and distributed clothing, including surplus army boots and greatcoats that were donated by the federal government.[36] Beyond the capital in Townsville, the names of society members were chalked underneath the town bridge, to be visible to the unemployed camping there.[37] In Adelaide, the Norwood 'conference' of the Ladies' Society of St Vincent de Paul, which boasted only twelve members, assisted 57 families. In 1930, they provided boots, blankets, 50 pairs of sheets, three eiderdowns, two mattresses, more than twelve parcels of second-hand clothing and 366 new garments. They made 225 visits to the sick and provided milk to several families. In Port Adelaide, expectant mothers were again provided with bedding, clothing and food. Schoolchildren were given boots, clothing, 'nourishment' and school-books. Of course, the spiritual needs of 'careless Catholics' were not forgotten either. Prayer books and Catholic literature were provided, infants and adults baptised, and masses offered for the living and the dead.[38]

Similar relief programs were run by the Protestant churches. The Church of England Men's Society based in Fortitude Valley, Brisbane, provided close to 100,000 free meals for unemployed single men in 1931. With support from farmers, businesses and the Queensland Railways Department, it also distributed clothing, operated a boot-repair service for men 'on the move' in search of work, and established a subsidised hostel, St Oswald's, at North Quay.[39] In Melbourne, the Anglican Church delivered social welfare through agencies such as the St John's and St Martin's Homes for Boys, the Mission to the Streets and Lanes, and the Community of the Holy Name, a ministry of Anglican sisters.[40] In Fitzroy, a priest, R.G. Nichols, extended a scheme he had initiated in the mid-1920s of providing hot meals—'penny dinners'—for hundreds of children at schools. His wife supervised the cooking while private individuals and traders donated the goods. This program was replicated in other parishes, from Prahran to Warrnambool and Adelaide.[41]

At least one initiative had an enduring impact on Australian welfare. An Anglican priest, Father Gerard Tucker, this time in Newcastle, established in 1930 the Brotherhood of St Laurence, with the aim of alleviating poverty. The organisation, which still endures, moved in 1933 to Melbourne, where Tucker's first project was a hostel for homeless unemployed men. In 1935 he devised a plan to relocate them and their families to a nearby farming community.[42] On the other side of the continent in Western Australia, the Anglican churches, after a 'tardy start, worked with auxiliaries and Toc H to run soup kitchens, men's teas and social evenings for the unemployed', while providing goods, and an employment service for immigrant workers. One Anglican deaconess recalled that in 1931:

we come to a shop where for some time we have paid for extra milk to be given to two of our poor friends . . . we ask again about Mrs W. She has 9 children, and the maximum sustenance only allows for 5 and she is far from strong; but we wonder if she is getting help from others? 'Oh no, I don't think so', says our friend at the shop . . . So once again we pay for the extra milk and wonder will we be able to do so again. Calling on Mrs W. who is bed, again we go on . . . then we stop at a terrace just opposite the school to inquire for an old couple, whom last week we got one of our friends to take in as they had nowhere to go. We paid for the first week's rent.[43]

The range of activities was similar among other churches. In Brisbane, the Methodists provided a total of 140,000 free meals in the eighteen months before November 1931, and ran their own hostel at Spring Hill.[44] In Melbourne, the Central Methodist Mission, with the aid of public subscriptions, provided a three-course meal to 130 homeless 'girls' every day in 1930–31, at the café adjacent to Wesley Church.[45] In Adelaide, the Methodist Mission, among other things, handed out second-hand clothing and military tunics. One man later remembered:

They would give them out at the back of the police station and there would be such a rush for them. I would grab a sleeve and someone else would grab a sleeve. We would finish up that were lucky to get a sleeve each [Laughs]. Rev. Willaston was marvellous the way he used to give out clothing. Without him I don't know how I would have got on . . . Sometimes he would come around and visit you, or send some of the mission women around.[46]

The Salvation Army, too, was, as ever, at the coalface of social need. As one itinerant man in Western Australia later commented: 'I've never been religious at all, not in any degree. But it was the Salvation Army who cheerfully bore the brunt of helping people in the depression. I give the Sallys full marks for their zeal.'[47] By 1930, the 'Salvos' were providing meals for 400 families a week in Brisbane.[48] In Semaphore, Adelaide, the Home League provided 1200 clothing parcels in early 1930.[49] In Melbourne, it provided nearly 370,000 free meals in seven months, May to December 1930, and opened the Gill Memorial Home in September 1929 to accommodate single homeless men.[50] The daughter of two Salvation Army officers in Melbourne later recalled that 'We never used to know when [our parents] were coming home of a night, sometimes they would be out half the night, finding these poor men.' Her mother also started a 'Give-out', which was, in effect, 'the first opportunity shop'. In a large barn in Abbotsford, she accumulated donations of clothing 'and stuff'. Everything was given a price, if only a penny or threepence. 'It was better to do that because in their mind they weren't accepting charity as such.' She remembered,

> [Mother] would hold the things up, and you'd hear 'Mrs Blake! Mrs Blake! Oh please, Mrs Blake!' She'd give it to the person she thought needed it most. And you'd hear a long drawn out, 'Ohhhhhhhh!' Somebody else had got it. I've never forgotten that 'Mrs Blake! Me! Me! Me!' and the 'Ohhhhh'.[51]

For all the churches' prodigious efforts at providing food, clothing and shelter, some Christian leaders became convinced that this was not enough. In late 1931, a Catholic Federation Employment Bureau was established in South Australia to try to place men in work.[52] In Sydney, Reverend Robert Hammond, the rector of St Barnabas Church on Broadway, established hostels for the unemployed and went on to found a settlement, Hammondville, near Liverpool in late 1932. Here families who had been evicted or were facing the threat of eviction from their current homes could establish themselves. The accommodation and the land they were allocated were not gifts but had to be paid for on a rent–purchase basis.[53] Beth McLean, who in 1933 taught at the school that the Department of Education established at Hammond's invitation, later commented:

> Cannon Hammond was quite a remarkable man, and he had a remarkable wife. He managed to interest an immense number of people in helping the Settlement . . . the people who went through that place were like the social register of Sydney. The Fibrous Plaster

Manufacturers and trade unionists co-operated to put ceilings in some houses. There was a strong community life. There'd be concerts and dances and there was even a Hammondville Younger Set.[54]

Similar ventures to Hammondville were a rural training scheme for boys at Abergowrie, north of Townsville, and Kuitpo Colony, south of Adelaide. The Queensland venture (later known as St Teresa's Catholic College) was inspired by the admirable, if impracticable, vision of the Catholic bishop of Townsville, Terence McGuire, that 'we should not have undeveloped land and unemployed labour'.[55] Kuitpo was the brainchild of Reverend Samuel Forsyth of the Central Methodist Mission in Adelaide, who also concluded that the way to avoid the demoralisation of the unemployed was to settle them on the land. After a public appeal in *The Advertiser*, and donations from the Adelaide social elite, in 1930 the mission rented property some 70 kilometres from Adelaide. Here the production of sheep, cows, pigs, poultry, fruit and clover intermingled with the clearing of vegetation, wood-chopping, car repairs, boot making, road making, blacksmithing and kitchen duties. Some 7000 men passed through the colony, which prided itself on making men productive members of the community by rescuing them from suicide, gaol and the degradation of unemployment.[56] Kuitpo also prided itself on being non-denominational: 'No man is asked his religion' boasted a promotional pamphlet.

This attests to a seeming—and surprising—lack of sectarianism in the non-government relief sector. An Adelaide meeting convened by Mayor Bonython in February 1929 included representatives of the Methodist City Mission, the Salvation Army and the St Frances Xavier Conference.[57] The Melbourne Ladies Benevolent Society boasted that seven of its 29 committee members in October 1930 were 'Roman Catholics'.[58] St Vincent de Paul, too, assisted the unemployed, homeless and poor irrespective of their religious affiliation.[59] Even where cooperation was lacking, Catholic and Protestant systems of relief seem to have operated in parallel rather than opposition. One interviewee remembered in the 1990s that while there was a sharp divide in Bookham, New South Wales, between Catholics and Protestants, there was 'no animosity': 'We'd all pull together to raise money; if there was a Catholic ball the Anglican women would help out and the Catholic women would help cater at the Anglican ball; but you didn't go to their houses.'[60] A historian of Geelong, Victoria, has also concluded that the 'sectarian differences were temporarily put aside', even if the barriers between the two communities were not broken down.[61]

As it happened, divisions within Protestant denominations could be as intractable. When various charities formed a coordinating agency in the Queensland Social Service League, they fell apart over the issue of whether they should raffle a car donated by General Motors. For the Methodists, Baptists and Salvationists a raffle was a form of gambling. It could not be deemed honest just because the money was being raised for the poor. Months later, the car was sold, although the vote approving this was close, thirteen to twelve, and the organising secretary almost resigned over the issue.[62] Such were some of the passions generated by the devil's choices of the Depression.

Part IV

MAELSTROM, 1930

CHAPTER 12

The tightening band of policy options

By January 1930, Scullin had concluded that Australia was facing 'a financial depression without parallel in the 30 years' life of the Commonwealth'.[1] The tariff increases he had introduced yielded little immediate benefit. On the contrary, imports ordered earlier continued to exceed exports, while the large shipments of gold went only some of the way to restoring the trade balance.[2] Unemployment continued to rise while the Commonwealth's budgetary situation worsened. As the level of London reserves dropped, the pressure on the exchange rate of the Australian pound intensified and the challenge of servicing Australia's debts reached the point where the government felt compelled to seek relief from the British government and, ultimately, defer to the advice of the Bank of England. With the visit of the bank's emissary, the judgemental Sir Otto Niemeyer, in mid- to late 1930, the pressure on Australian governments to adopt deflationary policies mounted. So, too, did the visceral opposition of the labour movement to such policy options.

The raw edge of the growing crisis continued to be unemployment. In late 1929, the federal government offered the states £1 million for roadworks, but this was a drop in the bucket compared with earlier public-works funding. While the ACTU demanded that the government fund the unification of railway gauges across states, in February the Loan Council decided it would have to cut expenditure to one half of the previous year and future programs would need to be funded from the domestic market rather than overseas borrowings.[3] The unemployment rate continued to escalate inexorably, and while Scullin asked the unions in January to prepare a scheme of unemployment insurance for application throughout the Commonwealth (fulfilling a promise he had made in the election campaign), this was never implemented.[4] Travelling to and from Canberra, Scullin was confronted by men tramping the roads looking for work. In the cities, the desperation was spilling over into violence. In Sydney in late February, protesters threatened to storm Parliament and clashed with baton-wielding police. In one case, a policeman was attacked with a 'knuckleduster' while another worker thrashed a policeman with a baton that he had grabbed.[5]

Caught within a tightening band of policy options, Scullin attempted to improve the balance of trade, first by reducing imports even further. In April, he announced what he conceded was a 'sensational' new scale of tariffs. Trade wars always carry the threat of retaliation and, by June, France and Italy had placed extra duties on imports from Australia. The British government, too, complained on behalf of their own manufacturers, especially in the clothing industries, whose exports to Australia were jeopardised. Still, Scullin argued, Britain could hardly urge Australia to put its house in order by balancing its international trading account and then criticise it when it tried to do so. The best contribution that Australia could make to the Empire's economic wellbeing was to make itself strong and prosperous. In time, however, Scullin had to concede that tariffs were doing little to create employment. Indeed, the maritime unions complained to him that the new tariffs had actually increased unemployment on the wharves.[6]

Second, Scullin tried to increase revenue from exports by encouraging farmers to 'Grow More Wheat'.[7] This proved to be a policy disaster. Farmers rushed to comply as the government guaranteed a fixed price for the 1930–31 crop of 4 shillings per bushel at country railway sidings. Growing wheat was depicted in a national advertising campaign as a patriotic duty, whereby farmers could increase their own wealth while performing an 'urgent national service'.[8] Banks were ready to lend more to those willing to take on the challenge. Ultimately some 18 million acres of wheat was planted—3 million more than the record planting of 1929—and, thanks to good autumn rains, the total yield was a 30 per cent increase on the average annual yield for the previous four years. But although Nationalist premiers had actually approved the plan, in July their colleagues in the federal Senate rejected Scullin's plans to create a compulsory national wheat pool to manage the sales. As they saw it, this reeked too much of socialism, denied farmers freedom of choice, and promised to be bureaucratic and inefficient. State legislation for compulsory wheat pools in Victoria and New South Wales also failed to gain the consent of sufficient numbers of wheat growers.[9]

More catastrophically, wheat prices collapsed internationally as other countries also rushed into overproduction. Soon farmers in Australia were paying more to produce their wheat than they could earn through sales. The government's options were few: if it fixed domestic wheat prices at a higher level than exports, or taxed flour, local food would be more expensive. The Commonwealth Bank, for its part, refused to liberalise banking policy on advances to farmers for the coming wheat season. Finally, in December 1930 the government managed to push through the *Wheat Advances Act*. By this time, the guaranteed price was only 2 shillings and 6 pence and the compulsory pool had been abandoned. Even this was too radical for the Commonwealth Bank, whose legal adviser, the young Victorian Robert Menzies, argued that the payment of a guaranteed price would infringe the interstate trade provision of section 92 of the Constitution. Farmers were left to negotiate whatever deal they could get. In the event, Australia's export income did rise substantially, given the volume of wheat and flour produced, but farmers were around 2 shillings poorer for every bushel they produced. The more enthusiastically farmers had responded to the 'Grow More Wheat' campaign, the greater had been their loss.[10] Their anger and need would resonate throughout politics in 1931 and beyond.

The wheat fiasco threw into relief a problem that paralysed the Scullin government throughout its term in office: its lack of a majority in the Senate. On this, and many other occasions in 1930–31, the Opposition parties would block legislation that Labor proposed in an attempt to manage the economic crisis. Should Scullin, then, have tried to cut through this Gordian knot by forcing a double dissolution soon after the election for the House of Representatives in October 1929? Anstey urged him to do so while Labor's stocks were still high. But the moment to challenge the Senate, if it ever existed, was let slip. Few in the Labor caucus had any appetite for another expensive election, which would have been the third in three years. Some feared being consigned to Opposition again by losing seats that they had been astonished to win in the 1929 election. Moreover, the conditions for a double dissolution set out in section 57 of the Constitution (that a piece of legislation has to be rejected twice by the Senate) were difficult to fulfil.[11]

The implications of living with a hostile Senate were soon apparent. Keen to progress Labor's agenda, Scullin introduced a raft of legislation aimed at investing the federal parliament with the power to amend the Constitution and to legislate on industrial relations, trade and commerce with the exception of state railways. But the bills for the necessary referendums were rejected by the Senate in May. The Senate also proved oppositional when, in early April 1930, Theodore introduced legislation to create a central reserve bank.[12] The Commonwealth Bank, as we have seen, had few central banking powers, and since it continued to act as a trading bank as well, it competed with private banks in ordinary banking business. Hence, as Page had discovered in 1924, the private banks would not deposit any considerable proportion of their reserves with the Commonwealth Bank. The argument for banking reform was strong and part of the ALP platform.

Theodore's banking bill passed through the lower house but it met a deluge of opposition in the Senate. Critics claimed that it was no time for radical change in financial institutions; the trading banks would not only be required to keep a proportion of their reserves with the central bank, they would also suffer from the more aggressive competition of the standalone Commonwealth Bank if it functioned as 'a people's bank'. Moreover, it was feared that the board of the new central bank would be open to political influence, having been nominated by government. In fact, the federal government already appointed the Commonwealth Bank board; but conservatives suspected that if Labor made the appointments, the directors might be sympathetic to the policy option that Theodore and other Labor radicals were already beginning to espouse: credit creation. As the young and energetic director of New South Wales Bank, Alfred Davidson, said: 'There is a large body in the Labour Caucus at Canberra which holds extraordinary theories in regard to money, credit and banking. They wish to make of the Reserve Bank a machine for manufacturing notes and credit, regardless of the consequence.'[13] Given the strength of the opposition, and some stalling in the Senate, the bill was eventually abandoned. Its failure contributed to the growing radicalisation of the left of the ALP and the difficulties Scullin faced in pursuing moderate policies.

Beyond all these domestic issues, the Scullin government was still confronted with the implacable problem of servicing Australia's debts in London. In January, the plan was to buy some time until the trade balance improved, by increasing the short-term debt through issuing another tranche of Treasury bills. The hope was that the easing of the strain on international liquidity after the New York stock market collapse would facilitate this course of action. But it soon became clear that there was little confidence in London about Australia's ability to pay her interest bills. Faced with the near-exhaustion of the Commonwealth Bank's sterling reserves, the government managed to persuade the trading banks in February to provide £2.95 million of their sterling reserves to reduce the overdrafts at the London Westminster Bank.[14] But this would provide only temporary relief and, on Gibson's advice, the government decided to ask the British government to defer temporarily the payment of £2.77 million, due on 31 March, towards Australia's war debt.

This request set in motion a chain of events that would become part of the mythology of the Great Depression.[15] The British government referred Australia's request for debt deferral to the Bank of England. In turn, the bank set about assessing Australia's creditworthiness. This was not inherently unreasonable, but it was clear that Bank of England officials were already predisposed to force a hard bargain with Australia. Not only did they harbour suspicions of any Labor government that might increase the money supply, but the deputy governor of the bank, Sir Ernest Harvey, who had advised Australia on central banking in 1927, also thought that Theodore's proposed changes to the Commonwealth Bank were 'fundamentally unsound in principle'.[16] The Bank of England was further concerned at what it saw as Australia's failure to conform to the rules of the gold standard: it had exported considerable gold reserves, but had not contracted the note issue. Finally, senior officials at the bank lacked any confidence that the Scullin government would undertake what they thought to be the adjustments in economic policy needed to correct Australia's exchange problem and address its relatively high costs of production.

After some discussions with Australian representatives in London, including Bruce, who had arrived on private business, the Bank of England asked the Australian government to provide wide-ranging details about policy and data.[17] What, for example, were the Loan Council's borrowing policies? What was the projected value of wool and wheat exports in 1929–30? Were the imminent tariff increases of a permanent or temporary character? Moreover, on 7 April Harvey suggested to Gibson, who as the head of Australia's proto-central bank was a natural point of contact, that it might be helpful if Australia sent to London some 'person or persons fully informed regarding all aspects of the matter, banking, economic and financial'.

The negotiations paused for two weeks, during which time it became clear that the New York stock market was as reluctant to advance money to Australia as was London. Then, on 7 May, Harvey wrote again to Gibson, setting out the Bank of England's concerns about the quality of the information it had received and the assurances it would require if it were to assist Australia. This time, while reiterating the option of Australia sending a special emissary to London, Harvey suggested that perhaps the Bank of England could arrange 'privately an intermediary to Australia if invited to do so'.

Gibson's response was remarkable. In a highly politicised five-page outburst, he attacked Australia's economic policies since his appointment to the Commonwealth Bank's board in 1924. In essence, he maintained that Australia could be saved only by 'the most drastic curtailment of borrowing with resultant deflation and a return to sound economic methods'. Australia needed assistance but should be forced to adopt a policy of self-reliance. The problem was that, while Scullin might be sincere in his desire to act, the party behind him would resist deflation, since this would lead to unemployment and a lower standard of living. If necessary, then, the government must be compelled, through being unable to borrow overseas, to 'carry the process through'.[18] Of course, Gibson concluded, he 'heartily' approved of the Bank of England sending an emissary to Australia. Later in May, he agreed that the best man for the job would be Niemeyer.

Finally, on 30 or 31 May, the Australian High Commissioner in London sent a message to Scullin proposing that the Bank of England send Niemeyer to Australia. Scullin had got wind of this possibility through Richard Casey (still acting as Australia's liaison officer in London), and when the cabinet discussed the London negotiations on 5 June, it agreed by consensus that it 'would cordially welcome' a representative of the Bank of England visiting Australia.[19] Niemeyer was duly invited.

Few decisions so shaped Australian policy development and Scullin's reputation in the months to come. Critics from Anstey to Lang would denounce the prime minister for bowing to the dictates of London's financial interests. The 'invitation' to Niemeyer was reportedly engineered by the Bank of England, which forced Niemeyer on Australia as a kind of bailiff. The archival record does not support this, nor Gibson's later claim that he arranged the visit.[20] Yet Scullin's voice was notably absent from the negotiations with London in April to May 1930, and his 'quick acquiescence was possibly a mistake'.[21] As the journalist Warren Denning put it, 'Whatever may have been the urgency of the reason, Mr. Scullin was never forgiven for bringing Sir Otto Niemeyer to Australia, or rather, for allowing him to come.'[22]

In Scullin's defence, it can be said that he had no option other than to work with the Bank of England if Australia were to avoid defaulting on the payments that were imminent—and default was an option he refused to consider, both in early 1930 and when Lang threw this gauntlet onto the table in 1931. It might also be noted that Niemeyer was only one of a succession of British economic and financial experts—Harvey in 1927 and the British Economic Mission in 1928—to whom Australians saw fit to turn in the decade after the war. Perhaps, then, the problem was not so much the invitation to Niemeyer as the way he behaved when he arrived. As the senior British Trade Commissioner in Australia would later say, Niemeyer 'lost his head a bit, was tactless and did some very stupid things'.[23]

Niemeyer's visit might have played out differently had Theodore not been forced to stand down as treasurer in July 1930. For some time, Theodore had carried more than a whiff of corruption.[24] When he transferred to federal politics from Queensland, his preselection for a safe seat in Sydney in 1927 had been tainted by allegations that the standing member had been bribed to resign—allegations that were not completely dispelled by a royal commission into the matter. Then there was the issue of Theodore's wealth. It was well known, so the Nationalist Senator Matthew Reid claimed in December 1929, that Theodore was rich. 'Where did this money come from?' when his fellow politicians were 'worth practically nothing?'[25] Rumour had it, too, that Theodore, while a parliamentarian in Queensland in 1915, had received a payment from the Melbourne bookmaker John Wren, on behalf of the licensed victuallers of Queensland, in return for which the Queensland government agreed not to interfere with the trading hours of licences for three years. According to the Nationalist Senator Harold (Pompey) Elliott, Theodore, Anstey and others had also been linked with Wren in the exploitation of mineral wealth in New Guinea.[26] Beyond this, Theodore was known to have been given, while premier of Queensland, preferential access to shares in the developing Mount Isa Mines.

Now, on 4 July 1930, Theodore found himself condemned by a royal commission, established by the Country and Progressive National Party Queensland government of Arthur Moore in October 1929 to investigate the purchase of the Mungana and Chillagoe mines by the Queensland government in 1922. The commissioner concluded, among other findings, that the price of £40,000 the government had paid for the mines had been highly inflated. Theodore, premier at the time, and other colleagues had been guilty of 'fraud and dishonesty in procuring the State' to purchase the Mungana mines. They had shared the 'fraudulently obtained' proceeds of the transaction between them.[27]

It was a political bombshell. When the news of the royal commission's findings hit Canberra, there was (as Denning put it) 'an almost sepulchral silence' in government lobbies; 'members in little groups discussed the affair in whispers, or walked about with troubled faces and nervous hands, wondering what it was all going to mean'.[28] Theodore denied all charges. He told Parliament on 8 July 1930 that they were 'damnably false'; the evidence was 'tainted and malicious'; the findings of the commission 'absolutely unjustified and biased'. He, Theodore, was the victim of 'a grave injustice'. The royal commissioner was 'a hired assassin', who had failed to make reasonable adjustments in the commission's schedule so that Theodore, who had been preoccupied with the preparation of the federal budget, could appear before it. As a result, Theodore was never cross-examined, nor had he made a written submission to the commission.[29] Even Billy Hughes, a master of public speaking himself, described Theodore's speech as 'a masterpiece'.[30] But the treasurer had no choice but to stand down until his name was cleared. He expected that this would take no more than two months. Scullin became treasurer temporarily in his stead.

The Queensland government, for its part, launched a civil action, claiming that Theodore and others had conspired to defraud the state when Mungana was sold. But—to look ahead a little—the case did not begin until July 1931. Theodore failed to give evidence under cross-examination and the outcome was inconclusive. The jury found in favour of all defendants, but this meant only that Theodore and his former cabinet colleague William McCormack had not been found guilty of being part of a conspiracy, not that they failed to benefit financially from the sale of Mungana. The taint of corruption remained, and with good reason. Theodore never provided an explanation for the frequent payments that, from 1920 on, he received from McCormack. To quote a forensic history of the Mungana affair, the balance of evidence is 'overwhelmingly' that Theodore did benefit from McCormack's proven involvement in the Mungana leases.[31]

Whatever the judgment as to Theodore's guilt or innocence, the scandal was a body blow for the Scullin government. Apart from his technical competence, Theodore was one of the few politicians who would offer alternative policy responses to deflation and retrenchment. As the editor of the

Australian Worker, Henry Boote, put it, Theodore had 'an unrivalled grasp of the problems of the monetary reform' that Labor needed to solve.[32] Furthermore, Theodore stood down only weeks before Niemeyer arrived. Had he remained treasurer, he would almost certainly have provided some counterweight to the deflationary advice that Niemeyer offered the Loan Council in August. Finally, Theodore would have acted as prime minister when Scullin left Australia in late August to attend the Imperial Conference in London. We can only speculate as to whether Theodore would have managed the increasingly fractious elements of the Labor Party in the last months of 1930 more ably than did the unfortunate James Fenton, but it seems probable.

Niemeyer arrived in Australia on 14 July 1930.[33] Landing in Fremantle, Western Australia, his delegation made its way to the east coast, where Niemeyer spent a week analysing data at the Commonwealth Bank. On 5–6 August, he met with the Loan Council to deliver his analysis. It was, as he told Bank of England colleagues, 'pretty formidable when marshalled in all its nakedness' in an effort 'to discourage shallow optimism'.[34] His starting point was Australia's indebtedness. For at least three years, the Commonwealth and almost all states had incurred budget deficits that were largely not provided for, other than by temporary methods of finance. They also had a heavy burden of external debt and internal securities that would mature within the current year. The yield from taxation was dropping substantially and could be expected to drop more. Australian credit was at a low ebb, lower than that of the other Dominions, and 'even lower than an [imperial] protectorate like Kenya'. The balance of trade was 'strongly unfavourable', given the drop in exports and low prices for wheat and wool. The exchange rate had depreciated and was maintained at current levels only by drastic tariff increases and the very rigid rationing of exchange by the banks, neither of which were permanent solutions. 'In short, Australia is off Budget equilibrium, off exchange equilibrium, and faced by considerable unfunded and maturing debts both internally and externally.' And why was Australia inflicted with this 'financial malaise'? Through a 'series of accidents, chiefly the liberality of lenders and accidental high prices' for its exports, Australia had maintained a standard of costs that the rest of the world had 'long since found to be impossible'. Australian productivity had lagged behind that of other competitor industrial countries. In essence, the standard of living in Australia had 'reached a point which is economically beyond the capacity of the country to bear, without a considerable reduction of costs resulting in an increased per capita output'.

Niemeyer concluded with a recipe for deflation. Australia's ability to fund its floating debt in London depended on, first, the Commonwealth and state governments balancing their budgets in 1930–31 and future years. Second, the Loan Council should raise no further loans overseas until existing short-term indebtedness had been 'completely dealt with'. The present loan program, even if funded from internal loans, should be reduced and confined to those projects that would yield revenue equivalent to their debt-servicing costs within a reasonable time. Finally, Niemeyer added a general exhortation on the need to reduce the costs of production.[35]

We have only Niemeyer's account of the impact of this jeremiad on the Loan Council. As he recalled, there was 'a painful pause, after which the State Treasurers [three of whom were also premiers], one after another, said that they agreed in principle both with what I said and with what I asked. Scullin said nothing, and indeed there was not very much that he could say.' As Niemeyer withdrew, however, the meeting descended—to use his words again—into 'the father and mother of a row . . . between the States as a body and the Commonwealth'. After many hours, the Council agreed that:

> they must do what I [Niemeyer] had asked for, but they were not going to sign anything, balance their Budgets or cut down their Loan programme unless the Commonwealth made equal sacrifices. They did not see why they should carry all the odium, while the Commonwealth did nothing to reduce its expenditure. Poor Scullin, who is a very decent little man, pitchforked into the Treasurer's position at about three weeks' notice and not master of his own party, had, I have no doubt a quite unpleasant evening of it.[36]

Essentially, however, it was agreed that the states would review their budgets to see how they might be balanced and then reconvene in Melbourne.[37]

This second meeting, held from 18 to 21 August, did not go at all smoothly. Scullin was confined to bed with a temperature of 39.4 degrees Celsius and attended only one day's proceedings, looking pale and tired and wearing a heavy overcoat and a scarf. He also presided over a four-hour cabinet meeting from his sickbed. Gibson attended for an hour and a half, advising that the governments must reduce their costs, as the limit of available bank credit was fast approaching.[38] Meanwhile, according to Niemeyer's diary, Fenton and Lyons were 'entirely at sea and like a couple of rabbits popping their heads occasionally out of the hole'. Lyons worried that the conference might be seen by the public as simply accepting Niemeyer's suggestions.[39]

Ultimately, the resolutions of the so-called Melbourne Agreement enshrined everything that Niemeyer had recommended: balanced budgets; a pause to overseas borrowings until short-term indebtedness had been dealt with; and the restriction of future public works financed by internal loans to those that were 'reproductive'.[40] It was the first commitment by Australia's political leaders to deflation. Yet this commitment was tentative, and it seems that the premiers, two of whom were Labor, thought they had no choice but to be seen as accepting Niemeyer's advice. One of Australia's Treasury bills in London was maturing within two weeks. Privately, Harvey had warned on 8 August that if the Australian governments refused to accept Niemeyer's recommendations, and he then left the country, the chances of Australia raising further money in London would be 'practically hopeless'.[41] In contrast, on 22 August—the day after the Melbourne Agreement was announced—Montagu Norman told Niemeyer that while he still mistrusted 'all Governments and Ministers', the Australian government should be able to borrow again 'under the moral responsibility for a time of the Bank of England'.[42]

News of the Melbourne Agreement, indeed, pushed the price of Commonwealth stock in London. On Niemeyer's advice, too, the London Westminster Bank, which had been pressing for substantial 'relief' for some months, agreed to reduce the overdraft of £7.9 million down to £5 million, and to carry this overdraft until 31 March 1931 (three months less than requested but better than nothing). A further shipment of £5 million of gold to London was arranged to strengthen the sterling reserves there.[43]

During the August negotiations, too, the Australian banks finally agreed, under a so-called Mobilisation Agreement, to create a central exchange pool that would allow the government to have first call on their overseas receipts of sterling and thereby finance Australia's immediate public obligations in London. But since Davidson and the Sydney private banks feared compromising their independence—Labor, after all, was theoretically committed to the nationalisation of banking, credit and exchange—the banks agreed only to provide £3 million per month from their receipts of London exchange. An amount equivalent to this would be deposited by the Commonwealth and state governments into the banks in Australia. It was a non-binding agreement from which banks could withdraw with one month's notice but, in the event, it remained in operation until wartime exchange control was introduced in 1939.[44]

The Melbourne Agreement bought Australia some breathing space in London, but it polarised opinion at home. Conservative politicians and the business community welcomed it as the necessary medicine for economic recovery.[45] 'No matter how we like being told,' a senior Sydney businessman said, the report was 'the truth, and if we tackle it properly and squarely we can come out of it sooner than we expect'.[46] The *Sydney Morning Herald* declared that 'The notion that Australia could keep herself, if she so desired, economically out of step with the rest of the world—that our standards of costly living and easy working could be preserved even if they isolated us from the world's trade and market—should now be definitely exploded.'[47]

On the other hand, the labour movement was outraged. Its longstanding distrust of bankers and financiers was given new oxygen.[48] The Melbourne Agreement was the craven capitulation of Australian politicians to the dictates of 'Money Power', the 'inner circle of great Capitalists' that controlled the banks and thus industry, as Anstey put it.[49] Scullin was allowing 'an outsider to dominate its financial policy' and the unions would 'fight tooth and nail' against Niemeyer's recommendations.[50] Hughes joined the chorus, writing in a pamphlet with the emotive subtitle, 'Bond or Free', that:

The heads of the Governments of Australia seemed to have been over-whelmed at the honour of sitting at [Sir Otto's] feet. They heard his lightest word with bated breath . . . When he lectured them upon public finance and economics, emphasizing their many and grievous errors; painting the future of Australia in a blackness that could almost be felt, and then wound up by telling them that their only hope was to turn over a new leaf, reduce the standard of the people's living; put aside their ill-advised ambitions to encourage Australian industries, and concentrate upon primary production—in which case THE BANK would help them—they humbly thanked him![51]

Meanwhile, across the country, associations advocating the ideas of the Scottish engineer Major C.H. Douglas sprang up in response to Niemeyer's visit. Maintaining that bank credit was an artificial creation, devised and controlled by bankers and financiers, proponents of Social Credit aimed to ensure that as much credit was available as the economy could effectively absorb, and that consumer demand was sustained by a more egalitarian distribution of income.[52] Resonating with Labor's distrust of Money Power, as well as with Christian values, the movement also appealed to rural regions, such as the Riverina, where banks were demanding foreclosures and the repayment of overdrafts.[53] In time, it would come to have some modest electoral success nationally and in states such as Tasmania and Queensland (see Chapter 32).

Niemeyer himself became the target of intense venom, his name a byword for harsh deflationary economics. In the eyes of the labour movement, he was the 'Pro-Consul of International Money Power', one of those 'cormorants and vultures of finance' intent on grinding down the workers of the world.[54] Dusting off its anti-Semitism, Sydney's *Labor Daily* denounced Niemeyer as the 'bailiff of London Jewry' while the Victorian *Labor Call* castigated the 'Shylocks, here and abroad . . . who rake off as much loot as they may in robbery interest rates and in profiteering on the sacrifices of people forced into bankruptcy'.[55] In fact, Niemeyer was not Jewish. He told the New Zealand politician Sir James Allen on 28 August, 'I don't happen to be a Jew or even much to like Jews so [the anti-Semitic campaign] merely amuses me.'[56]

Conservatives were mortified at this abuse of their distinguished British visitor. 'Much harm has been done to our country,' Latham told federal parliament, 'by the ill-founded criticism and ill-mannered abuse' levelled against the delegation.[57] The New South Wales Constitutional Association wrote to Norman apologising for 'the discourtesy' shown to Niemeyer. The views of certain politicians and newspapers, they claimed, 'do not represent the feelings of the people of Australia'.[58]

Niemeyer did not help himself. After his report was released in late August, he travelled around Australia and visited New Zealand.[59] Wearing a Homburg hat, dark suit, and a stiff short collar with rounded points, he was the very model of the modern British banker. He socialised almost exclusively with Australia's political or social elites—federal, state and municipal politicians, bankers, businessmen, journalists, railway commissioners, stockbrokers, and economists, including Giblin and Jim Brigden. Both of these men had contributed to an influential inquiry into the Australian tariff in 1928 and Brigden was now the first director of the Queensland Bureau of Economics and Statistics. Niemeyer was also entertained by state governors, dined at the gentlemen's clubs of Melbourne, Adelaide and Sydney, went to the races and football, played golf, visited the Barossa Valley and took up an invitation to visit a sheep station in northern New South Wales. As one parliamentarian said, Niemeyer's view that the Australian standard of living was too high was evidently based 'on the standard he himself enjoyed while living in firstclass hotels in the leading cities of the Commonwealth'.[60] His financial expertise was not matched by political nous. Only twice, according to the diary he kept of his mission, did he meet with trade union leaders, in Adelaide and Melbourne. It seems he never met anyone who was unemployed.

Furthermore, Niemeyer seems not to have liked what he saw of Australia. The countryside on the border of New South Wales and Queensland delighted him, but not so the Australians he met! Giblin was 'pretty disappointing'. The Australian government 'leaderless and stupid'. Australians had a 'pathetic' ignorance of economics. Victorian trade union leaders had views that were 'moderate though confused'. The president of Trades Hall in Adelaide was 'a nervous youth, crammed with undigested economics'; 'not much of a creature, but also not vicious'. Niemeyer's host on the sheep property was 'full of odd ideas'. In sum, as Niemeyer told the official representative of the British government in Australia, E.T. Crutchley, 'He had had a lot to do with bankrupt countries but have never seen one more utterly impotent to help itself.'[61] To Norman, he wrote, that while the Australian population was 'fundamentally sound':

> It is almost impossible to convey an adequate notion of the jarring elements at all times in this country . . . The ignorance of different sections of the population of one another's real feelings, problems and objects, the jealousies between political parties and between different wings of the same political party, and between the States, inter se, and as a body, with the Commonwealth, could hardly be equalled in a small cathedral town. With endless scrapping there is an extraordinary absence of constructive criticism. The personnel all round—political, administrative and banking—is, with rare exceptions, lamentable, a circumstance which is accentuated by the marooning of the Commonwealth Government and administration on a sheep run 200 miles from everywhere . . . the political leaders in general are listless and frightened and quite incapable of giving a lead. They are occupied half their time in saying that the present difficulty is not their fault but somebody else's . . . and the other half in trying to find ingenious ways by which somebody else should help them out.[62]

These views were expressed privately, in Niemeyer's diary and personal correspondence, but his condescension and disdain for all things Australian was surely evident in public. Incidentally, his impressions of New Zealand were only marginally more positive. While he said later that he had 'fallen in love' with the country, he concluded that the cabinet understood 'about one-quarter' of what he said. The leader of the Labour Party, Harry Holland was 'a fairly sound little man who might, if not in a minority, be doctrinaire and violent'. The chief justice was dismissed as 'a not very reassuring Jew'.[63]

As the criticism of his visit mounted, Niemeyer issued a public statement denying he had 'any interest in Australian politics'. 'He was not,' he said on

28 October, 'the agent of bondholders or British manufacturers, nor was he here to wreck Australian manufacturing industry, he was here to give advice— whether or not it was accepted was up to those who requested that advice.'[64] Norman argued that the animus against Niemeyer was 'political in character and was not representative of the attitude of those in a position to form a dispassionate opinion on the financial bearings of the advice tendered'.[65] But no one believed that economics was value-free, and Niemeyer's reputation was beyond rescue. Decades later, historian W.F. Mandle would write:

> When it is pointed out that at a farewell luncheon in Sydney on 13 November [Niemeyer] told a joke against the Bank of England . . . and that on the voyage from New Zealand back to Australia in September he became known as the kiddies' friend from his habit of playing with them and daily giving them sweets, an Australian would be apt to reply that Hitler was fond of dogs too.[66]

Still, Niemeyer at least could head for home. Scullin was left to deal with the political fallout of the visit.

CHAPTER 13

Losing control

The Melbourne Agreement that generated such controversy had a short life. Few of the state governments that endorsed it in August 1930 proved willing or able to implement it in the months that followed. Scullin chose to go to London to attend the Imperial Conference, and during his four-month absence the more radical elements of the labour movement mobilised to oppose the balanced budgets that would worsen the conditions of workers and the unemployed. Most importantly, in New South Wales the growing anger among the electorate brought the belligerent Lang to power in October 1930. By the end of 1930, consensus about economic policy was as remote as ever, Scullin's control over the ALP was slipping and the benefits, if any, of the Niemeyer visit for Australia's creditworthiness in London were in jeopardy.

The growing opposition to Scullin within labour circles was fuelled by his decision in August 1930 to reappoint Gibson as chairman of the Commonwealth Bank. Gibson's term was due to expire in October and his departure could not come soon enough for some in the Labor federal caucus.[1] Gibson had long been a disciple of limited government expenditure, he was committed to harsh deflation and he was opposed to increasing the money supply, an option that was gaining more advocates on the Labor left.[2] Still, Scullin went ahead with Gibson's reappointment for a second seven-year term, claiming to have the support of the majority of the cabinet. Beasley, who had reservations, was not at this meeting, and the wider parliamentary caucus was not consulted. In a gesture to Labor opinion, the government appointed to the bank's board a secretary of the Melbourne Trades Hall, Maurice Duffy, who had some financial expertise and had served on a royal commission into taxation in 1920.

In retrospect, the decision to retain Gibson seems to be one of Scullin's 'lost opportunities'. In the months to come, Gibson would continue to block the Labor government's attempts to stimulate the economy, placing an effective stranglehold on economic policy. In the circumstances of mid-1930, however, it is hard to imagine Scullin doing anything else. He was facing what we might now call a perfect storm. The Bank of England was making further credit in London conditional upon reassurances from Niemeyer about Australia's financial stability. Theodore had been forced to step down as treasurer. Scullin, who had temporarily assumed the role, had no formal expertise in banking or finance. His health was breaking down under the stress of governing. Moreover, there was no guarantee that a new chairman of the Commonwealth Bank would be any more open to innovative financial policies, since he would be selected by the existing directors of the board. Niemeyer—a far from unprejudiced observer, of course—told his Bank of England colleagues that there was no one 'to carry on' should Gibson, who was aged 68 and 'not in the best of health', break down. He helpfully suggested that the bank might send a soon-to-be-retired official to Australia 'on a holiday' to advise Gibson informally![3]

Gibson also had strong support within those sections of the Australian press for which he was the embodiment of 'sound finance'. The Melbourne *Herald* wrote on 22 August 1930:

in recent months the [Commonwealth] bank has been the fortress on whose fortunes the fate of Australia depended. The credit of the bank was the credit of the country . . . As the clouds darkened, and heroic, if not desperate, measures became necessary, they were taken by this quiet, unassuming man in whom his colleagues had implicit confidence. Fortunately for Australia at these critical times, the calibre of the man and the credit and the prestige of the institution of which he is the head, were known and appreciated in London, particularly at the Bank of England.

Members of the public also found reassurance in Gibson's presence at the bank. His private papers contain a letter from 'Widow':

I am taking the liberty of begging you not to inflate the not [sic] issue . . . It would just mean ruin and poverty for us all. If such a horror ever came, I would take my few belongings and go to New Zealand . . . Australia is looking to you to stand firm against the fools who are trying to run her further onto the rocks. For God's sake show yourself a man and save us.[4]

'Anxious' in Melbourne also wrote, begging Gibson 'on bended knees, not to agree to the merest hint of inflation. If you should give in to that blackguard Theodore, it will ruin Australia.'[5] For many middle-class Australians a cartoon depicting Gibson as the Beefeater at the Tower of London guarding a prisoner called 'Wild Cat finance', said it all.[6]

Little wonder, then, that Scullin decided Gibson's reappointment was a matter over which he would not stand and fight. This was particularly so since he was about to leave Australia to attend the Imperial Conference in London. In the past, these periodic meetings of the British government, the self-governing colonies and the Dominions of the British Empire had allowed Australian prime ministers to promote Australia's interests. But the timing of this conference could hardly have been worse for Scullin. Many in the press, Parliament and the labour movement thought his place was at home, trying to manage the economic crisis. The Melbourne *Herald* wrote of a 'joy ride' and ran a cartoon of a captain deserting his sinking ship. The *Sydney Morning Herald* declared that Scullin should not go to London since 'the tense position at home overrides any other duty'.[7] Beasley told Denning, 'Scullin is leaving his government behind him; he may not find it here when he returns.'[8]

Scullin, however, thought it was imperative for him to go to London. For one thing, this would allow him to explain Australia's financial position to its creditors. He also hoped (as it turned out vainly) to convince the

Imperial Conference that Britain should introduce more extensive tariffs to guarantee Australia a larger share of its imports. Beyond this, the conference was scheduled to discuss an issue that had been under review since the Dominions had demanded a greater role in imperial policymaking during World War I, the lessening of restrictions on the legislative freedom of the Dominions. The conference would agree on a set of resolutions that would be embodied in the 1931 Statute of Westminster, which confirmed that the Dominions were 'autonomous communities within the British Empire, equal in status, in no way subordinate to one another'. Finally, Scullin aimed to secure the approval of King George V for the appointment of an Australian as governor-general.

With some unease, then, the cabinet supported Scullin's leaving the country, taking with him Attorney-General Frank Brennan and the Minister for Markets and Transport, Parker Moloney. Scullin assured the public that he was 'not going to London as a supplicant at the feet of anyone. I am going to speak in the name of Australia, not as a mendicant, but as the representative of a great nation that has always paid its way, and will continue to do so.'[9] Even *Labor Call*, the official organ of the Political Labor Council of Victoria that was notable for its hyperbole, conceded that 'It is idle to pretend that under the prevailing circumstances Australia is the centre of financial gravity. Quite patently the centre is London. Labor . . . needed its Labor Prime Minister—its strongest man—at a notable conference (lest we be stabbed in the back) and at pivotal consultations.'[10] Little did *Labor Call* know that Niemeyer had written to Harvey on 8 August 1930:

> Now what I want is that you will do your best, when Scullin arrives in London, to prevent people encouraging him to think he can get large amounts of sympathy and considerable amounts of money in order that Australia may continue to live in luxury . . . I think I have convinced him in his heart that this is not possible . . . he has been living on a meagre diet, and I think this had a lowering effect . . . It is important that he should be kept in this state of body and mind, and that washy imperial sentimentalism and kind words meaning nothing should not undo the good work.[11]

'Give an Australian half a smile,' Niemeyer concluded, 'and he is off in Eldorado straight away.'

The domestic ramifications of Scullin's going to London were huge. Just as the absence of Billy Hughes in London in 1916 allowed the anti-conscription movement to gain an ultimately unstoppable momentum, so Scullin's absence meant that he lost control of the economic debate. Given that Theodore was in the wings, Fenton was appointed acting prime minister while Lyons became treasurer. Amiable though he was, Fenton was not up to the task. Principled and socially conservative, he was stolid, hardworking, slow-thinking and lacked a firm grasp of parliamentary procedure. He coped, so far as he did, by telephoning Scullin in London almost daily. Denning later recalled:

> Through the ether across half-a-world torn with its own distresses, for many nights . . . the voices of these two burdened men sped on the radio waves; words of hope and encouragement from Mr. Scullin, of woe and disaster from Mr. Fenton. Soon it became almost a standing jest in Canberra that Mr. Fenton was 'on the 'phone again'.[12]

Lyons, though in federal parliament for only a few months, proved far more able. But he displayed a growing policy conservatism and was soon at odds with the radicals in the cabinet and caucus.

The debate about the Melbourne Agreement played out differently at the federal and various state levels. Supporting Niemeyer's call for deflation was Queensland's Premier Moore, who had already launched a program of reducing government expenditure from both revenue and loans.[13] The South Australian premier, Lionel Hill, was also willing to conform. He was nominally Labor, but deferred to advice of Adelaide businessmen to compensate for his own lack of economic expertise. With nearly half of the state's income in 1930–31 being absorbed by repayment of external borrowings, he outdid even Nationalist premiers in advocating balanced budgets.[14] In Western Australia, James Mitchell, who had been premier in 1919–24 and was now returned to office in April 1930 at the head of a National–Country Party coalition, also 'faithfully absorbed' the need to 'batten down all expenditure', balancing budgets, cutting spending and wages, and reducing social services and subsidies.[15] Likewise, Tasmania's Nationalist premier, J.C. McPhee, a disciple of conservative financial policies and personal austerity—he was a teeto- taller and non-smoker—reduced public works expenditure in 1930–31 by 39.1 per cent.[16]

Yet if these premiers were on side, the Melbourne Agreement met fierce opposition in New South Wales and Victoria. In the latter state, Labor's Hogan, who was governing with the support of the Country–Progressive Party, initially favoured the agreement.[17] But his labour power base did not. Trade union militants at Trades Hall insisted that the Melbourne Agreement should be repudiated, the war debt renegotiated, the banks nationalised and state parliaments abolished. The central executive of the ALP, less radically, demanded assurances from all Labor parliamentarians that they would not support any wage cuts or dismissals. In December 1930, Hogan managed to push through Parliament a balanced budget, and the public-service salary cuts it involved, but he needed the support of the non-Labor parties to do so. To the fury of his critics the conservative upper house then exempted Supreme Court judges from the salary cuts. *Labor Call* took consolation in the thought that 'Labor in office is infinitely a better proposition for the workers than anti-Labor in office.'[18] But it was becoming hard to see the distinction, especially when police violently broke up protest meetings, such as that led by communists on the Yarra Bank in late October 1930.

In New South Wales, the conservative Bavin predictably supported the Melbourne Agreement's aspiration for balanced budgets. With his state's deficit greater than all the other Australian states combined, he had already introduced legislation for cuts in public servants' and politicians' salaries, the restoration of the 48-hour week and an income-tax levy of threepence in the pound for unemployment relief.[19] But this all came undone when Bavin faced the electorate in October 1930. Labor mounted a formidable campaign in which Lang's rhetorical powers took flight. While assuring the public that he recognised the sanctity of Australia's contracts to overseas creditors—'The Labour party sets its face against all repudiation'—Lang promised to defend the standard of living, guarantee wheat prices for farmers, fund public works for the relief of unemployment, restore the 44-hour week and reverse the cuts in social service payments.[20] This cornucopia of promises was embellished with vicious attacks on Niemeyer. The mention of the banker, Lang's biographer later wrote, brought 'a special twist to [Lang's] snarl, an extra rapidity to his swinging hands and stabbing fingers, and a conspiratorial tone to his staccato delivery'.[21] To cheering crowds, Lang claimed that the election was a fight to resist the domination of financial interests '12,000 miles away'.

> They have told you you are living too well; you are too well fed, too well clothed, and that you have to reduce your standard of living; and that you have to work longer and harder; and that you have got to cease endeavouring to make Australia a nation; your secondary industries must go to the wall, and you must revert to a primary production country only. If you are prepared to do that, to knuckle under, well, the Labour Party is not and will not![22]

Niemeyer's visit, Lang claimed, had been 'one of the most humiliating experiences to which a self-governing community had ever submitted'. Australia's premiers had been 'lectured and castigated . . . as though they were . . . school boys'.[23] He, Lang, was 'not prepared to accept this German Jew's commands'.[24] It was a message of defiance and hope that empowered the lowly, and when New South Wales voted on 25 October, Lang won by a landslide, with 55 per cent of the vote. It was 'the high point' of the political tide of Labor in 1929–30 and, in this state, at least, the Melbourne Agreement was dead.[25]

In the latter months of 1930, then, the lines were being drawn for the so-called battle of the plans that would tear Scullin's government apart in 1931. The issue was essentially this: if the deflationary medicine of the Melbourne Agreement was not acceptable, what mix of policy options should Australia adopt to address the economic crisis? The debate within Labor circles was the most vitriolic and fratricidal, but there were many other voices in the public sphere. Most notably, by mid-1930 a group of professional economists were emerging as an alternative source of advice to politicians. Economics was in its infancy academically in 1930, but the discipline gained a new status with the Depression, and economists emerged as the 'public intellectuals of the decade'.[26]

The intellectual leader of the group was Giblin, who had been a colleague of Lyons in Tasmania before taking up the chair of economics at the University of Melbourne. He had continued to be close to Lyons and became widely respected within the government for his advice on technical matters. Earlier than other economists, including Keynes and his student Richard Kahn in Cambridge, Giblin developed the important—and now universally employed—theory of the multiplier: that is, the concept that any stimulus to spending will lead to an increase in total spending by an amount several times as large as the initial stimulus.[27] Giblin also took on a public role, believing, as did some of his fellow economists, that the dynamics of the Depression needed to be explained to the public. In a series of ten 'Letters to John Smith' published in the Melbourne *Herald* in July 1930, he aimed to tell 'in simple language the facts' of Australia's economic position and especially to persuade readers of the need for wage reductions.[28] How successful he was in infusing the increasingly emotional and irrational public discourse with an element of rationality we can only infer.

As might have been expected, given the complexity of the economic crisis, Giblin and his colleagues were far from united on the question of appropriate policy responses. Edward Dyason, a prominent Melbourne stockbroker and founding member of the Economic Society of Australia and New Zealand, supported the expansion of the note issue, as did Giblin. Copland, at the University of Melbourne, was also a reflationist, although increasingly he sought to find a politically acceptable middle course between deflation and inflation.[29] More orthodox financial views were held by Edward Shann, an economist and historian who in 1930 published two influential works, *An Economic History of Australia* and *Bond or Free?* That same year, he was invited by Davidson to act as the Bank of New South Wales' economic consultant, the first economist to hold such a position in Australia. Similarly, Leslie Melville, who had been professor of economics at the University of Adelaide and was 'perhaps the most committed deflationist at this time', was appointed in 1931 as head of a new Research Department at the Commonwealth Bank, with Niemeyer's blessing.[30] Another two of this group of prominent economists were Jim Brigden and Torleiv Hytten, professor of economics at the University of Tasmania who served as the adviser to the Tasmanian government from 1929 to 1935 and would become chairman of the State Employment Council in 1932. Both tended towards economic orthodoxy, though with less dogmatism than Shann and Melville.[31]

Only weeks after the Melbourne Agreement was announced, Giblin, Dyason and Copland submitted to Lyons a plan that they believed would promote a more rapid recovery than would be possible under deflation. It would also meet the increasingly important political goal of distributing the burden of the loss of national income more equitably across all Australians. The main cause of the budget deficits that so troubled Niemeyer, the economists argued, was languishing industry. A drop in real wages was necessary if unemployment was to be reduced, but as soon as real wages were reduced, re-inflation would be essential. Industry and employment should be restored by 'sound monetary policy'—by which they meant a depreciation of the Australian pound, a maintenance of prices at the 1929 level, a note-issue expansion, over which the Commonwealth Bank would have control, and a graduated supertax on income.[32] As a 2006 analysis put it: '[This] is all quite familiar to the present day reader: give the central bank an inflation target, and let the central bank get on with it.'[33] The so-called Stabilisation Plan, however, which was given extensive newspaper publicity by Copland and Dyason, pleased neither the banks nor the conservative press, which took exception to the idea of 'managed inflation'.[34] Nor did it convince Scullin and Lyons, who pigeonholed the plan. The economists had to wait a few more months for their day to come.

Scullin had assumed when he left for London that Parliament would not sit in his absence. But when Fenton and Lyons learned that revenue in July and August had declined so much that the full year's deficit was likely to blow out, they decided to recall Parliament for a special session. Since all other measures to increase revenue and reduce expenditure had been exhausted, they concluded that there was no option but to reduce public-service salaries and social services, such as maternity allowances and pensions.

This produced a mutiny within the cabinet. Anstey and Beasley led the charge. In the New South Wales election campaign, Anstey had joined Lang in denouncing the Niemeyer mission, declaiming, 'These people do not want government [of] the people, by the people for the people, but government by finance for finance.'[35] Beasley threatened publicly to resign if the Melbourne Agreement were implemented. In an effort to nut out a compromise, a cabinet subcommittee was formed, but Gibson, who was invited to the meetings, made it clear that the Commonwealth Bank expected nothing less than strict adherence to the Melbourne Agreement. Between the rock of the bank and the hard place of the anti-Niemeyer labourites, Lyons' room to manoeuvre was shrinking. For the moment, however, the cabinet agreed on a cautious mix of salary reductions and increased expenditure on public works.[36]

These developments placed Scullin in an excruciating position in London. Norman told Niemeyer on 27 September that the statements of Labor leaders and unions were 'harmful' in London. Referring to Scullin's recent appearance at the League of Nations, where he had spoken in favour of disarmament, Norman quipped that 'some think Scullin . . . would be better employed in attending to his budget deficit than in declaiming high ideals in Europe or in London laughing at the idea of default'.[37] Norman was no more amenable when he and Harvey dined with Scullin at the Savoy Hotel on 2 October. The Savoy was the acme of British wealth and privilege, festooned with chandeliers, wood panelling, sculpted ceilings, views of the Thames and marble bathrooms. Even the most self-assured colonial might have struggled to feel confident, let alone one like Scullin who had never travelled overseas and was still feeling ill. The dinner conversation did little to put him at ease. According to Norman's account, Scullin opened by explaining that the proposed meeting of the federal parliament was being delayed, given the imminence of the New South Wales election. Yes, he knew 'the absolute necessity' for reducing costs, but he did not think it wise, or indeed possible, for his government to explicitly reduce wage levels. The only option was to reduce real wages by indirect taxation, such as sales taxes or increased customs. Scullin then shifted some of the blame onto his predecessors, claiming that Australian governments now trying to balance their budgets had to accommodate the heavy deficits of state railways that had lost traffic owing to the extensive program of road improvement in the 1920s.

When Scullin then stressed the need for more trade between Australia and the United Kingdom, and a new loan in London, Norman stalled. The prospects for Australian state and federal budgets, and their schemes for retrenchment and reducing the costs of production, he noted, were uncertain. 'The 'wild talk about repudiation' had placed a serious check on improved sentiment in London towards Australia. Scullin countered that these were the utterances of 'a few irresponsible extremists' who could not speak for the ALP, but acknowledged that 'failing drastic action', Australia ran a great risk of being driven into default. He then ventured on to another high-risk issue, Labor's plans for reforming the Commonwealth Bank, to make it 'an active competitive commercial institution'; 'it is not right that [the bank's] profits, which in his view have in the past been excessive, should all accrue to the private investor'. Norman, with all the gravitas of the Bank of England behind him, responded that 'such an attitude was directly contrary to responsible and informed opinion throughout the world and by adopting such a policy Australia would isolate herself from all the leading financial centres'.[38] Even on paper, 90 years later, the chill is palpable.

The admonitions of London bankers mattered little to the radicals in the federal Labor caucus. Emboldened by the voters' rejection of the Melbourne Agreement in the New South Wales election, they demanded a mild inflationary stimulus. Their argument ran thus: the money supply had been increased during World War I to assist the war effort. Why should it not now be increased to assist the unemployed? Bank credit did not rest on the assets of the individual banks, but on the total assets of the nation. The banks should thus 'release' the credit of the nation, maintaining the wages and spending power of the community and absorbing the unemployed by increased public-works expenditure.

Theodore now emerged as a champion of this approach. There was an element of political opportunism in this course. As a bitter opponent of Lang in the New South Wales ALP, of which Theodore was now part after winning Dalley in 1927, it suited him to offer a credible alternative to deflation. He also had a personal interest in white-anting Lyons, who had assumed his former role as treasurer. But Theodore, too, had an intellectual commitment to monetary policy options, having taken advice from R.F. Irvine, a former University of Sydney professor and now private consultant who advocated expansionary remedies.[39] 'I am convinced,' Theodore said in a series of articles in *The Worker* from late October on, that 'the acuteness of the depression in Australia is the outcome of [deflation]. The time has come when we should call an immediate halt to [this] and by reversing the monetary policy travel the other road for a while.' To critics who predicted doom from inflation, he gave assurances that credit expansion could be firmly controlled and checked at any stage.[40]

The federal caucus meetings in late October descended into chaos: what Denning described as 'scenes of bitter recrimination, with factions attacking the Ministry with the abandon of desperation, and attacking each other with equal ferocity'.[41] On 27 October, Fenton and Lyons proposed a range of financial measures consistent with the Melbourne Agreement, but Beasley moved a countermotion, to the effect that the caucus disagreed with Niemeyer and that the tariff and industrial policies of Australia were 'domestic matters to be determined by the people of Australia'.[42] Fenton soon lost control of the debate, which lasted from early evening on Monday 27 October until 6.20 p.m. the following Thursday! Eventually, on 30 October, the caucus passed a resolution that the Commonwealth Bank should finance the federal government for all services covered by parliamentary appropriations, provide £20 million for programs of public works, meet that portion of the internal loans maturing during the financial year that had not otherwise been provided for, and supply further funds for 'productive purposes in primary and secondary industries'.[43]

Even more controversially, on 6 November the caucus approved, by 22 votes to sixteen, a resolution by Anstey that the Parliament should postpone for twelve months the redemption of internal Commonwealth bonds worth £27 million that were falling due in December. It was a terrible call. Deferring the redemption would have done little to help relieve unemployment, but the very suggestion served to entrench Gibson's opposition to any moderately expansionist policy, while upsetting local owners of government bonds who wanted the chance of cashing them or converting them under new terms.

175

The Anstey resolution also alienated Fenton and Lyons. Fenton said that he would have to consider his position. Lyons, pale and trembling, shouted at the caucus, 'I will not do it . . . I will go out of public life first!' He left Canberra almost immediately, with his cabinet colleague Albert Green 'running after the departing train shouting, "for God's sake, Joe, don't do it [resign]!"'[44] Lyons did not resign, but it was only a matter of months before he would.

A formal split in the federal ALP was avoided for the time being, thanks to Scullin's intervention from afar. Telling Curtin that repudiation was 'dishonest and disastrous', he gave public assurances that the government would honour its obligations to bondholders, who were, in many instances, ordinary Australians. 'The sufferings of the people are now acute. They would become more acute and more widespread if confidence is shaken in the Government's honesty.' To the caucus he telegrammed that 'No self-respecting Government could agree [to defer the redemption of bonds]. Our Government floated a loan and guaranteed the public a safe investment. Thousands of people withdrew their savings from the Savings Bank to assist the Labour Government. To default on this loan would weaken the value of their investments [and] destroy public confidence.'[45] The caucus agreed to defer the question until Scullin returned, and unanimously passed a resolution denying any possibility of repudiation.

The previous day, Lyons had ignored the Anstey resolution and persuaded the Loan Council to proceed with the cash and conversion loan worth £28 million. The government desperately needed a good response from the public, but the terms were not especially attractive. So Lyons threw himself into the campaign with a vigour that gave him a new national prominence. On the radio and in the cinema, the lending of money to the government was proclaimed a patriotic duty and a national obligation as 'clear and inescapable as any issue faced in wartime'. It was not just 'a matter of sane, sound business—but a bond of honour', a vote of confidence and faith in the future of Australia. Citizens could play a role in vindicating 'the good name of Australia'.[46] Lest patriotism prove wanting, the loan was also presented by the Commonwealth Bank in sporting terms: it was a Test match, 'the greatest of all—to be won'.[47] It helped that Australia had won the Ashes in the United Kingdom earlier that year. This triumph had been achieved despite 'the discomforts of a cheerless English summer' that had not only required the visitors to adapt to the varying paces of different wickets but also to wear 'heavy underclothing under flannel shirts, and a couple of sweaters in addition' that still failed to keep them reasonably warm in the field, as the *Wisden Almanack* put it.[48] Banks, meanwhile, offered Australian investors liberal advances, up to 90 per cent. The corporate sector purchased bonds and allowed their employees to pay them off in instalments. At the climax of the campaign, 12 December, 'All for Australia Day', businessmen donated the whole of their day's takings to the loan, while Lyons intoned:

> I appeal to the people to make Friday a red-letter day in our post-war history and to realise the supreme patriotic duty that all men owe to their country and to themselves. Never since the dark days of the war has Australia been faced with such a critical position, never has there been a more urgent need for a spontaneous outburst of patriotism. If we do not now need the last man, we certainly do need the last shilling . . . Let the world know that the heart of Australia is sound, that her people possess the same fighting spirit in peace as they showed in war, and that they will not repudiate their obligations.[49]

It all worked. A month after the loan closed, it had been oversubscribed by £2 million. In reaching the target, the countless subscriptions of the small man and woman were as important as the large institutional subscribers. Many on reduced incomes drew on their savings to subscribe. It was possibly an even more remarkable national effort than the war and peace loans ten to fifteen years earlier. Whereas the enemy then had been tangible, now the threat was more nebulous: the loss of honour in the event of national bankruptcy.[50] Few Australians might have understood the technicalities of government financing, the implications of national insolvency, or how their subscriptions to the loan would help to avoid this fate. Yet it seems that the notion of unity in a national struggle still had considerable rhetorical power.

Now that the Melbourne Agreement's commitment to balanced budgets was defunct, the question arose as to what level of budget deficits could be tolerated.

This of course involved Gibson again. Towards the end of November, the cabinet forwarded to him the proposal that caucus had passed on 30 October: that the bank should 'release' credit by continuing to finance budget deficits and make available £20 million for expenditure on public works. For once, Gibson was willing to give a little ground. Realising that it was impossible politically for governments to achieve balanced budgets within the current financial year, he conceded that the bank would consider from month to month the finance needed to meet budget shortfalls. But on the question of funding public works, Gibson dug in. This, he argued, would be inflationary and, far from improving the situation, would 'definitely contribute towards plunging the country into more serious difficulties, and, if proceeded with, into financial disaster'. He wrote to the cabinet on 16 December: 'The [bank's] Board is fully seized with the responsibilities which have been placed upon its shoulders by Act of Parliament to administer and control the currency of this country in the interests of the people, and this is a responsibility which the Board has not the power to transfer to any other authority.' The board, he insisted, was not 'attempting to dictate the policy' of the government. But neither should the government's 'political exigencies' influence the board. This was of course a fiction. Financial and economic management were not hermetically sealed, separate spheres. In reality, too, Gibson's was 'a one-way principle'. While he asserted the right of the bank to be free from government interference, he expected the government to adhere to the principles of 'sound finance'—as the bank understood them.[51]

To add to the government's difficulties, the talk of repudiation in Labor circles meant that plans for negotiating a new funding loan of £10 million in London in December 1930 were cancelled. There was even serious doubt as to whether the bills that were maturing at the end of the year could be renewed. As ever, the Bank of England was sceptical. A poem, still held in the bank's archives, captured this whimsically:

> Ye Bankers of Old England
> Who sit at home at ease,
> List to the cry for help that comes
> From far-off Southern Seas.

Advance Australia Money,
So we don't have to sow,
But merely reap the benefit
Of the money that we owe,
And we'll pay you what you lend us
With the money that we owe.[52]

In the event, the bills were renewed by the Commonwealth Bank by private tender, but only after protracted negotiations and an interest yield of 5.25 per cent compared with the bank rate of 3 per cent.[53]

In all this turmoil, Scullin managed to score one notable success in London. He achieved his goal of securing the appointment of an Australian as governor-general. In the 30 years since federation, all eight governors-general had been British. All had been titled and, with the exception of the poet Lord Tennyson's son (1903–04), all had been British politicians, five of them conservative. As the term of Viscount Stonehaven was coming to an end in 1930, the Scullin government decided it was time to nominate an Australian.

The cabinet seems to have considered at least two possibilities.[54] One was Sir Isaac Isaacs, chief justice of the High Court, and the other the most distinguished of Australia's World War I commanders, John Monash. Other possibilities mooted in the press were Sir Harry Chauvel, the wartime cavalry leader; Matthew Charlton, the immediate past leader of the ALP; or Littleton Groom, the ex-speaker of federal parliament who had lost his seat in the 1929 election.[55] The cabinet opted in April 1930 for Isaacs. The news of this nomination left some in Australia aghast. Not only was Isaacs in his seventies, but he was Jewish (as for that matter, was Monash). The Anglo-Persian Oil Company's representative residing in Melbourne, W. Bird, said: 'Whatever our opinions may be in regard to having an Australian as G.G. that the first Australian G.G. should be a Jew and such Jew makes one's flesh creep. I have not met a single person who is in favour of his appointment.'[56] Less bigoted loyalists claimed that a distinguished and more detached figure from Britain would better secure the bonds of empire. Latham, never missing an opportunity to impute disloyalty to the ALP, claimed that the nomination of an Australian by Labor ministers who 'never had any real enthusiasm for the Empire and Great Britain' would 'sever an important link with what the great majority of Australians were still proud to call the Mother Country'.[57]

The nomination of Isaacs caused as much consternation in London. The constitutional position was unclear. The Imperial Conference of 1926, where the de facto independence of the Dominions had been recognised, had agreed that the governor-general was the representative of the Crown, not of the British government. As the King's representative, the governor-general should be appointed by the King. But who should provide the advice to the monarch on which he would act? And how was that advice to be tendered?[58] Was it, as some commentators suggested, a discourteous infringement of the royal prerogative for the Australian government to nominate only one individual?[59]

Given all these questions, Scullin agreed to defer discussion about the vice-regal appointment until he was in London. By the time he arrived, the names of various other potential vice-regal candidates were being canvassed. Almost all were lords. The exception was the British Field Marshal Sir William Birdwood, whom the King thought might be palatable to Australians because he had commanded the AIF for much of World War I. Moreover, Birdwood was thought to have adequate private means for the role, now that the costs of maintaining the vice-regal lifestyle in Australia had been reduced, with the closure of residences in Melbourne and Sydney as an economy measure.[60]

One thing was clear: the King was set against Isaac's appointment. Since the governor-general was his representative, he insisted that it was 'only right and fair' that he should know the man.[61] Moreover, the King claimed—somewhat speciously—that if an Australian were appointed governor-general, this would set a precedent that could prove difficult in South Africa and Canada. In these Dominions, he claimed, there was a distinct cleavage between 'two races'—the British and Dutch in South Africa, and the English-speaking and French-speaking in Canada—which would make it 'almost an impossibility' to find a generally accepted native-born candidate. Possibly this situation might be avoided if a citizen of one Dominion became governor–general in another, a solution that would affirm 'both the unity and autonomy of the component parts of the British Commonwealth'.[62]

This 'solution' had no appeal for Scullin and he held his ground. In a feisty interview in November, the King's private secretary, Lord Stamfordham, accused Scullin of holding 'a pistol to the King's head' by nominating only one man. To which Scullin countered that there were two precedents for this: South Africa and Ireland.[63] When Stamfordham responded that the governor-general appointed to South Africa was an Englishman, Scullin scored the obvious point: presumably if Australia had nominated 'an Englishman personally acceptable to the King', the issue of there being only one nomination would not have been raised. The objection was manifestly to Isaacs being Australian. As for Ireland, where James McNeill had been appointed on the recommendation of the Irish Free State government, Stamfordham threw up his hands saying 'excitedly': 'Do not talk to me about Ireland. That is a country of rebels and the man nominated for the position of Governor General was himself a rebel.' Scullin shot back: 'Am I to draw the inference that you accept the nomination of a Govt of rebels and the appointment of a rebel from amongst themselves, but if a country is loyal, such as Australia undoubtedly is, you refuse to accept . . . the appointment of an Australian born citizen whose loyalty has not been questioned?' Stamfordham then challenged Scullin to conduct a referendum in Australia to demonstrate public support for appointing an Australian. Scullin agreed, and even offered to hold an election on the issue. But would the King, he asked, wish the matter to be the subject of public propaganda and public controversy?

This seems to have been a trump card. When the Imperial Conference confirmed in November that a governor-general should be appointed on the advice of a Dominion government consulting initially with the monarch, Scullin met with the King. The now familiar arguments were rehearsed for some 45 minutes, but finally George V relented. He was, he said, a constitutional monarch and would accept the advice that Isaacs should be governor-general.

Its importance in Australian political history aside, this episode is noteworthy for the questions it raises about Scullin. Why did he refuse to bow before George V while eschewing open confrontation with Montagu and his colleagues at the Bank of England? Why was he willing to be more assertive at Buckingham Palace than at the Savoy? Perhaps it was because a form of nationalism that spurned the trappings of imperialism was core to the moderate Labor tradition, of which Scullin was part, in a way that opposition to capitalism was not.[64] Perhaps Scullin thought the conventions of vice-regal appointments were more negotiable than the law-like rules of the impersonal global financial system. Presumably, too, Scullin knew that aggravating the monarch would bring less dire penalties for Australia than defying the condescending bankers. Whatever his reasons, this victory did something to shore up Scullin's battered reputation within the restive labour movement at home. This was how Labor leaders were meant to behave with the British elites! As the Victorian *Labor Call* said: 'Let us hope that many more like appointments will be made, and thus show the world that Australians are equal, if not superior to, any imported pooh-bahs.'[65]

Fears that Isaacs's age and nationality would preclude him from fulfilling the vice-regal role proved groundless. He discharged his duties through the bleak Depression years with distinction, and far from severing the links with empire, he proved an ardent imperialist and king's man.

Scullin finally returned to Australia in early January 1931. Landing at Fremantle, he told a crowd in the packed Prince of Wales theatre:

> When I hear people say . . . that they are looking to the return of the Prime Minister to lift Australia out of its difficulties I feel very, very humble, because I realise that I have limitations. I realise that . . . no man, and no group of men, can lift Australia out of its difficulties'.[66]

It was hardly the stuff of inspirational leadership but it was realistic. In the year ahead, 1931, Australia would slip even more deeply into depression, and there was relatively little that 'good old Jim' Scullin, for all his decency and commitment to Labor principles, could do to protect the voters that had expected so much of him.

This unemployed man at a Perth demonstration in June 1930 demanding food, accommodation and medical attention seemed energised by his confrontation with police. (State Library of Western Australia, SLWA)

Sister Maurus Tierney serves a meal to unemployed men at the back of St Vincent's Convent, Sydney. Although leaders of the Christian churches failed to articulate a coherent or radical vision as to how to alleviate unemployment, they recognised the urgency of providing relief to victims of the Depression. (Congregational Archives of the Sisters of Charity, Australia)

Given the inadequacies of government support for the unemployed, the voluntary sector played a critical role in relief. Here the scale of the charitable effort is evident in this queue of men outside a Sydney soup kitchen in 1932. (*SMH*)

DEMORALISATION

Demoralised through malnutrition, thousands of the unemployed are losing the desire for anything better than they are getting."—News item.

SLOWLY SINKING IN THE QUAGMIRE.

The psychological impact of unemployment, especially for men without work for years, could be profound. The man in this cartoon is slowly sinking into the quagmire, losing his 'desire for anything better'. (11 February 1931, *AW*)

Government 'relief works' that provided some work for the unemployed tended to be concentrated in infrastructure—such as road construction, sewerage and water supply—and rural development. Here workers are digging a stormwater canal in Canterbury, New South Wales, 1933. (SLNSW)

With boots such as these, some of the unemployed struggled to perform the manual work that was demanded by most relief works programs. (SLNSW)

Labor premier of New South Wales, Jack Lang, in full flight, c. 1930. A powerful orator, his radical plan to default on at least some of Australia's debts would tear the ALP apart in 1931 and result in his own dismissal in 1932. (*SMH*)

THE BOMB THROWERS.

Stating that their unanimous judgment in the basic wage case would be handed out in typewritten form, the Judges of the Federal Arbitration Court hurriedly left the Bench, having been in the Court less than a minute.

The decision of the Commonwealth Court of Conciliation and Arbitration in January 1931 to reduce the basic wage in those industries covered by federal awards by 10 per cent outraged the labour movement. It was a political catastrophe for the Scullin government, even though the basic wage of workers under state awards was not necessarily cut. (28 January 1931, *AW*)

DEMONSTRATORS FLANKED BY TROOPERS MARCHING ALONG KING WILLIAM STREET—Placards, in addition to demanding beef in rations, bore such phrases as, "Class Against Class," "Down With Imperialism," and "Hands off China," while on a flag at the head of the procession were the crossed hammer and sickle, symbol of the Russian Soviet. Later these were converted into weapons of offence, when the clash with the police occurred. More than 2,000 were in the procession. (Other illustrations on Page 11.).

The 'beef riot', Adelaide, January 1931, protesting against the removal of beef from the 'sustenance' rations. The substitute, mutton, was considered inferior, in part because of its percentage of bone. Banners read: 'We demand the right to live' and 'Beef'. (SLSA)

Some of the huts erected by the homeless unemployed in Adelaide, c. 1930. They stretched nearly 2.5 kilometres from the back of the Zoo to the city weir. Many men remained in these huts despite periodic flooding and attempts by authorities to remove them. They were finally removed in 1938. (SLSA)

Two children in Surry Hills, Sydney, a suburb where families had long lived precariously close to the poverty line, June 1932. (*SMH*)

Some children were more fortunate, even in South Australia where the impact of the Depression was particularly harsh. Here a young girl plays with her doll and tea set in an Adelaide garden, c. 1930. (*SLSA*)

William Roberts, an 'original Anzac', evicted with his family from his home in Redfern, Sydney. Evictions of those families that could not pay their rent triggered some of the most violent clashes between police and protestors during the Depression. (SLNSW)

Home ownership, no matter how difficult the mortgage payments might have been, meant security and respectability for many families, as is attested by this image from Adelaide, in 1932. (SLSA)

Children at the government-run Moore River Native Settlement, Western Australia, in the early 1930s. During the Depression the Protector, Auber Neville, aimed to force Aboriginal people in the neighbouring regions to concentrate in this appalling settlement. (SLWA)

An older vulnerable worker, at Woodsdale, Tasmania, in 1930. (Tasmanian Archives)

Part V

◆

SURVIVING

CHAPTER 14

Sustenance

Whatever the disputes over economic policy, everyone agreed that governments must do something to help the unemployed. The efforts of the charities and churches, unceasing though they were, could not meet the growing need for food, clothing and other necessities of life. Hence, from 1930 on, governments across the country introduced legislation to establish systems of 'sustenance', soon to be known in the Australian vernacular as the 'susso'. At first these systems were 'tentative, ad hoc and unco-ordinated' and for the critical years of 1930–33 there was no national policy. Rather, sustenance was funded and delivered at the state and municipal level.[1] The help that the unemployed received was thus something of a lottery, depending on the budgetary situation, and to some degree the ideological position, of each state and local council. The sustenance programs were also marred by problems of delivery and an intrusive bureaucracy that fuelled resistance and protest from those who already felt that their governments were failing them. Nonetheless, the 'susso' provided a safety net of sorts and played a role in ensuring that those Australians most disadvantaged by the economic crisis survived.

All did not start well with the 'susso', as Victoria's example from 1930 reveals. In June, the Hogan government passed the *Unemployment Relief Act*, levying new taxes and setting aside £130,000 for sustenance. The balance of the

£1 million provided by the Act was allocated to relief works, it being widely agreed that it was preferable to give men work rather than a dole. Thanks to the conservative upper house, the Act gave the responsibility for distributing relief to charitable organisations and benevolent societies approved by the Charities Board of Victoria.[2] But as we have seen, these venerable institutions were already stretched to breaking point. The Melbourne Ladies Benevolent Society (MLBS) might have had a network consisting of some 28 loosely affiliated societies with a central council, but in some country towns there were no branches of this, or any other approved, charity. Moreover, the first grants from the government for sustenance were quite inadequate. By June–July 1930, the Brunswick branch of the MLBS was spending double the amount of its government grant in sustenance payments. The Northcote society was supporting 1125 unemployed people with a grant of £125.[3] The value of the grants distributed by various agencies varied widely across suburbs. Some country towns received nothing until well into 1931.

Within a week of the scheme being introduced, the MLBS suspended the distribution of sustenance. This tactic had been used before, but Premier Hogan now viewed it as a breach of the charities' obligations under the recent legislation. 'In effect [the MLBS] had gone on strike,' he said. 'In the industrial world when a body of men went on strike, their remuneration ceased. It would be interesting to know whether the pay of any of the persons responsible for this refusal and inaction had also ceased.'[4] This was too much for the middle-class ladies whose work, after all, was voluntary. The honorary secretary of the Essendon Ladies' Benevolent Society, Elizabeth Thomas, wrote to *The Argus* saying, 'The Premier forgot that he was dealing, not with men, but with committees of women who understand the purchasing power of 1/– [1 shilling], and who realised the absolute impossibility of continuing under conditions which simply made a farce of the whole scheme.'[5] She demanded an apology from the government and assurances that a workable scheme would be introduced before the distribution of sustenance resumed.

With *The Herald* running a series of front-page exposés, the Victorian government appointed a Minister for Sustenance, E.L. Kiernan, to bring some order to the system. No concessions were given to the MLBS, however, which resumed its work—albeit with some damage to its social capital—establishing food depots in central Melbourne and Carlton. Soon its staff were buckling under the strain of the 'deplorable' situation and the 'tremendous' time taken to check sustenance accounts.[6] In one week in September 1930, the MLBS was giving aid to 680 families in South Melbourne alone, a suburb that had been badly hit by the shipping and timber strikes of 1928–29.[7] Essentially, the MLBS could not readily make the transition from being a charitable agency to an instrument of government unemployment relief. It was not just its lack of infrastructure and funding, but also its reluctance to work cooperatively with other charities and its difficulty in crossing the class barrier.[8]

Few issues were as deeply emotive as food and housing, and soon the 'susso' galvanised the unemployed into more radical action. On 27 June, a large deputation from the Melbourne Trades Hall Council descended on Hogan's office complaining that the sustenance was 'entirely inadequate'. Dogs were treated better than unemployed single men, they claimed, as a crowd of nearly 4000 gathered outside and did their best to drown out the conversation.[9] In September, the increasingly militant Richmond Unemployed Association presented to its local council a petition of 500 signatures and a log of claims that included the distribution of food according to family needs, the allocation of relief work by roster rather than ballot, and the removal of women from the committees investigating applicants for sustenance.[10] The committee ladies refused to deal with male heads of households and it seemed that women were in control—a demeaning situation for men already emasculated by unemployment.

Protests turned aggressive in the following month when the MLBS decided that its depots in Carlton and North and South Melbourne would issue sustenance in kind, that is, in bags of food that the Society had previously purchased in bulk from grocers. This was supposedly a more economical use of sustenance funds, but many men wanted cash or, failing that, coupons that could be redeemed for goods over which they had some choice. The radicals among them blacklisted the Carlton depot—even though this meant denying food to others. Some of the 260 men who came to the Carlton depot on 20 October 1930 said that 'it was more than their life was worth to attempt to take bags of rations'. One woman pushed her way through the picket enforcing the blacklisting, hissing as she left with her bag of rations, 'You dare take this from me, you fools.'[11] The confrontation soon spread beyond the depot to Parliament House, where 'noisy and hostile' protesters howled Kiernan down when he tried to address them from the steps. When protesters tried to rush the minister, the police moved in to break the crowd up.[12]

The tensions continued in Richmond, where the relief depot had been blacklisted when this municipal council, too, insisted on supplying food direct rather than issuing coupons. Reportedly, some men were selling coupons for cash in local hotels. One unemployed man trying to gain entry to the sustenance room 'laid out three of his opponents' with black eyes: he had had training as a boxer.[13] Women breaking the pickets were hooted and their goods trampled in the gutter. One mother, crying bitterly that she and her family were starving, was escorted away with her parcel under police protection. Others evaded the picket by collecting rations from the town hall between 4 a.m. and 6 a.m. For a time Kiernan refused to reverse the decision for in-kind supply, earning himself the title of 'a second Mussolini' (he did, in fact, have some sympathy with fascist corporatist views).[14] As the stand-off continued, a full week of rations had to be destroyed. The conservative *Argus* lamented on 21 October: 'The action of the unemployed was indefensible and foolish. The food should have been used for their children instead of being wasted.' Eventually, however, the Victorian government gave ground and reinstated the system of vouchers that could be exchanged at a nominated grocer or butcher who then charged the government. The new arrangement was introduced first in the inner suburbs of Melbourne and progressively extended until by the end of 1931 it covered the whole state.[15]

The sustenance system established in other states had many features in common with Victoria, including the resistance they often generated.[16] Local politics and finances, however, ensured that there were significant variations in benefits and numbers across the states and over time (see Figure 14.1). Western Australia allowed the unemployed to receive two-sevenths of the dole in cash, rather than coupons. It was a greater proportion than any other state was 'prepared to trust to its unemployed'.[17] Queensland governments on both sides of politics restricted ration coupons to those for whom no relief work was available or who were physically incapable of heavy manual work.[18] The unemployed in South Australia suffered because of their state's

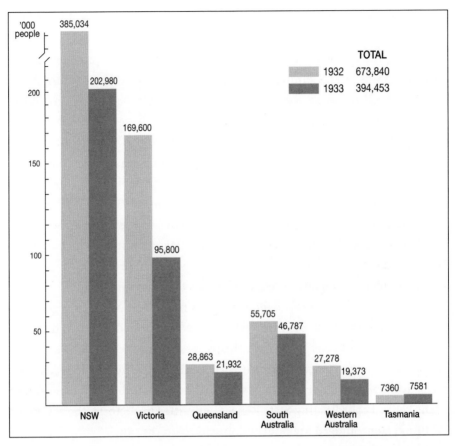

Figure 14.1: Approximate number of people in receipt of relief (sustenance payments) on 30 June 1932 and 1933

Note: The decline in numbers from 1932 to 1933 does not reflect a commensurate decline in employment but rather the tightening of relief administration, particularly in New South Wales after the defeat of Lang, and the introduction of relief works schemes.

Source: Bland, 'Unemployment Relief', p. 98.

impecunity. According to 1935 data, an unemployed married man with three children in South Australia received rations to the value of only 18 shillings and threepence, compared to 22 shillings ninepence in New South Wales, 27 shillings sixpence in Victoria and 35 shillings in Western Australia. South Australians called the dole 'the crumbs' or 'the chips'.[19] Little wonder, since the basic wage for men in South Australia in 1932–33 was a little above £3 (or 60 shillings) per week.

In all jurisdictions, the most significant of the goods provided under sustenance was food. Commonly the ration lists included bread, flour, meat, tea, coffee, cocoa, eggs, potatoes, rice, salt, oatmeal, barley, onions, milk, sugar, syrup, treacle, jam, condensed milk, butter, cheese and candles.[20] The meat could include loin chops, stewing steak, corned beef, offal (tripe, kidney and liver), sausages and mutton. This might seem a reasonable choice, but the quality and cuts of the meat could be poor. One deputation complained to the chief secretary of South Australia in December 1930 that the sausages provided were 'not fit for blackfellows'. A butcher whose feedback was then sought explained that 'he would give only one leg of mutton to each order, if he supplied them with two legs somebody else would have to go without . . . he would only have forequarters left and he tries to please everyone'.[21]

Initially, the dole rations contained little fresh fruit or green vegetables. But market gardeners, unemployed workers' groups, doctors and infant welfare officers all took issue with this, stressing (in the health profession-als' case) the importance of fruit in children's diets.[22] Vegetable seeds were made available as an alternative to standard items in Sydney.[23] The secretary of the central coordinating State Relief Committee in Victoria, the assiduous W. Bunker, encouraged Melbourne councils to do the same.

> We all know that vitamins and salts in green and root vegetables are essential to health, not only for adults but for growing children. To meet this want for their families men are to be seen on any market day appealing to stall holders for rejected or inferior vegetables, others overhaul vegetables thrown out either on the floors and ground and even in the bins set aside for clearance by municipal authorities.[24]

The council of Brighton, Melbourne, turned a public park into a vegetable garden in April 1931, with local companies donating fertiliser, equipment and even a horse.[25] Footscray Council developed a half-acre garden that produced some 2000 cabbages in the winter of 1932.[26] Mayors of various Melbourne suburbs visited local markets themselves, purchasing vegetables to be distrib-uted to the unemployed.[27]

The items on the sustenance lists were regularly adjusted, but the changes were not always for the better. In January 1931, beef was removed from the rations in Adelaide, to the chagrin of some of the unemployed who thought that the substitute mutton was inferior, in part because of its percentage of bone. About a thousand men, women and children marched in protest from Port Adelaide to the city, being joined on the way by a further thousand unemployed from the Labour Exchange. Carrying banners, placards and red flags, and singing revolutionary songs, they headed to the office of Premier Hill. The police intercepted them and violent street battles erupted. The batons and motorcycles of the police clashed with the wooden spikes, banner poles and other missiles from the crowd. Seventeen were admitted to hospital, including ten policemen. The violence and arrests of these 'beef riots' continued over subsequent days, ending in the presentation by the protesters of a wider log of claims to the chief secretary.[28]

A further grievance was the lack of flexibility in the rations lists. One family in Sydney had an oversupply of soap that it wanted to exchange for food. A country resident in New South Sales wanted kerosene and candles instead of some of the specified foods, because 'People in impoverished circumstances, living partly on the dole, without facilities for lighting, must necessarily see their children unable to do homework and forgo the pleasures of home life.'[29]

Even more contentious than the commodities provided was the question of eligibility for sustenance. The family unit was normally the basis of allocation, though the definition of this varied across states and with time. In Victoria in 1931, all members of the family living at home, irrespective of their age, were regarded as part of the family unit.[30] In New South Wales, the family unit originally comprised all children under 21 years of age. Given the strain this placed on family rations, it was later lowered so that children over fifteen could draw separate rations. In Queensland, the 'family unit' first excluded all boys over fourteen years of age, but included all dependent girls. In August 1931, the age for boys was raised to eighteen years, after which they were classified as single and required to travel in search of work in order to gain rations.[31]

The obligation on single men to travel, drawing rations from a different centre each week, was particularly aggravating. The rationale was that any man seriously looking for work should be willing to travel in search of it.

But this regulation condemned many men to a peripatetic life, their itineraries shaped by the need to reach another town on the particular day when rations would be distributed at the local police station. The impact on the young and on family life was so negative that ultimately, in June 1932, the Queensland government amended the 'travelling' regulation, allowing single unemployed men to draw rations at their place of residence. Still, the Minister for Labour and Industry in that state told a deputation of single unemployed men in January 1933 that 'the best way to emancipate yourself is to get married and thus become entitled to the privileges of married men'.[32] For many men marriage was out of the question until they had greater financial security.

Then there were various hurdles placed in the way of getting sustenance. Applicants needed to be registered as unemployed on a very regular basis at a labour exchange or the local police station.[33] Those seeking sustenance had to have been out of work for a given period. This varied by state, but in South Australia it was four weeks for a married man and eight weeks for a single man. Those temporarily out of work, for example over the Christmas break when some factories shut down, could not apply for relief in Victoria.[34]

Once approved for sustenance, and issued with the relevant documentation, the unemployed had to collect rations from an official depot or nominated suppliers. In Melbourne, it was thought that some women and girls were deterred from collecting sustenance because of the 'rather embarrassing comments' (presumably, sexual harassment) to which they were exposed when standing in long queues.[35] Car ownership was low and the cost of public transport well beyond many people's means. Hence, people could walk 'for miles and miles' to collect their rations.[36] One Sydney man recalled years later:

> You had to go No. 7 Wharf, Circular Quay and get your coupon, bring it back up to Railway Square, present it and it's a great big store, grocers shop with counters and that sort of thing they had built for the occasion . . . and take a bag with you . . . well you'd get just enough to keep you going', just, for the fortnight and then you'd go to the butcher's and you'd get meat and you'd have to cart it home. If you didn't have your fare to go home you walked.[37]

As the system became more developed, the number of depots in Sydney increased, to 77 in late 1931.[38]

Most frustrating for the unemployed were the regulations about 'permissible income'. Any income a family unit earned was offset against the value of its sustenance entitlement. 'Income' could include not just casual work but gifts of money, family endowment, rents from property and subtenants, and earnings from state-sponsored relief works. People receiving pensions, owning property or having bank savings were usually excluded, except in certain complicated circumstances.[39] Applicants for relief, then, had regularly to submit forms detailing their family's earnings and assets. If these exceeded a given threshold, the rations were lost. This catch-22 poverty trap was deeply resented. The communist-led Unemployed Workers' Movement (UWM) claimed:

Of all the most damnable regulations ever inflicted upon a body of workers it would be hard to find any that are more oppressive in their anti-working class character than the 'permissible income' regulations. These regulations are designed for the specific purpose of further putting the burden of the unemployed on the backs of the workers of industry, to rob the worker who has managed to save any monies during the time he was in employment, to deprive the sick, aged and returned soldiers of their paltry pittance . . . [as a result] boys and girls in employment leave their homes and make a break with the family tie.[40]

The Central Unemployed Committee of Melbourne, which represented a number of unemployed organisations, was more moderate in its language, but it, too, lobbied the government to withdraw the fortnightly income forms. It did not succeed.[41] In New South Wales, meanwhile, protest erupted when the authorities amended the forms in October 1931, requiring the application to be witnessed by an alderman, minister of religion, sergeant of police, town clerk or postmaster—not, as some critics quipped, the closest associates of many working-class unemployed! When, a year later, a 32-point questionnaire was issued, the aggravation was even greater. To quote one Sydney man's recollections:

One of the questions was 'Can you grow vegetables in your backyard? If not, why not?!' . . . The size of Sydney's slum backyards! [or, as his mate said] 'Ground unsuitable for cultivation.' 'Do you own any ducks, geese, livestock, dogs, pigs? If so how many?' Oh it was ridiculous and humiliating. So we burned them outside Paddington Town Hall.[42]

Strike action was contemplated on the coalfields. The steel town of Wollongong also saw protests, inspired, according to the press, by communist agitators from outside. The flames of the burning forms 'had hardly caught on' when the local police officer put his foot on them, and the crowd was dispersed, with three people being arrested for 'insulting the police'.[43]

The 'permissible income' questionnaires were not the only form of control. Like the charities, government officials were intent, for both ideological and budgetary reasons, on confining sustenance to the 'deserving' and most needy. In Victoria in August 1932, the police were required to notify authorities of anyone receiving rations who was convicted of 'drunkenness, larceny, disorderly conduct, etc.' Sustenance for the offenders was immediately cancelled.[44] Surveillance of various kinds was thus integral to the system. An Adelaide police officer described how:

> The inspector used to go around and visit the homes to see how [the unemployed] lived and enquire into all their personal affairs, rent, mortgage, debts, current accounts. If they came into the home and saw that you had a piano they would ask how long have you had that piano and whose it was. They would pick out artifacts and good paintings. If you had a car it was fatal.[45]

Such visits led one man, 'Disturbed', to protest to the Richmond Council in Melbourne: 'Are they supposed to [visit in the evening]: as it is unfair to others in the home as well as ourselves, to be disturbed at mealtimes by them calling on us.'[46]

In summary, to be eligible for sustenance, a family had to be well behaved and convincingly destitute. As the Perth government said on 20 June 1930, 'unemployment in itself is not a claim for Government sustenance, but if through unemployment the applicant has exhausted all his assets, except bare necessities and has thus been reduced to the position of not being able to secure food and meet his obligations, such as payment of rent, then and only then should his application be considered.'[47]

It is hard to escape the impression that the more Australian officials lost control over the big economic issues, the more intent they became with micromanaging relief. In Victoria in late 1930, all transactions had to be documented with receipts, and the local relief office had to report weekly to the central authorities. Anyone who lost his identification card could not gain sustenance.[48] Coupons could be redeemed only with nominated grocers who had to conform to agreed conditions and prices. They could not give the unemployed cash or any goods other than those listed on their orders. If they failed to comply, grocers were struck off the list of suppliers. The groceries themselves had be supplied in one parcel each week, not 'in dribs and drabs'. Bread, however, could be supplied 'in two or three portions each week as desired'. Applicants had to notify the relief committee 'immediately' when they obtained employment, but then had to make a fresh application for sustenance when that work ended.

These conditions were, admittedly, reviewed on a regular basis and at times liberalised. In Victoria, for instance, a double issue of sustenance was issued for one week before Christmas 1930 and 1931. The Victorian government also conducted a review of the relief system in early 1931, with a view to improving it.[49] But the tone did not change, and when in 1932 Wilfrid Kent Hughes, a forceful man who openly admired fascism, became Minister for Sustenance, the regulation of the system was tightened. On Kent Hughes' watch, Victoria attempted to link sustenance to relief works, forcing the unemployed to work for the dole.[50]

Not surprisingly, the regimes surrounding sustenance were seen by some of the unemployed as humiliating. The dole was the 'lowest form of help' and took away a man's pride, one man later recalled. Another chose to claim sustenance in Melbourne for only two or three weeks. 'I got that mad. I felt as if you had to crawl to them and I hadn't got to that stage where I'd crawl to anyone.'[51] In Adelaide, one of the unemployed waited for hours outside the relief office until he knew it was empty. Another man walked past the entrance to the office when he saw a friend coming down the street. On doubling back to enter the building, he found that his friend was already inside applying for relief.[52] Other people, often mothers, seem to have been more pragmatic. As the wife of one unemployed worker put it: 'We were glad to get [the dole] as we had children and we had to make sure they were looked after.'[53]

As so often with impenetrable bureaucratic systems, it was the low-level officials managing the allocation of rations who bore the brunt of the anger and frustration. While one contemporary account insisted that the officials acted with 'uniform courtesy', others claimed that little respect was shown to the unemployed.[54] Many years later, Clyde Cameron, aged eighteen in 1930 and later a federal ALP Minister for Labour, recalled:

> Every fortnight, applicants for food tickets would appear before an officer of the Unemployed Bureau and make the public confession that he or she was an inferior being . . . In the presence of everyone in the room, we were forced to announce that we were destitute, out of work, unemployable, and hungry. It was a terribly humiliating experience! We were not even treated like second-rate citizens. Instead, we were regarded as insects or vermin of some kind—bludgers on society—by public servants enjoying permanency of tenure with pay and perks that were the envy of all.[55]

Others, too, remembered the officials at the depots as being arrogant, herding men 'like sheep in a pen', snarling and throwing rations tickets at men waiting for their coupons.[56] Yet the clerks were easy targets, both in terms of their class and their function. The UWM might have deemed them 'an army of ration pimps', but they had the thankless task of mediating between the profoundly frustrated unemployed and the governments that insisted on the tightest surveillance of relief funds.[57]

All the bureaucratic scrutiny, however, could not prevent some rorting of the system. Men dodged from depot to depot to collect coupons; the 'twicers' or 'thricers', they were called. Many people did not fully divulge the income they and their families earned, or they claimed support to which they were not entitled. A random check by the South Australian Unemployment Relief Committee found that 25 per cent of those who were claiming an allowance for the supply of gas for cooking were not connected to a gas supply. Between 1931 and 1941, this state alone prosecuted and convicted almost 1200 people for obtaining rations illegally. No doubt there were many more who escaped notice.[58]

Predictably the press made good mileage out of what the *Sydney Morning Herald* called 'The Great Dole Scandal'. Imposters supposedly numbered in their thousands, while the cost to the New South Wales government of frauds was estimated in October 1932 to be between £400,000 and £500,000 per year. Ultimately, the New South Wales government would overhaul its rations system, converting to cash orders and, in an effort to prevent 'doubling', setting uniform issuing days and hours throughout the state. In rural areas, rations were issued only on Thursdays at 89 specified towns. After four weeks in a given town, a man had to reapply for relief as a local recipient.[59]

As with all systems of state control, there was also an element of informal surveillance. Motivated by resentment, self-righteousness or sheer meddle-someness, some Australians took it upon themselves to help regulate the system. One elderly man was denied sustenance in Sydney 'because he had been reported by some busybody as having been seen working'. It seems that he had been digging in his daughter's garden.[60] Two residents of Richmond provided details to the town clerk of the council of a single man receiving the sustenance of a married man, and of a man working at the gasworks and still taking the dole.[61] 'A ratepayer' wrote to the mayor of Brighton, Victoria, 'without any bitterness' to 'state a few true facts' about a family living at a given address in the neighbourhood. The wife kept a boarding house, the daughter worked and the husband had 'lost his jobs through drink'. But he still received help from the relief fund, boasting in the hotel that he did not need to work because he could get all he wanted for nothing. 'Can you wonder that people refuse to help when they see such glaring cases as this going on?'[62]

The 'susso' was in many respects a system that satisfied no one. This disaffection was almost inevitable, given the despair of the unemployed, the censoriousness of many of the more fortunate and the budgetary constraints on governments. What everyone wanted was that the unemployed should find work rather than rely on the dole. Yet for all the criticisms levelled at the 'susso', then and later, it did serve as something of a safety net. Without it, the situation of the unemployed would have been significantly worse. The core problem was that 'susso' was never enough. It always needed to be supplemented, not just by the efforts of charities and churches, but also by the self-help of local communities and the unemployed themselves.

CHAPTER 15

Community and family

All accounts of the Depression attest to the importance of communities and families in helping the unemployed to survive. The systems of social support that proliferated at the local level—municipal committees, trade unions, cooperative stores, associations of the unemployed, returned soldiers' organisations, school groups, philanthropists, and, as we have seen, charities and churches—cumulatively performed the role of building resilience through self-organisation and agency. Like the commemoration of World War I, the Depression attested to the importance of 'fictive kinship': that is, the social ties that relied on neither blood nor marriage.[1] But actual kinship ties were perhaps even more important. If nuclear and extended family units were functioning—and not all were—they provided shelter from the worst of the Depression by enabling people to pool resources and employ inventive strategies of self-help. Moreover, families, and the mothers who so often held them together, provided the emotional stability that was often the essence of individual resilience.

At the hub of the network of community support was the local council. Not only did federal and state governments devolve to municipalities much of the administration of sustenance—and, in time, of relief works programs— but councils were at the coalface of social distress. When people ran out of options, they turned to their mayors or that unsung hero, the town clerk. For example, a mother wrote to the Footscray Council in February 1932, asking if there were any blankets 'to spear':

> as i have got none for the children to cover themselves with my husband has been out of work for a long time . . . i would be very please to get them also any clothes as i have got no clothes for them to wear i would be very mutch oblige if you had any you could give me. I remain yours sin.[2]

Another mother wrote to the Preston Council, Melbourne, in November 1933 asking for clothing, bed linen and blankets for 'her eldest boy': he had lung trouble '& I am attending childrens hospital with him he is very delicate . . . I am very short of bed clothes & he must be kept warm . . . I would not ask you for anything if I was able to work. But I cannot. I have a little girl 8 years of age which has never walked.'[3] This same council took up with a state government department the 'sad' and 'very needy' case of a father seeking to secure a wheelchair for his invalid son. The man was unemployed and 'his boy, who has been taken out of hospital, is unable to walk . . . [and] is not likely to recover'.[4] Another desperate mother was referred to the Footscray council by the State Relief Committee; asking for a Christmas parcel in 1931 she wrote:

> My husband has been out of work now for over two years and we have had nothing but the sustenance to live on for over twelve months now. There are five of us three children and our two selves, it would be a God send to us if we could get one, all we had last Christmas was a peice of bread and corn beef. To make matter worse I have not one relation and my husbands people are all in poor circumstances and cannot help us, also I am disimposed myself expecting to go into the Women's Hospital next month.[5]

Such calls for help—and these are only a small sample from the rich archives of Melbourne's local councils—presented municipal authorities with intractable funding problems.[6] Food, the highest in the hierarchy of needs, was largely covered by the sustenance system, but there was always a need for more, and for other basic items such as clothing, fuel, blankets and the boots that were necessary for manual labour under relief works. As the Footscray branch of the Returned Sailors' and Soldiers' Imperial League Employment Bureau told the city mayor in April 1931, 'many of our Members are so badly shod that if we had a sudden call for Men for employment many would be unable to take advantage of the same for this reason'.[7] Councils thus ran appeals for second-hand boots and supported boot-repair workshops run by associations of the unemployed.[8] In Footscray, in the nine months between 1 October 1931 and 16 July 1932, some 3239 pairs of boots were repaired at five depots.[9] Occasionally the federal government provided worn-out boots, together with military clothing dyed from the original khaki.[10] The United Front of Employed and Unemployed in Sydney noted that it would have been better to have had new boots, clothing and blankets, not just the 'cast-offs of other people'.[11]

The need for clothing was visible everywhere in poorer suburbs. Children were going to school barefoot or wearing unsuitable clothing: in one case, an oversized overcoat, done up with safety pins, and no clothes underneath.[12] Collection boxes for second-hand clothing were placed in prominent streets and railways stations.[13] In Melbourne, if there was any surplus after local needs had been met, it was pooled centrally and distributed to points of greatest need.[14] In South Australia, supplies of clothing were augmented by prisoners in gaols, who made shoes for children in local schools.[15]

Firewood was another commodity provided locally. Many homes still had wood-fired stoves and open fireplaces rather than gas or electrical services, which were, in any case, beyond many people's means. Bathrooms often had chip heaters, or people washed by tipping hot water into free-standing pots set up in a kitchen or on an outside veranda. Many households washed their clothes in kerosene tins, boiling the water on fires in the backyard. The struggle to keep warm required endless improvisation: burning rags or newspapers, one page at a time; collecting fence palings and bits of timber from factories; picking up branches from paddocks; and retrieving driftwood from the sea, and coke and coal droppings from wharves and railways. Some families got donations of fuel from suppliers or deliveries from country friends or relatives.[16] In ten months, the Footscray Council issued 3736 tons of wood to 1800 people each week.[17]

With revenue from their rates declining and government grants requiring matching funding, councils relied heavily on local fundraising. Direct appeals for cash intensified and more collection boxes were left at hotels. When compassion ran dry, people were urged to 'enjoy yourself and help others'—at charity concerts, balls, dances, public lectures, community singing, bridge nights, theatre productions, euchre parties, harbour cruises, car races, football matches and bazaars featuring baby shows. The former Director of Education, Frank Tate, offered to give lectures in Brighton, Melbourne, on 'Life—in the Forest of Arden' and Shakespeare's *As You Like It*![18] How many came to hear him is not recorded. Possibly more appealing was a regatta at Brighton-Le-Sands, Sydney, that featured parachute jumping and boomerang throwing by La Perouse (Guriwal) Aboriginal Australians.[19] In Perth, the 1930 Royal Show's car park, which was under the control of Claremont Municipal Council, was operated by the unemployed and the proceeds given to the local unemployment relief fund.[20]

Much of this activity was driven by the same social elites whose voluntary work and patronage sustained the benevolent societies and church organisations. In Queensland, the governor's wife, Lady Goodwin, organised a regular sewing circle to provide garments for needy families.[21] In South Australia, Lady Hore-Ruthven (later Gowrie), another vice-regal partner, visited Port Adelaide to meet the local people and relief organisations. Her Lend-a-Hand Club, comprising 'a number of ladies who met regularly at Government House', distributed 3722 garments among the poor. With said ladies, Lady Hore-Ruthven also attended a 'sunshine afternoon', in the Port Adelaide Town Hall on 11 August 1932, when the wives of about 700 unemployed men were provided with afternoon tea.[22]

Various appeals were launched in the name of lord mayors. In Adelaide, Bonython urged the public to do their best 'to tide the poor and needy over the present critical period, and by doing so justify their faith in their fellow citizens, and bring to them an encouragement to face the future with confidence and hope'.[23] The Lord Mayor of Melbourne, H.D. Luxton, launched an 'S.O.S.' boots and clothing week in mid-1931, looking to councils for support and to radio stations and businesses for publicity. The Royal Automobile Club of Victoria provided motor transport for volunteers including boy scouts and girl guides.[24] This same Melbourne mayor promoted the concept of S.O.S. circles. Each municipality should form circles of 'enthusiastic ladies' to make clothes and collect second-hand clothing and footwear. These should multiply as each member of a circle of six recruited another circle of six. The aim, it was agreed, was 'to engender the spirit which was in existence during the war'.[25]

Typically, the wives of the mayors did much of the actual work of fund-raising. Mrs Bonython 'did not spare herself' in helping her husband. She organised committees of women working 'like Trojans in [the] philanthropic cause' to distribute food, clothing, firewood and blankets in Adelaide, while handling a stream of correspondence from the public.[26] In Footscray, the mayor's wife became president of the Unemployed Single Girls' Association, formed in early 1931 to provide women's clothing in certain wards of that city.[27] In Richmond, the lady mayoress organised multiple fundraising events, including, in September 1930, a million pennies fund that aimed to raise £3000 to £4000 in the following twelve months.[28]

Yet if these pillars of society provided leadership, the community efforts to alleviate unemployment had a wide social base. Almost every organisation with some civic role seems to have turned its hand to unemployment relief during the Depression years. To name only some: the National Council of Women, the Australian Red Cross (and its arm the Junior Red Cross), the YMCA, the YWCA, Toc H, Rotary, the Country Women's Association, the RSSILA and the National Council of Jewish Women.[29] The industrial labour movement also spawned its own plethora of associations to support the unemployed. The Central Unemployed Committee of Trades Hall, Melbourne, consisted of no less than 45 city unemployed organisations.[30] The capacity of the official union leadership to fund unemployment relief was limited, given that union revenue declined as many of the unemployed let their membership lapse. In Queensland, where the Moore government dismantled those clauses in industrial and rural awards that provided for union preference in employment, the once mighty AWU lost 54 per cent of its membership between 1927 and 1932.[31] Those unions that had property holdings struggled on, but many were forced to cut costs, cancelling annual picnics and May Day celebrations, and retrenching staff who might have developed programs to support the unemployed. In any case, the official position of the ACTU was that it was the duty of government to provide relief for the unemployed.[32]

Disaffected with official union leadership, many unemployed workers formed their own support associations. They lobbied councils not only for practical assistance but also for the right to hold fundraising events at public venues and to gain access to council meeting rooms and decision-making forums. These groups ranged across the ideological spectrum, each claiming to be the authentic voice of the unemployed. The Footscray Branch of the RSSILA Employment Bureau, for example, advised the local council that it viewed 'with great disfavour any section of returned soldiers having the right to collect without being under the strict supervision of the parent body and its responsible officers'.[33] In Richmond, the UWM claimed the mantle of leadership, accusing the mayoral relief committee of practising favouritism towards 'its pets' in the allocation of municipal funds. The council, in turn, formed its own counter-organisation of the unemployed in March 1931, providing it with a factory for accommodation and assistance with fundraising. The UWM was banned from attending council meetings or making deputations, and could not stand for the Unemployed Distress Relief Committee because of the requirement that all nominees supply ten signatures confirming that they were not members of the UWM or the Communist Party.[34]

Within this crowded landscape of community efforts, schools, too, were active players, especially those that saw it as their role to invest their students with a sense of civic duty and responsibility. The students and staff of the elite Geelong Grammar created an Unemployed Boys' Centre to assist the young unemployed of nearby Geelong.[35] The Anglican private girls' school Korowa, in East Melbourne, became

a hive of activity, [as] girls sacrificing their leisure worked to help those less fortunate than themselves—such is the spirit [the school magazine continued] fostered by the School. In the class-room and on the playing field, not for ourselves, or our small circle but working as one unit.[36]

Much of 1931 saw the girls 'busy knitting . . . socks, singlets and jumpers'.[37] In Preston, Melbourne, schoolchildren contributed to bazaars by writing essays on topics such as 'How I can help towards the future progress of Preston', and 'How the Future Development of Preston can be secured'.[38]

Then, there were the philanthropists, large and small, who donated cash, wages or in-kind assistance.[39] The owner of the Melbourne emporium, Sidney Myer, made a grant of £10,000 for unemployment relief that provided work for 1600 married men for nine days before Christmas 1931.[40] The Adelaide *News* and the Melbourne *Herald*—the latter controlled by the journalist who had made his name as Hughes' de facto public relations adviser in World War I, Keith Murdoch—ran public appeals for blankets. Some 52 municipalities in Melbourne benefited from one such appeal.[41] A pregnant mother of six children in Footscray made her claim by writing to *The Herald*, 'Their Father has been out of work for 2½ yrs & I find no way of getting any for them. I have got 1 double bed 2 single beds & 2 cots & have only got 1 thin blanket for each in fact the baby has only got a piece of blanket on his cot.'[42] Meanwhile, Murdoch's young wife, Elizabeth, employed local men to build a stone wall for the garden at the family property, Cruden Farm, near Langwarrin south-east of Melbourne. When the men asked for more work, she engaged them to build the farm's stone stables. 'The men were embarrassingly grateful for the work,' she said decades later, 'telling us it had been an absolute lifesaver for nearly a dozen families in Langwarrin.'[43]

Many acts of compassion were more modest but equally well intentioned. Help often came from neighbours, even those who could scarcely afford it.[44] A Preston councillor donated fifteen leather aprons for men to wear when unloading supplies of firewood, 'owing to the state of trousers worn by these men'.[45] A woman in Annuello in rural Victoria offered a load of mallee roots to the Richmond Council. 'Mallee roots,' she said, 'is the one thing we have plenty of.'[46] A baker in Townsville gave buns and bread to the unemployed with no expectation of payment.[47] That said, some small businesses saw the chance to commercialise charity. The company producing the cleaning products I-Kleen and Snowdrape used relief appeals as a marketing device.[48]

In retrospect, it is impossible to quantify the contribution that these diverse community initiatives made to the relief of social distress. No national records were kept as to how much money was raised, or by whom. Nor did any officials or researchers attempt to assess the efficacy of the various strategies employed in local fundraising. Clearly, the multitude of organisations competing for the charity pound generated inefficiencies, duplication and overlap. Authorities at state and municipal levels seem to have spent considerable energy policing the chaos: issuing licences to approved organisations; banning unauthorised collections and independent appeals through the press; chasing donations that had not been paid into official accounts; and warning the public to be on guard against fraudulent practices, such as fundraisers impersonating the mayor.[49]

Yet perhaps these community efforts should not be assessed in quantitative terms but recognised for their value as a source of societal resilience.[50] For all the political diversity of the community organisations, they were united around the common goal of mitigating the suffering of the unemployed. This community mobilisation differed from that of World War I, where the issue of conscription proved profoundly polarising. Moreover, community activism attested to the ability of Australians to organise, exercise agency and adapt in times of massive disturbance and change—all qualities that are recognised to be keys to resilience. Those who devoted their energies to fundraising might not have been able to do anything to change the impersonal forces of global economics, but they could respond to the stresses and shocks within their own neighbourhood. Their lives thus retained some of the coherence and meaning that strengthen resilience. The problems and demands that they confronted were worth investing energy in, worthy of commitment and engagement, and could be constructed as challenges that were welcomed rather than burdens.[51]

For those who benefited from the various community efforts, too, there were benefits beyond the material. It provided some reassurance that others in the community cared about their plight. Again this cannot be quantified, and memories of community support, it must be said, range from the enthusiastically positive to the bitterly negative. One woman speaking in the 1990s said that 'Wherever there was a problem most people around would rally to help in some small way . . . It was a caring time, although there was so very little to give.'[52] But not all communities pulled together, and self-interest must often have prevailed over compassion for the collective. An alternative memory is that 'Some wouldn't share but that's human nature.'[53] That said, the sheer scale and diversity of the community effort was such that most people would have been able to find an advocate on their behalf and access support that reflected a wider sense of humanity.

The agency that was evident within community organisations was also characteristic of the strategies of self-help that many families and individuals adopted to survive. Like so many aspects of the Depression, this capacity was contingent upon class and location. Take the home production of food: housing in the most disadvantaged working-class suburbs of the capital cities offered little space for growing and preparing food. Backyards were small and concreted and housed the outdoor toilet. Little use, then, for the vegetable seeds that councils provided, although one resident, in Rosebery in the inner city of Sydney, later described how 'We had some seeds which someone gave us . . . The yard of the house had never been used for a garden, unless many years before . . . We were compelled to borrow tools from some strangers up the street . . . Despite insects, cats and other enemies, we were able to grow some spinach, carrots, parsnips, lettuce, cabbages and radishes.' The problem was, she added, that: 'We had to move from this house shortly after, and were discouraged from ever starting again to grow vegetables, as we never knew when we would have to move on again.'[54]

In the more prosperous suburbs where homes were on larger blocks, the backyard was not the carefully landscaped site of leisure that it is today. Rather, it housed vegetable gardens, fruit trees and 'chooks' that were a ready source of eggs. Roosters were not yet proscribed as a neighbourhood nuisance. The son of an unemployed paper-hanger in Burnside, Adelaide, remembered: 'We had apricot trees . . . Mother made jam from them, and peach, fig, plum, nectarine . . . Fruit was preserved . . . And the ground in Burnside was extremely good soil and there wasn't anything you couldn't grow well. We grew most vegetables, potatoes and carrots, cauliflowers and cabbages and onions.'[55] If the soil was not good, aspiring suburban gardeners could collect the manure dropped by horses pulling carts that delivered bread, milk, vegetables and ice-blocks through the suburbs.

The home was not the only source from which to extract food. The waterways of Australia's capital cities had not yet been converted into stormwater drains or freeway valleys. Families grazed cows for milk along the river flats of the Yarra and Maribyrnong rivers in Melbourne. Some people sold milk illegally door to door. Others picked blackberries and mushrooms.[56] The creeks everywhere could be fished, as could the ocean. To quote one account of life in Birkenhead, near Port Adelaide:

> The fishboats used to come and tie up there and they used to sell sometimes you'd get 12 or 14 Tommies or Mullet for a shilling—and sometimes they used to come in there and have live Salmon—you get a big Salmon like that for about 6 pence and they used to bring in live crayfish— . . . we'd get a couple of nice crayfish for 2 shillings enough to feed us all—and they'd be alive, kicking when we carried them home.[57]

A barmaid living in Southport, Queensland, recalled that their home production—vegetables, mango tree, a chicken run and a cow—was supplemented by seafood. 'My brother . . . used to go and set crab pots and we'd always have lovely crabs . . . And we always had oysters.'[58]

For those who could not catch or grow their own food, daily diets were enhanced by careful shopping and bargain hunting. Meat could be bought cheaply from butchers or markets at closing time. Bakers and market stalls offloaded cheap stale bread and cakes, broken biscuits and bruised fruit. The daughter of a deserted mother remembered how:

> It was my job to go down to Prahran market and to get enough stuff for the whole family for a week. Mum would give me four shillings . . . At the last minute you could usually buy a full side of lamb for one and threepence. I'd go to the home-made pie-shop at closing time. You could get three baked rabbits for a shilling. The shopkeepers couldn't afford to leave anything, so they'd fill up big bags. They'd have sausage rolls and buns . . . And I'd take the pram round and get potatoes, thirty–three pounds [15 kilograms] a shilling.[59]

In the streets of the cities, too, hawkers, many of them unregistered, would sell cheap milk, butter, vegetables, jam, fish and rabbits. For many who lived through the Depression, their efforts at self-help were a source of lasting pride. To quote one later interview of a woman sharing accommodation with her extended family: 'We learned how to cook in those days. We fried, cooked, boiled, stuffed and made into sauce, just to vary the same cheap food a little. For instance, we bought the liver of an ox quite frequently because it was cheap and stuffed it and named it mock duck dinner.'[60]

Country dwellers were even more able to find alternative sources of food. Self-sufficiency had always been part of remote living and for some, little changed during the Depression. 'We always made our own bread, and had vegetables and plenty of meat from the farm because we couldn't sell it at good prices in those years . . . We were a lot better off than the city people. We ate well.'[61] Those making their living on farms owned livestock—cows, chickens, ducks, calves and lambs—and thus had ready sources of milk, cheese, butter and meat. Farmers commonly killed calves and lambs on a community basis, sharing the meat on rotation. Wheat farmers had grain on hand for bread making. Exchange of goods was a common strategy everywhere, but rural communities had more capacity than urban dwellers to barter goods: a bag of potatoes for half a lamb, fruit for milk and wheat, vegetables and honey for eggs, and a good horse for an old hack plus a sheep and a cow. Others resorted to eating wild pigs and native animals: kangaroos, birds, emus, bush turkeys and flying fox.[62]

Then there was the rabbit! Introduced into Australia with white settlement, this prolific pest numbered literally in the billions in the 1920s. By one estimate, there were 10 billion in 1920, as opposed to around 200 million today.[63] They caused immense economic damage—digging burrows, undermining fences, eating crops, competing with livestock and native animals for pasture—while causing massive soil erosion. But they were also a boundless source of food. One man surviving in the Victorian bush near Red Cliffs recalled that: 'They were like flocks of sheep. You'd put a trap down, catch a rabbit, skin it, cook, it, chuck what was left over away. Next meal, go down, catch a rabbit, skin it, cook it, chuck it away.'[64] Every meal, another recalled, was 'damned rabbit'.[65] But whatever the monotony, rabbits were a source of nutrition, high in protein and low in fat. Crates were brought down to the cities for distribution among those on sustenance.[66]

Moreover, rabbits could be sold for cash—it was an industry that required little capital—and their skins stitched by country women into bed covers, mats or baby clothes. The international market for rabbit skins had collapsed—by October 1930, London and New York had stockpiled bales of skins—but it picked up by 1933.[67] Some more entrepreneurial Australians thought that the rabbit might even be tinned for export! 'Here is a valuable food going to waste,' one man wrote to the federal government in 1934. 'Markets await this product both here and abroad. The raw material is cheap and plentiful. The scourge could and should be turned to profitable account. Rabbits could be a source of enormous wealth.'[68]

Whether it be in the country or the city, strategies of self-help often rested on that critically important figure in the family, the mother. Oral histories attest to this in a compelling way. To quote only a few examples: 'we never went short, because my mother was a good manager'.[69] 'Mother used to make everything. There wasn't anything she didn't make . . . She had all the responsibility of rearing us, making-do and making the money stretch, seeing we were well looked after.'[70] 'My mother was well-known as the best fruit tree pruner in the district . . . Mother made all our clothes, boys' trousers cut down from Dad's, and my dresses from bargain remnants or whatever she could find.'[71] 'My mother was marvellous in that she could turn her hand to anything; she could make a pound of potatoes go that far [by] supplement[ing] it with a bit of flour or whatever they did . . . in those days you would get a big bundle of bacon bones, maybe a pig's trotter thrown in . . . Mum used to cook that up and it spun out, [you] would just keep watering it down.'[72] Finally, Colin Thiele, who was a child of ten in 1930 and later authored *Storm Boy*, eulogised his mother as:

> the rallying figure for our survival. Her dairy cows (hand-milked twice a day by all of us) helped to provide a trickle of income through the fortnightly 'cream cheques' from the butter factory . . . my mother baked our own bread, made *kuchen* [cake], honey biscuits and scones . . . patched our work clothes with patches over patches.[73]

This is not to deny the importance of fathers in family dynamics, and the immense advantage of a family unit that remained intact and stable. Thiele also recalled his father repairing shoes or digging the backyard garden. But many men were absent seeking work, and it was mothers on whom the daily responsibility for feeding, clothing and nurturing family members fell. They were the 'ballast . . . the central force' that enabled the families around them to function.[74]

Women's socialisation predisposed them to perform these domestic tasks with the maximum efficiency. In the 1920s, Australian housewives, especially those in the middle class, were encouraged by organisations such as the Housewives' Association, the Country Women's Association and the Australian Women's National League to view their labour in the home as 'domestic science'. The housewife was expected to be an astute consumer, checking her purchases to ensure she was getting the best value for money, and the most healthy and wholesome foods for her family. Above all, she was meant to plan: menus, the household budget, and frequent trips to markets and shops. As one of the magazines aimed at a female audience, *The Woman*, said on 1 June 1921: 'The housewife in many instances needs to consider not only the high cost of food, but the high cost of carelessness in marketing, of carelessness in cooking, in sewing, and in preserving: in short to consider the high cost of waste of food that goes on in her ill-managed kitchen.'[75] These values were promulgated through domestic science courses offered in schools. This training was obligatory in high schools for those girls not intending to go to university and who were assumed to be waiting for marriage. Thus, 'getting by' and 'making do', balancing family budgets and cutting down on non-essentials were not just a matter of necessity during the Depression. They were valued behaviours that made the sacrifices required of mothers and their families not easy but a source of affirmation and validation.[76] At the local level, Australian women were doing what their governments were also requiring of themselves, living within their means.

CHAPTER 16

Health and resilience

During the worst years of the Depression, it was common for critics of the government to speak of Australians being 'on the verge of starvation' or 'facing starvation'.[1] The more radical press maintained that it was inherent in capitalism that the oppressed should either work or starve. *Labor Call* dubbed Kent Hughes the 'Minister for Starvation'. The mainstream press also ran stories at various times of Australians collapsing because of lack of food. The Melbourne *Argus* carried a report on 25 April 1931 that a woman had fainted in the street in Manangatang, in the remote Mallee, reportedly after not eating for two days. Another notorious case was the death of a young Melbourne woman in mid-1930. The *Labor Daily* had no doubts as to the cause: 'A few days ago a married woman died in the Melbourne Hospital. She had no right to die, for she was only 23 years of age, and she had no organic disease. But she was the wife of a worker who had for several months been denied work or sustenance. So she died of STARVATION!'[2] On closer examination—an inquiry was conducted into the woman's case—it emerged that this woman had a history of poor health and, according to the MLBS, had food in her house, from sustenance orders and neighbours, at the time of her death.[3]

Still, the idea of Australians being on 'the verge of starvation' was a politically powerful tool in the 1930s, invoked to castigate governments and mobilise the masses. It also found a place in later popular literature. The novelist Alan Marshall told of men wolfing 'like dogs' the cast-offs from

Melbourne restaurants: 'an unstable mound . . . girdled by a brown liquid' that included bones and scraps, all 'speckled with sodden tea leaves' and 'the black sand of coffee grounds'.[4] The spectre of hunger infused the histories of the Depression written from the 1960s on by labour historians with a political and emotional commitment to the victims of the Depression. A major collection of oral histories in 1978, for example, posed the question: '"Was it really so bad? Here? In Australia?" In fact . . . it was far worse.'[5]

But were Australians actually starving? While there is ample evidence of profound distress in the poorer suburbs of Australia's cities and in many parts of the bush, such data as we have about Australians' health in the 1930s suggest this did not necessarily translate into significant illness or premature mortality. Australia did not conduct any independent studies of public health such as were undertaken in Britain, but various official statistics and reports provide no evidence of widespread starvation.[6] As Table 16.1 shows, the major causes of death in 1931–32 were diseases of the heart, respiratory illnesses and cancer. Respiratory illnesses might be thought to indicate poverty, but tuberculosis rates declined, with the fastest rate of fall in the inter-war years occurring between 1930 and 1932. Pneumonia, sometimes called 'the poor man's adversary and the old man's friend', reached its lowest recorded level in New South Wales in 1932. Scarlet fever and diphtheria were prevalent in Victoria in 1931–32, but the case-to-fatality ratios rose only slightly for the state as a whole and fell to the lowest ratio ever in Melbourne and the Commonwealth in 1931–32.[7]

Notably, infant mortality, one of the most important indicators of public health, declined in the years of the Depression.[8] The birth rate itself declined by as much as 30 per cent between 1928 and 1934 in South Australia. This continued a trend already evident in the 1920s, and was probably caused by the deferral of marriage and the voluntary restriction of family size in the face of unemployment and changing lifestyles. The mortality rate for babies under one year also declined: from 57 deaths per 1000 live births to 44 in 1934.[9] This might be attributable to the greater opportunities for breast-feeding, cheaper dairy products and the dissemination of medical advice

Table 16.1: Major causes of death, Australia, 1929–33*

Abridged classification	1929	1930	1931	1932	1933
Infectious diseases†	2848	1897	2331	1763	2177
Tuberculosis (including tubercular meningitis)	3464	3258	3167	3004	2924
Cancer (malignant tumours) and other tumours	6588	6469	6934	7235	1018
Cerebral haemorrhage	3017	2810	2884	3021	3206
Diseases of the heart and circulatory system	11,734	11,272	12,919	13,700	14,780
Respiratory illnesses (bronchitis, pneumonia, etc.)	7149	5124	5669	5163	5748
Cirrhosis, liver, liver diseases, hernia and other digestive system	2167	2089	2029	2165	2161
Kidney disease and genitourinary system	4482	4193	4333	4519	4603

* Data not included for: 'Other general diseases', appendicitis, diseases of the skin and bone, diabetes mellitus, diarrhoea and enteritis, alcoholism, childbirth and pregnancy, 'criminal abortion', post-abortive sepsis, syphilis, diseases of nervous system and sense organs, locomotor ataxy, smallpox, malaria, homicide, accidental or violent death, congenital abnormality and premature birth, suicide, senility, and non-specified causes.
† Includes typhoid and typhus fever, measles, scarlet fever, whooping cough, diphtheria, influenza, and other infectious parasitic diseases.
Source: Year Book Australia, 1934, p. 823.

through the establishment of infant welfare centres and mothercraft clinics in previous decades.[10] States such as Victoria also made special food provision for expectant mothers and infants.[11] Maternal mortality, in contrast, remained high until 1937, when there was a significant fall, arguably associated with the availability of sulphonamides (antibiotics used to treat bacterial infections).[12] Deaths from abortions perhaps also declined, though this is hard to estimate (see Chapter 26).

As for children's health, some contemporary sources suggested that this might have actually improved. In 1932 the chief medical officer of the Melbourne Education Department investigated more than 43,000 inner suburban school-children, and, drawing comparisons with the recent past, concluded that

on the whole the children of the state have survived wonderfully the ordeal of the period of depression . . . With regard to physical defects,

213

the improvement previously recorded is still being maintained . . . Only 20 per cent to 30 per cent of children are now notified for defective teeth . . . Anaemia and rickets are each year definitively less, no doubt due chiefly to the more satisfactory feeding and hygiene of early life.

The weight of these children had also 'been maintained to a surprising degree'.[13] A 1938 report, by the Melbourne City Council Health officer, was more ambiguous. Some 31 per cent of children had been suffering from malnutrition in 1928, and this figure had increased in 1930 to 37 per cent, but by 1934 the malnutrition rates among infants in Melbourne's inner suburbs were lower than 1928. Rickets, caused by vitamin D deficiency and one of the most obvious markers of malnutrition, had all but disappeared.[14] That said, a doctor in Brisbane reported seeing 'a comparatively large' number of rickets cases in 1934, apparently among hospital admissions.[15] In South Australia, too, a 1930 report by the medical branch of the Education Department found that almost 15 per cent of children were suffering from malnutrition and, in that state at least, the rations were nutritionally inadequate.[16]

Notably, some studies suggested that average weight and height of children aged four to thirteen years increased in the fifteen years after 1922. Height is generally accepted as a reliable index of nutrition during a child's growing years.[17] It is significant, then, that although there were variations across suburbs, many Melbourne children aged 4 to 13 weighed and measured more in 1937–38 than Victorian children of the same age had over the period 1912–22. Many of them might have eaten too much bread, jam and salt and too few vegetables, but their calorific intake was probably bolstered by the free meals and milk provided to the most deprived children in kindergartens and primary schools. A 1935–36 report on more than 36,000 schoolchildren in Australia and New Zealand stated that, in the case of Melbourne:

during and since the depression, active measures have been taken in all directions to see that by some means or other those children who are not getting enough food in the house have it supplemented from outside. This has been done through the various charitable organizations. Some provide free meals for children and other food for the home; while the Sustenance Department of Victoria, for the past three years, has supplied free milk to necessitous children in all metropolitan schools, kindergartens and creches during the winter months. In addition, in many schools, during the worst of the depression, on the initiative of the head teacher or mother's club, special arrangements were made for the supply of extra food.[18]

The data from South Australia, however, suggest a less positive view: children in many age groups suffered a weight loss between 1926–29 and 1930–35.[19]

Most significantly, the Depression did not seriously disrupt the general trend of a decline over the twentieth century in mortality rates (that is the number of people per 100,000 of population who die in a given year). There is some evidence—albeit difficult to interpret—that mortality rates, particularly for older men, plateaued during the 1930s, the latter years particularly. It is 'difficult not to hypothesise some relationship' between this and the Depression. But if the decline in mortality rates for men stalled for several decades, there was no increase, and nothing to match the spike that occurred in 1919 when the 'Spanish flu' pandemic swept through the population.[20]

What seems clear, then, is that starvation did not stalk the streets of Depression Australia. This is not to deny that many people were hungry or malnourished. The sustenance rations, as we have seen, were not high in nutritional value.[21] High-risk groups—women and children who were deserted or abused, men struggling with chronic war injuries, families settled on remote uneconomic plots of farmland and the single unattached male who took to wandering the country in search of food and work—had a constant struggle to find reliable sources of food. But generally Australians did not starve.[22] The sustenance system, when supplemented by local governments, voluntary organisations, community initiatives and self-help, met at least the basic requirement of the majority of the unemployed for food. Beyond this, Australia's investment in infrastructure in the 1920s, though it may have contributed to external indebtedness, meant that some of the other essentials of public health—safe water and effective sewerage—were ensured in urban environments.

What about Australians' mental health? This is harder to be precise about, given the lack of recognition given to mental illness at that time. It seems self-evident that the effects of unemployment—the loss of self-respect and privacy when applying for relief, the problems of managing debt, the changes in family roles, the lack of purpose and status and sheer boredom—must have been damaging psychologically. As one group of unemployed in Canberra put it, their being 'social outcasts' aggravated their 'misery and distress'.[23] Fear has been called 'the mind-killer', and the sheer anxiety of anticipating unemployment must have been corrosive, even for those who ultimately kept their jobs.[24] One worker stitching clothing for Henry Bucks recalled how 'the boss would walk upstairs and your heart would be in your mouth and you'd think, "Oh, it's my turn to get put off."' Press reports noted that people were becoming 'exhausted mentally and nervously'.[25] Leading educators worried about the lasting harm that boys would carry for the rest of their lives if they could not gain employment when they left school.[26] Yet, for all this, admissions to 'mental hospitals', as they were then called, did not rise significantly in any of Adelaide, Melbourne or New South Wales. This might have been because such institutions were already overcrowded in Adelaide (and presumably other cities), and the stigma of admission to forbidding places such as Parkside psychiatric hospital—popularly called 'the loony bin'—was very high.[27]

The incidence of suicide in response to the Depression is again hard to determine. Press reports carried stories of a man blowing his head off after being dismissed from a property on which he had worked for three years; and a man taking poison while clutching a letter from his boss saying that 'the Depression has made it necessary for us to dispense with your services'.[28] The Sydney Harbour Bridge saw no fewer than 60 people jump to their deaths in the seven months after its opening in 1932.[29] The press linked some of these to unemployment.[30] Strikingly, too, the year 1930 saw the highest rate of Australian male suicide in the twentieth century.[31] This, too, suggests a correlation between economic hardship and suicide.

After peaking in 1930, however, the suicide rate declined a little in 1931 and 1932, the worst years for unemployment. Moreover, a close analysis of two of the most prominent suicides of the Depression years, that of General Harold 'Pompey' Elliott, commander of the 15th Australian Infantry Brigade in World War I, and Hugo Throssell, a Victoria Cross winner at Gallipoli, suggests that financial hardship was only one of a mix of factors that might have caused a man to take his life. Throssell accumulated ruinous debts in the years before he shot himself, but Elliott's financial position seems to have been secure, although, according to one of his advisers, this was not how he saw it. For these two men it seems that the impact of the Depression was to unleash the psychological damage that they had suffered in World War I—damage that had never been adequately treated in the 1920s. As later research into post-traumatic stress syndrome indicates, a second or later negative life event can have a severe impact on already traumatised individuals, making them less able to cope and more likely to develop chronic trauma symptoms. Thus, as the Depression denied life of any element of predictability and manageability and made returned soldiers more vulnerable, Elliott was plagued with nightmares, ghastly flashbacks and tormenting memories of the many young men who had died under his command in 1915–18. Though prominent in veteran affairs and politics, he felt impotent to do anything for those who had survived. His blood pressure rose and he suffered from diabetes. Throssell, too, experienced deteriorating health in the early 1930s. Having been diagnosed as 'restless and nervy', 'depressed', and subject to 'mental excitability' and sleeplessness in the 1920s, he developed considerable pain in his right eye because of a small fragment of metal embedded in his cornea during the war. He also suffered regular headaches, and then, when organising a last disastrous effort to retrieve his financial position, a rodeo in 1933, he broke two bones in his foot when it was crushed by a horse.[32]

The contemporary data about mental health thus leaves many questions unresolved. What might later oral history tell us? Here, too, we find complexities. Many of those interviewed decades after the Depression recalled the emotional damage that they or their parents endured: inferiority complexes, nervous dyspepsia, depression, anxiety and insomnia. They spoke of 'nervous wrecks', and men who 'never ever really recovered' from the humiliation they had endured.[33] Such symptoms were remembered as being worse in men: 'the men seemed to sag . . . They looked more beaten than the women.' Society expected them to be breadwinners, providing for their wives and children. White-collar workers and professionals were also recalled as being very vulnerable psychologically because 'the finer bred people' couldn't accept their loss of status.[34] Even if they did not have to seek the dole, they felt a 'bitter' disillusionment, seeing the Depression 'as a kind of betrayal of the ideal' that had followed World War I. 'That had been the "war to end all wars" and here was a different kind of war. An economic disaster that was killing just as many people. It was a world of emotional and mental depression, as well as economic depression . . . a tremendous atmosphere of despair.'[35]

There is, however, a competing set of memories that unsettles this narrative of widespread psychological damage. When Melbourne academic David Potts and his students conducted a series of oral histories from 1965 to 1986, many of their informants recalled the Depression as an essentially happy and fulfilling experience.[36] 'People were happier then.' Yes, they might have been 'hard up' and initially shocked, angered and deeply frustrated by the impact of the economic crisis on their lives, but although 'the bad was bad [it was] not necessarily dominating'. Instead, 'a positive culture of poverty' emerged: that is, 'a way of living positively in and beyond poor conditions'. Essentially, Potts argued it was a 'myth' to assume that the loss of work and income necessarily led to widespread psychological trauma. The unemployed were not, as so commonly depicted, demoralised and disempowered. Rather, they 'discovered new energies and initiatives' in the informal economy that sprang up, and new 'rewards in self-expression and self-esteem'. Freed from the 'drudgery of the average eight-hour day of work in the city, and sometimes dawn-to-dusk labouring on farms', the unemployed found solace in 'a richer and more varied life'. Family bonds were often strengthened by the crisis. Similar positive memories—of collective strength, self-help, cooperation, sharing, ingenuity—emerged as strong themes in another series of interviews conducted by students of the Australian National University in the 1990s.[37]

The fact that oral history can result in radically opposed accounts of Australians' mental health tells us much about the limitations of this source of 'evidence'. Its undoubted value is that it allows historians to hear the voices of those people and classes who did not leave written records of their experiences. During the Depression, Australians were not separated by vast distances from their families as they had been in World War I. They had little reason to keep diaries or write letters, unless they were appealing to authorities for help. But if oral history goes some way to capturing unrecorded experiences—and it is used liberally in this history for this reason—it is inherently selective, and can never claim to be representative in any scientific sense.[38]

Moreover, 'oral history' is, in fact, memory—and memory is always filtered through later life experiences, dominant cultural narratives and value systems. Most of the men and women interviewed by Potts and others were middle-aged or older at the time they gave their testimonies. With age comes perhaps a tendency to invest the past with positive value; or the need to validate the behaviour and values of youth. Earlier generations were thus remembered as being more resilient, more stoical and less self-centred than modern youth. They were less materialistic, harder working and more used to tolerating adversity. They knew how to value simpler things.[39]

Beyond this, the men and women who were interviewed in the second half of the twentieth century might have been predisposed to recall the Depression in generally positive terms because of their age in the 1930s. As young men, they might have been fitter and more able to deal with the rigours of unemployment, relief work or travelling around the country in search of work. As children, they were possibly protected from the worst ravages of the crisis by their parents, especially their mothers. Typically, children are unaware of their families' financial struggles and wider socioeconomic movements. As author Hugh V. Clarke recalled in his 1982 memoir of life in the Depression: 'At the time I was completely unaware of the worry which must have been consuming my parents. We had cricket, boxing and swimming at school and each lunchtime a pieman drove his horse and cart into the school grounds . . . we were never short of pennies to spend on his pies, rolls and cakes.'[40]

We are left then, with a range of opinions in oral history that is almost as diverse as the people interviewed. It is unlikely that the debates between 'optimists' and 'pessimists' about the experience of the Depression will be resolved on the basis of this 'evidence'. But the prevalence of more positive views in the hundreds of interviews that Potts and other scholars have conducted cannot be discounted. It suggests that, as in so many matters, there was no one Depression experience.

Subjective though it may be to say so, the diversity of responses to the Depression experience almost certainly reflected the degree to which Australians could draw on personal resilience. This is a term that needs to be used with caution.[41] Commonly, resilience is accepted to be the capacity of individuals to maintain stable, healthy levels of psychological and physical functioning when exposed to life-threatening situations. But such resilience is inherently difficult to 'test' or measure. There is no simple answer to the question as to why some people possess this quality while others facing the same stimuli do not. Yet it seems indisputable that some individuals are able in times of crisis and hardship to draw on a mix of variables that, singly or more usually collectively, protect them against the worst effects of trauma.

Among these variables are personal attributes and temperament. Some individuals seem to possess a positive self-concept and self-esteem: a hardiness that enables them to moderate the harm of extreme stress and to be flexible and adaptive in times of crisis. Some people even find stressful situations to be 'catalytic agents of resistance, or of more constructive responses'.[42] Take a contemporary of Elliott and Throssell, the South Australian Charles Hawker. Grievously wounded twice in World War I—he lost one eye, suffered nerve damage in one arm and was partially paralysed—he seems to have viewed his disability as a goad to achievement. As other returned soldiers succumbed to mental illness and suicide, Hawker ran his family's pastoral station, rode horses, drove an adapted car, became prominent in the RSSILA, and travelled widely across remote areas of Australia, Europe, Russia, China and Japan. In 1929 he was elected to federal parliament where he soon joined the ministry. Had he not died in a plane accident in 1938, he might have succeeded Lyons as prime minister. Everyone who met Hawker seems to have been in awe of his ability to remain positive, good-humoured and gregarious in the face of often excruciating and chronic pain. Perhaps some of Potts' 'optimists' were of Hawker's ilk.

Beyond personal attributes, resilience seems to be enhanced by positive childhood experiences, family stability and systems of social support. Those who, in contrast, are brought up within 'a multi-problem milieu'— parental criminality; poor parental supervision; cruel, passive, or neglectful attitudes; erratic or harsh discipline; familial conflict; large family size; and socioeconomic disadvantage—seem to be at greater risk of lacking resilience.[43] It is notable that Elliott had a somewhat impoverished and troubled childhood, living on a selection near Charlton, Victoria, where the family struggled to make a livelihood. His father was frequently absent, having an insatiable wanderlust, and when Elliott was only eight years old, his older brother became 'criminally insane', possibly because of a personality change that resulted from a fractured skull. One of Harold's sisters committed suicide after a bout of severe influenza.

During the Depression, family was, by many accounts, 'everything'.[44] In material terms, the family unit, as we have seen, was the basis of entitlement for sustenance, and functioning families had particular advantages in cushioning the impact of outside stresses. When one family member was out of work, another might bring in earnings. They could pool resources and energies. Adult children could return to the extended family when in desperate need. Companionate marriages provided emotional support, as did children. Of course, each child brought additional financial responsibilities and large families were very vulnerable to slipping into destitution. But the presence of children could also be a source of joy and a positive distraction. The family, furthermore, could be a place of entertainment—dancing and singing and playing musical instruments—when commercial venues were too expensive. Not surprisingly, then, in at least one oral history project the factor that seemed 'more than anything else' to have determined whether or not people believed they had had a 'good' or 'bad' Depression was the home-based family.[45]

Personal resilience was also enhanced by wider systems of social support and community resilience. As we have noted, the community efforts to provide food, clothing and other support met more than a physical need. They reassured individuals that there was a resource beyond themselves from which they could draw strength. Community entertainment, much of it self-made, served the same purpose, in that it generated the social capital that came from involvement and participation in group activity.[46] Farmers pitched together to build a hall for dances and parties in Ouyen, Victoria. People found the energy, even when out of work or living in shanty towns, to organise art, swimming, cricket and football clubs, and launch musical concerts, theatrical productions, fairs and bazaars.[47] Entries at the 1931 Royal Show in Adelaide were the highest ever, with the number of competitors rising from 800 in 1925 to 3000 in 1931, and some 2000 flower entries. About 200,000 people attended during the seven days of the event.[48] Meanwhile, 'community singing', the 1930s version of karaoke, flourished. Neighbourhood parties sprang up in the streets, in homes where people played cards, gave recitations or gathered around the piano, or in the camps that the homeless created. People played two-up in local backyards, or frequented illegal totes. Cinemas ran free screenings for the unemployed. Councils did the same, and let the unemployed use swimming pools without charge at certain times.[49] People congregated around shops whether they had money or not. They met in parks, on beaches, and at regattas and flower shows. They swapped tickets outside cinemas and escaped into the warm theatre's world of imported American materialism. And then, of course, Australians gathered together at those great communal festivals, football, rugby, cricket and horseracing fixtures. Australian Rules football set a new record of attendance in the midst of the Depression.[50] Sheffield Shield cricket, too, attracted large crowds, while Test cricket mesmerised many Australians, be they at the grounds, or listening to broadcasts at home or in the streets. Tellingly, two of the standout events of the Depression years in popular memory were the death of the racehorse Phar Lap in 1932 and the bodyline bowling cricket controversy in the summer of 1932–33 (see Chapter 33).

The sources of resilience for Australians thus were many. This is not to say that every individual was able to tap them effectively. Personal resilience is precisely that: personal. Many Australians, even those with access to the protective factors that enhance resilience, found the Depression to be an emotional disaster that was profoundly difficult to surmount. In Elliott's case, and presumably many others, class and status were not enough to ward off despair. Yet, clearly many other people did not succumb to the stresses of the Depression. The narrative of disaster that has dominated popular memory therefore needs to be complemented by one that acknowledges the capacity for resilience that many individuals discovered within themselves and their communities.

Part VI

WORK OF A KIND

CHAPTER 17

Searching for work

The search for work was *the* preoccupation of countless Australians throughout the Depression. Sustenance helped many of the unemployed survive, but everyone agreed that work was the better option. The unemployed wanted to earn a wage, to regain their autonomy and to avoid the humiliation of the dole. Governments and charities believed that work would improve the moral character of the working class, reduce their dependence on state budgets and minimise the potential for radical politics. From 1930 on, federal and state governments introduced programs of relief works; but given the lack of external loans to fund public works and the unwillingness of the Commonwealth Bank to release funds for such expenditure, there was never enough relief work in 1930–32 to allow men to work full time. Thus, finding work, like sourcing food and clothing, became a matter where government, community and individual efforts intersected.

The prospect of being sacked was terrifying. It could be the start of a long journey to find 'the job that didn't exist'.[1] The first step for the unemployed was to register at a labour exchange; but although registration was a requirement to receive sustenance, it was no guarantee of employment. In New South Wales, for example, only 49 per cent of men registered at state labour exchanges in 1930 gained work. In 1931 this figure slipped to 41 per cent, and it crashed to 30 per cent in 1932. Only in 1933 and 1934 did placement rates start to improve, but they were still only 66 per cent in 1934. For women, the rates of placement were worse: 23 per cent in 1931 and only 21.5 per cent in 1932. This was despite the fact that generally fewer women registered for employment—though there was a surge in female applicants for a brief time in New South Wales in 1931.[2]

Frantic for work, some people turned to private employment agencies. For a fee, Miss Ward's Employment Club at 26 Hunter Street, Sydney, would vet suitable applicants and advertise their availability for work. It was a subjective process. On 13 May 1932, the agency sought to place an 'Intelligent boy, age 18, College education, nice appearance, can drive car, has licence, ride, drive horses, assist housework and garden'. The same agency offered as a 'Scotch Cook-General', a 'middle-aged, nice woman, very good cook, makes oatcakes, cakes, scones, pastries, can take all duties, wait table well'.[3] No one knows what the success rate was for private agencies, but Miss Ward's was patronised with queues 'stretching into the street, and up to the first floor'.[4]

The 'Positions Vacant' columns in the newspapers were more accessible for many of the unemployed. Early in the day, they would gather outside newspaper offices, scanning jobs listed in a glass case on the wall. A rush would follow to the advertised place of employment. Commonly there would be tens, if not hundreds, more applicants than the number of vacant positions. Speed, then, was of the essence. In Adelaide, a man read in the newspaper of his friend's death. He jumped up from his breakfast, so his wife thought, to comfort the man's family. But then he said: 'I'm not going to see his wife. I'm out for his job'![5]

Alternatively, men would tramp the streets, applying for work even at places posting a 'No Vacancies' sign. They gathered at sites where casual work might be available. 'We stood around the wharves [of Sydney] from dawn, chilled in our grey woollen work shirts, awaiting a nod from the stevedore. It was a mighty important nod, for it meant a quid in your pocket or none.'[6] Some men fell victim to confidence tricks, paying a small fee to 'agents' who promised them work only to then disappear with their cash.[7] The most desperate—or perhaps adventurous—took to the country, walking vast distances or jumping illegally on trains, in search of casual work and handouts from farms and local towns (see Chapter 29).

If casual work happened to be available, it was usually part time and poorly paid. The Odd Jobs programs that local councils organised provided only temporary relief. Men and women might hold a number of casual jobs in succession: mixing, say, seasonal fruit picking with collecting and selling firewood, working in bars, pushing barrows in markets, carting sand, and offering cheap haircuts outdoors.[8] One young man who moved from state to state later explained:

> everyone was keen to be moving on, to go somewhere else. Over the ridge was going to be better . . . There must be somewhere where people work regularly . . . I got back to Tasmania in January 1932, and got two weeks work at the old job. A job came up on another newspaper, they were printing some religious magazine. It lasted six weeks, then there was nothing in printing. I got a job in a fishing trawler with an old Swede who was a mate of my father's. It was a ten day trip and you got only thirty bob a trip and keep.[9]

A common memory of the unemployed was door-to-door selling, notably of Electrolux vacuum cleaners:

> You could get that job fairly easily because there were so many people doing it . . . God, it was hard. We didn't have cars. You carried a bag that weighed thirty-five pounds with a vacuum cleaner inside from door to door with the dogs after you . . . It was a soul-destroying job.[10]

Much casual work was invisible to authorities. Women worked under their maiden names to avoid their family's earnings exceeding the limits of 'permissible income'. They made a few extra shillings through dressmaking, washing and ironing, babysitting, dish-washing at boarding houses, doing chores for neighbours and visiting patients in asylums.[11] In country districts, farmers' wives brought in extra money by running post offices, serving at local stores or teaching at schools. Their husbands supplemented farm income by droving, shearing, harvesting, picking fruit, taking contract work for fencing, digging dams and canals, and cutting sleepers. This underground economy was nothing new—it was how the labour market worked before the Depression—but now it risked penalties in terms of losing sustenance.

The more entrepreneurial, or perhaps foolhardy, among the unemployed started small businesses. One Adelaide man borrowed £54 from a money-lender and bought six cows to sell milk to his neighbours.[12] A Sydney woman, who had arrived from the United Kingdom only in 1927, created a modestly successful portrait studio. As her son recalled, she 'went wandering around Cremorne and Mosman, the more posh suburbs, knocking on doors doing these portraits'. Later, she set up her business in a Sydney arcade.[13] Obviously some Sydney residents could still afford such indulgences. Another relatively successful enterprise was selling flowers: there was always a demand from funerals.

But many ventures failed. Hugh Clarke's father lost the hotel he owned in Toowoomba as a result of heavy debts. He then opened a lending library in Brisbane, with a loan from a friend. He purchased books from families who were selling their libraries to get a few pounds. '[W]e lurched away', Clarke later wrote, 'with cases full of law books' from one barrister's home. Business was slow, however, and when the library was relocated to a 'dim and dingy' shop in an unsuitable location in South Brisbane, 'it was a disaster . . . hours would go by without a single customer entering the shop.'[14]

Failure, as we have already seen, was a common story. Bank credit was tight, and landlords could be inflexible when rents fell due. Money lenders, to whom the more desperate turned for liquidity, often charged exorbitant interest rates, perhaps 100–150 per cent, or even more.[15] In 1929–30 there were more bankruptcy proceedings than in the previous six years combined. The number increased in 1930–31 before slowly declining (see Figure 17.1). One man later recalled that he lost three businesses in succession: at one stage 'we were able to paper a wall with summons for debt'.[16]

A lower-risk business was hawking. Normally the selling of goods in public places required a licence. In Victoria, where the fee was £1 a year with a £20 surety, the number of licensed hawkers doubled between the mid-1920s and 1932.[17] Many other people took to the streets without registering: selling

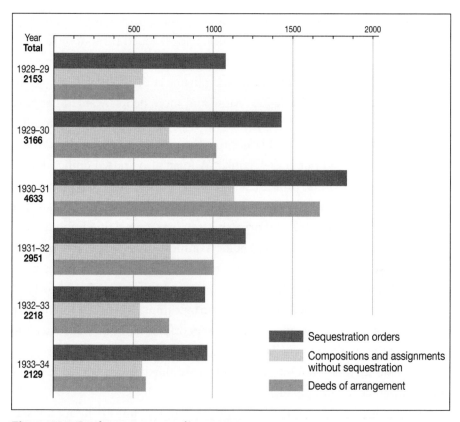

Figure 17.1: Bankruptcy proceedings, 1928–34

Note: A 'sequestration order' was one passed by a court declaring bankruptcy, in which a trustee managed assets on receipt of this order.

'Composition and assignment without sequestration' refers to provisions in the *Bankruptcy Act 1924* for 'two intermediate states of insolvency, permitting an agreement with creditors and discharge of the debtor without bankruptcy proceedings and without the sequestration of the debtor's property'. The more formal was 'Composition and assignment without sequestration', under which a meeting of creditors was called, to which the debtor submitted a statement of his assets and liabilities. The acceptance was not valid until confirmed by a subsequent meeting and was open to court challenge. 'Deeds of arrangement' was a more informal agreement between debtor and creditor for the distribution of the debtor's assets in discharge of his debts: Everett, 'Trading under the Laws of Australia', p. 36.

Source: Parliament of Australia, *Sixth Annual Report*, p. 3.

bootlaces, pencils, haberdashery, stationery, magazines, wood, kindling, and fruit bought cheaply from the market. They trooped from door to door, offering home-made food—jams pickles, pies, cakes and confectionery—fish, eggs and, of course, rabbits. According to one childhood memory: 'Mum started selling jams and pickles . . . More and more people wanted her jam, so my mother loaded the pram up with the baby laying [sic] down, a toddler sitting on the front and a box of jam across the middle . . . we children would sometimes take a load out after school.'[18] Women also crafted doilies, hand-kerchiefs and milk covers, while men fashioned kookaburras from pine cones, pot plant stands from kerosene tins, and toast racks from wire. Hawking was so widespread in some suburbs that retailers complained about their own trade being undercut.[19] Householders 'almost under siege' put up signs saying 'No hawkers or canvassers', but people still kept coming 'in streams'.[20] In country towns, meanwhile, farmers' wives sold butter and eggs to local residents and food to relief workers in nearby camps. In coastal towns, like Townsville, young men would scrape oysters off the harbour walls, stealing out at night with a hurricane lamp and a sharp screwdriver, despite regulations forbidding this.[21] Rabbits, as already mentioned, were peddled for their skins, as were foxes and possums.

Predictably, in this unregulated black economy, not all items for sale were of merchandisable quality. Some men later boasted of selling dust marketed as flea repellent, shampoo made of soap powder, and metal polish concocted from a mixture of nitric acid and mercury. 'It looked beautiful. You'd demonstrate it on an outside tap. Of course the next day the thing would go black, but that didn't worry us because we could sell it for one and six a bottle!'[22]

In the search for work, it helped to have advocates on your behalf: a trade union official; a friend of the family who might refer you to an employer; or a special-interest lobby group. Returned soldiers benefited from the ongoing advocacy of the RSSILA. At the local level, this formidable organisation formed a variety of employment bureaus to lobby councils for work and relief for returned soldiers.[23] Nationally, it used its privileged access to government to defend one of the core policies of Repatriation: namely, that returned soldiers should have preference in employment.

This right had never been unlimited. In the years after World War I, many businesses had exploited loopholes in the legislation about preferential employment to evade their obligations. Even in the public sector, where the principle was applied more rigorously, veterans complained that they had been consigned to temporary public-sector positions or appointed well down the promotion ladder.[24] Still, preference was an entitlement of considerable value, especially as unemployment started to rise. It was manifestly at risk when governments started looking for cuts in public-sector salaries.

For a brief time, in early 1930, it seemed that returned soldiers might lose this status.[25] The Scullin government was under great pressure from the labour movement to reverse the setbacks incurred in the battles with the Bruce–Page government, and announced in May 1930 that it would reinstate the preference for unionists in employment. As Scullin told federal parliament, union preference was 'the policy of this Government, and has been the policy of the Labor party ever since it has been in existence'. Returned soldiers, he maintained, would not be disadvantaged by a change in policy, since if they were union members they would be covered by an arbitration court award and be free from exploitation by contractors. The greatest service to returned soldiers was 'the maintenance of a strong industrial organization to protect their rights'.[26]

It was not an argument that convinced many conservatives. Politicians, the press and, naturally, the RSSILA rushed to defend the principle of preference for ex-servicemen. This, they argued was not just a policy issue, it was a matter of 'national honor'.[27] Invoking a language that was infused with notions of duty and the sacred, they claimed that the nation owed a special debt to the men who had volunteered to serve in World War I. Any change in veterans' entitlements would represent 'a distinct breach of faith', 'a repudiation of the solemn national pledge' given to the survivors of World War I.[28] Faced with this morally charged language, Scullin met with the president of the RSSILA, Gilbert Dyett, with whom he had a close personal relationship. He then announced on 7 May 1930 that his government would retain the existing system of preference. He justified this 'graceful retreat' by claiming that Dyett had assured him that all returned servicemen offering themselves for work in the Commonwealth were already union members. Dyett, indeed, had always advocated that they should be.[29]

Scullin's options were, in fact, limited, as they were on so many policy matters at this time. The votes of at least some returned soldiers had helped Labor come to power in 1929, and Scullin judged that the Senate would disallow any regulation giving preference to, say, waterside workers over returned soldiers.[30] Preference in employment was not, as he saw it, an election-winning issue. As Scullin told the caucus, it was 'not big enough to fight the Senate & go to the Country'.[31] Indeed, it was probably *too* big an issue, given how deeply the mythology of Anzac was already entrenched in the national culture. The public debate about preference coincided with Anzac Day 1930, which marked the fifteenth anniversary of the landing at Gallipoli. Across the nation, the Anzacs were exalted for their 'glorious deeds' when they stormed the 'shattering heights' of 'Deathless Gallipoli' in Australia's 'baptism of fire'.[32] This rhetoric and the debates about preference signified that the term 'returned soldier' had become a 'site of memory' that embodied a powerful representation of national unity, pride and sacrifice. The 'returned soldier' was the man who, by volunteering to serve in the AIF, had placed the nation above all other allegiances and sectional interests, including unionism. Moreover—and this was key to the protection of veterans' employment rights—the 'returned soldier' now embodied all the qualities that the Australian nation needed in the time of economic crisis. 'The spirit of Anzac,' the *Canberra Times* wrote, 'was its unselfish sacrifice for country. This is the spirit which is needed in Australia to-day more than all else.'[33] General John Monash developed a similar theme:

one found Australia in a worse position than ever before in her history. What is the basic cause of this condition? It can be summed up in one word—'selfishness'. The fundamental lesson taught by the Great War was co-ordination, and one solid undivided effort by millions of men and women united in a common objective to make the world safe for democracy. The soldiers of Australia and the rest of the British Empire though composing all shades of religious and political opinion submerged their individual beliefs in that of patriotism and love of liberty—they united in this common objective. Can we not do the same today?[34]

It must be stressed that this status of the 'returned soldier' as a revered imagined collective did not mean that individual veterans were quarantined from the hardships of the Depression. Far from it. The numbers of returned soldiers who benefited from preference in public-service employment were relatively few. They were concentrated mainly in the Department of Repatriation, where they were thought to have a natural sympathy for dealing with fellow veterans. Ex-servicemen in other sectors of the economy fell into what the RSSILA newspaper in New South Wales, *Reveille*, called 'the cruel vortex of unemployment'.[35] Thanks to their war wounds, many returned soldiers struggled to perform the manual work that relief programs required. The Department of Repatriation estimated that in August 1931 some 28,500 men were suffering from gunshot wounds, 6500 from heart conditions, 2900 from tuberculosis, 3250 from war neurosis and mental illness, 129 from blindness, and a further 30,000 from other diseases and disabilities. Some 3150 were lacking limbs.[36] Amputees were at a particular disadvantage when competing for work with able-bodied men, and 'apart from any disabilities incurred during War service, age is beginning to tell'.[37]

The national press and the files of the charitable organisations thus record many stories of indigent returned soldiers and their families. Among them was a veteran camping on the banks of the River Torrens, Adelaide, who wrote to Bonython asking for a pair of shoes to replace his own, which were 'in a deplorable condition'.[38] In Port Lincoln, the RSSILA reported in early May 1929, some months before the New York stock market crash, that a returned soldier was living off the pickings from a municipal rubbish dump: he was later committed to a 'mental home'.[39] *Reveille* claimed that 1931 was 'the bitterest year in the story of the A.I.F.' Adopting the language of war it said:

A pitiless campaign it was, with no honest tangible enemy to face and grapple with; no quickening excitement of the crowds' cheers and flattery; no high falutin' promises and eulogies from High Places; no honourable scars, or quick despatch in hot blood under the open sky;

but a welter of silent fights, forlorn hopes and desperate stands against invisible forces of misery, starvation and diseases, led by that most merciless of all the War Lords—General Unemployment.[40]

Two year later, *Workers' Art Magazine* published a sardonic poem, 'Anzacs', in the aftermath of Anzac Day:

Anzacs! Anzacs! Let the cannons roar:
Let the Chaplains bleat about that Austral blood-drecht shore:
But the men who 'scaped the 'glory' of a hero's death are here,
With their stomachs pincht [sic] with hunger, and their eyes be-smit
   with fear;
Their nerves all gone to Blazes, and their hopes all swept to Hell . . .
Liars, Thieves and Hypocrites, What about your pact?
The Heroes are not all interred: Now's the time to act.[41]

Still, if many individual ex-servicemen suffered deep distress and disadvantage during the Great Depression, the status of 'returned soldier' as an imagined collective was affirmed. Not only was preference in employment preserved as a principle in 1930, but 'the returned soldier' was also one of the very few cohorts to be given some exemption from government budget cuts in the following year. When the deflationary Premiers' Plan was introduced in mid-1931, and the pensions of many Australians were cut, the 'returned soldier' was once more spared the worst of the retrenchment, since he had already made the sacrifices that were demanded of all citizens in time of national crisis.

CHAPTER 18

Relief works

As the search for work became more desperate, everyone looked to governments to provide employment. In response, state governments introduced 'relief works' or in some cases required men to work for the dole. But given the desire to balance budgets, the reluctance to increase taxation and the lack of the external loans that had previously funded public works, the funds to provide employment were always inadequate. Men were not offered full-time work, or even, at times, work at award wages. Relief works, like sustenance, thus became a cause of contention and protest. Nevertheless, across the country, roads and bridges were built, forests were cleared, sewerage and water systems constructed, and rural settlements developed. They still stand as a testament to the labour of the men who had no option but to accept relief work during the Depression.[1]

In the early stages of the Depression, the Scullin government believed that relief works, like sustenance, should be largely the responsibility of the state governments. It confined its direct role in unemployment relief to the FCT, the Northern Territory and a few small projects in the states. It did, however, make a series of ad hoc grants to the states. In December 1929, it managed to find £1 million from funds set aside for the construction of main, trunk and arterial roads under the Federal Aid Roads Agreement. These were assigned to the states to disburse 'in the best interests of the unemployed', as Scullin put it.[2] A further federal grant of £1 million was made available in June 1930. This was meant to be distributed to the states on a population basis, but with the agreement of the premiers at the Melbourne conference in August, a considerable proportion of the available funds was reallocated to South Australia, which was in a dire financial position. Then, with the approach of Christmas—a time that was always recognised to require an extra effort to support the unemployed—a further £500,000 was granted by the Commonwealth to the states.[3]

It fell to the states and municipalities in 1930 and beyond to raise the vast majority of the funding for relief works.[4] This depended upon their willingness to levy special taxes, which varied across the states. Western Australia spent considerable sums on sustenance and relief work. Victoria employed more than 11,000 men on projects in 1932–33 alone.[5] In Queensland, the Moore government spent nearly £2 million on relief work in the two years 1930–31 to 1931–32.[6] In contrast to the larger states, South Australia levied no special taxes and could do little to employ men on public works, although some local governments did introduce relief projects. In late 1933, South Australia had not even managed to fully use its allocation under the Federal Aid Roads Agreement.[7] Tasmania, too, made only modest use of relief works to employ those out of work.[8]

As unemployment grew, the pressure on the Scullin government to fund relief works mounted but, as we have seen, in 1930 Gibson would not agree to providing Commonwealth Bank credit for such purposes. Only in October 1931, after the Premiers' Plan had been agreed upon, did the Commonwealth Bank agree to release some funding for existing 'reproductive' works: that is, those projects that would generate sufficient revenue to cover the long-term rate of interest on the loans and make a contribution to the statutory sinking fund. It also allowed local municipalities to apply directly for loans for unemployment relief and to grant £3 million worth of credit to help wheat growers. With Christmas and a federal election approaching, Scullin also drew on consolidated revenue to fund works for the renovation of Commonwealth property.[9] Only £250,000 was allocated, but men were employed across the country on projects such as erecting telephone lines in Mount Isa, repairing installations at Jervis Bay, and renovating buildings and plants at the Cockatoo Island works in Sydney Harbour. This last project was in Theodore's electorate of Dalley, which gave Opposition parliamentarians further ammunition to allege corruption on the treasurer's part (see Chapter 25).

When the United Australia Party (UAP) took power with Lyons at the helm in 1932, it agreed to provide further funding to the states for reproductive public works.[10] But the money came with strings attached. Each state was required to establish an employment council consisting of state and federal representatives. In New South Wales, where Lang was facing dismissal for his policies of repudiation (see Chapter 32), federal officials dealt directly with local municipalities. In all cases, relief works could proceed only after being vetted by these employment councils, the relevant state and federal treasurers and the Commonwealth Bank. Perhaps to no one's surprise, the bank often raised objections. In September 1932, another committee, a Commonwealth Advisory Committee on Employment, was established to coordinate the work of the state councils and to ensure their compliance with government policy. Given this cumbersome system, little money was spent under the scheme before the end of 1932. Some money remained unspent even at the end of 1934.[11]

Federal funding for relief works continued with the early signs of economic recovery in 1933. Once the banking sector was persuaded that orthodox financial policies were being followed, the Lyons government was able to float a series of recovery loans. Lyons claimed in Parliament in October 1933 that with these funds, and the 'practically doubling' of federal revenue, some £2.5 million was available, 'the bulk of which will be expended on providing employment'.[12] The following year, the Commonwealth funds for relief works increased by 5 per cent over the previous year. Lyons also moved in late 1934 to formulate a national plan for the amelioration of distress of unemployment. Part of that plan was an invitation to premiers to provide schedules of public works that might be suitable for relief. Yet the amount provided for relief works was never enough.[13] In 1935–36 relief expenditure provided full-time employment for only 55,000 of the estimated 300,000 unemployed.[14]

◆

What was the funding, such as it was, spent on? The priority for the federal government was to give work to men who were unemployed. The grants were not to be used to purchase materials and heavy machinery, nor to keep people in employment who might otherwise have been made redundant, as the Brisbane City Council, for one, hoped to do.[15] To the irritation of business, the grants were also used to fund public, not private works, though it was sometimes difficult to differentiate between public and private benefit. For example, £15,000 was allocated to assist in the development of the Moonta and Wallaroo mining fields in South Australia.[16] Most importantly, the grants were to fund relief works that would be reproductive.

The problem was that many of the unemployed were unskilled, and the work they were fit to perform was not always 'productive'—at least in the short term. Reafforestation could take twenty years before it realised any significant return. Exceptions were made in this case and Victoria planted more than 2 million softwood trees and created nearly 1000 kilometres of firebreaks.[17] But other projects that had a long-term value fell foul of the 'reproductive' criterion. Among these was the proposal of the South Australian government to spend £12,000 on a new chemistry building at the University of Adelaide.[18]

Generally, relief works were concentrated in the areas of road construction, sewerage and water supply. Sewerage was favoured because it could generate revenue as soon as the pipes were connected. Most of Perth's inner suburbs—to cite only one example—were sewered in the 1930s.[19] As for road construction, Victoria boasted in late 1931 that it built or repaired 825 kilometres of roads. These included the Boulevard along the Yarra River, St Kilda Road, roads around Albert Park Lake, tourist roads to Marysville, Warburton and Healesville, and sections of the Great Ocean Road, an iconic project that had started years earlier as a war memorial.[20] Some road construction opened up isolated and previously neglected regions. In Queensland, the Mount Nebo scenic route was constructed inland from Brisbane, while the Mount Spec road was carved through the hills of the Paluma ranges north of Townsville.[21] In New South Wales, the Hume Highway was improved between Sydney and Goulburn, while in the as yet half-empty FCT, the Federal Highway and other roads were developed.[22] As for water projects, to name only a few of many implemented across the country: Illawarra region's water services were upgraded, a 48-kilometre diversion was dug to deliver water from the Glenelg River to the Wimmera–Mallee districts; and the water supply to the Kalgoorlie goldfields was replaced.

Beyond these infrastructure projects, railway tracks were reconditioned, swamps and saltpans reclaimed, hospitals built and refurbished, sporting ovals levelled, swimming pools, bowling and golf greens installed, and public gardens and school grounds beautified. In Brisbane, the Grey and Story bridges were constructed and a new campus for the University of Queensland developed at St Lucia. In Melbourne, the precinct of the Shrine of Remembrance, which would be opened in 1934, was landscaped, while land was reclaimed at Fishermans Bend, a major industrial area at the mouth of the Yarra. In New South Wales, additions were made to the refrigerating chambers at the district abattoir at Newcastle. The list of these monuments could go on. Many still stand—although the labour of the relief workers is rarely acknowledged today in plaques or other heritage markers. One of the few exceptions is the John Forrest National Park east of Perth, where the work of some five hundred unemployed workers in cutting wood, and building terraces, garden beds, shelters and a weir is recorded on heritage boards.[23]

Rural development was a priority for many governments. This was partly because authorities thought it was prudent to remove potentially restive unemployed men from the radicalising influences of the city.[24] As the town clerk of Blayney, near Bathurst, said when seeking government subsidies to develop the river flats of that town for vegetable farming: 'There is an old adage that Satan finds some evil for idle hands to do, and our idle citizens are likely to become so much breeding ground for communistic propaganda.'[25] In Adelaide, the response of the authorities to the 'beef riot' of January 1931 was to force unemployed men to relocate to isolated work camps in the country. The establishment of Blackboy Hill camp outside Perth was also thought by *The Worker* to be possibly 'a shrewd move on the part of the Government to put [the unemployed] where they will be less in the public eye, and so far away that they will not concentrate in the city and take part in . . . a riot'.[26] In sum, rural relief works were thought by both sides of politics to be a form of social control.

More positively, rural development was expected to improve Australia's balance of trade by increasing exports, and it resonated with the dream of closer settlement that continued to inspire Australians' imagination, the failures of soldier settlement notwithstanding. Members of the public bombarded the prime minister with suggestions for relief projects that often read like Brady's *Australia Unlimited*. One resident of Toowoomba wrote to Lyons on 4 April 1932:

> Rough lands near railways could be utilised for poultry, especially turkey raising, which could be made quite profitable. Fox proof fences would be necessary, but no other costly improvements. There is practically no limit to the number of people who could be placed on the land. The main thing would be to see that the prospective settlers were adapted for the life . . . this country needs more population.[27]

Other correspondents suggested a host of projects: the erection of telegraph and telephone works in the Tamworth district; the ballasting of the transcontinental railway from Port Augusta to Kalgoorlie; the construction of silos and reservoirs; the planting of forests; alluvial gold mining; and the painting of drill halls in Sydney.[28] One letter writer explained to Lyons that:

> [My plan] is <u>incredibly</u> simple to put into operation and will not hurt anyone financially . . . It would benefit the whole of the Commonwealth financially & would automatically <u>wipe out unemployment</u> without any further acts of any kind. Bear in mind it is not a scheme, but a <u>sound plan</u> . . . I have much more I would like to say but must refrain until I have reply from you as a guarantee that future communications will be to <u>you only</u>, until the whole plan has been put before you.[29]

Alas, we do not know if this offer was taken up and the 'sound plan' ever disclosed.

Western Australia's Mitchell was a particular enthusiast for rural development; his nickname acquired during his earlier term of office was 'Moo-cow' Mitchell. The premier established a new dairy farming district at Nornalup on Walpole Inlet, about 120 kilometres west of Albany. Eighty-two farms were settled by hand-picked unemployed men. Smaller settlements were established at Nannup, North Albany and Busselton.[30] Across the continent in Victoria, settlements were developed in Beech Forest near Colac, Heytesbury in the Western District, and southern and east Gippsland. Most were engaged in dairying; the others in mixed farming. The Queensland government supported banana farming and settlements at Upper Mudgeeraba (Gold Coast), Kenilworth (Sunshine Coast), and Mount Mee and Mount Pleasant in the Moreton Bay region. In South Australia, settlements were created near Willunga and Mount Compass, Echunga in the Mount Lofty ranges, and Barmera on the Murray River. Only New South Wales had no illusions about the ability of small-scale rural development to absorb unemployment. It preferred to allocate funding to the employment of rural workers on existing farms, to fund private building construction and repair; and to develop training and employment schemes for women and youths.[31]

These various settlements had mixed success. Where the soil was fertile, as in the Adelaide Hills, dairying and mixed farming proved profitable. Nornalup became one of Mitchell's more successful enterprises. But ultimately land settlement often came at a disproportionate cost.[32] Meanwhile, other plans for unemployment relief in the country, such as paying farmers and graziers to employ men on their properties, tended to founder, given that the farmers often lacked the capital to spend on development projects. Other proposals never advanced beyond thought bubbles. The Unemployed Workers' Union of Concord in Sydney condemned one such scheme proposed in early 1931 as 'vicious':

those down and out, grasping at any straw, would be coaxed or economically forced into a living hell during the winter months. Many men of experience in every line of primary production spoke very strongly against the foolishness of the mattock and spade suggestion unless to dig the graves of those who die of exposure during the winter.[33]

One of the more ill-conceived use of funds was the support given to thousands of Australians to prospect for gold. Prospecting needed little capital or organisation, and gold never lost its allure. Rumours abounded that all the major fields in Western Australia, including the Golden Mile, were merely outliers of some massive reef to be found further out in the wilderness. Then a promising patch of alluvial gold was found at Larkinville, south of Coolgardie. In January 1931, a lucky Jack Larcombe mined the biggest nugget ever found in Western Australia, the 'Golden Eagle' weighing 32 kilograms. Men poured into Kalgoorlie, some having their fares and sustenance paid by the Perth Labour Bureau.[34] The Victoria Cross winner Hugo Throssell joined them, hoping this might be his financial salvation, but 'the specks of gold that occasionally turned up in the pan weren't enough to meet the cost of food and water'. As his son, Ric, later wrote: 'There was always a chance that tomorrow there'd be something. If you gave up too soon . . . But each day it was the same: dust and flies, nothing but the mocking glint of new chum's gold.'[35] The government support for gold prospecting in Victoria, meanwhile, proved 'virtually the same as paying the unemployed in lottery tickets for digging holes out in the bush'.[36] One man who set out from Richmond, Victoria, became so 'absolutely destitute' that he appealed for clothing and boots from his council at home.[37]

It is difficult to assess the value of all of this activity in terms of relieving unemployment. No precise data about the numbers employed on relief works or the amounts paid to workers were recorded nationally, and state records are uneven. But we know that these works programs were never on a scale to absorb all the unemployed, even on a part-time basis. Moreover, they might arguably have inhibited Australia's economic recovery. In causing a shift from full-time public works to part-time projects, relief works might have delayed the revival of full-time employment. Governments in effect 'robbed Peter to pay Paul'.[38] Still, in the circumstances of 1930–32, when public-works funding was profoundly constrained, the rationing of work was possibly the only feasible option politically. As far as we can tell in the absence of formal public opinion surveys, many Australians thought that part-time work was better than none. The relief works programs were the target of much criticism, as we shall soon see, but no one suggested their abolition. Presumably then, relief works, if not aiding recovery, did mitigate the impact of the Depression on many Australian men and, since they were breadwinners, on the women and children who depended upon them.

CHAPTER 19

Protest and grievance

Unemployed men and women all wanted work, but not necessarily on the terms of the relief works programs. A man who refused to work at the direction of state or municipal authorities could forfeit his right to the dole. Beyond this, relief work was only part time, the rates of pay were often below the awards determined by arbitration, working conditions could be primitive, and jobs in the country involved long absences from home. Thus the relief works programs, though welcomed by some, were often the source of organised protest. Like food depots, they became the site at which unemployed Australians directly faced the power of the state, were reminded of their own lack of power, and gave voice to their anger and frustration.

The first grievance, inevitably, was how the money for relief works was allocated. Federal politicians were deluged with complaints about perceived inequities, a kind of 'grant envy'. If Lithgow had received £2500, the Workers' Industrial Union of Australia (the miners' union) in the Illawarra district asked on 15 June 1931, could they, too, be given 'somewhat the same amount', since they had many more unemployed?[1] The Sydney municipality of Holroyd was afraid that it might be 'left out' in the handing-out of grants.[2] The Ryde ALP Unemployment Relief Council, also in Sydney, suggested that it would be best to distribute grants in proportion to the number of unemployed in each municipality.[3] Other shires despaired of ever winning a grant, having submitted 'application after application'.[4]

More common were the complaints about how the relief work was allocated among the unemployed themselves. This played out in two ways. The more radical elements in the labour movement objected to the element of compulsion: the fact that men in some jurisdictions had to accept relief work or forfeit sustenance. Many other men (and their families) welcomed the chance to work, but resented the irregular and part-time nature of relief work. Normally it was only two or three days a week. Rationing of work was one way of ensuring some rough equality—'the only way to make each and all bear their share of misery', as one Brisbane worker put it.[5] A Canberra wife lectured Scullin on 2 April 1931 that the authorities 'should not give one ½ the men constant work, & let the other ½ starve, they should all bear the burden, everyone is satisfied to do their part when times are bad if the responsible men do the right thing'.[6]

There were also hierarchies of eligibility for relief work. In Victoria, preference was given in the *Unemployment Relief Act* of 1930 to unemployed married men, particularly those with children, and to 'persons on whose earnings other persons are ordinarily dependent for support'. Thanks to the lobbying of the Country Party, at least 30 per cent of the places on country work were set aside for unemployed men from the country. In Queensland, farmers and their sons were excluded from relief work and could not be classified as unemployed as long as they retained possession of their farms.[7] Everywhere, it seems, union members received no systemic preference. The suggestions of unions and other associations that their membership lists should be used as the basis for work rosters seem to have fallen on deaf ears.[8] So, too, did the claims by returned soldiers that they should be given preference for relief works. They had kept their established right to preference for public-sector jobs and some local councils gave them priority for casual work, a practice which, critics claimed, was prejudicial to men who had been too young to enlist in World War I.[9] But this preference did not extend to new relief works, which, the Treasury argued, were to be distributed 'fairly among all classes in the community'.[10]

The relief works usually employed men, but various work projects were initiated on behalf of women. Sewing depots were set up in Victoria and New

South Wales for women who were allocated two half-days of work per week in return for food relief and a modest payment. In Queensland, a 'housecraft training school' was established for unemployed single women to train them as domestics. More than 1200 women were trained in cooking and dress-making between October 1931 and June 1939. But only about a fifth of these women were known to have gained employment in households other than their own.[11]

Perhaps the most contentious issue was the question of pay. As far as the union movement was concerned, men should be paid at the rates specified by relevant arbitration awards. The Scullin government agreed and told state governments that award rates of pay for relief workers were mandatory, as far as federally funded relief works were concerned.[12] Relief works in the FCT conformed with this.[13] At the state level, however, award rates did not neces-sarily apply. In Victoria, the rates of pay for state-funded projects were linked to the urban and rural costs of living.[14] Then, in 1932 many of the unemployed were required to work for the dole. In other states, policies regarding wage rates fluctuated with changes of government, but generally the rationing of work meant that relief workers earned less than the basic wage. Take Queensland as an example: in 1936 more than four-fifths of relief workers were employed for fewer than three days each week, the average being just over two days. A man with a wife and one child thus earned about 33 shillings a week at a time when the basic wage in Brisbane was 67 shillings.[15]

The working conditions on relief programs were a further source of grievance. While many projects were located in or near the capital cities, others were more remote. To judge by press reports, relief workers were transported to the sites by truck or train. Workers assigned to a camp beyond Benambra, north-east of Omeo in Victoria's remote high country, travelled 274 kilometres by train without any food, then went by truck, over often rough road, for the rest of the journey. 'A mob of sheep [would be] treated with more respect,' one local grazier said.[16] Other workers travelled to Wilsons Promontory, 250 kilometres south-east of Melbourne, in an open truck, getting bogged three times; their bedding was soaked.[17] Access to the Mount Spec roadworks in north

Queensland was so primitive that a payroll escort carrying the Christmas pay for the workers was subjected to an armed hold-up.[18]

Almost all the relief work was manual labour, taxing men whose physical fitness had been eroded by months of hardship or chronic war injuries. One man refused to accept an assignment because he was a plasterer who had 'never done bush work in my life and am not in the Best of Health'.[19] Many found it a struggle to cope. Hands became painfully blistered. Men digging deep irrigation channels in Western Australia suffered 'clay-shovelers' fracture', when clay clung to their shovels at the peak of a high toss. The jarring caused pain or seizure, and sometimes long-term damage.[20] Men working at quarries near the old goldmining centre of Cracow in central Queensland had to break up huge boulders with 3-kilogram hammers, then 'overhead shovel' the broken stone into lorries. By the end of the working day, they were coated with dust and stone fragments.[21] Injuries were common—although there were few reported fatalities. Press reports tell of a man being killed from a tree falling the wrong way during scrub clearing and another dying of pneumonia after working in bad weather.[22]

Living conditions in work camps fuelled the discontent of many workers. Camps like Broadmeadows, to the north of Melbourne, and Blackboy Hill, east of Perth, were run on semi-military lines (both had been training camps for the AIF during the war). At Blackboy Hill, regulations governed every detail of life, from working and sleeping hours to eating times and personal hygiene.[23] Liquor and gambling were forbidden. 'Objectionable conduct' could lead to expulsion from the camp. Men complained about sleeping on stuffed chaff bags infested with vermin.[24] Blackboy Hill was soon dubbed 'a concentration camp' by *The Worker*.[25] Broadmeadows, too, became a site of considerable unrest (see Chapter 28).

In rural Victoria, some work locations had little lighting and no washing facilities.[26] The drinking water was sometimes brackish from bores, or muddy from dams. The lavatories were basic: a hole dug in the ground, perhaps protected by tin sides; 'pits with old tentflys for roofing and sides'. In the Chiltern Forest camp, Victoria, the toilet was a trench. With no disinfectant available, it soon deteriorated into 'a state of corrupt filth . . . the flies from this cesspool used to alight on all the food we tried to consume'.

Then there was the weather. Men had work in the rain, with little chance of drying their clothes before the next day's work. If deployed near the coast, they were buffeted by cold winds. In the mountains around Mount Buffalo, they battled snow. To quote one complaint from Beech Forest, near the Otways in Victoria:

> The first 2½ days we stuck it out in rain, and came to a wet and dreary cold camp. The camp conditions at the end of two days were awful; without doubt, the equal of a pig-sty, mud and slush everywhere. The entrance to the mess hut where we eat is a slimy pond, and although fern stumps have been laid down, the muck oozes over the top. We have no complaint with the Overseer or Gangers. They are treating us as men should do . . . We ate our dinner in the rain.[27]

If winter rains brought misery, summer would bring heat, flies, dust or sand. Whatever the workers' ailments, there was little medical support close by. One worker claimed that he had to walk more than 3 kilometres to see a doctor after he had broken two ribs working in the gravel pits at Penshurst near Warrnambool.

The battles were emotional, too. Men in rural camps were separated from their families and the routines of normal life. As one unemployed labourer whose sixth child was due to be born, said: 'You had to go where they sent you; there was no compassionate leave or excuse for not going.'[28] Given the distances and the cost of travel, relief workers could not return home regularly, even though they might be working only two or three days a week. On the days without work, the hours dragged. The nights were dreary and monotonous.[29] Men appealed through the press for books, magazines and sporting material. They resorted to gambling: two-up, card games and betting on horse races broadcast on the radio.[30] Some men, the Melbourne Trades Hall Council feared, were driven by idleness 'into habits which were not conducive to their welfare'. A camp observer in Western Australia also concluded that free time left 'a leaderless legion open to temptation'. The evidence is thin, but there are allusions in later memoir material to prostitutes and 'sexual perversion'.[31]

Given the strain on family relations, some wives and children joined their partners at the work sites. This could simply spread the hardship.

A local doctor, practising at Harvey, 140 kilometres south of Perth, thought that the wives were 'naturally sad and depressed about the end of all their financial hopes, with their home gone'.[32] A young woman with two young children recalled her anguish when she arrived at a camp near her husband's work. The site was strewn with garbage. The latrine stank and the dirt floors became a quagmire when it rained. The fireplace was flat on the ground, and it was impossible to light a fire in heavy rain. Drunken brawls in the camp were unnerving; and there was little privacy. Gradually this woman tried to organise a group of wives to clean up the site and improve the condition of some children—they were covered with sores, and had swollen eyes and matted hair—but she was told by another mother to 'get to buggery, and keep your hands off my bloody kids'.[33]

But camp life was not always as demoralising. In time, some of the camps settled into better-organised communities with neatly aligned, serviceable tents. Workers developed vegetable gardens, even flowerbeds. They formed sporting teams, held concerts, sang around camp fires, and visited local towns for concerts, dances, sports meetings and euchre parties. And if rural and coastal environments made life rugged, they also offered bushwalking, fishing and relaxation in the sheer beauty of nature. One project engineer at Tongala, Victoria, concluded that, 'The fellows were pretty happy to get away from the city, especially those that came from the inner suburbs.'[34]

Even if some experiences were positive, relief works were often the trigger for militant protest. In Victoria, this issue became a core part of unemployed politics.[35] In dispute were not only the working conditions, but also the sub-award rates of pay and the policy of making men work for sustenance: that is, paying them in kind by crediting their hours of work against their entitlement for sustenance. 'Working for the dole', which was introduced by the Hogan government in late 1931 and intensified by Kent Hughes in 1932, smacked of the economic conscription that unions had resisted so passionately during the wartime debates of 1916–17. The UWM spoke of 'Slave Labour for Coolie Wages' and 'Vicious Chain Gang Legislation'.[36] The Central Unemployed Committee (CUC) argued that the link between relief work and sustenance 'strikes a vital blow at the freedom of the subject . . . we are faced with an attempt in Victoria to remove the freedom of contract and an effort made to conscript the labor power of the unemployed'.[37] Meanwhile, an aggrieved worker penned a poem for *Workers' Art Magazine* in 1933:

> Now work for the dole, you bastards,
> Take that gleam of hope from your eye.
> Just work for the dole, you bastards,
> Or watch your children die . . .
> So dig out the sewers, you bastards,
> Up to your knees in slime.
> Some day we know you'll resist us,
> But we'll keep you down for a time.[38]

The more conservative AWU tried to resolve the question of award wages through the state and Commonwealth arbitration systems, but radical elements of the labour movement resorted to public protest: demonstrations, clashes with truncheon-wielding police, and angry delegations to politicians. The CUC and the UWM also launched a succession of 'dole strikes'. Particular projects were declared 'black' and men instructed to refuse to respond to government call-ups for work. To cite only two examples of many: in Geelong in mid-1932, the men summoned to one pick-up threw their notice cards through the gateway and shouted at the labour bureau official, 'we don't want your work . . . Give the police the job.' This inspired, so the *Geelong Advertiser* recorded, 'wild cheering from the big crowd of unemployed . . . and cynical laughter was the only reply to [the Labour Bureau official's] reminder that the men concerned would be refused sustenance in consequence of their action'.[39] In Port Melbourne, during a sustenance strike of mid-1933 only ten of 485 men called for work accepted. By the end of July, every unemployed man from Port Melbourne had been struck off sustenance and the job was closed.[40]

These protests made some difference. A number of municipal councils that were controlled by the ALP refused to implement the work-for-sustenance policy or withdrew projects in the face of protests. The state government made some concessions: increasing the rate of sustenance and relaxing the regulations surrounding permissible income. Yet ultimately the dole strike proved to be a limited tool. Many strikes started well, with large numbers of men refusing the call-up, possibly because they felt intimidated. In Essendon in August 1932, when the council decided to enforce work for sustenance, mayhem broke out: 'As each name was called,' *The Age* reported, 'there was much shouting and boo-hooing from the [400 strong] crowd. When the man who was called showed any inclination to respond, there were derisive cries and urgings to refrain.'[41] But many desperate men, especially those who were married, accepted work on whatever terms; and the Victorian government seemed to have little trouble filling its quotas. The strike was a fragile weapon in times of mass unemployment.

Dole strikes, too, reinforced negative perceptions among those inclined to believe that the unemployed were work-shy. Kent Hughes complained that relief projects were marred by 'lax supervision', 'flagrant loafing' and a low standard of efficiency.[42] When relief workers at the Maroubra sandhills in east Sydney threatened a stoppage unless award rates were paid, some journalists chastised them for 'poor gratitude'; they failed to appreciate the 'very earnest effort' that was being made by their government to give them 'the wherewithal for bodily sustenance until something better offers for them'.

> The action of the Government had actually been to appeal to the manhood of the men—to give them the right to say they were earning the relief monies received, rather than having them on a charity list for the dole. Actually the work of levelling sandhills in any other circumstances would be an extreme farce, and the men well know it.[43]

The Bulletin, meanwhile, carried a cartoon of 21 October 1931 depicting a group of working-class men smoking their pipes outside the dole depot, with a caption reading, 'Anybody could fill our bellies by makin' us work. What we gotta demawned is somebody to fill our bellies wivout work (Loud applause).'[44] The public could also be judgemental. As the son of the federal attorney-general, Frank Brennan, said when recalling a demonstration of the unemployed in Melbourne:

We watched them march up Bourke Street about twenty abreast, a most impressive and rather fearful sight. They were very silent, very ominous, and most of them were pushing their bicycles. And I recall a woman standing beside me saying, 'If they're so poor, why don't they sell their bicycles?' I was only about thirteen at the time, but I remember thinking, 'Oh, Christ Almighty!'[45]

Yet in any balance sheet of the relief works protests, we need to acknowledge that they had the value of investing protesters with agency and a voice. There was the solidarity of collective action—the purposefulness of planning, the exhilaration of large marches, the catharsis of confrontation with the police, and the sense of community that came from supporting those who lost their rations as a result of dole strikes. Protest is generally energising, and anger infinitely sustaining. As one Melbourne activist said, 'we activists had no time . . . If you wasn't attending some conference in the city at the Trades Hall, you was organising the unemployed or working on the [Fishermans] Bend having deputations to the Minister for Sustenance, interviewing estate agents, trying to stop evictions.'[46] Or to quote a man from Brisbane: 'I was engrossed in the Unemployed Movement in Brisbane. It became my life. There was always something to do.'[47] Most importantly, protest against relief works reinforced the belief that the relief workers were not crushed. They still had the ability to fight and organise.

The same can be said of the grassroots opposition that flared up within the relief work camps. When angry about their conditions, men would down tools or write letters of complaint to the press.[48] Camp welfare committees were established to champion workers' rights and respond to over-officious or poor management.[49] Gang supervisors who overstepped the mark were labelled 'Mussolini' or 'King Kong' and brought to order. An old unionist on a forest job at Erica, near Mount Baw Baw in Victoria, described a situation in which the supervisor 'thought he had a gang of inexperienced men. He didn't. He got a bit high. And so did the men. Anyway, he got displaced . . . The unemployed elected a committee and put all their complaints to the authorities.'[50]

251

Resistance could also be informal. If a worker lacked power, he could always resort to the time-honoured tactic of 'going slow'. To quote one later account: 'Our public register, she says to me one day, "Many's the time I've seen you leaning on your shovel, Mr. Smith." "Well, yes", I said, "There's a reason for that", I said. And she said, "What's that?" "The money isn't adequate. How would you like to be out there shovelling and the money isn't adequate?"'[51] In Western Australia, meanwhile, a newspaper reporter, having faked his way into a camp, asked his tent mate if the work was hard. "'Aw, no," he grinned. "Not if yer works yer 'ead."'[52]

Progressively, governments acknowledged the need for change. Guarantees of cleanliness and sanitation in camps were included in Victorian legislation. Workers were provided with new boots, first-aid kits, drying facilities and better sleeping quarters. Their grievance about having to walk long distances to reach their workplace without payment was acknowledged and they were granted paid 'walking time'. The relief workers were, after all, employees of the state, with voting rights, and their capacity to mobilise the press and public sympathy meant that their voice could not be silenced.

The story of relief works is thus a mixed one: on the one hand, the programs generated a deep sense of grievance, frustration and anger that fuelled resistance among the unemployed. On the other, this resistance was eroded by the willingness of others to accept the work on the terms it was offered to them. We know little about the numbers in each of these cohorts, but the protesters had a high public visibility that sustained the pressure on governments. At the risk of forfeiting such benefits as the state offered, these men exercised their right to protest against the erosion of workers' conditions and rights. If the response of the state was inadequate, it was not implacable. Concessions were given and over time the scale of relief works expanded. But the core problem with the relief works system remained the shortage of funding. And little could be done to change this while deflation remained the economic orthodoxy and prevented any stimulus of the economy.

Part VII

THE NADIR, 1931

CHAPTER 20

The battle of the plans

By early 1931, the Melbourne Agreement was in tatters, and a new battle of the plans erupted in policymaking circles. At the risk of oversimplification, the options in contention were deflation, as advocated by Niemeyer and demanded by Gibson and other disciples of 'sound finance'; monetary expansion and economic stimulus, as proposed by Theodore and radicals within the ALP; or repudiation of some elements of Australia's external debts, as championed by the recently elected Jack Lang. Some mix of deflation and stimulus was also proposed. Ultimately, Scullin had very little, if any, capacity to 'choose' between these options. In the first half of 1931, he found himself caught between the same irreconcilable forces that had dogged him in 1930: the financial conservatism of Gibson and the Commonwealth Bank board backed by the demands of London creditors; the opposition of the conservative Senate; the internecine factions of the ALP; and the groundswell of protest, not only from the unemployed but from increasingly disaffected conservatives. Scullin was an able politician but there was no way he could square this circle.

On two critical matters decisions were taken out of Scullin's hands. The first was the rate of exchange of the Australian pound for the pound sterling. Nothing approaching a national policy on this matter existed, since the setting of the exchange rate was in the hands of the private banks and the currency market.[1] When the Depression started, the Australian pound was held at parity with the pound sterling, but its value began to slip as Australia's holdings of sterling exchange rapidly depleted at the end of 1929. In March 1930, the trading banks were forced to agree to a modest devaluation, the rate being set at £104 and 2 shillings to £100 sterling.[2] Opinion among the banks about further unpegging of the exchange rate was divided. Some bankers believed that remaining on the gold standard was the indispensable condition of 'sound' economic policy (even though Australia had, in effect, left the gold standard in late 1929). Devaluation, it was feared, could lead to an inflationary cycle. The interest bill of the Loan Council abroad would also rise substantially, which would probably result in increased taxation and a delay in achieving the grail, as Gibson and others saw it, of balanced budgets and reduced costs of production.

Alfred Davidson at the Bank of New South Wales, however, concluded that the Australian pound should not be held at an artificially high level. This violated the principle of a free-market economy and the unrestricted interplay of 'natural economic laws'. His thinking on monetary matters was influenced by Shann, whom Davidson had come to know well when he had been in Western Australia earlier in his career and with whom he maintained a regular correspondence. Davidson also came to believe that devaluation, which would make Australian exports less expensive to foreign buyers, was preferable to subsidies as a means of supporting Australia's struggling primary industries. Those financial institutions that had practically all their balances in rural areas dependent on export revenue agreed, as did leading lobby groups for primary producers, such as the Graziers' Association of New South Wales and the Producers' Advisory Council.[3]

By late 1930, the move to devaluation was becoming irresistible. With the adoption of the Mobilisation Agreement in August, the banks whose sterling reserves were being absorbed struggled to maintain the current exchange rate. The very public fracas within the ALP in November and December about credit expansion also triggered a mild flight from the currency. Then on 9 December Lyons, in his capacity as acting treasurer, asked Gibson to devalue for the benefit of primary industries. Some banks still resisted, but finally Davidson took the initiative. With the Sydney wool sales scheduled for 6 January 1931, he increased the Bank of New South Wales' exchange rate. The other banks had to follow. As they had expected, the outside market then immediately increased the rate, outbidding the banks by several points. In late January, the rate settled at £130 Australian to £100 sterling. This was maintained till the following December.

In retrospect, this devaluation of the Australian pound seems a positive development and one that might have accelerated Australia's recovery if embraced earlier.[4] With exports priced more competitively, primary producers were able to sell more and thereby offset the impact of low global commodity prices. Devaluation, together with favourable seasons, helped many farmers and pastoralists to continue on the land. The banks that financed them were also shored up and the risks of a crisis in banking such as afflicted the United States was mitigated. Finally, the increased cost of imports with devaluation encouraged import replacement and gave some stimulus to the manufacturing sector.

The second development in January 1931 beyond the government's control was the reduction of the basic wage. In August and September 1930, the commissioners of various state railways, which were among the largest government employers in New South Wales and Victoria, had applied to the Commonwealth Court of Conciliation and Arbitration for what amounted to a reduction of existing wage rates. In the following months, the court widened the scope of its inquiry to consider the basic wage more generally. On 22 January 1931, it finally handed down its judgment: the basic wage in those industries covered by federal awards should be reduced by 10 per cent for a period of twelve months.[5]

In making this momentous decision the court, which received submissions from unions and economists such as Copland and Irvine, was well aware of the impact that any further reduction of wages might have on workers' purchasing power and consumer confidence. But this was not the era for stimulus packages. The court accepted the argument that the decline in national income as a result of the global crisis demanded a readjustment of costs across the board: from government to production and services to rents, dividends and interest. Manufacturing enterprises were at risk of becoming 'very precarious' unless there was some stabilisation of prices. Moreover, it was considered essential to reduce the production costs of the primary producer, who was carrying more than 'his share of the burden' of the crisis.

The decision of the court applied only to workers under Commonwealth awards, and not all states followed its lead in cutting the basic wage of workers under state awards. The effect of the judgment was thus confined to about half the workforce. In some states, the real basic wage increased.[6] But the decision was still a political catastrophe for Scullin. The *Australian Worker* dubbed the Arbitration Court's decision as 'pauperizing the worker . . . No longer can we boast that Australia leads the world in the material welfare of the masses.'[7] A spate of union resolutions held the Scullin government accountable for 'allowing' the court to act as it did. The decision should not be proclaimed or gazetted, and 'these Judges who in such a brazen-faced manner robbed our wives and children and presented the result of the theft to the employers' should be dismissed from the court. The ACTU thought that Scullin should call a national emergency.[8] The New South Wales Trades and Labor Council even voted to launch a general strike—though other unions thought that this would be madness.[9] One unionist, a seaman, moved at a meeting of the Trades Hall Council in Melbourne that 'in view of the impotency of the workers to improve their class position on their present basis of organisation, this Council calls upon all workers to become organised consciously and politically for the abolition of capitalism'.[10] Such rhetoric might have made the proposer feel better but it was hardly practical politics.

The federal government could do very little. The attorney-general, Brennan, immediately applied to the court to postpone the introduction of its order, on the grounds that the government itself was planning ways to address one of the court's concerns: the equitable distribution of the burden of loss and of spending power across all sections of the community. But the court rejected his application.

At this already turbulent time, Scullin took the decision to reinstate Theodore as treasurer.[11] The shadow of Mungana was still present, since the civil case being launched by the Queensland government was months away. But many in the ALP thought this a political stunt anyway. There was no candidate for treasurer who came near matching Theodore's competence, and Lyons had asked to be relieved of the role. Moreover, Scullin was attracted to some elements of Theodore's case for a limited expansion of credit, and he knew that he had to do something to engage with the increasingly radical demands of the New South Wales party. The benefits of reinstating Theodore seemed to outweigh the risks.

The caucus was not so sure. After a long and acrimonious debate, the vote was carried by an extremely close margin. Curtin welcomed Theodore back: 'At last this Government will fight for something,' he concluded privately.[12] But others, such as the Methodist lay preacher Norman Makin, were concerned at the ethical implications of reinstating a man who had not yet been cleared of the charges against him. Radicals, such as Yates, Anstey and the member for Werriwa, Hubert (Bert) Lazzarini, suspected Theodore's motives, seeing his embrace of expansionary policies as a means of getting back into office. On the conservative side of the caucus, Fenton and Lyons had their own reasons for opposing Theodore's reinstatement. On 4 February 1931, they both resigned their cabinet positions.

Press opinion was divided. Some thought Theodore's presence would strengthen the cabinet, but critics claimed that Scullin had used Fenton and Lyons, only to then dump them. Some publicity was given to a letter by the Labor member for the farming constituency of Angas in South Australia, Joel Gabb, who resigned from the ALP. He declared that he had lost confidence in Scullin as leader, particularly in view of his 'ingratitude' to the men who had stood by him in his absence 'to the great danger of their political lives'. (Gabb, it might be noted, would later show an inclination to extreme right-wing politics.) The *Sydney Morning Herald* argued:

> There can be little stability left in a Cabinet whose leader, while resolutely declaiming against inflation of the note issue for Govern-ment purposes, insists on having as Treasurer a man who must soon answer grave charges in the courts, who only recently advocated gross inflation . . . and who said only a week ago that the Commonwealth

Bank can release extensive credits to the Governments whenever it chooses.

Scullin, it claimed, had destroyed confidence in his leadership and made his future uncertain. 'A new great rift has opened in the Labour party, not unlike the fissure in the mountain walls near Katoomba.'[13]

The Scullin government was disintegrating. On 31 January 1931, it suffered a massive loss in a by-election in Parkes, a Sydney electorate that then had the Canterbury Racecourse at its centre. The sitting Labor member, Edward McTiernan, had retired after being nominated for the High Court by the caucus in December 1930. Scullin had opposed the nomination, not just because he wanted to avoid any suggestion of political interference in High Court appointments, but also because he feared that by-elections would give the Opposition the chance to reduce his majority and allow the radical elements of Sydney Labor to install their own candidates. His fears were justified. Parkes had traditionally been a Nationalist seat, held by Labor only since 1929, and in the by-election the swing to the Nationalist candidate was more than 14 per cent. The message seemed to be that the voters were fearful of fiscal experimentation, repudiation and uncontrolled inflation. Should the Scullin government pursue such policies, it would surely be defeated at the next election.

Against this backdrop, the battle of the plans erupted in a long and fractious conference of the premiers spanning most of February. When discussions between the government and the Commonwealth Bank had come close to deadlock in December, all parties had agreed that a workable plan was needed. Early in the New Year, the Loan Council established an expert committee of state under-treasurers (principal advisers to state ministers) and Gibson to provide advice to a later meeting of premiers. The resulting committee report was a deflationary document, full of strictures against monetary expansion and 'dangerous inflation'.[14] It recommended budgetary balances in 1931–32, reductions in government expenditure and the costs of production, all involving, it conceded, 'the severest sacrifices'—though not necessarily by those making the recommendations.

When the premiers' conference met on 6 February, Scullin opened with a tour d'horizon of the economic situation. The 'essential need of the moment is to revive industry as a whole, so that our people may be provided with work'.[15] But when asked by Lang what the federal government's plan was, he said he had none: the point of the conference was to evolve one.[16] Woe betide any chair who does not know what the preferred outcomes of a meeting might be! On the second day, Theodore took charge of the debate, producing an economic plan whose existence Scullin had denied the previous day: namely, an expansionary monetary policy that would stimulate production, reduce unemployment and restore prices to their 1929 level. The premiers, some of whom may not have understood much of Theodore's economics, adjourned for a day to consider his plan.

This pause in proceedings proved momentous. Lang had seemed conciliatory when Theodore spoke, but when the conference reconvened on 9 February he was more truculent. Castigating the conference for its 'shilly-shallying', he claimed that the heart of the nation's affliction was the burden of its interest payments. Australian governments should cease to pay interest to British bondholders until such time as Britain had dealt with the Australian debt on terms comparable to those of her own debt to the United States. Interest on government borrowings in Australia should be reduced to 3 per cent and the government should abandon the gold standard in favour of a currency based on the wealth of the country, a so-called goods standard.

This was not the platform on which Lang had stood in October 1930, and his motives now seem to have been political as much as economic. A lonely and aloof man, always suspicious of others, he viewed politics primarily in terms of power and conflict between personalities. He had long seen Theodore as a rival, even if he supported his reinstatement as treasurer because credit creation might help New South Wales' finances. Lang also discerned in 'repudiation' of debt a rallying point for the dispossessed that might shore up his already eroding electoral popularity. In the three months since he had been elected, Lang had tried to increase his government's revenue by approving new state lotteries and raising the special tax for unemployment relief that had been introduced by the Bavin government. Lang had also passed legislation to protect tenants from being evicted or losing their property when they failed to pay rent. The fiscal difficulties of New South Wales remained huge, however, especially as Lang refused to cut public-service wages or to reduce award rates for those employed on government relief work. The discontent within the state ALP was such that a movement dedicated to applying Labor's socialisation plank was proving hard to contain.[17] The 'Lang Plan', then, served at least two needs. Powerfully resonant with Labor's populist discourse against 'Money Power', it provided an 'economic rainbow' to chase, as Ben Chifley put it.[18] It also positioned Lang as the hero of the unemployed, and countered the appeal of the more radical members of the labour movement. For a time it seemed that it might even project Lang into national leadership of the ALP.

If it was powerful politics, the Lang Plan was unworkable. As Theodore said,

> Mr. Lang could, it is true, take the first step [of refusing to pay interest]; but how could he continue to finance his governmental arrangements thereafter? Where could he get the money to enable him to do so? If he could rid himself of the obligation to pay the Commonwealth his proportion of the interest he would certainly have that amount to play with . . . What other funds could he get?[19]

The premiers, too, rejected the Lang Plan. But given that the alternative plan proposed by Theodore would need the support of the Commonwealth Bank, the conference paused as the treasurer headed to Sydney to try to secure agreement.

To no one's surprise, Gibson proved inflexible. He insisted that the bank would only support the government if it scaled down expenditure and cut pensions. The trading banks, too, made it clear that reductions in interest rates would only be made if government finance was placed on a 'sound' footing. The stand-off between the government and banks was now entrenched, and Theodore raised the stakes. If the banks would not expand credit, then he would try to amend the *Commonwealth Bank Act* to allow an increase in the fiduciary note issue—that is, that portion of the note issue that was protected by reserves or assets of a non-metallic character, such as commercial bills of exchange or government securities. In this way, he could raise £18 million for relief works and assistance to the wheat-growing industry. It was a radical proposal and the support of the premiers was highly conditional. The conference ended after seven days of argument with nothing approaching the national plan that Scullin wanted.

All the time the chaos in New South Wales intensified. To Scullin's misfortune, the death of a sitting Labor member, John West, forced another by-election, this time in East Sydney on 7 March. Scullin expected, as the federal party leader and prime minister, to lead the campaign, but the New South Wales ALP executive defied him, announcing that it would campaign on the basis of the Lang Plan, not the Scullin–Theodore one. Moreover, it would expel from the party any parliamentarian who did not support the Lang candidate, Eddie Ward. Scullin, in turn, told the caucus that he 'was not going to take dictation from any one section of the movement' and threatened expulsion for anyone promoting the Lang Plan.[20] It was 1916 again, all the fury and frustration at seismic events beyond anyone's control turning inwards, fuelling a destructive brinkmanship that escalated beyond control. Ten members of the federal caucus linked their fortunes to Lang, underlining the direct danger of Lang's mutiny to the Scullin government, especially in view of the revolt on the right of the party led by Lyons and Fenton. A spill of cabinet positions followed in early March, and Beasley, Anstey and the Senate leader, J.J. Daly, were all dropped from the ministry. Beasley challenged Scullin for the leadership but polled poorly. The new cabinet was more supportive of Scullin, but not one of the five new men (a third of the ministry) had spent more than five years in federal parliament.[21]

As Scullin's government fractured, Ward won the East Sydney by-election. The swing against Labor was not as dramatic as in Parkes, allowing Scullin to claim that the vote was not an endorsement of repudiation. Lang had attracted huge crowds when he spoke, but the increase in the Nationalist vote from 31.47 per cent in 1929 to 44.24 per cent in 1931 could be read as a censure of him as well as the federal government. The split fracturing the ALP was now unstoppable. It was formalised on 12 March when Scullin refused to admit Ward to the federal caucus, the logic being that since Ward had not campaigned on federal Labor policy, he could not take part in the business of the Federal Parliamentary Labor Party.[22] After yet another incredibly fractious caucus meeting, Beasley and six supporters walked out, forming a Lang Labor group in both houses of federal parliament. Two days later, Theodore was expelled from the New South Wales branch. On 27 March, the federal conference of the ALP meeting in Sydney expelled the New South Wales branch and formed a new state ALP branch under federal authority. There were now two Labor parties in New South Wales.

With good cause the press began speculating that the government might fall. When Theodore introduced his bill for the fiduciary issue on 4 March, Latham immediately moved a vote of no confidence. The Scullin government, he claimed, was vacillating and pandering to the extremists on the left. By advocating 'politically controlled inflation' it would place Australia on the road to 'repudiation, national dishonour, ruin, and disaster'. Latham's colleagues joined the chorus of abuse. Scullin was 'a ginger-bread Prime Minister', a 'whimperer', a failure as a leader of the Australian people, and Australia's 'prime political acrobat and contortionist'; 'in tongue, he was a lion, but in heart he was a mouse'. The government had 'trumpeted its intention around the earth; it is always going to do something, but it has done nothing. It has no policy.' Hughes, as ever, went for the jugular: 'What the Labour Party badly needs is a leader; it is without one.' To which a Scullin supporter quipped: 'What the right honourable member [Hughes] needs is a party'![23]

Scullin managed to survive the vote of no confidence. The Lang Labor group supported him, it seems because Lang concluded that it was preferable at this point to keep Scullin in power. But neither Fenton nor Lyons supported Scullin. Lyons made a memorable speech, saying that he could only support 'honest' finance and government, instead of 'visionary schemes [that] will avail us nothing'. He could not be 'untrue to the people' he represented.[24] Scullin's victory, then, was a hollow one. As *The Times* of London said, 'For Mr. Scullin it was . . . almost worse than defeat, for it was secured only by an appeal to the secessionists, who although they voted with the Government, cannot be counted upon to keep Mr. Scullin in office . . . The Government cannot prolong its uneasy existence much longer.'[25] Indeed, it would not last out 1931.

CHAPTER 21

Populism and secession

The ferment generated by the battle of the plans did not simply tear the ALP apart. It also generated a remarkable mobilisation of new political forces at the grassroots level. While the unemployed protested against sustenance, relief works and, as we shall see, evictions of tenants from their homes, a host of new political organisations emerged on the right of politics in 1930 and 1931. Many of these 'citizens' movements' gave voice to a deep frustration with the political parties that seemed impotent in the face of the economic crisis. For a few heady months, the populism of these movements appeared to challenge the existing political system, as did the paramilitary movements with which they were associated. The very physical shape of the nation was also contested, as activists across the country demanded the creation of new states and secession as the answer to their economic woes. Ultimately, however, the potential for radicalism of the citizens' groups dissipated as the more traditional forces of the right mobilised to realign the non-Labor parties in a new, more powerful form, the United Australia Party, and to enlist Lyons to this cause.

Citizen's movements were not new on the Australian political landscape. In earlier decades, an array of non-party conservative groups, educational associations and protest movements had campaigned for diverse causes, including empire, defence, immigration, women's rights and sectarianism.[1] In the aftermath of World War I, the fear of socialism and Bolshevism fuelled further movements, such as the Sane Democracy League and clandestine paramilitary units, of which we shall hear more. The deepening of the Depression, however, triggered an explosion of such activism. In 1930–31 a plethora of organisations sprang up, claiming that the existing political system had failed and needed to be transformed to meet the national crisis.

In some ways this activism had the character of 'a populist revolt against the conservative establishment'.[2] For all their diversity, these movements shared the belief that is at the heart of populism: that society is separated into two homogeneous and antagonistic camps, 'the pure people' versus 'the corrupt elite'.[3] If Australia were to recover from the Depression, political and moral rejuvenation was needed through a reawakening of the citizenry. The citizens were stoic, hardworking and willing to put the interests of the collective above their own—they thought 'nationally instead of individually'. Politicians, in contrast, were preoccupied with 'sectional' or 'class interests'.[4] Furthermore, they were slaves to 'machine politics', thanks to the preselection of parliamentary candidates and the enforcement of party platforms through candidate pledges and block voting in Parliament. The party system thus fuelled the division of Australia into classes 'based on wealth or social position', and if the system did not change, 'there would be no end but revolution and disaster'.[5]

In essence, the political system needed transformation. The specific proposals varied across the movements, but among them were the following: proportional representation should be introduced to ensure that no one party dominated Parliament; Parliament should be 'restored' as a 'deliberative' assembly, comprising 'responsible representatives of the people'; cabinets should be elected by Parliament, and parliamentarians should be allowed to vote according to their conscience. Country regions should have more devolved power. As for economic policy, businesses should be liberated from the shackles of government control and the burdens of excessive taxation. Economic policy should be placed in the hands of independent experts, who would 'disinterestedly examine' questions of taxation, wages and the tariff, and restrain the extravagance of governments and their tendency to pander to sectional interests.[6]

Given their distrust of traditional parties, these movements claimed to be above politics. But they were not. Although they were as critical of the

Nationalist party machine as of Labor, their values aligned strongly with those of mainstream Australian conservative liberalism. They celebrated patriotism, imperialism, loyalty, thrift, honour, self-reliance, individualism, private enterprise, efficiency and—most importantly in 1931—'sound finance'. They were almost hysterically anti-communist and, in New South Wales, implacably anti-Lang. Inflation and repudiation—two of the options under consideration in the battle of the plans—were anathema to them. These movements still claimed to be apolitical because they thought their opinions were 'akin to natural laws' that transcended politics. Like many who favour the status quo, they assumed that their values aligned with the national interest while those of their opponents did not. Thus the citizens' movements have usefully been described as 'anti-political political thought'.[7]

Opinions differ as to what motivated the Australians who led and joined these movements. Members were drawn from professional groups, large and small businessmen, disaffected members of the rural community and restless returned soldiers. The organisations fared well in the urban areas of South Australia, Victoria and New South Wales, but had varying success in rural areas. Their phenomenally rapid growth in early 1931 indicates that they tapped a groundswell of anger and despair from 'below'. But—and herein lay their weakness as populist movements—their leaders were often drawn from established political and social elites. By one estimate, about a third of the leaders of the Australian movement had served in the AIF, and half of them had done so at commissioned or non-commissioned level. A significant number were also active in the dense network of overlapping voluntary work, community organisations and unemployment relief. Almost all were male.[8] Most were well off, but anxious.

An early, and quintessential, example of these movements (of which we can only consider the most important here) was the Citizens' League of South Australia.[9] Begun in the Balfours café in Adelaide in October 1930, it originated within the Constitutional Club of South Australia, one of a national grid of clubs formed in the mid-1920s to campaign for industrial law and order. The league was led by a former AIF officer, E.D. Bagot, a British-born imperialist who protested against Isaacs' appointment as governor-general. A domineering personality, Bagot also professed an admiration for Mussolini, whose works he circulated. 'There was never a time in the political history of the country,' he claimed, 'so fraught with immediate danger as the present, nor when so many people were crying out for a strong leader who would "cleave through party politics" and establish law and order in our social system.'[10] The man whom Bagot, and many others, had in mind was their military hero Monash, although quite readily Bagot would settle on the decidedly unmilitary figure of Lyons.

The league's political program combined morally charged principles such as the cultivation of national sentiment, equality of sacrifice and service as a civic duty, with a commitment to national unity along non-party lines. It tolerated moderate Labor opinion and showed a practical concern for the unemployed. Change, it believed would be achieved by the mobilisation of public opinion: 'We are a conscience,' Bagot claimed, 'a sentiment, a force, the force of public opinion, public sentiment, public conscience, which awakened at last by the crisis that confronts us, attempts to make itself both heard and felt.'[11] A sophisticated mix of populist tactics was employed to attract recruits. 'Monster rallies' packed the Adelaide Town Hall, members were awarded gold badges and brooches if they encouraged others to join, and countless thousands of dodgers, letters and circulars were distributed. Soon nearly 22,000 people—6.7 per cent of the total registered voters in South Australia—joined across 93 metropolitan and 60 country branches.[12] Some of these members were secretly enrolled as special constables to support the South Australian police in maintaining essential services in the case of industrial unrest. Bagot aspired to much more: a nationwide movement based on the Constitutional Clubs across the country. But despite his best efforts, the league failed to take off in Queensland, where citizens' movements, like the Vigilants, proved short-lived, perhaps for lack of leadership. In Western Australia and Tasmania, the focus of conservative mobilisation was more, although not exclusively, on secession.[13]

In Victoria and New South Wales, the conservative mobilisation also took different forms. Even though Bagot lobbied in Melbourne for a Victorian version of the Citizen's' League of South Australia, he failed to secure the cooperation of the Melbourne Citizens' Committee, an elite group of businessmen who had supported Lyons during the loan campaign in late 1930.

Instead, on 19 February 1931 in a Melbourne Town Hall bedecked with Union Jacks and Australian flags, Melbourne's civic leaders launched the Australian Citizens' League. One month later, this organisation adopted the name and objectives of the All for Australia League that had arisen independently in New South Wales. Under a banner that proclaimed 'National Integrity, Security and Sacrifice', the renamed Australian Citizens' League attracted a membership by end of May 1931 of 80,000 across 320 branches.[14]

The All for Australia League in New South Wales owed its existence to the panic triggered among conservatives by Lang's election in October 1930. This initially inspired the formation of the Producers' Advisory Council (PAC), a rural-based movement led by graziers who were calling for lower costs of production, tariff reductions and special assistance for the rural sector. When the PAC met with almost instant success—in January 1931 alone it addressed a total of 40,000 people in 40 meetings across the New South Wales countryside—several Sydney businessmen were inspired to form a similar organisation in the city. On 12 February 1931, the All for Australia League was launched. As in Melbourne, its leaders were business and professional men, all Rotarians. Its executive included Major General Gordon Bennett, commander of the 2nd Division of the AIF and president of the Chamber of Manufactures, who would later become notorious for leaving Singapore shortly before it fell to the Japanese in February 1942.

The All for Australia League enjoyed an immediate popularity, though more so in Sydney than in rural areas. The New South Wales countryside was something of 'a crowded ideological space' by early 1931, with a number of populist groups and paramilitary forces competing for members.[15] Still, by the end of June, perhaps 130,000 citizens of New South Wales were wearing the badge of a six-point star with a double A in the centre.[16] The New South Wales branch of the league soon aspired to form its own party running its own candidates. So much for opposition to traditional political party structures!

For all their popularity, these citizens' movements achieved comparatively little. The months in which they exploded were ones of remarkable political fluidity. After Lyons' resignation from cabinet, it seemed that he might form a new centre party, claiming ground from both the Nationalists and moderate Labor. Bagot, among others, hoped that this party might be built on the foundations of the citizens' leagues, and a conference in Adelaide on 9–10 April courted Lyons with this aim in mind. But the Nationalist powerbrokers in Melbourne had other ideas. The Group, an informal association of Melbourne financiers and business figures, saw Lyons as the possible leader of a reconfigured Nationalist Party. At the very time the All for Australia League was being created, they approached Lyons suggesting that he leave the Labor Party.[17]

For Lyons, the thought of severing the associations of a lifetime with Labor was deeply distressing. But his decision was effectively made for him when the Tasmanian Labor conference censured him for disobedience of caucus, and Theodore proceeded with the Fiduciary Notes Bill. When Lyons spoke against this in Parliament, he emerged as 'the ideal representative' for the Australian right. He could be depicted as a man who placed the good of the nation above the claims of his party, appealed to his conscience and elevated duty and service above personal ambition and self-interest. All this erased from conservative minds the memory of Lyons' opposition to conscription in 1916–17, his Irish nationalism—he had described the leaders of the 1916 Easter uprising as misguided heroes and had supported Home Rule—and his strong Catholic faith.[18] Instead, he was now a potential saviour of 'sound finance' with considerable electoral appeal.

The main obstacle to the plan to enlist Lyons was Latham who, for all his rather cold public persona, had proved an effective Opposition leader in federal parliament. He was understandably reluctant to forfeit his chances of being prime minister, chances that were looking more promising every day as Scullin's government spun out of control. But after a fortnight's resistance, Latham agreed to defer to Lyons. Personal feelings, he said in a considerable act of self-effacement, could not stand in the way when a national emergency arose.[19] Lyons, so his wife Enid would have it, was genuinely distressed: 'Why should Latham do this for me?' he asked her time after time.[20] But he accepted Latham's withdrawal, nonetheless, and on 17 April became leader of the Nationalist Opposition. His elevation was applauded by leading public figures, the business community and the anti-Labor press, including Keith Murdoch. As it happened, the head of the Melbourne *Herald*'s political bureau in Canberra, J.A. Alexander, came from Devonport, Lyons' home town; he had reported on state politics while Lyons was Tasmanian premier and had consulted closely with him in the early months of 1931.[21] In Adelaide, meanwhile, the *Advertiser and Register* described Lyons during the April conference as follows:

The picture thousands carried away from the meeting was of a solid, clear minded man of the people, whose simple conception of right and wrong had been bred in the normal atmosphere of family life, whose measure of life was the welfare of a gallant wife and a household of happy children [there were ultimately twelve Lyons children, two of them born in 1931 and 1933] . . . Here was someone who thought and felt as they did, who had a home like them to lose or save, talking to them in a conversational way.[22]

The party Lyons now led soon took a new name, the United Australia Party (UAP). With this title it genuflected to the citizens' movements and their claim to unite Australians across class and social divisions. Lyons coopted just enough of the populist style of the citizens' movements to 'wrap them into a centre-right political framework'.[23] But names aside, the parliamentary UAP was a creature much like its Nationalist predecessor. Lacking a national vision, it never developed a mass or federal base. In many ways it remained the creation of its finance committees, the National Union in Victoria and the Consultative Council in New South Wales. These groups were everything the left suspected them to be: small, secretive, powerful, and able to exploit personal connections behind the scenes to raise funds and ensure that the 'right' men entered Parliament. Even one Nationalist veteran quipped that what began as a movement 'to replace incompetent politicians by capable business and professional men . . . finished by placing those same politicians more firmly in the saddle'.[24] As for the wider agenda of parliamentary and electoral reform that the citizens' movements advocated, this too dissolved.

Indeed, with the creation of the UAP, the citizens' movements collapsed. In Victoria, the All for Australia League decided to cooperate in the creation of the UAP under the leadership of Lyons. Ultimately, their opposition to party politics proved less compelling than the immediate goal of unseating the federal ALP government. Bagot, too, accepted this logic and was effectively reined in by leading South Australian conservatives, including the indefatigable Charles Hawker, who created an Emergency Committee: that

271

is, a front of the Liberal Federation, the Country Party and various non-party organisations that would field candidates for the next federal election. The All for Australia League in New South Wales held out longer, elevating anti-party purity above pragmatic electoral concerns, but the issue of whether or not to cooperate with other conservative parties was a source of growing internal disunity. By October 1931, the league was so starved of funds and members that it agreed to cooperate with the Nationalists.

The rapid collapse of the citizens' movements begs some explanation. First, it was critical that the new leader whom conservatives were seeking to fill the vacuum of national leadership emerged fortuitously in the form of Lyons. Second, the citizens' movements suffered from structural weaknesses. As with many manifestations of populism, their ideology was 'thin-centred'.[25] This is not to deny that the movements had some elements akin to the fascism that was a feature of European politics during the inter-war years: for example, they appealed to national unity and self-sacrifice, they demonised the 'other' of communism, and they flirted with corporatist economic ideas. Like fascists, too, they elevated idealism as a driving transformative force over substantive policy. But the term 'fascism', which does not conform readily to any fixed template, fails to capture the essence of the citizens' movements.[26] They were positioned firmly within the Anglo-Australian conservative tradition. This meant that, after their initial burst of populist-style activity, they were readily assimilated into the existing conservative traditions and party structures. Third, the citizens' movements were not led, as many movements of the truly radical populist right have been over the past century, by political 'outsiders'. Rather they—and the paramilitary forces that arose at the same time—were largely the creations of men who were already members of the political and financial elites of traditional conservatism. When these men chose to, they were willing and able to defuse the radical challenge of the citizens' movements while reaping the manifest electoral advantages of their populism.

The Country Party refused to have any part of this reconfiguration of the Nationalists. Page argued in his inimitable fashion that 'the mob behind the Lyons–Nationalist Coalition are all big Melbourne manufacturers and stockbrokers, and would have no more mercy on us than on Latham, whom they have buried alive.'[27] Hence, while the Country Party agreed that it would cooperate with the UAP with the aim of restoring confidence and rehabilitating Australian industry, it insisted that it remain a discrete entity. Only after the election of September 1934 did it form a coalition with the UAP, and this arrangement lasted less than five years.

Page's personal feelings aside, the Country Party had good reason to go it alone in 1931, given the depth of the anger of rural Australia. Primary producers, as we have seen, were under siege, thanks to the loss of export income, high production costs and the tariffs that Scullin piled on in an effort to dampen imports. The wheat-growing regions were also seething about the 'Grow More Wheat' campaign, the full disaster of which became apparent just as Lang's plans for repudiation became known. Across the country, primary producers demanded stronger provincial government, lower tariffs, less taxation and reduced government intervention. To this was added, as the Depression worsened, a demand that the constitutional relationship between Canberra and the states and regions be renegotiated. For many in the country districts, the federation of 1901 was unfinished business. Not only should there be further adjustment of the financial relationships between the Commonwealth and the states, but the map of Australia should also be redrawn.[28]

The movement to create new states was particularly strong in New South Wales, in the primary-producing and export-dependent regions of New England, the Riverina and the Monaro. The New England movement was the most deeply rooted, dating back to colonial times when Queensland separated from New South Wales.[29] The demand for greater autonomy had simmered during and immediately after World War I, when the cause was championed by Page, whose home town was Grafton in the Northern Rivers region. The agitation abated a little in the 1920s, when two royal commissions failed to recommended change,[30] but the Depression refuelled the sense of grievance. Resources were supposedly being drained from the put-upon country to the bloated city. Vast amounts of taxpayers' money were being spent on a bridge in Sydney and too little on irrigation, country roads, railways and ports. Freight was too expensive; secondary industry was too concentrated in the capital; and the primary producers, the creators of the nation's wealth, had too little say in economic policy.

Lang's threat of repudiation invested the demand for a carving up of New South Wales with a passionate intensity. In early 1931, conferences convened in Armidale and Maitland to start the process of drawing the boundaries of the new state and framing a constitution. The optimal size of the new state was a matter for considerable debate. Data was marshalled from other countries of comparable size to demonstrate that Australia had too few states for its land mass.[31] The United States had 48 states and two federal territories, Australia five states and two territories. Brazil was only slightly bigger than Australia, yet it had twenty states.[32] Switzerland, with its cantons, communes and a federal parliament, proved that decentralised government worked.[33]

Any new Australian state, it was agreed, needed to be compact, homogeneous and easily managed.[34] Some advocates thought that Victoria, like Goldilocks' third bowl of porridge, was about right: large enough for self-government and able to generate a sound taxation base, but small enough for effective administration. The population of northern New South Wales was also just right; as great as that of Western Australia and almost entirely white and of British extraction. People of 'British race' supposedly had shown themselves peculiarly fitted to govern themselves, and the New England region and the north coast (which would form part of any Northern or New England state) had already produced a crop of state and federal politicians who had held or were holding cabinet rank.

But what should the boundaries of the new Northern State be? Clearly one should be the existing Queensland border. The rich and diverse primary industries of New England, around Tamworth, Armidale and Grafton would be the state's heartland. But should the industrial and mining regions of the lower Hunter and Newcastle be included? Whatever its boundaries, the new state should be large enough to offset 'the preponderance of influence' of the capital city on national affairs. Most especially New Englanders should not be stained with the dishonour of repudiation. Page, still campaigning tirelessly for the cause, declared that 'The people of Northern N.S.W. refuse to have any part or lot in this matter of default.' They have 'no other course but to cut adrift from N.S.W.'[35] More dramatically, he argued, drawing on his medical expertise, 'this political disease' was like appendicitis. 'Amputation is the only way to save clean and wholesome tissue from the gangrene of extravagance, communism

274

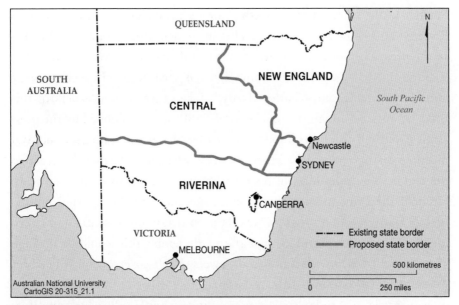

Map 21.1: One proposed version of new states for New South Wales, c. 1931
The rump state around Sydney is not named in the original.
Source: David Henry Drummond Papers, UNE&R Archives, V3013.

and repudiation that is eating into the metropolis.'[36] A handbill for a petition to the federal parliament seeking a new state put this mix of issues succinctly:

> If you are against Repudiation
> If you are opposed to Communism
> If you are tired of the domination of the Big City
> If you have faith in New England and its People
> Sign! Sign!! Sign!!![37]

Another handbill asked New Englanders:

> Are you going to let a handful of Industrial Communists . . . commit you irrevocably to Repudiation, Communism and the disruption of Australia? Are you going to calmly see your own unemployed without work, whilst the money that ought to be providing work for them, and business for your town, [is] drained away to the Big City?[38]

Further to the south of New South Wales, a campaign for an autonomous Riverina also gained momentum. This movement, too, had a long history. In the period before 1921, the most frequent demand was for annexation to Victoria. In 1931 the separatist campaign was spearheaded by a charismatic local timber merchant, Charles Hardy.[39] Like other citizen leaders of this time, he was also a mainstay of the local RSSILA. Soon dubbed by the press as the Cromwell or John Hampden of the Riverina, Hardy addressed monster meetings on the banks of the Murrumbidgee attended by farmers from across the region. 'Fire smoulders in his deep-set blue eyes, with their sleepy lids. His bold, direct manner is reflected in his speech,' the press reported approvingly.[40] Hardy's actual program was light on detail, but essentially it called for the Riverina to control its own affairs. Preferably this would be through a provincial council with unfettered powers of self-government. If need be, it would be by secession from Australia. Like other citizens' groups, the movement claimed to be 'strictly non-political', but Hardy, who sometimes professed to be a fascist, detested Lang.[41] Somewhat ominously, he hinted that the Riverina would be prepared, in the event of a national emergency, to use force, employing a 'silent division' to maintain 'orderly self-government'.[42]

The Riverina movement had a vast reach, stretching from Tumut to Albury and from Griffith to Deniliquin, but Hardy, ambitious and hyper-energetic, also headed a loose confederation of organisations across the state. He swooped around New South Wales by air, rail and road, causing the less militant rural separatist leaders in New England to come to see him as a threat.[43] His demagogic rhetoric also attracted the attention of the police and the Commonwealth Investigation Branch. But ultimately Hardy's rhetoric proved to be more puff than revolution. The Riverina Movement was eventually subsumed into the UAP. In August 1931, Hardy became chairman of the United Country Movement, another of the regional networks that had arisen to advocate strong provincial government. Elected to the Senate as a United Country Party candidate in December, his taming was complete.

Yet if Hardy became respectable, the agitation for new states was too great to be ignored. When a UAP government took office in coalition with the Country Party in mid-1932, Premier Stevens agreed to hold a royal commission to consider whether any of the proposed new autonomous regions, including the Monaro and the western regions anchored on Dubbo, would be sustainable.[44] Eventually, in 1935, Commissioner H.S. Nicholas ruled that while the abnormal economic conditions made it impossible to form accurate estimates as to the financial position or prospects of each of the areas, the northern area of New South Wales could be sustainable as a new state, as long as it included the large urban centre of Newcastle. Nicholas, however, rejected the case for an autonomous Riverina. He favoured a larger state that would include the central west, the Riverina and the whole of the western division, which, if left on its own, would lack the resources and population to be viable.

This seemed a victory at least for New England, but no action was taken, given the significant and contentious constitutional issues involved. As economic conditions improved, and Australia faced war again, the question of New England's statehood remained unresolved. Three decades and one

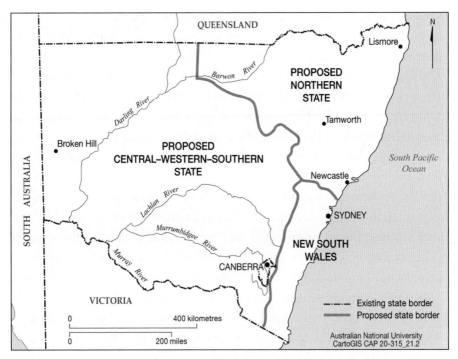

Map 21.2: New South Wales subdivision as suggested by the 1934 Nicholas Royal Commission

Source: David Henry Drummond Papers, UNE&R Archives, V3013.

unofficial referendum later, it was finally put to the vote in 1967. The vote went 54 per cent against, in part because, in accordance with Nicholas's report, the proposed boundaries included Newcastle and the Lower Hunter. This effectively spelled the end of the campaign, though it would bubble up from time to time in later years.

The 'independence' movements that the Depression fuelled in other states would also fail. Tasmania had a brief flirtation with secession. Continuing to be resentful about high tariffs, their state's lack of control over customs and excise revenue, and the restraints on freedom of interstate trade, some Tasmanians established a Dominion League. Its journal trumpeted 'Freedom for Tasmania' from the 'Federal nightmare'.[45] Somewhat fancifully, given that their population was around 227,000 in 1933, Tasmanian secessionists also aspired to control 'war and other functions'.[46] There were shades of the fictional Grand Duchy of Fenwick's aspiration to wage war with the United States here. The movement petered out without having had any influence on either the National Party or other citizens' movements across Bass Strait.

More serious was the challenge from Western Australia.[47] This state had been a reluctant member of the federation in 1901. The vote had been swung in favour by those people from other states who had arrived during the goldmining boom in the 1890s. Many in rural districts remained opposed to federation, and the flame of secession had been kept alight throughout the 1920s by the indefatigable *Sunday Times*. The arguments for autarky were familiar economic ones: the control of the Commonwealth was 'intolerable'; the tariff and federal customs duties favoured the more industrialised eastern states; the sugar embargo satisfied pressure groups at the expense of consumers; and Western Australia could more readily gain access to the overseas money market if it were free from the controls of the Loan Council. In some ways London seemed closer than Canberra. One Mrs F.A. Pratt wrote to the *West Australian* on 8 April 1933: 'To the mothers of Western Australia I send out an S.O.S. call to be true to your British traditions . . . Our Ship of State is sinking fast overloaded with cargo packed in the interests of Eastern States monopolists, providing work for the children of the East but leaving your sons and daughters helpless.'[48] No one conceded that the federal financial

Eric Campbell, the leader of the paramilitary movement, the New Guard, and his colleagues give the fascist salute at a meeting in New South Wales, 17 December 1931. Campbell's avowed aim was to unseat the Lang government, if need be by force. (*SMH*)

This grainy image is probably a restaging of the famous episode in Victoria's free speech campaign, when the young communist artist Noel Counihan defied police by speaking from a cage in Phoenix Street, Brunswick, May 1933. (State Library of Victoria)

Earle Page, leader of the Country Party, and his wife, Ethel, in the early 1930s. Though not always in formal coalition with conservative forces, Page opposed Labor policies and championed the rights of rural Australians, especially in his own New England, New South Wales, which sought to become a new state. (*SMH*)

Prime Minister Scullin meeting the people, at Coogee, New South Wales, during the campaign for the election of December 1931 that brought an end to his troubled government. (*SMH*)

Joe Lyons (left) and John Latham, c. 1931. Although an effective leader of the Nationalist Party in Opposition, Latham conceded to Lyons the leadership of the new United Australia Party created in April–May 1931. (*SMH*)

The United Australia Party was a hybrid of non-Labor forces. Here Lyons, the General of Finance, sits astride the horse of Capitalism, mobilising his forces: 'Somersaulting Billy' Hughes (in Little Digger uniform); the All for Australia League (as drummer); the Nationalist Party ('Pension Stealer'); and the Country Party ('Labor Renegade' and 'Wage Reducer'). (29 April 1931, *AW*)

The anti-Labor forces are now making every effort to present a united front.

THE GENERAL: "Everybody's welcome to join our ranks. We're not particular who they are, so long as they'll help us to defeat the workers."

Cave-dwellers, including a toddler, at Kurnell, Sydney, in the 1930s. Other homeless families resorted to makeshift accommodation in camps on the outskirts of cities and towns, or took to wandering the country in search of work and food. (NLA)

A group of families in Happy Valley camp, La Perouse, Sydney. Though originally makeshift, this camp ultimately became well organised, with residents developing communal facilities and attracting the support of the local golf club and Sydney's social elites. (SLNSW)

A key element in resilience and survival was self-help, including producing food at home. Here a woman tends her garden at Happy Valley camp. (SLNSW)

A family, part of a group settlement, with their maize crop, at Tingledale, Western Australia, c. 1929. Western Australia's Nationalist Premier James 'Moo-cow' Mitchell (1919–24, 1930–33) was an enthusiast for rural development through assisted immigration and unemployment relief programs. Other state premiers, too, saw primary industry as critical to unemployment relief and economic recovery. (SLWA)

Relief workers (here probably at Blackboy Hill camp, outside Perth) had none of the comforts of home. Among the deprivations of relief work, which unemployed men were often required to accept, were sometimes primitive living conditions and separation from families. (SLWA)

Some Australian communities turned inwards, resenting the outsider in times of economic competition. Here local people in Cairns, driven primarily by irritation at the 'invasion' of itinerant workers, attacked those who had occupied the Parramatta Park showground, in July 1932. (Queensland Police Museum)

Captain Bill Woodfull ducks to avoid a rising ball from Harold Larwood in the acrimonious Ashes 'Bodyline' series of 1932–33. The passion unleashed in this controversy owed something to wider tensions between Australia and Britain throughout the Depression years, including over the question of Australia's debt crisis. (Getty)

The Depression fuelled secession movements in both Tasmania and Western Australia (the latter a reluctant member of the Australian federation in 1901). In April 1933, Western Australians voted two to one in favour of leaving the federation, and late in 1934 four delegates headed for London, armed with the proposed flag for their new state. (SLWA)

Prime Minister Joe Lyons' electoral appeal owed much to his image as a family man. At the Lodge, Canberra, in the 1930s, with wife Enid and their children. (NLA)

compact of 1928 gave Western Australia favourable treatment, or that it was improbable that a small Dominion, already burdened with debt, could carry much weight in international monetary circles.

Western Australia's Dominion League, formed in May 1930, soon attracted some 30,000 members. As the popular protest swelled, the streets of Perth were filled with motorcades and processions flying a new flag, a Union Jack with a black swan in a gold circle at the centre. Enthusiasts tried their hand at poetry, for want of a better word for it:

> Rise Westralia!
> Grand of Old, be Grander Yet ...
> From the Leeuwin to the line—
> this bit of the world belongs to us!
> Westralia! Westralia! Wave o'er Australia free![49]

Premier Mitchell was not enthusiastic, however. Not until April 1933 was the question of secession finally put to a referendum. Lyons made the journey across the continent to present the federation's case and required a police escort when in Perth. He was shouted down at a meeting in the Theatre Royal, where the official stage party, including wife Enid, was pelted with pennies. Hughes also made several appearances and seemed very much in his metier. Never more energised than when engaged in rancorous debate, he told a rowdy meeting in Fremantle Town Hall: 'if you vote for secession you are the biggest goats that ever lived. You have been let into a booby trap.'[50]

Many Western Australians ignored Hughes. On 8 April 1933, they voted two to one to leave the federation. But once more, all the passion and activism achieved little. Labor's Philip Collier, who returned as premier in the state election held the same day as the referendum, adopted that effective stalling tactic of forming a committee, to frame a submission to the British parliament. It was not until September 1934 that the secessionists set sail for London, armed with their flag and an 8-metre-long petition 'handsomely housed in a polished jarrah case'.[51] Some nine months later, a Westminster parliamentary subcommittee judged the Western Australian case invalid. The federation could only be dissolved with the consent of both parties to the contract. Canberra, of course, was not going to give its consent, and the issue died.

By 1935, the worst of the Depression was over. The urgency had gone out of the state's grievances, especially since a Commonwealth Grants Commission had been established in July 1933 to advise the Commonwealth on the payment of special grants to states in recognition of their fiscal differences. Early in its existence, the commission adopted the principle for determining a special grant as being the amount necessary to allow a state to function at a standard not appreciably below that of other states.[52] Essentially, then, the function of secession as a safety valve for Western Australian economic anxieties had dissipated. The issue soldiered on, however, across the decades. In 2020, during the Covid-19 pandemic, a Facebook page posted a map of Australia with the eastern half of the continent coloured red and dubbed 'Filthy Virus Ridden Eastern States'. A caption worthy of the 1930s asks: 'has anyone noticed how the world hasn't collapsed now we have a border. How much better will it be once we stop haemorrhaging money to Canberra.'[53]

Despite their brief life and limited achievements, the various movements of the early 1930s remain an important part of the story of Australia's Depression—and indeed, of the history of the development of Australian conservatism. Their populism triggered the reconfiguration of the Nationalist Party in a way that would prove to be electorally popular. In retrospect, too, they can be seen as foreshadowing the reorientation of liberalism under Robert Menzies in the 1940s towards the 'forgotten people' of the Australian middle class. During the Depression itself, the citizens' movements also gave conservative Australians a means of voicing their anxieties. The tens of thousands who rushed to join one or other of the organisations presumably found a sense of belonging in their mass meetings and local busyness. Their participation in grassroots activism, if only short-lived, provided a safety valve in the most chaotic years of the Depression. If dramatic at times, however, the disaffection on the right of politics was accommodated and never seriously challenged the structures of the democratic state. The same might be said, with some qualification, about the paramilitary movements with which the citizens' movements were often intermeshed and aligned.

CHAPTER 22

Taking up arms

The citizens' and secessionist movements were the more respectable face of the mobilisation of conservative Australians during the Depression years. In 1930–31 a number of paramilitary forces also emerged, in Victoria and New South Wales especially. They, too, were intent on countering communism and defending the established order against the radicalism of Lang. But they were willing to do this, if need be, by force. In the event, they did not resort to violence, since one of their primary objectives in New South Wales, the removal of Lang from power, came about by other means in May 1932. None of these paramilitary forces, for all their rhetoric and physical clashes with their political opponents, took up arms in a way that actually challenged the institutions of the state. Nor, for that matter, did any of the forces that the radical left formed to defend themselves against the military-style mobilisation of the right.

Like the citizens' movements, the conservative paramilitary groups were not new.[1] At various times over the past two decades, citizens had mobilised, or been called upon, to defend the 'social order' from the so-called excesses of disloyalty, industrial action and communism. During major strikes, such as that in Brisbane in 1912 and the general strike of 1917, special squads of volunteers and 'constables' had been recruited to keep essential industries functioning. When the police went on strike in Victoria in 1923, the government authorised the formation of a special constabulary force of 5000 men to replace the strikers. In the immediate aftermath of World War I, too, a network of loyalist organisations took it upon themselves to defend Australia from the alien influences that were 'foreign to the true spirit of Australia'.[2] The King and Empire Alliance, launched in 1920, and that other staunchly loyalist organisation the RSSILA, did not advocate violence, but there were regular clashes between loyalists and returned soldiers at public meetings.[3]

Behind the scenes, more clandestine groups were also created by those conservatives intent on making themselves available to defend the established order. Their early history was shrouded in secrecy, but the British author D.H. Lawrence, in his novel *Kangaroo*, written after a visit to Australia in 1922, depicted a system of 'Diggers' Clubs' formed by returned soldiers for paramilitary activities. *Kangaroo* was allegedly fictional, but its characters bore such a striking resemblance to prominent figures of the Sydney right that it is reasonable to conclude that Lawrence encountered a secret army connected with the King and Empire Alliance.[4] A central character of the novel, Jack Callcott, seems to have been based on W.R. Scott, who was involved in a dramatic storming of the socialist platform in the Sydney Domain in May 1921. 'Kangaroo' himself—Ben Cooley—seems to have been modelled on the commander of the 2nd Division, Sir Charles Rosenthal. It seems likely, then, that a tight coterie of businessmen, shop owners, graziers, professionals and returned soldiers waited in the wings to be called upon to defend the state in the event of a national crisis. They were ready, indeed eager, to act during the 1925 seamen's strike, when Prime Minister Bruce asked Scott to select 500 ex-AIF men to assist police if needed.

In Victoria, similar clandestine planning led to the formation of a White Army. This was a shadowy network of interconnected cells that included the Melbourne University Rifles as potential shock troops. Possibly the White Army was led by the prominent World War I staff officer and, from 1925, chief of Victorian police, Thomas Blamey, or by the even more distinguished veteran Sir Cyril Brudenell White.[5] The evidence for these claims is largely circumstantial and often disputed, but there is little doubt that the movement in Victoria was closely associated with former members of the AIF and the inter-war militia. Donovan Joynt, winner of the Victoria Cross in August 1918 and an inaugural member of the veteran-family support group Legacy, was part of the White Army in the Dandenong Hills. Edmund Herring, a future chief justice of Victoria and World War II commander, was regional commander of the White Army on the Mornington Peninsula.

As the political tensions worsened in 1930–31 and Lang threatened repudiation, these secret movements acquired a more public face and a wider membership. Victorians formed, in early 1931, the League of National Security (sometimes known variously as the League of National Safety, the White Army, the Volunteer Defence Force, or even the New Guard after the New South Wales organisation of that name). The aims of the league were not entirely clear, but its main purpose was to stand ready to counter radical threats.[6] On 6 March 1931, the movement staged a rural mobilisation for this purpose. This day was being marked around the world as International Unemployment Day and, as evening fell, hundreds of men in the Mallee and the Wimmera took up their guns and agricultural implements to defend their towns.[7] Supposedly, a red army was marching on Ballarat and Geelong; an insurrection was brewing in the camp of the unemployed on the Murray at Mildura; rioting was breaking out in Melbourne and police officers had been killed. Sectarianism was added to this rumour mill. The Irish Catholics were suspected in some towns of being in league with the unemployed and the communists. They were purportedly planning to sweep through the region, rifling banks and destroying property. Piano cases of rifles were being shipped into convents in the dead of night! It was all somewhat hysterical—almost like *la grande peur* that swept France in 1789.[8] After hours spent up gum trees waiting for communists, or weeks spent protecting bridges, silos, weirs and pumping plants from imagined sabotage, the men mobilised in March went home. In left-wing memory, they have been accused of staging 'a trial run at a coup'.[9]

The League of National Security occasionally projected their activities across the border into New South Wales.[10] But the paramilitary space in that state was dominated by different and ultimately more notorious forces: the Old Guard and its progeny, the New Guard. The Old Guard was a secret network of conservative organisations, the precise character and structure—and indeed the very existence of which—has been debated by historians.[11] A compelling case has been mounted, however, that with Lang's election in 1930 a structured movement emerged in Sydney led, like the All for Australia League, by the city's commercial and military elites. A key figure was the general manager of CSR, Philip Goldfinch. At least one of that company's warehouses in Pyrmont was used to stockpile arms and ammunition. The Bank of New South Wales, meanwhile, provided the Old Guard with an overdraft of £12,000.

While its origins were in Sydney, the Old Guard soon spread to the countryside, where through personal networks and enmeshment with the RSSILA and the PAC, it recruited wealthy graziers, country-town professionals, small businessmen, bank managers, stock and station agents, soldier-settlers, even the rural working class. This was the same socioeconomic cohort that peopled the citizens' movements, and presumably many men joined more than one organisation. The precise numbers in the Old Guard are difficult to calculate given that the organisation insisted on extreme secrecy and took various names locally, but a considered estimate would be close to 30,000.[12]

Leaders of the Old Guard claimed that their aims were purely defensive. Their role was to 'assist the Civil Power in the event of any riot or revolution taking place'.[13] Like that other imperially minded organisation the Boy Scouts, the Old Guard aimed 'to be prepared': poised to seize strategic locations if the Lang government was unable to meet its financial commitments and collapsed, if the unemployed were inclined to revolt, or if a Bolshevik revolution erupted. To meet these contingencies, members of the Old Guard were organised into hierarchical military units, usually under an ex-AIF officer, and assigned particular military-style duties—the 'front line', staffing, finance, medical services, ciphers, supplies and transport. Some were drafted into an elite corps of shock troops knows as the 'Starmen'. It was almost the Great War again: maps to be surveyed, plans drafted, communications systems maintained, signals coded and deciphered, and logistical challenges mastered. To be sure, there were no Germans or shrapnel, but there were the class enemies, the communists. As the president of the Canowindra RSSILA in New South Wales, Frederic Hinton, said on Anzac Day 1931, 'We soldiers are not going to stand for a movement by an outside body to spoil this land of Australia . . . Just as the men were prepared to give or gave their lives in the 1914–1918 period, so would they do it again.'[14]

Some members of the Old Guard thought that its approach was too reactive, too timid. Hence, in the first months of 1931 a breakaway movement, the New Guard, was formed by a decorated World War I officer, well-established lawyer and senior officer in the militia, Eric Campbell.[15] Like other conservative organisations of the time, the New Guard was committed to 'unswerving loyalty' to the throne and empire, 'sane and responsible government', the liberty of the citizen, a moral renaissance in public life, and the suppression of 'disloyal and immoral elements' in government and society. Campbell also recommended a paring-down of the state sector, and an end to machine party politics. Privately, he advocated government by a 'commission of disinterested gentlemen'.[16] But unlike the Old Guard, which Campbell deemed to be full of 'cold-footers', the New Guard adopted a more aggressive, militant and 'virile' approach. Gone was the secrecy. Campbell brought out into the open his quest to 'put the Commos where they belonged'.[17] At a mass rally in July 1931, he told an overflowing audience of 3000 that 'Communist activities, more fatal to the future of Australia than the most deadly pestilence . . . must be stamped out ruthlessly and without mercy'.[18] Thereafter Campbell delivered a series of radio addresses and published a journal, known first as the *New Guard* and later *Liberty*.

Poaching members from the Old Guard, Campbell also created an impressively organised, mobile and tightly knit force. Mass recruitment began in April 1931, and although Campbell habitually inflated the numbers, the police estimated that there were eventually 36,000 members in Sydney. The movement was far less successful in the country, with perhaps 3000 members. Recruits were organised into territorially based units, supported by a mobile division of private vehicles, armoured cars, motor lorries and motorcycle despatch riders. A naval and air squadron was also raised. The New Guard paid particular attention to the gathering of intelligence and the identification of strategic and vulnerable points in various districts. One sleuth claimed that he was secreted beneath the floorboards of Lang's sister-in-law's house where, equipped with a dictaphone, he hoped to catch the premier visiting for 'immoral purposes'![19]

The New Guard appealed strongly to the middle class and small-scale businessmen.[20] Nearly all of its founders were ex-officers in their late thirties.[21] The Old Guard, annoyed at its poaching of members, thought it was led by a 'lot of no-hopers' and that Campbell projected 'a certain *nouveau riche* brashness'.[22] But among its stars were the aviator Charles Kingsford Smith, some Nationalist politicians, and leading business figures in industry and agriculture. All the same, the New Guard never gained the endorsement from the traditional establishment that the Old Guard or other secret paramilitary organisations did. Campbell offered leading positions in the movement to Monash, Bennett and Rosenthal, as well as Aubrey Abbott, a Country Party parliamentarian and member of the Old Guard, and Sir Henry Braddon, a prominent businessman, financier and member of the Council for Prevention of the Relief of Unemployment. All declined.[23]

Nor did the New Guard ever enjoy the tacit sanction from the authorities that the Old Guard did. Instead, it was subjected to a coordinated campaign of surveillance by the state and Commonwealth agencies and harassment by the New South Wales police, led by ambitious Glasgow-born W.J. (Bill) MacKay. This was partly because the New Guard was not willing to lie in wait but was more openly provocative, operating at the margins of legality. It regularly disrupted working-class meetings with the aim of 'mopping up Communist and other reptile meetings', as one divisional commander put it.[24] In late 1931, Campbell declared that unless Lang vacated office by 26 January 1932, the New Guard would tip him out. He claimed to be willing to restrain police if they were 'disloyal' enough to try to enforce Lang's socialisation plans. All communists were told to leave Australia by 29 February 1932 or they would be forcibly removed. The labour leader Jock Garden was also assaulted at his home in May 1932, though whether this was by members of the New Guard, as was thought at the time, or was engineered by police in an effort to discredit the movement has been debated.[25] Woken early in the morning, and enticed outside by men pretending to be police, Garden warded off his attackers by calling for his sons to bring his gun and letting loose the family Airedale terrier.[26]

◆

Given that one of the fundamental guarantees of a liberal democratic society is the monopoly of force by the elected government, the paramilitary forces of the Depression years have inspired considerable controversy. One commonly debated question—as with the citizens' movements—is the degree to which they were fascist. There is no simple answer, since, as we have seen, fascism is an elusive concept. Certainly the paramilitary movements displayed certain elements that distinguished European fascist movements of the 1930s: rabid anti-communism; intense nationalism; a sense of being a united body of loyal citizens threatened by hostile influences in their midst; and, in the case of the New Guard, a cult of violence. Many members flirted with illiberal ideas and saw the solution to Australia's problems as 'strong government', possibly under an authoritarian leader. But neither the White Army nor the Old Guard saw their role as seizing power for themselves by unconstitutional means. Rather, they saw themselves as adjuncts to conservative power. The director of the Commonwealth Investigation Branch, Major H.E. Jones, described the Old Guard in 1932 as 'loyal and highly influential citizens upon whom we have to rely on in an emergency'.[27]

The character of the New Guard is more ambiguous. In boasting that it would unseat a democratically elected premier, Lang, the movement was inherently unconstitutional. It has commonly been described as 'fascist', 'semi-fascist' or 'fascist in inspiration'.[28] This was not just because of its public style, such as its violent attacks on left-wing meetings, and the use of uniform and the Nazi-style salute at rallies. Campbell also claimed to be a 'fascist'—although rather confusingly he explained that this was because he was a democrat who believed in 'government by the general will'.[29] In 1933 he met fascist leaders in Europe and the following year made the case for fascism and Mussolini's corporate state in a publication, *The New Road*.[30] If Campbell had authoritarian inclinations, however, he did not speak for the whole of the movement, and his orientation towards European fascism was more marked after the decline of the New Guard than when the movement was at its apogee in 1931. Moreover, for all its professed willingness to use whatever means might be necessary to unseat Lang, the New Guard never articulated coherent plans to radically restructure Australian society or to overthrow traditional power elites.

Significantly, nothing came of the plans in any of the paramilitary movements to install a national leader with emergency powers that transcended the rule of law. At times Monash was suggested for this role. One 'Old Digger' wrote to *The Bulletin*, 'General Monash is one of the greatest organizers the world has ever seen, and with the advice of financiers, backed up by drum-head court martials, he would save Australia within three years.' The Western Australian Liberation League (who liked to be known as Blackshirts) also called on Monash and 5000 ex-servicemen to seize power in Canberra.[31] But Monash himself would have none of it. As he wrote to Major General Harold Grimwade, a wartime colleague and commander of the 4th Division Australian Military Forces from 1926 to 1930: 'If ever the time should come that an English-speaking community alters its system of government and abandons the present democracy, I feel convinced that this would come about by constitutional means and not by the methods of violence so familiar in Latin countries.' When approached by three prominent businessmen to establish himself as a national leader, Monash declared that he had no ambition to 'embark on High Treason', usurping parliamentary power and upsetting the Constitution.

> What would you say if a similar proposal were made by the Communists and Socialists to seize power for the benefit of the proletariat and the extinction of the bourgeoisie, as they have done in Russia? Would you not call that Revolution and Treason to the Crown and the Constitution? Depend upon it, the only hope for Australia is the ballot-box and an educated electorate.[32]

If historians have struggled to classify the conservative paramilitary movements, the labour movement of the day had no doubt that the New Guard, at least, was 'fascist' or 'semi-fascistic'.[33] They mobilised their own forces against the class enemy. For the most part, the trade unions continued to work within established democratic practices, the ACTU conducting interminable debates, not about arming the workers but about passing resolutions, drafting amendments to resolutions and forming deputations to political leaders.[34]

But the strike battles of the late 1920s had spawned a Labor Defence Corps on the mine fields, and in March–April 1931, the New South Wales labour movement created the Australian Labor Army (ALA). Holding a major demonstration in Sydney's Domain, conducting drills on Sydney's north shore, and convening meetings in country towns such as Newcastle, within a few weeks it claimed to have a membership across the state of 40,000 and a Women's Auxiliary.[35] The members of the ALA seem, however, never to have been equipped with anything more menacing that the army's badge, a red star on a white background.

The Communist Party, for its part, created its own proto-military force, the Workers' Defence Corps (WDC).[36] Active during the 1929 lockout on the Hunter Valley coalfields and the timber strike of the same year, this force was revived in 1931. It was organised around secret cells, with hierarchical layers of command operating at district and state levels. Later, it would adopt a more flexible guerrilla-style mode of operation, with units as small as eight men. Among the Sydney ranks of the WDC were men with impressive radical credentials: one was of Irish descent 'well versed in the traditions of the republican army', while another boasted a decades-long association with Russian anarchism.[37] In preparation for armed clashes, the WDC accumulated stolen weapons: police revolvers, truncheons and poles; and ammunition pilfered from militia depots. According to an undercover police officer who infiltrated the WDC, it had plans to rob banks, shoot or bash the police, torch the houses of rich landlords evicting tenants, seize Bunnerong Power Station (then in Matraville, Sydney) and even to 'pop off' Lang and Garden. Though Garden was a former communist, and under attack from the New Guard, he was seen as an apostate because of his support for Lang.[38]

Yet for all its big talk, the WDC operated in a defensive manner. Its main aim was to provide protection for pickets at dole and other strikes, and to support speakers and demonstrators that were under public attack. Like the UWM, it also came to the aid of Australians resisting eviction. On one notable occasion, during the Bankstown riots of February 1932 (see Chapter 27) the WDC fought off a motorised column of the New Guard. But rarely, if ever, did it seek out set-piece battles with the Old or

New Guards. Like the Communist Party itself, it remained 'defiant rather than insurrectionary'.[39]

Indeed, the capacity for left-wing mobilisation was constrained by the vulnerability of the Communist Party of Australia itself. Though a monstrous bogey in conservative nightmares, the CPA was tiny.[40] It had perhaps at most 2000 members in December 1931. Many of its members were probably 'on paper only'. From this small base the party reached out to the masses by running a stable of newspapers and establishing several 'fraternal' organisations, or 'fronts', of which the WDC and the UWM were two. An agrarian section encouraged farmers to fight foreclosures and resumptions by banks, while the Militant Minority Movement (MMM) established cells within unions and factory committees encouraging workers (usually employed) to engage in collective action, as opposed to relying on arbitration. The Pastoral Workers' Industrial Union, a rival to the AWU, which led a strike by pastoral workers against wage reductions in 1930, was an example of its work.[41]

The liability of the CPA's small size was compounded when it shunned collaboration with moderate labour socialists and trade union leaders. Under the prevailing 'Third Period' doctrine espoused by Stalin, these members of the labour movement were castigated as 'social fascists': agents of a barren parliamentarianism and an obstruction to the revolutionary consciousness of the working class. This doctrine, which would catastrophically divide the left-wing opposition to Nazism in Germany, led Australian communists to denounce Trade Hall officials as 'vermin doing the bosses work'.[42] Hence rather than pooling resources to maximum benefit, the CPA competed with other agencies assisting the unemployed, and alienated even the few left-wing unions, such as the Australian Railways Union, that had previously given them some support. The ALP, in turn, forbade any of its members from being associated with the UWM, while members of the MMM were often sacked, frequently with the collusion of trade union officials. The CPA, meanwhile, had virtually no electoral base. In the federal election of 1931, the best vote the communists could muster was 2.32 per cent in Queensland.[43]

The CPA increasingly functioned as a closed elite, focused inwards. Countless hours were spent in a penitential self-criticism and 'cleansing' of its ranks. Who was guilty of infractions of party discipline or lax performance? Some sections had more expulsions than recruitments. Fearing infiltration by government agents, party members also became obsessed with secrecy—using pseudonyms, changing meeting venues frequently, and discouraging casual conversations among members. They had reason to be paranoid. The police and many within the political elites might have supported, or turned a blind eye to, the mobilisation of the right, but they devoted huge efforts to silencing communism and other left-wing activism. In Melbourne and Sydney, several municipal councils denied radical groups the use of council facilities for meetings. Forced into public spaces, the communists were then refused permission to hold street meetings.[44] In the country, suspected subversives were given a deadline by which they must leave town.[45] The police intervened only when this illegal action seemed likely to turn into lynching.[46] State and federal governments also invoked a variety of offences—unlawful assembly, loitering, offensive behaviour, insulting police, resisting arrest, vagrancy, possession of 'weapons and documents'—to arrest communists and other demonstrators.

By the end of 1930, many of the CPA's national leaders were in gaol. But the repression did not ease. Branches of the party were infiltrated by police spies and placed under surveillance by the Investigation Branch of the Commonwealth Attorney-General's Department. The Victorian police—the commissioner, Blamey, it will be recalled, was prominent in the White Army—established special squads to investigate communist activities and public gatherings of the radical unemployed. Leaving 'a trail of broken heads and bruised bodies' around Melbourne, they raided the communist hall, the Matteotti Club (named after the Italian anti-fascist) and the speakers' forum at the Yarra Bank. They broke up 'unauthorised' marches and meetings of the UWM.[47] On 6 April 1932, the Victorian police clashed with a procession of unemployed proceeding along Flinders Street to join a demonstration of the UWM and the CUC scheduled to coincide with the opening of the parliamentary session. After a brawl, several of the demonstrators were admitted to hospital.

The following month, the federal government amended the *Commonwealth Crimes Act*, making it an offence to provide assistance to any association defined as 'unlawful' by the High Court or the Supreme Court of a state. Property owners were deterred from renting premises or meeting venues to communists. The publications of the CPA were progressively censored or banned, as was postal transmission of their materials. The threat of deportation hung over naturalised Australians who fell foul of this or other legislation. Several public employees who visited Russia as delegates of the Friends of the Soviet Union were sacked on their return.[48]

Few incidents captured the escalating cat-and-mouse game between the authorities and communists more dramatically than the public speech made by the young communist and artist Noel Counihan in Phoenix Street, Brunswick, Melbourne, in May 1933.[49] This lane was a traditional site for public meetings, especially on Friday nights when shoppers were out late. Blamey, however, was determined to muzzle this activity. Denied the extensive powers that he asked for from the Victorian government, he invoked the obstruction clause of the *Traffic Act*. Supposedly, public speaking in Phoenix Street constituted a 'potential' obstruction, even though it was a dead end down which cars rarely drove. Over 1932–33, a succession of speakers were arrested and fined at this site: not just communists but also trade unionists and ALP politicians, including the sometime acting premier Tom Tunnecliffe. Finally, on 19 May, Counihan outwitted the police by being smuggled into Phoenix Street inside a steel mesh cage bolted onto a wagon. Police were distracted as this happened by a decoy, 'Shorty' Patullo, who delivered a speech on the top of a tram, only to be chased by police up a side street where he was shot in the thigh. Counihan all the while gave a 25-minute speech, as the police used an improvised battering ram to try to smash the cage in which he stood. The assembled crowd joined the affray, counting down the police and chanting, 'Out you bastards. Out!' Eventually, Counihan surrendered and was fined, though he successfully appealed against this. Patullo was also fined and gaoled for a month.

The issue of free speech that Phoenix Street enshrined was important not only to communists like Counihan. A crescendo of opposition from the trade unions and Freedom of Speech leagues forced the Victorian government to rein in the police. Over Blamey's protests, a new *Street Meetings Act* was passed in August 1933 giving protesters in the streets protection from conviction if they were not causing 'undue obstruction' given 'the amount of traffic which was actually at the time on the footpath, street or road'.[50] It was a significant concession from the state, and a statue in Sydney Road, Brunswick, now marks the victory for the people—not that the casual passer-by would readily identify it as such. It is a bell-shaped cage, draped in a cloth, with a bird perched on top, seemingly ready to fly.

Given the powerful forces aligned against the radical left, and especially against the CPA, it might be asked whether communism really posed the threat the right-wing militia claimed. Was the communist bogey inflated in order to justify a conservative mobilisation? Was the response to communism 'an over-reaction touched by paranoia' or a 'steam roller being used to crack a nut'?[51] Again, there is no simple answer. The definition of what constitutes a threat is always socially constructed, and social or political groups may be perceived as a threat when objectively they are not. Hence, while it seems clear today that the minuscule CPA had no chance of mounting a revolution and overthrowing capitalism, conservative Australians saw it differently. Lenin, after all, had managed to seize control of a whole country from a minority position in Petrograd. Moreover, the CPA spoke the language of revolution and sabotage, for example, in suggesting they might attack the power supply of Adelaide or provoke a general uprising in Broken Hill. They also openly sought to wrest control of the trade unions from more moderate elements of the labour movement—a strategy that alarmed Labor politicians as much as it did conservatives, and that began to bear more fruit in the late 1930s.

The question that we should probably ask is not whether the threat from the communists was 'real', imagined or exaggerated: but why the invocation of the communist 'threat' motivated so many conservative Australians to action. Almost certainly it was because of the tendency of communities in crisis to create social outcasts as a means of reinforcing their internal cohesion: 'Never do the members of a community feel closer to each other than when called to face a common threat to their shared values.'[52] In any society, the definition of a threat also reveals who has the power to assert their values and to punish those who do not subscribe to them. Thus the demonising of communism during the Depression years in Australia was an assertion of power by traditional conservatism, an assertion that defused radical movements on the right as well as the left in 1931. The transference of blame and anger onto communists enabled 'the group to continue to function'.[53]

The ethics of such scapegoating might be troubling. Yet for all their anti-democratic potential, the paramilitary movements ultimately inflicted relatively little damage on the fabric of Australian political life. Yes, the New Guard burned Union Jacks and the Red Flag, fought to control public space, and clashed with the radical left at rallies. But this level of violence was qualitatively different from that inflicted upon German society by Nazi and communist paramilitary movements in the death throes of democratic government. In *only ten days* in July 1932, the Prussian authorities reported more than 300 acts of political violence in which 24 people were killed and almost 300 injured.[54] Australia endured no such systematic onslaught on law and order. It is telling that the act for which the New Guard was, and remains, most famous was pure theatre. On 19 March 1932, Francis de Groot, a Dublin-born antique dealer and senior member of the New Guard Council of Action, upstaged Lang at the opening of the Sydney Harbour Bridge by charging in on horseback and cutting the ribbon before the premier could do so (see Chapter 32).

We will never know if the conservative movements would have taken up arms had Lang continued unchecked on his path of repudiation and had the more radical elements of Labor triumphed in the federal policy debates. There is some evidence—albeit to be treated with considerable scepticism—that the New Guard was poised to launch a coup and even contemplated kidnapping Lang and his cabinet in the first months of 1932.[55] But the radical right did not need to act. In mid-1931, Scullin bowed to the forces demanding deflation and agreed to the Premiers' Plan. Six months later, he was removed from power by a democratic election. In May 1932, Lang also was brought down, in his case by the exercise of vice-regal power. Force was never needed, and without their energising bête noire in the form of Lang, the paramilitary movements gradually faded away.

CHAPTER 23

In office but not in power

While citizens' protests were erupting in the first months of 1931, the battle of the plans continued at the national level. From February to May 1931, Scullin and Theodore did all they could to get control of the policy agenda: managing Australia's debts in London, dealing with the fallout of Lang's new embrace of repudiation, and trying to secure parliamentary support for injecting the economy with a monetary stimulus. But the opposition of Gibson, the banking sector, the state premiers and the Nationalist majority in the Senate proved insurmountable. With default on Australia's debts excluded as a policy option, and the Commonwealth Bank dictating monetary policy, the federal government concluded that it had no choice but to compromise and bow to the forces demanding retrenchment and deflation.

No sooner had the premiers' conference in late February ended than Lang began to make good on his threat to reduce or default on interest payments. First, the New South Wales Treasury asked its Commonwealth counterpart for funding to the tune of nearly £750,000, for the purposes of covering interest commitments or capital repayments. But the Loan Council, on which the other states were represented, refused to give any assistance until such time as Lang guaranteed that he would honour his state's interest obligations.[1] Undeterred, Lang, buoyed by the East Sydney by-election on

15 March, defaulted on the interest due to the Commonwealth on advances made for closer settlement. Two days later, he introduced legislation reducing the interest payable to bondholders in New South Wales to 3 per cent. When the bill was rejected by the Legislative Council on 25 March, Lang told Scullin that his state would not be able to meet the interest owing to Westminster Bank and the Bank of England on 1 April. His logic? If he remitted this money to overseas bondholders, an equivalent amount of credit would be withdrawn from primary and secondary producers. Moreover, Lang claimed—erroneously—that the foreign loans Australia had taken out imposed an obligation on the lenders to buy 'exported' goods at 'reasonable prices': 'our creditors', he told a lunch gathering of the Royal Agricultural Society on 1 April, 'have failed in their duty to buy the products at [such] prices'.[2]

No one was certain what the legal responsibilities of the Commonwealth government were for debts owed by the states. But the consensus of opinion was that Canberra had to pay. With the approval of the other five states, Scullin authorised the payment of New South Wales' interest bill. When the news broke in London, the House of Commons erupted in cheers.[3] The Secretary of State for the Dominions, James Thomas, called Scullin to congratulate him.[4] The stock market, too, responded favourably, and the *Financial Times*, while cautioning against Theodore's 'unsound inflation plan', welcomed the restoration of confidence in Australian affairs.[5]

While meeting the obligations of New South Wales, the federal government also scrambled to manage short-term debts in London. In early March, some £5 million of Treasury bills matured. Given Australia's low credit standing, the Commonwealth Bank had no choice but to pay them off in order to avoid default. This meant, however, that the bank ate further into its dwindling sterling reserves. The amount of gold it now held was depleted to the point where it was close to the minimum legal requirement to underpin the note issue. Theodore thus added to his already contentious legislative agenda a bill to abolish the statutory gold reserve and secure greater control over gold for the government (see below).

With these actions the Scullin government made emphatic its rejection of the Lang Plan. Any form of default on Australia's external debts was not a policy option it was prepared to consider. It is worth asking why.

During the Great Depression, many other countries sought readjustments to their servicing of their external borrowings. All but four Latin American countries—Argentina, Honduras, Haiti and the Dominican Republic—defaulted on their borrowings, particularly from US banks, in the early 1930s.[6] Germany, too, in the summer of 1933 declared a moratorium on the transfer of interest payments, thus triggering another tortured renegotiation of its war-related debts. It is, of course, perilous to make comparisons between different countries' indebtedness. To paraphrase Leo Tolstoy, each debtor country is unhappy in its own way. But Scullin's reluctance to try to negotiate some form of deferral or reduction in interest payments is striking. If he had suspended interest payments, it has been estimated, about £36 million a year would have been released to be spent internally on unemployment relief, while easing the pressure on other government expenditure. Perhaps one-half of the unemployed might have been absorbed by this means. Instead, Scullin let the City of London 'dictate the rules of the game'.[7]

Presumably Scullin believed that the impact of default on Australia's credit rating would be intolerable. Not only would he have found it virtually impossible to win the support of the local banking sector, but the prospects of further government borrowing in London would also have been severely damaged, perhaps for an indefinite period. Foreign investment in the private sector might also have been seriously undermined. In all likelihood, too, the Australian pound would have lost further value. There might have been a run on the currency. Australian assets in London might also have been frozen, or imports from Australia to the United Kingdom blocked. In retrospect, it also seems that if Australia had defaulted it would have struggled to negotiate the favourable trade terms it secured at the Ottawa Imperial Conference of 1932. Yet how real was the risk of sanctions from the United Kingdom? No matter how querulous the London banks, some in that city had sympathy for the members of the empire who had been devastated by the collapse of global trade in primary commodities. Keynes told Prime Minister Ramsay MacDonald in 1930 that it was in Britain's interests to increase 'world trade as a whole':

I hope that we shall stretch a point if necessary to help Australia out of her difficulties . . . She has perhaps learnt her lesson. In any case a time when wool and her exports generally are at these disastrous prices is not a time to choose for pressing her too hard. She ought to send us some more gold—say £10,000,000 to £15,000,000—to help with *our* problems. Subject to that we ought to meet her necessities.

In September 1931, Keynes also suggested that, as a partial solution to the international debt problem, Britain 'might take shipments of goods, reckoned at more reasonable prices (say 25 per cent higher) than present world prices, from such countries as India, Australia, Canada, Argentina, Germany, etc., the proceeds to be credited against the interest dues of these countries in London'.[8]

The reluctance of the Scullin government to consider default can only be explained if we look beyond the pragmatic to the emotional. As the horror that Lang generated in conservative circles indicates, 'repudiation', no matter how modest, violated the powerful contemporary value of honour. The Melbourne *Age* declared on 30 March 1931:

Australia is feeling as would any decent family if it woke some morning to discover that one member had brought upon it disgrace. It hurts terribly . . . Our Australian nation was founded by self-reliant, self-respecting men. The record for sterling honesty which they set up their sons have regarded with pride, and have sought to maintain. Last week that record was besmirched and for all time the name of J.T. Lang will be associated with the despicable work . . . A generation will not serve to wipe out the stain . . . Whatever his other political creed the duty of every Australian is now to stand loyally together in a common antagonism to the defaulter.[9]

Scullin himself was greeted with 'a storm of clapping' when he told the same Royal Agricultural Society luncheon that Lang addressed on 1 April, 'If we dishonour our bond to Great Britain—our best customer—we would not only dishonour our nation, but we would destroy our market. Our national loss would be greater, and poverty and misery would increase.' Lang, in contrast, was met with a 'cold but respectful silence'.[10] Likewise, a manifesto in May 1931 by Adelaide church leaders (including the Roman Catholic archbishop) read:

We are concerned with the moral and spiritual issues, as distinct from the political issues, involved in the actions of some of our responsible Governments at this time. The avowal of repudiation [of debts], the gross lowering of moral standards of Parliamentary and public life, and the recall of the Commonwealth Treasurer [Theodore] (whether he be innocent or guilty) . . . constrain us to appeal to our fellow-citizens for loyalty to those moral principles which are the only basis of true nationhood.[11]

Even *Labor Call* accepted that while the blame for Australia's crisis lay with non-Labor governments and the banks,

The contracts have been made and the conditions must be observed. The success of social life depends upon people's goodwill and confidence . . . Even though sharp practices have been the order of the day, and the way is hard and the cost is great, it always pays to be strictly honorable in our dealings with one another, either individually or collectively . . . Labor will always honour Australia's obligations, even though it has been tricked into being committed to them.[12]

As with the issue of preference for returned soldiers, then, 'honour' proved once more to be powerful trope. It had an additional emotional power so far as repudiation was concerned because it resonated with that other dominant value, 'loyalty'. Australia's debts, after all, were owed to the 'Mother Country'. In the chaos of the Depression, Australians were in no state of mind to contemplate rupturing the imperial networks on which white Australians had depended since 1788. On the contrary, as international trade collapsed, capital supplies were ruptured and the parity between the Australian and British pound was lost, national solvency must have seemed 'the last remaining anchor'.[13]

If default was not a policy option, Scullin was now prepared to back Theodore's plan, and from late March 1931 the treasurer tried to push through a raft of enabling legislation. The centrepiece was the Fiduciary Notes Bill, whereby

the money supply would be increased. A further Bank Interest Bill would empower the treasurer, acting on the advice of a newly created Bank Interest Board, to vary the rates of bank interest and discounts. Theodore presented his controversial economic plan to Parliament on 17 March. Australia, he argued, needed a new monetary policy. The Fiduciary Notes Bill, he explained, would allow the issuing of some £18 million in Treasury notes of which £6 million would be used for the relief of wheat farmers and £12 million for the immediate creation of employment through reproductive works. With some 40,000 men employed, their increased purchasing power would stimulate demand in industry. To those anxious about the confidence in such currency—and Theodore conceded that the banks viewed the proposal with 'hostility'—he said that the convertibility of the Australian pound into gold was already an illusion. Yet this had not shaken the trust of the public in the Australian currency. Neither would the proposed fiduciary notes issue do this, since it would be backed by the intrinsic wealth of the country.

Theodore conceded that there was some risk of inflation, but this could be controlled. It need not cause mayhem as it had in Germany because the government there had resorted to inflation as a means of relieving the country of the 'tremendous and crushing obligations' of reparations. In France, there had been 'a certain measure of inflation' but this had not destroyed the currency. On the contrary, France's current financial position was better than any other European country. The Opposition might think that Theodore's plan was 'wholly unorthodox . . . an experiment in the realm of the dangerous', but England had operated a form of fiduciary currency for many years under the management of the Bank of England within the framework of the British *Currency and Banknotes Act 1928*. Moreover, Theodore claimed, somewhat speciously, many of Australia's leading economists—Copland, Dyason and Giblin—had recommended in the past 'almost everything that the Government has been contending for'. So, too, had various international experts. Theodore cited Keynes to the effect that 'if wages are cut all round, the purchasing power of the community as a whole is reduced by the same amount as the reduction of costs; and . . . no one is further forward'. He even held aloft a copy of Keynes' *Treatise on Money*. Supposedly, this was the first copy of this work in Australia, sent at Theodore's request from London soon after its publication.[14] Though this book would not register in academic discussion until the second half of 1931, and most reviews did not appear until 1933, Theodore now declaimed, 'It will stand for fifty years as a guide to the intellects of the nations on this subject.' Finally, Theodore turned on the banks:

> They may take the stand that in the matter of monetary policy they and not the Government are to decide . . . But, I ask, is that the correct attitude? Is it sound that in so vital a matter the affairs of the nation should be left to a handful of bankers in the community—that they alone should assert control and influence in such a matter, and that governments and parliaments can be pushed aside and dictated to in regard to it?[15]

Theodore's speech was a tour de force that seemed, to judge by the interjections, to be beyond the understanding of many of the Opposition. But as Theodore's parting shot indicated, his plan for a fiduciary notes issue met with the implacable opposition of the banking sector—and even some of the economists he cited. The National Bank spoke of the treasurer's 'quack remedies and stimulants'. Its director, Sir Ernest Wreford, said that 'Australia was financially sick, and will not get well by drinking the financial champagne of further borrowing or note inflation.' Davidson considered the theories of many in the Labor caucus in Canberra in relation to money, credit and banking to be 'extraordinary'. Collectively, the banks financed the mass circulation of a pamphlet by Archibald Grenfell Price, an Adelaide polymath, called *The Menace of Inflation*. It had the endorsement of the economists Shann and Melville. [16] Copland and Giblin also distanced themselves from Theodore's ideas, Copland arguing that they would destroy confidence and lead to a flight of capital. As he saw it, Theodore's plans did not address the fundamental problem of the unfavourable relationship between export prices and domestic costs and the need for substantial expenditure cuts, including wage cuts (a point he had already made in the January Arbitration Court case).[17] Giblin used one of his John Smith commentaries in the *Herald* to attack the 'foolishness' of printing notes or releasing credits. The only solution, he argued, to 'an outside problem which is causing an inside problem' was an interim cut in real wages. Giblin conceded privately that while Theodore's plan was intrinsically 'reasonable and sensible', it was at odds with the dominant psychological mood.[18] The only one of the leading economists who supported Theodore's plan was Irvine, ever the dissident.

By far the most important of Theodore's critics was Gibson. On 11 March, Theodore had written to the Commonwealth Bank accusing it of providing some £900,000 to banks in South Australia and Western Australia for the relief of farmers—even though it had rejected an earlier request from the Loan Council for £6 million for that very same purpose! Theodore now demanded that the bank make £3.5 million available to the Commonwealth to assist farmers, and provide a further million for the relief of unemployment. At the same time, Theodore pushed ahead, without Gibson's approval, with the preparation of the legislation for the abolition of the statutory gold reserve, introducing on 24 March a bill that would allow the treasurer to dispose of the gold reserve to the amount needed to cover Australia's debts in London.

The confrontation came to a head when on 2 April Gibson refused to provide the funds that Theodore requested, and furthermore delivered an ultimatum to the Loan Council. Given that governments had failed to check the drift in their finances, Gibson warned a point was being reached 'beyond which it would be impossible for the [Commonwealth] Bank to provide further financial assistance for the Government in the future'. Moreover, the bank had decided on a limit of £25 million of Treasury bills and overdraft finance within Australia, and since the finance already provided by the bank amounted to £18 million, only £6.8 million would be available for deficit service. Under the existing rates of expenditure, this would cover about two months.

Scullin and Theodore brooded over their reply for the best part of a fortnight. Then, on 15 April, Theodore delivered a broadside. Gibson's latest communication, he claimed, was 'an attempt on the part of the Bank to arrogate to itself a supremacy over the Government in the determination of the financial policy of the Commonwealth, a supremacy which, I am sure, was never contemplated by the framers of the Australian Constitution, and has never been sanctioned by the Australian people'. There was no possibility, Theodore explained, of Australia's governments reducing their expenditure quickly enough to balance their budgets before the bank's limit for deficit funding was reached. Thus all governments would be forced by the bank's attitude to default in their contractual obligations. He conceded that the banks were not responsible for the decline in national income and prices, but they had aggravated the situation by blindly following the overseas banks into a policy of contraction. The government knew that Australia needed to reduce costs, but economy alone could not achieve budget equilibrium or commercial prosperity. A fundamental change in monetary policy was required to restore internal prices and commercial activity. Hence the government intended to proceed with its parliamentary program.[19]

It was a remarkable situation. The government and the Commonwealth Bank had irreconcilable positions on monetary policy. Each claimed the right to determine it. The problem was that in 1931 there was no machinery for resolving this impasse in the government's favour. Some years later, in 1937, a banking royal commission would recommend that, in the event of an irreconcilable conflict between the federal government and the bank as to what was in the nation's best interests, the government should take responsibility for the proposed policy. The bank should see it as its duty to accept and implement policy.[20] This principle was enshrined in legislation when the Labor government of Ben Chifley passed the *Commonwealth Bank Act* in 1945. It was further affirmed when the Reserve Bank of Australia was created in 1959, separating the trading and savings bank functions of the Commonwealth Bank from its role as a central bank. While the independence of the Reserve Bank from the political process in the operation of monetary policy was confirmed, it was established that if there was an irreconcilable difference, the government had primacy—on the condition that it present to Parliament the reasons for its disagreement with the Reserve Bank.[21] This provision has never been invoked. Disagreements between governments and the Reserve Bank triggered some discussion about invoking clause 11 in later decades, but in the event, one side or the other backed off.[22]

In the midst of this policy wrangling, a major Australian bank was forced to close its doors. The Government Savings Bank of New South Wales was one of the largest savings banks in Australia. With 189 branches and more than a million accounts, it managed the savings of many small depositors while offering loans for home mortgages, farming development and small businesses.[23] With the onset of the Depression the bank, like other financial institutions, lost funds as people facing unemployment and wage cuts drew on their savings. But it was the political battles in New South Wales that triggered a crisis. Lang's anti-bank rhetoric during the election campaign in October 1930 led to a sharp fall in deposits. So, too, did the equally irresponsible claims by the Opposition that Lang, if elected, would commandeer the banks' funds to finance his expansionary policies.[24] Withdrawals continued to grow during the loan conversion campaign of December 1930 as anxious depositors sought safety in alternative forms of investment.

The situation stabilised for a brief time, but then in February 1931 Lang released his sensational plan. Moreover, during the East Sydney by-election, Bavin quoted Theodore as predicting a run on the bank, and Lang introduced his bill to reduce the rate of interest paid on government securities. When Lang finally defaulted on interest owed to British lenders on 1 April, withdrawals again surged. Double-page press advertisements reassuring the public that their money had the backing of all the assets of the government of New South Wales seemed only to fuel the anxiety. With the bank's cash reserves exhausted, Lang announced on 21 April that the Government Savings Bank might amalgamate with the Commonwealth Savings Bank. Unfortunately, the Commonwealth Bank's public response was non-committal.[25] Not only did Gibson distrust Lang's 'political insanity' but the Commonwealth Bank also had no experience in acting as a lender of last resort for a bank that had a crisis of liquidity rather than insolvency. The run on the New South Wales Savings Bank accelerated on 22 April until the bank suspended payments.[26]

Few things cause greater anxiety for the public than a bank failure. For many Australians their deposits in a bank represented not just personal financial security. Saving was a civic virtue, a testament to their capacity for self-denial, thrift and their willingness to contribute to the national welfare.[27] As the *Canberra Times* reminded its readers: 'among the vast number of depositors, exceeding one million in number excluding accounts of small amounts, there are the pennies and sixpences of nearly 140,000 schoolchildren. These children will long remember why they can neither add to or withdraw their savings accounts today.'[28]

Thus, even though the New South Wales parliament quickly approved the amalgamation of the failing bank with the Commonwealth Savings Bank, the news that bank funds were being frozen sparked a further run, this time on the Commonwealth Savings Bank. On 2 May, queues stretched from the crowded chamber of the bank in Castlereagh Street some 27 metres along the footpath. Most of the anxious crowd were women, and their numbers were so great that the bank had to extend its opening hours.[29] Yet, importantly, the panic about banks did not spread more widely. On 4 May, Gibson went on radio to assure Australians that the Commonwealth Bank was in the 'strongest possible position' and would 'never close its doors so long as the nation itself stands'.[30] With his Scottish accent and claim to official authority, he conveyed a calming image of frugality and practicality. In the days that followed, depositors who desperately needed cash were given limited access to their funds. It would be months before the amalgamation between the collapsed bank and the Commonwealth Bank was finally completed, but the depositors' money was secure.

Only two other small trading banks failed in Australia during the 1930s. One, the Primary Producers' Bank of Australia, accounted for less than 0.5 per cent of Australian bank deposits. When wound up, it was able to almost fully pay out its customers, most of whom were farmers. The second, the Federal Deposit Bank, was more of a building society and accounted for 0.2 per cent of Australian bank deposits. Once it was taken over by another financial institution, its depositors were paid in full in instalments over a number of years.[31] Australia's banking system thus proved itself more robust than during the 1890s depression, when more than half the trading banks of note issue suspended payment and a large number of non-bank financial institutions failed.[32]

Australians, then, did not experience the disastrous collapse of banks that afflicted the United States during the Great Depression (see Chapter 8). The Australian banking system was oligopolistic in structure. Thanks to a period of consolidation after 1917, there were only nine trading banks (excluding

the Commonwealth Bank) of any size in the early 1930s. After further amal-
gamations in 1931, only three large savings banks remained. This prevented
the scenario in which a large number of potentially weaker banks brought the
whole system into jeopardy. Moreover, the Australian banks were less exposed
to risk in the years before the Great Depression than they had been during the
speculative boom of the 1880s. For a variety of reasons they chose to maintain
a high level of reserve ratios (that is, the proportion of customers' deposits
that they held as reserves in the form of cash rather than lending out). The
standard was around 20 per cent in Australia compared with 8–9 per cent
in the United States in the late 1920s.[33] While this had the effect of reducing
the supply of money in the community, it also served to contain the banks'
exposure to liquidity risks and insolvency.

Politics, as German chancellor Otto von Bismarck famously put it, is 'the art
of the possible, the attainable—the art of the next best'. The US economist
and intellectual J.K. Galbraith later modified this: 'Politics is not the art of
the possible . . . It consists in choosing between the disastrous and the unpal-
atable.' By May 1931, Theodore and Scullin, for all their frustration, had no
choice but to accept this. They could not make Gibson budge. The Nationalist majority in the Senate stood like some modern-day Cerberus at the gates
of what they saw as the Hades of reforming legislation. There was no chance
of the upper house approving the fiduciary notes issue legislation, which
was the only hope of Theodore's monetary expansion. Finally, the premiers
were not willing to support the Commonwealth's stand. This became clear
at a Loan Council meeting at the end of April. With Gibson attending one
of its sitting days, and Lang absent, the council agreed it should try again to
devise an economic plan that would receive general support. It established
a subcommittee of three premiers to consult with economists and report
on what further action should be taken. Somewhat remarkably—or was it a
gesture of defeat?—the federal government refused to take part.

With this, the Theodore Plan effectively collapsed. Even the vestige of
the plan to which the premiers agreed, an internal loan to assist the wheat
industry and relieve unemployment, failed to eventuate. Gibson, as ever,

stalled in his negotiations with the trading banks to underwrite the loan. Soon this proposal would be overtaken by the compromise agreement of June 1931 on which all parties, including the federal government, finally reached consensus: the Premiers' Plan.

CHAPTER 24

The Premiers' Plan

The Premiers' Plan was a compromise, not just between the warring politicians and the Commonwealth Bank, but also between the economists who were called upon to play a major role in shaping the policy recommendations. Since it was essentially deflationary, the Premiers' Plan was hardly the outcome to the battle of the plans that Theodore wanted. The labour movement, too, saw the plan as a lamentable surrender to the forces of capitalism and 'sound finance'. But at least the plan could be sold to the electorate as enshrining the important value of 'equality of sacrifice'. Whether it set Australia on the road to economic recovery is debatable, but it provided the stability that had been manifestly absent from Australian policymaking in the first half of 1931.

The subcommittee that the Loan Council established in May to develop a plan did not include the federal government but it was at least bipartisan. That said, the Labor representative, South Australian Premier Hill, was hardly a man to provide radical advice. Noted for his vanity and vacillation, he told Theodore during the deliberations about the Premiers' Plan, 'I can't really make up my mind'—to which Theodore had snapped, 'You bloody old woman, you haven't got a mind to make up.'[1] The real intellectual work for the new plan was delegated to an advisory committee of economists: Copland, Giblin, Shann and Melville. This was the first time in Australian history that professionals outside the public service were drawn upon by government to such a degree.

If the plan was largely the work of these economists—and hence was sometimes called the Copland Plan—it was nevertheless shaped by an acute sensitivity as to what would be politically acceptable to the public, the banks and the Senate majority.[2] To ensure that the premiers, too, were on side, the economists' committee included the under-treasurers as well as Commonwealth Treasury officials.[3] The key goal of the plan was to restore budget equilibrium: that is, a situation where total revenue equalled total expenditure in a given financial year. But economists and politicians alike were concerned that the real loss of income as a result of the Depression had fallen unequally on different sections of Australian society. Now was the time to find remedies that shared the burden as equally as possible. The term, 'equality of sacrifice', of course, 'changed with every speaker who used it' and was something of an illusion, given that every Australian started from a different economic base.[4] A flat-rate percentage cut was inherently inequitable, since it had a more severe impact on those Australians who were on lower salaries or pensions.[5] Everyone agreed, however, that bondholders, public servants and pensioners, as well as wage-earners, had to make their contribution to national recovery.

The premiers convened on 25 May to consider the report of the subcommittee of economists. There was an air of expectation in the press. 'This conference is regarded as undoubtedly the most vital in the history of the Commonwealth,' a Perth newspaper stated. '[It] is expected to mark the turning point in Commonwealth Government policy, as five States have unanimously endorsed the plan of the sub-committee.'[6] The federal leaders, however, approached the conference with a good deal of scepticism. Theodore opened by arguing that the recommendations of the report went beyond the authority of the Loan Council. The states responded that 'if the Scullin Ministry was unwilling to accept the odium of making reductions so strongly recommended by the experts the only course open to it was to make way for an administration that would not shirk this duty'.[7] After this initial sparring, Scullin took the lead. It helped to defuse the emotionally charged atmosphere that the conference had access to detailed data and the budget estimates prepared by each of the states. During the conference, too, representatives of banks, insurance companies, stock exchanges and the legal profession were constantly in session, providing advice on any technical issues that arose.[8]

What finally emerged after three weeks of deliberations was an integrated package of measures, intended to be indivisible and to last for three years. First, it was agreed that all adjustable government expenditure—that is, wages, salaries and pensions, including war pensions—should be reduced by 20 per cent.[9] An exception was to be made for old-age pensions, which were to be cut by 12.5 per cent. Some discretion was also left to the state governments as to how to distribute the 20 per cent cut across income groups. Second, the internal debts of the governments would be converted on the basis of a 22.5 per cent reduction of interest. This included existing loans, which would be converted 'voluntarily'. Third, taxes would be increased by the states and the federal government. Fourth, rates of interest on deposits and advances would be reduced. Fifth, there should be relief for private mortgages. All these economies, it was estimated, while significantly reducing the budget deficits, would still leave a gap of £13 million to £15 million which would require some borrowing. How this would be arranged was a matter for the Loan Council and Commonwealth Bank to negotiate.[10]

Copland would later claim that the plan, for which he took much credit, charted a middle course between deflation and inflation.[11] On the whole, however, the package made for deflationary economics.[12] Most obviously, it excluded any notion of monetary expansion that had been at the heart of Theodore's recommendations. Nor did the plan have any explicit program to generate employment, which Scullin thought was 'a fundamental weakness'.[13] But despite their reservations, Scullin and Theodore accepted the Premiers' Plan and supported the necessary legislation as it passed through Parliament. This might be seen as a capitulation, but the harsh reality was, as one of Scullin's ministers Parker Moloney put it, that Labor was in office, not in power.[14] Throughout the premiers' conference Scullin was seen 'walking in short, nervous steps and always worried'.[15] He claimed that he would not have given the Premiers' Plan a minute's consideration if he had not thought that the alternative was default by the end of July. In that month, so he told Jack

Holloway, the government would be able to pay only twelve shillings in the pound (a pound comprised twenty shillings) for all its liabilities, including to bondholders, pensioners and public servants.[16]

Theoretically, the federal government could have gone to the voters. Theodore might have sent the Fiduciary Notes Bill back to the Senate, where it had already been rejected, and used the second veto to trigger a double dissolution. But this would have taken three months, by which time finance from the Commonwealth Bank might have been cut off. Moreover, the prospects of the ALP's winning any federal election were remote. The party was so divided that agreement on anything approaching a united national platform was impossible and its public support was clearly collapsing. On 9 May, the Nationalists won the Tasmanian state election in a landslide, with John McPhee campaigning for expenditure cuts over Labor's expansionary policies. Some in the labour movement thought that it would be better to relinquish national power than accept deflation, but moderates considered that it would be 'abhorrent to the workers and disastrous to the country' to hand the reins of power back to the Nationalists.[17]

The other compelling reason to accept the Premiers' Plan was that it broke the deadlock between the federal government, the Commonwealth Bank and the Nationalists. Lyons, Latham and the leader of the Opposition in the Senate, George Pearce, were incorporated into the discussions in the third week, hence the plan was guaranteed to get through Parliament. Gibson brought the trading and savings banks on side, even though some of them were uncomfortable with the intrusion of economists into the world of policy advice.[18] In fact, during the protracted stand-off over budget policy, the Commonwealth Bank had expanded credit significantly.[19] Furthermore, when Theodore abandoned the Fiduciary Notes Bill and the Bank Interest Reduction Bill, Gibson gave some ground on the matter of the gold reserve. On 17 June, the Commonwealth Bank Bill passed all stages in both houses. The statutory reserve was reduced to 15 per cent, although it was agreed that the former minimum reserve of 25 per cent would be restored over a period of four years. Enough gold was then able to be shipped to London to cover the Treasury bills maturing on 30 June. The Bank of England agreed to provide an advance while the shipment was on its way.

311

But—and it was a big 'but'—the premiers' consensus about the Premiers' Plan did not include Lang. His mood fluctuated from genial and cooperative to terse and sullen. As he saw it, neither economists nor Treasury officials should usurp the right of politicians to make economic policy. He would later call Copland a 'torchbearer for the Niemeyer Plan'.[20] Lang did eventually agree to sign up to the plan, but only on the condition that the conversion of the government loans should precede any cuts in government expenditure. Child welfare and widow's pensions should be exempt from any cuts.[21] In a flamboyant public gesture, Lang also proposed to reduce every person in his government's employ to a maximum salary of £500 per annum, thus protecting the lower-paid public servants. It would give him great pleasure, he told a press reporter, to go after the better-paid 'tall poppies'.[22]

In the wider community, the reaction to the Premiers' Plan was predictably mixed. Within the labour movement it widened the already yawning divisions. The Federal Labor Executive, the state ALP executives and the ACTU all opposed the cuts. Two federal ministers resigned from cabinet. Eventually, the majority of the federal caucus was brought around to supporting the plan, though not without a long debate stretching over two days.[23] When the necessary slate of legislation was being debated in Parliament, Anstey accused the government of 'crucifying the very people who raised its members from obscurity and placed them in power'.[24]

I know of no blow which is harder to bear than the blow of a friend, and of no stab which goes so deep as the stab from the hands of one's own companions. What would Christ have thought as He hung on the cross if the nails that pierced His hands and feet had been hammered in by His friends; if the sword that pierced His side had been driven by His friends; if the sponge of vinegar had been held to His lips by His friends? These things were done to Him not by His friends, but by His bitterest enemies.[25]

Curtin, too, when debating the bill to convert government loans, denounced the plan as being essentially the work of the Opposition: 'the Government is continuing to use the sword of office against the people who returned it to power.'[26]

I refuse to be guilty of what is worse than the surrender of a political faith. When a person surrenders, he gives up his sword, and ceases to be a combatant. But this Government has not surrendered its sword; it is continuing to use it and to use it against the interests of the very people in whose interests Ministers were put into power. I would not complain, even if pierced to the heart, if it were done in clean and open combat with the political sword of honorable members opposite; but I more than object to an assassin burying his dagger in my back, and a poisoned dagger at that. That was an action of which even Brutus was incapable.[27]

The labour press also viewed the pension cuts with 'invincible repugnance'. As the *Australian Worker* put it, this was 'scraping the butter off the bread of old age pensioners and war-broken veterans'.[28] None of the proposed cuts would 'dissipate' the depression afflicting Australia. They might balance budgets, but 'What is needed, before Australia can be saved, is greatly increased consumption of commodities. The people must be enabled to buy the goods with which the shops, warehouses and factories are now glutted.'[29] *Labor Call* was, as ever, more inclined to hyperbole. It refused to accept 'one of the greatest confidence tricks ever attempted by anti-Labor at the expense of the workers'. Any members of the caucus who supported this anti-Labor policy were in 'a state of fear or paralysing ignorance'. Alas, experience through the ages 'always has shown that the slave is as hard a taskmaster as he whom the slave has displaced, and whose whip he wields'.[30] Yet for all this outrage, a special conference of the party in late August grudgingly accepted the plan, albeit with some unhelpful qualifications.[31]

The reaction of business and financial interests to the Premiers' Plan was generally more positive. There seemed to be some revival in business confidence in Australia.[32] But some conservatives claimed that the reduction in interest rates was tantamount to repudiation. The Melbourne stockbroker Staniforth Ricketson, who was a member of the Group and honorary treasurer of the All for Australia League, declared that the plan 'outLangs Lang'. Menzies dubbed it 'the Lang Plan with hypocrisy'.[33] He claimed he would rather see every Australian citizen die of starvation than fail to honour contractual debts in their entirety. Some might have said that Menzies was not one to talk about starvation!

In the event, the conversion of the loans proceeded successfully in August 1931. As in December 1930, a mass public campaign was mounted, backed by the triad of Scullin, Lyons and Gibson, that embodied the new consensus. Australians once more were urged to suffer hardship and sacrifice in a 'test of national pride'.[34] This was, the press crowed, 'almost the greatest conversion in the history of the world' in which 'all will stand together'.[35] Again Australians trusted their savings to their government, even though they were receiving a lower return. Out of a total internal debt of £558 million, £541 million was voluntarily converted.[36] The small balance of the internal debt was later converted compulsorily, with some exemptions being allowed for cases of personal hardship or where people needed capital for pressing commitments.

In the all-important money market of London, meanwhile, the Premiers' Plan aroused some suspicions that Australia might try to reduce the interest paid on external debts as well as internal debts. Scullin, as ever, reassured London that Australia would meet its external obligations. This indeed was the purpose of the Premiers' Plan. This seemed to settle the unease and Australia gained a further reprieve when on 20 June the United States' Hoover administration announced a one-year moratorium on inter-governmental war debts. With its own repayments deferred, Britain agreed to suspend payments of principal on Australian debts for 1931–32. Still, now that Australia's sterling reserves were virtually non-existent, it again struggled to pay off its Treasury bills held by the Westminster Bank, due for renewal on 30 September. The long-suffering bank renewed them for three months.[37]

There was one notable exemption to the 'equality of sacrifice' mantra that infused the Premiers' Plan: the returned soldiers. Initially war pensions were to be included in the 20 per cent cut proposed by the plan. They were an obvious target for economies. The scheme had become fiendishly complex and expensive, with three main groups of Australians being beneficiaries: not just the men who had been left incapacitated by their war service, but also the wives, mothers and children of soldiers who had died as a result of the war, and the dependants of incapacitated men whose pensions were supplemented.[38] The rise in unemployment led to a surge in applications for support from Repatriation, although after 1930 the numbers then contracted, for some unknown reason.

The returned soldiers' lobby groups had been concerned about the vulnerability of their pensions for some time.[39] The RSSILA's indefatigable Dyett lobbied the premiers when they convened for their conference in May 1931, urging them 'not to touch soldiers' pensions until every other avenue of savings had been explored . . . war pensions should be considered sacrosanct as a natural corollary of the promises made by the people both during and subsequent to the war'.[40] But the original version of the Premiers' Plan did list pensions as being subject to the 20 per cent cut. This was expected to achieve a £1.29 million saving from a total annual Repatriation budget of around £8 million.[41]

When this news broke, Dyett went onto the offensive. He immediately met with Scullin and convened, in the relatively remote Canberra, a meeting of veterans' groups that had the emotive power of representing the most grievously wounded soldiers: not just the RSSILA, but also the Limbless Soldiers' Association, the Tubercular Soldiers' Association and the Blinded Soldiers' Association.[42] Without hesitation Scullin agreed to their suggestion to refer the matter to a specially created War Pensions Enquiry Committee. This would identify the best way to find the required economies in war pensions 'with the least possible hardship to war pensioners'.[43] The members of this committee were exclusively ex-servicemen. The sole economist, Giblin, was himself a veteran, wounded three times and the winner of the Military Cross and Distinguished Service Order in 1917–18.

The mantra of 'equality of sacrifice' worked to this group's advantage, since it resonated with the debates of wartime. In 1914–18 the labour press had interpreted 'equality of sacrifice' to mean that all classes should share the economic burdens of the war. Price rises generated by wartime inflation should be controlled, while the bloated plutocrats of 'Money Power' should be prevented from profiteering.[44] For the loyalists, however, 'equality of sacrifice' meant military conscription. As *The Age* had said during the plebiscite campaign of 1916: 'in the absence of conscription there can be no equality of sacrifice in this war. One household generously gives three, four or five of its members to the cause of the Empire. Another keeps back all its eligible sons.'[45] The *Sydney Morning Herald*, likewise, asked in the second campaign of December 1917: 'Was it a fair thing in a democratic country that a few should suffer for others who would not go? Was that equality of sacrifice?'[46]

This militarised version of 'equality of sacrifice' now served to make cuts in war pensions unacceptable. The volunteer of World War I had already made his sacrifice and should not be asked to do more. To quote the Nationalist Senator James Guthrie, addressing Parliament in July 1931, 'Have not these men who, in fighting for our liberty, lost their eyesight or their limbs, or contracted tuberculosis or some other disease, made sacrifices for which they can never be repaid?'[47] Many disabled soldiers, others noted, were now in middle age, and were already 'carrying more than their fair share of the burden in the present distress'.[48] The rate of war pensions, which were not indexed to the cost of living, had not been adjusted since 1920, and whereas bondholders were being asked to make a voluntary contribution to the nation through the loan conversion, the cuts to soldiers' pensions were to be mandatory.[49] As with the issue of preferential employment a year earlier, this debate was also infused with the language of a sacred obligation: to quote a Country Party parliamentarian, Roland Green, 'soldiers' pensions should be sacrosanct... a definite promise was made to the men who went to the War'.[50]

Scullin again readily deferred to the power of this rhetoric. The War Pensions Enquiry Committee recommended in late June 1931 that four classes of war-pension recipients be exempt from any cuts: disabled (or incapacitated) ex-soldiers, sailors and nurses; war widows; children of soldiers whose death was due to war service; and widowed mothers of unmarried soldiers whose death, again, had been due to war service.[51] The benefits paid to other recipients—parents, children and wives of ex-servicemen who were still living; brothers and sisters of deceased servicemen; war widows who had remarried; and certain other classes of dependants—should be reduced. Furthermore, the payments for ex-servicemen's children should be a flat rate rather than the current graduated scale that provided more for older children. In addition, women who had married returned soldiers, and children who were born after 1 October 1931, should no longer be regarded as dependants, although children born after that date might be exceptions where the father's death was considered to be due to war service.[52] Even with these adjustments, the savings did not amount to the scale of economies that the government required.[53] The committee, therefore, undertook to identify additional savings through further technical adjustments in Repatriation benefits.

This was the first time that some categories of war pensions had been reduced purely on the ground of the inability of the nation to meet the bill, but it was the only significant adjustment to the Premiers' Plan. Scullin once again privileged soldiers over other Australians, acknowledging how powerful the 'returned soldier' had become as a site of collective memory, though this was not the language that he or other politicians of that day used. Moreover, since the final pension cuts fell mostly on the families of returned soldiers who were still living, it was the memory of the war *dead* that was affirmed as core to the political culture of 1931.

What, if anything, did the Premiers' Plan do to assist Australia's recovery from the Depression? If we believe Copland, it was the reason that 'Australia came out of the depression earlier than most other countries'. He was unapologetic about the makeshift nature of the plan—it being the product of a number of divergent and sometimes opposing forces of political and economic opinion—but he claimed that no other country had done as much as Australia in its economic readjustment. Copland spent considerable time promoting the merits of the Premiers' Plan with what his fellow economist Shann quipped was a 'demagogic egotism'.[54]

Assessments of later scholars diverge, often radically. On the one hand, it has been argued that Australian economists displayed considerable political aplomb and some 'native genius', even 'a penchant for social experimentation in dealing with economic problems'. They thereby helped to navigate the nation 'through the Charybdis of repudiation and the Scylla of deflation'. 'As a piece of economic architecture, the plan provided the platform for Australia's economic recovery even though it was, in fact, quite deflationary.'[55]

Alternatively, the significance of the Premiers' Plan has been discounted. Like other key policy responses of the federal government to the slump, it is thought to have 'probably had only minor impacts on the broad course of economic events'. This was partly because there were limits to what could be achieved by internal adjustments such as wages, interest rates and government spending, the key priorities of the Premiers' Plan. Moreover, some elements of the plan worked against each other.[56] One leading economic historian has gone so far as to conclude that 'economic policy played little part in shaping the course of the depression in Australia. What was gained by exchange devaluation and by deficit financing in 1930–1, for instance, was almost certainly lost in 1931–2 following the fall in public expenditure after the adoption of the premiers' plan.'[57]

Yet if the benefits of the Premiers' Plan are debated, it does not necessarily follow that the alternative, in the form of a more expansionary fiscal policy or looser monetary policy, would have been any more effective. If Scullin and Theodore had somehow managed to overcome internal resistance and adopt policies aimed at boosting domestic demand and creating employment, they would probably have soon hit external constraints. The increased demand for imports fuelled by this stimulus might have worsened the balance-of-payments crisis. Foreign holders of Australian debts would then have been even less inclined to extend Australia's loans, foreign exchange reserves would have been further depleted and the currency subject to further devaluation. Possibly, then, Australian policymakers had little choice but to do what they did—wait for recovery elsewhere in the world.

CHAPTER 25

Scullin's end

Politically, Scullin was a 'dead man walking' after the announcement of the Premiers' Plan. Although his government managed to shepherd the required legislation through Parliament, the damage to the government's political base was terminal. He could retain power only as long as the Langites did not cross the floor of Parliament. Moreover, even though the Premiers' Plan garnered support beyond Labor circles, it became mired in state politics and the resistance of the banks. The plan, too, made little difference to unemployment levels, which continued to rise. Although Australians responded when asked to contribute to national recovery by converting their loans to the government to a lower rate of return, many were now prepared to desert the Scullin government. In December 1931, they were given the chance to do so—and they did it in droves.

Policy is only as good as its implementation. The decisions of the Premiers' Plan required an enormous amount of legislation at federal and state levels. The path through the federal parliament was relatively smooth, given the support of the Nationalists. At the state level, much depended on who was in power. In the three states where the ALP was in opposition—Queensland, Western Australia and Tasmania—the divisions in the Labor ranks did not impede the progress of the plan. Since the states had some discretion as to how the 20 per cent cut in public-sector wages was to be applied, some opted for a flat reduction, others for a sliding scale.

In the Labor states, things were predictably tumultuous. In South Australia, 'Slogger' Hill had to rely on the support of the conservative opposition after the local Labor movement expelled him and 21 other parliamentarians who supported the Premiers' Plan. Victoria's Premier Hogan also confronted fierce opposition from local ALP branches and the ALP Central Executive, which instructed all state parliamentarians to vote against the plan. Facing accusations of 'unthinkable treachery', Hogan did manage to push the legislation through in September 1931, with eleven caucus members dissenting.[1] Salary and pension cuts were most severe for those on higher salaries and rates.[2] An open split in the ALP loomed but was avoided for a time, thanks to the intervention of Arthur Calwell, the Victorian Labor Party branch president who had already headed off the Langites. But when the Scullin government was defeated in December, and Labor's representation outside Melbourne was wiped out, the balance of the Victorian party shifted against the Premiers' Plan.

Predictably, the passage of the Premiers' Plan was also turbulent in New South Wales. Lang found himself walking a tightrope, needing to dissociate himself from the plan for populist reasons and to contain the challenge from the more radical Socialisation Units within the local ALP. But New South Wales remained dependent on financial support from the Commonwealth. With its deficit predicted to be £11 million, the state needed £500,000 in July and a further £3 million in August to September.[3] Lang tried to increase taxes dramatically, but the bill was defeated in the Legislative Council, that bastion of conservative power that Lang had long been intent on destroying. In the first week of August, then, on what the press dubbed 'Black Thursday', some 23,000 New South Wales public servants, including 11,000 teachers, were not paid their salaries.[4] Lang had no option but to rejoin the Loan Council. Since some of the premiers took strong exception to his return, he agreed to once more accept responsibility for the payment of interest on New South Wales debts. The Loan Council advanced New South Wales some £500,000 of scarce Treasury bills.[5]

Lang also tried at the end of July to implement the idea mooted at the premiers' conference of limiting the 20 per cent cut required by the Premiers'

Plan to those public-service employees with salaries of more than £500 per year. Salaries lower than that would not be touched. The tax imposed by the Bavin government would also be repealed on salaries below £250 per year. But again the Legislative Council rejected the bill. Lang finally resorted to a more orthodox plan to graduate the cuts across all salaries in a way that achieved the overall reduction of 20 per cent. His state budget at the end of August brought the projected deficit for 1931–32 to within £0.5 million of the figure the premiers' conference required.[6] Lang thus continued more or less in compliance with the Premiers' Plan—although the New South Wales budget deficit soon blew out dramatically because of a drop in taxation revenue and increased expenditure on unemployment relief.

The quid pro quo of the states reducing their expenditure was the banks agreeing to reduce interest rates. The response of the banking sector to the Premiers' Plan was generally positive, but when detailed discussions began, they quibbled about the size and the timing of the reductions in interest rates. With the exception of the Commonwealth Bank, which moved swiftly to reduce rates on both deposits and advances, the banks prevaricated in a way that suggested they were willing to make profits at the expense of the wider community. It was, admittedly, far from clear, given the elasticity of the concept of 'equality of sacrifice', whether the banks or the depositors were the ones expected to bear the pain of lower interest rates. Scullin had no doubts that it should be both and threatened the banks with legislative action. At the state level, too, pressure was brought on the banks, including through legislation that reduced or placed moratoriums on mortgage interest payments.

Whatever the challenges of implementing it, the Premiers' Plan was effectively the policy framework for budget planning in the second half of 1931 and beyond. But it offered no strategies for dealing directly with the most urgent and troubling aspects of the Depression: unemployment and the desperate straits of wheat farmers. Unemployment continued to rise in 1931 until it peaked in 1932. Yet another attempt, in July 1931, to assist the farmers, by creating a compulsory pool and fixing domestic prices, was rejected by the Senate even though it had the support of the Country Party.

In an effort to find some way forward, the Loan Council appointed yet another committee to consider 'production and employment'. Headed by John Gunn, formerly director of the Development and Migration Commission, and including economists Giblin and Brigden, the committee handed down its rapidly compiled report in early September.[7] Its key recommendations were that Australia's banking credit must be used to maintain the wheat grower in production, continue existing levels of employment on public works and provide enough stimulus to 'set moving the gradual revival in business and enterprise for which conditions appear to be nearly ripe'. The premiers agreed and decided to raise £8 million, of which £5 million could be spent on new public works and £3 million on wheat bounties.

Yet once more Gibson tried to exercise a veto. He was already maintaining a constant vigil on government spending, scrutinising any requests from the Loan Council for finance to ensure that they would not blow out government budget deficits. Now he claimed that the Commonwealth Bank board could not approve any additional credit. His argument, as before, was that it could not exceed the limits on the note issue provided for under existing legislation.[8] Gibson's rigidity on credit expansion was particularly maddening after all the compromises of the Premiers' Plan, but it seems that the strain of the previous years was taking its toll. With a frail body, Gibson would suffer several long bouts of illness in 1932–33 before dying in January 1934. He was not alone in feeling the stresses of central bank management. As we have seen, his counterpart at the Bank of England, Montagu Norman, suffered a nervous collapse in the midst of the European financial crisis of mid-1931. With the prospect of Britain leaving the gold standard looming, Norman resorted to apocalyptic predictions—hyperinflation, a collapse in currency values, food shortages, soaring prices, strikes and riots. He became easily distraught, panicky, erratic and incapable of making decisions.[9]

The new impasse between Gibson and the governments was resolved at a tense meeting between the premiers and the banks. There it was agreed that the Commonwealth Bank would provide the requested £3 million for a wheat bounty but it would release only £2.25 million for 'reproductive' works that were in progress up to 31 December. Local authorities were invited to apply to the bank for grants for their own relief works. In the coming months, the implementation of the wheat bounty would prove technically and administratively messy, but eventually it was paid, giving the wheat industry some modest federal government assistance after many months of abortive legislative initiatives.[10] Towards the end of 1931, wheat and wool prices at last began to rise, providing some relief for the beleaguered primary industries— although prices would seesaw in subsequent years (see Figure 34.1 below).

Any benefits that these export industries had gained from devaluation were offset when, as Australia's sterling reserves started to rise, the Commonwealth Bank decided to revalue the Australian pound. Davidson argued strongly for the rate to remain at £130 Australian to £100 sterling. Some of the leading economists also issued a manifesto in November 1931 arguing the case for the exchange rate to remain where it was. But the Commonwealth Bank decided in early December to reduce this to £125. Gibson, it seems, might once again have been swayed by advice from Niemeyer.[11] It was a decision that did little to improve the prospects of an export-led recovery.[12]

With the Commonwealth Bank vetoing significant increases in government-funded relief works, Scullin appealed to private industry and the Australian public. In early November 1931, he launched a Prosperity Campaign. Employers were urged to take on more workers, if only for the weeks before Christmas. The public were again exhorted to buy Australian goods. 'National recovery', the press trumpeted, 'depends upon your help.'[13] In the spirit of the Premiers' Plan, the Opposition supported the appeals to public action. Page went on Brisbane radio to ask 'the man on the land' to provide work 'even if it is only one man for a short period'.[14] Lord mayors took up the campaign, linking up with each other across the states via radio.[15] Sidney Myer chose this moment to make his donation of £10,000 to enable married men with families to work for two weeks before Christmas.

All this was hardly a panacea for mass unemployment but, like the loan conversion campaigns, it aimed to tap Australians' civic-mindedness while boosting morale. 'Great good', the Melbourne *Age* said, might come from the campaign 'if the citizens can only be induced to adopt an optimistic mood, and have faith in their country'.[16] Some of the public seemed unconvinced, however. Scullin told a Melbourne suburban audience in November that 'we are slowly but surely emerging on the other side of the valley of depression. For the first time since I have been Prime Minister I can see daylight ahead in Government finances.' To which an interjector famously replied, 'You must have very good eyesight.'[17]

Whatever Scullin's upbeat demeanour, his hold on government was slipping. The coup de grâce was delivered by Lang Labor. It is not clear why Lang decided at this point to bring the federal government down. Possibly he feared that the tide of popular and party opinion was turning in Scullin's favour with the first (if faint) signs of some economic improvement. Possibly, too, Lang feared that some of the Beasley group might choose to return to the mainstream ALP, weakening his aspirations for federal influence. His position in New South Wales was also potentially precarious, given the state's financial difficulties. Other Labor dissidents, meanwhile, seemed unable to live any longer with the compromises of power. Better to lose office than govern in a way that violated Labor's core principles. As Lazzarini put it, when explaining why he was withdrawing his support for Scullin:

> It was because for two years we had had from the Government nothing but vacillation and exhibitions of hopeless ineptitude that we decided to take the step we did, being quite indifferent whether the Government remained in office or not. So far as we can see, it matters little to the unemployed whether the present Government remains in office, or the Opposition is returned.[18]

In early November, two of Lang's followers in the Senate, J.P.D. (Digger) Dunn and Arthur Rae, accused Theodore of political graft in the allocation of the government's unemployment relief grants.[19] Some of the recent funding had been allocated to the Cockatoo Island dockyard, which was near the treasurer's electorate of Dalley. Supposedly, Theodore's organisers were collecting names giving residents of Dalley preference for relief work. Theodore strenuously denied the charges, but Dunn, like 'a political bulldog . . . [had] sunk his political teeth into Mr. Theodore's political leg, and [refused] to let go'.[20] So, too, had Beasley, who raised the charges relating to Cockatoo Island in the House of Representatives, asking that a select committee of both houses be appointed to investigate them. When Scullin refused to agree to this or to the royal commission that Dunn had demanded, the Beasley group joined with the Opposition to vote the government out of office. It was a fratricidal—indeed suicidal—move. *Labor Call* wrote bitterly of the 'bovine stupidity of men who call themselves Langites in the name of Labor, and who allied themselves with anti-Labor'.[21] Beasley would carry for the rest of his political career the sobriquet 'Stabber Jack'.

The election campaign that followed has been described as a 'campaign of terrors' more than a 'campaign of promises'. Each side solicited support because of the dangers of the other side winning power.[22] Scullin cited his government's record, such as it was. Claiming to have maintained the nation's honour through lifting the 'dark cloud of national default', he highlighted the reduction of imports through tariffs and the reversal of the adverse balance of trade. Australians were asked to invest the government 'with the power to continue its labour for the economic rehabilitation of the nation'.[23] There were few vote-catching promises. If re-elected, Scullin would reintroduce the Central Reserve Bank Bill, amend the arbitration system and persevere with trying to get more funds from the banks for unemployment relief.[24]

Using the radio to reach a national audience Scullin toured the mainland eastern states, visiting Melbourne, Adelaide, Ballarat, Colac, Geelong, Ararat, Benalla, Horsham, Wangaratta, Albury, Sydney, Tamworth, Warwick, Toowoomba and Brisbane.[25] There was little chance of any incumbent government being re-elected in the depth of the Depression, but the prime minister carried the additional burden of the ALP's internal feuding. A Sydney meeting erupted into 'a storm of hooting' from Lang supporters at the mention of Theodore who sat smiling on the platform.[26] Scullin, in turn, condemned the Langites as betrayers of the labour movement, denouncing them as an offshoot party that followed the policy named after one man. The Lang Plan was 'just the old "hobo" idea of not paying your debts'.[27] Not that that deterred Lang. At a rally in the Domain, he told a crowd of 80,000 that the people of Australia were more important than bankers' profits:

the bankers' policy was that all extravagances must be cut out. What were the extravagances? The bankers declared that widows' pensions were an extravagance; workers' compensation was an extravagance; old age and invalid pensions and maternity allowances—all these were extravagances from the bankers' standpoint.

Was the crowd willing to work for the bankers' policy? The response was a 'resounding "No" from all parts of the assemblage, accompanied by a fresh outburst of cheering' as Lang resumed his seat.[28]

As Opposition leader, Lyons had no difficulty making the case for change. With UAP money behind him, he made a 'talkie' to be shown at cinemas before setting off on a nationwide campaign trail (though he did not go to either Queensland or Western Australia). His message? The Premiers' Plan for which Labor was claiming credit had been forced on them 'virtually at pistol point' by the Opposition, the premiers and the Commonwealth Bank. If Labor won the election, the outcome would be inflation and political control of banking and the currency.[29] The UAP, in contrast, would do everything in its power to balance the budget. A victory for the UAP would also presage the downfall of the detested Lang government. 'The Langites are Mr. Theodore's next-of-kin, and Communism is akin to both,' Lyons claimed, with a total disregard for the factional feuding in New South Wales.[30] Like Nationalist politicians before him, Lyons also played the imperial loyalty card. The election slogan was 'Tune in with Britain'. 'Remember,' Lyons said on election day, 'that when you are voting for us you are voting for the maintenance of the British tradition in finance and Government.'[31] 'Trust the United Australia Party as the British people trusted the United British Party. Turn a deaf ear as they did to proposals for financial tricks and devices.'[32]

When Australians voted on 19 December, they gave vent to the explosive frustration and despair of the past two years. Labor was routed. Although Scullin won almost 60 per cent of the votes in his own inner-city electorate in Melbourne, elsewhere the swing to the conservative parties was massive. In the House of Representatives, the UAP, the Country Party and the Emergency Committee of South Australia won 54 seats. Federal Labor lost 32 seats, crashing to only fifteen, fewer than the Country Party (with sixteen). Lang Labor, too, lost seats, being reduced to four. Of the eighteen Senate seats contested, the UAP and Country Party gained fifteen; the ALP three. Only in Queensland did Labor have any gains. Here the unpopularity of the Moore government and the low profile of the Lang faction meant that the ALP picked up two seats and each of the three Senate vacancies. Unsurprisingly, the worst state for Scullin was New South Wales, where the ALP won only three of the 23 seats it contested. Eddie Ward lost the seat of East Sydney that he had won in the bitter by-election earlier that year. Lazzarini and Chifley were also defeated. Most notably, Theodore lost Dalley to a Lang Labor candidate, Sol Rosevear, a future speaker of the House of Representatives. It was Labor's worst electoral performance since 1917 and, like that, a testament to the price of disunity in politics.

Scullin accepted the humiliating popular verdict with remarkable grace. The 'people have spoken', was his first comment, 'and theirs is the deciding voice'. To the crowd gathered at Richmond Town Hall on 30 December he said,

> I have no bitterness in my heart as a result of the election. We have been passing through strange and bitter times . . . In the same circum-stances and on the same rocky path I would take the same steps as those that I took before. Our motives were not to win popularity, but to save Australia . . . I was not exhilarated when I was returned at the head of the Government two years ago. I am not downcast now.

Perhaps Scullin was relieved to be free of the burden of trying to govern without any real power. In January 1932, he told a reporter. 'I feel like a school kid going on holidays.'[33] Yet Scullin did not quit political life, as defeated political leaders normally do today. He would stay on as leader of the Opposition until October 1935, when he resigned the leadership to Curtin. He remained in Parliament until December 1949 as a respected elder statesman and confidant to Labor prime ministers.

Theodore, in contrast, decided that his stunning defeat 'finishes me with politics'. His loss was particularly personal, as Lang exulted over what he called 'the most crushing and humiliating defeat it was possible to imagine.

He wasn't even a runner-up.'[34] (An unknown UAP candidate had come second.) Theodore had also lost faith in the 'fool workers' who formed Labor's traditional constituency.[35] Two days after Christmas, he wrote to Henry Boote, editor of the *Australian Worker*, 'The people are fickle and irresponsible. They reward the political treachery of Lyons, Fenton, McGrath, Price, Gabb and Guy (What a crop of rats this time!) and they turn out Parker Moloney, Cunningham, Brennan, Chifley . . . whose defeat leaves the Labor Party poor indeed.' A year later, he told Curtin that he had known in 1931 that he was not winning the people over to his proposed changes in monetary policy:

> The power drunk Lang faction, with the aid of their paper, and job patronage, and a liberal use of political lucre . . . [corrupted] the Labor movement in NSW . . . Simultaneously the Nationalists, playing on the fears and childish dreads of the major portion of the people in the matter of currency inflation, succeeded with the aid of the Press, the banks and the Senate, in creating a widespread hostility against the Government and the policy we had formulated.[36]

It was the classic lament of a reserved intellectual whose rationality and measured logic proved no match for populist demagoguery—although Anstey, too, despaired of the electorate that had abandoned them. 'It is not the enemy that scares me,' he wrote to a friend. 'It is the hopeless spineless mob you try to save . . . They are hopeless—they have only the instincts of slaves, and in them there is no hope—and I am finished.'[37]

Theodore naturally had his supporters. Letters of condolence poured in after the election from people across the political spectrum. One assured Theodore that 'a greater miscarriage of justice has never besmirched the history of Australian politics. From a parched garden of weeds you cultivated a rich soil bearing blossoming trees from which you would have plucked the fruits of your labours in a few more months.'[38] Another typical response, in this case from a press gallery journalist, read:

> I want to say how sorry I am that you were defeated in the Dalley election—sorry not only on personal grounds, but also because the national Parliament will be much poorer without you . . . Labor's own

stupidity and wrangling, the bitterness & spite within the party, are responsible in large measure for the present position. . . . Do not take your defeat too much to heart. The people are notoriously fickle. Many excellent men have gone down . . . but they will come again.[39]

Nothing would persuade Theodore to stay. Resigning from politics, he joined forces with the young Frank Packer to pursue a career in newspaper publishing. The lure of mining continued—but now it was gold in the South-West Pacific. When war with Japan came, Curtin, now prime minister, recalled Theodore to lead the Allied Works Council, organising resources for war-related projects. As ever, Theodore proved forceful and competent, but the bitterness of the Depression years lingered as he clashed with his old antagonists Beasley and Ward, and proved willing to invoke punitive labour regulations that angered the unions.

The man who became Australia's new prime minister, Lyons, had little of Theodore's charisma and intellectual power. He has been described as 'possibly our most reluctant Prime Minister', but he was the man for the times.[40] Plump, with a shock of unruly hair and a high-pitched voice, his personality seemed elusive and enigmatic. His nickname, the 'tame Tasmanian', was telling. (He was the first, and only Tasmanian, to be prime minister.) Yet it seems that calmness was what Australians wanted after a torrid two years of Labor politics. Lyons, the family man, projected an image of integrity and reliability. He was 'Honest Joe', and it was mainly said without irony. He embodied a consensual style of politics, presiding over a cabinet in which several men eclipsed him in terms of their drive, education and international experience. Above all, he had the human touch. Menzies described him as 'essentially a man of the people':

He understood ordinary men and women, and they understood him. He was a family man with many children. He was a comparatively poor man, with no silly social pretensions. The instinctive feeling he evoked from the public was that he could be trusted to do his best for the unfortunate, and for households grievously afflicted by the Depression . . . In his own undemonstrative way, he illustrated the moral force of leadership.[41]

This was the man who would lead Australia for more than seven years, through the remaining years of the Depression, and then the years of recovery. The task helped to kill him.

Part VIII

ON THE MARGINS

CHAPTER 26

Women at risk

Certain sectors of society were especially vulnerable during the Depression, despite official efforts to guarantee 'equality of sacrifice'. Of these, women formed one of the larger groups. Thanks to the gendered nature of work, women's wages were generally lower than men's. Any pro rata cuts or rationing of hours thus had a more severe impact on them. Importantly, too, as we have seen, the systems of sustenance and relief works generally favoured men, and particularly married men. The family unit was the place where a woman was expected to be provided for. But if this was the arena in which a woman was meant to be secure, it followed that she was at considerable risk when that family unit did not exist, disintegrated or became dysfunctional.

Several cohorts of women were particularly vulnerable: single women without family support, women in abusive relationships, and women whose marriages broke down. The chances of a woman marrying in the 1920s had been affected to some degree by the gender imbalance resulting from World War I. In 1933, there were 98 men for every 100 women aged 35 to 39.[1] Now, the Depression brought a steep decline in first marriage.[2] Even though marriage increased a man's dole and his eligibility for relief works, and although two people could often live almost as cheaply as one, many Australians chose to defer marriage. The crude marriage rate (that is, the number of marriages per 1000 of mean annual population) declined from 7.93 in 1927 to 5.96 in 1931 before slowly rising to 8.70 in 1937.[3] Long engagements were partly a matter of class expectations. As one woman later explained, 'Until the young man had the house furnished and the girl had her full trousseau, all her sheets, towels and pillow-slips, they didn't get married. Nothing was on cash orders, though we used lay-bys.'[4] For many people there was simply no choice. As one man later recalled: 'I gave away the idea of getting married, although I was the type who would normally marry and rear kids . . . A single bloke or a single girl could scratch along, but to inflict it on kids, the misery! You couldn't do it.'[5]

An unmarried woman often returned to her parental home when she became unemployed. But if she lacked this refuge, her situation was potentially precarious. Women's access to sustenance varied state by state. 'Minister for Starvation' Kent Hughes in Victoria was convinced that 'whilst domestic work was available at any wage under any conditions anywhere in Victoria, the Government was not obliged to provide assistance to unemployed women'.[6] In Queensland, women were entitled to six shillings of rations per week, although the value of this was less than one-sixth of the female basic wage in the early 1930s. Here, as elsewhere, women could face more stringent eligibility requirements. Officials subjected them to searching interviews, thinking they should be dependent on a male breadwinner or should seek board and lodgings through domestic service. By 1931, however, the government decided that all unemployed females, irrespective of age, could be included in the relief family of any 'intermittent worker', and that this man's 'weekly amount of work increased in proportion to such added claims'. Women were provided with free transport to enable them to return to the parental home, where they could be included as part of the 'relief family'.[7]

The situation of single unemployed women troubled many women's associations and activists. In early 1930, the Victorian National Council of Women and the Young Women's Christian Association (YWCA) organised a 'Helping Hand' Bureau to place unemployed women in domestic service.[8] Since there were more applicants than positions, council members themselves agreed to take on 'house-helpers' to ease the strain. The labour activist Muriel Heagney, and the president of the Central Council of Benevolent Societies, Jessie Henderson, also organised a 'Girls' Week' fund, and then established the Unemployed Girls' Relief Fund. Some 21 work centres were established around the city, employing by late 1931 more than a thousand 'girls' who were homeless and around 2300 who lived with their relatives. The organisation boasted that it met every application from unemployed girls belonging to families in which all members were unemployed. In 1932 these female workers produced 4000 items of clothing per week and vast quantities of jam, a favourite of amateur food production. The plan was originally to sell the garments commercially, but instead they were distributed to the unemployed. Some were sent to the industrial suburb of Yarraville with the message, 'They carry with them the sympathy of the girls for their fellow workers, and the hope that these dark days will soon pass.'[9] In 1932 the production line was supplemented by three-week training courses for domestic service.

Similar schemes were established in other states. The women's committee of the Queensland Social Service League set up a headquarters at the South Brisbane Town Hall, where women again created garments that were distributed to unemployed families. With a workforce averaging 30 between January 1930 and November 1931, some 11,061 garments were produced. In 1931 the government introduced a House Craft Training scheme, which conducted classes in cooking, dressmaking and home nursing for approximately 40 women each month.[10]

In New South Wales, Labor and non-party women's organisations lobbied the state government from early 1930 to arrange hostels for homeless women and to provide relief works, possibly by renting or purchasing factories, creating sewing centres and giving work to tailoresses and the like. Scullin, too, was petitioned by the women's branches of the Trades Hall, Sydney, to pay attention to 'the pitiable and hopeless outlook of single women, also the middle-aged, who are totally or partially supporting themselves'. As was its practice, the federal government referred the matter to the state Unemployment Relief Councils. Some £25,000 was allocated to meet the needs of unemployed women, girls and youths.[11]

All of these initiatives were framed by traditional understandings of what was 'women's work'. The trade unions and others did not welcome women competing with unemployed men in traditionally male areas of employment. Occasionally a more unusual proposal arose, such as establishing a large cooperative shop in Sydney to be run by unemployed women, selling products such as dairy goods, food, drapery and clothing. But even this relief work was in the traditional area of textiles and food preparation. Commonly, they offered only one to two days of work per week and rates of pay that were too low to give women any financial security.

Women did not accept their plight without protest. In Sydney, a number of women protested at a public meeting attended by Governor Philip Game in September 1930. When he entered the hall, they refused to stand. One woman called out that they were 'too tired after looking for work all day'. When Game exhorted the crowd to make sacrifices, a girl's voice was heard from the back: 'How much do you get a year anyhow, and how much will you sacrifice?' The conservative Minister for Labour and Industry told a persistent heckler, 'You did not take advantage of the help which was offered you, but slept in the Domain and spent your money on something else.' Other speakers were howled down, as was a motion expressing appreciation of the steps taken by the committee for the relief of unemployed women, girls and youths.[12]

The concern to find women work was driven partly by anxiety about the moral dangers of poverty. Whereas the unease about unemployed boys was often expressed as a problem of morale, in the case of girls it was morals.[13] Women, if destitute, might become vulnerable to sexual exploitation. Either they would have extramarital relations, resulting perhaps in unwanted pregnancies, or, worse, they might slip into prostitution. Hence women's organisations were constantly focused on providing single women with 'safe' supervised accommodation: church hostels, boarding houses and private homes.

The unwanted pregnancy was not just a disaster for single women. Women with large families dreaded having yet another child to house and feed.[14] One woman reportedly claimed that it was better 'to give your old man a few shillings to see someone down the street' than risk another pregnancy.[15] Hard data is lacking, but clearly backyard abortionists and some private medical practitioners were willing to help women with unwanted pregnancies.[16] 'The abortion trade flourished,' one woman later claimed, 'because to have kids was so awful really. You had enough problems just to live. There was a friend of the family who made a good living out of abortions.'[17] Women also reportedly tried to bring on miscarriages by taking Epsom Salts, walking long distances carrying kerosene tins full of water, or jumping off chairs piled on high tables.[18] 'People had abortions or they gave themselves abortions,' one woman later recounted;

> when I was about thirteen, a lady up the street had brought a miscar-
> riage on, and she wasn't sure whether it had all come away. So she
> wrapped it in a newspaper and brought it down. My grandmother put it
> on the kitchen floor and checked it, and said 'yes, everything is right'.[19]

There were also occasional reports of infanticide.[20] Yet for all that, it is claimed that the rate of deaths from abortion declined.[21]

How many destitute women slipped into prostitution is also difficult to know. Many towns had well-established 'red light' districts. The brothels in Hay Street and elsewhere in Kalgoorlie were 'a legendary feature of life', 'an important social institution for the local men who patronised them, [and] . . . a source of amusement and gossip for "respectable" townsfolk'.[22] Roe Street in Perth saw the number of brothels rise during 1930 from 50 to 70.[23] In Sydney, one of the more notorious 'madams' reportedly managed 20 to 30 brothels in the 1930s. Melbourne also had a significant trade, especially in St Kilda, while Queensland tolerated brothels, albeit under police registration and regular health checks. Adelaide, predictably for 'the city of churches', had stiffer legislation and less public prostitution.[24]

The established brothels did not necessarily reveal the full extent of pros-titution. Many sex workers presumably avoided these established institutions, with their madams and pimps and their associations with organised crime, in Sydney particularly, by working independently and casually. For the historian, these casual sex workers are virtually invisible, except on the occasions they came to the notice of law enforcement. There are only clues. The Brisbane Commissioner for Public Health suggested that the Depression triggered an increase in street walkers and the 'clandestine' sex worker.[25] In New South Wales, the government passed legislation at the end of 1929 widening the definition of vagrancy applicable to women and making consorting with prostitutes an offence punishable with up to twelve months' imprisonment. Did this suggest 'a panic response to the female employment crisis'?[26]

On the subject of prostitution, oral history is contradictory. Some recalled that the taboos against sex work held up under economic pressure. Close-knit communities acted as watchdogs to prevent young girls from 'hawking the body'. Others, to the contrary, remembered the market for paid sex being flooded and prices dropping to as little as sixpence per time. Women, it is claimed, bartered sex for food, rental arrears and other commodities. One hawker claimed to have been offered sex for a couple of rabbits. Another man recalled inviting a woman whom he met on the street to come home with him:

> I said: 'I'm broke, I couldn't even take you home on the tram, but if you'd like to walk home there is a bed and something to eat'. So she came home to Drummond Street and she was there a fortnight. She washed our clothes, cooked whatever there was, did the ironing. Of course, she came into bed with me. She didn't have to, but she didn't mind.[27]

Of two things, at least, we can be confident. First, the forces propelling a woman to resort to prostitution were far greater for working-class women than those from the middle class. Second, prostitution did little to address women's poverty. As male purchasing power declined, weekly wages for sex workers (at least in Hay Street) declined to as low as £1, as opposed to a peak in war years of £15.[28] Many women probably got less.

Perhaps the most vulnerable of all women in the Depression years were those trapped in violent marriages. The abuse of wives was extensive in early twentieth-century Australia, though much of it went unreported.[29] Life in the home was thought to be a private domain beyond the purview of the state. World War I probably increased the levels of domestic violence, partly because of the large number of men who suffered what would now be called post-traumatic stress disorder; and partly because the war, and the Anzac legend it spawned, celebrated violence as integral to male identity. Even men who did not serve in the war were socialised into this model of masculinity.

Of course, this did not mean that all returned soldiers and all men were violent in their personal relationships. The causes of domestic violence are so complex that we should be cautious about inferring a direct nexus between domestic violence and war service. In the public discourse of the 1920s, however, this nexus was often assumed to exist. When returned soldiers came before the courts for attacking or murdering their wives, this violence was commonly attributed to their being 'nervous wrecks'. Alcoholism and drug dependence were also thought to be contributing factors.

It seems logical that the Depression would have increased the levels of domestic violence. Studies of masculinity point to a link between a man's sense of diminished personal power and his being abusive. Unemployment and poverty inherently challenged a man's sense of being in control and eroded his identity as the head of the family and the breadwinner. The anecdotal evidence of the Depression years certainly attests to cases of domestic abuse. The Melbourne Ladies Benevolent Society recorded 'a very sad case' of 'a girl married at the age of 18 to a worthless man who ill-used her. She is now 21 and has three children . . . The man's conduct had been so unspeakably cruel that . . . steps should be taken to protect the mother and the children.'[30]

Presumably, too, many marriages came under severe strain. Money, or the lack of it, generated tensions within family units, while unemployment forced many men to leave homes for long periods. Either they went 'on the track' searching for work outside the cities, or they were sent on relief works, perhaps in distant locations. As one worker later recalled: 'I will never forget the first time I had to go away on sustenance work. It was a bitterly cold morning. I had my old army kitbag over my shoulder. I can still see my wife, baby in arms, two small children beside her, watching me out of sight down the street.'[31] As we have seen, some women followed their husbands, but commonly the man's absences threw the full burden of family care onto the mother. Over the months, her fortitude could be worn down. In Kylie Tennant's reportage *The Battlers* (1941), the wife of the main character, Snow, starts a new relationship while he is 'on the track'.

If the environment was conducive to marital breakdown, however, we know little about its actual incidence and trends during the Depression.

Intriguingly, the consumption of alcohol went down during the Depression. With purchasing power reduced, there was a 50 per cent fall in the early 1930s in the national per capita consumption of spirits and a 20 per cent drop in beer consumption.[32] Sales of wine were also depressed within Australia (though exports doubled).[33] Convictions for drunkenness declined from 97.5 per 10,000 inhabitants in 1928 to 60.9 in 1932.[34] Temperance associations took heart from this, believing that many of those who had stopped drinking for economic reasons 'will continue as abstainers when normal conditions return, and young persons who have not acquired the drink habit will have passed the most dangerous recruiting age'.[35]

But alcoholism was far from eradicated. One woman interviewed decades remembered that her father, a heavy beer drinker and punter, would belt her and her brother with the knuckle end of a belt before locking the boy in a shed all night. On one occasion, he killed the family cat by smashing in its head. On others, he would break crockery or threaten to kill his wife and himself. A few years later, he did in fact suicide, leaving a family that had lived on 'shredded nerves'.[36] Yet another (then) child recalled a father as a 'roaring, raving drunk'. He 'was not only mean, but he was violent. We lived in terror of him. Sometimes we were locked out because of his violence and we slept in the Park'.[37] Less dramatic, but still memorable for a teenage son in Townsville, was being sent out from home to see if he could find his drunken father's dental plate 'among last night's vomit'![38]

The strains on many marriages are perhaps reflected in the statistics for divorce, though these are hard to read.[39] From a peak of 2087 divorces Australia-wide in 1929, the numbers dropped to 1761 in 1930, 1969 in 1931 and 1714 in 1932. Thereafter, the numbers slowly increased to 3137 in 1939.[40] Likely, the relatively low rate of divorce in the early 1930s was attributable to the social stigma attached to divorce, the religious prohibitions on it, especially for Catholics, and the need to prove a marital offence. Given the time it took to secure a divorce under the laws of the day, the rise of divorce in the late 1930s might attest to relationship breakdowns some years earlier.

Yet presumably, given their lack of access to financial and legal resources, many poorly educated women took the calculated risk to stay in the family home. At least there they might gain access to sustenance rations and enhance their children's chances of being fed and housed. But there were other, more troubling, reasons why women remained in their marriages, even when these were abusive and violent. Fear of bodily and emotional harm if they tried to leave was one. Constant insults, criticism and physical violence are also known to eat at the self-esteem of victims, reducing their capacity to judge their situation rationally and causing them to believe that they, not their abusers, are to blame.[41] Many of the women most at risk during the Depression might thus have 'worn anxiety like a thick robe for so long' that they found it hard to take it off.[42]

CHAPTER 27

Losing your home

Another group of Australians especially at risk were those who lost their homes. As unemployment mounted, many families found it impossible to service their mortgages or to meet rental payments. Men, women and children were driven onto the street, with whatever possessions they might have managed to accumulate or save. Without shelter they slipped easily from hardship to destitution. Evictions thus became one of the most powerful images of the Depression. The desolation of the dispossessed encapsulated in an especially vivid form the misery and humiliation of unemployment. Homelessness galvanised activists in a way few other issues did; and the sites of evictions became a key public space in which these radicalised unemployed challenged the power of the authorities and the police.

Home ownership was not yet the 'Australian Dream' it would become in the post–World War II decades; but in 1933 more Australians owned or were purchasing private dwellings than were renting.[1] Many homeowners were middle-class, self-made men who had made their way up the social ladder by study or business. Their wealth was not ostentatious. The salaries of most middle-class managers and semi-professionals in Melbourne in the 1930s ranged between £500 and £700 per year. In the 1920s, a seven-bedroom brick villa in Camberwell or Canterbury, the heartland of middle-class Melbourne, might cost £1575; a five-roomed wooden house, on a quarter-acre block, £795.[2] For many of the middle class, this hard-won status was precarious. So, too, was that of the skilled and semi-skilled workers—people such as those in South Australia who, with wages between £220 and £300 per annum, were enabled by the Thousand Homes Scheme of the 1920s to purchase bungalows in suburbs such as Colonel Light Gardens.[3] Those who continued to be tenants aspired to the security and respectability that owning homes such as these would bring.

The story of how homeowners coped with the Depression is a hidden one, partly because, among the middle class at least, 'a high premium was placed on emotional control', self-discipline and the stoic endurance of suffering. As one child later put it: 'None of us were allowed to cry—to have a few quiet tears . . . the loud sobs that children do—you just had to learn to control them—you were not to cry.'[4] Fierce pride also prevented many professional people from admitting how deep was their financial distress and humiliation as the Depression worsened. But when their clients fell away, bad debts accumulated and public-sector salaries were cut, these homeowners struggled to meet their financial commitments. By June 1930, one-third of all people with homes mortgaged to the State Bank in South Australia were in arrears. By 1932–33, this had grown to two of every three mortgagors. In the mid-1930s, some home purchasers in that state owed more than they had initially borrowed.[5] One woman in Ascot Vale, Melbourne, explained to the manager of the local branch of the State Bank in March 1931 that her husband had been out of constant work for two years, and now at best, got two days' work a week. Her son had done no work for a year. She had asked another son in Adelaide for £20: 'as soon as things look up I could keep up the payments then, so trusting you will give me a chance I will do my best, it is worrying the life out of me because I am afraid they will take the house from me'.[6]

Banks were often accommodating of their clients' situation, recognising that they could not demand money when it was simply not there. Banks reduced payments, charged interest only and even tolerated non-payment of mortgages for some time—although they descended on the anxious homeowner every few months to assess their financial position. Some later memories of the banks are quite positive: they were 'lenient' and 'very fair'.

'I really owe the bank a lot, they helped us through the Depression,' one person later recalled. But as ever, there was the alternative view: the banks were 'very harsh' and 'bloody bandits'.[7]

Given the threat that homelessness posed to social stability and community health, state governments at various times legislated for the relief of mortgagors: moratoriums, extensions of repayment periods, reductions in interest rates, and prohibitions on home and farm foreclosures.[8] Conservatives fretted at this 'organised, legalised attack on property', but generally there was bipartisan support for intervention on the part of the state.[9] Everyone agreed that nothing would be gained by annihilating debtors. Mass foreclosures would only push property values down and lenders would recover little from a forced property sale.

Still, many Australians with mortgages were unable to cope. In South Australia, it has been estimated that at least 10 per cent of all people purchasing homes who had loans with the State Bank lost their properties.[10] In Victoria, State Bank loans fell by 13 per cent and building society loans by 10 per cent, many of which might have been from foreclosures.[11] In some cases, those in default had to vacate their premises and allow the lending institution to put tenants in the dwellings and use the rent to pay arrears. Some 'homeowners' simply walked away from their property, 'going bush' to escape their liabilities.

Those renting their home were in an even more precarious position. Rents actually declined, possibly by up to 30 per cent on their pre-Depression levels in South Australia.[12] But so, too, did the income of many tenants. Some landlords, like the banks, seem to have tolerated the situation, if unwillingly. They chose to accept part payment, or to get their tenants to do work in lieu of rent. They seized some of a tenant's assets as a means of recovering arrears, although in New South Wales distraint was prohibited from late 1930.[13] Some tenants were allowed to stay on rent-free. At least if a property was occupied, it was not vandalised or taken over by squatters.[14]

Many landlords, however, chose not to forgo rental payments. Nor could they always afford to. Not all landlords were big rentiers or stereotypical slum landlords—though there were some of these. Many were widows or retired people relying on perhaps only one investment property as a source of their income.[15] As the chief secretary in the Victorian Labor government, Tom Tunnecliffe, told a deputation of unemployed Geelong men in 1932, 'Often times the landlord class like the tenant was a struggling individual.'[16] Hence, many tenants faced eviction as the economic crisis deepened. In Melbourne, the numbers of warrants issued for eviction rose by 235 per cent from 1930 to 1931, increasing a further 173 per cent in the following year.[17]

In these circumstances, some tenants simply packed up their belongings and made a 'moonlight flit', leaving their debts behind them. One family, according to a relative, 'would have to shift regularly overnight with a little two-wheel barrow and place [their] belongings on that . . . they would move from place to place overnight'.[18] Other tenants, however, stayed in their accommodation until they were literally thrown into the street. This was the Depression at its most pitiless, and the prospect of families huddling on the pavement with their meagre furniture, possibly in the rain, mobilised the unemployed to action. The densely populated working-class suburbs of the capital cities—Bankstown, Newtown, Redfern, Glebe, Leichhardt, Brunswick, Fitzroy, Collingwood, Richmond, Footscray, South Melbourne, Bardon, Spring Hill, Red Hill, Hobart centre, Port Adelaide, Victoria Park and Fremantle—became battlegrounds. Landlords, real estate agents, bailiffs and police confronted the dispossessed and their champions.[19] The UWM was at the vanguard of this opposition. For this communist-led movement, evictions served as the 'main point of struggle' whereby the party could progress its wider objective of 'bringing about a complete change in the social system'.[20]

The forms of resistance were many. Deputations armed with petitions demanded that local and state governments freeze rents or reduce rates and land taxes, so that landlords could tolerate arrears in rents. If a family's possessions were about to be requisitioned, 'flying squads' or 'bailiff gangs' removed the furniture before the landlord arrived. When well organised, as in Perth, this operation might take as little as ten minutes.[21] Sometimes the furniture of the evicted family would be dumped at the local town hall in protest. In the case of one family in Brunswick, Melbourne, where the father was a Gallipoli veteran, the town hall pillar was inscribed: 'An Anzac fought for his home in 1915. Evicted 1931.'[22] In Hobart, various articles of household furniture were deposited on the steps of the town hall by a crowd bearing banners saying 'Heroes, 1914–18, Paupers, 1932' and 'Unemployed family thrown into gutter in pouring rain'.[23] At the more violent end of the spectrum, protesters vandalised houses that had been forcibly evacuated, breaking windows, smashing doors and walls, and flooding premises by wrenching off taps. Some Melbourne homes from which tenants had been evicted mysteriously burned down.

As with the rations system, much of the anger about evictions was directed against those enforcing the system. Some bailiffs and landlords took to carrying arms or sought police protection while trying to serve a warrant that gave them the legal authority to enter a house and eject the tenant. Agents controlling properties were intimidated.[24] The windows of every real estate agent in Richmond, Melbourne, were smashed in August 1931 after an eviction had been enforced in neighbouring Burnley. Noel Counihan (of the Phoenix Street cage incident) recalled the predicament these agents faced:

[A] demonstration would generally be called to take place at the estate agent's office . . . If you had several hundred people outside and six to a dozen came into your office you simply had to talk. So it was often put to him that it was very much in his interests and the interests of his office if he rang the landlord and asked him to call off the eviction and of course he often did. This was a display of force. We stood there until he did.[25]

The most violent confrontations occurred when police enforced an eviction order. In suburbs with dense housing the often-outnumbered police could not use their horses. The anti-eviction forces, for their part, developed siege tactics. In Sydney's Redfern in May 1931, members of the Anti-Eviction League lay in wait for the local agent and police after padlocking the front door of a house in Douglas Street, where a family had been tenants for twelve years. A red flag was hoisted on the balcony from which the wife of the tenant initially watched proceedings. The police smashed the front door with a sledgehammer, stormed the premises and drove the pickets out through the back door. A fight, complete with revolvers and batons, then erupted when the protesters tried to remove the tenant's furniture from a waiting van. The wife 'stood in one of the bare rooms sobbing bitterly'.[26]

In Bankstown the following month, an eviction in Brancourt Avenue escalated into 'one of the fiercest street fights ever recorded in Sydney's history'. Here protesters barricaded the house with sandbags and barbed wire, and armed themselves with axe handles, iron pipes and garden forks.[27] A hail of stones and bricks greeted the police, who responded with at least nine shots, wounding two men. According to one press report, 'Some of the anti-evictionists presented a sorry sight, and several had to be supported by the police.'[28] Seventeen men were arrested. Two days later, these scenes were repeated at 143 Union Street, Newtown. One of the protesters who occupied the house stated that:

a volley of shots came through the back door . . . A bullet hit the wall close to my head and the plaster spurted out and hit me in the face . . . I was hit on the head with a baton by one of the police. The baton split. Another policeman then hit me and his baton split also, I was knocked down. They said 'fancy breaking good weapons over a bastard like you'. . . . When I reached the backyard they knocked me down and one said 'Put the bracelets on this Russian Bastard' . . . [Later] When I reached the charge room one policeman hit me in the face, blackened my eyes and cut my lip.[29]

Another activist who testified for the legal proceedings that followed the riot claimed:

I am a returned soldier and served right through the War with the British forces. I mention this only because the Police behaved like they were men going over the Top. They seemed to be out of control & this was probably due to the liquor which we could smell on them. Whenever we captured prisoners at the Front we treated them as men and not as beasts. There was no brutality over there to compare with the police brutality at Newtown.[30]

Further testimony alleged that the police continued to kick and punch protesters after their arrest.

[My] kicked knee [B. Urbanski testified] has given me trouble since and almost continuously I feel a stinging pain . . . [a doctor] told me that the injury to the knee was permanent and there was no use in treating it in any way as the ligaments of the knee had been displaced by the kick and had grown on or become attached to the wrong place . . . I had two teeth loosened by the punch on the mouth. For a long time I carried them in my mouth but continual and unavoidable use of them made them worse and I had to remove them.[31]

Allegations of police violence were perhaps to be expected from radical activists who dubbed the day of the Newtown riot 'Bloody Friday'.[32] Even the conservative *Sydney Morning Herald* reported, however, that the defenders in the Newtown fighting had been 'dragged, almost insensible, to the waiting patrol wagons'.[33] So heavy were the casualties—one man was shot when he raised a bayonet to the police and two suffered fractured skulls—that at the end of June 1931 the political bureau of the Communist Party had to caution restraint.[34] Still, it was notable—and, for the peace of Australia's cities, fortunate—that no one died of their injuries, either in Sydney or in the anti-eviction riots in other cities. The only fatality seems to have been a bystander in Newtown, Sydney, who suffered a heart attack in his excitement.

The risks were considerable but the eviction riots were performative politics at its most energising, staged for the local community, the press and the government. Large crowds gathered to watch the confrontations between rioters and police. The protests were sometimes family events, with women and children watching on, even participating enthusiastically.[35] 'News of the encounter spread round the neighbourhood like wild-fire,' the *Sydney Morning Herald* reported of the Bankstown battle. 'The noise of the conflict could be heard a quarter of a mile distant.'[36] People travelled across Melbourne to join protests in that city. Brunswick streets became blocked with 'a seething mass of humanity'.[37] In Preston, the police needed to cordon off entire streets. In Newcastle, New South Wales, when 60 police arrived to enforce an eviction order, they met 'a number of women [who] emerged from the house screaming loudly . . . Even when the police had possession of the house, these women and girls returned again and again to fling execrations at the men in uniform.'[38]

But if the riots were galvanising they were not, as some communist activists hoped, 'the beginning of a revolution'.[39] To be sure, a Bankstown house was renamed 'Eureka Stockade' and communists played a prominent role in the riots, but in retrospect, the eviction riots seem to have had some of the elements of the food riots of earlier centuries. While they were certainly political in inspiration, they were local in focus, communally based and founded on a moral economy that, in this case, asserted the right to a home.[40] Some of the activism was spontaneous. The crowds at the first Brunswick eviction, in July 1930, were swollen simply because a march of the unemployed happened to be passing nearby. At other times, protesters were mobilised with little advance notice by bicycle squads pedalling round the district, ringing their bells and exhorting others to join the fight. Messages would be chalked on the pavement, giving details of the site of an imminent eviction. All this challenged the state's control of public space, but it was not Petrograd in November 1917. As one activist said after listening to a long exposition on the global capitalist crisis at a UWM meeting, 'Brilliant bloody analysis but I used to keep thinking: how do you get back to the rank and file?'[41]

The response of the Australian state also diluted the radical potential of the eviction riots. Certainly the police violence was excessive and multiple arrests followed each eviction. The courts, too, could be partisan. The magistrate presiding over a case arising from a riot at Fitzroy, Melbourne, after complimenting the police 'on the manner in which they had carried out unpleasant duties', dressed down the defendants:

The trouble with you people, who are not sufficiently educated to understand what is going on, is that you follow blindly and take part in something that does not concern you. You interfere with other people's affairs instead of minding your own business. It is the fault of many persons themselves that they are not working at present . . . This hooliganism is going to be stopped.[42]

Typically, the police were not held to account for their violence but some protesters received gaol sentences. After a lengthy legal process involving three trials, fourteen men arrested in the riot at Bankstown were sentenced to twelve months in prison.[43]

Yet the arrests of the rioters did not always result in convictions, given the considerable public support for the anti-eviction cause.[44] Proceedings against sixteen men arrested at a Newtown riot were dropped after the jury could not reach agreement.[45] A public outcry greeted the prosecution of the 21 men arrested for malicious damage of property during an anti-eviction riot in Clovelly, Sydney. A government inquiry was held and several men released.[46] Meanwhile, to the north in Newcastle, a committee headed by the mayor spoke out in defence of 30 men arrested during a riot at Clara Street, Tighes Hill, in June 1932. An outspoken priest and future bishop, Ernest Burgmann, also denounced the police brutality.[47] Twenty of the men on trial were acquitted. The remaining ten, whose fate the jury had left undecided, were retried at Singleton, but the new jury acquitted two of them and failed to reach a verdict on the others. To the delight of the press, the trial descended into a Gilbert-and-Sullivan farce. A member of the jury became ill, two of the accused had appendicitis, the counsel for the defence caught the flu, the judge had an attack of laryngitis, one of the police on the indictment accidentally shot himself and the sheriff's officer collapsed with kidney trouble. To cap it all, when a 'choice consignment of fruit' was sent from a hotel to the jury, it was mistakenly given to the prisoners, 'who consumed the contents of the hamper with great gusto'.[48] With a little help from luck and ineptitude, the checks and balances of the democratic system functioned. The judiciary and popular opinion acted as a brake on executive power.

Moreover, the militancy of the eviction rioters was diluted by some measure of success. Far fewer evictions took place than the number of warrants authorising them.[49] In Melbourne in 1931, some 2168 warrants were issued but only 692 executed; in 1932, some 1651 of 3756 were executed.[50] Presumably landlords were dissuaded from proceeding to eviction by the fear of suffering public exposure, bad press and property damage. The newspaper coverage of the evictions increased the moral pressure on the authorities. What politician could stand idle when journalists described tenants sheltering from the rain on the footpath thus: 'the children's clothes were wet through and the men's mackintoshes glistened as the police held [back] the angry crowd of men'?[51]

Local councils, too, found alternative housing for some victims of eviction. This was usually temporary, but the surviving documentary record reveals councils to be troubled, anxious, even compassionate rather than heartless. In the case of the Brunswick veteran mentioned earlier, a council van delivered his furniture to his new accommodation. The Sydney Council made the old Redfern Fish Market available for housing the unemployed.[52] State governments, too, as mentioned, chose to take some responsibility for those facing homelessness. In Western Australia, the conservative Mitchell government legislated in July 1931 to reduce rents by 22.5 per cent unless permission for an increase was officially granted.[53] Lang did likewise in late 1931, while in April 1932, the Hogan government in Victoria, under pressure from councils and unions to address the housing issue—and facing an election—agreed to provide eight shillings a week in rent allowance for those who were utterly destitute and had been evicted from their homes.[54] The police were instructed to anticipate evictions and find suitable houses into which evicted tenants could move. South Australia, however, did not provide rent assistance until August 1934, when state government departments provided one day's work a week for unemployed men facing eviction.[55]

None of this, of course, addressed the wider problem of homelessness, and government intervention often came a year, if not two, after the first eviction riots. Furthermore, evictions never really ceased.[56] Even after the windows of estate agents had been smashed across Richmond, the rate of evictions did not slow. In less than four months in early 1932, there were 241 evictions in that suburb.[57] Moreover, if the Victorian government's rent allowance was a win for the eviction rioters, it failed to keep up with rising rentals as the economy started to recover—although in 1934 the Victorian government did allow tenants to keep the subsidy while earning a small income.[58] Meanwhile, in Western Australia unscrupulous landlords were able to find loopholes in the Mitchell legislation, benefiting from the fact that the legislation did not cover short-term leases.[59]

Thus, for all the dramatic efforts of the anti-eviction forces and the attempts of governments to deal with the need for shelter, many of those who lost their homes found that they had to rely on their own resources. As with the battle to supplement the official and charitable supplies of food, Australians navigated their crisis of housing through self-help, stoicism and resilience.

351

CHAPTER 28

Without a home

The future of people who lost their homes depended, as did so much of the Depression experience, on the resources they could mobilise. Some were able to rely on their family or some form of community support. But many of the homeless found themselves on the margins of society, squatting in abandoned buildings, sleeping rough, living in controlled institutions or swelling the camps or shanty towns that sprang up in urban spaces and on the edges of towns. But if the homeless were marginalised, they were not without strategies for coping and remaining resilient. Nor were they invisible. The camps in which they found themselves forced to live generated a mix of responses typical of the Depression years: official and charitable support, and intrusive social control; but also anxiety, suspicion and resentment on the part of local communities in which the homeless sought refuge.

Where did people go when they lost their home? The more fortunate fell back on their families. Couples with children moved in with grandparents. Siblings took each other in. Single children returned to the family home. Younger children might be sent to live with more affluent relatives on farms, where accommodation and food were available at little cost.[1] Sometimes those with no blood links pooled their resources to make housing affordable. This reliance on 'fictive kinship' was nothing new. It had pre-dated the dole and other forms of welfare. Important though it was, however, the extended-family option brought its tensions: crowded accommodation, lack of privacy and intergenerational incompatibility.

An alternative for the evicted, as we have seen, was to keep moving from one rented place to another. The new housing might be cheaper and worse. A whole home might be replaced by rooms in a boarding house or one of the dosshouses or hostels run by charitable institutions and private individuals. It was a regime of constant insecurity, an anchorless way of living. As a child living in South Australia later recalled: 'we would come home from school and everything would be packed up and a chappy would come around with a horse and dray just after dark and he and Dad and Mum would pack everything on to this dray and off you would go to this other house'.[2]

Beyond this, the homeless could squat in unoccupied buildings. Conditions were sometimes appalling. One couple visited by a health inspector in Alberton, South Australia, lived in a small unlined shed only 2.3 metres high. There was no window and no fireplace. Their sleeping arrangements consisted of a double bed with an old stained flock mattress. The pillows, too, were stained and had no slips. All the blankets were old and torn. One of the family, a two-year-old child fathered by another man who provided no support, lived with an aunt, while the mother was expecting a second child: 'very ill clad . . . and without undervests, shoes and stockings', she feared that her children would be 'taken from her'.[3] Another building owned by the South Australian Harbour Board was occupied by eighteen unemployed men. The basement had 'a considerable quantity of water' and rubbish. 'Each floor was very dark and on the first floor a strong smell of urine was noticeable.' The street frontage was scattered with ash, paper, tins and rags that, being wet and damp, attracted large numbers of flies.[4]

The worst outcome was living on the streets. Some evicted families suffered this fate, if only for a short time. When two families with eleven children were evicted from a house they had been sharing in Port Adelaide, the four parents sent the children to relatives while they slept on one double bed in the street.[5] Another family, in Sydney, sheltered under a tarpaulin for a week, with neighbours supplying hot meals and a kerosene tin filled with coke to keep them warm. One returned soldier was so distraught that he placed his Gallipoli star and other campaign medals on top of his furniture stacked in the street, to show how poorly diggers were being treated. His wife 'broke down and just sat in the gutter with tears streaming down her tired face'.[6]

Such families ultimately relocated, even if this was to shanty towns or primitive natural shelters, such the caves in the Sydney cliffs overlooking the Pacific Ocean. But for some men the streets remained 'home'. Little has been written about the history of homelessness and vagrancy in Australia, but a range of intersecting factors seem to have made certain people vulnerable: the availability of affordable housing, family support, physical health, class and cultural background.[7] Many returned soldiers, disabled by the physical and psychological legacy of the war, had slipped into homelessness well before the Depression years. As the supply of cheaper lodgings for single men dried up, they took to sleeping in public places, parks and gardens.

Across the country, 'cities' of the homeless emerged in public spaces. The Sydney Domain had a long history, dating back to the 1890s depression, of housing destitute 'Domain Dossers'. In February 1931, the *Sydney Morning Herald* reported that in the early hours of the morning scores of homeless people could be seen in the Outer Domain

> lying on the bare ground, their bodies wrapped in nondescript garments, ranging from woollen materials to old newspapers. Some sleep with head and face exposed; others curl themselves into huddled bundles from which neither head not feet can be seen . . . Some men wash themselves thoroughly at the drinking fountains.[8]

In Perth, the homeless congregated at the Esplanade, waiting for their food rations and then turning the ground into an insanitary 'quagmire littered with refuse of all descriptions'.[9] In Melbourne, the unemployed camped in the railway carriages at Jolimont, near the Melbourne Cricket Ground.[10] In Adelaide, one police officer recalled that he would

> come across men sleeping in lavatories, in parklands, in the ditches and in the sheds. In waterways around the public reserves. They would run around the town carrying a wheat bag . . . Some slept in cemeteries, in empty houses and shops, in ceilings, lanes and doorways, banks of

the Torrens, drainage pipes, empty railway coaches and railway yards. We used to have to go and clear them out . . . It was pathetic to urge them on.[11]

In Port Augusta, the homeless occupied construction pipes, one end blocked with corrugated iron, tarpaulins or wooden planks. One itinerant man claimed that they made 'admirable little homes'.[12]

These homeless men spilled onto the streets in the day, begging for food and cash. It was easy to construct them as social deviants. While the *Sydney Morning Herald* noted in September 1930 that 'Many of those who have swelled the ranks [of beggars] are obviously the victims of the financial crisis, honest, unfortunate beings, reluctantly driven to the quick charity of the passer-by as a last resource,' it also continued: 'Now a new army is augmenting their ranks. The newcomers are furtive, quick people, darting and dotted in the jostling crowds. It is a terrible army, a leaderless, lost legion. Aloof from each other, they march gutter, pavement, road, by-way, nowhere but seeking, insistent, remorseless.'[13]

Poverty, it was feared, was turning men to crime. Children were reportedly being organised by Fagan-like characters into gangs that extorted money from the public. In bare feet and ragged clothes they played on the public's sympathy by singing songs to 'their destitute mother'.[14] To quote the *Sydney Morning Herald* again:

Lurking in an alley-way, a man pushes his stunted child forward to offer onion pickles, home-made toffee. 'Has the gentleman a coin? . . . sick mother . . . Please sir!' Thin faces dart from the doorways—ties, hand-kerchiefs, face cream, shoe laces, posies, fish that waggle fins; unshaven chins, unwashed necks, collarless, shirtless, sockless, tense faces: 'Buy, buy, buy, give, give, give' . . . eager, thrusting, tenacious, imploring.[15]

It is difficult to know how much such impressions were indebted to reality, how much to Dickens' *Oliver Twist*. Still, the police and courts tried to make the homeless less visible. Men sleeping in Melbourne's railway carriages were arrested for trespass and vagrancy. An unemployed man in Adelaide was imprisoned for three months in January 1931 for being without sufficient means of support. A young man who had been sleeping on the banks of the Torrens, existing on the fish he could catch, was sent to Magill Reformatory for two years when he stole a pocket mirror from a woman.[16]

Some authorities decided that the solution to this social threat and the manifest need of the homeless for shelter was to establish officially run camps. In the FCT, for example, many labourers had been thrown out of work when construction of the national capital came to a virtual standstill. Housed in camps stratified by occupational status, the men suffered from Canberra's bitter nights; 'with 'winter coming on', their representatives wrote in 1930, 'the poor fellows are in for a hard time'; many of them were not in very good health and were living 'on a very small dole given out by the FCT's Returned Soldiers' League'.[17] Their numbers were inflated as itinerant workers started to arrive from other regions, penniless and hungry. The authorities responded by offering accommodation at Parkes Barracks, situated between Commonwealth Bridge and Scotts Crossing. With a septic-tank service, washing and bathing facilities, good cubicles and a mess house with two stoves, the site had the advantages, from the perspective of official-dom, of being 'reasonably distant from any residential area, and not too far from the Labor Bureau'.[18]

The South Australian government, for its part, made accommodation for the homeless available in 1931 in the Exhibition Building, a massive structure dating from the 1880s (and demolished in 1962). Located at the heart of the city and close to the Torrens River where many humpies had sprung up, it housed up to 500 men, organised into two separate camps. The arrange-ment had little to recommend it. The men had to vacate the building during the day and sought shelter in the nearby public library, museum and art gallery. The camp became a 'human pigsty', to quote one leader of the unem-ployed. The death of one of the occupants was attributed to the camp's miserable conditions. Far from pacifying the unemployed, the camp fuelled a higher level of political activism. As single men with little to lose, the unemployed demanded blankets, leather for boot repairs and better-quality food from the cafés where their meal tickets could be used.[19]

The camp that the Victorian government established for single men in December 1930 also proved to be a hotbed of unrest rather than a safety valve for the overcrowded accommodation in the city.[20] Ironically named 'Better Days' camp, it was housed in a former recruitment centre from World War I at Broadmeadows, 20 kilometres to Melbourne city's north. From an official perspective, this was conveniently isolated and distant from where most people lived and worked. The accommodation consisted of sixteen corrugated-iron huts, each housing 30–40 men, with bunks fitted with straw paillasses. The camp's commander, J.J. Scanlan, a decorated colonel of the AIF, ran the site on military lines. While Broadmeadows 'was not the Gulag', Scanlan imposed strict regulations for cleanliness, early rising and meal times. He encouraged wholesome entertainment: boxing, wrestling and athletics—but, of course, no gambling. Men had to perform camp duties in return for their accommodation.

Most controversially, anyone who showed radical or assertive tendencies was disciplined, either serving time in the camp gaol or being expelled from the camp. In time, Broadmeadows became, to quote one resident, 'a seething cauldron of dissatisfaction, discord and unadulterated misery'. Scuffles broke out in early 1931 when some men refused to accept relief work in the country. Radical supporters from the outside community threatened to march on the camp in solidarity. Finally, in February 1931, the police launched a dawn raid, removing 95 men on suspicion of political unreliability. Two were later shown to be communists. Some months later, 167 men walked out of the camp in protest at the treatment of a man who had abused Scanlan when caught removing wood from the kitchen without authority. Allegations of brutality and corruption in the distribution of rations and clothing fuelled the discontent until, in late 1932, the camp was finally closed. It had served the government's purpose of sustaining single unemployed men at a low financial outlay, but the political cost was considerable. It is a little overstrained to claim, as one historian has, that at Broadmeadows 'the set of human rights ostensibly inherent in a democracy had ceased to have meaning'.[21] But the men who had to accept accommodation at a government facility undoubtedly paid a price in terms of their privacy, dignity and autonomy.

For many of the homeless, the only choice was to relocate to unofficial camps on the perimeters of the capital cities and in countless country towns. The precise number of these shanty towns will never be known. They varied greatly in size and quality. Many were improvised, created to meet a temporary need and then dismantled as the occupants moved on. At the worst, the conditions were dire. One regional newspaper reported of the camp in the northern New South Wales town of Casino in July 1931 where more than a thousand people were living: 'Campers had horses, which roamed indiscriminately about, while the many tents contained three or four dogs and cats. People walked bare-footed through the accumulated filth. Household rubbish was thrown indiscriminately between the tents, despite the fact that a pit had been constructed for the refuse.'[22] Housing was often primitive, at least in the early stages of the development of many camps. Humpies were gouged into hillsides; their floors were hard earth. Shacks and furniture were cobbled together from pieces of timber, bags, bricks, kerosene tins, sheet iron—'any usable material at all'.[23] The 'kitchen' might be in the open, as were the toilets.

At Platts Channel, Mayfield, Newcastle, the houses were built on stilts, with the high tide lapping under them. The toilet was a hole in the floor; the waste dropped into the Hunter River.[24] At Rosewater near Port Adelaide, the camp created in 1928 had tidy canvas tents, but refuse littered the site and an open stormwater drain was used as a latrine.[25] When rain fell, the latrine, tents and huts were flooded. Then there were the insects, mosquitos, spiders and snakes. Flinders Street camp, Port Kembla, was located in a swampy drainage easement where typhoid and dysentery were endemic. In the summer months, swarms of flies and the heat spread infection and the children especially were vulnerable to gastric disorders.[26]

Still, life in the camps was not unmitigated horror. The residents had some freedom and were spared the immediate threat of eviction. Their housing, if initially primitive, improved with time. Many of the unemployed, after all, had worked in the construction industry. Extensions were added to 'homes' and walls were whitewashed. Wives aspiring to domesticity decorated interiors with flowers in jam jars or bottles. Since camp-dwellers could draw rations and accept relief work, they had adequate sources of food. Vegetable gardens were common, if the soil allowed. Near Menindee in outback

New South Wales, 'Many ingenious devices were invented to raise water from the river for household use and to irrigate the beds of tomatoes, beans, peas, carrots and cabbages that grew in rich loamy soil on the banks of the Darling River.'[27] Some campers claimed in retrospect to have enjoyed the natural environment, the bushwalking, the fishing and the clean air. The humpies and shacks were even remembered as 'comfortable'—given names such as 'Tranquillity Haven' and, perhaps more ambiguously, 'This'l Do'.[28]

The hardships of camp life were also mitigated by collective action. In the larger and more permanent camps, central committees managed affairs.[29] They pooled ration coupons; made bulk purchases of food; distributed clothing and other goods donated by charities; rostered maintenance work; regulated entry into the camp; and mediated in disputes, including marital ones.[30] They arranged entertainment to relieve the corrosive boredom of unemployment: lending libraries, card evenings, dances and sporting matches. Happy Valley near La Perouse in Sydney was an exemplar. It had a bulk store, an oval for soccer and rugby, and a marquee with wooden floor, piano and gramophone.

Camp committees also mediated relations with the outside world, sending deputations to governments and councils. Local authorities knew that it was not in their interests to ignore the shanty towns, given their potential threat to public health. A small group of sixteen families camped along the edge of the Canning River, south of Perth, was thus provided by the Roads Board with a tap located a short distance from the camp. The Health Department helped install some communal sanitation.[31] The council of Armidale, New South Wales, likewise provided the evicted unemployed with free water and sanitary services.[32] Happy Valley became the focus of attention for the philanthropically inclined Sydney social elites. The camp's marquee was the gift of the wife of a newspaper magnate, Lady Marcie Fairfax. The neighbouring golf links agreed to connect water to the camp from their source. At least this stopped campers walking across their beloved greens! The Mayor of Randwick, a member of the golf club, opened a subscription list among the members to purchase a fishing boat, nets and gear for the camp.[33] A first-aid hospital was donated by one Mrs Charles Salon, while a bevy of Sydney dignitaries launched a fundraising carnival, on the camp's behalf, in a packed Paddington Town Hall.[34] The ubiquitous governor, Philip Game, and his wife were patrons of the fund and visited the camp in June 1931. Game commended the residents on their 'great experiment on social lines', and their choosing 'to live in the open instead of pigging it in the city'. Even more fatuously, Lady Game said that she 'could settle here and be happy myself'.[35] But she seems to have shown no inclination to move out of Government House.

Elsewhere, relationships between camp-dwellers and local communities were more troubled. The local population saw the men in the camps as competitors for work. Ratepayers and councils fretted at the impact of the 'mushroom slums' on property values. In the New South Wales town of Dubbo, it was suggested that trees should be planted on the edge of the unsightly shanty town, 'Tin Town', to obscure it from the view of visitors.[36] Once more, the clusters of unemployed were thought to raise crime rates. Police in Brisbane suspected that the Crystal Palace hostel was operating an illegal still, even though it was under the jurisdiction of the Presbyterian Church. The committee denied this accusation, claiming that it was payback for some of its members supporting relief workers on strike for better conditions.[37] Still, many camps carried a social stigma that was painful for those whose self-image of respectability jarred with their material deprivation. Children were heckled on the way to school: 'Get back where you belong—you dirty little camp kids.' Or they were forbidden from playing with local children. Decades later, one woman recalled that as a girl from the camps she had been 'Snubbed by people who were ill-mannered, illiterate, and sometimes smelling from unwashed bodies, but who still had jobs.'[38]

Community tensions erupted dramatically in the north Queensland town of Cairns in July 1932.[39] Some 150 unemployed men were camped in the showground at Parramatta Park, near the centre of town. They were not local unemployed, for whom there might have been some sympathy, but itinerant workers from other parts of Australia. They were viewed, as the town mayor put it, as 'invaders'. Moreover, since they were led by a radical activist from outside, Jack McCormack, the campers were easily constructed as 'enemies of society', defying constitutional authority and fomenting strife. Indeed, the Red Flag flew from the grandstand.

Matters came to a head when the grounds were required for the agricultural show, an event that Cairns had let lapse in the 1920s but had revived in 1931.[40] The local council offered to accommodate the unemployed in temporary accommodation, a shed covered with tarpaulins at the back of one of the wharves. Water and sanitation facilities were accessible nearby.[41] McCormack refused. The unemployed, he claimed, were entitled to the same accommodation as the town authorities might expect for themselves. The battle lines were drawn at a public meeting early in July. McCormack insisted that 'he wanted the unemployed taken notice of. They were at present occupying dog and cattle stalls and were now threatened to be pushed out to make room for prize fowls; but to heave them out would not be easy, because the unemployed might resist.' He warned that 'if the law of the land were not to give the unemployed justice, then the unemployed must adopt the law of the jungle'. In Frank Hardy's semi-fictional account of the battle, McCormack is depicted as daredevil agitator, provoking the townspeople while the local party member seeks compromise.[42] The response of the mayor, however, was non-negotiable: 'When the representatives of the unemployed inferred that their interests were paramount to those of the citizens of Cairns, he would say definitively that they were not . . . No section of the community shall be allowed to flout the interests of the whole community.'[43]

The town leaders lobbied the state government to resolve the situation. Could it fund the better-quality accommodation that the unemployed demanded? Alternatively, could it evict them from the showgrounds? But the Labor premier, William Forgan Smith, refused to take responsibility, claiming that local initiatives should be funded by voluntary subscriptions. Legal action, he said, was the better way to relocate the unemployed. As preparations for the show stalled, and extra police were deployed from Innisfail, the town seethed with rumours. Members of the RSSILA and the Catholic Church were reportedly being urged to 'get down and do over the unemployed'. A local brewery manager told his employees, 'Don't come to work on Monday morning unless you've been down at Parramatta Park getting into the unemployed.'[44]

Finally, on the morning of Sunday 17 July, two days before the show was to begin, hundreds of citizens, led by the mayor and local businessmen, joined the police in evicting the squatters from the showgrounds. The brawl involved weapons of wood, iron bars, concrete, cane knives, and even a gelignite bomb that failed to explode. About a hundred people were injured, seventeen of whom required hospitalisation. A young teenage observer remembered the police cars taking the injured swagmen away in cars; some of them were 'unconscious with blood streaming from their head . . . and their arms hanging out the car window'.[45] Outnumbered by perhaps five to one (the numbers vary), those men who had survived the brawl uninjured were then chased out of town, though they were allowed back later to retrieve their possessions.

The agricultural show then proceeded and was deemed 'an outstanding success'.[46] Four of the unemployed campers, including McCormack, were sentenced to gaol, but they were later found not guilty on appeal. The dynamic communist lawyer Fred Paterson, committed to defending the socially disadvantaged and willing to offer his services pro bono, acted in their defence. Paterson would later serve on both the Gladstone and Townsville city councils, and was the first communist to be elected to the state parliament when he won the state seat of Bowen in April 1944.

It is tempting to see the Cairns riot as another manifestation of the earlier right-wing mobilisation in the southern states. Certainly it was framed in ideological terms. The Townsville branch of the UWM described the attackers as 'the Fascist element of Cairns'. The attackers themselves spoke the language of anti-communism and law and order. On 18 July, the *Cairns Post* declared the riot a 'red-letter day' in the town's history:

> The challenge given to the Law, to Society, and to Citizenship, by the extreme nomadic element that had taken possession of Parramatta Park, resulted in the Law, Society and Citizenship vindicating themselves, and making a splendid gesture to the whole State . . . The violent conduct of the extremists and the dangerous weapons they employed . . . proves to what extent this element will go.[47]

Yet there is scant evidence that the vigilantes were members of a paramilitary movement like the Old or New Guard. Their attack on the camp seems to have been driven primarily by frustration and irritation with the itinerant workers—and with a government in Brisbane that left them to resolve local disputes. Put simply, they were not going to let these 'invaders' deny them their show! The state home secretary implied as much when he declared that the police should not have acted as 'a "basher gang" for the convenience of any individual or show committee'.[48] The significance of the Cairns riot was indeed its parochialism. Community solidarity, as we have seen, was often a source of resilience for many Australians during the Depression. But it also functioned to exclude the outsider. As communities turned inwards in times of economic competition, priority was given to their own. Compassion, as ever, had its limits, and it often ended at the town boundary.

CHAPTER 29

On the track

The most vulnerable of the homeless were those who left the cities or the more established camps and went 'on the track'. Most itinerant swagmen, as far as we know, were working class but they included a sprinkling of desperate professional men. They were driven primarily by the need to find work, although some were escaping marital conflict and obligations. Young men also left home as a rite of passage. Women and children followed their husbands and fathers. Many had a restless, even compulsive, urge to keep moving. All believed that their lifestyle and chances of survival would be improved if they left the slums and disappointments of city life behind. They were usually wrong.

The single man on the move was nothing new, as the semi-official national anthem, 'Waltzing Matilda', attests. For decades, the swagman—or 'whaler', 'sundowner' or 'hobo'—had been a mythologised figure of the Australian bush. 'Humping his bluey' or living 'on the wallaby', he survived on practically nothing, camping in the open, stealing or cadging food from others and doing stints of casual labour. He was often the driftwood of society: the labourer without skills, the worker who was too old or incapacitated to compete, or the man whose trade had been wiped out by changes in technology or taste.

The Depression swelled their numbers, adding women and families to the mix. We do not know precisely how many there were, but in South Australia over 10,000 more men and 3000 more women left the city to go to the country than vice versa—a migration that was a reversal of the pre-Depression drift to Adelaide. The numbers in other states were probably greater, given that the South Australian government did not provide 'track' rations to people travelling from town to town.[1] An old-time swaggie complained that the new travellers were 'like a swarm of locusts. The country is bare after they pass.'[2]

Life 'on the track' meant constant movement. Travellers' lives were dominated by the regulation in some states that rations could not be collected in the same town on successive weeks. This could involve nightmare journeys, such as that described in Kylie Tennant's *The Battlers*, a novel based on her first-hand experience of punishing walking tours with the unemployed. Her main characters drive their horse-drawn van through the night when the wind is 'a charging elephant' and the empty plains 'under empty skies' are coldly brutal. They dare not stop. 'They would miss their dole; and if they did that, what would become of them?'[3] Sometimes men had to have a minimum residency in the state in which they were claiming rations, so they swapped cards at the borders and used someone else's name to collect rations.

The search for work also drove travellers on. News spread across the countryside of employment opportunities, such as fruit-picking or sewing wheat bags. But often the travellers arrived to discover that preference had been given to local men or that others had got there before them: there were 'more bloody bagmen out there than bags of wheat'.[4] They started the journey again. 'We agree,' two travellers wrote in a Broken Hill newspaper in March 1931, 'that work is almost a myth, but somewhere there must be a job a silver lining to the dark clouds under which we have travelled so many weary miles.'[5] If work was found, it was seasonal or casual work. With no union protection, men had to accept rates of pay below the award. They could do almost anything in a day's work: milking cows, hoeing a vegetable garden, backing up a horse team, digging holes for fence posts and cutting timber. 'We worked them from daylight till dark,' one primary producer later recalled.[6] Many worked for their food alone: a loaf of bread and a half a sheep in return for doing a day's washing on the farm.[7] The food could range from 'huge meals' of excellent quality to the almost inedible. One farmer fed a man on 'boiled wheat and rabbits day after day'.[8]

The vast distances of rural Australia posed massive challenges. The epic journeys of the American Okies that John Steinbeck immortalised in *The Grapes of Wrath* are justly famous, but some Australians travelled further: for example, from Kalgoorlie to Broken Hill via Mount Isa, a distance of some 8000 kilometres.[9] The more fortunate had some form of mobility: cars, horse-drawn vehicles, bicycles or motorbikes. Kylie Tennant, this time in her 1935 debut novel, *Tiburon*, captured the miscellany vividly:

> Sulkies loaded high with tents, household gear, children and bedding—with perhaps a spare horse, and certainly a dog or so, trotting behind. Battered old motortrucks, bottle-oh carts and cars belonging to pedlars of soap, brushes and tinware . . . Dusty men pushed their bicycles up the rise, while others came tramping with their 'nap' on their backs and the remains of last week's dole slung over their shoulders in sugar-bags.[10]

Those without vehicles hitched rides from others. But many walked. Tom Combey, who made his way from Brisbane to Mount Isa and back in a vain search for work, covered over one thousand kilometres on foot.[11] For such men their patched shoes and their blistered feet joined food as gnawing obsessions.

Predictably, men resorted to the illegal use of trains—or as it was known, 'jumping the rattler'. Their preference was to try for a goods train on which they could force an entry into box cars or crawl under tarpaulins. A 'Battler's Ballad' captured the dangerous moment of trying to catch a moving train:

> Then you see the green light flashing and you hear the bumpers crashing
> And you see the great big engine rushing by,
> With your swag held at the ready, your nerves are not so steady
> For you know you've got to take her on the fly.
> Then your swag you try to throw in but the flaming thing won't go in
> Bounces off the truck and hits you and you fall,
> Pick the remnants of your swag up, pick your billy-can and bag up,
> And you say, 'I missed the bastard after all.'[12]

Anecdotal evidence testifies to men losing limbs while trying to jump onto a train.[13] Once on the train, the conditions could be rugged. Squeezed among crates and livestock, men had no toilet facilities or comfortable places to sleep. One man stood a whole night with a mob of cattle, holding his case in the air, trying to keep his gear off the muck on the floor.[14]

'Jumping the rattler' brought the swagmen into direct confrontation with the authorities. Not only was travelling without paid tickets illegal, but some men prised open crates and stole food on the trains. Special detectives, railway officials and police all tried to reduce the losses. They kicked and belted the tarpaulins wherever they could see a lump.[15] Station masters moved along the side of a goods train at night, rattling stones in a billy can and asking, 'Any room in there mate?' The unsuspecting traveller who answered yes was arrested.[16] The latter story was possibly apocryphal, repeated so often that it became legendary. But one way or another, many riding the trains were charged with trespass and sentenced to time in gaol.[17] For all that, some police are remembered as not taking formal action against the travellers. They were glad to see the men leave their town or, if the numbers of men jumping on a train were high, they knew they could do little to stop them.

The police were in an ambiguous position, responsible for law enforcement but also in country towns charged with distributing the rations and relief work that were critical to the travellers' survival. They had duties of care to both their governments and the travellers. To quote Tennant's *The Battlers*, they stood 'between the devillings of the "dole chasers" on the one hand and the deep sea of the Chief Secretary's files and enquiries on the other'.[18] The police were also members of the community, responsible for defending the property and security of local residents. Travellers raided gardens, shoplifted and stole livestock.[19] Swagmen became drunk and disorderly, including through drinking cheap alcohol laced with methylated spirits. Even when orderly, the travellers had an unsettling presence within the community. They occupied public spaces, sleeping under bridges, at racecourses, and in deserted houses, schools, sheds, sports and showground pavilions, and railway station rest rooms. They slept rough, even in tropical rain.[20]

Some police seem to have negotiated the contradictions of their positions with humanity. In Peterborough, South Australia, the local police officer established a swagman's shelter where men could camp for three days. He gave each man a pair of rabbits to live off before they moved on; 'we were all very happy', one traveller said.[21] Some officers were flexible, not wanting to be bothered with the paperwork of rations or to make difficulties for the unemployed. Other police combined law enforcement with charity. Tom Combey's diary records that he was taken off a train by a local policeman:

> On arriving at the police station we were introduced to the 'Sergeant' who inquired if we had any tucker, & on being informed that we really did have about a quarter of a loaf of bread and about ½ lb meat, called out to Mary [his wife] 'hurry Mary and get these hungry bagmen a feed.' The 'feed' consisted of sausages, plenty of bread and butter and tea. Justice was surely done to those sausages.[22]

Another man, picked up for vagrancy on his way to Dubbo, later recalled:

> And so lo and behold the next morning [the police officer] took me down to the station. We had tomato sandwiches. About a foot high they looked like. And water. And he gave me a voucher for tucker, a coupla ounces of tobacco, ten bob, and told me to get out of town within two hours. So I was quite happy about that one.[23]

If men were ultimately convicted for vagrancy, some justices of the peace, according to one police officer, fixed the period of internment so that the men were released in time to collect their rations and then move on.[24] While in gaol, they were provided with food, blankets, hot water and facilities to wash clothes. Life could be worse.

Yet the relationship between the unemployed and the police was often adversarial. Oral histories are replete with memories of police being pernickety in administering rations, or of men getting 'vagged' (arrested as vagrants) and pushed out of town straight after dole day.[25] Police are recalled as dogs, animals and 'just like Nazis'. They reportedly harassed travellers, tipping the contents of their bags onto the ground, kicking their billies and frying pans into the fire, and throwing bags into rivers to discourage men from sleeping under bridges. They hounded men who tried to organise the travellers for better conditions.[26] According to one hearsay account, a sergeant walked up and down a rations queue, saying:

'Isn't it about time you got some work. You must have been able to find something by now.'

And he came to one young woman and he said to her, quite smug 'didn't I see you at the pictures the other day with a young man', she said 'yes, I suppose that's right' and he said 'Well, I don't know,' he said, 'can't you get some, ah, some financial type help from him,' more or less telling the girl that she should prostitute herself.[27]

In Tennant's *The Battlers*, the activist trying to organise a Bagman's Union declares that 'For all the police care, we can die on the road; yes, and we do die on the road—of starvation, and cold, and despair.' The police in this account threaten men with losing their dole if they refuse to work at sub-award rates for local farmers.[28]

The range of attitudes among police mirrored the ambivalence of the wider society. One the one hand, the travellers were seen as objects of pity and charity. Large farming towns set aside a fenced-in area on the outskirts of town, with tin sheds, showers and lavatory. The YWCA in Cairns established a hostel for transient boarders.[29] Some farming families left the door to small huts on their properties unlocked or placed food at the back door for anyone travelling past.[30] '[Y]ou could always get a feed in the country,' one traveller later recalled. Others claimed 'the vast majority of farmers gave handouts', or that 'Overall people were very helpful.'[31]

On the other hand, there are stories of the travelling cohorts being shunned. As we saw with the vigilante-style riot at Cairns, the travellers were seen as an 'alien infiltration'. Their class background and their appearance—unkempt, dishevelled, unshaven and dirty—had the effect of dehumanising them, a tragically common plight of the victim. To quote Tennant, 'They were worn, hard-faced, loud-voiced women for the most part, and the children, whining about their skirts, were all suffering from running colds and sores.' The local police officer in *The Battlers* ruminates that it is 'easy enough to pick a traveller by the sharpened, hungry face of him. He is either toothless or his gums have drawn back from his teeth, giving him the look of a wolf. His lips have drawn back dry and cracked and stiff in a perpetual half-snarl; the skin of his face is stretched taut as vellum over the projecting bones and is burnt almost black by the sun.'[32] Those owning pastoral properties feared, with good reason, that the hungry travellers might steal their sheep, chickens and turkeys—or worse, their daughters. Since many of the travellers were single men, or married men with families in their cites, they posed a sexual threat. They painted lewd images of naked women on the bridges where they slept and exchanged ribald stories around campfires. A farmer thus offered one traveller work on the condition that he keep away from his daughter. Young swagmen were warned off when they tried to take out local girls. That said, some did meet women whom they married.[33]

Positioned between these extremes of kindness and ostracism, many travellers claimed in retrospect that those of lower social status treated them more humanely. 'The poor are always the most generous to the poor.'[34] Another recalled that when he asked for overnight accommodation in Port Macquarie, 'the rich pub . . . knocked me back and a poor little broken-down place where the publican was serving in the bar, cooking the meals . . . gave me a room and told me to have a meal in the morning!'[35]

More important to the travellers' survival were probably their own social networks. Despite their peripatetic life, travellers kept in touch with each other through the word-of-mouth relay, 'the bush telegraph'. They tracked each other's movements. They helped each other and shared local knowledge. Phillip Law, later an eminent Antarctic scientist, went bush during one university vacation and encountered an itinerant hawker who gave him 'a rundown on all the farmhouses and property owners in the district, noting those that were kind and would give you a feed—and those who were not and would set the dogs on you'.[36]

In this world apart, the travellers created new lives and communities. A 'brotherhood' was established along the Coorong, in South Australia, formed of men who had started from Adelaide with the idea of walking to Melbourne but stopped to live off rabbit, duck and fish until, with the onset of winter, they moved on.[37] Frank Huelin, a young immigrant from the United Kingdom who quickly became itinerant, wrote in 1973 that after returning to the track after visiting city relatives: '[We] were happy, exhilarated by the thought of returning to what had become our "normal" mode of living. Before many days had passed we were back in our old stamping ground—the wheat country of the central west, Forbes, Cowra, Young, Grenfell . . . Once again we were meeting mates.'[38] Ted Waight recalled that although the person living a comfortable, well-ordered life might look at begging and scrounging food as dreadful and incomprehensible, 'to us, on the "outer" it was the only way. We had to adjust, and we did. Actually it was fun, a challenge.'[39] George Parr likewise wrote to his fiancée from Rockley south of Bathurst, New South Wales, on 2 February 1932: 'the three of us are thoroughly enjoying ourselves, as this is a life we have never experienced before, and one never knows what is going to happen or turn up next. As regards to our health, we declare that we have never felt better.'[40]

The more euphoric statements about 'the romance of the swag' need to be treated with some caution. Not only does the passage of years tend to sentimentalise the past, but memories of life on the track were mediated through the discourse of mateship, which, thanks to the bush mythology and the Anzac legend, had become deeply embedded in Australian popular culture by the 1930s. The travellers were not necessarily prone to community. Their lifestyle inclined them to independence and self-reliance. According to Tennant, there was also clear stratification among the travellers: 'the young bagmen on foot or with bicycles did not mix with the men with families and sulkies; and the families spoke only to other families. Caste was caste, and the nice distinctions must be preserved between the settler in the hut and the temporary occupants of a tent.' Still, Tennant's novel also attests to the 'simple, easy friendships founded on mutual respect' that formed between travellers.[41] Her main character, Snow, revels in the independence and autonomy on the track, but comes to accept his relationships with originally unwanted companions, Dancy/The Stray, the busker and even the unlikeable Miss Phipps.

If they developed a community of sorts, the travellers did not form any wider organisation that might have given them political agency. For all their anger about the society that had consigned them to destitution, they presented little organised resistance. Admittedly, some travellers argued with their employers, demanding better conditions, and when itinerant workers were congregated in regional towns, the UWM had some success in channelling their discontent.[42] Party members met men off the rattlers in Townsville, fed them and offered them room to sleep in their office. Itinerant workers did not fit easily into Marxist theory—they were not really a lumpen proletariat in the sense of their being the lowest, most disreputable and apolitical stratum of the industrial working class—but 'they were always welcome' in the homes of party members—or so it has been claimed.[43] At times this association could fuel activism and resistance.

But a 'bagman's union' founded in north Queensland does not seem to have gained traction nationally. Most travellers seem to have been so focused on the daily struggle for survival that their horizons shrank to the next camp, the next town and the next rations day. Boredom, isolation and grinding poverty dampened their sense of agency. Beyond this, the itinerant workers lacked political or industrial power because they were precisely that: itinerant. Their nomadism virtually forbade effective collective action. They had no workplace around which to organise. They rarely congregated in a critical mass and they had little labour that they could withhold to bring pressure on employers, let alone political elites. There was something surreal—and almost pathetic—about the bagman's union meeting at which 'Some of the hotheaded and youthful members . . . suggested that every swagman in this State throw down his swag and refuse to walk the bush roads or jump the "rattler". It was finally decided that all members refuse to call at the squatter's station to have their bags filled.'[44] It is hard, then, not to conclude that the exodus of so many Australians from the cities to the countryside achieved what many in conservative circles hoped it would: the diffusion of the radical potential of the Depression's victims.

CHAPTER 30

Aboriginal Australians

More vulnerable even than the men and women 'on the track' were Australia's Aboriginal peoples. Nearly a century and a half of relentless colonisation had consigned them to a position of profound disadvantage. Violence, disease, poverty and dispossession of their traditional lands had caused their numbers to decline to the point where even some reputable sources—though not all—assumed that they were a 'vanishing race', on the point of extinction.[1] The Depression inevitably increased the vulnerability of these already marginalised peoples. The response of some authorities and local communities to the destitution of Aboriginal peoples was to intensify already draconian government controls, forcing them into reserves against their will. Yet at the same time, the ill-treatment and suffering of the 1920s and 1930s added momentum to an already budding activism for Aboriginal civil, social and economic rights that continues to this day.

The precise numbers and locations of Aboriginal Australians during the Depression years are not known, given the lack of reliable censuses.[2] But the greatest concentrations were in Queensland, Western Australia and the Northern Territory. Wherever they were, Aboriginal Australians were denied full civil rights. Each of the states, from the mid-nineteenth century on, had established 'Protection' regimes, the provisions of which varied.[3]

373

In the first decades of the twentieth century, these systems of control had become more organised, institutional and bureaucratic. Not all people who identified as Aboriginal were 'under the act'. But at their extreme, Aboriginal boards and public-service Protectors, such as Auber Neville in Western Australia, Cecil Cook in the Northern Territory and John Bleakley in Queensland, controlled virtually every detail of Aboriginal people's lives: where they lived, where they worked, what they were paid, who they married and what they ate. Few Aboriginal children were guaranteed education of any quality or length. In more settled areas, they could be excluded from white schools on the insistence of a few parents. Most heinously, the Protection regimes removed children of mixed descent from their parents. Whether this constituted 'genocide' has been much debated, but it is beyond dispute that many family units were torn apart by authorities who believed that the removal of children would be in their best interests and of little consequence to their mothers.[4]

Beyond these formal controls, Aboriginal peoples faced a powerful 'caste barrier' because of their skin colour. In cities, they met fewer restrictions, but in rural locations they were denied access to shops, businesses, churches, community organisations, social clubs and swimming pools. In a 'new spatial politics of exclusion and entry', white Australians sought to confine Aboriginal people to reserves on the outer perimeters of their towns.[5] They needed Aboriginal labourers, and so required them to live nearby, but they also found these workers to be a source of discomfort, disdain and even fear.

Well before the Depression hit, then, many Aboriginal Australians were trapped in a cycle of poverty. In settled areas, the men were congregated in unskilled and casual seasonal employment: working as labourers, stripping bark, pulling corn, erecting fencing and digging potatoes. They also found employment as shearers on farms or as manual labourers on local council projects and the railways.[6] In many of these roles they received wages below the award, or were paid a mix of cash and in-kind: beer, flour or alcohol at inflated prices.[7] The trade unions (with some variations) 'paid lip service to the special obligations owed to Aborigines but acquiesced in the imposition of inferior conditions'.[8] On the vast pastoral estates of outback Australia, conditions tended to be better. While some features of Aboriginal workers' lives were oppressive, they retained a relative autonomy. If work on the station decreased, they could return to their traditional lands where they could access natural waters and game, while enjoying a sense of liberty and space. Moreover, those Aboriginal men employed in mustering and droving boasted skills in bushcraft and orienteering that were recognised to be of considerable economic value.[9]

Aboriginal women were commonly employed in domestic service. Teenage girls were 'apprenticed' to such work by Protection authorities, who believed that domestic service might absorb them into the white working class while exposing them to the 'uplifting' influence of respectable families.[10] These young women had little freedom to leave their place of employment, no matter how crushing was their loneliness or distress at their distance from their families and communities. They often worked long hours and their wages could be paid into trust accounts over which the Protector had control.[11] They received little education other than training in the home. The conditions under which these young women, and even children, worked have been likened to slavery.[12]

Young Aboriginal women, be they in suburban homes or on pastoral stations, were also vulnerable to physical and sexual abuse. Interracial relationships were condemned by white and black activists alike, but many women became ensnared in casual or semi-permanent sexual liaisons, not just with white employers but, in Broome, with Japanese pearlers.[13] Between 1912 and 1938, some 11 per cent of those apprenticed to domestic service in New South Wales became pregnant. In urban situations, the figure was 17.15 per cent.[14] Girls in domestic service in Melbourne frequently had to return to the reserve at Lake Tyers to bear illegitimate children.[15]

In certain situations, Aboriginal women might have had some agency in these sexual relationships. In the Northern Territory, there was a significant gender imbalance, which meant that Aboriginal women were in considerable demand as sexual and domestic partners for white men, despite regulations prohibiting such relationships. But in white suburban homes the asymmetry of power between the domestic servants and their employers and their sons made any notion of 'consent' hollow. There is ample evidence that the New South Wales Aborigines Protection Board was implicated in the sexual abuse of apprentices. In contrast to South Australia, where fathers were pursued for maintenance and Aboriginal mothers allowed to keep their babies, the New South Wales Board viewed with suspicion girls who alleged that they had been sexually abused in their place of employment. The response could be punitive if the girls named a respectable man as their abuser. They could be sent to a harsh 'industrial institution' or to a mental asylum. Moreover, the children of these interracial liaisons were transferred at birth to the care of the Child Welfare Department, while the young mother could be sent back into service or to a reserve or mission.[16]

Given their systemic disadvantage, low socioeconomic status and lack of education, the position of many Aboriginal people during the Depression was precarious. Their casual and seasonal work dried up, and the support they could access varied from state to state. In Victoria, where the numbers of Aboriginal workers were relatively low, the unemployed could access sustenance and work relief programs. So, too, in South Australia residents of Aboriginal missions were eligible for government rations, though at a scale lower than the white unemployed.[17] But in New South Wales they were denied the dole, while in Western Australia they were referred to the Aborigines Department for assistance.[18] Often Aboriginal men and women congregated in shanty towns or were forced to move into government missions and reserves, where the numbers of destitute people grew.[19]

The situation in Western Australia has been well documented, in part because a royal commission into Aboriginal conditions was held in 1934.[20] It is a story without redemption. Although the demands on the Aborigines Department grew with rising unemployment, the annual grant from the government was cut. The ration scales for Aboriginal people declined until in 1931 the basic weekly ration for meat was 680 grams.[21] No systematic efforts were made to provide Aboriginal men with relief work. Indeed, in several districts men were actually put off relief works schemes on account of 'their colour'. In his annual report for 1931, Neville concluded: 'At no time in the past fifteen years and, I believe, in the State's history have conditions been so hard for the natives, particularly in the south west . . . No section of the community has suffered more from the effects of the financial depression.'[22]

Shanty towns proliferated to house the unemployed. In the south of the state, some 50 of these were situated on private or crown land.[23] To the dismay of authorities, camps also mushroomed in the environs and suburbs of Perth—in Swanbourne, Midland Junction, Caversham, Guildford, Lockridge and near the Fremantle cemetery. In these camps, Aboriginal men and women eked out an existence, making and selling brooms and wooden props for clotheslines, collecting and selling old bottles, carting and gardening. Even by the low standards of the Depression, conditions in some Aboriginal settlements were deplorable. Magistrate Henry Moseley, who headed the 1934 royal commission, said that the camps along the Great Southern Railway were 'without exception . . . a disgrace'. Some huts were 'worse by far than the kennel some people would provide for their dogs—whole families of 9 or 10 being huddled together in abject squalor, with no beds to lie on, no cooking or eating utensils worth the name, no proper facilities for washing, and dressed in clothes a tramp would despise'.[24] Little, if any, assistance was given by authorities to provide these camps with basic amenities, such as rubbish collection and sanitation. At one camp there were two latrines for more than 120 people. Sometimes water had to be carted long distances by hand.

The incidence of illness within Aboriginal communities was high. Respiratory problems, stomach and bowel ailments, and eye and skin diseases were chronic. In 1933 ten children died of whooping cough in camps in the south. In Derby to the north, there were 85 cases of leprosy in six months in 1933–34 alone. Throughout the state, cases of venereal disease remained untreated, even in children.[25] The mortality rates of Aboriginal women during childbirth were also high: in 1936 only eight of 24 hospitals in the south were willing to take Aboriginal women during their confinement. Only in 1935 were 'native' hospitals established at Broome and Wyndham, and a leprosarium at the Sunday Island Mission at Derby.[26] In the interim, those suffering from leprosy at Beagle Bay settlement, north of Broome, were taken to Darwin, in many cases against their will. As they awaited the arrival of the lugger that would transport them, their spokesmen were kept in chains. Then, as author and historian Mary Durack described it:

The leave-taking of the twelve who were packed on board [the lugger *W.S. Rolland*] was one of the most pathetic incidents in the mission's history. The more advanced half-caste and part-Filipinos among them, hoping to encourage the terrified full-blood victims, made brave attempts to be merry, as though setting off on a holiday cruise. One had an accordion and played a jaunty air, but as the lugger pushed out to sea a high-pitched keening of tribal lament went up from both the ship and the shore, and even the captain, a hardened old sea-dog, could not restrain his emotion.[27]

Neville thought—as did authorities elsewhere—that the 'solution' to this social disaster was to concentrate the Aboriginal people in government settlements and reserves, if need be, by force. He ordered the residents of the semi-permanent Walebing camp near Moora in the Wheatbelt to move to the Native Settlement at Moore River. They refused, on the grounds that they would have no chance of getting work at Moore River and would be unable to take their dogs and horses. When Aboriginal men were then suspected of drawing rations while earning money during the shearing season of 1931, Neville closed down the rations depots in Moora and the surrounding district. After five months without these supplies, the Aboriginal people had no choice but to move into Moore River, in February 1932.

The same pressure was applied to those people settled about 3 kilometres from the town of Northam. Relationships between the Aboriginal residents and the local town became toxic from late 1931. White men openly demanded sex from Aboriginal women, drunken brawls broke out and police harassed the Aboriginal campers for petty crime. The camp residents maintained that their dogs were being poisoned and their horses stolen. The town authorities, in turn, claimed that the camp, located in a riverbed opposite the sanitary depot and the rubbish dump, posed a health threat. As it happened, this was Premier Mitchell's electorate, and state elections were to be held in April 1933. In January, in a move of questionable legality, the Aboriginal campers were rounded up by police, detained overnight and transported by train to Perth and then to Moore River. Those who refused to leave their drays, horses and dogs behind were allowed to travel overland to the settlement under police escort.[28]

The Moore River settlement that awaited them was 'a woeful spectacle'.[29] The numbers had grown from 300 to 500 between 1929 and 1933, but departmental expenditure on the site had fallen. According to Moseley's report, the dormitories in the compound were dilapidated and 'vermin ridden' to an extent which 'makes eradication impossible'.[30] Apart from a sewing room, where clothing was made for 'indigent natives throughout the State', there was no equipment for any kind of vocational training. No vegetables were grown at the settlement and the rations of meat, fruit and eggs were inadequate. The 'hospital', such as it was, lacked a labour ward. An official inspection of children in 1934 revealed an alarming incidence of dwarfism, endocrine imbalance, precocious and delayed puberty, hypothyroidism, disorders of the alimentary system, skin disease, nasopharyngeal disease and malnutrition.

Such conditions reduced some individuals to apathy or fatalism. In 1936 one young Aboriginal man told the journalist (and later Liberal politician and governor-general) Paul Hasluck, who had been on the staff of the royal commission: 'A lot of these young fellows won't work more than they need to. What's the use if they do. You work hard but you can never get anywhere. You try to improve your place but you still never get anywhere, can't get any of the privileges the white people get.' But some at Moore River absconded to marry, others simply to find freedom. Neville declared the environs of the camp a prohibited area, to prevent outsiders 'enticing' inmates to get out.[31] The compound was equipped with a detention centre, 'the boob'. In this small 'room' there was scarcely a gleam of light and little ventilation. People could be incarcerated here for up to fourteen days. 'It is barbarous treatment,' Moseley wrote in 1934, 'and the place should be pulled down.'[32] As for the camp more generally, Mosley concluded that 'this should be removed to some other site immediately'. Not that this meant that he sympathised with the Aboriginal residents. The camp, he wrote, housed 'useless, loafing natives, content to do nothing and always ready to entice the compound girls to the camp. It would be better that the grown-up people should be sent away and the children taken from their parents and put in the compound [for young people]'.

It is easy—and just—to demonise Neville and Moseley but, as we have seen, local white communities demanded segregation. Thus, when Neville planned to reopen the Carrolup reserve (it had been closed in 1922 as an economy measure and the residents moved to Moore River), white residents complained that their land would lose value, and their women and children would be threatened. The campers' dogs would worry 'white' stock and their fires would destroy local crops.[33] Similarly, efforts by Christian churches to establish or develop missions at Narrogin, Gnowangerup and Badjaling met opposition from town residents, as well as from Neville. As it was, the Aboriginal people themselves opposed forced segregation—'a natives' reserve means imprisonment', the civil rights leader and farmer William Harris claimed in 1931—and the plan to reopen Carrolup was abandoned in late 1931 because of cost considerations.[34]

White prejudice, of course, was not unique to Western Australia. In New South Wales, townspeople also waged campaigns to remove Aboriginal communities from their vicinity. From 1933, the Aborigines Protection Board began to force Aboriginal people into confinement in reserves. Exploiting groundless fears that Aboriginal people could spread a virulent blinding infection to the rest of the population, the board managed in 1936 to secure amendments to the *Aborigines Protection Amendment Act* (the so-called 'Dog Act'). These gave it additional powers to forcibly relocate Aboriginal people to reserves if they were living in unsanitary or undesirable conditions. The proportion of the known Aboriginal population living under managerial control rose from 15 per cent in 1927 to 33 per cent in 1936. That said, the policy of 'concentration' was implemented very unevenly given the shortage of funds.[35]

Yet if prejudice was deeply entrenched, there were at times more positive stories. In late 1933, news broke about the appalling living conditions of some 70 Aboriginal people at Framlingham reserve about 25 kilometres from Warrnambool, Victoria.[36] There was no water supply, no sanitation and no made roads. The humpies were the usual earthen-floored, one-roomed structures, divided internally by a bagging screen. These conditions seemed especially grievous because several of the residents had served their country during the Great War. Some of them were of mixed descent and 'closely resemble[d] pure-blooded whites', as the Melbourne evening tabloid *The Star* put it.

Perhaps for these reasons, the exposé struck a nerve with the Victorian reading public. While some responses were racialised and paternalistic, food and grocery orders were sent to Framlingham residents. A school was opened under the oversight of local churches and service clubs, including Toc H, Apex, Rotary, the Country Women's Association and the Girl Guides. The local Warrnambool community also worked with the state government to introduce a scheme that gave the Framlingham people security of tenure over reserve land, and allowed them to farm and build houses there. This 'remarkable and idealistic plan of individual citizenship' was in many ways a product of its time: it was conceived by whites, and the land parcelled out was held tenuously under a lease governed by strict rules and policed by a local board of management. Over the next decade, the relationship between Aboriginal residents and local and state authorities became severely strained. It was not until 1970 that the community gained the reserve land as communal freehold. Still, if flawed, these developments of the 1930s were, 'a small, but significant victory' for the Aboriginal people.[37]

The Framlingham project attested to a growing public activism demanding better conditions and human rights for Aboriginal people. This, it needs to be said, pre-dated the Depression and cannot be attributed solely to it. The first Aboriginal activist group, the Australian Aboriginal Progressive Association, was founded in 1924 by an Aboriginal waterside worker, Fred Maynard, who was influenced by international civil rights activists, including the Jamaican Marcus Garvey.[38] The association demanded the restoration to Aboriginal peoples of their traditional lands, the abolition of the control exercised by Aboriginal boards, an end to the removal of Aboriginal children, and a royal commission into Aboriginal affairs in New South Wales. Ultimately it had more than 600 members in New South Wales.[39] Across the continent in Western Australia, William Harris created an extensive network of politically adept activists, which in 1926 became known as the Native Union. Its deputation to the premier in 1928 claimed that 'the Protector [Neville] was the worst enemy the natives had, and if allowed to continue in control would soon be responsible for the extermination of the race.

The department which was established to protect the blacks was really killing them out.[40]

The consciences of white humanitarians were also increasingly troubled, not just by the long history of Aboriginal dispossession and mistreatment but by egregious acts of violence on the frontier, such as the Forrest River massacre of 1926 in the Kimberley and the Coniston massacre of 1928.[41] In the latter case, more than 60 Aboriginal people in the Central Desert region were killed in reprisal for the murder of a white trapper. Organisations such as the Australian Federation of Women Voters, the National Council of Women, the National Missionary Council, Australian Aborigines' Amelioration Association and the Victorian Aboriginal Group added weight to the push for reform. Paternalistic, middle class and Christian, they lobbied for better education for Aboriginal people, an end to the removal of children and the assumption of responsibility for Aboriginal policy by the federal government.[42] The Communist Party, too, called for an end to forced labour, the abolition of Protection Boards—'capitalism's slave recruiting agencies and terror organisations'—the cessation of discriminatory practices within trade unions, and even the creation of independent Aboriginal republics in central, north and north-west Australia.[43]

If not originating with the Depression, this activism was given an additional momentum by the economic crisis. In the 1930s, the 'Aboriginal problem' became almost daily news.[44] Arguably, the impoverishment of the Depression sensitised more white Australians to the Aboriginal experience of disadvantage: 'the effect of dislocation, loss of self-esteem and the general "wondering as to where the next meal was coming from"'.[45] In the 1930s, too, professional anthropologists joined the humanitarian lobbyists as advocates for Aboriginal justice. A.P. Elkin, an Anglican minister and (from 1934) professor of anthropology at the University of Sydney, published academic research and voluminous letters and articles for the popular press on race relations and the problem of prejudice. He became president of the Association for the Protection of Native Races and vice-president of the Aborigines Protection Board of New South Wales (from 1940 the Aborigines Welfare Board). Elkin would be later criticised for embracing Assimilation and

382

eschewing confrontation with government, but he played a major role in championing the Aboriginal cause.

Another anthropologist, Donald Thomson, worked extensively as a representative of the Commonwealth government with the Yolngu people in Arnhem Land. He notably took up the Aboriginal cause in the notorious Caledon Bay case of 1932–33, when five Aboriginal men in the Northern Territory were convicted (one to hanging) for the murder of five Japanese trepang fishermen, a white police officer and possibly two other white men.[46] Later, in World War II, Thomson would command a coastwatching unit in Arnhem Land that employed Aboriginal men, Solomon Islanders and a Torres Strait Islander.

The 1930s also witnessed further growth in advocacy organisations led by Aboriginal activists themselves. Among them were the Victorian Australian Aborigines' League (1934), Northern Territory Half-Caste Progressive Association (mid-1930s) and the New South Wales Aborigines Progressive Association (1937).[47] The latter was founded in response to the amendments to the *Protection Act*, and was led by William Ferguson, an Aboriginal shearer, Labor Party member and AWU unionist in Dubbo with strong links across white and Aboriginal unemployed organisations. In 1934 William Cooper, a Yorta Yorta man resident in Melbourne, founded the Australian Aborigines' League. Among its demands were Aboriginal voting rights, federal control of Aboriginal affairs, an end to segregation in schools and to child removal, and—here we see a specific response to the Depression—equality in relief works. In a dramatic and symbolic gesture in 1937, Cooper compiled a petition with between 1800 and 2000 signatures from Aboriginal people all over Australia calling for civil rights and Aboriginal representation in Parliament. He aimed to send it to King George V, but the federal government refused, arguing that it was not a matter for the King constitutionally. Like other activists, Cooper was dismayed that the service of more than a thousand Aboriginal men in World War I had done nothing to improve the civil rights of Aboriginal people. Cooper's own son, Daniel, had been killed in action in Belgium in September 1917. He wrote to the federal Minister for the Interior, John McEwen, when war once again threatened in 1939:

I am father of a soldier who gave his life for his King on the battle-field and thousands of coloured men enlisted in the A.I.F. They will doubtless do so again though on their return last time, that is those that survived, were pushed back to the bush to resume the status of aboriginals . . . We submit that to put us in the trenches, until we have something to fight for, is not right.[48]

Perhaps the most memorable of the achievements of Cooper, Ferguson and the president of the Aborigines Progressive Association, Jack Patten, was the 'Day of Mourning' declared on the 150th anniversary of the British landing in Australia on 26 January 1938. Patten told the Aborigines All-Australian Conference on the day: 'While the white man is enjoying the celebrations we mourn over the frightful conditions under which the aborigine has existed and is existing today on this continent, which once belonged to our forefathers.' The conference condemned the 'callous treatment' of Aboriginal people by white Australians, and demanded full citizenship and equality within the community. [49] One regional newspaper commented, 'It is strange to hear the aborigines speaking up for themselves. One had almost forgotten they had a voice.'[50]

Governments knew it was time to listen. After a conference of Chief Protectors and boards in Canberra in 1937, Aboriginal policy began to shift from 'Protection' to 'Assimilation'. In 1939 McEwen proposed what he called a new deal for Aboriginal people. His aim was to meet their immediate physical and health needs, supply education and training for useful community services, and promote civic and religious instruction. The status of Aboriginal people would thereby be raised to the point where they qualified for the privileges and responsibilities of full citizenship. All these were worthy aims, but Assimilation assumed that over time all persons of Aboriginal birth or mixed blood would come to live like white Australians. In this view, little in Aboriginal culture was of value to either the peoples themselves or the wider white community that hoped to absorb them. The future of the Aboriginal people lay in their conforming to the standards of whites. The Depression, for all its exposure of the appalling disadvantage of Aboriginal Australians, had not changed this deep prejudice within Australian society.

CHAPTER 31

The new immigrant

Crises tend to generate insularity. Countries with poor economic performance are known to develop negative attitudes towards immigration, as economically vulnerable individuals fear competition from outsiders for jobs and scarce material resources. The cultural and ideological values of the 'foreigner' may also be seen as threatening the host society's world view.[1] Australia's ethnic homogeneity, engineered by the White Australia policy, meant that xenophobia was not a source of major social disruption in the Depression years, but still the doors were closed to new immigrants. Established European communities in north Queensland and Western Australia especially found themselves the object of suspicion, while even immigrants from the traditional source, the United Kingdom, had good reason to complain about the situation in which they found themselves.

The immigration programs that had been central to the vision of national development in the 1920s did not survive the onset of the Depression. At the start of 1931, the Scullin government announced a halt to the immigration of 'aliens' until the country's economic situation improved.[2] Alien immigrants had to obtain landing permits and these were issued only to 'very close dependent relatives of persons already settled here' or people who could bring in 'a considerable amount of capital'.[3] Quotas were placed on intakes from Italy, Greece, Poland, Czechoslovakia, Estonia and Balkan countries.[4]

Those immigrants who had recently arrived in the country attracted some suspicion and resentment. The press carried reports of foreigners accepting under-award rates for woodcutting, road repair and fruit picking.[5] Local businesses and governments alike encouraged consumers to buy Australian-made goods.[6] This was partly an economic argument: if local industries were not supported, how could Australian men find employment?[7] A member of the Labor federal caucus said in December 1930: 'every migrant should be banned until something had been done for Australia's unemployed'.[8] But it was also partly tribal. The Australian Natives' Association, an organisation of the white native-born, argued that even foreign films had 'ill-effects, from the economic, moral and patriotic viewpoint'.[9] So, too, did foreign art, 'which led some people to see merit only in performers who had foreign names'.[10] Such views were extreme, but not unusual: one historian has called inter-war Australia 'the quarantined culture'.[11]

Even recent immigrants from Great Britain could find themselves marginalised. They were of the same racial stock as the vast majority of Australians—some 98 per cent of the population in 1933 were born either in Australia or the British Isles—and they were British subjects, the status of all Australians at that time. Many Australians did not differentiate between British and Australian workers, while public authorities spoke of them as one and the same.[12] But the Anglo–Australian relationship, like any familial one, was a mix of deep affection and niggling irritation. Niemeyer's visit inflamed the negatives, at least among the labour movement. Factory signs declared 'No Pommies need apply', while a woman recently arrived from the United Kingdom remembered: 'My sister and I started at the Lincoln Mills, but the girls were very nasty to us. They would shout "Go home Pommy, we don't want you here" and stick their tongues out and put their fingers up to their nose.'[13]

One group of British immigrants felt particularly disadvantaged: namely, those whose passage to Australia had been funded by the assisted immigration schemes of the 1920s and who had settled on the land. Many were in financial difficulties even before the Depression began. As countless soldier-settlers discovered so painfully, the land allocated under such schemes was too poor or small to be productive. Debts accumulated, commodity prices collapsed and properties were overvalued. With the onset of the Depression, British immigrants who had been settled on holdings in Murrabit, Tongala and Shepparton in Victoria concluded that they had been victims of 'a confidence trick'. Conditions in Australia had been 'grossly misrepresented' in the official literature they had been given back home, and the promises of support from the Victorian government had not materialised. 'Bitterness and resentment [were] the natural result,' the British Overseas Settlers' Association of Victoria claimed in June 1929.[14] Settlers in South Australia felt much the same. One wrote to his local parliamentarian on behalf of a group of 505 'distressed migrants' on 31 October 1930:

> we were grossly misled by certain posters and pamphlets printed for the Federal Government for the purpose of enticing us to leave our own country and family circle to come to these shores. I, myself, saw pictures depicting an Australian wheat crop with the heading 'yours in three years' . . . I, with a wife and young family was naturally anxious for opportunities for them, and I have been receiving Government rations for nine months as my reward . . . now I have nothing and am destitute.[15]

Such was the chorus of complaints that the Victorian government established a royal commission into migrant land settlement. Its report in 1933 confirmed many of the complaints: the land provided was not always suitable to allow farmers to make even a frugal living; the choice of land did not live up to the expectations raised in chirpy promotional literature; and the government did not fulfil its obligations to provide the immigrants with training and supervision. Even allowing for the impact of an unusually long drought and the collapse of wheat prices, the government had failed the immigrants by settling them in the Mallee.[16]

These 'stranded migrants', as they called themselves, started to campaign for their repatriation to Britain at the Australian government's expense. One of their leaders wrote to Scullin:

> why should we be kept here like convicts (nay, worse than that) . . . we were all hoaxed away from our homeland (the land of milk & honey) by

misleading and untruthful propaganda we were shipped out here like the 'Babes in the Wood'. Australia wanted money and the unprincipaled British Government threw out a bait for the Commonwealth to bite . . . we ask for bread & we receive a stone [sustenance] . . . I did not realise when I sold up my home that we had returned to the days of slave-dealing . . . if you can't repatriate us deport us, as even that would be a god-send to many of us. [17]

Another immigrant appealed to the state's obligation to veterans:

[My husband] met with a serious accident in being thrown from a horse while droving a cow nearly two years ago & has been incapacitated from working his farm since then, owing to injuries to head & spine. He had been a soldier in the Great War with the B.E.F. [British Expeditionary Force], serving in France, and the after effects intensify the present trouble.[18]

This sense of grievance was only fuelled by advertisements continuing to appear in the British press, even in November 1930, inviting British immigrants to come to Australia.

Some Australians sympathised with the 'distressed' British. Although the immigrants were sometimes seen as rats deserting a sinking ship, they attracted large audiences to their meetings in Adelaide.[19] The Western Australian parliament claimed that 'hundreds of [the immigrants] are going hungry and practically naked'.[20] Trades Hall in Melbourne also thought that Australia had a moral obligation to repatriate those who had been induced to immigrate 'by the grossly misleading promises' of the Bruce–Page government.[21] The ALP in Kalgoorlie agreed, on the assumption that the repatriation of the British would be matched by the return of Australians who were destitute in England.[22]

The Commonwealth government, however, was unsympathetic. State governments, which complained that unemployed immigrants were a serious drain on sustenance funds, were reminded that they had actively sought the British immigrants in the first place. They could not now expect the federal government to cover the expense of repatriation.[23] More importantly, Australia might have to refund to the British government the amount it contributed to the original passage of immigrants as well as the assistance granted to the states under the £34 million agreement.[24] London was inclined to agree. The immigrants lobbied the British government, and even the King, maintaining that they would readily find employment or family support at 'home'.[25] But the British representative in Australia said it would be 'a matter of sheer impossibility' to reabsorb considerable numbers of migrants. Unemployment in the United Kingdom was already over 2.5 million.[26] All the British Treasury wished to see was the 'final end of the absurd £34 million agreement', which did indeed lapse in 1930.[27]

In July 1931, a group of immigrants under this agreement sent a delegation to meet with Scullin in Canberra, sleeping on the roadside on their way.[28] They claimed to represent some 1262 immigrants and their families in South Australia and 5000 in Victoria. But Scullin told them they had a duty to remain in Australia.[29] As his government saw it, they were citizens of both Australia and the British Empire (this dual status had been confirmed by London after earlier immigrant complaints). They must accept 'a share of the difficulties which may occur in a Dominion through local or world-wide circumstances'.[30]

Non-British immigrants faced different problems. Their numbers were not great, the largest cluster being the Italians, at close to 27,000 according to the 1933 census. But as the xenophobia of World War I had shown, 'aliens' were always an easy target. This was so even in regional areas, such as the goldfields of Western Australia and the sugar-cane fields of Queensland, where the impact of the Great Depression was not at its worst. Kalgoorlie and Boulder already had a history of hostility to southern European workers, with returned soldiers rioting in 1919 after one of their number was fatally stabbed by an Italian. The local RSSILA leadership, too, had long called for limits on southern European immigration.[31] Now, in early 1934, explosive violence erupted against the Italian and Slav communities when an Italian barman at one of the local hotels in Kalgoorlie assaulted a popular local figure, George Jordan. A good footballer, 'prominent in all manly sports', Jordan later died from a fractured skull.[32] Hundreds of 'infuriated men' then targeted the immigrant community. Some 60 houses and 55 camps were damaged or destroyed, two hotels and a club burned down and ten business premises wrecked and looted.[33] The police seemed powerless to control the mob, while the fire brigade trying to extinguish the flames of the burning buildings was greeted with derisive hoots and jeers. The 'foreigners' fought back, brandishing rifles and daggers at the rioters. Two, or possibly three, lives were lost.[34] It took three days for order to be restored and a week before the goldmines reopened.

The rioters were probably only a small minority of the miners, whose racist views were fanned by the RSSILA.[35] The AWU remained committed to admitting members regardless of their nationality. Lyons, to his credit, declared that 'all right thinking Australians would view with contempt the action of those miners . . . who were responsible for the riots'. His government 'deplored such scandalous happenings in civilised communities', a generous description of Kalgoorlie in the 1930s.[36] Yet the Western Australian government offered only limited compensation to the victims, providing materials to rebuild homes, but not businesses, destroyed in the riots.[37] Yugoslav workers remained segregated in Boulder, just south of Kalgoorlie. According to one press report, the wrecked premises of the Croatian–Slavonic Society were not restored since the government did 'not believe in the cultural advance of foreign-born workers'.[38] The eruption of violence attested to the fact that, as the *Sydney Morning Herald* put it, 'The mob spirit is always dormant— waiting only for something to waken it into activity.'[39]

Among those targeted during the Kalgoorlie riots were immigrants from Italy.[40] During the 1920s, some 23,000 Italians (three-quarters of whom were male) had entered Australia as the United States imposed quotas on migration to that country.[41] Some men chose to repatriate as the Australian economy deteriorated, but new immigrants continued to arrive in 1930.[42] In November, the federal government decided it was time to stop the flow. Two shiploads of Italians were prevented from disembarking in Sydney on the grounds that their entry 'would probably aggravate the unemployment situation'.[43] The ban was dubious legally, since the migrants' papers were in order and some on board the ships were naturalised Australians. Italian representatives in Australia campaigned on their behalf, and the Italian press declared the immigrants'

exclusion 'immoral and inhuman'. Australia and Italy, after all, had been allies during World War I. Critics also noted the paradox of the Australian labour movement, which preached internationalism but ostracised Italians. Nonetheless, the ships departed for Italy with most of their passengers still on board. A few decided to jump ship, only to be given sentences of six months' detention followed by deportation.[44]

There remained a significant community of Italian Australians, especially on the sugar-cane fields in Queensland. This community of 'white aliens' had grown after Chinese and Pacific Islanders had been excluded with the introduction of the White Australia policy after federation. Partly as a result of chain migration, they numbered more than 8000 by 1933, the highest concentration of Italians in any Australian state.[45] Residing mostly in Innisfail, Ingham, Ayr and Cairns, they often dominated cane-cutting gangs. Employers believed that Italians would 'work right through the season without a hitch' and they rarely resorted to industrial action.[46] Through hard work and the pooling of resources, Italians also managed to purchase their own farms and plantations.

This competition from the 'olive peril' had already triggered hostility in the 1920s. The RSSILA, angered that the Italians were acquiring plots of land from unsuccessful returned soldiers, had called for mass Italian deportation, while the Sydney *Labour Daily* reported in April 1924 that the 'whole of Northern Australia is a volcano which may burst into an eruption of racial feud at any time'.[47] In 1925 the Queensland government launched a royal commission into so-called alien intrusion. Chaired by an Ingham police magistrate who was an active member of the Anti-Alien League, it concluded that while northern Italians were 'a very desirable class of immigrant', those from the southern regions of the Mediterranean—Sicilians, Greeks and Maltese—were far less so. The Greeks were thought not to make good settlers; they added nothing to the wealth or security of the country and engaged in no useful work that could not be better performed without their assistance.[48]

As the Depression set in, white wage labourers, their numbers swollen by itinerant workers from the south, moved into the sugar industry 'with proprietorial aggressiveness'.[49] A coalition of the AWU, the ALP and the RSSILA—odd bedfellows united by White Australia—established a British Preference League in Giru, south-east of Townsville, in February 1930.[50]

Spreading to ten other towns, the league campaigned for a 'British Australia with all that that implies'. It actually meant the progressive exclusion of aliens from the workforce of the sugar industry, British control of farm ownership, a ten- rather than five-year requirement for naturalisation, and tests for language skills before naturalisation. Even more significantly, in terms of industrial relations on the sugar-cane fields, the AWU negotiated a 'gentlemen's agreement' with the Australian Sugar Producers' Association and the Queensland Canegrowers' Council—but not CSR, which dominated the industry. The agreement was that 'British' quotas in the workforce were to be increased at the expense of workers born overseas.

The racism driving these initiatives was unapologetic. The president of the Innisfail chapter of the British Preference League wrote to the local parliamentarian arguing that:

> There can be no denying that the trend of affairs in this Far North constitutes a definite menace to Australian ideals. In a population of about 100,000 there are 7,000 of one foreign race [Italian], and double that number of other races—black, yellow and 'piebald'. Many thousands of these people who are naturalised know neither oral nor written English . . . the sinister aspect is that their influence has increased all out of proportion.[51]

Truth accused foreigners of having 'obnoxious habits'—they guzzled down raw eggs—and unpatriotically sent money out of Australia.[52] In fact, remittances home were substantial, but the Italians also injected much into the local economy. Still, the ever-venomous *Smith's Weekly* in late March 1930 described Innisfail as the 'Nightmare City of North Australia', 'a town of dreadful dagoes . . . a filthy foreign scum oozes from its highways'. It claimed that Italian cutters gained preference over British because they bribed farmers to employ them.[53] Less emotional, but no less political, were the claims that the use of 'alien' labourers in the sugar industry at the expense of Australians threatened to jeopardise the import embargo on which the industry depended for its viability. Even in London, a member of the House of Commons questioned the privileged position of Queensland sugar in the Commonwealth market vis-à-vis West Indian sugar, given the supposed alien control of the Queensland industry.[54]

The Italian community in north Queensland fought back.[55] Their Foreign Cutters' Defence Association, one of a number of organisations, questioned the legality of the 'Gentlemen's Agreement'. They petitioned the Queensland government and the governor-general for its abolition or alteration, and for British justice for naturalised Australians. They mounted a newspaper counter-attack, denouncing the *Smith's Weekly* article as 'scurrilous and vulgar', and declaring in a timely history lesson that 'We do not wish to say anything against the race from which the Australians spring, but it is well known that civilisation springs from around the Mediterranean sea.' In Italy itself Mussolini's brother penned two newspaper articles denouncing anti-Italian developments in the Queensland cane fields.

At times the ethnic tensions erupted into local brawls in which shots were fired and sticks, bottles and razors brandished. In something of a comic opera, a shopkeeper in Innisfail ran an Australian flag up a pole outside his store every time the Italian flag was flown at the adjacent vice-consul's head-quarters. When the insignia were stolen from this Italian establishment, Canberra despatched federal investigators to investigate the possible pene-tration of the town by anti-fascists. Nothing sinister was uncovered and the insignia were later found along a riverbank. Mussolini was duly informed: honour was restored.

The question of British preference in employment continued to divide the communities of north Queensland. Another sugar inquiry, held in 1931, heard a range of views, positive and negative, and found in the Italian workers' favour: 'it would appear impossible', it found, 'to recommend any procedure to delimit [alien] penetration which . . . would be ethical in conception, and equitable and practicable in enforcement'. Italian purchases of land were arguably to the benefit of 'strategic outposts in the north'. If Italian cane cutters could secure work from their compatriots and Australian farmers, 'it is difficult to see how they can be denied'.[56] Australian chauvinism, nonethe-less, had a qualified victory. From 1930 to 1934, the number of British cutters in the industry increased by 47 per cent, while alien cutters increased by only 4 per cent.[57]

In time, some Australian and Italian workers were brought together by the common enemy of Weil's disease. Spread by rats and lacerations in cane cutters' limbs, the symptoms of this illness were dire: a high temperature, brown furred tongue, loss of appetite, headaches, body pain, depression and, in the more extreme cases, jaundice, bleeding gums, bloodstained vomit and urine, and even death. The disease was especially prevalent in cane fields cut by Italians. In 1934 to 1935, 4000 workers, united across ethnic lines, demanded that the sugar be burned before cutting.[58] To judge by the admittedly partisan novel *Sugar Heaven*, written by the New Zealand–born communist author Jean Devanny, who organised the women's auxiliaries during the strike, the various national groups displayed mutual tolerance and respect.[59] One fictional unionist asks, 'Why in hell they [the Italians] don't learn the language better than they do beats me', only to be told, 'They would have learned English quickly enough if we hadn't isolated them.'[60] A central female character has a sexual relationship—albeit tinged with her chauvinism—with an Italian worker, described as 'tall, fair-skinned, but of black hair and eyes, a handsome son of the Middle Italy peoples'.[61] In this fictional representation, physical passion and ideological conviction trump parochialism and xenophobia—although Devanny refrained from making her hero the squat and swarthy Italian of racial stereotyping.

Many of the rank-and-file Italian workers affected by Weil's disease had fled fascism in Europe. Infuriated by the conservatism of the 'bosses union' of the AWU that opposed strike action, some looked to communist leadership. So, too, did those Australians who opted to go on strike. In the event, the strikers did not win, but progressively cane burning was introduced throughout northern Queensland. With improved health measures, the development of an effective serum and rat-control programs, Weil's disease was largely overcome.

Yet the Italian community remained vulnerable. Although British preference for employment on the cane fields was relaxed in the mid-1930s and more Italians were allowed to enter the country, especially between 1937 and 1939, the traditional foes of a liberal immigration policy remained hysterical about the supposed threat that aliens posed to racial homogeneity. Ultimately, when Italy became Australia's enemy in 1940 and the threat of an 'enemy within' raised its ugly head once more, Italian community leaders in the cane-growing district were among the first to be thrown into internment camps.

Part IX

CLIMAX, 1932

CHAPTER 32

Lyons' first six months

For many Australians 1932 was no better than 1931. Although the first glimmers of economic recovery could be detected in Australia and some other countries, the all-important indicator of unemployment peaked at around 30 per cent of unionists in the second quarter of the year. Two-thirds of all breadwinners received an income in 1932–33 that was less than the basic wage.[1] Governments continued to provide, and even to increase, sustenance and relief works, but the Commonwealth Court of Conciliation and Arbitration refused a union request in June to restore the 10 per cut in the basic wage. Moreover, the political chaos that had marked 1931 spilled over like some tsunami into the first half of 1932. The election of December 1931 brought stability at the national level but in state politics the battles over policy continued until the incumbent governments—all of them—were eventually thrown out of office. Most dramatically, the challenge that Lang posed to the federal government's financial orthodoxy reached a climax in New South Wales in May 1932, and with this, the premier was dismissed by Governor Game—one of only two occasions in Australian history when vice-regal power has been employed to dismiss a democratically elected leader.

The United Australia Party that led Australians through this difficult year continued to be somewhat improvised. In Tasmania and Western Australia, the non-Labor parties retained their old Nationalist title and organisation, while in Queensland, South Australia and Victoria the UAP operated as a (not always stable) hybrid with the country parties. It was to Lyons' credit that he held the party together at the federal level. With only two years' experience in federal politics, he initially drew on the expertise of political stalwarts such as Latham and Bruce, the latter of whom had reversed the humiliation of 1929 by regaining his seat of Flinders in the landslide of 1931. Bruce became assistant treasurer in the first Lyons cabinet (the prime minister held the position of treasurer himself); but he would soon take on more senior roles, representing Australia at the Ottawa Imperial Conference of 1932 and renegotiating Australia's debts in London. In 1933 he would become Australia's high commissioner in London, a post he held until 1945. Latham, making the best of his loss of the leadership, assumed several cabinet roles, including attorney-general and External Affairs minister. He would represent Australia at the 1932 disarmament conference in Geneva and the reparations conference at Lausanne. Two years later, in 1934 he would tour South-East and North Asia, the first such initiative by an Australian Minister for External Affairs and a testament to the growing importance of the region to Australia's trade. In 1934 he left politics and in October 1935 became chief justice of the High Court.

Notably, there was no place in the first Lyons cabinet for the Country Party. With his massive electoral win in 1931, Lyons did not need a coalition. He did offer Page three places in the ministry, but places that he, Lyons, would choose. Page retired to the back bench 'with all the dignity he could muster'.[2] The coalition of non-Labor parties that would dominate post-1945 politics was not formed until after the 1934 election, when the Country Party again held the balance of power; and even then the alliance would crack in 1939–40. For the moment, in 1932, with an unassailable majority in both houses of federal parliament, Lyons faced none of the vetoes that had blocked almost every policy initiative of Labor. A relative calm returned to federal politics.

The opposite was the case in New South Wales. On 29 January 1932, Lang told the Loan Council that New South Wales would again default on some of its interest payments due in London and New York. While the state would be able to pay about half, the Commonwealth Bank would need to provide the balance.[3] But the political landscape had changed since 1931, when the Loan Council came promptly to New South Wales' rescue. Now, with Lyons at the helm, it protested that Lang had not reduced his expenditure in accordance with the Premiers' Plan. Moreover, the New South Wales state budget was tracking well beyond the planned deficit. Nearly half of the projected national deficit was to be from this state.[4] Thus Lyons and Bruce decided to let New South Wales default for a time, exposing the people of that state to the shock of being classed as defaulters. Only two weeks later did the Commonwealth pay the outstanding interest owed by the state.

By now, as Senator Pearce (now Minister for Defence) said, the federal government was 'determined that this sort of thing must stop, and at once'.[5] On 18 February, it passed an unprecedented piece of legislation, giving the federal government the power to recover money directly from New South Wales' revenue, should that state fail to meet its interest obligations.[6] The Act also resolved the ambiguity that had existed in 1931, clarifying that the federal government was responsible for meeting the interest payments of a state that defaulted on its external obligations. Lyons told Parliament:

> On previous occasions, when the Commonwealth Government paid the amounts due by New South Wales immediately, the full effect of the default by New South Wales was not realized either in Australia or abroad. So long as the Commonwealth was prepared to step in and shoulder the burden no one worried. . . . But for the sake of Australia's future credit, and to protect the holders of New South Wales bonds, the position had to be faced definitely, and final action taken to obviate similar happenings in the future.[7]

To this, Lang countered that if Canberra gained the power to commandeer the state's money, New South Wales would no longer have the revenue to pay for essential services, including unemployment relief. There would a 'complete breakdown of the State Government as a going concern'.[8]

In the midst of this increasingly tense impasse, the Sydney Harbour Bridge was opened on 19 March 1932. Lang, never one to shy away from publicity, decided that he should cut the ribbon—even though the King reportedly preferred that this be done by the governor-general, Isaacs, or failing that, by Governor Game bedecked in full Royal Air Force uniform and service decorations.[9] The New Guard had its own ideas, however. One of its members, Francis de Groot, managed to join the Light Horse escort of the official party, then dramatically charged in on a decrepit horse and sliced through the ribbon.[10] The bridge, he declared, was open 'on behalf of the respectable citizens of New South Wales'. Captured by a photographer, this was the moment that would dominate memories of the New Guard, but the governor thought the stunt 'a somewhat childish gesture'. He wrote to King George V, it 'did not attract much attention at the time and would have attracted less, had not the Announcer in charge of the wireless drawn attention to it'.[11] Lang was still able to have his moment in the sun when the ribbon was restored to its due place and cut once more. De Groot was promptly arrested, and initially deemed to be insane, but then charged with maliciously damaging a ribbon that was the property of the Government of New South Wales worth £2, offensive behaviour and using threatening words to the police.[12] In turn, de Groot served a writ on the New South Wales police, alleging wrongful arrest and ultimately securing an out-of-court settlement.[13]

A few weeks later, another headline story distracted Australians even more. On 5 April 1932, the celebrated racehorse Phar Lap died suddenly in the United States. This massive champion, standing at 1.74 metres tall with a deep chestnut coat, had a remarkable track record. In 1930 he won fourteen consecutive races, including a Melbourne Cup in which he carried a massive handicap of 68 kilograms. The only horse to have started as outright favourite in three successive Melbourne Cups, Phar Lap had even survived an assassination attempt, when a gunshot was fired from a car as the horse was leaving the Caulfield racecourse. A bet on the races offered many Australians a chance to relieve the misery of the Depression. They might not be able to afford the entry fees at the racetrack, but they could place a twopenny or shilling wager, either legally or through one of the off-track bookmakers whose businesses boomed in the 1930s. But Phar Lap was more than the prospect of a winning bet. He was a source of hope and national pride, his very strength and humble origins attesting to Australians' ability to triumph against the odds. Audiences across the nation followed his major wins by radio and relived them via the 'talkie' newsreels at the local cinemas.

Hence, when the news broke that the horse had died in California, the nation was plunged 'into mourning'.[14] Sydney's *Sun* newspaper office was inundated with calls from an incredulous public.[15] What had killed this powerful champion? Colic? Enteritis? Contaminated feed? Or, as many suspected, US gangsters who saw the 'Red Terror' as a threat to their profits after his spectacular victory at the Agua Caliente Handicap in Tijuana, Mexico? The debate has never been resolved. Though arsenic was detected in Phar Lap's hair as late as 2011, it is unclear how it got there. As with the premature death of any iconic figure, conspiracy theories fuelled the legend. Meanwhile, various institutions scrambled to claim Phar Lap's remains. His huge heart— at 6.35 kilograms, it was at least one and a half times that of the average racehorse—went to the Institute of Anatomy in Canberra; his skeleton to the Dominion Museum in New Zealand (the country where he was foaled); and his mounted hide to the National Museum in Victoria. In later years, Phar Lap's stuffed body was moved to the new Melbourne Museum, where for a few months in 2010 it was reunited with his skeleton on loan from New Zealand. Phar Lap's heart now resides in the National Museum of Australia in Canberra, while the phrase 'a heart as big as Phar Lap's' is embedded in the national language to signal staying power and courage. In cinematic memory, meanwhile, the horse has been translated into 'a longshot', 'a cross between a sheep dog and a kangaroo' that 'came from nowhere' to 'beat all odds to become legend' and a 'hero to a nation'.[16]

As Australia mourned Phar Lap, the position of Lang became, in his own words, 'desperate'. He challenged the constitutional validity of the federal government's new legislation, taking the matter to the High Court where he hoped that the judges with Labor backgrounds, Edward McTiernan and H.V. ('Doc') Evatt, would swing the decision in New South Wales' favour.[17] But the majority of the High Court supported the Commonwealth. Further-more, the court refused to allow Lang to appeal to the Privy Council against what the premier saw as the destruction of states' rights. The federal government then directed that all New South Wales tax payments be made to the Commonwealth treasury. A few days later this was extended to other forms of state revenue, such as betting, racecourse admissions and entertainment taxes.

The drama mounted as Lang locked the doors of his state Taxation Department and impounded documents relating to state income-tax assessment, so that the federal government's tax office could not deliver assessment notices. A guard of men recruited from unemployed members of the Timber Workers' Union was posted outside the state tax office. All government departments were instructed not to pay income into banks and to make collections wherever possible in cash. The Treasury vaults were soon awash with banknotes. Money was brought in by train from country centres and 'all day there was a constant stream of cars arriving in front of the Treasury Building, disgorging officials carrying satchels full of money which they hurried down into the lower recesses of the building where receipts were given by Treasury officials who had abandoned their other duties to become banking officials'. Members of state parliament had to go to the treasury to get paid, while the head of the Teachers' Federation was entrusted with all the pay for teachers. Lang later wrote, with masterly understatement, that these measures were 'at best improvisations and could not be continued on a permanent basis'![18]

Lang's tactics immediately triggered further legislation from the federal government aimed at blocking loopholes. In response, Lang pushed through the state parliament, in an all-night sitting on 11–13 May 1932, the Mortgages Taxation Bill. Imposing a 10 per cent tax (or capital levy) on all mortgages to be paid within fourteen days of the commencement of the Act, it would have resolved the government's immediate revenue problems, but only by placing great pressure on insurance companies, which advanced huge sums on mortgages. For Lang it was a time of war. Just as 'after the Franco–Prussian War . . . the French people were asked to surrender their gold to pay the invader . . . we were faced with the alternative of either paying the invaders or throwing them out'.[19]

The 'invader', however, had no intention of retreating. Lyons immediately rushed through both federal houses further legislation that nullified the New South Wales Act in order to preserve 'the peace, order and good Government' of Australia with respect to taxation, insurance and trade. This was, as the Melbourne *Herald* put it, 'a step unprecedented in Australian history', but Lyons claimed that the 'financial and economic stability of the whole of Australia is endangered by what Mr Lang has done'.[20]

This tit-for-tat saga was abruptly and dramatically ended when, on 13 May, Game intervened. The governor had not been given officially a copy of the circular in which Lang had instructed state government officials to ignore the Commonwealth proclamation requiring them to pay revenue into the Commonwealth Bank, but an accountant in the Lands Department, R.H. Beardsmore, leaked the document to him.[21] On 12 May, then, Game asked Lang either to confirm that his circular was within the law or to withdraw it.[22] Lang could have given ground, especially as Game's ultimatum coincided with the passing of the controversial tax legislation, but the premier's response was curt: the circular 'cannot possibly be withdrawn'. This has been described as Lang's 'virtual suicide note'.[23] The following day, Game summoned the premier to Government House and dismissed him. 'My position,' he explained in writing, 'is that if my Ministers are unable to carry on essential services without breaking the law my plain duty is to endeavour to obtain Ministers who feel able to do so.'[24] Parliament was prorogued, and Game commissioned the leader of the leader of the Opposition, Bertram Stevens, to form a caretaker cabinet until elections were held.

It was an unprecedented exercise of vice-regal power, matched only by the later dismissal of Gough Whitlam by Governor-General John Kerr in 1975. Game's motives have been much debated. His most severe critics depict him as an authoritarian who consciously plotted to overthrow Lang.[25] But this seems unduly conspiratorial. Certainly, Game, who had arrived in Sydney in May 1930, had a personal preference for conservative politics. He sent the Nationalist Bavin 'a line of personal sympathy and regret . . . and admiration' when the premier lost the October 1930 election. He would later describe Bavin's subsequent resignation in March 1932 as 'a knock-out'.[26] There is also no doubt that, under pressure from the media and conservative lobbyists, Game contemplated the possibility of removing Lang from office well before May 1932. To offset this, however, there is ample evidence that Game respected the constitutional convention that, as governor, he should accept the advice of his ministers as long as they had a popular mandate and acted within the law. 'I am here,' he wrote privately in December 1931, 'as an umpire but I have to abide by the rules of the game. I can't give a Government out, when they are keeping their wicket up, just because the side that is fielding don't like the way they bat.'[27] Thus, while Game blocked Lang's efforts in 1931 to swamp the Legislative Council with large numbers of new members, he ultimately agreed to increase the numbers by 25. Game's thinking, as he told Lang, was that while he disagreed with the advice, he could not demand Lang's resignation: 'Were I to do so it would inevitably give rise . . . to a popular outcry that I was taking sides, and I cannot put the King's representative in that position.'[28]

Moreover, it is clear that until the day of Lang's dismissal, Game maintained a working relationship with the premier. At times he even expressed a grudging admiration for him. He wrote to King George V in March 1931:

To give Mr Lang his due he is a leader, and can carry the people with him and does not appear to forfeit their confidence, even when he fails to make good his many and rash promises. He seems to have some magnetic power over them which induces them to accept his assertions as true however palpably absurd and false they may be . . . The whole business is such a tragedy. They are a fine people at heart and even the extremists are, I believe, mostly activated by good motives at bottom, though there are exceptions.[29]

This was a far cry from the acerbic critique of Australia offered by that other representative of the British establishment, Niemeyer, in 1930.

Lang's increasingly confrontationist tactics seem to have slowly tipped the balance for Game. On 11 March, the New Guard presented the governor with a petition to the king requesting that the government be removed. Forwarding this to London, Game raised with the Dominions Office the question as to whether he might dismiss Lang. At the same time, he consulted with the chief justice and senior Sydney lawyers.[30] The advice from the lawyers was supportive, but that from London inconclusive. Game hesitated, telling a civic reception at Narromine in the central west in early March that although public affairs were in a 'chaotic condition', New South Wales had had self-government for 75 years and 'it is the duty of the people and not of the State Governor to find a way out of the trouble'. But in a final and ambiguous caveat, Game added, 'I will help as much as I can . . . to bring about a state of peace.'[31] According to his wife, this speech provoked '*fury everywhere*':

> the *Bulletin* had a really vile article as well as the cartoon [depicting the Governor as Pontius Pilate washing his hands], so that Mr. Scullin actually got up in the House and said that they very much regretted this attack on the Governor . . . rumours were spread everywhere that [Game] was in Lang's pay and took a huge sum to make those extra members [of the Legislative Council]! The letters, anonymous and otherwise, were particularly unpleasant.[32]

We shall never know the precise point at which Game decided to act, but his conversation with Lang on 12 May was probably decisive. Without the assurances that he demanded from the premier, Game decided that he did have the legal power, as governor, to act rather than condone illegality.

Was Game's intervention constitutional? Probably, yes, although this question, too, is open to debate.[33] On the one hand, the precedents within the British Empire established that the governor of a self-governing colony did have the power to dismiss his advisers. But on the other, this right was not unlimited, and it seems that before Lang's dismissal the 'illegal action by a ministry had not *per se* been a ground of dismissal'.[34] The advice of the Dominions Office was a bureaucratic 'bet each way'. If the governor himself was not personally involved in illegality, it considered, Game could constitutionally allow his ministers to commit allegedly illegal acts until such time as a court had decided whether or not they were legal. But alternatively, if a governor decided that he could not permit an illegal act, he could seek other advisers (that is, another ministry), provided that he was sure of obtaining ministers who would have a majority in Parliament. As it happened, Game did not receive this advice from London before he acted. Nor did he allow the legality of Lang's actions to be again tested in the courts—the path that Evatt strongly judged to be more appropriate in his 1936 study of the relationship between the King and the Dominions.[35]

Perhaps the most important point is that the constitutional status of Game's decision was not widely challenged at the time. To be sure, the *Labor Daily* claimed that Game

allied himself with the invading forces in N.S.W., and dismissed the Labor Government from office on the most flimsy of pretexts. No more treacherous and tragic defeat was ever written to a gallant fight than the wretched chapter recording the fall of the one Australian political leader who stood out against the attempt of the financial institutions to reduce the wages and conditions of the Australian people to the level of slaves.[36]

But this newspaper had long served as 'Lang's own publicity vehicle', and a more common public response to Lang's dismissal was jubilation.[37] The *Sydney Morning Herald* wrote on the day of Lang's dismissal:

The Lang Government is devoting itself very assiduously to the work of revolutionary Communists . . . [it] is to all intents and purposes, at the point of war with the federal Government and the remainder of Australia . . . The matter is no longer one of party politics; it is a question of reducing to obedience to the law the leader of a Government which is defying the law.[38]

Michael Bruxner, the leader of the Country Party in New South Wales, rejoiced that 'the electors . . . would now have a chance to make the country permanently safe'. The president of the Graziers' Association declared, 'The news will be as life-giving rain after an "old man" drought.'[39] The conservative Melbourne *Argus* ran the headline 'The Shadow of Anarchy Passes':

Out of the tumult a consoling fact arises. The people of New South Wales, and the people of Australia, are back to the British tradition of law . . . Mr. Lang and Mr. Garden have drunk at the fountain of Russian Bolshevism. They see in themselves pocket editions of Lenin and Stalin, exercising, in the name of democracy, a cruel and ignorant tyranny. That phase has run its course.[40]

While such exaggeration was increasingly par for the course in Depression politics, when Game and his wife went to the opera—admittedly, no working-class stronghold—a few days after the dismissal, the audience rose and burst into wild cheers.[41] Privately, too, Game received many letters of support, including one from an Anglican leader in Melbourne who saw divine intervention at work: 'God has given you great courage and much wisdom and marvellous patience . . . Australia is very proud of you and very grateful to you for what you have done.'[42]

Most strikingly, Lang did not resist his dismissal. Game told the King that the premier was 'entirely courteous and personally friendly' throughout their final interview.[43] As Lang left Government House, he was observed by Lady Game to be 'looking a completely defeated man in his old grey hat—very grey himself too, for he had been up all night'. To her, it seemed that Lang was almost relieved at his dismissal. Lady Game wrote to her mother that she could not 'at all understand how a clever man like Lang could do such a thing, or commit this illegality, unless for the purpose of provoking his own dismissal and Philip [Game] is inclined to think that he *did* wish it'.[44] Others thought the same, the *Sydney Morning Herald* speculating that Lang was perhaps 'inviting dismissal'.[45]

Lang himself professed some relief, telling a reporter, 'Well, I am sacked, I am dismissed from office. I have attempted to do my duty, but now I must be going. I am no longer Premier but a free man.'[46] It was a stark contrast to Whitlam's defiance and controlled anger on the steps of Parliament House on 11 November 1975, 'Well may we say "God save the Queen", because nothing will save the Governor-General!' Lang's acquiescence sat oddly with his own belligerent public style and aggressive factional politicking. But he was a man of great contradictions; to quote Game in a letter to the King five days after the dismissal, Lang 'is a difficult man to understand, and I do not pretend to understand him. I have come to think he is a living Jekyll and Hyde, and there is certainly a large element of good and of great courage in him which one cannot but admire.'[47]

Yet if Lang went quietly on the day, he would later create a potent and enduring mythology. In his 1970 memoir, he portrayed himself as the victim of powerful commercial and banking interests that were intent on generating a constitutional crisis between the government and the governor. Game, like Lyons, was 'acting under pressure from London'. As evidence of this, Lang claimed that in their final confrontation Game was 'tense, taut and obviously ill at ease':

> Throughout the interview he gave me the impression of a man being forced to do a job for which he had no relish . . . I have never seen a more ill-at-ease man, as if what he was doing was contrary to his own will. The Governor had been handed the assassin's dagger and, as one brought up in the traditions of the British civil service, and Royal Air Force, it never entered his mind that he could refuse to carry out his orders.[48]

Well might Game have been tense, but Lang might have misread the reasons for it. Appealing though the notion of a British-led 'coup' might have been to Lang's supporters, the documentary record—or at least that which survives— does not support it.

Lang also claimed in retrospect that he briefly entertained the idea of turning the tables on Game and arresting him for acting illegally. Governor Bligh, after all, had been arrested during the Rum Rebellion of 1808 by officers of the New South Wales Corps. But Lang claimed to fear that such resistance would bring bloodshed. While he had no doubt that the New South Wales police would carry out his orders, and his supporters would 'rally to the defence of their elected government', the federal government might send in the defence forces. Supposedly, it had already put all of Sydney on alert, distributing arms and ammunition to the various military and naval bases, and recruiting 'peace officers' to supplement the Commonwealth Police Force.[49] Lang even claimed that if he had defied the authority of the King, as represented in Game, he would have given an 'open invitation' to the Royal Navy to intervene. British warships might have arrived off Sydney Heads and shelled the city. 'So, rather than risk civil war and have bloodshed in the streets of Sydney, I decided to accept the dismissal.'[50] It was all rather melodramatic but Lang must have been conscious of the dangers posed by the Old and New Guards, which might well have acted had he not been deposed.

Whatever the reasons for Lang's acquiescence, it helped to ensure that the public took the news of the dismissal 'very quietly'. The police reported to a relieved Game that

> the soap box oratory in the Domain . . . was the mildest for many weeks last Sunday. There has not been the slightest sign of any violence of any kind whatever . . . This is a result [Game said] I hardly dared to hope for as even such level headed observers as the Chief Justice felt that a violent end to the tension was almost inevitable.[51]

Perhaps the public welcomed an end to the political turmoil of the past few months. Perhaps they were distracted by the tragic news on 14 May that the kidnapped infant son of the celebrated US aviators Charles Lindbergh and Anne Morrow Lindbergh had been discovered dead by the side of a road in New Jersey. Most probably the public accepted that their verdict on Lang's dismissal could be delivered through democratic processes. As the *Daily Mail* said: 'The Governor has cut the knot, and thereby restored self-government to the people . . . No genuine democrat, whatever may be his party allegiance, can object to this solution.'[52]

The people of New South Wales had their chance to vote on 11 June 1932. In the election campaign, Lang denounced 'the hand of the assassin, swift and unerring' that had seized the people's freedom from them. Vast crowds attended his rallies, preceded by processions of brass bands and children bedecked in fancy dress. Some 200,000 people gathered in Sydney around Central Railway Station and the Haymarket on 5 June. City traffic came to a halt as the march surged along George Street, Liverpool Street, Oxford Street and Flinders Street, taking two hours to pass a given point. Reaching Moore Park at 3 p.m., the crowd was harangued by Lang from the back of a lorry with his wife and daughter at his side. His speech covered all the familiar themes: the iniquity of the Premiers' Plan and the banks; the ill-treatment of New South Wales by the Commonwealth; even the conscription crisis of 1916–17. 'Today they are out on another conscription campaign. It is not only your sons, but daughters, too, who are to be taken from your fireside.'[53] The crowd responded by carrying a motion declaring that 'LANG IS RIGHT', while a euphoric Jack Beasley predicted that the Lang government would not only retain all its seats but also increase its majority.

It was all self-delusion. On election day, Lang Labor was reduced to 24 seats as opposed to the 55 seats it had won in 1930. It lost all of its country, non-mining electorates, the first time since labour parliamentary action began in 1891 that it failed to win a rural seat. In his own western Sydney seat of Auburn, Lang's vote fell from 75.8 per cent in 1930 to 52 per cent.[54] It was an emphatic rejection of all that he had stood for in the past months, although he could take some consolation from the fact that Lang Labor polled 40 per cent of the vote while Federal Labor gained only 4 per cent, and no seats.

Like Scullin, the man whose government he had unseated, Lang did not leave politics after this crushing defeat. Although he never regained his electoral appeal—in 1932–38 he lost two more state elections, both to Stevens—he remained a major player in Labor factional and federal politics well into the next decade. But if Lang lingered on, the plan that took his name did not. Repudiation of Australia's debts was never again on the political agenda.

The dismissal of Lang has understandably dominated narratives of 1932 politics, but the devastation of Labor occurred in other states in these torrid months. In South Australia, Lionel Hill, after his expulsion from the ALP in August 1931, formed a 'national government' with the Liberal and Country League that had emerged from the 1931 Emergency Committee. In August 1932, this agreement collapsed, and after six months of ineffectual government Hill appointed himself agent-general in London with a generous financial package—a well-trod path for politicians past their use-by date since colonial days.

In Victoria, the Trades Hall Council and the party's central executive continued to attack Ned Hogan for his commitment to the Premiers' Plan.[55] In March 1932, he suffered a nervous collapse and left for the clearly popular destination of London. In his absence, the acting premier Tom Tunnecliffe refused to assure Parliament that he would continue to implement the Premiers' Plan, and on 13 April 1932 lost a parliamentary vote of non-confidence. The ensuing election, fought in the shadow of Lang's crisis, witnessed a 'spectacular shattering' of the minority Labor ministry. Three ministers who supported the Premiers' Plan resigned. Hogan, believing that Tunnecliffe had betrayed him, fuelled the disarray with messages from London. The Victorian Central Executive, he later claimed, had 'assassinated' his government.[56] *The Age* saw it as 'another case of suicide' by Labor.[57] Tunnecliffe was even physically attacked at a May Day rally on the Yarra Bank. Speaking from the back of a lorry, he was first shouted down and then struck on the head and shoulders with 'a loaded rubber hose' (presumably a hose packed with metal to maximise the force of the blow). He and his colleagues on the platform escaped only when the driver of the lorry dispersed the rioters by driving into them. Possibly this violence was led by communist outsiders, but it testified to the irreconcilable divisions within the labour movement. A cartoon in the Melbourne *Herald* depicted Tunnecliffe as the puppet of a 'trades hall junta' who were directing him across stepping stones labelled Destruction of Plan, Unemployment, Reputation and Chaos. The destination on the far bank of the river was 'Lang Land'.[58] In contrast to Labor's chaos, the Opposition leader, Stanley Argyle, a medical doctor, reassuringly promised stability, 'a workable Parliament' and a continued commitment to the Premiers' Plan.[59] When the election was held on 14 May 1932, just as the news of Lang's dismissal was breaking, the voters chose the plan. Labor lost almost half its seats in what was its worst defeat since 1907.

A bloodletting of ALP expulsions, including of Hogan, followed. Some rejoiced that Labor was the better for being freed from 'a false and dangerous position' that had been created by the supporters of the Premiers' Plan. 'At any time Labor has everything to gain and nothing to lose by keeping on the straight and narrow path laid down by the workers' everyday struggle against the inhuman exploitation and victimisation enforced by the capitalist owners of industry,' *Labor Call* wrote on 19 May 1932. 'Labor will ultimately come into its own when the time is due.'[60] But that time would not come for many years.

Queensland was the only refuge for Labor. Here in June 1932, Forgan Smith ejected Moore, who had not only pursued the Mungana allegations against Theodore but had enthusiastically supported the Premiers' Plan. The Scottish-born Forgan Smith, who was a critic of the plan, would soon emerge nationally as a strong voice in favour of policies that would revive confidence in industry and provide employment.[61] Labor's success in Queensland was attributable to the fact that the local economy was not as devastated by the Depression as those of other states. It also owed much to the relative lack of factional disputes within the party. With the AWU dominating the union movement and the Forgan Smith government, the threats from Lang Labor and the communists were readily quashed.[62] So, too, was the challenge from advocates of Douglas Social Credit led by a psychiatrist who had been injured by mustard gas in World War I, Julius Streeter. In the Queensland election of 1935, Social Credit would gain more than 7 per cent of first preferences—its best result in any Australian election—but thereafter it lost traction.[63] Most importantly, Labor in Queensland had the great advantage of not being in power in the first years of the Depression. All the political parties holding government on 1 January 1929 were dismissed by the voters or destroyed by policy disputes over the next four years. Tasmania's Nationalists clung on only until 1934. There was no advantage in being the incumbent government.[64] Rather, like generals at the start of a long war, few politicians could survive the losses and casualties of the Depression.

CHAPTER 33

Debt, imperial preference and cricket

With state politics in turmoil, the priority of the Lyons government in 1932 was to implement the Premiers' Plan: balancing budgets; keeping a cap on wages and pensions; and cautiously releasing funds for relief works. Essentially, economic recovery was a matter of waiting for world trade to revive and improve Australia's balance of trade. It was hardly an inspiring plan for recovery, but the federal government saw increased imperial trade as a solution and fought hard at the British Empire Economic Conference held in Ottawa in August 1932 for better access for Australian products to the British market. Such success as it had was attributable to the negotiating skills of Bruce, who found his metier once more in imperial circles. After Ottawa, Bruce undertook the slow but critical task of renegotiating the terms of Australia's debts in London. These financial and trade matters had none of the drama of Lang's dismissal or eviction battles, and certainly could not match the furore of the bodyline bowling cricket controversy of 1932–33. But by the end of the first year of the UAP government, some of the settings for Australia's recovery were in place.

The challenge of the Premiers' Plan was that it needed all states to cooperate in balancing budgets. But by April 1932 it appeared that the combined deficits of the states and the Commonwealth in 1932–33 would balloon beyond the targets set in mid-1931. If budgets were to be balanced by 1933–34 as the plan required, further substantial economies would be needed. Gibson, as usual, took it upon himself to remind the Loan Council of this.[1] Claiming that the Commonwealth Bank had been called upon to make more finance available than anticipated, he warned Lyons in June that 'the bank's ability to continue to finance [deficits] was fast approaching a point which the Board is unable to envisage without serious embarrassment and which might be easily disastrous'. The bank would not be able to finance deficits in excess of £6–7 million for the year 1932–33.

Gibson cried wolf once too often. By mid-1932, the premiers included men who had just won convincing elections and had powerful mandates. At the premiers' conference in June, Forgan Smith and Stevens both spoke out against the futility of policies that were based exclusively on cost reduction. 'Budgets could not be balanced,' Stevens said, 'until employment was restored and people had a reasonable opportunity of earning a living.'[2] The banks might claim that they would have less capacity to assist industry if governments gained access to their funds, but in reality the banks were embarrassed by the lack of demand for advances and were placing excess quantities of cash in government securities. What was needed was a rise in the internal price level, which could be achieved by devaluation, lower tariffs and a judicious expansion of public works. Forgan Smith agreed that a vigorous program of public works and policies to revive business confidence was needed.

These arguments won the day. In a compromise motion that did not specifically mention the politically toxic Premiers' Plan, the premiers committed themselves to reducing their budget deficits and meeting their interest obligations. But they also agreed on action to revive industry and employment.[3] A national recovery loan of £15 million would be floated over a period of three years and the proceeds would be used exclusively for the relief of unemployment under the state employment councils. After a lengthy meeting of Gibson and the Loan Council, the official deficit figure across all states for 1932–33 was set at £9 million.

Given that the Commonwealth had concluded the year 1931–32 with a small surplus, Lyons agreed to allow the finance that was servicing this deficit to go to the states. The Commonwealth would cover its needs by reducing old-age and invalid pensions further and adjusting public-service salaries and wages downwards in accordance with the fall in the cost of living. These pensions were in some ways an easy target. In the Premiers' Plan they had been reduced by only 12.5 per cent, not the standard rate, and the real income of pensioners had risen slightly as retail prices had fallen. Moreover, as so often, some of the public assumed that social welfare benefits were being abused. The relatively liberal *Age*, for example, deemed the federal government's bill for war, old-age and invalid pensions to be 'a terrific load'. The numbers had kept rising while lax administration and 'systematic political pandering' were a 'national scandal'. How many of the 'army' of 240,000 old-age and invalid pensioners, *The Age* asked, had gained their benefits through 'subterfuge or brazen imposition'?[4] Why, the Commonwealth auditor-general also queried, were elderly Australians getting pensions when their children could support them without difficulty? And why should pensioners bequeath their homes to their children rather than compensate the state for the cost of their benefit?[5]

For the pensioners, naturally, the perspective was very different. 'Old-Age Pensioner' in Western Australia wrote to the press: 'It is six years since I had any new clothes, as I have been beholden to friends for their cast-off things. Surely there are a few who possess sufficient of the milk of human kindness in their composition to put a word in for us.'[6] Another 'pensioner' suggested that if the cost of pensions was 'too much of an expense and nuisance', Lyons might consider building a chamber similar to that used by the Dog's Home in London, 'where unclaimed dogs suffer a painless death'. He could 'put all the old age and invalid pensioners in it and turn on the gas . . . This would be more humane than condemning them to an existence of semi-starvation and rags.'[7]

Some Labor politicians suspected that Lyons justified the cuts to pensions by deliberately underestimating the revenue that the government would earn in the 1932–33 financial year. Indeed, in the second half of 1932 the amount generated by customs and tariffs did improve, to the point where in November, Lyons thought the federal government might again bring in a surplus. He thus announced a raft of initiatives to help the beleaguered wheat industry, including a significant reduction in federal land tax. Almost incredibly, Gibson tried yet again to exercise a veto. Given that government deficits had been 'financed by temporary accommodation from the Bank', he said on 13 December, any surpluses should be used to reduce these. At the very least, the Bank board should be consulted before budget surpluses were applied to other purposes. Even for a government that was ideologically sympathetic to the banks, this attempt to dictate fiscal policy was too much. Lyons made it clear to Gibson that there were limits to the banks' influence over government policy. Gibson backed down.[8]

In retrospect, it can be seen that this was a point at which power over the formation of economic policy began to shift away from the banks, finding ultimately a new and more appropriate balance in the government's favour. But in the interim, Gibson joined with other banks to force the Loan Council to reduce the amount of the national recovery loan agreed upon in June that would be allocated to unemployment relief. One-half would be assigned to reduce the funding that the bank was providing to the states. After considerable wrangling, the loan was launched early in November—only to fail miserably. Some 63 per cent of subscriptions were left in the hands of the underwriters. Both the government and the banks blamed each other, and probably the terms on which the loan was offered were too low to attract subscribers. Whatever the reasons, the failure of the loan meant that, for the moment, the government's plans for relief programs were disrupted, as were Gibson's hopes of reducing the floating debt in the immediate future. Once more, policymaking faltered because of the inability of politicians and bankers to agree.[9]

No one doubted that the real key to Australia's recovery was an improvement in its terms of trade. Given Australia's historic trading patterns and the resort of many countries to economic nationalism, this meant primarily, though not exclusively, more trade with Great Britain. Hence Lyons despatched to the British Empire Economic Conference in Ottawa in July and August 1932 a high-powered delegation including Bruce and the Minister for Trade Henry Gullett.[10]

Its brief was to secure preferential access to the UK market for a limited range of Australian commodities. This did not include wheat and wool, even though these were vital exports. In the case of fine wool, Australia already dominated the global market; in the case of wheat, it was assumed that, since the empire as a whole produced more wheat than it consumed, quotas on imports to Britain would simply displace foreign wheat to other markets where it would then compete with surplus Australian exports. Instead, Australian demands at Ottawa focused, first, on meat (mutton, lamb and beef). In 1932 the United Kingdom accounted for four-fifths or more of world imports of butter, pig meat and beef, and about 95 per cent of mutton and lamb.[11] In meeting this demand, however, Australian meat, had to compete with that from countries such as Argentina, whose chilled beef was superior to the Australian frozen product and more easily transported across the Atlantic. Second, Australia sought to retain the existing duties on British imports of foreign pig lead and crude zinc; and, finally, it wanted stronger protection for Australian sugar, wine, eggs, certain fruits and butter (although it left the lead in the negotiations on the last to New Zealand).

Tariff schedules do not make for riveting reading, but the proceedings at Ottawa were high drama. Despite many months of preparation, the British delegation arrived without a coherent strategy or a united front. In 1931, Britain had finally broken with its longstanding tradition of free trade and adopted its own general tariff. Imperialists, such as Chancellor of the Exchequer Neville Chamberlain, believed it was essential that the conference should reach agreements that demonstrated imperial integration in a world of beggar-thy-neighbour economic nationalism. Others, like the president of the Board of Trade, Walter Runciman, and the Secretary of State for Dominions, J.H. Thomas, resisted undue concessions to the demands of the Dominions. At various times during the conference these men threatened to resign.

Relationships between the British delegation and the Dominions were also strained to breaking point. The imperial lion found much to aggravate her in the manners of her insistent cubs. Chamberlain wrote in the personal diary he kept during the conference that the Canadian prime minister, Richard Bennett, who was hosting the conference, 'has stretched our patience to the limit. He, has insulted us personally . . . He has been threatening & bullying in his manner, shifty & cunning in his methods, palpably untruthful, passionate & unreasonable. He has throughout poured out to the press a constant stream of defamation of the Brit. del. while continually informing us that he never touched the press.' Bennett was intent on 'wrecking' the conference even though 'failure meant the end of the Empire'. Only the British delegation's 'unalterable patience & firmness', Chamberlain wrote, with a healthy dose of self-commendation, made agreement possible.[12]

Negotiations with Bruce were also stormy. He approached the conference thinking he was embarking on a 'suicidal job', and when the British refused to introduce a duty on foreign meat, he threatened to walk out and to tell the world 'of the treachery he had met'.[13] The British delegation reacted with 'strong indignation'. Thomas seethed about 'insults' and 'blackmail'.[14] Stanley Baldwin, now the Lord President of the Council in the British National government and heading the British delegation, begged Bruce to stay, arguing that Australia's insistence on a duty on mutton and lamb 'would quite possibly break up the [British] National Government' and 'would imperil the possibility of the Conference being a success, with disastrous results to the British Empire and the whole world'.[15]

It was all a trite far-fetched, and Bruce continued to hold out, at times speaking 'rather hotly', until a compromise agreement was reached. But then Bruce learned that New Zealand had been allocated a greater quota of lambs than Australia.[16] Thomas recalled:

> After we'd got all the bloody Dominions to initial their bloody agreements, in marched Bennett with the whole of his Cabinet and raised some point about their bloody Dominion. We wrestled all over the floor until about two in the morning and finally agreed. No sooner had we done so than in storms Bruce and said that New Zealand had stolen five thousand tons of his bloody lambs.[17]

When New Zealand conceded some ground, agreements were signed whereby Britain agreed to limit its imports of lamb and mutton from foreign suppliers. Empire supplies would enter the British market duty free and without any restrictions until July 1934. In turn, Australia and New Zealand would limit their shipments voluntarily during 1933.

The Australian delegation also agreed, under Article 10 of the final agreement, to allow British imports to enjoy 'reasonable competition' with local manufacturers in Australia. With this goal in mind, Australia's Tariff Board would review all protective duties. No duties on British goods would be increased without a prior recommendation from the board, and the surcharges and prohibitions on British goods introduced by Scullin in 1930 would be repealed as soon as possible. Australia also agreed to give British exports a fixed margin of preference over foreign goods according to an agreed formula.

This was enough to placate Chamberlain. 'In spite of the anxieties they caused us,' he wrote to his wife Annie, 'I have no complaint to make of the Australians or the New Zealanders. They had to think of their difficulties with their own people who were expecting much more than was reasonable.'[18] Of Bruce, Chamberlain said: 'Though he is a bit long winded and tedious sometimes, nothing could be better than his general attitude. He goes for the big things and doesn't allow himself to be trammelled by preconceived opinions if a good case against them is put to him.'[19]

Some Australian historians have claimed that the Ottawa conference was 'a great triumph' in which, through superior negotiating skills, Australia 'got almost everything it requested in return for very few concessions'.[20] But if it was successful economic diplomacy, did imperial preference actually assist Australia's recovery from the Depression? A positive assessment is that Ottawa agreements proved of real value to Australia. They allowed Australia to increase primary production and exports, and to fend off the growing pressure within Britain in the mid-1930s for agricultural protectionism. Moreover, Australia was able to maintain tariff-free entry for the bulk of its exports to the United Kingdom beyond the five-year time frame of the original Ottawa agreement. By 1938, the United Kingdom was importing more than twice the volume of products from Australia than it had in 1929, although the prices for Australian primary produce were low.[21]

On the debit side of the ledger, mutton, lamb and beef, the beneficiaries of the Ottawa negotiations, accounted for only about 5 per cent of Australia's exports in the early 1930s.[22] Australia's dominant export, wool, was left outside the framework of imperial preference, and was arguably made 'particularly vulnerable to retaliatory action by non-British countries', such as France, Italy and Belgium. As these countries encountered difficulties with their balance of payments in the mid-1930s, they limited imports from British countries. The impact of this on wool prices is not known, but it 'must have negated part at least of the small addition to export prices obtained in 1932. A more negative assessment is thus that Ottawa had only 'a minor impact on the pace and shape of Australia's recovery'.[23]

Whatever the benefits to Australia of Ottawa, the returns for Britain exporters were fewer. While Australia did reduce tariffs on British goods, it never fully implemented Article 10 relating to domestic competition.[24] This was a matter of constant aggravation to British officials, especially as Australia kept hectoring London about meat and butter in the years that followed Ottawa. But for London it was a devil's choice. British exporters suffered from the squeeze on imports that competed with Australian industry but British rentiers benefited from Australia's generating the sterling reserves needed to service its external debts.

Debt continued to be both a financial challenge and a political liability for the Lyons government. All Australians had now made sacrifices in the form of lower interest rates, but creditors in London continued to be paid interest rates in the range of 5–6.5 per cent. This was despite the fact that interest rates in London fell after Britain's departure from the gold standard in mid-1931 and Chamberlain had managed to convert £2000 million worth of British war debt owing to the United States from 5 to 3.5 per cent in one operation.[25]

Hence, after Ottawa, Bruce went to London to negotiate the conversion of Australia's existing debts to a lower-interest rate basis.[26] Months of hard-hitting negotiations with the British Treasury, the Bank of England and the underwriter Nivison & Co. followed. Bruce's first challenge was to convert a New South Wales loan of £12.4 million that matured in November 1932. The underwriters initially claimed they could not offer terms that were satisfactory to the Australian government. It seemed, Lyons complained to Bruce, that despite all of Australia's efforts to restore her credit and keep faith with the bondholder, the British were more willing to help Europe and other countries in financial difficulties, even though some of these had defaulted. There was a public impression that 'Australia, though a Dominion, is expected to rely entirely on her own standing in the market and is not extended any material sympathy or recognition of her special efforts for rehabilitation.'[27]

Eventually, the New South Wales loan was successfully converted at a rate of 3.5 per cent interest, an achievement that Bruce described as 'almost incredible'.[28] It is not entirely clear how the mood in London was turned around, but it probably helped that the English financial press commented favourably on Australia's reconstruction efforts. Possibly, too, Bruce's patrician style helped to reassure those in the City who were prone to see Australia as a wayward irresponsible child. The *Australian Worker* thought as much:

Our Mr. Bruce, by the persuasive employment of his English Johnnie accent, and some well-timed kow-towing in imperialistic quarters, has been able to get a New South Wales conversion loan of £12,000,000 underwritten on the London market at a slightly reduced interest. And we are all of us expected to be exuberantly glad. The Tory newspapers are effusive in expressions of joy, and leading exponents of U.A.P.ism are going about this sad old world with their features wreathed in smiles.[29]

Bruce's next aim was to convert £84 million of stock owned by British bondholders, starting with the conversion of £43 million of the highest-interest-bearing stock in a single operation. This was a massive conversion and the British government, the Bank of England and Nivisons all recommended a series of smaller operations at three- to four-month intervals. By early 1933, negotiations had reached an impasse. Lyons and the Loan Council insisted that 'a comprehensive scheme to secure relief was a national and political necessity', given the only thing that had enabled Australia to maintain its interest payments was a series of almost unprecedentedly good seasons for exports. If this changed, default would be 'inescapable'.[30] If more satisfactory terms could not be secured in London, Langism might reassert itself. But if Lyons was trying 'to frighten the British into submission', it did not work.[31] In May 1933, Bruce told the British that if they did not support the proposed conversion of £43 million, he would try to convert £80 million in an even larger operation. The British cabinet refused and Chamberlain threatened to block any attempt at conversion by continuing the embargo on optional conversions that he had introduced in early 1933 to stop the flight of capital from London. On 12 May, Chamberlain told Bruce testily that he was 'tired of Australia coming and threatening to default'.[32]

As so often, London had the stronger hand in this high-stake game. Bruce had no choice but to convert loans in smaller operations than he and his government wanted. Still, by February 1934 Bruce had completed the entire £84 million conversion, and further conversions followed in later years.[33] This took some pressure off government budgets and made considerably more manageable the debt servicing that had so crippled Australian governments in the early years of the Depression. The deeply contentious policies of deflation seemed to have brought some rewards in the London money market at least. But the benefits to individual Australians were not immediately obvious—at least not to *Labor Call*, which declared that the reduction of interest rates

> certainly does not mean that the workers in the immediate future would receive an increase in their wages, or that money that is not paid out as interest will be spent in providing them with additional work . . . whether interest rates to be paid are either high or low, the workers have nothing to gain either one way or the other . . . The real reason why interest has been reduced . . . has been because of the inability of the borrowers to pay the rates originally agreed upon. Either a reduction had to be made or almost certain repudiation or default had to be faced.[34]

Every shilling that Australia paid in interest, this Labor press claimed, still bore 'the robber stamp upon it'.[35]

The tensions in the debt negotiations attest to the deep ambiguity in the relationship between Australia and Britain throughout the Depression years. Be it Niemeyer's 1930 visit or Bruce's haggling in Ottawa and London, the British tended to see the Australians as demanding, irksome and unwilling to accept responsibility for their own economic plight. Australians, particularly those on the left, viewed the British as unsympathetic, overbearing, condescending and, in the case of the City banks, exploitative. Neither side, of course, questioned the importance of imperial unity. Indeed 'loyalty' remained a dominant value in the Australian political culture, even for Labor governments. But as with any family, there were many tensions in the imperial relationship—all the deeper for the length and intimacy of the relationship.

This tension exploded in early 1933 in a remarkable controversy about that quintessentially imperial sport, cricket. In the early years of the Depression, Australians had taken great heart from the performance of the young Don Bradman. Often dubbed the best batsman of all time, Bradman's average during the 1930 tour of England had been a staggering 139.14, in a game where an international Test average of 50 marked a batsman as in the front rank.[36] During one day at Leeds, he had scored 309 runs, still a record for the sport. But the phenomenon of Bradman led the British captain of the next 1932–33 Ashes team, Douglas Jardine, to embrace new tactics—leg theory or, as it soon became known, bodyline bowling. This meant that fast bowlers aimed the ball at the body of the batsman, in the hope that when he defended himself, he would deflect the ball into the hands of one of a ring of predatory fielders on the leg side. To deliver this approach, the touring English team included four fast bowlers, among them Harold Larwood, a former coalminer who was blessed with remarkable accuracy, speed and stamina. Jardine, in contrast, was a child of the British Raj (he was born in India and educated at an elite school) who had made no friends among the irreverent Australian crowds on his earlier tour in 1928–29. His clipped accent and harlequin cap, from an Oxford University club, reeked of the British class system that riled so many Australians. It was as if Niemeyer had returned to Australia in cricketing creams.

Bodyline tactics would shock Australians, not least because they limited Bradman's effectiveness, forcing him to duck, weave and move about the crease. They were also intimidating and ethically dubious, in that batsmen at that time wore limited protective gear. The controversy simmered in the early days of the series. Without undue use of bodyline tactics, England won the First Test. Bradman did not play because of a contractual dispute with the Australian cricket authorities. In the Second Test, the series was levelled.

Although Bradman, to the dismay of the crowds, was dismissed for a duck on the first ball of the first innings, he mastered the English bowling to score 103 not out in the second.

It was the Third Test in Adelaide that brought matters to boiling point. On the second day, one of Larwood's deliveries hit the Australian captain Bill Woodfull on the heart, and, to the fury of traditionally sedate South Australians, Jardine persisted in positioning his fielders in a bodyline position. Police had to be deployed on the boundary. Woodfull batted on, sustaining several more blows, but when he finally returned to the dressing room, he was met by one of the English managers, who enquired after his health. Woodfull retorted with what the BBC later described as 'for some years, the 25 most famous words in sport': 'I don't want to see you, Mr Warner. There are two teams out there. One is trying to play cricket and the other is not.'[37] Someone—it has never been conclusively proven who—leaked this to the press. This 'amazing outburst' became headline news across the nation and caused 'uproar' in the United Kingdom.[38]

Tensions escalated the following day when another Australian batsman, Bert Oldfield, the team's wicketkeeper and a less able batsman than Woodfull, suffered a fractured skull while trying to defend himself against Larwood's bowling. The ball, as it happened, was a conventional delivery, but the huge crowd reacted so violently that the English cricketers debated arming themselves with the stumps as weapons should the pitch be invaded. As the British author Ronald Blythe has put it: '*Wisden*, in the exalted language taken for granted by cricketers, says, "the plan of the [bodyline] campaign was to reduce Bradman to mortal limits". To the crowd which watched it looked more as if Bradman and his colleagues were to be reduced to mortal remains.'[39] In the event, the pitch was not stormed, but at end of the fourth day's play the Australian Board of Control for International Cricket did something arguably worse. On 18 January 1933, it sent a cable to the Marylebone Cricket Club (MCC), cricket's ruling body, stating that bodyline bowling was 'unsportsmanlike ... Unless stopped at once likely to upset friendly relations between Australia and England.'[40]

What greater insult could there be than to call an Englishman unsportsmanlike! If a cable had arrived at Lords accusing the English Eleven of cannibalism, 'it could hardly have produced greater horror'.[41] The MCC, a bastion of the English establishment, 'deplored' the Australian cable, coming to the defence of Jardine and Larwood, whose tactics it had earlier approved, and suggesting that the remainder of the tour might be cancelled unless the insult was withdrawn. The MCC probably knew that the Australian board could not bear the financial penalty of cancellation.

Soon a diplomatic crisis loomed as the press in both countries stoked the fires. It seemed that the very future of the empire was at stake—or at least the future of Anglo-Australian trade. The governor of South Australia, Alexander Hore-Ruthven, who happened to be in London, met with Dominions secretary Thomas and later warned him of the significant impact the bodyline dispute might have on consumer demand in Adelaide for British goods. The people of South Australia he said, tended towards insularity: 'The slightest hint from an outsider that all is not perfection causes offence at once. The narrow and confined outlook of the people is in inverse proportion to the breadth and expanse of the country.'[42] Less patronisingly, if somewhat implausibly, a journalist in Hong Kong reported that the bodyline controversy had cost Australian businesses in China some deals.[43] Lyons, too, told the Australian board that Australia might suffer economic hardship if the British public boycotted Australian trade.

Ultimately, the Australian board cabled the MCC, withdrawing the offensive charge. It maintained its opposition to bodyline bowling but confirmed that it did not regard the sportsmanship of the British team to be in question. Honour was saved. The tour continued with Larwood still using bodyline but less frequently than before. Larwood even was cheered when he scored 98 runs as nightwatchman in the Sydney Test. England won the series, 4–1.

Victory came at a price. Jardine led the next English tour to India, though not without some further controversy, but he retired from first-class cricket the following year. According to his daughter, he felt abandoned by the MCC.[44] As for Larwood, while the MCC eventually revised its rules regarding bodyline, it asked him to apologise for his bowling tactics. He refused, on the grounds that he had been following his captain's instructions. Larwood never played for England again. He did, however, emigrate to Australia in 1950, where he renewed contacts with some of his former opponents. Only in 1993, when Larwood was 88 years old, was he recognised with an MBE. Almost a decade later, a statue of him was unveiled at Kirkby-in-Ashfield, close to his birthplace.

Larwood might have found acceptance in the country that once howled for his blood, but in Australian popular memory, the bodyline series became enshrined in the hall of British infamy: not as perfidious as the bungling of Gallipoli, of course, or as heinous as the sacrifice of Australian troops on the Western Front, but still 'The Day England Declared War on Australia'.[45] The mix of unemployment and imperial mistrust that invested the bodyline issue with such emotion in 1933 was soon to pass, but even in 1984 an ABC program could claim that to this day, 'Douglas Jardine remains the most hated man ever to set foot in Australia.'[46] It might have been some consolation to Niemeyer had he been able to hear it.

Part X

RECOVERY, 1933–37

CHAPTER 34

Economic recovery

From 1932, the Australian economy started to recover from the Depression. This process was gradual and uneven, and to those who remained unemployed it must have seemed intolerably slow. Unemployment rates remained high throughout the 1930s, condemning some Australians to corrosive and demoralising long-term unemployment. Tragically for this generation, it was only the onset of another global war that brought about full employment in Australia, in 1941. Yet if we allow for the persistence of unemployment, it is clear from other economic indicators that Australia's Depression started to ease much earlier. The reasons for this, however, are, like so many other aspects of the Depression, a matter for ongoing debate.

Anyone seeking a simple answer as to what caused Australia's economic recovery will be disappointed. Multiple factors are often cited: the rise in exports of commodities, especially after the 1932 Ottawa agreement; Australia's departure from the gold standard and the devaluation of the Australian pound; the stimulus provided to local production and manufacturing by tariff protection; the decline in local costs with lower wages; and increases in productivity. But if this list is more or less agreed, there is no consensus as to the relative weight to attach to the various factors.[1] Most assessments of a specific cause of recovery require qualification. For example, the devaluation of the Australian pound in 1931, which has been described as a powerful influence over Australian recovery, was followed by a later revaluation (though still not to parity with the pound).[2] Wage reductions that were intended to lower costs were not universally applied across all states. Wage changes might be also seen as reactions to the Depression rather than initiators of production and employment.[3]

Moreover, if the volume of certain critical exports rose, their prices also fluctuated and, at times, stagnated (see Figure 34.1). The export price of wool, for example, seesawed. It rose in 1933–34 thanks to demand from European and Japanese woollen textile industries, but then dropped again. The introduction of the ill-conceived Trade Diversion Policy in 1936 (see Chapter 35) did little to stabilise wool exports, given that it triggered embargoes from the emerging and important Japanese market. As for wheat, the price rose at the end of 1931, but then remained stationary for the next four years. An international conference between major wheat producers, brokered by the Monetary and Economic Conference in July–August 1933, failed to achieve any significant constraints on production and exports or to increase wheat prices.[4] In 1934 a survey of wheat farmers found that only 56 per cent of the sample of 3277 had sufficient assets to cover their debts.[5] As late as 1935, the Commonwealth had to pass legislation restructuring farmers' debt obligations. But even at the end of the decade, many farmers were still struggling to cover costs. Those who made surpluses tended to use these to reduce their debts to the banks, so that arguably the multiplier effect of any moderate rise in export income was weak.[6]

An issue that attracts considerable debate is the role manufacturing played in Australia's recovery. The conventional view, articulated at the time by Copland and Giblin, and later by economic historian Boris Schedvin, was that manufacturing growth was 'the driving force in expansion' from late 1932 on.[7] In Schedvin's view, one of the early signs of recovery in 1932–33 was a pronounced rise in activity in the textiles industry, especially in Victoria, where the bulk of the mills were located. The centre of industrial production then shifted decisively towards the metals groups of industries, notably the iron and steel industries based at Port Kembla and Newcastle. By early 1934, the output of steel outstripped the peak of the 1920s, and by the end of the

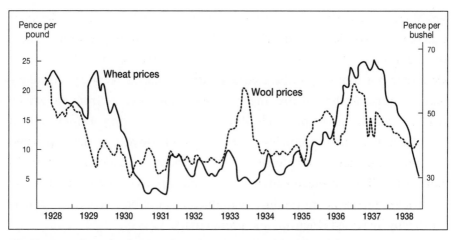

Figure 34.1: Export, wheat and wool prices, monthly, 1928–38
Source: Schedvin, *Australia and the Great Depression*, p. 292.

1930s it was nearly three times the 1929 figure. Although less spectacular, there were other important advances in engineering and metal-using industries, producing items such as industrial equipment, domestic appliances, excavating equipment, wire netting, machinery for sugar refining, steam boilers and engines, industrial refrigeration and light machine tools. The sale of motor cars was slow to regain the levels of the late 1920s, but there was still a substantial increase in the Australian component of many vehicles. With more vehicles being assembled locally than in the 1920s, the demand grew for accessories: axles, springs, shock absorbers and gears. Finally, there was a rise in production of galvanised sheet iron used, for example, in the construction of new factories and cheaper housing.[8]

The importance of manufacturing in the Australian economy is undeniable, but other scholars question its *relative* importance in Australia's recovery, vis-à-vis the expansion in agricultural production and exports.[9] Less than a quarter of real GDP growth over the recovery, it has been estimated, originated in the manufacturing sector. If the national income accounts are considered, as opposed to labour force figures, the contribution of manufacturing to recovery might be deemed less significant.[10] A further point of debate is what caused the growth in manufacturing in the 1930s. Was it attributable, as Schedvin argued, to 'a boom' in import substitution? If so, how do we explain the lag between the tariff rises of 1929–30 and the devaluation of the Australian pound in January 1931, and Australia's recovery? These interventions might have shored up the manufacturing sector in 1930–32 but were they not too early to be credited with Australia's recovery? An alternative argument, then, is that the spark for recovery came from elsewhere: namely, from a mix of price adjustments and cost cutting at home, which gave Australian manufacturing increased competitiveness; the expansion of domestic demand; and changes in the economy's technology matrix. In sum, 'Australia's continued march towards industrialisation was based not on artificial inducements to produce manufactures, but on lower costs, underwritten by increased efficiency and productivity.'[11]

The debate about causes notwithstanding, it is evident that, by some important indicators, Australia was starting to pull out of the Depression in 1933. By 1934, Australia's aggregate production of goods and services (GDP), which had fallen around 10 per cent between 1929 and 1931, had returned to 1929 levels.[12] As we have seen, by 1932–33, the Commonwealth managed to bring in a small surplus, while the states concluded the year with a lower deficit than anticipated. The grail of 'budget equilibrium' was also achieved by 1934–35, one year after the target date of the Premiers' Plan. From 1933–34, Lyons also began to remove a large proportion of the taxation provisions imposed in the context of crisis management during 1930–31. By 1935, many, though not all, of the emergency measures had been removed. The states, too, though forced to give priority to the reduction of deficits, abolished or reduced their special unemployment taxes and made some marginal reductions in income taxation.[13] Public investment recovered slowly, but by 1937–38, private investment had trebled from its trough in 1931–32, and over that period public investment had roughly doubled.[14]

Yet for many Australians, the benefits of recovery were slow in coming. The earnings for the majority of wage-earners were not readily or fully restored.[15] From 1933–34, the Commonwealth began to reverse the earlier reductions that had been made in public-service salaries and wages and in old-age and war pensions. Although these remained below pre-Depression rates, the real income of these groups had been more or less restored because of the fall in retail prices. The Commonwealth Court of Conciliation and Arbitration, while rejecting the unions' application in 1933 for the restoration of the 10 per cent cut in the basic wage, adopted a different price index for making cost-of-living adjustments. This had the effect of increasing the average wage by 4 per cent. In the following year, it restored the 10 per cent cut in real wages but at the same time adjusted the 'Harvester wage' principle to mean that the 'average' family unit whose 'normal needs' should be met by a basic wage was set at four, rather than five people. In many ways this reflected the decline in the size of families since Justice Higgins' famous judgment of 1907, but the traditional principle of basing wages on a worker's 'needs' was becoming secondary to the capacity of industry to pay.[16]

Most problematically, unemployment remained high throughout the 1930s. The statistics are not entirely satisfactory, but in 1939 and 1940 it was still over 9 per cent.[17] A study made in late 1936 of unemployed men registered at labour exchanges in New South Wales revealed that two-thirds had been out of regular work for at least three years. In 1939, a National Register of males aged 18–64 found that one-quarter of the 224,000 unemployed men had been out of work for more than a year.[18] Fearing social unrest, governments continued to offer relief works, with the amount being allocated from revenue and internal cash loans increasing from approximately £12.1 million in 1930–31 to a peak of approximately £19.1 million in 1935–36.[19] But this was part-time employment, not the full-time work many men and their families craved. The unskilled were, as ever, the most vulnerable. At least some of the chronic unemployment was due to the significant shift during the Depression from the construction industries to the manufacturing sector, which required a higher proportion of skilled labour.[20] Even as economic activity picked up, the income gap between the skilled and unskilled that had opened up in favour of the higher paid during the slump was not narrowed.[21]

Long-term unemployment was a source of despair for many men and their families. Few things were more corrosive than being deemed 'unemployable'. As one man, whose poorly educated and barely literate father was out of work until 1938, later recalled:

Still graven on my mind are pictures of him sitting on the wood heap with his head in his hands after he had chopped for hours for the sake of something to do; my mother's haggard face as she asked him night after night, 'Did you get a job today?' I still hear the sadness of her voice as she told us there was only bread and jam for 'pudding'—sometimes not even that.[22]

To quote another memory:

Hanging about the house all day, [my father] took to sitting in his big armchair, gazing into space when he wasn't reading the newspapers. Or, for a change of scene, he would sit at the kitchen table while Mum was cleaning or cooking. He would sit there with nothing to do, and now and then drum his fingers on the table . . . Sometimes he would get up and stand at the back door, staring out at nothing.[23]

It was one of the great mockeries for this generation of Australians that it took a new war to give them work. When a new army, the 2nd AIF, was raised in late 1939, some the men who rushed to volunteer were unemployed or underemployed. We do not know the precise number, and clearly many volunteers had motivations other than security of employment: patriotism, fear of Nazi expansionism, a sense of duty, a desire to emulate their fathers' service in World War I and so on. They resented the stigma of being dubbed 'economic conscripts', as Eddie Ward called them.[24] But still, it is likely that, as one man recalled:

red, white and blue patriotism discreetly hid some other things . . . things such as the dole and ration chits and blokes humping their swags in search of work all over the country, camping in railway yards of every country town until the police moved them on . . . It wasn't until you'd been in the army a while that you realised how many had been on the bones of their arse, scrounging feeds and living under the stigma of being unemployed.[25]

For those who chose not to join the armed forces, either in 1939 or later years, secure employment came with the mobilisation of the nation for

434

war. Output, demand, real income and living standards all rose in response to the new national crisis. Australia very quickly moved from a situation where resources were underutilised to one of virtual full employment. By 1942, the agricultural industry had a market so large it could hardly cope with meeting the needs of civilians, the defence forces, neighbours in the Pacific and the troops of Australia's new ally, the United States. The demands of war for munitions also stimulated manufacturing and more technologically advanced, capital-intensive industries, giving many workers, including women, the chance to acquire new high-level skills.[26] As one farmer later said: 'It took the war to make us prosperous. As far as we were concerned, it was a wonderful thing. The war set us up.'[27]

CHAPTER 35

An emergency government without an emergency

While the Australian economy gradually recovered, the governments that came to power in the crisis years proved generally stable. Non-Labor parties held office in New South Wales until 1941, in Victoria until 1945, and in South Australia until 1965. Labor administrations continued in Western Australia until 1947, in Queensland until 1957, and in Tasmania until an astonishing 1969. At the federal level, the makeshift UAP managed to provide national leadership until 1941. This stability did not necessarily mean political stasis. The more visionary of state politicians, on both sides of the political divide, tried in the years of recovery to reshape their local economies and reduce their future vulnerability to external economic shocks. The drive for development so evident in the 1920s continued wherever possible. But at the federal level, the innovation in social policy that the Depression had shown to be urgent was stifled by budget constraints, conservative timidity and, from 1936 on, the threat of a second war.

In recovering from the Depression, each of the states had a distinct trajectory. In Western Australia, the Labor government of Collier returned to power in April 1933 when economic recovery was already in train, especially in gold production and the dairy industries. Collier's immediate preoccupation was the vote for secession, an issue he handled adroitly. He also maintained the commitment to rural development that characterised all Western Australian administrations of the time. Effective in fighting for money in Canberra, Collier seemed eventually to lose interest in governing—he had already been premier for six years in the 1920s—and, in poor health, he stood aside for John Willcock in August 1936. A model of 'sound finance' with a fondness for balanced budgets, Willcock continued agricultural development and the construction of public works, although he did not provide full-time employment for men on relief works, or introduce a shorter week for the state's workforce. Later in the decade, Willcock encouraged the diversification of his state's economy and fostered the development of a range of small secondary industries.[1] He retained power almost until the end of World War II.

South Australia, in contrast, entered a period of long conservative rule in the mid-1930s. After Hill departed for London, a hopelessly divided Labor fielded no fewer than three parties in the April 1933 election. The 'official' ALP won only six seats and Lang Labor three, while a group of those expelled for advocating the Premiers' Plan won a further four. The new Liberal and Country League government under Richard Butler ensured that South Australia was the first of all states to balance its budget, and spent much time—not all of it productive—trying to reach a consensus on how to assist the depressed wheat and dairy industries. Butler also started the process whereby a significant amount of secondary industry was attracted to South Australia over the next three decades. He offered concessions to Holden's Motor Body Builders when it threatened to move to Melbourne in 1935 and incentives to BHP to build a blast furnace at Whyalla. This strategy was continued under Butler's successor in 1938, the formidable orchardist Thomas (later Sir Thomas) Playford. By 1965, South Australia had the highest per capita value of secondary production of all the states.[2] Like Collier in the west, Playford was highly effective in winning funding from Canberra, but his hold on power for a remarkable 26 years and 125 days was ensured by a gerrymander heavily weighted in favour of rural seats. For those born in Adelaide in the middle of Playford's long reign, the world seemed fixed in some immutable order: Playford was premier, Menzies prime minister, and God presided over all from heaven.

In another of the 'small' economies, Tasmania, the Nationalists lost power to Labor in 1934. The new premier, Albert Ogilvie, was a divisive figure, combining verve, panache and fluent oratory with abrasiveness, cynicism and a 'Theodore-like reputation for unscrupulousness'.[3] But in many ways he was a remarkable success. With his treasurer, Edmund Dwyer-Gray, advocating a variant of Douglas Social Credit theories, Ogilvie increased public spending, borrowed more money and expanded the role of government: improving education, providing cheaper home loans, stimulating tourism and rebuilding the Royal Hobart Hospital in flamboyant style. With assistance from the new Commonwealth Grants Commission (discussed later in this chapter) and the Loan Council, Ogilvie pushed ahead with the completion by 1938 of a hydroelectric power station at Tarraleah. Employing a large workforce in an inhospitable climate on the alpine central plateau, this construction doubled Tasmania's generating capacity. In 1936 the Associated Pulp and Paper Mills was established at Burnie, a business that would dominate the town's life for the next 50 years. In the 1937 election, Ogilvie achieved a 13 per cent swing and won an unprecedented 58.67 per cent of the vote.[4] But he died suddenly in 1939 of a heart attack at the age of 49, only ten weeks after Lyons.

Across Bass Strait in Victoria, the UAP's Stanley Argyle held power for less than three years with the slender majority he had won in May 1932. Lacking an imaginative spark, he increased the number of those employed on relief works, but only by paying rates that were under award (although they were higher than those for sustenance without work). Among other emergency measures, Argyle charged fees at the state high schools and adjusted the payments owing to the government under the various closer settlement schemes. In Opposition, Labor continued to feud, tainted by its supposedly corrupt associations with the sporting entrepreneur John Wren, scandals in Richmond and Collingwood, and ongoing threats from Trades Hall militants to form an alliance with Lang.[5]

In 1935, with little hope of returning to power in its own right, the Victorian ALP formed an alliance of convenience with the United Country Party. In an agreement, purportedly brokered by Wren, Labor supported the government of Albert Dunstan, which, in turn, passed legislation congenial to Labor, such as increasing sustenance payments and providing full-time work for the unemployed. This pragmatic arrangement was a testament to the party's lack of confidence, its 'harking back to an age when Labor had not yet fully conceived of itself as a party of government'. John Cain, who assumed leadership of the party in 1937 and who viewed Labor's subservience to Dunstan as a betrayal of party traditions, explained his party's dilemma: 'I do not want a Labor Government at the moment because a Labor Government cannot do as much as can be accomplished by supporting the present alignments of parties.'[6] Victorian Labor did not return to power in its own right until 1945, and even then as a minority. A ministry in 1943 lasted only four days before being replaced by a coalition of the Country Party with the UAP.

In New South Wales, the Stevens–Bruxner government, secure in power after trouncing Lang in June 1932, addressed the most egregious social problems by offering relief works rather than simply issuing the dole, and progressively refining the legislative protection for tenants and mortgagors. One of the early Australian politicians to be aware of Keynesian economics, Stevens saw public finance 'as an instrument and a servant; not an altar on which social stability and human happiness should be sacrificed'. Still, in order to get single teachers back to work, he sacked married women whose husbands were in employment.[7] New South Wales' patterns of borrowing, the source of so much trouble in the Depression years, were gradually changed, so that after 1937 more loans were raised locally than overseas.

Finally, in the relatively unscathed Queensland, Forgan Smith, flushed with his success in shaping national policy in June 1932, launched an ambitious public works program. Under the influence of economist Jim Brigden, who had been brought to Brisbane by Moore in 1929 to establish a Bureau of Economics and Statistics, Smith believed that public expenditure—consolidated revenue, high rates of taxation and loans from institutions such as the Australian Mutual Provident Society—would provide the solution to unemployment. But it was primary industry that Forgan Smith saw as the core of Queensland's recovery. He clung to this ruralism even though secondary industry had a greater capacity to absorb labour. Much time and energy was spent on settling the urban workless on the land, until by 1937 the levels of failure in, say, the banana settlements and tobacco growing were so high that the policy was abandoned. A strong personality who assumed his views would prevail—'Foregone' was his nickname—Forgan Smith was nonetheless popular with the electorate. He won the 1935 election by a 40-seat margin, although the Douglas Social Credit candidates won 7 per cent of the vote. Forgan Smith retired in 1941, but the ALP continued in power for a further sixteen years.[8]

At the national level, the UAP governed for a decade before it fell apart. After the landslide victory of 1931, Lyons won two other elections, in September 1934 and October 1937, albeit with reduced minorities. His success was due partly to his continued capacity to project to the public a reassuring presence and personality. Not only did he make frequent radio broadcasts in the days before talkback radio was ubiquitous, but he travelled across the nation in an effort to gain visibility in the local press and party organisations. Sensitive to the centrifugal tendencies in the UAP and the federation, Lyons held cabinet meetings in all states.[9] Sometimes he used air travel, a mode of transport that spoke of modernity but that was also risky. Charles Hawker died in a plane crash in 1938, as did Henry Gullett, two other federal ministers and the Australian chief of staff in a crash outside Canberra in August 1940. One of the towns Lyons visited in his travels was Gundagai, where in November 1932 he unveiled the statue of the dog on the tuckerbox. A monument to local pioneers, this diminutive statue provided the occasion for a prime ministerial homily about self-reliance. The locals should not lean too readily on government, lest they come 'very close to communism'. Lyons' name was soon, if briefly, scratched off the plinth, whether as an act of vandalism or protest we do not know.[10]

There was, of course, more to Lyons than sheer affability. He emerged as a unifying figure: a Labor politician who had found a meeting ground with conservatives; a Catholic who led a Protestant-dominated political party; and a leader who originated from a peripheral state to provide national leadership. Above all, Lyons staked his claim to leadership on values—decency, integrity and family life. He might have left the ALP, but he still projected an image of being committed to humanising society and ameliorating poverty, inequality and social distress. As writer and erstwhile journalist for the *Australian Worker* Dame Mary Gilmore said: 'I would still feel I voted Labour if I voted for him . . . His heart was with the people, and it neither changed with position nor wavered with circumstance.'[11]

Strikingly, Lyons managed to maintain cordial relationships with his former ALP colleagues, including Scullin. Whereas Hughes was detested as 'the rat' when he left the party in 1916, the personal hostility towards Lyons within the party was largely confined to the Lang group (whom Lyons called 'larrikins' and a 'mob of scoundrels').[12] Somehow Lyons' betrayal of the ALP seemed less heinous than Hughes', even though deflationary budget cuts violated some of the labour movement's deepest values. This might again have been a matter of personality. Lyons had none of Hughes' extremes of frenetic passion, rages, ruthlessness and abrasiveness. But perhaps military conscription, which was literally a matter of life and death, made apostasy on this matter beyond pardon or understanding. Lyons, unlike Hughes, continued to wear his loathing of war on his sleeve, especially as the world became more dangerous.

Lyons had three further skills essential to political survival. First, he was 'a positively brilliant Parliamentarian', to quote Menzies, who entered federal parliament in 1934.[13] Second, Lyons could hold his government together. Over the period 1932–39, almost all the original core of the UAP ministry resigned or left to follow other professional careers. This change of personnel, and the ebbing of the immediate threat of the Depression, did bring internal tensions: distrust between liberals and conservatives, demarcation disputes, and bitter rivalries between ambitious contenders for leadership, such as Menzies and (Robert) Archdale Parkhill. Through all this, Lyons maintained control of his cabinet. Even those who took issue with his policies did so without rancour. For example, when Hawker resigned in September 1932 after the government refused to reduce parliamentary salaries further, he told the prime minister that his consideration for his subordinates 'always made you such a likeable leader personally to work under'.[14]

Finally, Lyons was able to forge a productive relationship with the other major non-Labor force, the Country Party. In the election on 15 September 1934, the UAP lost its absolute majority as both the ALP and Country Party increased their numbers of seats. After a faltering start, the UAP and the Country Party joined forces. Page became deputy prime minister and his party was allocated two full portfolios. It was a marriage of convenience, with deep disagreements over tariffs (which Lyons agreed to review) and rural policies. But Page, who entered the government as the prime minister's severest critic, became Lyons' most loyal ally and his greatest supporter in cabinet. He wept when Lyons died suddenly in office in April 1939, and turned viciously on the man he held partly responsible for the prime minister's demise, Menzies, accusing him publicly of cowardice for not serving in World War I.

Yet if Lyons was able to hold on to power as the Depression ebbed, his government did little in the way of policy innovation. As Paul Hasluck famously put it, it was 'an emergency government that lasted longer than the emergency'.[15] Lyons might have been a 'subdued radical'—a generous judgement, for there was little that was radical about him—but, given the UAP's inherent conservatism and his consensual style, he made no attempt to achieve substantive and transformative change.[16] He widened the responsibilities of the federal government only when rural, economic or social needs were so pressing that they could not be ignored. His cabinet was often focused on administrative minutiae, the contemporary practice being that cabinet was largely responsible for coordinating and supervising federal government administration.

In Lyons' first term, public finance was kept well under control and little was done to stimulate the economy other than creating a psychological climate for expansion. A major policy initiative, developed by Giblin, was the formation in 1933 of the Commonwealth Grants Commission. The previously ad hoc, acrimonious and highly charged debates about the allocation of grants to states were thereby assigned to an ongoing independent source of advice.[17] Still, when Lyons went to the electorate in September 1934, he admitted that his policy position was practically unaltered from that of 1931, although there would be some changes to meet new circumstances. The old bogeys of Langism, communism and 'extremism' were dusted off once again and used to demonise Labor and the radical left.

This strategy backfired shortly after the election, when late in 1934 the government tried to prohibit the Austrian–Czech communist journalist Egon Kisch from entering Australia to attend the All-Australian Congress Against War and Fascism. Kisch jumped 5 metres from the deck of his ship in Melbourne, broke his leg and was promptly put back on board. When he finally landed in Sydney, he was given a dictation test, the administrative mechanism whereby a person seeking entry to Australia could be tested in a European language of an official's choice. Since Kisch was fluent in many languages, he was tested in Gaelic! On failing the test, he was sentenced to six months' imprisonment. The High Court set the conviction aside, however, on the grounds that Gaelic was not a European language. After further negotiations, Kisch left Australia voluntarily in March 1935, while the Lyons government suffered considerable reputational damage and criticism from champions of free speech for its draconian use of the law.

In his second term, Lyons' legislative record was thin. Pensions were progressively restored to former levels. Under pressure from the Country Party, the marketing of primary produce was reorganised in the interests of producers, and, as we have seen, rural debtors received assistance. Progressively, tariffs on many items that disadvantaged primary producers were reduced. But plans to increase employment through the unification of railway gauges, water and sewerage schemes, housing and reafforestation did not progress far. On 30 July 1935, *The Age* would write:

From whatever angle the position is examined, the evidences of neglect, procrastination and indecision can be discerned. Political virility seems to have been extinguished with the last election . . . The Lyons–Page Ministry is rapidly sinking into the rut of an uninspired routine Conservative Administration. Few Governments have derived so much self-satisfaction from doing so little.[18]

Consistent with this, the Lyons government failed to introduce the reforms to the banking sector that the struggles over economic policy in 1930–32 made so manifestly overdue. In 1935, Lyons responded to an irresistible groundswell by establishing a royal commission into the banking, monetary and exchange systems. After a very public airing of the issues, in 1937 the commission recommended that there must be machinery to ensure close and cordial relationships between the Commonwealth Bank, the Loan Council and the Commonwealth government. The independence of the bank was affirmed, but the primacy of Parliament over monetary policy was also confirmed. In the event that the differences between the bank and the government were irreconcilable, the bank should carry out the policy of government.[19] The central bank should also hold the surplus foreign exchange reserves of the private banks, and the private banks should be obliged to keep deposits with the central bank up to any percentage approved by the treasurer.

Thanks to lobbying from the private banks, which continued to resist central bank control, Lyons did not take significant legislative action. Still, the appointment of Sir Harry Sheehan as governor of the Commonwealth Bank in February 1938 brought more harmonious relationships with government than in the wilderness days of Gibson. Sheehan had previously been secretary of the Loan Council (1923–32) and secretary of the Treasury from 1932. In 1938–39, the bank even proved willing to engage in Keynesian policies to ensure that the banking system and the public had adequate funds; these included supporting deficit finance on the security of Treasury bills, and increasing its bond holdings through effective open-market operations.[20]

One of the few progressive policy initiatives of the Lyons government was the planning for a national insurance scheme. The existing pension scheme, which was funded from consolidated revenue, would be replaced by one to which employees and employers contributed. Richard Casey, back from London and, from 1935, treasurer, believed that 'a more kindly state' should remedy the lot of the unfortunate through 'a practical, instead of a visionary socialism'. He was also convinced of the need to reduce the significant drain of pensions on the federal budget.[21] But progress on the national insurance scheme was slow. Menzies for one, believed that if old-age pensions were regarded as a birthright, Australia might become a nation of mendicants.[22]

The drag of the government on social reform, in the wake of the misery of the Depression, frustrated some within it. F.H. Stewart, successively Minister for Commerce and Parliamentary Under-Secretary for Employment, had a strong personal commitment to social insurance. A wealthy Sydney businessman, a leading philanthropist and a man of deep religious convictions, he visited the United Kingdom (at his own expense) to investigate its schemes, submitted a report to Lyons and campaigned in the press. When the government seemed unduly dilatory in acting on his report, he resigned in March 1936 and went on to lead a small informal group of UAP parliamentarians who championed a policy agenda of 'social betterment'.[23]

The policy weakness of the Lyons government was particularly evident in the Trade Diversion Policy announced in 1936.[24] This was the brainchild of Gullett, one of Lyons' more erratic colleagues, who decided to impose new prohibitive duties on imports from so-called 'bad customers': that is, those nations who had an unfair or unfavourable trade advantage over Australia. One of the targets was the United States, with which Australia did have a negative balance of trade. But the other—oddly—was Japan, which had become Australia's second-best customer in terms of the volume of trade and was an important purchaser of wool. In recognition of this burgeoning trade, Australia had appointed a trade commissioner to Japan in 1935 and, at the very time that the Trade Diversion Policy was introduced, was negotiating a treaty of friendship, commerce and navigation.

What, then, motivated the change? One rationale for the duties on Japan was to give preference to British imports of cotton and textiles to Australia. Lyons had been almost harassed by this lobby group while he was visiting Britain in 1935, and a mission from the Manchester Chamber of Commerce had come to Australia in 1936 with the aim of improving its access to the Australian market. Since Page was in London trying to negotiate a greater share of the British market in meat and butter than Australia had won at Ottawa, preferential treatment to British exporters of cotton goods seemed an appropriate quid pro quo. The opposition to Japanese imports was also partly strategic. As it posed a growing threat in the region, Japan's penetration of the Australian domestic market seemed unnerving. Could it be that the Japanese, by undercutting British prices, were trying to isolate Australia economically, even politically, from Britain? In the case of the United States, Gullett hoped that the increased protection against the American imports would stimulate the expansion of the local automobile industry by compelling American motor vehicle manufacturers to establish some production in Australia if they wished to hold their share of the market.

The problem with the policy was that tariffs against Japan hurt Australia as well. As might have been anticipated, the Japanese retaliated by seeking alternative sources of wool and wheat, and imposing their own duties on Australian products. The Lyons government soon moved to abandon the policy, but the damage was done. While the Trade Diversion Policy succeeded in reducing Japanese textile imports into Australia, Japanese direct purchases of wool also declined (the Japanese attended auctions through proxies from other countries).[25] The year 1937–38 saw Australia's first trade deficit with Japan, and trade between the two countries would not return to the pre-1936 level until the 1950s. Possibly—though this is speculative—by excluding Japan from a key market, Australia also fuelled that nation's aggressive pursuit of raw materials in the Asia–Pacific region in the lead-up to war. A contemporary critic suggested as much on New South Wales radio in October 1936:

> at the very moment when it is becoming clear that the British Fleet can no longer be relied upon to defend Australia, and when Britain is preoccupied with recurring crises in Europe, at that very moment we are rushed into provocative action against Japan—action which will tend to make her desperate. Is that in the interests of Australia? Or of Britain?[26]

The last term of the Lyons government from 1937 to 1939 was a time of transition, out of the Depression and into war. Foreign and defence policy dominated the agenda, as Japan, Germany and Italy progressively exited the League of Nations and threatened the status quo in Europe and Asia. These topics are not core to the Depression narrative, but self-evidently the shadow of economic recovery hung over rearmament. Lyons became an unqualified supporter of the British policy of appeasement (making significant concessions to potentially aggressive powers in order to avoid armed conflict), and, as far as the recovery of the economy in the mid- to late 1930s allowed, the government encouraged defence production at home.[27] But the fear of slipping back into recession was ever present and the increases in defence expenditure and the pace of rearmament were 'determined by the level of economic recovery rather than by the level of international threat'.[28] Lyons, too, resisted any proposal to reintroduce compulsory military service. That said, Lyons and Casey were eventually willing to run deficits and increase taxation in the late 1930s in an effort to fund rearmament. Moreover, the government encouraged the development of Australian industry, local technology and munitions production that would prove of great value in the war effort to come: heavy artillery shells, aircraft bombs, depth charges, mines, optical equipment and naval stores that had hitherto been sourced from overseas.[29] The Lyons government also established, in 1936, the Commonwealth Aircraft Corporation in Port Melbourne, which would build under licence, first, an American plane, the NA-16 aircraft, which in its Australian iteration was known as the Wirraway; and then, at the height of Australia's crisis in 1942–43, a fighter, the Boomerang.

Social welfare policy, however, languished. The national insurance scheme was finally passed by Parliament in late 1938, despite 'the utter condemnation' of the ALP of the principle of individual contributions to pensions by invalids, the elderly and widows.[30] But the policy unravelled in the face of opposition from a formidable array of medical practitioners, communists, grassroots organisations and those who thought the priority in government expenditure should be defence. After months of fruitless discussions, the cabinet decided in March 1939 not to proceed with the insurance scheme before re-examining it. Menzies, who had already been manoeuvring to be Lyons' successor, resigned in protest. While not issuing a direct challenge to Lyons, he made pointed public comments about the lack of national leadership. Through 1938–39, his claims were advanced in the newspapers of Sir Keith Murdoch, previously an enthusiastic supporter of Lyons.

Lyons had long wearied of the stresses of the prime minister's role. In late 1932, after some lengthy and emotional parliamentary sittings, he begged Latham to take over the prime ministership. In October 1933, after another parliamentary battle, he said to his wife, Enid, 'I wish they'd defeat us, and we'd be out of our misery and get a little happiness.'[31] In 1937, he told

Enid, 'I've really reached the point where I could cheerfully leave it all aside.' In May 1938, he bemoaned: 'It is just dreadful to come back to what awaits me here [in Canberra] but I suppose one day it will come to an end.'[32] In late 1938, he and Enid started to prepare for his retirement, sending the youngest children back to Devonport to be cared for by their older sisters until their parents rejoined them. In 1939 Lyons reportedly told a Tasmanian associate, 'I should never have left Tasmania; I had real mates there, and was happy; this set-up is killing me.'[33]

The end came in the first week of April 1939, when Lyons suffered a coronary occlusion. He died, aged 59, on 7 April, fittingly Good Friday. Enid was at his side. He was the first prime minister to die in office. (Curtin would die of heart and other complications in July 1945, and Harold Holt would go missing in the surf near Portsea in December 1967.) Lyons' body lay in state at St Mary's Cathedral, Sydney, where it was viewed by 45,000 people until it was taken by destroyer for burial in Devonport, Tasmania.[34] At a mass at St Patrick's, Melbourne, the administrator of the cathedral said:

> The Prime Minister is dead, and the nation is stricken with grief. Well may we grieve, for we have lost not only our leader, but one who, as a statesman, as a husband, and as a father, has been an inspiration to all . . . Born of the people, he was naturally humble and courteous. But this unassuming man came to be regarded as a born leader of men. He will be numbered among the great ones of Australia.[35]

In fact, Lyons is one of Australia's less celebrated prime ministers. Statues to Lyons and the indefatigable Enid can be found in Devonport, Tasmania. A worn plaque marks the cottage in which Lyons was born in the town of Stanley, Tasmania. His bust appears in the Prime Ministers' Avenue in Ballarat, Victoria, along with everyone else's, and he merits a tree in another local tribute to Australian prime ministers, the Corridor of Oaks in Faulconbridge, New South Wales. But in the national capital of Canberra, now bedecked with memorials and statues of various kinds, it is Labor politicians John Curtin and Ben Chifley who stride across the public space towards Old Parliament House from the Kurrajong Hotel. Lyons' admirers must be content with a suburb named after him in 1965. This is perhaps not surprising, given that

Curtin and Chifley led Australia during the national crisis of war and drove the agenda of post-war reconstruction. But it also attests to the relative insignificance of the Great Depression compared to warfare in the national collective memory that the man who led the nation out of its most severe economic crisis has a lower profile.

So, for that matter, does the unfortunate Scullin. He also merits a Canberra suburb (gazetted in 1968), a place in prime ministerial galleries, and a large cross over his grave in the Melbourne cemetery. Erected by the federal executive of the ALP, the Federal Parliamentary Labor Party and the ACTU, the cross is inscribed with Scullin's words, 'Justice and Humanity demand interference whenever the weak are being crushed by the strong.' There are other tributes in Victoria: a humble park in Trawalla (opened by Gough Whitlam in 1971), and a modest obelisk erected on the side of the Western Highway by the Trawalla Progress Association in March 1969 to mark Scullin's birthplace. But beyond this, the prime minister of the Great Depression has little place in the public landscape.

The triumph of Labor in wartime, just a decade after the fratricidal strife of 1930–32, was possible only because it managed to regroup and rebuild the federal party quite rapidly. Given the entrenched factionalism and the legacy of Lang, it was a painful process, involving torturous negotiations and much recrimination about past disputes. Unity was paramount, but not at the price, Scullin believed, of allowing Lang to become the federal leader. He had his own reasons for animus against the man who brought him down, but he was concerned, too, for the careers of those who had supported him in the battle of the plans. If Lang assumed a national role, the waves of dissension would ripple across the ALP in all states.

Still, the reunification of the party in New South Wales was finally achieved, thanks to the efforts of Curtin and Chifley. The latter, Lang's principal opponent in New South Wales, damaged his voice permanently in a torrid and bitter campaign for the seat of Auburn in 1935. The Langites were readmitted to the federal party in early 1936. Lang still retained the leadership of the now official New South Wales ALP until 1939, and for years thereafter continued to be a force in Australian politics. Elected to the federal parliament for a term in 1946–49, he was a trenchant and bitter, if solitary, critic of Curtin and Chifley, whom he denounced as 'the right wing of the Conservative Party'.[36]

While the ALP was being reconstituted, Scullin tried to keep the attention of voters on Labor's policies: the maintenance of tariff protection for Australian industries; banking reform; support for the unemployed and wheatgrowers, including via a compulsory wheat pool. But the ALP, as we have seen, performed poorly in the 1934 election. For Scullin it was a crushing result. He was already showing signs of profound strain. For the first time in 30 years of public speaking, he lost control at a public meeting. In Malvern, Melbourne, in early 1934, he jumped from the platform to punch a man who accused him of lying about the basic-wage reductions. His performance in Parliament was nothing like that of his heady days of 1928–29, when he brought down the Bruce–Page government. After a sequence of illnesses, he resigned the leadership in October 1935. Notifying Parliament, he made 'a patently exhausted yet dignified figure'. Beasley, who had done so much to destroy his government, conceded that Scullin had been 'a fearless fighter in the exposition of what he believes to be the right course'.[37]

Somewhat surprisingly, Curtin narrowly won the following ballot for national leadership of the ALP. It was not a strong field of candidates.[38] Forgan Smith was mooted as a possibility, but he did not want to swap his role as premier for the dispirited and divided federal opposition. Makin was an option but he was in London attending the silver jubilee of King George V's reign and could not muster support. Frank Forde, who had been a principal architect of tariff policy under Scullin, seemed the most probable candidate. But Jack Holloway, now holding the seat of Melbourne Ports, thought Curtin the better choice and rallied support for him within the caucus—on the proviso that Curtin promise to remain sober (which he did). Curtin was recognised as a more dynamic orator and, in contrast to Forde, had been a critic of the Premiers' Plan. Since he had been living in Western Australia, he was also untainted by the ructions of Victoria and New South Wales in the early 1930s, and could project something of the image of a mediator. Still, Curtin defeated Forde by only one vote—a vote that seems to have been a proxy from the Victorian radical Maurice Blackburn, who actually disliked Curtin. The feeling was mutual.

Curtin immediately threw himself into reinvigorating and rebuilding the federal ALP. He toured the country by rail, offering a message of optimism for the labour movement. He appealed to the socialists within the party with a mix of idealism and pragmatism, aiming to achieve 'the maximum of Socialistic benefits within the limits of the capitalist system'.[39] But just as it seemed that the rifts of the Depression years were being bridged, foreign policy issues threatened to split the ALP again. The tension between Catholicism and socialism had always been present within the party. It became acute when Italy invaded Abyssinia (now Ethiopia) in 1935, fatally undermining the already fragile collective security of the League of Nations. The Spanish Civil War of 1936–39 also pitted the forces of the Catholic fascist General Francisco Franco against the left-leaning Popular Front of the Republic. The division of opinion within the ALP on this issue was so profound that Curtin stayed silent on what was for many in the labour movement 'the supreme issue' for ideologues in the 1930s.[40]

Labor made little progress in the 1937 federal election, when it won only two additional seats in the House of Representatives, but the results were more encouraging in the Senate. Under Curtin's leadership, Labor was emerging once more as a credible alternative government. This was not least because Curtin played a prominent role in the increasingly fraught debate about defence policy from the mid-1930s. Rather than reiterating the now anachronistic mantras about general disarmament, or endorsing the increasingly unrealistic imperial defence strategy that gave priority to the British naval base at Singapore, Curtin joined senior army officers in articulating the case for a more self-reliant defence policy, framed around a modern air force and an army capable of defending continental Australia. For Curtin, as for Lyons, this did not involve conscription.

Labor's time would finally come in late 1941, when the UAP, now under the able but arrogant Menzies, fell apart under the stresses of disastrous military defeats in Greece and Crete. Brought to power by a vote of Parliament rather than an election, Curtin was thrown almost immediately into the daunting task of leading the nation in the face of Japanese attack. But with this new crisis would come the opportunity for the ALP to address the problems that the Great Depression had thrown so starkly into relief. In its visionary program of post-war reconstruction, the ALP could finally pursue 'the light on the hill', as Chifley would memorably put it. Again the irony was bitter. Australians who fought or were born during World War I and who were catapulted into the economic catastrophe of the Great Depression had to endure another war before significant social reform was possible. Many thousands did not live to witness it.

EPILOGUE

A resilient nation

We return now to the questions that opened this book. How did Australia's social and political systems adapt and survive the most severe economic crisis in the nation's history? What were the sources of resilience that sustained Australians who had already endured the trauma of World War I?

These questions can be answered at several levels: national institutions, the community and the individual. As far as Australia's institutions are concerned, the democratic system generally proved robust. This was despite multiple challenges. The political elites faced often visceral opposition and relentless criticism for their failure to protect the living conditions of Australians from the global economic shock. The political party system was subjected to a major assault by the populist citizens' movements that exploded in 1931. The growth of conservative paramilitary movements threatened one of the fundamental guarantees of a liberal democratic society, the monopoly of force by the state. Meanwhile, at the other end of the political spectrum, radical activists and the militant unemployed took regularly to the streets, clashing with public authorities and the police in the extra-parliamentary sphere. Commonly, it was claimed that capitalism was close to a state of collapse. Yet ultimately, none of this mobilisation on either side of politics brought about any structural changes in the political system.

Partly this was because radical systemic change was rarely the aim of this protest. Despite the conspiratorial air of the paramilitary movements, they did not aspire to replace the status quo with a new form of government. Their role, as they saw it, was to contain communism and restore conservative and 'responsible' financial government, in New South Wales particularly. Once Lang was dismissed, these movements were starved of their political oxygen and withered away. So, too, with the other populist conservative movements. Their rhetoric was one of substantial change—the reform of party politics and even the installation of an executive form of government under a charismatic leader—but they proved to be ideologically thin and easily incorporated into the traditional non-Labor political movement. None of the movements on the right could claim to be fascist, even allowing for the flirtation with fascism of the New Guard's Eric Campbell in later years. It should be remembered, too, that the mobilisation of the conservative right was most prominent in New South Wales and Victoria. Dominant though these states were economically—and central though they have been in Australian historiography of the politics of the Depression—they were not the whole of Australia.

On the left, the level of activism and protest was impressive, but again lacking in revolutionary intent. The outbursts of public violence were frequent, including demonstrations against evictions, pickets of sustenance depots and 'strikes' against relief works. But many of these protests were local in focus, communally based, spontaneous and impulsive. The Communist Party, which managed to seize the leadership of some of these protests, might have seen them as the herald of revolution, but they were not. They were focused on redressing specific grievances, such as wage rates, the processes for allocating sustenance, or living and working conditions in the camps created to house the unemployed. Only occasionally was the battle against the New Guard taken to the streets.

Why the unemployed failed to take more revolutionary action has been much debated. Was it their lack of political experience and revolutionary consciousness; their fragmentation and demoralisation as a result of unemployment; and/or the repression and control exercised by the Australian state, the police and middle-class charities? None of these elements can be discounted, but we should not conclude that the unemployed were 'quiescent'.[1] They responded to the crisis, but in a way that was consistent with the historic reluctance of the Australian labour movement to mount radical challenges to the country's institutions or economic system. Past victories for the workers had been won not only through direct action but also through accommodation with the state. The creation of the ALP by the union movement implicated it fully in the parliamentary system, while it had long been dependent—some would say, unduly dependent—on the system of arbitration and conciliation for the maintenance of the standard of living under capitalism. Labor's ideological commitment to socialism was ambiguous, and it feared communism as much as did the conservatives. Hence, no matter how devastating the levels of unemployment and working-class distress, the response of the labour movement to the Depression was largely to work within the existing structures. The government at the federal level and in several instances at the state level was, after all, Labor. Huge energies were thus poured into trying to influence these governments—through petitions, deputations, and resolutions at state executives and party congresses—and when these proved ineffective, threatening non-compliant parliamentarians with the loss of their preselection and expelling them from the ALP. Refracted through personal ambition, factionalism, corruption and intimidation though these methods might often have been, they did not challenge the broader democratic tradition. Few seriously questioned the legitimacy of the popular vote as expressed in elections. Even Lang's dismissal and election defeat were accepted, including by the premier himself. Some purists might have thought it better to be in Opposition rather than betray Labor principles in office, but the ALP always regrouped to fight another election.

The only movement that explicitly advocated the destruction of the existing democratic system was the Communist Party. Its influence undoubtedly grew through the UWM's leadership of the protests, especially the eviction riots, but this never translated into a revolutionary threat to the established order. In the face of constant state repression and Moscow's directive to shun 'social fascists', the CPA remained small and focused inwards. If anything, its major function in the Depression was to reinforce the energy of its opponents by providing them with a target onto which to deflect their anger, and thereby affirm the superiority of their own role and values.

The resilience of the political system also owed much to the capacity of Australian governments and politicians to adapt to the economic crisis.

To be sure, it did not always seem that they were doing so. The policy responses at the federal and state level were faltering, uncoordinated and deeply circumscribed by deflationary economics. The Scullin government was incapable of policy innovation in the face of the unyielding troika of the Commonwealth Bank, the conservative Senate and the bankers in London. But for all that, Australian governments across the political spectrum did respond: by creating systems of sustenance and relief works, providing legislative protection for mortgagors and tenants, and, albeit often ineptly, seeking to assist the struggling export industries. Moreover, as the Depression worsened, they accepted that policymaking was not the exclusive domain of politicians but required the input of professional economists. Many of the policies thus devised arguably did little to assist recovery or to meet the huge social need, but for the first time the Australian state accepted that the alleviation of poverty was more than a matter for charities and voluntary organisations. This principle, and the incorporation of specialist opinion into government planning, would flower little more than a decade later in the Curtin and Chifley governments' post-war reconstruction program.

Furthermore, the leaders of Australian political and social elites proved able to reconfigure their organisational structures at various times during the economic crisis. The UAP might have been a somewhat synthetic creation of Melbourne's business community, but it served the immediate purpose of recapturing national power for the non-Labor forces nationally. While it struggled under Lyons to articulate a coherent ideology, it foreshadowed the powerful appeal that Menzies would make in 1942 to the 'forgotten people', those of the Australian middle class who survived the Depression through hard work, individualism and independence. As for the ALP, it had inflicted upon itself grievous wounds for the second time in fifteen years, but it showed a remarkable ability under Curtin in the mid- to late 1930s to regroup and rebuild so effectively that it would not only govern in wartime but also prove highly innovative in social, economic and foreign policy.

The resilience of Australian democracy also owed something to the account-ability of Australian leaders at all levels to their publics in the Depression years. Local councils were at the heart of the delivery of sustenance and relief work, and their records attest to constant, if often contentious, engagement between their officials and the public. The unemployed—or at least those who were not avowedly communist—had access to and representation on a plethora of local committees. State parliamentarians, too, were regularly on the hustings, and in the case of the ALP, answerable to state executives and party congresses. For federal politicians, visibility was a greater challenge, given the huge distances and the embryonic state of air travel. Radio and film helped bridge this to some extent, but still politicians travelled, often at the cost of their physical and emotional health. They appeared in public halls or on the back of trucks, shouting themselves hoarse and fielding a torrent of vitriolic abuse and opprobrium. They were often unable to respond to specific grassroots demands, but these were not leaders who hid behind media managers, dashed for cover surrounded by security men when an angry crowd appeared, or uttered soundbites from the cloistered confines of Parliament House.

What of resilience at the collective and individual level? We should be wary of generalisations. As we have seen, the impact of the Depression varied significantly across class, region and economic sector. Some industries suffered much higher levels of unemployment than others. Each of the states had its own distinctive economy. The urban professional and middle classes and the owners of large pastoral properties suffered less than the rural poor and the industrial working classes. Australians with capital and interest-bearing assets enjoyed greater protection than those on wages or the dole. The mantra of 'equality of sacrifice' that so infused the policy debates of 1930–32 was powerful for the very reason that the burden of the Depression was, in reality, unequal. For some Australians, then, finding resilience was less of a challenge than for others.

Clearly, too, the impact of the Depression on Australians' health was variable. For the most vulnerable Australians who lived in abject poverty, the struggle to find reliable sources of food was a constant challenge, taxing resilience to the extreme. But this was not a universal experience, and there is no evidence of widespread starvation. By some important indicators, the physical health of Australians improved. As for their mental health—one of the key indicators of resilience—the data do not permit any meaningful conclusions to be drawn about the degree to which the anxiety and stresses of the Depression caused serious mental disorders. A more nuanced, less pessimistic view of the impact of the Depression on balance seems warranted.

Yet even if we allow for this, we have to account for the resilience of the many thousands of Australians for whom the Depression *was* a catastrophe—those who struggled with dire poverty, poor health, chronic financial insecurity, gnawing anxiety, and the loss of self-esteem that came with being unemployed, often for years. We should also not discount the possible impact on the mental equilibrium of those who were relatively affluent but lived in fear of losing their status and standard of living. It seems that all these people drew their strength from a mix of community and personal systems of support. The mobilisation of Australian society during the Depression was impressive. In addition to the programs provided by the state were those of municipal committees, charities, churches, schools, professional organisations, trade union collectives and returned soldiers' organisations, to name only the most important. This powerful philanthropic impulse might have been prone to social control and moralising judgements, but we cannot discount its practical and emotional value. It did not always reach those at risk on the margins of society, especially Australia's profoundly disadvantaged Aboriginal peoples, but for many men and women the support of local communities bridged the gap between state aid and their needs. It also communicated a sense of compassion, collective endeavour and unity in the face of suffering. For those who were active in the public sphere, this mobilisation also encouraged a sense of agency, self-organisation and purpose in a seemingly chaotic world. To paraphrase the Dalai Lama, compassion is not a luxury; it is a necessity without which humanity cannot survive.

No form of community was as important to societal resilience as the family. Be it nuclear or extended, a functioning family provided practical support and emotional security at a time of extraordinary dislocation and acute anxiety. Once more, the experience was variable. Middle-class families with their larger homes and backyards had a considerable advantage in creating alternative economies, but even in the urban slums, shanty towns and desperately poor regional areas, the family, with the tireless maternal figure at the core, provided a refuge for the homeless, the opportunity to pool resources and the chance for inventive strategies of self-help.

Finally, there was personal resilience. Despite the problems of defining this term and identifying its sources, it is clear that many individuals were able in times of profound crisis and hardship to draw on a mix of personal attributes, temperament and environment to ward off the worst effects of trauma. In retrospect this generation of Australians inspires a certain awe. Many of them had lived through World War I, losing sons, fathers and husbands to the great maw of industrialised warfare. Many carried terrible physical and mental injuries from that conflict and the cruel pandemic that followed it. Their children grew up in the shadow of this grief and loss. Moreover, even the less damaged and more affluent of Australians had a standard of accommodation and living far lower than today's. Their economic decline during the Depression started from a lower base. Yet, when faced with the greatest economic crisis in the history of capitalism only a decade after World War I, they accommodated the humiliation of unemployment, the reduction in their standard of living, the anxiety of profound financial insecurity, the shattering of personal expectations, and the deferral once more of marriage and child-bearing. Many tolerated living conditions that seem intolerable today. Then they faced another global war that would again take their sons, husbands and fathers, and threaten them with the nightmare of foreign invasion.

Somehow the vast majority of them, across classes, regions and gender, found the resilience to survive. They endured, 'made do' and even found something positive in the memory of this struggle. How they did so we will never fully understand, but almost certainly they were sustained by a value system that privileged stoicism, independence, self-reliance, personal responsibility and even resignation. Their expectations of life were simply lower. They accepted hardship, sacrifice and suffering as a part of life. Happiness was not an entitlement and they were not seduced by vapid platitudes that their dreams would come true if only they had the courage to pursue them. Many fell back on the assurances of the still dominant Christian faith that the struggles of this world were an intrinsic part of the human condition, leading to rewards in the life to come. Men, women and children with these values made up the Australian nation in 1929, and if 'Australia' proved to be resilient during the Great Depression, it was surely because its people were so.

APPENDIX: Federal and state elections, 1927–37

	Commonwealth	NSW	Victoria	Queensland	South Australia	Western Australia	Tasmania
1927		8 October 1927 Nationalist/ Country Party (Thomas Bavin)	9 April 1927 Minority ALP (Edmond Hogan)		26 March 1927 Liberal Federation (Richard Butler)	26 March 1927 ALP (Philip Collier)	
1928	17 November 1928 Nationalist (Stanley Bruce)		22 November 1928 Nationalist (William McPherson) after vote of no confidence in Hogan				30 May 1928 Nationalist (John McPhee)
1929	12 October 1929 ALP (James Scullin)		30 November 1929 ALP (Edmond Hogan)	11 May 1929 Country and Progressive National (Arthur Moore)			
1930		25 October 1930 ALP (Jack Lang) Dissolved 18 May 1932 Caretaker government (Bertram Stevens)			5 April 1930 ALP (Lionel Hill, later Robert Richards)	12 April 1930 Nationalist– Country (James Mitchell)	

461

	Commonwealth	NSW	Victoria	Queensland	South Australia	Western Australia	Tasmania
1931	19 December 1931 UAP (Joseph Lyons)						9 May 1931 Nationalist (John McPhee, later Walter Lee)
1932		11 June 1932 UAP–Country (Bertram Stevens)	14 May 1932 UAP–Country (Stanley Argyle)	11 June 1932 ALP (William Forgan Smith)			
1933					8 April 1933 Liberal and Country League (Richard Butler)	8 April 1933 ALP (Philip Collier)	
1934	15 September 1934 UAP–Country (Joseph Lyons)						9 June 1934 ALP (Albert Ogilvie)
1935		11 May 1935 UAP–Country (Bertram Stevens)	2 March 1935 Country (Albert Dunstan) with ALP support	11 May 1935 ALP (William Forgan Smith)			
1936						15 February 1936 ALP (Philip Collier; from 19 August 1936, John Willcock)	
1937	23 October 1937 UAP–Country (Joseph Lyons)		2 October 1937 United Country (Albert Dunstan)				20 February 1937 ALP (Albert Ogilvie)

ACKNOWLEDGEMENTS

The Australian Research Council provided generous funding from 2016 to 2020 for my research for this book. This support allowed me to aspire to write a national history of the Great Depression, one that captured the experiences of Australians across diverse cities and regions.

I was privileged to have an able team of research assistants, many of them scholars in their own right, who played an invaluable role in my research. Given the closure of interstate borders during the Covid-19 pandemic, I was unable to complete some of the research myself, as planned. My thanks go to Bianka Vidonja Balanzategui, Jodie Boyd, Carolyn Collins, Mark Cryle, Patricia Curthoys, Clair Greer, Glenda Lynch, Eamonn McNamara, Andrew Messner and Shannyn Palmer. Working in capital cities and regional towns, they unearthed far more material than I was able to do justice to in this general history. There are rich resources still to be tapped by students and historians in the future.

Most especially I thank Paul Dalgleish in Canberra, whose knowledge of the byways of the National Archives of Australia was exceptional, and who made countless trips to the archives and the National Library of Australia on my behalf, including during the many Melbourne lockdowns of the Covid-19 pandemic in 2020–21. His support was always generous, quickly provided and invariably informed and helpful.

I must also thank the staff of the many libraries, archives and historical associations I consulted. Pre-eminent among these were the National Archives of Australia, the National Library of Australia, the Noel Butlin Archives Centre (Australian National University), and the state libraries and archives. The value of Trove's digitised newspapers and the Australian Parliament's ParlInfo are inestimable. History can only be written if records of the past have survived.

We are beholden to all those men and women who preserve this evidence, often with grossly inadequate financial support, and to those countless volunteers who maintain local history records across the country. As much as any historian, they are custodians of the nation's past.

Writing can be a solitary occupation, but the support and advice of colleagues along the journey is crucial. Any general history is built on the work of earlier scholars, and, as my notes indicate, I drew heavily on their research and insights across the decades. As always, I am also indebted to the Strategic and Defence Studies Centre, Australian National University, for providing an environment that privileges research, scholarship and collegiality. Frank Bongiorno (School of History, College of Arts and Social Sciences, ANU) was generous beyond imagining: reading a very long draft manuscript; sharing his prodigious knowledge of Australian political and labour history; and offering countless thoughtful, perceptive and incisive comments. Sincere thanks are also owed to Selwyn Cornish, College of Business and Economics, ANU, for his freely given advice on the mysteries of banking and economic theory, and willingness to read a draft version of the book. Sam Furphy (School of History, ANU) offered his deep expertise on the history of Aboriginal people in the inter-war years, while Aditya Balasubramanian (also of ANU's School of History) contributed greatly valued insights as an economic historian. James Cotton (University of New South Wales, Canberra) was always willing to share his encyclopaedic knowledge of inter-war politics and political personae. Charlie Fox travelled Perth and its environs, identifying sites where the Great Depression has been commemorated—and not.

Book production is always onerous. I thank CartoGIS, ANU, and particularly Jenny Sheehan, for the maps and figures. At Allen & Unwin, Elizabeth Weiss, Angela Handley, Nicola Young and Stephen Roche provided exemplary support: eagle-eyed editorial correction; judicious, informed and encouraging commentary; and the shepherding of this book through the publication process.

Finally, thanks go my family, Diana, Caroline, Julia and their partners and children. In the time that I was writing this book I was blessed with grandchildren. I dedicate this book to them. They fill my writer's life with joyous distractions. They are my hope for the future of the nation I have sought in my research and writing to understand.

ABBREVIATIONS

ABC	Australian Broadcasting Commission (later Corporation)
ACT	Australian Capital Territory
ACTU	Australasian (later Australian) Council of Trade Unions
ADB	*Australian Dictionary of Biography*, National Centre of Biography, ANU
AIF	Australian Imperial Force
ALA	Australian Labor Army
ALP	Australian Labor Party
ANU	Australian National University
AWU	Australian Workers' Union
BHP	Broken Hill Proprietary
CPA	Communist Party of Australia
CSR	Colonial Sugar Refining
CUC	Central Unemployed Committee (Melbourne)
FCT	Federal Capital Territory
MBE	Member of the Order of the British Empire
MCC	Marylebone Cricket Club
MLBS	Melbourne Ladies Benevolent Society
MMM	Militant Minority Movement
NAA	National Archives of Australia
NA(L)	National Archives (London)
NBAC	Noel Butlin Archives Centre, Australian National University
NBER	National Bureau of Economic Research
NLA	National Library of Australia, Canberra
PAC	Producers' Advisory Council
PROV	Public Record Office Victoria
RSSILA	Returned Sailors' and Soldiers' Imperial League of Australia (later RSL)

SLNSW State Library of New South Wales
SLQ   State Library of Queensland
SLSA   State Library of South Australia
SLV   State Library of Victoria
SLWA   State Library of Western Australia
SROWA State Records Office of Western Australia
SRSA   State Records of South Australia
UAP   United Australia Party
UWM   Unemployed Workers' Movement
WDC   Workers' Defence Corps
YMCA   Young Men's Christian Association
YWCA   Young Women's Christian Association

GLOSSARY OF TERMS

assets things that have earning power or other value to their owner.

autarky the concept that a country should be self-sufficient and able to obtain all essential goods and services from the domestic or a bloc economy.

balanced budget the situation when the total public-sector expenditure is equal to the total government revenues over a given period.

balance of payments a statement of all economic transactions between private citizens or government agencies in one country and all other countries in the world over a particular period.

balance of trade the difference between the monetary value of a nation's exports and imports over a certain period.

bonds securities issued by governments, companies and other organisations as a way of raising capital, and on which interest is paid.

Bretton Woods a conference held at Bretton Woods, New Hampshire, United States, in 1944, which established the international monetary system after World War II and set up the International Monetary Fund and the World Bank.

budget deficit the situation when the total public-sector expenditure exceeds the total government revenues over a given period.

central bank an institution that manages a country's monetary system, by setting interest rates, managing the money supply and by acting as a lender of last resort to commercial banks.

constant prices a way of measuring the real change in output. A year is chosen as the base year. For any subsequent year, the output is measured using the price level of the base year.

creditor a person or institution that lends money to a borrower—for example, by making a loan or buying a bond or providing some other form of credit.

current account the record of a nation's transactions with the rest of the world—specifically its net trade in goods and services, its net earnings on cross-border investments, and its net transfer payments—over a defined period of time, such as a year or a quarter.

debt service the payment of interest and principal due on a debt.

deflation a persistent fall in the general price level of goods and services. It can result in a slump in demand and a shrinking money supply.

devaluation a fall in the value of one currency against other.

exchange rate the rate at which one currency is exchanged for another.

exports sales to customers external to a nation.

fiscal policy a government's policy on public spending, taxation, and any other government income or assistance to the private sector.

free trade trade between countries that occurs with few or no trade barriers.

full employment a situation where all who seek employment can find it.

GDP gross domestic product, a measure of economic activity in a country, calculated by adding the value of all goods and services produced in the economy over a given period of time, usually a year.

GNP gross national product, another measure of economic activity in a country, calculated by adding GDP to the income earned by residents from investments abroad, less the corresponding income sent home by foreigners who are living in the country.

gold standard the monetary regime under which a national currency was fixed and could be freely converted into gold. Currencies were linked internationally at fixed rates of exchange and gold shipments were the ultimate means of balance-of-payments settlements.

gross private domestic investment the amount of money that domestic businesses invest within their own country.

hot money money that is held in one currency but is liable to switch rapidly to another currency in search of the highest available returns.

hyperinflation inflation that occurs at an extremely high rate.

imperial preference a system of reciprocal tariffs or free trade agreements between units of the British Empire.

imports purchases of foreign goods and services.

inflation rising prices that erode the purchasing power of a unit of currency.

infrastructure facilities such as roads, ports, railways, water and electricity that enable social and economic life.

interest the price you have to pay to borrow money.

Keynesian economics a branch of economics, based, often loosely, on the ideas of John Maynard Keynes, which believes in active government intervention and is suspicious of market outcomes.

lender of last resort the role played by a central bank whereby it lends to banks in financial difficulties or takes control of a troubled bank, thus minimising the risk of a bank run by reassuring depositors that their money is safe.

loan conversion when a loan rolls over, or converts, to a different loan structure after a certain term.

macroeconomic policy policy relating to an economy as a whole, concentrating on economy-wide factors, such as interest rates, inflation and unemployment.

microeconomics the study of the individual pieces—people and businesses—that together make an economy.

monetary policy using changes in the money supply, including changes in interest rates in order to stimulate or slow down economic activity.

multiplier an economic factor that, when increased or changed, causes increases or changes in many other related economic variables.

national debt the total outstanding borrowing of a country's government (usually including national and local government).

nationalisation when a government takes ownership of a private-sector business.

oligopoly an industry with only a few firms.

open-market operations operations in which a central bank buys and sells securities in the open market, as a way of controlling interest rates or the growth of the money supply.

protectionism opposition to free trade, intended to protect a country's economy from foreign competitors.

recession period of slow or negative economic growth, usually accompanied by rising unemployment.

reflation policies to stimulate demand and thus boost the level of economic activity.

reserve ratio the fraction of its deposits that a bank holds as reserves.

reserves money in the hand, available to be used to meet planned future payments or if some other need arises; for a bank, reserves are those deposits it retains rather than lending out.

sinking fund a fund in which money is set aside for the gradual repayment of a debt.

'sound finance' a dominant conservative philosophy that believed in balanced budgets, low inflation, reductions in government expenditure and minimal government interference in the banking sector or economy.

sterling reserves the amount held by banks in sterling (British) currency.

tariff a tax on goods produced abroad, imposed by the government of the country to which they are exported.

terms of trade the ratio between a country's export prices and its import prices—how many units of exports are required to purchase a single unit of imports?

Treasury bill a short-term government debt backed by the Treasury, used to manage fluctuations in the government's short-run cash needs.

NOTES

Introduction: Australia's Great Depression

1 I acknowledge a profound debt to C.B. Schedvin, whose classic *Australia and the Great Depression* (first published 1970) was an indispensable source for this book and is often cited.
2 'Melbourne Renters Struggling in Lockdown Urge Government to Bring Back Eviction Moratorium', *Guardian*, 4 June 2021.
3 David Taylor, 'JobKeeper and the Coronavirus Stimulus Bill Has Been Slashed, but What Can We Do with the Extra Cash?, ABC News, 26 May 2020, <www.abc.net.au/news/2020-05-26/jobkeeper-missing-60-m-what-next/12283554>.
4 'Coronavirus: Time for Us to Summon the Anzac Spirit', *Australian*, 6 April 2020.

Chapter 1: The soldiers come home

1 Beaumont, *Broken Nation*.
2 Horne, 'Demobilizing the Mind'. The related ideas of 'cultural mobilization' and 'political mobilization' have been developed in recent French and Anglo–American scholarship especially, but are by no means uncontested.
3 The article, 'The Habit of Killing', originally published in Britain, was published in the left-wing Victorian paper *Labor Call* in February 1920, and re-run in the Brisbane *Worker* on 24 June 1920. For 'agog', *Soldier*, 1916, see Garton, 'Demobilization and Empire', p. 131.
4 Stanley, *Bad Characters*, p. 174; Ekins, 'Fighting to Exhaustion', pp. 112–13.
5 Lake, 'The Power of Anzac', pp. 197–8.
6 Thirkell, *Trooper to the Southern Cross*, p. 121.
7 McMullin, *The Light on the Hill*, p. 117.
8 Curson and McCracken, 'An Australian Perspective', pp. 103–4.
9 Garton, 'Demobilization and Empire', p. 136.
10 The definitive account is Evans, *The Red Flag Riots*.
11 'Peace Day Rejoicings', *Age* (Melbourne), 21 July 1919.
12 'Assault on the Premier', *Age*, 22 July 1919.
13 E.W. Gordon and L.D. Song, quoted in Kaplan, 'Toward an Understanding of Resilience', in Glantz and Johnson (eds), *Resilience and Development*, p. 52.
14 For further discussion, see Beaumont, 'Remembering the Resilient', pp. 140–1, 145–8.
15 Carroll, *My Ninety Years*, p. 38.

16 For discussions of the importance of the strength of the state, see Edele and Gerwarth, 'The Limits of Demobilization', pp. 4–8; and Gerwarth and Horne, 'The Great War and Paramilitarism in Europe', pp. 267–73.

17 I owe the term 'culture of defeat' to Wolfgang Schivelbusch, *The Culture of Defeat*.

18 Edele and Gerwarth, 'The Limits of Demobilization', p. 7.

19 'Meet the *Freikorps*', National World War II Museum, New Orleans, <www.nationalww2museum.org/war/articles/meet-freikorps-vanguard-terror-1918-1923>.

20 Edele and Gerwarth, 'The Limits of Demobilization', pp. 6–7. On Britain, see Lawrence, 'Forging a Peaceable Kingdom', pp. 557–89.

21 See Crotty and Edele, 'Total War and Entitlement', esp. p. 20.

22 F. Berkes and C. Folke, quoted in Pendall et al., 'Resilience and Regions', p. 74. See also A.S. Marsten and M. Rutter, in Kaplan, 'Toward an Understanding', p. 20.

23 See especially Scates and Oppenheimer, *The Last Battle*; and Lake, *The Limits of Hope*.

24 For a deeply moving account of disabled soldier-settlers, see Scates and Oppenheimer, *The Last Battle*, pp. 161–72; for letter about leg, p. 165.

25 Lake, 'Power of Anzac', p. 213.

26 This argument is developed at length by Blackmore, *The Dark Pocket of Time*, esp. pp. 194–6.

27 Garton, *The Cost of War*, p. 87.

28 Crotty, '"What More Do You Want?"', pp. 52–71. For general histories, see Kristianson, *The Politics of Patriotism*; Crotty, 'The Returned Sailors' and Soldiers' Imperial League of Australia', pp. 166–86; and Sekuless and Rees, *Lest We Forget*. For Dyett, the most comprehensive work is Sturrock, 'Gilbert Dyett'.

29 Crotty and Edele, 'Total War and Entitlement', p. 21.

30 Blaikie, *Remember Smith's Weekly?*, pp. 158–9.

31 Garton, 'Demobilization and Empire', pp. 133–4. The British state, in contrast, offered only 'modest compensation' to disabled veterans and relied for the reintegration of veterans on voluntary and philanthropic efforts (Cohen, *The War Come Home*, pp. 4–5). For a detailed comparative analysis of repatriation in various countries, see Crotty, Diamant and Edele, *The Politics of Veteran Benefits*.

32 Garton, *The Cost of War*, pp. 83–4.

33 See, for example, Lack (ed.), *Anzac Remembered*; Andrews, *The Anzac Illusion*, esp. pp. 60–3, 84–91, 144–7, 214–15; Seal, *Inventing Anzac*; Moses and Davis, *Anzac Day Origins*, esp. chs 7 and 8; Holbrook, *Anzac*, ch. 2.

34 For coherence and meaning as factors in resilience, see Kaplan, 'Toward an Understanding', p. 49.

35 For the classic account of the war memorial movement, see Inglis, *Sacred Places*, esp. ch. 4; for names, p. 182.

36 'Anzac Day 1930', *Canberra Times*, 25 April 1930.

Chapter 2: Politics reshaped

1 Pendall et al., 'Resilience and Regions', pp. 77–8.

2 For the earlier history of liberalism, see Walter with Moore, *What Were They Thinking?*, pp. 99–102, 136–9; and Brett, *Australian Liberals*, pp. 9, 17, 24–34.

3 Fitzhardinge, *The Little Digger*, pp. 213–14.

NOTES

4 McMullin, *The Light on the Hill*, p. 127.

5 Walter with Moore, *What Were They Thinking?*, p. 103.

6 Gollan, *Revolutionaries and Reformists*, p. 12.

7 Bowden, 'The Rise and Decline of Australian Unionism', p. 59.

8 'Unions Defy Expectations to Report Membership Growth in Pandemic', *Sydney Morning Herald*, 22 July 2020.

9 See Turner and Sandercock, *In Union is Strength*, p. 77. The definitive history of the OBU is Hearn and Knowles, *One Big Union*.

10 For a useful summary of the 'dependency' argument, see Gahan, 'Did Arbitration Make for Dependent Unionism?', pp. 648–98.

11 Gollan, *Revolutionaries and Reformists*, p. 10.

12 Macintyre, *The Reds*, p. 119. The account that follows draws on this definitive history.

13 Ibid., p. 21.

14 The classic work on which this account draws is Graham, *The Formation of the Australian Country Parties*, pp. 55–142.

15 For Page's rise, see Wilks, *'Now Is the Psychological Moment'*, ch. 2.

16 O'Farrell, *The Catholic Church*, p. 233.

17 'St Patrick's Day', *Ballarat Star*, 20 March 1920.

18 'The Federal Elections', *Register* (Adelaide), 28 November 1919; 'Dr. Mannix and Protestant Federation', *Daily Examiner* (Grafton, NSW), 24 November 1919.

19 'Expelled M.P.', *Sydney Morning Herald*, 29 November 1920.

20 Fisher, 'Lacking the Will to Power?', p. 224.

Chapter 3: War and the economy

1 Bongiorno, 'Post-war Economies'. See also Dyster and Meredith, *Australia in the Global Economy*, pp. 80–1.

2 For the negotiations regarding wool, see Tsokhas, 'W.M. Hughes, the Imperial Wool Purchase and the Pastoral Lobby', pp. 232–63. The terms on which the imperial government purchased the Australian wool clip were largely determined by the Australian government in consultation with wool-grower representatives and the major wool brokers.

3 Sendziuk and Forster, *A History of South Australia*, pp. 113–14.

4 Scott, *Australia During the War*, pp. 556, 564.

5 Macintyre, *Oxford History*, p. 212.

6 Schedvin, *Australia and the Great Depression*, p. 56.

7 Yule, in Connor, Stanley and Yule, *The War at Home*, p. 54.

8 Connor, 'The War Munitions Supply Company', p. 805.

9 Statistica, 'Number of artillery shells produced by British forces during the Battle of the Somme in 1916, <www.statista.com/statistics/1022824/british-artillery-shells-produced-during-the-somme/>.

10 McLean, *Why Australia Prospered*, pp. 147–8.

11 Yule, 'Organization of War Economies (Australia)'.

12 Yule, *The War at Home*, p. 57; Copland, *The Banking System of Australia*, p. 52.

13 Copland, *The Banking System*, p. 52.

14 Scott, *Australia During the War*, pp. 499–502.

15 Tsokhas, '"A Pound of Flesh"', p. 14.

16 Carter, *The Price of Peace*, pp. 49–51.
17 Tooze, *The Deluge*, pp. 38, 40.
18 Scott, *Australia During the War*, p. 486.
19 Fitzhardinge, *The Little Digger*, p. 387.
20 The account that follows draws on Tsokhas, '"A Pound of Flesh"', pp. 12–26.
21 Ibid., pp. 15–16.
22 Ibid., pp. 17–18.
23 Ibid., p. 20.

Chapter 4: Recovery and development

1 King, 'The Tarring and Feathering of J.K. McDougall', pp. 54–67.
2 Fitzhardinge, *The Little Digger*, esp. pp. 447–51.
3 Ibid., p. 498.
4 Cumpston, *Lord Bruce of Melbourne*, p. 21.
5 Lee, *Stanley Melbourne Bruce*, pp. 17–22.
6 Cotton, 'William Morris Hughes', pp. 103–14. See also Sales, 'W.M. Hughes and the Chanak Crisis of 1922', pp. 392–405; and Bartrop, *Bolt from the Blue*.
7 Fitzhardinge, *The Little Digger*, p. 516.
8 Murray, *The Confident Years*, pp. 141 ff.
9 For a full development of this argument, see Merrett and Ville, 'Tariffs, Subsidies and Profits', pp. 46–70. For the inter-war years, see Bongiorno, 'Search for a Solution', pp. 64–87. See also Maddock and McLean, *The Australian Economy*, p. 41.
10 Population statistics that follow are taken from Vamplew (ed.), *Australians: Historical Statistics*, pp. 36, 41.
11 Production statistics for New South Wales and all states, ibid., pp. 79–81, 88, 92–3.
12 Costar, 'Labor, Politics and Unemployment', p. 9.
13 Fitzgerald, *A History of Queensland from 1915 to the 1980s*, p. 65.
14 Sendziuk and Foster, *A History of South Australia*, p. 116.
15 Gibson, *Tolley*, p. 63.
16 Snooks, 'Development in Adversity', p. 239.
17 State Library of Western Australia (SLWA), 'The Land: Pastoral Stations 1901–1939', <https://slwa.wa.gov.au/wepon/land/html/pastoral2.html>.
18 Reynolds, *A History of Tasmania*, p. 238.
19 Ling, *Commonwealth Government Records about the Northern Territory*, p. 19.
20 Notes of 4th Meeting, Imperial Economic Conference 1923, London, 9 October 1923, cited in Cotton (ed.), *Documents on Australian Foreign Policy*, p. 312.
21 Brady, *Australia Unlimited*, p. 101.
22 Geographer Griffith Taylor, University of Sydney, cited in Macintyre, *Oxford History*, p. 199; Phillips and Wood, 'The Australian Population Problem', p. 16.
23 Wickens, 'Australian Population', p. 62.
24 The following summary draws Drummond, *Imperial Economic Policy*, esp. ch. 3.
25 There were no Catholic initiatives supporting British immigration until the late 1930s, when some English Catholic boys came to work on a vast property at Tardun near Geraldton, WA.
26 Jill Roe, 'Booth, Mary (1869–1956)', *ADB*; Gill, *Likely Lads*, pp. 167, 142, 149.
27 Gill, *Likely Lads*, pp. 5, 15.

28 Macintyre, *Oxford History*, p. 200; Australian Bureau of Statistics, 'Trends in National Fertility Rates', 3301.0 Births, Australia, 2008, <www.abs.gov.au/AUSSTATS/abs@.nsf/0/CB88996A50DAF915CA25766A00120D19?opendocument>.
29 Drummond, *Imperial Economic Policy*, pp. 119–20.
30 Gill, *Likely Lads*, p. 21.
31 Ibid., p. 89.
32 For a discussion of how many such children there were, see Parliament of Australia, *Lost Innocents*, pp. 61–2.
33 *Lost Innocents* states (p. 76) that, of the 38 submissions that reported assault, all but four instances occurred between 1947 and 1963. All but 14 occurred in the Christian Brothers institutions in Western Australia, which started to receive child migrants only late in the 1930s.
34 For an overview of imperial preference in the 1920s and 1930s, see Tsokhas, 'Protection', pp. 65–87.
35 Lee, *Stanley Melbourne Bruce*, p. 39. For McDougall's important but little-known role, see Way, 'F.L. McDougall and Commodity Diplomacy', pp. 93–110.
36 Drummond, *Imperial Economic Policy*, p. 29.
37 The account that follows draws on Barnes, 'Bringing Another Empire Alive?', pp. 61–85; Meredith, 'Imperial Images', pp. 30–6; and Self, 'Treasury Control', pp. 153–82.
38 Self, 'Treasury Control', pp. 156–7.
39 Barnes, 'Bringing Another Empire Alive?', p. 62.
40 Ibid., p. 71.
41 Meredith, 'Imperial Images', pp. 33–4; Barnes, 'Bringing Another Empire Alive?', p. 66.
42 An assessment of the Empire Marketing Board's effectiveness can be found in Constantine, 'Bringing the Empire Alive', pp. 219–24.

Chapter 5: The voracious borrower

1 Schedvin, *Australia and the Great Depression*, pp. 3–4; Maddock and McLean, *The Australian Economy*, p. 53.
2 The Colonial Stock Act 'empowered trustees in Great Britain to invest in colonial inscribed stocks even when they were not otherwise permitted to do so by the terms of their trust deeds': see Jessop, 'The Colonial Stock Act of 1900', p. 154.
3 Schedvin, *Australia and the Great Depression*, p. 98.
4 The Bank of England and Treasury feared that, unless the London capital market was cleared of foreign loans, there would be upward pressure on the bank rate and a denial to the British government of the capital that might have been needed to counter speculation against sterling: Tsokhas, 'Anglo-American Economic Entente', p. 622.
5 Schedvin, *Australia and the Great Depression*, pp. 5–6.
6 The British-Australasian Society, quoted in 'Queensland's Pastoral Rents', *Age* (Melbourne), 28 August 1920.
7 'Mr. Theodore and Sir R. Philp', *Advertiser* (Adelaide), 27 September 1920.
8 Attard, 'Financial Diplomacy', p. 117.
9 'American Loans', *Newcastle Morning Herald and Miners' Advocate*, 7 July 1925.
10 Attard, 'Financial Diplomacy', p. 116.
11 Schedvin, *Australia and the Great Depression*, pp. 100, 96.

12 Ibid., p. 3.
13 Schedvin, 'The Long and the Short', p. 10.
14 For further useful detail, see Schedvin, *Australia and the Great Depression*, pp. 76–95.
15 Coleman, Cornish and Hagger, *Giblin's Platoon*, pp. 32–4.
16 Cornish, *The Evolution of Central Banking in Australia*, p. 3.
17 For the early history of the Loan Council, see Gilbert, *The Australian Loan Council*, chs 5–7; for the details of the 1927 financial agreement, pp. 88–91.
18 'Help Your Government', 27 August 1923, National Archives of Australia (NAA), A2487 1924/2003.
19 Nairn, *The 'Big Fella'*, pp. 99–100.
20 Gilbert, *The Australian Loan Council*, pp. 85–6.
21 Attard, 'The Bank of England', p. 68.
22 Schedvin, *Australia and the Great Depression*, pp. 97–9.
23 Quoted in Attard, 'The Bank of England', p. 69.
24 Quoted in Gilbert, *The Australian Loan Council*, p. 79.
25 Schedvin, *Australia and the Great Depression*, pp. 98–9.
26 Richmond, 'S.M. Bruce and Australian Economic Policy', p. 248.
27 'Australia's Economic Position', *Advertiser* (Adelaide), 2 July 1927.
28 Attard, 'Financial Diplomacy', p. 121.
29 Attard, 'Financial Diplomacy', pp. 117–18; Tsokhas, 'Anglo-American Economic Entente', pp. 623, 628.
30 The Report of the British Economic Mission of 7 January 1929 is found at NAA, A5954/1 28/67.
31 Copland, *Australia in the World Crisis*, p. 13.

Chapter 6: Recession

1 For Newcastle, see Gray, *Newcastle in the Great Depression*, pp. 11–17.
2 Ahamed, *Lords of Finance*, p. 3.
3 Lack, *A History of Footscray*, pp. 270–4.
4 Rev. S. Archer Harris, Salvation Army, to Secretary, Archer Relief Fund, 22 October 1928, Public Record Office Victoria (PROV), Richmond City Subject Correspondence files, VPRS 16668/P/0001 unit 28.
5 Richmond Ladies' Benevolent Society to Mayor, 29 October 1928, ibid.
6 C. Blazey, Town Clerk, 'Mayor of Richmond's Unemployed Relief Fund', nd, ibid.
7 Blazey to R.C.C. Social Club, 24 November 1928; and Archers Pty Ltd to Blazey, 1 November 1928, ibid.
8 Blazey to Marshall Shoe Company, 20 July 1928, ibid.
9 Secretary, Reynolds, Smith, Mitchell & Co., to Town Clerk, Richmond, 6 September 1928; and William Horfsall Pty Ltd to Blazey, 12 September 1928, ibid.
10 Frank Wiles to Mayor of Richmond, 8 September 1928, ibid.
11 Salvation Army Officers' Quarters to Blazey, 25 August 1928, ibid.
12 *Southern Cross* (Adelaide), 23 December 1927.
13 Marsden, *A History of Woodville*, p. 193.
14 'S.A. Unemployed Procession to Govt. House', *Northern Standard* (Darwin), 19 February 1929.

15 Town Clerk's Department (C15), Annual Reports (S21), 1928, Adelaide City Council Archives.
16 Town Clerk's Department (C15), Annual Reports (S21), 1929, Adelaide City Council Archives.
17 'Old Bill of 1929', *Mail* (Adelaide), 26 January 1929.
18 Report of Finance Committee, 30 June 1930, South Australian Soldiers' Fund, State Library of South Australia (SLSA), SRG 79.
19 Dickey and Martin, *Building Community*, pp. 61–2, 71.
20 See City of Port Adelaide Mayor's Reports for 1926–1927 to 1928–1929, Corporation of the Town of Port Adelaide, State Records of South Australia (SRSA), GA257.
21 'Help Wanted', *Recorder* (Port Pirie), 11 February 1929.
22 'Unemployed in Port Augusta', *Transcontinental* (Port Augusta), 17 August 1928.
23 'Serious Problem: Relief for Unemployed', *Daily News* (Perth), 31 July 1928; Premiers' Department—1928—Conference of representative citizens to discuss unemployment, August 1928, State Records Office of Western Australia (SROWA), Cons 1496 1928/0709.
24 H.C. Sewell, quoted in J.S. Battye to Under Secretary of State for Lands, Perth, 7 January 1929, NAA, A786 B61/1.
25 F.W. Clayton to J. McPhee, premier, 12 February 1929, Tasmanian Archives, PD1/1/460 files.
26 Bill Ince and children, Ken and Margaret, quoted in Lowenstein, *Weevils in the Flour*, pp. 51–3.
27 Linn, *Community of Strength*, p. 153.
28 Quoted in 'Mallee Settlers', 28 February 1929, in Torpey, *The Way it Was*, p. 69.
29 'The Man on the Land', 5 September 1929, ibid., p. 74.
30 Macintyre, *Oxford History*, p. 245.
31 The account that follows draws on Lee, *Stanley Melbourne Bruce*, pp. 50–75; and Gifford, 'The Effects of the British Seamen's Strike', pp. 73–87.
32 Gifford, 'The Effects of the British Seamen's Strike', p. 76.
33 Lee, *Stanley Melbourne Bruce*, p. 50.
34 'Mr. Bruce's First Election Message', *Age* (Melbourne), 19 September 1925.
35 Murray Perks, 'Charlton, Matthew (1866–1948)', *ADB*.
36 Robertson, *J.H. Scullin*, p. 137.
37 'Port Melbourne Battle', *Sunday Times* (Perth), 4 November 1928.
38 'Allan Whittaker: Victim of Capitalism's Assassins', *Workers' Weekly* (Sydney), 22 February 1929; 'When a Trade Unionist is the Victim', *Workers' Weekly*, 19 April 1929.
39 'Citizens Defence Brigade', *Register* (Adelaide), 1 October 1928; 'Answering the Call', *News* (Adelaide), 1 October 1928.
40 'Defence Brigade', *Advertiser* (Adelaide), 1 October 1928; 'Reminiscent of Wartime', *Advertiser*, 2 October 1928.
41 'Answering the Call', *News*, 1 October 1928.
42 For the election campaign, see Robertson, *J.H. Scullin*, pp. 145–50.
43 Ibid., p. 150.

Chapter 7: Over the cliff

1 For the timber strike, see Dixson, 'The timber strike of 1929', pp. 479–92.
2 'Arbitration. Unions Asked to Resist', *Maitland Weekly Mercury*, 23 February 1929.
3 Louis and Turner, *The Depression of the 1930s*, p. 26.

4 Macintyre, *The Reds*, p. 155.

5 Broek, 'Trouble on the Bay', p. 4; 'Ballot-burning Demonstration', *Lithgow Mercury*, 28 March 1929; 'Effigy of Judge Lukin Burned', *Daily Telegraph* (Sydney), 28 March 1929.

6 Matt, quoted in Lowenstein, *Weevils in the Flour*, p. 74.

7 Broek, 'Trouble on the Bay', p. 7. For the role of gender relations in sustaining industrial action, see Broek, 'Partners in Protest', pp. 145–63.

8 Turner and Sandercock, *In Union Is Strength*, p. 82.

9 'Communist Menace. Mr Bavin's Warning', *Brisbane Courier*, 30 March 1929.

10 Macintyre, *The Reds*, p. 155.

11 F.R.E. Mauldon, speaking to the Economic Society of Australia and New Zealand, 24 May 1929, University of Melbourne Archives, Economic Society of Australia and New Zealand, 1975.0102.

12 The following account draws on Dixson, 'Rothbury', pp. 14–26; Evans, '"Murderous coppers"', pp. 176–200; and Gollan, *The Coalminers*, pp. 189–96.

13 'Coal Situation', *Queensland Times* (Ipswich), 23 March 1929.

14 Wilks, '*Now Is the Psychological Moment*', p. 175.

15 The account that follows draws on Fitzhardinge, *The Little Digger*, pp. 569–85; Lee, *Stanley Melbourne Bruce*, pp. 88–92.

16 For details of the Australian Party, see Fitzhardinge, *The Little Digger*, pp. 591–9.

17 Schedvin, *Australia and the Great Depression*, p. 128.

18 Conference of Commonwealth and States Ministers, Canberra, 28–30 May 1929, NAA, A9504 3.

19 Lee, *Stanley Melbourne Bruce*, p. 85.

20 Ibid., pp. 86–7.

21 For the lobbying, see Fitzhardinge, *The Little Digger*, pp. 577–9; and Lee, *Stanley Melbourne Bruce*, pp. 89–90.

22 Millmow, 'The Patrician and the Orator', p. 55.

23 Ibid., p. 64.

24 Lee, *Stanley Melbourne Bruce*, p. 90; Fitzhardinge, *The Little Digger*, p. 579.

25 'Mr Scullin's Speech', *Sydney Morning Herald*, 20 September 1929.

26 Millmow, 'The Patrician and the Orator', p. 58.

27 'Industrial Control', *Examiner* (Launceston), 27 September 1929.

28 Quoted in Millmow, 'The Patrician and the Orator', p. 58.

29 Lee, *Stanley Melbourne Bruce*, p. 86.

30 D.J. Davies, General Secretary of the Miners' Federation, and Theodore, quoted in Robertson, *J.H. Scullin*, p. 167.

31 Ibid., p. 170.

32 Ibid., p. 167.

Chapter 8: What caused the Great Depression?

1 Ahamed, *Lords of Finance*, p. 309.

2 Crafts and Fearon, 'Lessons', p. 291; Stephen A. Schuker's critique of Robert Boyce's *The Great Interwar Crisis and the Collapse of Globalization*, in *H-Diplo Roundtable Review*, p. 24. This useful symposium also includes contributions by Talbot C. Imlay, Jonathan Kirshner and Kenneth Mouré, and a response by Boyce.

NOTES

3 See Kirshner and Boyce in *H-Diplo Roundtable Review*, pp. 7, 34–5; on globalisation, see Boyce, *The Great Interwar Crisis*, p. 3.

4 Tooze, *The Deluge*, p. 303.

5 Schedvin, 'The Long and the Short', p. 4.

6 Boyce, *The Great Interwar Crisis*, esp. pp. 18–21, 428–30.

7 Crafts and Fearon, 'Lessons', p. 289.

8 See, for example, Kindleberger, *The World in Depression*, pp. 291–2. This view is given qualified support in Boyce, *The Great Interwar Crisis*, pp. 12–13.

9 Quoted in Ahamed, *Lords of Finance*, p. 173.

10 Ahamed, *Lords of Finance*, pp. 91, 319.

11 Ibid., p. 149.

12 Ibid., p. 12.

13 Eichengreen, *Golden Fetters*, pp. 5–8.

14 Ahamed, *Lords of Finance*, p. 87.

15 Ibid., p. 69.

16 Cornish and Coleman, 'Making a Land', pp. 20–8.

17 The classic critique is that of John Maynard Keynes, 'The Economic Consequences of Mr Churchill', which consisted of three articles that originally appeared in the *Evening Standard* of 22, 23 and 24 July 1925. For a recent analysis, see Morrison, 'The 1925 Return to Gold'.

18 Crafts and Fearon, 'Lessons', p. 290.

19 Schuker in *H-Diplo Roundtable Review*, p. 23.

20 Romer, 'What Ended the Great Depression?', pp. 781–3.

21 The statistics in this and the following paragraph are taken from Crafts and Fearon, 'Lessons', pp. 291–2.

22 Ahamed, *Lords of Finance*, pp. 389, 391.

23 Crafts and Fearon, 'Lessons', pp. 297–8.

24 Quoted in Saint-Etienne, *The Great Depression*, pp. 14–15.

25 Crafts and Fearon, 'Lessons', p. 293.

26 On tariffs and the contraction of world trade, see Hynes, Jacks and O'Rourke, 'Commodity Market Disintegration in the Inter-war Period', pp. 120, 141; and Madsen, 'Trade Barriers', pp. 848–68.

27 Kindleberger, *The World in Depression*, p. 291.

28 James, *The End of Globalization*, p. 68.

29 The account that follows draws on James, *The End of Globalization*, pp. 53–69; Eichengreen, *Golden Fetters*, pp. 264–85; and Boyce, *The Great Interwar Crisis*, pp. 299–323; for 60 per cent, see James, p. 53.

30 Tooze, *The Deluge*, p. 494.

31 Quoted in Saint-Etienne, *The Great Depression*, p. 16.

32 Tooze, *The Deluge*, p. 494.

33 Tooze, *The Deluge*, pp. 495–6; Schuker in *H-Diplo Roundtable Review*, p. 24.

34 Bordo, Goldin and White (eds), *The Defining Moment*.

35 Boyce, *The Great Interwar Crisis*, p. 315.

36 Ibid., p. 317.

37 Crafts and Fearon, 'Lessons', p. 295.

38 Eichengreen, *Golden Fetters*, p. 284.

39 Schuker, in *H-Diplo Roundtable Review*, p. 22.
40 Crafts and Fearon, 'Lessons', p. 296.

Chapter 9: Scullin's poisoned chalice

1 Robertson, *J.H. Scullin*, p. 179.
2 Denning, *Caucus Crisis*, p. 22.
3 Schedvin, *Australia and the Great Depression*, p. 119.
4 Denning, *Caucus Crisis*, p. 20.
5 Geoffrey Serle, 'Curtin, John (1885–1945)', *ADB*.
6 Cook, 'The Scullin Government', p. 44.
7 Ibid., pp. 57–8, 68.
8 Letter from Hon. A. Poynton, *Advertiser* (Adelaide), 2 November 1929.
9 Cook, 'The Scullin Government', p. 58.
10 Robertson, *J.H. Scullin*, p. 177.
11 Neville Cain, 'Theodore, Edward Granville (1884–1950)', *ADB*.
12 'Mr Scullin. Links with Church', *Canberra Times*, 17 December 1930.
13 'The Church and Catholic Politicians', *Southern Cross* (Adelaide), 17 April 1930.
14 Robertson, *J.H. Scullin*, p. 210.
15 O'Farrell, *The Catholic Church*, p. 258.
16 Cook, 'The Scullin Government', pp. 8–9.
17 McMullin, *The Light on the Hill*, p. 134.
18 MS of article written for *Current History*, Theodore Papers, National Library of Australia (NLA), MS 7222, Box 1, Folder 2.
19 McMullin, *The Light on the Hill*, pp. 136–7.
20 Schedvin, *Australia and the Great Depression*, p. 121; Ian Turner, 'Anstey, Francis George (Frank) (1865–1940)', *ADB*.
21 Turner, 'Anstey'.
22 Anstey, *Red Europe*, p. 176.
23 Bede Nairn, 'Beasley, John Albert (Jack) (1895–1949)', *ADB*.
24 'Factors in the Slump', *Canberra Times*, 30 October 1929.
25 'Criticising and Advising the Government', *Advertiser* (Adelaide), 30 October 1929.
26 Robertson, *J.H. Scullin*, p. 185.
27 House of Representatives, 21 November 1929.
28 Robertson, *J.H. Scullin*, p. 183.
29 'For Talkies. Ministers Appear', *Sydney Morning Herald*, 25 October 1929.
30 'What of the Water-front?', *Daily News* (Perth), 11 November 1929.
31 'Federal Matters: Shipping to Tasmania', *Northern Miner* (Charters Towers, Queensland), 14 December 1929.
32 House of Representatives, 21 November 1929.
33 John Latham, House of Representatives, 21 November 1929.
34 Quoted in 'Destroying Australia's Defence', *Daily Mercury* (Mackay, Queensland), 20 November 1929.
35 'Defence Position', *Telegraph* (Brisbane), 7 November 1929.
36 Wilcox, *For Hearth and Homes*, pp. 92–3.
37 'National War Memorial', *Mercury* (Hobart), 30 November 1929.

NOTES

38 'Yates Yells', *Sun* (Sydney), 22 November 1929; 'Mr. Yates Critical', *Barrier Miner* (Broken Hill, NSW), 23 November 1929.

39 House of Representatives, 21 November 1929.

40 'Stringent Money Market', *West Australian*, 30 November 1929.

41 Macintyre, *Oxford History*, p. 255.

42 'Labour's Tariff', *Argus* (Melbourne), 23 November 1929.

43 Robertson, *J.H. Scullin*, p. 196.

44 Schedvin, *Australia and the Great Depression*, p. 122.

45 Ibid., pp. 113–14.

46 Ibid., pp. 113–15.

47 Ibid., pp. 121–6; Robertson, *J.H. Scullin*, p. 193. Scullin later claimed that Australia had in effect been off the gold standard before this, because the imbalance between imports and exports had reached a point at which the exchange rate was kept at par only by extravagant borrowings overseas.

48 'Gold Reserves', *West Australian*, 3 December 1929.

49 Quoted in 'Control of Gold', *West Australian*, 3 December 1929.

50 Shann and Copland, *The Crisis in Australian Finance*, p. xii.

51 'Mr. Theodore's Campaign', *Western Argus* (Kalgoorlie, WA), 1 October 1929.

52 Evans, '"Murderous Coppers"', p. 185.

53 Dixson, 'Rothbury', pp. 21, 24.

54 Robertson, *J.H. Scullin*, p. 202.

55 House of Representatives, 12 December 1929; Robertson, *J.H. Scullin*, p. 200.

56 Cook, 'The Scullin Government', pp. 146–7.

57 'The Conference', *Sydney Morning Herald*, 23 December 1929.

58 Macintyre, *The Reds*, p. 156; Gollan, *The Coalminers*, p. 196.

59 George and Freda Teerman, quoted in Lowenstein, *Weevils in the Flour*, p. 79.

60 'Dole Withdrawn', *Singleton Argus*, 12 March 1930.

61 Walker, *Coaltown*, p. 126.

Chapter 10: The unemployed

1 Commonwealth Year Books, cited in Louis and Turner, *The Depression of the 1930s*, p. 89. Schedvin, *Australia and the Great Depression* (p. 47), cites the figure of 28 per cent for unemployment in 1932.

2 On divisions in the Queensland trade union regarding work pooling, see Costar, 'Labor, Politics and Unemployment', pp. 254–5.

3 Galenson and Zellner, 'International Comparison of Unemployment Rates', pp. 449–50, 478–82.

4 The figure given by Michael Cannon in *The Human Face* (p. 16) of more than 50 per cent unemployed has no supporting data and is not confirmed by other sources.

5 Spenceley, *The Depression Decade*, p. 43; Macintyre, *Oxford History*, p. 253; Schedvin, *Australia and the Great Depression*, p. 461.

6 Schedvin, *Australia and the Great Depression*, p. 211; Potts, *The Myth*, p. 9.

7 Broomhill, *Unemployed Workers*, p. 21.

8 'Depression in Building Trade', *Advertiser* (Adelaide), 13 April 1929.

9 Broomhill, *Unemployed Workers*, p. 21.

10 Ray Tonkin, J.D. Somerville Oral History Collection, SLSA, OH 10/2, p. 25.
11 Spenceley, *The Depression Decade*, p. 44.
12 Mackinolty, 'Sugar Bags Days', pp. 29–30; data based on NSW Year Books and the NSW Statistical Register. For the recovery of textiles, see Schedvin, *Australia and the Great Depression*, p. 11.
13 Broomhill, *Unemployed Workers*, p. 23.
14 According to Saunders and Lloyd, 'Arbitration or Collaboration?' (p. 127), only fifteen of 55 workers at Hitchcock's, a brass-finishing firm in Carrington Street, in the Adelaide CBD, were retained in the early 1930s.
15 L.J. Haysom, quoted in Spenceley, *The Depression Decade*, p. 45.
16 Broomhill, *Unemployed Workers*, p. 23.
17 Broomhill, 'Unemployment and the Great Depression in Adelaide', p. 7.
18 Spenceley, *The Depression Decade*, p. 49.
19 Broomhill, *Unemployed Workers*, p. 26.
20 'Adelaide, Do You Remember . . . the John Martin's Christmas Pageant?', *Advertiser* (Adelaide), 15 November 2015; 'Gay Pageant in City', *News* (Adelaide), 18 November 1933; 'Street Pageant Delights Crowds', *Advertiser*, 20 November 1933.
21 Spenceley, *The Depression Decade*, p. 48.
22 Broomhill, *Unemployed Workers*, p. 27, citing Report of the Public Service Commissioner.
23 Mackinolty, 'Sugar Bag Days', p. 31.
24 Spenceley, *The Depression Decade*, p. 49.
25 Ibid.
26 Mackinolty, 'Sugar Bag Days', p. 55.
27 Quoted ibid., pp. 58–9.
28 A.H. Burnet to Premier B. Stevens, 19 February 1934, NAA, A786 L43/1; Broomhill, *Unemployed Workers*, p. 27.
29 For free dental treatment in Brighton, Victoria, see Report to Council of the Unemployed Conference, 27 July 1931, PROV, Brighton City General Correspondence, VPRS 14629/P0001 unit 7.
30 *Elder, Smith and Co.*, p. 49.
31 Broomhill, *Unemployed Workers*, p. 9.
32 Cannon, *The Human Face*, p. 214, citing relevant Commonwealth Year Books; Potts, *The Myth*, p. 10.
33 Broomhill, *Unemployed Workers*, p. 7.
34 Alex, quoted in Lowenstein, *Weevils in the Flour*, p. 312.
35 Potts, *The Myth*, p. 10.
36 Cottle, *Life Can Be Oh So Sweet*, p. 37.
37 Statistician's Report, Census of the Commonwealth of Australia, 30 June 1933, p. 309.
38 Cottle, *Life Can Be Oh So Sweet*, p. 36.
39 *Year Book Australia, 1932*, p. 620; *Year Book Australia, 1933*, p. 552.
40 *Year Book Australia, 1932*, p. 633.
41 Spenceley, *The Depression Decade*, pp. 51–2.
42 Way, *A New Idea Each Morning*, pp. 129, 132.
43 Costar, 'The Great Depression: Was Queensland Different?', pp. 34–5.
44 'The President's Message to Country Women', *Housewife*, October 1930, p. 27, SLSA. For earlier opposition to the sugar embargo, see Foley, 'The Women's Movement', pp. 121–2, 159–60.

45 On Weil's disease, see Penrose, 'Medical Experts and Occupational Illness', pp. 125–43.

46 Mackinolty, 'Sugar Bag Days', pp. 91–3.

47 Ibid., p. 94.

48 Broomhill, *Unemployed Workers*, p. 16.

49 Letter A.H. Burnet to Premier B. Stevens, NSW, 19 February 1934, NAA, A786 L43/1.

50 Julius Forth, quoted in Lowenstein, *Weevils in the Flour*, p. 171.

51 Census of the Commonwealth of Australia, 30 June 1933, Part XXVI, Unemployment, p. 1778.

52 Mackinolty, 'Woman's Place . . .', p. 101.

53 Quoted in Kath Macdermott, 'Public Service/Policy', The Encyclopedia of Women & Leadership in Twentieth-Century Australia, <www.womenaustralia.info/leaders/biogs/ WLE0446b.htm>.

54 Quoted in Spenceley, *The Depression Decade*, p. 48.

55 Foley, 'The Women's Movement', p. 105.

56 Ranald, 'Feminism and Class', pp. 273–4; Theobald and Dwyer, 'An Episode in Feminist Politics', pp. 59–77.

57 'Unemployment', *Advertiser* (Adelaide), 30 July 1927.

58 Jessie, quoted in Lowenstein, *Weevils in the Flour*, p. 134.

Chapter 11: The voluntary sector to the rescue

1 Rathbone, *A Very Present Help*, p. 162.

2 Minutes of General Committee Meeting, 28 September 1931, Melbourne Ladies Benevolent Society (MLBS), State Library of Victoria (SLV), Box 3211/4, MS 12414.

3 Peel, 'Charity, Casework', p. 83.6.

4 For discussion of this term, see Beaumont, 'Whatever Happened to Patriotic Women?', pp. 273–86, esp. p. 285.

5 Mrs M.E. Orr, 'For Unemployed Women', c. January 1931, NAA, A458 AL502/3.

6 Quoted in Fox, *Fighting Back*, p. 83.

7 Bush, 'Crisis of Moral Authority', p. 116.

8 Quotations from the relief files of the Adelaide Benevolent Society, which are a rich source of case notes and visitor reports (see SLSA, SRG 573 46/1).

9 Minutes of General Committee Meeting, MLBS, 28 January 1930, SLV, Box 3211/2, MS 12414.

10 Minutes of General Committee Meeting, 25 March 1930, ibid.

11 Singley, '"Skilful Handling and Scientific Treatment"', p. 96.

12 Annual Report, 1930, Benevolent Society of New South Wales, State Library of New South Wales (SLNSW).

13 Minutes of General Committee Meeting, MLBS, 17 December 1929, SLV, Box 3211/2, MS 12414.

14 Peel, 'Charity, Casework', p. 83.2.

15 Singley, '"Skilful Handling and Scientific Treatment"', p. 92.

16 Charity Organisation Society of Melbourne, quoted in Peel, 'Charity, Casework', p. 83.2. See also Spenceley, 'Social Control', p. 236.

17 Gleeson, 'Catholic Charity', p. 70.

18 Singley, '"Skilful Handling and Scientific Treatment"', p. 95; Peel, 'Charity, Casework', p. 83.8.

19 John Clemens, quoted in Lowenstein, *Weevils in the Flour*, p. 155.

20 Fred Daly, 31 May 1994, John Knott Depression interviews, Noel Butlin Archives Centre (NBAC), Z562, Box 2/1.

21 This argument is developed in Spenceley, 'Social Control', pp. 232–51.

22 For divisions within the Melbourne Ladies Benevolent Society, see Bush, 'Crisis of Moral Authority', ch. 4.

23 Peel, 'Charity, Casework', pp. 83.5, 83.9. See also Singley, '"Skilful Handling and Scientific Treatment"', p. 97.

24 F.M.L. Thompson, quoted in Spenceley, 'Social Control', p. 233.

25 Notice of Bassendean Road Board and Bassendean Unemployment Relief Committee, 21 November 1930, SLWA, Nedlands Relief Committee Papers.

26 *Australian Lutheran*, 15 May 1931, p. 113.

27 Costar, 'Christianity in Crisis', pp. 209–10.

28 Cowdell, 'The Anglican Church', p. 86.

29 See Peter, 'Social Aspects' (p. 189) for the views of the *Catholic Press*.

30 Costar, 'Christianity in Crisis', p. 208.

31 For the Catholic Guild for Social Studies in Adelaide, established in early 1933, see John Mitchell, 'Catholic Response to the Depression', Box 137, Adelaide Catholic Archdiocesan Archives; and seminar paper by Ms Rafferty, 'Catholics and Social Issues in South Australia in the 1930s', ibid., 1985, esp. pp. 5–16.

32 Nicholls, 'Australian Protestantism', p. 220.

33 Peter, 'Social Aspects', p. 158.

34 Quoted ibid., p. 154. The centenary history of the Presbyterian Church in Queensland argued that social service was not a forte of the church in that state (Costar, 'Christianity in Crisis', p. 205).

35 Gleeson, 'Catholic Charity', pp. 73–4.

36 Singley, '"Skilful Handling and Scientific Treatment"', p. 93; Costar, 'Christianity in Crisis', p. 205.

37 Maguire, *Prologue*, p. 108.

38 Report of the Ladies' Society of St Vincent de Paul in Australia and New Zealand, 1930, St Vincent de Paul Society, Adelaide Catholic Archdiocesan Archives, Series 4505, Box 546.

39 Costar, 'Christianity in Crisis', p. 204.

40 Darling, 'The Church of England in Melbourne', p. 11.

41 Pear, 'Muscular Christianity', pp. 8–9.

42 Ruth Carter, 'Tucker, Gerard Kennedy' (1885–1974), *ADB*.

43 Cowdell, 'The Anglican Church', pp. 90–2.

44 Costar, 'Christianity in Crisis', p. 204.

45 Report on the Relief of Unemployed Girls, 5th August, 1930 – 30th June, 1931, PROV, Footscray City General Correspondence, VPRS 8291/P0001/87.

46 W.G. Waye, quoted in Broomhill, *Unemployed Workers*, p. 94.

47 Patrick, quoted in Lowenstein, *Weevils in the Flour*, p. 346.

48 Singley, '"Skilful Handling and Scientific Treatment"', p. 93.

49 *War Cry*, 10 January 1931, records held at Salvation Army Melbourne Heritage Centre.

50 *War Cry*, 3 January 1931. For the Gill Memorial Home, see Lamm, 'The Role of the Salvation Army', pp. 16–19.

51 Hannah and Arthur, quoted in Lowenstein, *Weevils in the Flour*, pp. 253–4.

52 'Catholic Federation Employment Bureau', *Southern Cross*, 6, 13, 27 November 1931.

53 Quinn Shwan, 'Hammondville—Where's That?', University of Sydney, History Matters, <https://historymatters.sydney.edu.au/2019/09/hammondville-wheres-that/>.

54 Beth McLean, quoted in Lowenstein, *Weevils in the Flour*, p. 165.

55 Regnaud, *Abergowrie College*, pp. 99–104.

56 Ida M. Forsyth, *National Waste and the Kuitpo Industrial Colony*, Papers of Samuel Forsyth, SLSA, PRG8/7.

57 'Scheme by Lord Mayor', *Advertiser* (Adelaide), 28 February 1929.

58 Melbourne Ladies Benevolent Society, Meeting of 7 October 1930, SLV, Box 3211/3, MS 12414.

59 Gleeson, 'Catholic Charity', p. 73.

60 Anthony J. Martin, 11 May 1994, Knott Depression interviews, NBAC, Z562, Box 2/1.

61 Swain, 'Besmirching our Reputation', p. 58.

62 Costar, 'Christianity in Crisis', p. 207.

Chapter 12: The tightening band of policy options

1 Robertson, *J.H. Scullin*, p. 227.

2 Schedvin, *Australia and the Great Depression*, p. 130.

3 For the report of an ACTU Committee chaired by Jock Garden, 27 February 1930, see Louis and Turner, *The Depression of the 1930s*, p. 43. For the Loan Council, see Shann and Copland, *The Crisis in Australian Finance*, p. 11.

4 Robertson, *J.H. Scullin*, pp. 230–1.

5 'Wild Scenes', *Sydney Morning Herald*, 27 February 1930.

6 Robertson, *J.H. Scullin*, pp. 237–8.

7 For further detail, see Schedvin, *Australia and the Great Depression*, pp. 146–53.

8 Scullin, quoted in Robertson, *J.H. Scullin*, p. 229.

9 Cathcart, *Defending the National Tuckshop*, pp. 18–19.

10 Ibid., p. 19.

11 For discussion as to when Scullin might have forced a double dissolution, see Robertson, 'Scullin as Prime Minister', pp. 34–6.

12 The account that follows draws on Cornish, *The Evolution of Central Banking*, pp. 172–6.

13 Schedvin, *Australia and the Great Depression*, p. 174.

14 Holder, *Bank of New South Wales*, p. 668.

15 A detailed account of the prelude to Otto Niemeyer's visit is to be found in Attard, 'The Bank of England', pp. 66–83.

16 Quoted ibid., p. 76.

17 In the interim the Commonwealth Bank did find the exchange for the war debt payment, possibly, Attard argues, on the basis of a credit from the Bank of England: 'The Bank of England', p. 74.

18 Ibid., pp. 78–80.

19 Ibid., p. 80.

20 Millmow, 'Niemeyer', p. 149.

21 Robertson, *J.H. Scullin*, p. 248.

22 Denning, *Caucus Crisis*, p. 78.

23 Quoted in Attard, 'The Bank of England', p. 82.

24 Unless otherwise stated, the account that follows draws on a definitive analysis of the Mungana affair, Moore, *The Curse of Mungana*.

25 Matthew Reid, Senate, 3 December 1929, quoted in 'The Senate', *Brisbane Courier*, 4 December 1929.

26 'Inquiry Urged', *Brisbane Courier*, 11 April 1930. Further details can be found in Fitzgerald, '*Red Ted*', ch. 7.

27 Moore, *The Curse of Mungana*, p. 205.

28 Denning, *Caucus Crisis*, p. 80.

29 Theodore, House of Representatives, 8 July 1930.

30 Quoted in McMullin, *The Light on the Hill*, p. 161.

31 Moore, *The Curse of Mungana*, pp. 215, 301.

32 H.E. Boote to Theodore, nd [late 1931?], Theodore papers, NLA, MS 7222, Box 1, Folder 1.

33 Unless otherwise stated, the paragraph that follows draws on Niemeyer's diary from 13 August to 23 October 1930, reproduced in Love, 'Niemeyer's Australian Diary', pp. 267–77; and Millmow, 'Niemeyer', pp. 149–53.

34 Niemeyer telegram, 7 August 1930, Bank of England Archives, OV13/48.

35 Niemeyer's statement to the Loan Council was released to the press after his meeting with Commonwealth and state ministers in Melbourne from 18 to 21 August. It is reproduced in Shann and Copland, *The Crisis in Australian Finance*, pp. 18–31. The implication there and in some newspaper reports is that the speech was given in Melbourne, but it is dated 5 August and thus was first presented to the Loan Council.

36 Niemeyer to Sir Ernest Harvey, 8 August 1930, Bank of England Archives, OV13/48.

37 Minutes of Ninth Meeting of the Australian Loan Council, 5–6 August 1930, NAA, A6001 vol. 1.

38 Robertson, *J.H. Scullin*, p. 263.

39 Love, 'Niemeyer's Australian Diary', p. 268.

40 'Conference of Commonwealth and State Ministers, held in Melbourne from 18th to 21st August 1930', NAA, A461 748/1/263.

41 Harvey to Niemeyer, 8 August 1930, Bank of England Archives, G1/291.

42 Norman to Niemeyer 22 August 1930, ibid.

43 Schedvin, *Australia and the Great Depression*, pp. 184–5.

44 Ibid., p. 138; Minutes of Ninth Meeting of the Australian Loan Council, 5–6 August 1930.

45 'Economic Crisis. The Niemeyer Report. Welcomed by Business Community', *Age* (Melbourne), 23 August 1930.

46 'Niemeyer's Report True', *Daily Pictorial* (Sydney), 25 August 1930.

47 'Stand of the States', *Sydney Morning Herald*, 21 August 1930.

48 On 'Money Power' in labour politics, see Love, *Labour and the Money Power*.

49 Anstey, *Money Power*, p. 18.

50 'Labour Action', *Sydney Morning Herald*, 23 August 1930.

51 Hughes, 'Sir Otto Niemeyer's Report: Bond or Free' (1930), quoted in Louis and Turner, *The Depression of the 1930s*, p. 65.

52 See Berzins, 'Douglas Credit and the A.L.P.', passim; Batt, 'Tasmania's Depression Elections', pp. 115–20.

53 Perkins and Moore, 'Fascism', pp. 278–9.
54 'The Cat Comes Home', *Labor Call*, 10 September 1931; 'cormorants', Anstey, quoted in 'Vultures of Finance', *Labor Call*, 9 October 1930.
55 *Labor Daily*, quoted in Louis and Turner, *The Depression of the 1930s*, p. 133; 'A Financial Christ', *Labor Call*, 9 October 1930.
56 Bank of England Archives, OV59/18.
57 Latham, House of Representatives, 14 November 1930.
58 Letter to Bank of England, 30 October 1930, Bank of England Archives, OV13/48.
59 The paragraphs that follow draw on Love, 'Niemeyer's Australian Diary'.
60 David Riordan, House of Representatives, 18 November 1930.
61 Quoted in Millmow, 'Niemeyer', p. 152. For the visit to Adelaide, see Niemeyer to Bank of England, 8 September 1930, Bank of England Archives, G1/291.
62 Niemeyer to Norman, 1 September 1930, ibid.
63 Niemeyer to Lord Bledisloe, 21 September 1931, and 'New Zealand Diary', pp. 8–9, 11, Bank of England Archives, OV59/18.
64 Quoted in Mandle, *Going it Alone*, p. 82.
65 Norman to F.A. Maguire, President, NSW Constitutional Association, 17 December 1930, Bank of England Archives, OV13/48.
66 Mandle, *Going it Alone*, p. 74.

Chapter 13: Losing control

1 Robertson, *J.H. Scullin*, p. 259.
2 In November 1918 Gibson had chaired a royal commission that advocated economies in Commonwealth government expenditure and the formation of an 'efficiency Board': Cornish and Coleman, 'Making a Land', p. 5.
3 Niemeyer to Bank of England, 30 July 1930, Bank of England Archives, G1/291.
4 'Widow' to Sir Robert Gibson, nd, SLV, Papers of Sir Robert Gibson, MS MS SEQ, Box 1(c).
5 Ibid.
6 Copy held in Papers of Sir Robert Gibson, Box 2(c).
7 'Mr. Scullin's Place is in Australia', *Herald* (Melbourne), 19 August 1930; McMullin, *The Light on the Hill*, p. 163.
8 Denning, *Caucus Crisis*, p. 38.
9 'Will Not Be a Supplicant in London', *Observer* (Adelaide), 21 August 1930.
10 'Scullin's Mission', *Labor Call*, 28 August 1930.
11 Niemeyer to Harvey, 8 August 1930, Bank of England Archives, OV13/48.
12 Denning, *Caucus Crisis*, p. 83.
13 B.J. Costar, 'Moore, Arthur Edward (1876–1963)', *ADB*; F.T. Grove, 'Queensland and the Moore Government', p. 86.
14 Ray Broomhill, 'Hill, Lionel Laughton (1881–1963)', *ADB*; Hopgood, 'Lang Labor in South Australia', p. 164.
15 Bolton, *A Fine Country*, pp. 112–13.
16 Batt, 'Tasmania's Depression Elections', p. 112.
17 The account that follows draws on Strangio, *Neither Power Nor Glory*, pp. 186–92.
18 'The Hogan Government Vindicated', *Labor Call*, 18 December 1930.

19 'The Pruning Knife', *Age* (Melbourne), 26 March 1930; Parliament of New South Wales, '1930 to 1939—Depression and Crisis', <www.parliament.nsw.gov.au/about/Pages/1930-to-1939-Depression-and-Crisis.aspx>.

20 Nairn, *The 'Big Fella'*, pp. 202–5; 'New South Wales Elections', *News* (Adelaide), 16 October 1930; 'Final Appeals', *Sydney Morning Herald*, 24 October 1930.

21 Nairn, *The 'Big Fella'*, p. 204.

22 'Mr. Lang in Goulburn', *Goulburn Evening Penny Post*, 3 October 1930.

23 'Mr. Lang's Policy Speech', *Age*, 23 September 1930.

24 'Monaro electorate', *Braidwood Review and District Advocate*, 30 September 1930.

25 Robinson, *When the Labor Party Dreams*, p. 39.

26 Coleman et al., *Giblin's Platoon*, p. 131.

27 For discussion of the multiplier, and the claim that Giblin developed the concept earlier than, and independently of, Keynes, see Coleman et al., *Giblin's Platoon*, pp. 85–90, 93–6, 98–9.

28 Ibid., p. 134.

29 Harper, *Douglas Copland*, p. 164.

30 Coleman et al., *Giblin's Platoon*, p. 114.

31 See Schedvin, *Australia and the Great Depression*, p. 219.

32 Ibid., p. 222; Coleman et al., *Giblin's Platoon*, pp. 114–17; Cain, 'The Australian Economists', pp. 1–28.

33 Coleman et al., *Giblin's Platoon*, p. 116.

34 Holder, *Bank of New South Wales*, p. 693.

35 Cited in Love, 'Frank Anstey', p. 139.

36 Schedvin, *Australia and the Great Depression*, p. 190.

37 Norman to Niemeyer, 27 September 1930, Bank of England Archives, G1/291.

38 'Australia', 2 October 1930, Bank of England Archives, G1/291.

39 For Irvine, see Cain, 'Australian Economic Advice', pp. 20–5.

40 Quoted in Robertson, *J.H. Scullin*, pp. 290–1.

41 Denning, *Caucus Crisis*, p. 65.

42 McMullin, *The Light on the Hill*, p. 164.

43 Schedvin, *Australia and the Great Depression*, p. 191.

44 Denning, *Caucus Crisis*, p. 84.

45 Robertson, *J.H. Scullin*, p. 282.

46 'Conversion Loan', *Queensland Times* (Ipswich), 21 November 1930; 'Conversion Loan', *Cobram Courier*, 4 December 1930. For honour, Schedvin, *Australia and the Great Depression*, pp. 201–2.

47 Schedvin, *Australia and the Great Depression*, p. 201.

48 'The Australian team in England, 1930', *Wisden*, <www.espncricinfo.com/wisdenalmanack/content/story/155208.html>.

49 'What Success Would Mean', *Sydney Morning Herald*, 12 December 1930.

50 I owe this insight to Schedvin, *Australia and the Great Depression*, p. 202.

51 Ibid., pp. 195–6.

52 'Absit Invidia', Bank of England Archives, G1/291.

53 Schedvin, *Australia and the Great Depression*, p. 186.

54 We have only one account of their deliberations, that of Solicitor-General Robert Garran.

55 'Lord Stonehaven's Successor', *Sydney Morning Herald*, 24 March 1930.

56 W. Bird to Lord Greenway, Anglo-Persian Oil Company, 30 April 1930, National Archives, London (NA[L]), DO121/43.

57 Quoted in *Times* (London), 25 April 1930, copy in NA(L), DO 121/42.
58 Memorandum from Officer, July 1930, Cotton, *Documents on Australian Foreign Policy*, pp. 656–7.
59 *Observer* (London), 27 April 1930, copy in NA(L), DO 121/42.
60 Casey to Scullin, 21 November 1930, Cotton, *Documents on Australian Foreign Policy*, p. 682.
61 Note by E.J.H. (Harding?), 15 April 1930; Lord Passfield to Sir W. Jowitt, 16 April 1940, NA(L), DO 121/42.
62 Casey to Scullin, 21 November 1930, Cotton, *Documents on Australian Foreign Policy*, p. 684.
63 The following draws on Notes by Scullin on interviews with Stamfordham and the King, Cotton, *Documents on Australian Foreign Policy*, pp. 684–6.
64 Kirk, '"Australians for Australia"', pp. 102–3.
65 'New Governor-General', *Labor Call*, 4 December 1930. When Isaacs retired in January 1936, Australian governments of both persuasions reverted to old habits. It was not until 1965 that it became standard practice to appoint an Australian.
66 Robertson, *J.H. Scullin*, p. 293.

Chapter 14: Sustenance

1 Snooks, 'Robbing Peter to Pay Paul', p. 5.
2 'More than a Million Allocated', *Herald* (Melbourne), 26 August 1930. The account that follows draws on Fox, *Fighting Back*, pp. 89–91; Bush, 'Crisis of Moral Authority', pp. 120–34; and McCalman, *Struggletown*, pp. 151–61.
3 Bush, 'Crisis of Moral Authority', p. 124.
4 'Sustenance Position', *Age* (Melbourne), 21 June 1930.
5 'Ladies' Benevolent Societies Part', *Argus* (Melbourne), 23 June 1930.
6 Minutes of the Executive Committee Meeting of the MLBS, 29 July 1930, SLV, MS 12414, Box 3211/3.
7 Minutes of the Executive Committee Meeting of the MLBS, 23 September 1930, ibid.; '680 Distressed Families Assisted in Week', *Herald*, 4 September 1930.
8 For further details, see Bush, 'Crisis of Moral Authority', pp. 131–3.
9 'Relief Distribution', *Newcastle Morning Herald and Miners' Advocate*, 28 June 1930; 'Inadequate Sustenance', *Mercury* (Hobart), 28 June 1930.
10 'A Noisy Deputation at Richmond', *Age*, 16 September 1930; Fox, *Fighting Back*, p. 99; McCalman, *Struggletown*, p. 159.
11 'Relief Depot Still "Black"', *Herald*, 20 October 1930; 'Carlton Relief Depot "Black"', *Herald*, 18 October 1930.
12 'Hostile Crowd', *Brisbane Courier*, 21 October 1930.
13 McCalman, *Struggletown*, pp. 160–1.
14 'Relief Depot to Remain "Black"', *Herald*, 8 November 1930; 'Food Destroyed', *Northern Star* (Lismore), 12 November 1930.
15 Fox, *Fighting Back*, p. 105.
16 In April 1930, Darwin witnessed similar activism to Melbourne when a hundred unemployed invaded the government resident's office, demanding work or full sustenance instead of the £1 a week dole they were receiving (see NAA, A1 18913/4202 for details).
17 Bolton, *A Fine Country*, p. 98.

18 Costar, 'Labor, Politics and Unemployment', p. 192.

19 Broomhill, *Unemployed Workers*, pp. 42, 82–3, includes comparative data citing Australia, *Labour Report 1935*. A summary of sustenance rates by state in 1933–34 can be found in 'Treasury Officers' Report', Premiers' Conference Matters, NAA, CP 103/11 828.

20 As an example, see Circular by Minister in Charge of Unemployment Relief, Melbourne, 28 November 1930, PROV, VPRS 14629/P/0001 unit 7.

21 Decisions of Acting Chief Secretary on Deputation from Unemployed re Meat Ration etc., letter from Acting Chief Secretary to Unemployment Relief Council, 20 January 1931, Chief Secretary's Correspondence, SRSA, GRG/24/6/00000/738, File 59/1931.

22 For unemployed workers' associations and doctors, see H. Marshall, Unemployed Workers' Movement, Footscray, to J. Gent, Town Clerk, 19 November 1931, and Minutes of Conference of Representatives of State School Mothers' Club and School Committees, 9 December 1931, PROV, VPRS 8291/P/0001 unit 88.

23 Peter, 'Social Aspects', p. 73.

24 W.R. Bunker State Relief Committee, 'Supply of Vegetable Seeds for Citizens Receiving Sustenance', 9 November 1931, PROV, VPRS 8291/P/0001 unit 85.

25 Report of Brighton Council to Unemployed Council, 'Unemployment Relief', 27 July 1931, PROV, VPRS 14629/P/0001 unit 7.

26 Summary of Relief Activities at Council's Depot, 16 July 1932, PROV, VPRS 8291/P/0001 unit 85.

27 Footscray Unemployed Rank & File Relief Association to Town Clerk, Footscray, PROV, VPRS 8291/P/0001 unit 83.

28 Broomhill, *Unemployed Workers*, pp. 176–7.

29 Both ration examples cited in Peter, 'Social Aspects', pp. 73–4.

30 Sustenance Department, Victoria, 'To Relief Committees Operating Under the New System of Distribution of Government Sustenance', 12 October 1931, PROV, VPRS 17453/P/0001 unit 31.

31 Bland, 'Unemployment Relief', pp. 100–1.

32 Costar, 'Labor, Politics and Unemployment', p. 195.

33 Broomhill, *Unemployed Workers*, p. 82.

34 E. Kiernan, Chief Secretary's Office, 12 December 1930, Minister in Charge of Sustenance Circular, 11 December 1931, PROV, VPRS 16668/P/0001 item 30.

35 A.V. Stenning, State Relief Committee to Town Clerk, Footscray, PROV, VPRS 8291/P/0001 item 85.

36 Edna Ryan, Sydney, quoted in Cannon, *The Human Face*, p. 286.

37 Allen Cox, New South Wales Bicentennial Oral History Project, SLNSW, MLOH 48.

38 Peter, 'Social Aspects', p. 71.

39 For example, Sustenance Department Victoria, 'To Relief Committees Operating Under the New System of Distribution of Government Sustenance, 12 October 1931, PROV, VPRS 17453/P/0001 unit 31.

40 W.R. Mackenzie, Report to the United Front Conference of Employed and Unemployed, 14 February 1932, NBAC, Jack and Ruth Davison Papers, P117–6.

41 Unemployed Bulletin no. 28, 19 April 1932, PROV, Preston City General Correspondence, VPRS 4540/P/0000 unit 177.

42 Jocka [sic] Burns, quoted in Lowenstein, *Weevils in the Flour*, p. 210.

43 'Demonstration Fails', *Newcastle Morning Herald and Miners' Advocate*, 5 November 1932.

44 F.R. Frawley, Department of Labour, Circular 25/32, 10 August 1932, PROV, VPRS 4540/P/000 unit 177.

45 Broomhill, *Unemployed Workers*, p. 45.

46 'Disturbed' to Blazey, 28 January 1931, PROV, VPRS 16668/P/0001 unit 30.

47 Letter from Department of Industries, 20 June 1930, Unemployment, General File, Perth City Council 1930–, SROWA, CONS 3054 1930/0093.

48 This paragraph draws on a circular by Minister in Charge of Unemployment Relief, 28 November 1930, PROV, VPRS 14629/P/0001 unit 7.

49 Chairman, Chief Secretary's Office to Blazey, Richmond Council, 14 January 1931, PROV, VPRS 16668/P/0001 unit 30.

50 See Spenceley, "'The Minister for Starvation"', esp. pp. 139–44.

51 Potts, *The Myth*, p. 143.

52 Broomhill, *Unemployed Workers*, pp. 42–3.

53 Potts, *The Myth*, p. 144.

54 Ibid., p. 145.

55 Cannon, *The Human Face*, pp. 246–7.

56 Potts, *The Myth*, p. 145.

57 Report to the United Front Conference, p. 3.

58 Broomhill, *Unemployed Workers*, pp. 107–8.

59 Peter, 'Social Aspects', pp. 75–9.

60 Charles Murray, quoted in Cannon, *The Human Face*, p. 275.

61 H.V. Jones, 25 September 1931, and Anonymous to Blazey, 28 September 1931, PROV, VPRS 16668/P/0001 unit 30.

62 Letter to Mayor, 7 November 1931, PROV, VPRS 14629/P/0001 unit 7.

Chapter 15: Community and family

1 For the role of fictive kinship in war remembrance, see Winter, *Sites of Memory*, ch. 2.

2 Mrs D.M. Mcarthur, 14 February 1932, PROV, VPRS 8291/P/0001 unit 85.

3 Mrs A. Dever to Councillor Johnson, 24 November 1933, PROV, VPRS 4540/P/0000 unit 177.

4 Town Clerk to F.M. Frawley, Sustenance Department, 18 July 1932, ibid.

5 Mrs A. King, 21 December 1931, PROV, VPRS 8291/P/0001 unit 85.

6 Unless otherwise stated, the account that follows relies on the rich archives held in the Public Record Office of Victoria (PROV) for the Brighton, Footscray, Preston and Richmond city councils. It is assumed that the range of activities in these Melbourne suburbs was similar to those in other locations for which the archival record is not as copious.

7 Letter, Footscray Branch of the RSSILA Employment Bureau, 24 April 1931, PROV, VPRS 8291/P/0001 unit 85.

8 'Collingwood Workless Self-Supporting', letter from General Unemployed Association to Town Clerk, Brighton, 1 May 1931, PROV, VPRS 14629/P/0001 unit 7; Lord Mayor's appeal for boots and clothing, 1st to 9th July 1931, PROV, VPRS 8291/P/0001 unit 85.

9 Summary of Relief Activities at Council's Depot, 16 July 1932, PROV, VPRS 8291/P/0001 unit 85.

10 Fraser, *Working for the Dole*, ch. 1, p. 2; Minister in Charge of Sustenance to Blazey, 13 May 1931, PROV, VPRS 16668/P/0001 unit 30.

11 Minutes of Meeting of United Front of Employed and Unemployed, 7 April 1932, Papers of James Normington Rawling, NBAC, N57/421.

12 Memory of Patricia Ireland, 28 May 1993, Knott Depression interviews, NBAC, Z562, Box 3/1.

13 Press release, 'Unemployment Relief: Footwear Appeal', *Southern Cross*, 13 June 1931, in PROV, VPRS 14629/P/0001 unit 7.

14 A.V. Stenning, State Relief Committee, to Town Clerk, Footscray, 28 August 1930, PROV, VPRS 8291/P/0001 unit 85.

15 Edna Ward, interview, 23 October 1990, J.D. Somerville Oral History Collection, Mortlock Library of South Australiana, OH111/2.

16 Potts, *The Myth*, pp. 85–6.

17 Summary of Relief Activities at Council's Depot, PROV, VPRS 8291/P/0001 unit 85.

18 Unemployment Relief Scheme, nd (July 1930?), PROV, VPRS 14629/P/0001 unit 7. For Tate's earlier role in funding the reconstruction of the Villers-Bretonneux school, see Fathi, *Our Corner of the Somme*, pp. 55–9.

19 'Regatta at Brighton', *Sydney Morning Herald*, 7 October 1930.

20 'Royal Show', *West Australian* (Perth), 4 October 1930.

21 Costar, 'Christianity in Crisis', p. 207.

22 Mayor's Annual Report 1932–1933, City of Port Adelaide, 1934, Corporation of the Town of Port Adelaide, SRSA, GA 257.

23 'Lord Mayor's Relief Fund Announcement', Adelaide City Council Archives, Lord Mayor's Unemployment Fund Correspondence, SPF 154A:01.

24 Lord Mayor to Mayor of Footscray, '"S.O.S." Boots and Clothing Week', 18 June 1931, and W.H. Bunker, State Relief Committee, to Mayor of Footscray, 29 May 1931, PROV, VPRS 8291/P/0001 unit 85.

25 Bunker to Mayor of Footscray, ibid.

26 'For Those in Need', *News* (Adelaide), 12 May 1930.

27 Town Clerk to Secretary, State Relief Committee, 23 April 1931, PROV, VPRS 8291/P/0001 unit 85.

28 Letter, Town Clerk Blazey to E.L. Kiernan, Assistant Chief Secretary, 10 September 1930, PROV, VPRS 16668/P/0001 unit 29.

29 For example: for CWA, Pagliano, *Country Women*, p. 63, where the CWA is cited as working with the Queensland Social Services League; for Rotary, Hunt, *The Story of Rotary*, pp. 39–44; for the Red Cross, Stubbings, *Look What You Started*, p. 259, and Oppenheimer, *The Power of Humanity*, p. 72.

30 A.S. Monk, 'Central Unemployed Committee', 11 April 1932, PROV, VPRS 4540/P/0000 unit 177.

31 Costar, 'Labor, Politics and Unemployment', pp. 139–40.

32 Minutes, All Australian Trade Union Congress, 4 March 1930, 23 September 1932, NBAC, N147/587.

33 F. Clark to Mayor and Councillors of City of Footscray, 24 April 1931, PROV, VPRS 8291/P/0001 unit 87.

34 Nomination form, PROV, VPRS 17453/P/0001 unit 31. For details of the disputes in Richmond, see McCalman, *Struggletown*, pp. 161–3.

35 'Boys' Employment Movement, Geelong', *Corian*, December 1934.

36 Editorial, *The Palm Leaf*, November 1930, p. 3.

37 *The Palm Leaf*, November 1932, no page numbers given.
38 Mayor of Preston's bazaar flyer, late 1932, PROV, VPRS 4540/P/0000 unit 177.
39 Unemployment Relief Scheme, nd, PROV, VPRS 14629/P/0001 unit 7.
40 Letter H.L. Wootton, Deputy Town Clerk, Preston, to Town Clerk, Preston, 10 December 1931, PROV, VPRS 4540/P/0000 unit 177.
41 Bunker, State Relief Committee, to Town Clerk, Preston, 7 April 1932, ibid.
42 Mrs R. Rayner to editor, *Herald* office, 19 April 1932, PROV, VPRS 8291/P/0001 unit 85.
43 Quoted in Cannon, *The Human Face*, p. 269.
44 See Potts, *The Myth*, pp. 92–3.
45 Town Clerk, Preston to Sustenance Department, 18 July 1932, PROV, VPRS 4540/P/0000 unit 177.
46 Mrs W.R. Anderson to Mrs Crowley, 10 June 1931, PROV, VPRS 16668/P/0001 unit 30.
47 John Vernon Shaw, cited in Pearn, *A Scottish Chain*, p. 121.
48 'Assist Your Local Distress', nd, PROV, VPRS 8291/P/0001 unit 83.
49 C.C. Blazey to Chief Commissioner of Police, Melbourne, 28 May 1932, PROV, VPRS 17453/P/0001 item 31.
50 The analysis that follows draws on Berkes and Ross, 'Community Resilience', pp. 5–20.
51 Kaplan, 'Toward an Understanding', p. 49.
52 Lola Meech, 19 May 1991, Knott Depression interviews, NBAC, Z562, Box 1/1. For a similar view about 'the constant willingness to share the little' people might have, see Smith, *Australian Battlers Remember*, p. 215.
53 Keith Brown, 25 April 1993, Knott Depression interviews, NBAC, Z562, Box 2/1.
54 Quoted in Potts, *The Myth*, p. 37.
55 Ibid., p. 38.
56 Ibid., p. 39.
57 Interview, George Alexander Andrews, 22 October 1990, Mortlock Library of South Australiana, J.D. Somerville Oral History Collection, OH111/1.
58 Quoted in Potts, *The Myth*, p. 39.
59 Sylvia Fletcher, quoted in Lowenstein, *Weevils in the Flour*, p. 303.
60 Potts, *The Myth*, pp. 40, 42.
61 A 'Settler', ibid., p. 119. For self-sufficiency living off the land, see Adams, *Crocodile Safari Man*, pp. 39–47.
62 Potts, *The Myth*, p. 119.
63 'The Rabbit Problem', Rabbit Free Australia, <www.rabbitfreeaustralia.com.au>.
64 Tom Hills, quoted ibid., p. 425.
65 Cecil Curtis, quoted in Lowenstein, *Weevils in the Flour*, p. 358.
66 See Town Clerk, Richmond, to Secretary for the Railways, 27 April 1931, PROV, VPRS 16668/P/0001 unit 29.
67 For the international market, see Munday, *Those Wild Rabbits*, pp. 144–5.
68 A.H. Burnet to Hon. B.S.B. Stevens (?), 19 February 1934, NAA, A786 L43/1. See also Eather and Cottle, '"As Good as Cash All the Time"', pp. 125–48.
69 Potts, *The Myth*, p. 41.
70 Barbara Wawn, quoted in Lowenstein, *Weevils in the Flour*, p. 115.
71 Bernice Lorraine Ranford, quoted in Cannon, *The Human Face*, p. 280.
72 Robert Overton, 5 June 1992, Knott Depression interviews, NBAC, Z562, Box 2/2.

73 Cannon, *The Human Face*, pp. 295–6.
74 Baird, *Phosphorescence*, p. 123.
75 Quoted in Foley, 'The Women's Movement', p. 109.
76 This discussion draws on Foley, 'The Women's Movement', pp. 182 ff.

Chapter 16: Health and resilience

1 This conclusion is based on a keyword search of the National Library of Australia's Trove database for the three years from 1 January 1930 to December 1932.
2 'Died of Starvation', *Labor Daily*, 23 July 1930. Upper case in the original.
3 Potts, *The Myth*, p. 26. See also the Minutes of the United Front of Employed and Unemployed, 7 April 1932, where reference is made to children 'dying of starvation' in Balmain, and UWM, 'Crimes against the Unemployed', pp. 10–13, papers of James Normington Rawling, NBAC, N57/421.
4 Quoted in Potts, *The Myth*, p. 47.
5 Lowenstein, *Weevils in the Flour*, p. xiii.
6 British works included G.C. McGonigle and J. Kirby, *Poverty and Public Health* (London, 1936); B.S. Rowntree, *Poverty and Progress* (London, 1941); and John Boyd Orr, *Food, Health and Income* (London, 1936–37).
7 Smith, 'Australian Public Health', pp. 101–2.
8 Potts (*The Myth*, pp. 27, 345), cites *Year Book Australia, 1934* to claim that the general infant mortality rate dropped by 25 per cent between 1923–26 and 1930–33.
9 Australian Bureau of Statistics, 'Australian Social Trends, Family Formation: Trends in Fertility, 1996', 4102.0 Australian Social Trends, 1996, p. 36; Broomhill (*Unemployed Workers*, p. 89) claims that in South Australia the number of infantile deaths 'increased markedly at the beginning of the Depression'.
10 Smith, 'Australian Public Health', p. 99: Deacon, *Managing Gender*, p. 211.
11 Department of Labour to Town Clerk, Preston, 16 June 1932, PROV, VPRS 4540/P/0000 unit 177.
12 The significance of sulphonamides in preventing puerperal fever, a major cause of maternal death, has been disputed: see Loudon, 'Puerperal Fever', p. 488.
13 Spenceley, 'The Social History', p. 43.
14 Ibid., p. 44.
15 Smith, 'Australian Public Health', p. 101.
16 Broomhill, *Unemployed Workers*, pp. 89–91.
17 For height as a nutritional index, see Wu, 'How Severe was the Great Depression?', p. 131.
18 Quoted in Spenceley, 'The Social History', pp. 44–5.
19 Broomhill, *Unemployed Workers*, p. 90.
20 Taylor, Lewis and Powles, 'The Australian Mortality Decline', pp. 31–3; Magnus and Saskowsky, 'Mortality over the Twentieth Century in Australia', pp. 103, 109. The data suggesting no increase in the death rate conflict with Broomhill's conclusion (*Unemployed Workers*, p. 88) that there was an increase in the death rate in South Australia, from diseases 'associated with poverty', in some years of the Depression.
21 For further discussion, see Broomhill, *Unemployed Workers*, pp. 85–91.
22 This a consistent theme in the interviews conducted by students of John Knott in the 1990s (now held at NBAC, Z562): the food might have been monotonous, but it was adequate.

NOTES

23 Parkes Barracks Unemployed Association to Minister for Home Affairs, Canberra, 24 November 1931, NAA, A6272 E175.

24 'Mind-killer': Frank Herbert, *Dune.*

25 Potts, *The Myth*, pp. 308–9, 316.

26 J. Darling, principal of Geelong Grammar School, cited in 'Unemployment: Effects on Boys', *Townsville Daily Bulletin*, 19 August 1932.

27 Broomhill, *Unemployed Workers*, p. 72; Potts, *The Myth*, pp. 315–16; Smith, 'Australian Public Health', p. 104.

28 Potts, *The Myth*, pp. 317–18.

29 Annie Stevens, 'Skint: Making Do in the Great Depression', Sydney Living Museums, <https://sydneylivingmuseums.com.au/stories/skint-making-do-great-depression>.

30 For example, 'Jump into Harbour', *West Australian* (Perth), 31 October 1932; 'Jump from Sydney Harbour Bridge', *West Australian*, 15 December 1932; 'Jump Off Bridge', *Maryborough Chronicle, Wide Bay and Burnett Advertiser* (Queensland), 7 December 1932.

31 Joanne Simon-Davies, 'Suicide in Australia', 16 May 2011, Parliament of Australia, <www.aph.gov.au/About_Parliament/Parliamentary_Departments/Parliamentary_Library/FlagPost/2011/May/Suicide_in_Australia>.

32 For further detail, see Beaumont, 'Remembering the Resilient', pp. 148–9.

33 Bill Nicholls, quoted in Lowenstein, *Weevils in the Flour*, p. 248; Lola Meech, 19 May 1991, Knott Depression interviews, NBAC, Z562, Box 1/1.

34 Broomhill, *Unemployed Workers*, pp. 39, 42.

35 Father James Murray, 21 July 1991, Knott Depression interviews, NBAC, Z562, Box 3/1.

36 The paragraph that follows is drawn from Potts, 'A Positive Culture of Poverty', pp. 3–14. Potts developed his arguments extensively in his 2006 book, *The Myth*.

37 Knott Depression interviews, NBAC, Z562.

38 For discussion of the problem of sampling, see Spenceley, 'The Social History', pp. 35–41. Joanne Scott and Kay Saunders attempted to refute David Potts' arguments by conducting their own set of interviews in Queensland ('Happy Days are Here Again?', pp. 10–22), but Spenceley took issue with the small size of their sample, their failure to identify the various balances of population incorporated into their interviews, and the undue negativity of the conclusions they drew, given the comparatively more generous welfare system in Queensland (pp. 46–7).

39 For examples of these attitudes, see Potts, *The Myth*, pp. 158–60; Keith Brown, 25 April 1993, Knott Depression interviews, NBAC, Z562, Box 2/1, Alice Olney, 4 May 1991, ibid., Box 1/1; George Alexander Andrews, 22 October 1990, J.D. Somerville Oral History Collection, Mortlock Library of South Australiana, OH111/1, p. 36.

40 Clarke, *The Broke and the Broken*, p. 29.

41 The following discussion draws on Kaplan, 'Toward an Understanding of Resilience', passim; Reid and Botterill, 'The Multiple Meanings of "Resilience"', pp. 31–40; Windle, 'Critical Conceptual Measurement Issues'.

42 E.W. Gordon and L.D. Song, quoted in Kaplan, 'Toward an Understanding', p. 52.

43 E. Losel, T. Bleisener and P. Koferl, quoted ibid., p. 39.

44 Robert Overton, 5 June 1992, Knott Depression interviews, NBAC, Z562, Box 2/2.

45 Potts, 'A Positive Culture', p. 9.

46 For the importance of social capital in disaster response and recovery, see Aldrich and Meyer, 'Social Capital and Community Resilience', pp. 254–69.

47 Potts, *The Myth*, pp. 132–3, 179–95, 283–4; 'Workers' Art Club', *Workers' Art Magazine*, April 1933, Papers of John Patrick Kavanagh, NBAC, N336/79.
48 Royal Agricultural and Horticultural Society of South Australia, Report for the Year ended December 1931, SLSA.
49 City of Port Adelaide Mayor's report, 1932–33, p. 10, City of Port Adelaide Enfield Library Archive.
50 Potts, *The Myth*, p. 186.

Chapter 17: Searching for work

1 Clyde Cameron, quoted in Cannon, *The Human Face*, p. 244.
2 Mackinolty, 'Sugar Bag Days', p. 64, data from NSW Year Books, 1932–33.
3 *The Land*, 13 May 1932.
4 J. Forth, quoted in Mackinolty, 'Sugar Bag Days', p. 66.
5 Quoted in Broomhill, *Unemployed Workers*, p. 34.
6 George Farwell, *Requiem for Woolloomooloo*, Sydney 1971, quoted in Mackinolty, 'Sugar Bag Days', p. 72.
7 Les Fletcher, quoted in Lowenstein, *Weevils in the Flour*, p. 371.
8 Potts, *The Myth*, p. 96. For haircuts, see Cannon, *The Human Face*, p. 251.
9 John, quoted in Lowenstein, *Weevils in the Flour*, p. 126.
10 Simon Bracegirdle, quoted ibid., pp. 129–30.
11 Cannon, *The Human Face*, p. 252.
12 Broomhill, *Unemployed Workers*, p. 104.
13 Simon Bracegirdle, quoted in Lowenstein, *Weevils in the Flour*, p. 127.
14 Clarke, *The Broke*, pp. 33–4, 42.
15 Broomhill, *Unemployed Workers*, p. 96.
16 Les Fletcher, quoted in Lowenstein, *Weevils in the Flour*, p. 371.
17 For further details, see Potts, *The Myth*, pp. 97–100.
18 Quoted ibid., pp. 98–9.
19 Ibid., p. 101.
20 James Murray, 21 July 1994, Knott Depression interviews, NBAC, Z562, Box 3/1.
21 MacDonald, *Random Recollections*, 29.
22 Dave Bowen, quoted in Lowenstein, *Weevils in the Flour*, p. 250.
23 See, for example, Footscray RSSILA Employment Bureau to Mayor, Footscray, 24 April 1931, PROV, VPRS 8291/P/0001 unit 85.
24 Garton, *The Cost of War*, p. 91.
25 For more detailed exposition of the argument that follows, see Beaumont, 'The Returned Soldier', pp. 8–20.
26 Scullin, House of Representatives, 2 May 1930.
27 'Preference to Soldiers is a Pledge of Honor', *Age* (Melbourne), 1 May 1930.
28 'Adelaide Protests', *Age*, 2 May 1930; 'Preference to Returned Soldiers', *Age*, 2 May 1930.
29 Scullin, House of Representatives, 7 May 1930.
30 Minutes of Committee of Management, Waterside Workers' Federation, NBAC, 16 May 1930, T62/1/2.
31 Weller (ed.), *Caucus Minutes*, p. 369.
32 'Anzac Day', *Riverina Recorder*, 26 April 1930; 'Anzac Day', *Weekly Times* (Melbourne),

26 April 1930; 'Anzac Day', *Advertiser* (Hurstbridge, Victoria), 25 April 1930. These are three of many such statements in the press.

33 'Anzac Day 1930', *Canberra Times*, 25 April 1930.

34 Quoted in 'Anzac Day Memorial Service', *Northern Standard* (Darwin), 25 April 1930.

35 *Reveille*, 31 April 1930.

36 Seventeenth Annual Report and Financial Statements of the Australian Red Cross Society, 1930–31, University of Melbourne archives, L61/24, p. 7.

37 P. Phelan, RSSILA Newcastle sub-branch, to Lyons, 14 April 1932, NAA, A458 C502/3 pt 3; letter, R. Mansfield, Limbless Soldiers' Association NSW, Employment Bureau, ibid.

38 Adelaide Benevolent Society Relief files, SLSA, SRG 46/1.

39 'Soldiers Discuss Unemployment', *Port Lincoln Times*, 24 May 1929.

40 *Reveille*, 31 December 1931, quoted in Peter, 'Social Aspects', p. 227.

41 Papers of John Patrick Kavanagh, NBAC, N336/79. Underlining in original.

Chapter 18: Relief works

1 The best sources on relief works are Bland, 'Unemployment Relief', pp. 97–111; Snooks, 'Robbing Peter to Pay Paul'; and Fraser, *Working for the Dole*.

2 Fraser, *Working for the Dole*, p. 10.

3 Ibid., pp. 10–11.

4 Fishbank, 'Relief during the Great Depression' (p. 228), estimates that the federal government provided only 4.3 per cent of the total government funds spent on relief.

5 Snooks, 'Robbing Peter', p. 31. This is an estimate and the data for earlier years is not available.

6 Costar, 'The Great Depression', pp. 38–9; Costar, 'Labor, Politics and Unemployment', p. 199.

7 Fraser, *Working for the Dole*, p. 55.

8 Snooks, 'Robbing Peter', pp. 13–14.

9 *Appropriation (Unemployment Relief) Act*, November 1931.

10 The relevant legislation was the *Loan (Unemployment Relief Works Act)*, 28 May 1932. For a summary, see 'Prime Minister's Department, 'Unemployment', 19 October 1933, NAA, A458 BB230/16.

11 Schedvin, *Australia and the Great Depression*, p. 338.

12 Lyons, House of Representatives, 25 October 1933.

13 For the increase, see Snooks, 'Robbing Peter', pp. 2–3.

14 Schedvin, *Australia and the Great Depression*, p. 340.

15 See the discussion in NAA, A458 D502/6, particularly Scullin to Premier of Queensland, 6 March 1931. For further opposition to using relief funds to keep in employment men who already had work, see Notes of a Deputation of the Operative Painters' Union with Minister for Defence, 22 March 1930, NAA, A458 C502/3 pt 1.

16 Schedvin, *Australia and the Great Depression*, p. 338.

17 The data for Victoria that follows is taken from Statement by Premier E.J. Hogan, Summary of Works Undertaken at a Cost of £1,735,743, 18 December 1931, PROV, VPRS 14269/P/0001 unit 7. See also Snooks, 'Robbing Peter', p. 16.

18 Schedvin, *Australia and the Great Depression*, p. 338.

19 Snooks, 'Robbing Peter', p. 13.

20 Cannon, *The Human Face*, p. 110.

21 'Making a New Scenic Road for Brisbane', *Telegraph* (Brisbane), 8 August 1931; Wegner, 'Hinchinbrook', p. 17.
22 A.J. Christie, Civic Administrator, to Secretary, Department of Home Affairs, 26 June 1930, NAA, A430 G180.
23 I am very grateful to Professor Charlie Fox, University of Western Australia, who toured the environs of Perth researching this matter on my behalf. Enquiries to various state heritage agencies and local history societies produced little, if any, evidence of public commemoration of the Great Depression.
24 This argument of social control is developed in Spenceley, 'The Broadmeadows Camp', pp. 57–73.
25 Attachment to Robert Grantham, Town Clerk, Grantham, to Lyons, 20 April 1932, NAA, A786 L43/1.
26 *Worker*, 'Must Go into Camp', 6 June 1930.
27 John Fitzpatrick to Scullin, 4 April 1932, NAA, A458 C502/3 pt 3.
28 All examples come from correspondence in NAA, A458 C502/3 pt 1 and pt 3.
29 Chas H. Bayley to Lyons, 12 April 1932, A458 C502/3 pt 3. Underlining in the original.
30 Bolton, *A Fine Country*, pp. 123–4.
31 Snooks, 'Robbing Peter', pp. 14–15.
32 Bolton, *A Fine Country*, p. 124.
33 Letter, President, Unemployed Workers' Union, Concord, to Dr Richard Arthur, 17 March 1931, NAA, A458 C502/3 pt 2.
34 Bolton, *A Fine Country*, pp. 124–5.
35 Throssell, *My Father's Son*, p. 114.
36 Snooks, 'Robbing Peter', p. 16.
37 George Gray to Mayor, Richmond, 11 July (?), PROV, VPRS 16668/P/0001 unit 30. By April 1931, Victoria had allocated £15,000 to men wanting to undertake prospecting work (Memorandum, Deputy Chairman, Unemployment Relief Works Board, to Acting Premier, 16 April 1931, PROV, VPRS 11687/P/0001 unit 74).
38 Snooks, 'Robbing Peter', p. 22.

Chapter 19: Protest and grievance

1 District President, Workers' Industrial Union of Australia, to H.P. Lazzarini, Parliament House, 15 June 1931, NAA, A458 C502/3 pt 2.
2 Town Clerk, Holyroyd, to P.E. Colman, Parliament House, 11 June 1931, ibid.
3 J. Beasley to Mr Eldridge, Parliament House, 2 February 1931, ibid.
4 Warringah Shire Council to Archdale Parkhill, Parliament House, 12 June 1931, ibid.
5 W. Bruce to Lyons, 18 February 1932, NAA, A786 L43/1.
6 Mrs Kelly to Scullin, 3 April 1932, NAA, A461 F351/1/7.
7 Costar, 'Labor, Politics and Unemployment', p. 195.
8 Fox, *Fighting Back*, p. 194. State Secretary (Queensland), Carpenter and Joiners of Australia, to Scullin, 24 November 1931, NAA, A458 C502/7.
9 For returned soldiers' lobbying, see correspondence in NAA, A458 C502/7; Fox, *Fighting Back*, p. 194.
10 Secretary to General Secretary RSSILA, Melbourne, 19 July 1932, NAA, A458 0502/8; 'Federal Case', *Herald* (Melbourne), 13 November 1931.
11 Snooks, 'Robbing Peter', p. 18.

12 See, for example, Matters Submitted to All Australian Trade Union Congress Meeting of 20 September 1932, ACTU Minutes, NBAC, N47/587; Telegram, Scullin to Premier, Adelaide, 8 June 1930, NAA, A458 AJ 502/3; Fraser, *Working for the Dole*, ch. 1.

13 H.C. Brown, Department of Interior, to Secretary, Prime Minister's Department, 2 May 1934, NAA, A461 F351/1/7.

14 *Unemployment Relief Amendment Acts*, 31 December 1930 and 30 June 1932.

15 Costar, 'Labor, Politics and Unemployment', p. 194.

16 'Official Bungling', *Age* (Melbourne), 10 February 1931.

17 'Grave Relief Camp Charges', *Herald*, 17 August 1931.

18 Fielding, *Queen City of the North*, p. 67.

19 Letter, William Pritchard to Mr Harris, 14 August 1931, PROV, VPRS 16668/P/0001 unit 30.

20 Potts, *The Myth*, p. 221.

21 Cannon, *The Human Face*, p. 112.

22 Potts, *The Myth*, p. 222.

23 Bolton, *A Fine Country*, pp. 107–8.

24 'Men Leave Blackboy', *Daily News* (Perth), 1 December 1930.

25 'Unemployment: Blackboy Camp Depot', *Daily News*, (Perth), 2 June 1930; *Worker*, 6 June 1930, copies held in SRWA, CONS 1496 1930/0349.

26 Details and quotations that follow are taken from 'Additional Cases Supplied by Witness,' A.E. Monk, PROV, VPRS 11563/P/0001 unit 118.

27 Ibid.

28 Quoted in Potts, *The Myth*, p. 220.

29 This paragraph draws on Potts, *The Myth*, pp. 229–34.

30 'Relief Camp Men Want Sporting Material', *Herald*, 27 February 1931.

31 Potts, *The Myth*, p. 233.

32 Bolton, *A Fine Country*, p. 213.

33 Potts, *The Myth*, p. 231.

34 Ibid., p. 234.

35 The paragraphs that follow are drawn from Fox, *Fighting Back*, chs 6 and 7.

36 Fox, *Fighting Back*, p. 164.

37 A.E. Monk, Secretary, Central Unemployed Committee, to Town Clerk, 2 July 1932, PROV, VPRS 17453/P/0001 unit 40.

38 'Working for the Dole', *Worker's Art Magazine*, April 1933, Papers of John Patrick Kavanagh, NBAC, N336/79.

39 Quoted in Fox, *Fighting Back*, p. 203.

40 Ibid., p. 171.

41 Ibid., p. 167.

42 Potts, *The Myth*, p. 227.

43 See 'Strikes and Relief Works', *Braidwood Review and District Advocate*, 29 July 1930 and 'The Relief Works', *Daily Express* (Wagga Wagga), 24 July 1930, both of which relate to a stop work on the Maroubra sandhills.

44 Reproduced in Peter, 'Social Aspects', following p. 80.

45 Niall Brennan, quoted in Lowenstein, *Weevils in the Flour*, p. 204.

46 Tom Hills, quoted ibid., p. 403.

47 Mick Healey, quoted ibid., p. 411.

48 Letter to the editor, 'Lake Cotta Camp Conditions', *Age*, 15 August 1931. For stop-work meetings at Blackboy Hill camp, see Bolton, *A Fine Country*, p. 179.
49 For a strike over discrimination against men who arrived late for work, see 'Relief Workers Strike', *Newcastle Morning Herald and Miners' Advocate*, 6 November 1930.
50 Potts, *The Myth*, p. 225.
51 Cited ibid., p. 224.
52 Bolton, *A Fine Country*, p. 209.

Chapter 20: The battle of the plans

1 The discussion of the exchange rate that follows draws on Schedvin, *Australia and the Great Depression*, pp. 155–68, and Holder, *Bank of New South Wales*, pp. 679–86.
2 Robertson, *J.H. Scullin*, p. 227.
3 Tsokhas, 'Business', p. 43.
4 Butlin and Boyce, 'Monetary Policy', pp. 11–12.
5 The judgment can be found in Shann and Copland, *The Crisis*, pp. 102–46. For a detailed analysis of the argument behind this decision, see Schedvin, *Australia and the Great Depression*, pp. 216–17.
6 Sheldon, 'State-level Basic Wages', pp. 249–77.
7 'Ten Per Cent and the Trail of Bruce-Page', *Australian Worker*, 28 January 1931.
8 'Union Resistance', *Labor Call*, 29 January 1931.
9 Quoted in Cook, 'The Scullin Government', pp. 362–3.
10 'Trades Hall Council', *Labor Call*, 29 January 1931.
11 The following account draws on Robertson, *J.H. Scullin*, pp. 304–21; McMullin, *The Light on the Hill*, pp. 167–73; and Nairn, *The 'Big Fella'*, pp. 220–30.
12 McMullin, *The Light on the Hill*, p. 169.
13 Editorial, *Sydney Morning Herald*, 28 January 1931.
14 The report can be found in Shann and Copland, *The Crisis*, pp. 146–81.
15 Robertson, *J.H. Scullin*, p. 306.
16 Great Conference of Commonwealth and States, copy in Frank Anstey Papers, NLA, MS 6245.
17 For detail on the 'socialisation units', see Martin, '"Bucking the machine"'.
18 Quoted in Schedvin, *Australia and the Great Depression*, pp. 230n.
19 Ibid., p. 229.
20 McMullin, *The Light on the Hill*, p. 170.
21 Robertson, *J.H. Scullin*, p. 314.
22 Nairn, *The 'Big Fella'*, p. 228.
23 Robertson, *J.H. Scullin*, pp. 319–20.
24 Lyons, House of Representatives, 13 March 1931.
25 Quoted in 'The No-Confidence Motion', *Age* (Melbourne), 16 March 1931.

Chapter 21: Populism and secession

1 Matthew Cunningham's 'The Reactionary and the Radical' offers a comprehensive account of these movements.
2 Robinson, 'The All for Australia League in New South Wales', pp. 36–7, 40.
3 A very useful analysis of populism, and the problems of defining it, can be found in Cas Mudde and Cristóbal Rovira Kaltwasser, 'Populism', *The Oxford Handbook of Political*

Ideologies, <www.oxfordhandbooks.com/view/10.1093/oxfordhb/9780199585977.001.0001/oxfordhb-9780199585977-e-026>.

4 Cunningham, 'The Reactionary and the Radical', p. 92.

5 Matthews, 'The All for Australia League', p. 143. For the critiques by individual citizens and letter writers, see Dickenson, '"God Give Us Men"', pp. 87–105.

6 Cunningham, 'The Reactionary and the Radical', p. 103.

7 Loveday, 'Anti-political Political Thought', pp. 136–47.

8 Cunningham, 'The Reactionary and the Radical', pp. 123, 125–6.

9 Some of the other movements to emerge were the 'Who's for Australia?' League, the Political Reform League, the Young Patriots' Association, the United Australia Association, the Soldiers' and Citizens' Party, the Empire Loyalty League, and the Farmers' Production Association. In Victoria and South Australia there was a revival in 1930 of the Kyabram Movement, an agrarian reform movement of the late nineteenth century, but this proved short-lived.

10 Lloyd, 'The Formation', p. 64.

11 Ibid., pp. 65, 68.

12 Cunningham, 'The Reactionary and the Radical', p. 118.

13 See ibid., p. 95, for strike-breaking force, and pp. 120–3 for further details on other states. Among the minor movements to spring up in Western Australia were the Groper Non-Party Movement, the Australian Unity League and the Australian Liberal League.

14 Matthews, 'The All for Australia League', p. 140.

15 Cunningham, 'The Reactionary and the Radical', p. 124.

16 Matthews, 'The All for Australia League', p. 139.

17 A detailed account of negotiations with Lyons can be found in Hart, 'J.A. Lyons', pp. 91–4; and Hart, 'Lyons: Labor Minister', pp. 44–51.

18 Brett, *Australian Liberals*, p. 101.

19 Latham to A. Pratt, cited in Hart, 'J.A. Lyons', p. 113.

20 Lyons, *So We Take Comfort*, p. 181.

21 Lloyd, *The Rise and Fall*, p. 141.

22 Quoted in Brett, *Australian Liberals*, p. 105.

23 Cunningham, 'The Reactionary and the Radical', p. 172.

24 Quoted in Macintyre, *Oxford History*, p. 269.

25 Mudde and Kaltwasser, 'Populism'.

26 See Roger Eatwell, 'Fascism', *The Oxford Handbook of Political Ideologies*, <www-oxford handbooks-com.virtual.anu.edu.au/view/10.1093/oxfordhb/9780199585977.001.0001/oxfordhb-9780199585977-e-009>.

27 Hart, 'J.A. Lyons', p. 116.

28 Presidential address, AGM, South Australian Chamber of Manufactures, 19 November 1930, SLSA, 380.099423 C443b.

29 Neale, 'New States Movements', p. 14.

30 A federal royal commission into new states in 1924–25, and one on the Constitution in 1927.

31 'Separation: The Case for New England', Lecturette no. 1, David Henry Drummond Papers, University of New England & Regional Archives (UNE&R Archives), A248 Box V3011.

32 S. Kingsbury, *A Sydney Critic's Catechism of the New State*, 1932, New England State Movement Pamphlets and Newspaper Clippings, UNE&R Archives, A1 Box 13.

33 Ellis, 'Why New States are Vital to Australia', Office of Rural Research and Development, Canberra, 1948, New England State Movement Pamphlets and Newspaper Clippings, UNE&R Archives, A1 Box 15.

34 The paragraphs that follow synthesise arguments that feature regularly in the rich archive of the Drummond Papers (UNE&R Archives, Boxes V3009–3014) and the New England State Movement Pamphlets and Newspaper Clippings, UNE&R Archives.

35 '"Time Opportune"', *Northern Star* (Lismore), 18 February 1931; 'Provisional Govt. for Northern N.S.W.', *Macleay Argus* (Kempsey), 20 February 1931.

36 Cited in Lloyd, 'The Formation', p. 62.

37 Drummond Papers, Box V3011.

38 'The New England Separation Movement', Drummond Papers, Box V3011.

39 This paragraph draws on Andrew Moore, 'Hardy, Charles Downey (1898–1941)', *ADB*.

40 'Organising for the Western State', *Sun*, 2 March 1931, copy in New England State Movement Pamphlets and Newspaper Clippings, A1 Box 13.

41 'Riverina Movement', Drummond Papers, Box V3011.

42 Quoted in Cathcart, *Defending the National Tuckshop*, p. 38.

43 Cooper, 'The Armidale Electorate', p. 52.

44 Letter E.S.B. Stevens to Lt-Vol. E.J. Munro, United Country Movement, Drummond Papers, Box V3014.

45 *The Dominion*, 30 April 1931.

46 Lloyd, 'The Formation', p. 59.

47 A useful account can be found in Bolton, *A Fine Country*, pp. 116–20, 184–5, 235–6, 249, 256, 262–3.

48 Bolton, *A Fine Country*, p. 254.

49 Lloyd, 'The Formation', p. 58.

50 Bolton, *A Fine Country*, p. 253.

51 Ibid., p. 262.

52 Australian Government, Commonwealth Grants Commission, <www.cgc.gov.au/about-us>.

53 Western Australian Secessionist Movement, <www.facebook.com/WASecessionist Movement>.

Chapter 22: Taking up arms

1 The definitive accounts are Moore, *The Secret Army and the Premier*, and Cathcart, *Defending the National Tuckshop*.

2 Cathcart, *Defending the National Tuckshop*, p. 96.

3 See 'Sydney Loyalists', *Warwick Daily News* (Queensland), 9 May 1921; 'The Disturbance in the Domain', *Bowen Independent* (Queensland), 28 May 1921.

4 Moore, *The Secret Army and the Premier*, pp. 41–50, provides a good analysis of the debate about *Kangaroo*.

5 Michael Cathcart is convinced of Blamey's role (*Defending the National Tuckshop*, pp. 56–9), but Blamey's biographer John Hetherington denies this. David Horner judges the evidence against Blamey to be circumstantial, although 'by training and instinct he was an autocrat' ('Blamey, Sir Thomas Albert (1884–1951)', *ADB*). Keith Amos (*The New Guard Movement*, p. 11) credits Brudenell White with organising the White Army, but Jeffrey Grey considers the evidence for White's leadership also circumstantial: 'A man

of sensitivity and intellect, he believed in the rule of law ('White, Sir Cyril Brudenell (1876–1940)', *ADB*).

6 For discussion of the problem with determining the League of National Security's aims, see Cathcart, *Defending the National Tuckshop*, pp. 59–60.

7 See Vodicka, *Coup d'État!?*; and Cathcart, *Defending the National Tuckshop*, pp. 10–17.

8 I owe this comparison to Cathcart, *Defending the National Tuckshop*, p. 23.

9 Armstrong, 'The Secret History of Fascism in Australia'.

10 Cathcart, *Defending the National Tuckshop*, p. 59.

11 The case for the existence of the Old Guard, made by Andrew Moore, was critiqued by Evans ('"A Menace"'). Moore mounted an effective rebuttal in 'Superintendent Mackay and the Curious Case of the Vanishing Secret Army'.

12 Moore, *The Secret Army and the Premier*, p. 88.

13 Ibid., p. 87.

14 Ibid., p. 114.

15 For the creation and operations of the New Guard, a foundational account is Campbell, *The Rallying Point*.

16 Amos, *The New Guard*, p. 27; Moore, *The Secret Army and the Premier*, p. 144.

17 Moore, *The Secret Army and the Premier*, p. 141; Amos, *The New Guard*, p. 24.

18 Moore, *The Secret Army and the Premier*, p. 143.

19 Ibid., pp. 147–8.

20 Moore, 'The New Guard and the Labour Movement', pp. 57–8.

21 Amos, *The New Guard*, p. 26.

22 Moore, *The Secret Army and the Premier*, p. 140.

23 Ibid., pp. 154, 144.

24 Ibid., p. 147.

25 See Evans, '"A Menace"', pp. 76.13–76.15, and Moore, 'Superintendent Mackay', pp. 72.12–72.13.

26 'Jock Garden', *Kyogle Examiner*, 6 May 1932.

27 Quoted in Moore, 'Red Devils and White Reaction', p. 166.

28 Cunningham, 'Australian Fascism?' (pp. 375–93) provides a useful analysis of the literature on the New Guard and fascism. See also Moore, *The Secret Army and the Premier*, pp. 138–9.

29 Quoted in Cunningham, 'Australian Fascism?', p. 375.

30 Campbell, *The New Road*. For the New Guard after 1932, see Moore, 'Discredited Fascism', pp. 188–206.

31 Cathcart, *Defending the National Tuckshop*, p. 41.

32 Serle, *John Monash*, pp. 519–20.

33 'Assistance Not Required', *Australian Worker*, 23 September 1931; 'Row in the "New Guard" Camp', *Australian Worker*, 11 November 1931.

34 Minutes are to be found at NBAC, N1467/587.

35 'An Australian Labor Army to Be Formed', *Labor Daily*, 19 March 1931; 'Labor Army Makes Big Strides', *Labor Daily*, 15 April 1931; 'Successful Women's Meeting', *Labor Daily*, 4 May 1931. For drills on the north shore, see Peter, quoted in Lowenstein, *Weevils in the Flour*, p. 95.

36 Moore, 'Red Devils and White Reaction', p. 169; Moore, 'The New Guard and the Labour Movement', pp. 60–1.

37 Macintyre, *The Reds*, p. 210; Moore, 'Red Devils and White Reaction', p. 170.
38 Moore, 'Red Devils and White Reaction', p. 171.
39 Macintyre, *The Reds*, p. 210.
40 In Tasmania a branch of the CPA might have been established only in 1930: see Tkaczuk, 'Communists and the Great Depression in Tasmania', p. 26.
41 Tsokhas, 'Shifting the Burden', pp. 40–3; Moore, 'The Pastoral Workers' Industrial Union', pp. 61–74.
42 Macintyre, *The Reds*, p. 197.
43 Ibid., pp. 184–6, 200–1, 220.
44 Fox, *Fighting Back*, p. 226.
45 For example, 'Communists in Bourke', *Townsville Daily Bulletin*, 14 November 1931; 'Dubbo Decision', *Sydney Morning Herald*, 21 November 1931.
46 Macintyre, *The Reds*, pp. 212–13.
47 Fox, *Fighting Back*, pp. 226–8.
48 Macintyre, *The Reds*, pp. 214–15.
49 The account that follows draws on Fox, *Fighting Back*, pp. 230–6.
50 *Street Meetings Act, 1933* (Vic), AustLII, <http://classic.austlii.edu.au/au/legis/vic/hist_act/sma1933186>.
51 For the debate on this question, see Hirst, 'Communism and Australia's Historians', pp. 26–31, quotations at pp. 26, 31. Andrew Moore's response is found in 'Red Devils and White Reaction', esp. pp. 165–7, 176–7.
52 Tsoukala, 'Boundary-creating Processes', pp. 137–41.
53 Douglas, *Scapegoats*, p. 6.
54 See Childers and Weiss, 'Voters and Violence', pp. 482–3.
55 See Moore, *The Secret Army and the Premier*, pp. 177–83.

Chapter 23: In office but not in power

1 The following account draws on Schedvin, *Australia and the Great Depression*, pp. 232–6; and Nairn, *The 'Big Fella'*, pp. 229–33.
2 Nairn, *The 'Big Fella'*, p. 231.
3 'The Default of N.S.W.', *Mercury* (Hobart), 1 April 1931.
4 'Mr. Lang's Default', *Kalgoorlie Miner*, 1 April 1931.
5 Cited in 'Australia Will Pay', *Townsville Daily Bulletin*, 1 April 1931.
6 Eichengreen and Portes, 'Dealing with Debt', pp. 21–4; Jorgesen and Sachs, 'Default and Renegotiation', pp. 21–2.
7 Schedvin, *Australia and the Great Depression*, pp. 253–4.
8 Quoted in Markwell, 'Keynes and the Depression in Australia', p. 14.
9 'The Challenge of Default', *Age* (Melbourne), 30 March 1931.
10 'No Default', *Sun* (Sydney), 1 April 1931; 'Mr. Scullin, 'Default Would Increase Distress', *Sydney Morning Herald*, 2 April 1931.
11 'A Church Manifesto: Combined Protest Against Lang Policy', *Age*, 8 May 1931.
12 'Australia's Social Contracts', *Labor Call*, 2 April 1931.
13 Schedvin, *Australia and the Great Depression*, p. 255.
14 For Theodore and Keynes, see Hawkins, 'Ted Theodore', pp. 91–110, and Markwell, 'Keynes and the Depression in Australia'.

15 Theodore, House of Representatives, 17 March 1931.

16 Millmow, *The Power of Economic Ideas*, pp. 80, 83.

17 Cain, 'The Australian Economists', p. 25.

18 Millmow, *The Power of Economic Ideas*, pp. 85–6.

19 Schedvin, *Australia and the Great Depression*, p. 242.

20 Commonwealth of Australia, *Report of the Royal Commission into the Monetary and Banking Systems*, p. 206.

21 Clause 11, *Reserve Bank Act 1959*.

22 I owe this insight to Selwyn Cornish, Australian National University.

23 Polden, 'The Collapse', p. 52. This account also draws on Fitz-Gibbon and Gizycki, 'A History of Last-resort Lending'.

24 Lang claimed this in *The Great Bust*, p. 235.

25 For judgements on the role of the Commonwealth Bank, see Polden, 'The Collapse', pp. 65–70.

26 *Royal Commission into the Monetary and Banking Systems*, p. 144.

27 Brett, *Australian Liberals*, p. 92.

28 'A Lesson in Bank Wrecking', *Canberra Times*, 28 April 1931.

29 'Run on Commonwealth Bank', *Week* (Brisbane), 6 May 1931.

30 'Telegraphic News', *Braidwood Review and District Advocate* (NSW), 5 May 1931; 'Run on Commonwealth Bank', *Week* (Brisbane), 6 May 1931.

31 Fitz-Gibbon and Gizycki, 'A History of Last-resort Lending'.

32 A detailed comparison of the financial systems in the depressions of the 1890s and 1930s can be found in Fisher and Kent, 'Two Depressions, One Banking Collapse'. pp. 6–7. This concludes (p. 45): 'Although there was a boom of sorts leading up to the 1930s depression, the same factors which led to financial instability during the 1880s were more muted, or operating in the opposite direction during the 1920s. For example, the rise in the share of bank credit to GDP was smaller and started from a lower base; the share of building activity in GDP was much lower, although there was still a sizeable increase in property prices; the ratio of trading bank advances to deposits was rising only slowly from a low base and capital inflows were not sustained at the same levels, nor for as long, as during the 1880s; a greater proportion of bank assets were being held in the form of government securities during the 1920s; and in contrast to the 1880s, trading banks were increasing both capital and retained earnings at a faster rate than their total assets.'

33 Schedvin, *Australia and the Great Depression*, p. 209.

Chapter 24: The Premiers' Plan

1 Macintyre, *Oxford History*, p. 270.

2 Millmow, *The Power of Economic Ideas*, p. 88.

3 For the various views within the group of economists, see Schedvin, *Australia and the Great Depression*, pp. 244–6.

4 Bland and Mills, 'Financial Reconstruction', p. 167.

5 See, for example, Edward Riley and Edward Holloway, House of Representatives, 25 June 1931.

6 'Great Task Faces Premiers' Conference', *Daily News* (Perth), 25 May 1931.

7 'Loan Council', *Sydney Morning Herald*, 25 May 1931.

8 Schedvin, *Australia and the Great Depression*, pp. 246–7.

9   The committee adopted as its standard the fall in the Commonwealth basic wage since 1928: 10 per cent through the Arbitration Court order and 10 per cent through a cost of living adjustment (Schedvin, *Australia and the Great Depression*, p. 244).

10 Macintyre, *Oxford History*, pp. 270–1.

11 Copland, *Developments in Economic Thought*, p. 11.

12 Millmow, *The Power of Economic Ideas*, p. 91.

13 Robertson, *J.H. Scullin*, p. 340.

14 'Converting the Nation's Internal Debt', *Australian Worker*, 1 July 1931.

15 McMullin, *The Light on the Hill*, p. 174.

16 Robertson, *J.H. Scullin*, pp. 340, 342.

17 'Wage cuts and Pension Reductions Opposed by Federal Labor Executive', *Australian Worker*, 24 June 1931.

18 Millmow, *The Power of Economic Ideas*, p. 113.

19 Neville Cain, 'Theodore, Edward Granville (1884–1950)', *ADB*.

20 Lang, *The Great Bust*, p. 344.

21 Schedvin, *Australia and the Great Depression*, pp. 248–9.

22 Robertson, *J.H. Scullin*, p. 341.

23 'Wage Cuts and Pension Reductions Opposed by Federal Labor Executive', *Australian Worker*, 24 June 1931; 'Premiers' Plan Accepted by Federal Caucus', *Labor Daily*, 17 June 1931. For the caucus debate, see Cook, 'Labor and the Premiers' Plan', pp. 100–1.

24 Quoted in McMullin, *The Light on the Hill*, p. 175.

25 Anstey, House of Representatives, 8 July 1931.

26 'Federal Session', *Sydney Morning Herald*, 25 June 1931.

27 Curtin, House of Representatives, 24 June 1931.

28 'A Warning Labor Cannot Heed', *Australian Worker*, 17 June 1931.

29 'Will the Premiers' Plan Save Australia?', *Australian Worker*, 10 June 1931.

30 'Reductions Must Be Opposed', *Labor Call*, 25 June 1931.

31 'Wage Cuts and Pension Reductions Opposed by Federal Labor Executive', *Australian Worker*, 24 June 1931.

32 Millmow, *The Power of Economic Ideas*, p. 109.

33 Coleman et al., *Giblin's Platoon*, p. 121.

34 See Scullin's broadcast speech, 'The Hour of Sacrifice', *Age* (Melbourne), 12 August 1931.

35 'Loan Conversion', *Advertiser* (Hurstbridge, Victoria), 14 August 1931.

36 Louis and Turner, *The Depression of the 1930s*, p. 57.

37 Schedvin, *Australia and the Great Depression*, pp. 278–9.

38 The best account of the technicalities of the evolving pensions system is Toose, *Independent Enquiry into the Repatriation System*, esp. pp. 25–32.

39 On 30 August 1930, for example, *Reveille* trumpeted, 'hands off pensions'.

40 'Should Be Considered Sacrosanct', *West Australian*, 27 May 1931.

41 The account of the 1931 pensions debate in the following paragraphs draws on the Second Interim Report of the Special Committee to Consider Questions Relating to War Pensions, and Scullin to Dyett, 19 June 1931, NAA, A461 B382/1/2 pt 1. For greater elaboration of the arguments, see Beaumont, 'The Returned Soldier', pp. 19–23.

42 Details of the RSSILA lobbying and meeting with the government can be found in Dyett to R. Muish, President Queensland Branch RSSILA, 13 July 1931, NLA, MS 6609 Box 43 5042B 1, and Federal Executive RSSILA, Circular no. 107/31, 3 June 1931, NLA, MS 6609 Box 457.

43 Scullin, House of Representatives, 26 June 1931; Soldiers' Pensions' press reports, NLA, MS 6609 Box 521.

44 See Beaumont, *Broken Nation*, pp. 41, 143–5.

45 No title, *Age*, 16 September 1916.

46 'Equality of Sacrifice', *Sydney Morning Herald*, 7 December 1917.

47 James Guthrie, Senate, 3 July 1931.

48 T.W. White, House of Representatives, 24 June 1931.

49 Paul Jones, House of Representatives, 24 June 1931.

50 Roland Green, House of Representatives, 19 June 1931.

51 Report of the War Pensions Enquiry Committee, Part I, NAA, A461 B382/1/2 pt I.

52 Lloyd and Rees, *The Last Shilling*, p. 246.

53 Skerman, *Repatriation in Australia*, p. 65.

54 Shann, cited in Millmow, *The Power of Economic Ideas*, p. 92.

55 Millmow, *The Power of Economic Ideas*, pp. 110–11, citing Neville Cain and W.R. Maclaurin.

56 Valentine, 'The Battle of the Plans', pp. 169–70.

57 Schedvin, *Australia and the Great Depression*, p. 373.

Chapter 25: Scullin's end

1 For a detailed account of Victorian politics, see Strangio, *Neither Power Nor Glory*, pp. 194–202.

2 Government Printer, 'Beneficial Results in Victoria following the Adoption of the Premiers' Plan', PROV, VPRS 14269/P/0001 unit 7.

3 Nairn, *The 'Big Fella'*, p. 243.

4 'Salaries Not Paid', *Sydney Morning Herald*, 7 August 1931.

5 Nairn, *The 'Big Fella'*, pp. 246–7; Schedvin, *Australia and the Great Depression*, p. 270.

6 Schedvin, *Australia and the Great Depression*, pp. 271–2.

7 Gunn's report, 'Employment and Production', can be found at NAA, A458 AR502/3 pt 4.

8 Gibson to Scullin, 8 September 1931, NAA, A458 AS502/3. This file also contains details of discussions between the premiers and the banks.

9 Ahamed, *Lords of Finance*, pp. 424–5.

10 Schedvin, *Australia and the Great Depression*, pp. 277–8, provides details of the complexities.

11 Millmow, 'Douglas Copland and the Aftershocks', pp. 29–30.

12 For details of the bank debate and the thinking behind the revaluation, see Schedvin, *Australia and the Great Depression*, pp. 280–2.

13 'Prosperity Campaign', *Swan Leader* (WA), 20 November 1931.

14 'Prosperity Campaign', *Age* (Melbourne), 18 November 1931.

15 'Prosperity Campaign', *Age*, 3 December 1931.

16 'Prosperity Campaign', *Age*, 14 November 1931.

17 Robertson, *J.H. Scullin*, p. 363.

18 Quoted in Robertson, *J.H. Scullin* p. 370.

19 For details, see Dunn, Senate, 12 November 1931.

20 'Tea for Two in the Bedroom', *Sun* (Sydney), 20 November 1931.

21 'Federal Elections', *Labor Call*, 3 December 1931.

22 *Round Table*, quoted in Head 'Economic Crisis and Political Legitimacy', p. 22.
23 Robertson, *J.H. Scullin*, p. 371; 'Final Appeals by Party Leaders', *Sydney Morning Herald*, 18 December 1931.
24 'The Pitiful Failure of Joseph Lyons', *Australian Worker*, 9 December 1931.
25 For details of Scullin's election schedule, see Robertson, *J.H. Scullin*, pp. 371–5; 'Political Pellets', *Labor Daily*, 7 December 1931.
26 'Labour Meeting in Sydney', *Argus* (Melbourne), 10 December 1931.
27 Robertson, *J.H. Scullin*, p. 374.
28 'Labour Rally', *Sydney Morning Herald*, 14 December 1931.
29 'Mr. Scullin's Policy', *Cairns Post*, 3 December 1931; '"Condemns Itself"', *Advocate* (Burnie, Tas.), 3 December 1931.
30 '"Defeat Scullin"', *Newcastle Morning Herald and Miners' Advocate*, 18 December 1931.
31 'Mr. Lyons', *West Australian*, 19 December 1931.
32 See White, *Joseph Lyons*, p. 134.
33 All quotations from Robertson, *J.H. Scullin*, pp. 377–9.
34 Fitzgerald, *Red Ted*, pp. 307–8.
35 Cain, 'Theodore, Edward Granville (1884–1950)', *ADB*.
36 Quotations from Fitzgerald, *Red Ted*, p. 311.
37 Love, 'Frank Anstey', p. 140.
38 Thomas Hagahan (?) to Theodore, 21 December 1931, Box 1, Folder 1, Theodore Papers, NLA, MS 7222.
39 W. Farmer Whyte, Federal News Service, 18 January 1932, ibid.
40 Andrews, *Joseph Lyons*, p. 78.
41 Menzies, *Afternoon Light*, p. 125.

Chapter 26: Women at risk

1 Australian Bureau of Statistics, 2071.0 Reflecting a Nation: Stories from the 2011 Census, 2012–2013, <www.abs.gov.au/ausstats/abs@.nsf/Lookup/2071.0main+features952012-2013>.
2 Carmichael, 'So Many Children', p. 103.
3 *Year Book Australia, 1938*, p. 391.
4 Betty, quoted in Lowenstein, *Weevils in the Flour*, p. 347.
5 Albert Robinson, quoted ibid., p. 149.
6 Foley, 'The Women's Movement', pp. 347–8.
7 Scott, 'Making Ends Meet', pp. 55–6.
8 The details that follow are drawn from Foley, 'The Women's Movement', pp. 345–51; and Report of Relief of Unemployed Girls, 5th August 1930 to 30th June 1931, PROV, VPRS 8291/P/0001 unit 87.
9 Letter Muriel Heagney to Sustenance Committee, Yarraville, 28 April 1931, PROV, VPRS 8291/P/0001 unit 87.
10 Costar, 'Labor, Politics and Unemployment', p. 198. See also Scott, 'Making Ends Meet', p. 55.
11 President, Trades Hall, Sydney, to Scullin, 13 June 1930; Premier's Office to Mrs M.E. Orr, 30 September 1930; and Bavin to Acting Prime Minister, 30 September 1930, NAA, A458 AL502/3.
12 'Unemployed Girls', *Singleton Argus* (NSW), 10 September 1930.

13 Kennedy, 'Segregation for Integration', p. 41.

14 Perkins, 'Crime' (p. 174) cites a Queensland report of 1934–35 that estimated that 14 to 18 per cent of puerperal deaths were due to abortion and most of these were married women.

15 Cannon, *The Human Face*, p. 255.

16 McCalman, *Sex and Suffering*, pp. 202–6.

17 Jessie, quoted in Lowenstein, *Weevils in the Flour*, p. 133.

18 Jessie, quoted ibid., p. 134; Shirley, quoted ibid., p. 414.

19 Barbara Wawn, quoted ibid., p. 117.

20 Chief Secretary's Correspondence, SRSA, GRG24/6/00000/738, File 89/1931.

21 Smith, 'Australian Public Health', p. 100.

22 McKewon, *The Scarlet Mile*, p. 42.

23 Frances, 'The History of Female Prostitution', pp. 49, 51.

24 Bongiorno, *The Sex Lives of Australians*, pp. 182–4.

25 Scott, 'Making Ends Meet', pp. 57–8.

26 Golder and Allen, 'Prostitution in New South Wales', p. 19.

27 Potts, *The Myth*, pp. 102–3.

28 Frances, *Selling Sex*, p. 212.

29 The following draws on Elizabeth Nelson's 'Civilian Men and Domestic Violence', pp. 97–108, and 'Victims of War', pp. 83–106.

30 Minutes of the General Committee Meeting, 19 April 1933, SLV, MS12414, Box 3211/5.

31 Potts, *The Myth*, p. 148.

32 Smith, 'Australian Public Health', p. 102.

33 Gibson, *Tolley*, p. 64.

34 *Year Book Australia, 1934*, p. 299.

35 South Australian Temperance Alliance, Annual Report 1932, SLSA.

36 Potts, *The Myth*, p. 155.

37 Miriam Tonkin, quoted in Lowenstein, *Weevils in the Flour*, p. 232.

38 MacDonald, *Random Recollections*, p. 23.

39 Day, 'Divorce in Australia', p. 59.

40 Vamplew, *Australians: Historical Statistics*, p. 47.

41 Jason Whiting, 'Eight Reasons Women Stay in Abusive Relationships', Institute of Family Studies, <https://ifstudies.org/blog/eight-reasons-women-stay-in-abusive-relationships>.

42 Pernell Plath Meier, <www.goodreads.com/author/quotes/20768409.Pernell_Plath_Meier>.

Chapter 27: Losing your home

1 *Year Book Australia, 1938*, p. 365.

2 McCalman, *Journeyings*, pp. 70–3.

3 Broomhill, *Unemployed Workers*, p. 120.

4 McCalman, *Journeyings*, pp. 82, 85.

5 Broomhill, *Unemployed Workers*, pp. 121, 126.

6 Fox, *Fighting Back*, p. 145.

7 Potts, *The Myth*, p. 63.

8 Legislation, often amended, included Western Australia's *Tenants, Purchasers and Mortgagors' Relief Act 1930*, New South Wales' *Moratorium Act 1930*, Queensland's *Purchasers of Homes Relief Act 1930* and *State Housing Relief Act 1930*, Victoria's

Unemployed Occupiers and Farmers Relief Act 1931, and South Australia's *Crown Debtors Relief Act 1934*.

9   'The Rights of Property', *Sydney Morning Herald*, 27 December 1930.

10 Broomhill, *Unemployed Workers*, p. 124.

11 Potts, *The Myth*, p. 58.

12 Broomhill, *Unemployed Workers*, p. 129.

13 Ibid., p. 133; Fox, *Fighting Back*, p. 146; 'State Session New Legislation', *Sydney Morning Herald*, 12 December 1930.

14 See, for example, Deputy Town Clerk Minute, 'Premises 110a Albion Street', 3 February 1933, City of Sydney Archives, 4072/32.

15 Fox, *Fighting Back*, p. 141; Bolton, *A Fine Country*, p. 175.

16 Fox, *Fighting Back*, p. 142.

17 Ibid., p. 140.

18 Potts, *The Myth*, p. 59.

19 Unless otherwise stated, the details of the eviction riots that follow are taken from Cannon, *The Human Face*, pp. 42–8; Fox, *Fighting Back*, pp. 143–60; and Potts, *The Myth*, pp. 53–9.

20 Macintyre, *The Reds*, p. 197; Unemployment Workers' Movement Rules and Constitution, NBAC, N57/421.

21 Bolton, *A Fine Country*, p. 175.

22 'Excited Scene at Brunswick', *Age* (Melbourne), 25 April 1931.

23 'Procession Through Streets', *Examiner* (Launceston), 23 April 1932.

24 See, for example, 'A Footscray Demonstration', *Age*, 20 February 1931.

25 Fox, *Fighting Back*, p. 149.

26 'Revolvers and Batons in Eviction Riots', *Sun* (Sydney), 30 May 1931.

27 'Fierce Fight at Bankstown' *Lithgow Mercury*, 17 June 1931. See also Cottle and Keys, 'Anatomy of an "Eviction Riot"', pp. 186–200.

28 'Fierce Clash', *Daily Examiner* (Grafton), 18 June 1931.

29 William Hawkins statement in Papers of Phillip Thorne, NBAC, P15/8–9.

30 Garbett statement in Thorne Papers.

31 B. Urbanski, in Thorne Papers.

32 'Bloody Friday in Newtown', John Patrick Kavanagh Papers, NBAC, N336–67.

33 'Desperate Fighting', *Sydney Morning Herald*, 20 June 1931.

34 Macintyre, *The Reds*, p. 193.

35 For example, 'Footscray Eviction', *Argus* (Melbourne), 13 August 1931.

36 'Hand-to-hand Battle', *Sydney Morning Herald*, 18 June 1931.

37 *Brunswick-Coburg Gazette*, in Fox, *Fighting Back*, p. 153.

38 *Newcastle Sun*, in Cannon, *The Human Face*, p. 46.

39 'Hand-to hand Battle', *Sydney Morning Herald*, 18 June 1931.

40 Taylor, 'Food Riots Revisited', p. 483.

41 Quoted in Macintyre, *The Reds*, p. 196.

42 'Fitzroy Eviction', *Argus*, 18 August 1931.

43 'Eviction Riots at Bankstown', *Western Argus* (Kalgoorlie), 1 November 1932.

44 See Notes of Cases for I.C.W.P.A (International Class War Prisoners Aid), NBAC, Thorne Papers.

45 'Newtown Riots', *Sydney Morning Herald*, 24 October 1931.

46 Notes of Cases for I.C.W.P.A.

47 Macintyre, *The Reds*, p. 194.

48 'Newcastle Conviction Case', *Australian Worker*, 24 May 1933.

49 Potts, *The Myth*, p. 57.

50 Fox, *Fighting Back*, p. 140.

51 *Footscray Advertiser*, cited in Potts, *The Myth*, p. 65.

52 Town Clerk, Roy Hendy, to Under Secretary, Department of Agriculture, 18 July 1932, City of Sydney Archives, 4072/32.

53 Bolton, *A Fine Country*, p. 176.

54 For pressure from councils, see Town Clerk, Preston Council, to Tunnecliffe, 10 March 1932, and from unions, Unemployed Bulletin no. 28, 19 April 1932, PROV, VPRS 4540/P/0000 unit 177.

55 Broomhill, *Unemployed Workers*, p. 136.

56 Fox, *Fighting Back*, pp. 139–40.

57 Letter, Town Clerk, Richmond, 7 May 1932, PROV, VPRS 17453/P/0001 unit 31.

58 Fox, *Fighting Back*, p. 156.

59 Bolton, *A Fine Country*, p. 176.

Chapter 28: Without a home

1 For oral history confirming the importance of the extended family, see Potts, *The Myth*, pp. 59–60.

2 Broomhill, *Unemployed Workers*, p. 134.

3 Health Inspector to Town Clerk, 6 July 1929(?), Port Adelaide Library, Local History Archives.

4 Report by Health Officer, 5 September 1929(?), ibid.

5 Broomhill, *Unemployed Workers*, p. 135.

6 Cannon, *The Human Face*, p. 42.

7 O'Brien, 'National Shame/National Treasure', pp. 173–4.

8 'Bag Town', *Sydney Morning Herald*, 25 February 1931.

9 Letter Town Clerk to Commissioner of Police, 23 August 1930, Perth City Council, 1930–, Unemployment General Filing, SRWA, CONS 3054 1930/0093.

10 Les Barnes, quoted in Lowenstein, *Weevils in the Flour*, p. 217.

11 Broomhill, *Unemployed Workers*, pp. 162–3. For vagrancy laws, see Kimber, 'Poor Laws', p. 542.

12 Ted Waight, 'On the Track', Mitchell Library, SLNSW, MLMSS 5608, p. 4.

13 'Beggars Increase', *Sydney Morning Herald*, 12 September 1930.

14 'Organised Begging', *Northern Miner* (Charters Towers, Queensland), 23 March 1931.

15 'Beggars Increase', *Sydney Morning Herald*, 12 September 1930.

16 Broomhill, *Unemployed Workers*, p. 163.

17 Henry Miller for the unemployed soldiers of White City Camp, to F. Anstey, Minister for Repatriation, 1 May 1930, NAA, A6272 E301. In 1925 three 'permanent' camps had been erected: White City near Civic Centre, Capitol Hill, and Causeway (Anne Gugler, 'Canberra Camps, Settlements & Early Housing', <https://canberracamps.webs.com>).

18 A.J. Christie, Civic Administrator to A. Blakeley, Minister for Home Affairs, 17 May 1930, NAA, A6272 E301.

19 Broomhill, *Unemployed Workers*, pp. 161–2.

20 The account that follows draws on Spenceley, 'The Broadmeadows Camp', pp. 53–73.
21 Ibid., p. 70.
22 'Unemployment', *Toowoomba Chronicle and Darling Downs Gazette*, 30 July 1931.
23 Vera Deacon, quoted in Cannon, *The Human Face*, p. 254. See also Tom Galvin, quoted in Lowenstein, *Weevils in the Flour*, p. 418; Dave Bowen and Sally, quoted ibid., p. 249.
24 Vera Deacon, quoted in Cannon, *The Human Face*, pp. 254–5.
25 Report on Unemployed Camp, Port Adelaide Library, Local History Archives.
26 Richardson, *The Bitter Years*, p. 71.
27 Potts, *The Myth*, p. 280.
28 Ibid., p. 276.
29 Ibid., pp. 283–5; Costar, 'Labor, Politics and Unemployment', p. 270.
30 See, for example, 'Not Found Genuine', *Sun* (Sydney), 19 June 1931.
31 Bolton, *A Fine Country*, p. 177.
32 'Camping Ground', *Armidale Express and New England General Advertiser*, 6 May 1931.
33 'Unemployment', *Sydney Morning Herald*, 15 June 1931; 'Governor's Visit to La Perouse Camp', *Sydney Morning Herald*, 10 June 1931.
34 'Three Halls Full', *Daily Telegraph* (Sydney), 9 June 1931.
35 Potts, *The Myth*, p. 272; 'The "Happy Valley" Camp', *Australian Worker*, 24 June 1931; 'Governor Visits Happy Valley', *Daily Telegraph* (Sydney), 10 June 1931.
36 Jessie Davies, 'Tin Town: A Forgotten Shanty Town in Country New South Wales', ABC News, 9 August 2018, <www.abc.net.au/news/2018-08-08/remembering-dubbos-tin-town/10071892>.
37 Costar, 'Labor, Politics and Unemployment', pp. 270–1.
38 Potts, *The Myth*, pp. 287–8.
39 Unless otherwise cited, the account of the Cairns riot that follows is taken from Costar, 'Controlling the Victims', pp. 6–7; Bottoms, *Cairns*, pp. 406–14; Walmsley, 'The Battle of Parramatta Park', pp. 1–3; Scott, '"A Place in Normal Society"', pp. 137–9.
40 'The History of the Cairns Show', <https://cairnsshow.com.au/history-cairns-show>.
41 Scott ('"A Place in Normal Society"', p. 137) claims that the unemployed squatted in the showgrounds after the Cairns council failed to honour its promise to provide shelter for the travelling unemployed, but contemporary press reports do not confirm this narrative.
42 Macintyre, *The Reds*, p. 239.
43 'Men in Possession', *Townsville Daily Bulletin*, 8 July 1932.
44 George Bliss, interviewed in Fox, *Depression Down Under*, p. 72.
45 Ernie Silvester, quoted in Bottoms, 'The Battle of Parramatta Park', p. 5.
46 'The History of the Cairns Show'.
47 Editorial, *Cairns Post*, 18 July 1932.
48 'Over 100 Injured', *Telegraph* (Brisbane), 18 July 1932.

Chapter 29: On the track

1 Broomhill, *Unemployed Workers*, pp. 154–5.
2 Potts, *The Myth*, p. 238.
3 Tennant, *The Battlers*, p. 72.
4 Mick Healy, quoted in Lowenstein, *Weevils in the Flour*, p. 326. For preference given to local men, see Parr, 'Letters to Clare', pp. 113–14.

5   'Men Travel 5000 Miles in Search of Work', *Barrier Miner* (Broken Hill, NSW), 2 March 1931.

6   Potts, *The Myth*, p. 239.

7   *Murray Pioneer*, quoted in Broomhill, *Unemployed Workers*, pp. 158–9.

8   Potts, *The Myth*, p. 239.

9   'Men Travel 5000 Miles in Search of Work', *Barrier Miner*.

10 Tennant, *Tiburon*, p. 7.

11 Tom Combey diary, NBAC, P80/ALL.

12 By Jack Wright, quoted in Lowenstein, *Weevils in the Flour*, p. 337.

13 Potts, *The Myth*, p. 248; Jack Henry, quoted in Lowenstein, *Weevils in the Flour*, pp. 409–10.

14 Potts, *The Myth*, p. 247.

15 Ibid.; John, quoted in Lowenstein, *Weevils in the Flour*, p. 124.

16 'Men Travel 5000 Miles in Search of Work', *Barrier Miner*.

17 Potts, *The Myth*, p. 250.

18 Tennant, *The Battlers*, p. 23.

19 See, for example, Perkins, 'Crime', p. 121.

20 Basil, quoted in Lowenstein, *Weevils in the Flour*, p. 370.

21 Broomhill, *Unemployed Workers*, p. 157; Ted Waight, 'On the Track', Mitchell Library, SLNSW, MLMSS 5608, p. 4.

22 A similar memory of the police and wives providing food can be found in Donald Tuckwell, 23 May 1993, Knott Depression interviews, NBAC, Z562, Box 2/1.

23 Quoted in Potts, *The Myth*, p. 250.

24 Bert Grummitt, quoted in Lowenstein, *Weevils in the Flour*, p. 263.

25 Potts, *The Myth*, p. 243.

26 Tom Hills, Jack, and Cecil Curtis, quoted in Lowenstein, *Weevils in the Flour*, pp. 404, 238, 358; Potts, *The Myth*, p. 248; George Bliss, in Cannon, *The Human Face*, p. 238.

27 John Jenkins, 1 June 1993, Knott Depression interviews, NBAC, Z562, Box 2/2.

28 Tennant, *The Battlers*, pp. 147, 107–8.

29 Report, YWCA/HOSTEL/REP/2, James Cook University, Townsville Special Collections.

30 Alan Crawford, 9 June 1992, Knott Depression interviews, NBAC, Box 2/3; information about Nhill from Frank Bongiorno, ANU.

31 Potts, *The Myth*, pp. 242–3.

32 Tennant, *The Battlers*, pp. 35–6.

33 Potts, *The Myth*, pp. 252–3.

34 Bill Ince, quoted in Lowenstein, *Weevils in the Flour*, p. 268.

35 Simon Bracegirdle, quoted ibid., p. 129.

36 Phillip Law, quoted in Cannon, *The Human Face*, p. 265.

37 Broomhill, *Unemployed Workers*, p. 157.

38 Huelin, *Keep Moving*, pp. 135–6.

39 Waight, 'On the Track', p. 3.

40 Parr, 'Letters to Clare', p. 122.

41 Tennant, *The Battlers*, pp. 92, 75.

42 Macintyre, *The Reds*, p. 194.

43 Menghetti, *The Red North*, p. 113.

44 'On the Track', *Townsville Daily Bulletin*, 18 January 1930.

Chapter 30: Aboriginal Australians

1 For discussion of contemporary debates about the numbers and future of Aboriginal people, see Holland, *Breaking the Silence*, pp. 80–94 (ebook version).

2 For discussion of numbers, see Richard Broome, *Aboriginal Australians*, p. 172; Markus, *Governing Savages*, p. 22.

3 So-called 'frontier' administrations trying to manage large Aboriginal populations had different practices from the more densely white-populated eastern states.

4 Markus, *Governing Savages*, p. 22. For discussion of genocide, see vol. 25 of *Aboriginal History*, 2001.

5 Goodall, *Invasion to Embassy*, p. 208.

6 Hodson, 'Nyungars and Work', p. 73.

7 Charles Rowley, cited in Curthoys and Moore, 'Working for White People', p. 9. For labour practices on the far south coast of New South Wales, see Castle and Hagan, 'Dependence and Independence', pp. 158–62; the mid-north coast of New South Wales, Morris, 'From Underemployment to Unemployment', pp. 506–8; and Queensland and other states, Rowley, *The Remote Aborigines*, passim.

8 Andrew Markus, 'Talka Longa Mouth', p. 142.

9 Ann McGrath, *Born in the Cattle*, pp. 44, 148. See also Curthoys and Moore, 'Working for White People', p. 12.

10 Unless otherwise stated, the account that follows draws on Haskins, '"A Better Chance"?'; and Robinson, '"We Do Not Want One Who Is Too Old"'.

11 See Haskins, '& So we are "Slave Owners!"', pp. 147–64.

12 Robinson, *Something Like Slavery*.

13 Parliament of Western Australia, *Report of the Royal Commissioner* (Moseley report), p. 7.

14 Haskins, '"A Better Chance"?', pp. 45, 43.

15 Rowley, *Outcasts in White Australia*, p. 58.

16 See Haskins, '"A Better Chance"?', esp. pp. 44–9.

17 Eckermann, *Kooniba*, p. 158.

18 Goodall, *Invasion to Embassy*, pp. 215–17.

19 Legislative Assembly, New South Wales, 'Aborigines: Annual Report of Board for Protection of, for the year ended 30th June 1931, p. 1; Queensland Command paper, Report upon the Operations of the sub-departments of Aboriginals . . ., Brisbane: Government Printer, p. 4; Parliament of South Australia, *Report of the Chief Protector of Aboriginals*, p. 4: all reports held at Australian Institute of Aboriginal and Torres Strait Islander Studies, Canberra.

20 Unless otherwise stated, the account that follows draws on Haebich, *For Their Own Good*, pp. 284–314; and Hodson, 'Nyungars and Work', pp. 73–92.

21 Rowley, *Outcasts*, p. 49.

22 Haebich, *For Their Own Good*, pp. 285–6.

23 The larger camps were near Gnowangerup, Narrogin, Williams, Wagin, Pingelly, Badjaling, Brookton and Beverley.

24 Moseley Report, p. 8.

25 Ibid., p. 10.

26 Rowley, *Outcasts*, p. 301.

27 Durack, *The Rock and the Sand*, p. 231.

28 There was 'trouble' when the Northam people arrived at Moore River, and some of the so-called ringleaders were sent back to Northam on the condition that they keep away from the town (Rowley, *Outcasts*, p. 100).

29 Moseley Report, p. 11.

30 Ibid., p. 12.

31 Rowley, *Outcasts*, p. 99.

32 Moseley Report, p. 12.

33 Haebich, *For Their Own Good*, pp. 297–8.

34 Ibid.

35 Goodall, *Invasion to Embassy*, pp. 230–5.

36 The description that follows draws on Broome, '"No One Thinks of Us"'.

37 Broome, '"No One Thinks of Us"', p. 21.

38 For further details, see Maynard, 'The Rise of the Modern Aboriginal Political Movement', pp. 113–34. A more extended study is Maynard, *Fight for Liberty and Freedom*.

39 'Formation of the AAPA', National Museum of Australia, <www.nma.gov.au/defining-moments/resources/formation-of-the-aapa>.

40 George G, 'Australia's First Aboriginal Civil Rights Group', Medium, 20 November 2018, <https://medium.com/the-junction/australias-first-aboriginal-civil-rights-group-ef6380010ad9>.

41 An important study of white humanitarian activists before and during the Depression years is Holland, *Breaking the Silence*.

42 Foster, 'Contested Destinies' pp. 103–25.

43 Markus, 'Talka Longa Mouth', pp. 148–50.

44 Holland, *Breaking the Silence*, p. 19 (ebook version).

45 Maynard, *Fight for Liberty*, p. 124.

46 Egan, *Justice All Their Own*; Holland, *Breaking the Silence*, pp. 47–9 (ebook version).

47 Stanton, 'The Australian Half-Caste Progressive Association', pp. 37–46. This association sought not just rights for all Aboriginal people but recognition of 'part-Aborigines' as a discrete group.

48 Quoted in Maynard, 'The Rise', p. 131.

49 '"Day of Mourning"', *Age* (Melbourne), 27 January 1938.

50 'Aborigines "Day of Mourning"', *Daily Advertiser* (Wagga Wagga), 28 January 1938.

Chapter 31: The new immigrant

1 See Billiet, Meuleman and de Witte, 'The Relationship between Ethnic Threat and Economic Insecurity', pp. 135–61.

2 'Alien Immigration Restriction', *Kalgoorlie Miner*, 1 January 1931.

3 Scullin to J.A. Loughnan, Richmond ALP branch, 25 June 1931, NAA, A458 Q154/19. For immigration policy during the Great Depression, see Roe, *Australia, Britain and Migration*, ch. 7.

4 'Migration Ban', *Northern Star* (Lismore), 5 January 1931.

5 Potts, *The Myth*, pp. 305–6.

6 See, for example, correspondence in NAA, A458 B502/6. For use of Australian-made materials, see correspondence between the Associated Country Sawmillers of NSW and Scullin, May–June 1932, NAA, A458 P502/8.

7   'Australian Natives' Association', *Advocate* (Burnie, Tasmania), 21 April 1930.

8   'Ban on Migrants', *The Week* (Brisbane), 12 December 1930.

9   'Problem of Foreign Films', *Horsham Times* (Victoria), 3 March 1931, reporting on the Annual Report of the Victorian Board of Directors of the ANA.

10 'Australian Musicians', *Age* (Melbourne), 24 May 1930.

11 Williams, *The Quarantined Culture.*

12 See, for example, '100 per cent British', *Herald* (Melbourne), 11 March 1931; 'Preference to Australians', *Age*, 30 June 1931.

13 Potts, *The Myth*, p. 306.

14 British Overseas Settlers' Association of Victoria to Bruce, 26 June 1929, NAA, A786 G61/1.

15 S. Hill, J. Meynell and W. Breakwell to F.J. Condon, MLA, 31 October 1930, NAA, A458 Q154/19.

16 *Report of the Royal Commission on Migrant Land Settlement*, Melbourne: Government Printer, 1933.

17 Mrs W.S. Murdoch, British Migrants' Association, to Scullin, 8 December 1931 (?), NAA, A458 Q154/19.

18 D. Bailey to W.P. Hill, MHR, 3 August 1931, ibid.

19 'Repatriation of Migrants', *West Australian*, 11 July 1931; Hill to Scullin, 7 May 1931, ibid.

20 Mitchell to Scullin, 14 July 1931, ibid.

21 W.J. Duggan, Trades Hall Council, to Scullin, 16 June 1931, ibid.

22 J. Lawler, Trades Hall, Kalgoorlie, to Scullin, 11 May 1931, ibid.

23 F. Daly for Prime Minister, to Mitchell, 23 July 1931, ibid.

24 Arthur Blakeley for Prime Minister, to J.C. Eldridge, 31 August 1931, ibid.

25 'British Settlers Who Want to Return Home', *Herald*, 26 February 1931.

26 E.T. Crutchley to Scullin, 31 July 1931, NAA, A458 Q154/19.

27 Drummond, *Imperial Economic Policy*, p. 131.

28 'Repatriation of Migrants', *Argus* (Melbourne), 23 July 1931.

29 'British Migrants Refused Repatriation Request', *Advertiser and Register* (Adelaide), 23 July 1931.

30 Daly for Prime Minister to Hill, 17 October 1931, A458 Q154/19. This file contains considerable correspondence about the immigrants' citizenship.

31 Gregson, '"It All Started on the Mines"?', pp. 22–4.

32 'Kalgoorlie Outbreak Followed News of His Death', *Mirror* (Perth), 3 February 1934.

33 'Kalgoorlie Riot Damages', *Newcastle Sun*, 22 February 1934.

34 'Crowds Riot', *Kyogle Examiner* (NSW), 2 February 1934.

35 Gregson, '"It All Started on the Mines"?', p. 36.

36 'Kalgoorlie Riot', *Wingham Chronicle and Manning River Observer* (NSW), 6 February 1934.

37 'Inadequate Compensation', *Telegraph* (Brisbane), 7 August 1934.

38 'Kalgoorlie Riot Aftermath', *Red Star* (Perth), 27 July 1934.

39 'The Spirit of the Mob', *Sydney Morning Herald*, 6 February 1934.

40 The following account of Italians in north Queensland draws primarily on Evans, *A History of Queensland*, pp. 176–7; Douglass, *From Italy to Ingham*, passim; Henderson, *Little Italy*, passim; and Menghetti, *The Red North*, passim.

41 Evans, *A History of Queensland*, p. 176.

42 Douglass, *From Italy to Ingham*, p. 165.

43 'Notwithstanding Depression Migrants Still Come', *Daily Standard* (Brisbane), 28 November 1930.

44 Douglass, *From Italy to Ingham*, p. 166.

45 Ibid., p. 168.

46 Henderson, *Little Italy*, p. 126.

47 Quoted in Menghetti, *Red North*, p. 55.

48 'Aliens in the North', *Worker* (Brisbane), 4 June 1925.

49 Henderson, 'More than Rates', pt I, p. 108.

50 'Italians Protest', *Cairns Post*, 10 April 1930.

51 Quoted in Douglass, *From Italy to Ingham*, pp. 170–1.

52 'Sending Money out of Australia', *Truth* (Brisbane), 5 January 1930.

53 Henderson, *Little Italy*, p. 126.

54 Douglass, *From Italy to Ingham*, p. 172.

55 Unless otherwise stated, the following paragraphs draw on Douglass, *From Italy to Ingham*, pp. 174–86.

56 Parliament of Australia, *Reports of the Sugar Inquiry Committee*, pp. 10, 13.

57 Douglass, *From Italy to Ingham*, p. 178, 186.

58 For the strike about Weil's disease, see Griggs, *Global Industry*, pp. 627–8.

59 On women's auxiliaries, see Menghetti, *The Red North*, p. 52.

60 Devanny, *Sugar Heaven*, p. 58.

61 Ibid., p. 81.

Chapter 32: Lyons' first six months

1 Macintyre, *Oxford History*, p. 275, citing the 1933 census.

2 Ibid., p. 298.

3 Gilbert, *The Australian Loan Council*, p. 154.

4 Nairn, *The 'Big Fella'*, p. 254.

5 'State's Default', *Sydney Morning Herald*, 4 February 1932.

6 *Financial Agreement Enforcement Act 1932*.

7 Lyons, House of Representatives, 18 February 1932.

8 Lang, *The Turbulent Years*, p. 186.

9 Lady Game, cited in Foott, *Dismissal of a Premier*, p. 204.

10 For a full study of de Groot, see Moore, *Francis de Groot*.

11 Game to King George V, 29 March 1932, Copies of letters to King George V, Game Family Papers, Mitchell Library, SLNSW, MLMSS 2166 (Safe 3/59).

12 'Captain de Groot', *Toowoomba Chronicle and Darling Downs Gazette*, 22 March 1932.

13 Moore, 'Another Wild Colonial Boy?', p. 140.

14 Museums Victoria, 'Phar Lap: A True Legend', <https://museumsvictoria.com.au/melbournemuseum/whats-on/phar-lap>.

15 'Tragic News of Phar Lap', *Sun* (Sydney), 6 April 1932.

16 Phar Lap (1983) trailer, YouTube, <www.youtube.com/watch?v=pXFJY_2DPo8>.

17 Lang, *The Turbulent Years*, pp. 185, 187.

18 Ibid., pp. 189–90.

19 Ibid., pp. 195, 197.
20 'Nullifying Lang Law', *Herald* (Melbourne), 13 May 1932.
21 Game to King, 18 May 1932, MLMSS 2166.
22 The correspondence between Game and Lang was published in the *Sydney Morning Herald* as 'The Illegal Circular', 14 May 1932.
23 Stone, *1932*, p. 279.
24 'The Illegal Circular', *Sydney Morning Herald*.
25 For a traditional critique, see Cain, *Jack Lang and the Great Depression*.
26 Game to Bavin, 26 October 1930, and Game to Bavin, 30 March 1932 (?), Mitchell Library, SLNSW, ML MSS 2166; Cain, *Jack Lang*, p. 292.
27 Game to John Macphillamy, 30 December 1931, Macphillamy Papers, Mitchell Library, SLNSW, MLMSS 5926.
28 Quoted in Evatt, *The King and his Dominion Governors*, p. 158.
29 Game to King, 18 March 1931, MLMSS 2166.
30 Seven King's Counsels confirmed Game's position, Memorandum 11 April 1932, Game correspondence, 1929–1935, ML MSS 2166.
31 'Governor's Opinion', *Sydney Morning Herald*, 4 May 1932.
32 Lady Game to her mother, quoted in Foott, *Dismissal*, p. 212.
33 A useful analysis can be found in Ward, 'The Dismissal', pp. 160–70.
34 Ibid., p. 163.
35 Evatt, *The King*, p. 168.
36 'Lang Sacked at Moment of Victory', *Labor Daily*, 14 May 1932.
37 McMullin, *The Light on the Hill*, p. 145.
38 'Lang Taxation', *Sydney Morning Herald*, 13 May 1932.
39 'Summary', *Sydney Morning Herald*, 14 May 1932; 'Public Opinion', *Sydney Morning Herald*, 14 May 1932.
40 Cited in 'Press Comment', *Sydney Morning Herald*, 14 May 1932.
41 Foott, *Dismissal*, p. 215.
42 Letter T.W. Melbourne to Game, 17 May 1932, MLMSS 2166.
43 Game to King, 18 May 1932, ibid.
44 Foott, *Dismissal*, pp. 212–13.
45 'The Longest Lane', *Sydney Morning Herald*, 14 May 1932.
46 Stone, *1932*, p. 292.
47 Game to King, 18 May 1932, MLMSS 2166.
48 Lang, *The Turbulent Years*, pp. 186, 205–6.
49 'Dramatic Climax Is Due', *Daily Standard* (Brisbane), 13 May 1932.
50 Lang, *The Turbulent Years*, pp. 208–9.
51 Letter to King, 18 May 1932, MLMSS 2166.
52 Quoted in 'Press Comment', *Sydney Morning Herald*, 14 May 1932.
53 Nairn, *The 'Big Fella'*, p. 265.
54 Ibid., pp. 265–6.
55 This account draws on Strangio, *Neither Power Nor Glory*, pp. 198–200.
56 Hogan, *Memoirs*, p. 9.
57 'Not for Class or Party', *Age* (Melbourne), 27 April 1932.
58 *Herald* cartoon, 21 April 1932, held in Papers of T. Tunnecliffe, SLV, MS MSB315.
59 'Wants Mandate', *Herald* (Melbourne), 7 May 1932; 'Sir Stanley Argyle at Sale', *Gippsland Times*, 12 May 1932.

60 'Labor and the Elections', *Labor Call*, 19 May 1932.

61 'W Forgan Smith, Condemns Deflation', *Daily Standard* (Brisbane), 29 June 1932.

62 Costar, 'Labor, Politics and Unemployment', p. 108.

63 A detailed study is Brockett, 'Douglas Social Credit in Queensland'. The Social Credit Party won 4.6 per cent of the vote in the 1934 national election but won no seats.

64 Head, 'Economic Crisis and Political Legitimacy', p. 14.

Chapter 33: Debt, imperial preference and cricket

1 The following paragraphs draw on Schedvin, *Australia and the Great Depression*, pp. 320–30.

2 'Employment First', *Newcastle Morning Herald and Miners' Advocate*, 30 June 1932.

3 'Stevens Urges Something More Than Economy Cuts', *Newcastle Sun*, 29 June 1932.

4 'Our Army of Pensioners', *Age* (Melbourne), 14 July 1932.

5 'Review of Pensions', *Age*, 2 August 1932.

6 'Old-Age Pensions', *West Australian* (Perth), 29 August 1932.

7 'Old Age and Invalid Pensions', *Telegraph* (Brisbane), 15 August 1932.

8 Schedvin, *Australia and the Great Depression*, pp. 321–3.

9 Ibid., pp. 330–1.

10 For the Ottawa Conference, see Drummond, *Imperial Economic Policy*, chs 5–9; Cumpston, *Lord Bruce*, pp. 97–100; Lee, *Stanley Melbourne Bruce*, pp. 100–2, and Rooth, 'Ottawa and After', pp. 133–57.

11 Rooth, 'Ottawa and After', p. 135.

12 Chamberlain diary, 16, 20 August 1932, Papers of Neville Chamberlain, University of Birmingham Library, GB 150, NC2/17; Self, *The Neville Chamberlain Diary Letters*, vol. III, *The Heir Apparent, 1928–33*, Aldershot, Hampshire: Ashgate, 2002, p. 343.

13 Cumpston, *Lord Bruce*, p. 98; Attard, 'The Limits of Influence', p. 327.

14 Chamberlain diary, 15 August 1932.

15 Lee, *Stanley Melbourne Bruce*, p. 101.

16 Chamberlain diary, 18 August 1932.

17 Cumpston, *Lord Bruce*, pp. 98–9.

18 Self, *The Neville Chamberlain Diary Letters*, p. 343.

19 Chamberlain to Annie, 10 August 1932, Papers of Neville Chamberlain, University of Birmingham Library, GB 150, NC1/26/473.

20 John O'Brien and Kosmos Tsokhas, quoted in Rooth, 'Ottawa and After', p. 137.

21 Ibid., pp. 143–8, 151.

22 Ibid., p. 137.

23 Schedvin, *Australia and the Great Depression*, p. 371.

24 See Drummond, *Imperial Economic Policy*, pp. 391–408, and Attard, 'The Limits of Influence', pp. 325–43.

25 Lee, *Stanley Melbourne Bruce*, pp. 102–3.

26 For details of the debt negotiations, see Lee, *Stanley Melbourne Bruce*, pp. 102–4, Attard, 'Financial Diplomacy', pp. 125–6, and Schedvin, *Australia and the Great Depression*, pp. 354–9. Apart from the conversions, the Commonwealth raised three new long-term loans in London between 1929–30 and 1939 (Gilbert, *The Australian Loan Council*, p. 191).

27 Schedvin, *Australia and the Great Depression*, p. 355.

28 Attard, 'Financial Diplomacy', p. 125.

29 'The Deadly Curse of Interest', *Australian Worker*, 5 October 1932.

30 Lee, *Stanley Melbourne Bruce*, p. 103.

31 Stone, *1932*, p. 376.

32 Lee, *Stanley Melbourne Bruce*, p. 104.

33 Attard, 'Financial Diplomacy', p. 126.

34 'Reduced Interest Rates', *Labor Call*, 13 October 1932.

35 'The Loan Truth Is Out', *Labor Daily*, 18 October 1932.

36 For the bodyline controversy, see especially Sissons and Stoddart, *Cricket and Empire*; and Frith, *Bodyline Autopsy*.

37 Greig Watson, 'Bodyline': 80 Years of Cricket's Greatest Controversy, BBC News, <www.bbc.com/news/uk-england-nottinghamshire-21013615>.

38 'Amazing Outburst', *Canberra Times*, 16 January 1933; 'M.C.C. and Woodfull-Warner Incident', *Kadina and Wallaroo Times* (South Australia), 18 January 1933.

39 Blythe, *The Age of Illusion*, p. 122.

40 Quoted in 'Bodyline', National Museum of Australia, <www.nma.gov.au/defining-moments/resources/bodyline>.

41 Blythe, *The Age of Illusion*, p. 122.

42 Frith, *Bodyline Autopsy*, pp. 248–9.

43 Ibid., p. 382.

44 ABC, 'Bodyline—It's Just Not Cricket', YouTube, <www.youtube.com/watch?v=tE0fjST5S3U>.

45 'The Day England Declared War on Australia' is the subtitle of Derriman, *Bodyline*.

46 ABC, *Bodyline*, episode 1, YouTube, <www.youtube.com/watch?v=R4qJbqsTGoY>.

Chapter 34: Economic recovery

1 A thorough analysis of the various factors can be found in Gregory and Butlin (eds), *Recovery from the Depression*.

2 On the role of currency depreciation, see Eichengreen, 'The Australian Recovery of the 1930s', p. 57.

3 Gregory, 'Overview', in Gregory and Butlin, *Recovery from the Depression*, p. 21.

4 Way, *A New Idea*, pp. 147–51.

5 Davidson, 'Agriculture and the Recovery from the Depression', p. 287.

6 Schedvin, *Australia and the Great Depression*, pp. 293–4.

7 Ibid., p. 291.

8 Ibid., pp. 301–9.

9 See Davidson, 'Agriculture and the Recovery from the Depression', esp. pp. 287–8.

10 Thomas, 'Manufacturing and Economic Recovery', p. 248.

11 Ibid., pp. 263–4, 271.

12 Gregory, 'Overview', p. 7.

13 Schedvin, *Australia and the Great Depression*, pp. 324–5.

14 Pincus, 'Australian Budgetary Policies', p. 186.

15 Macintyre, *Oxford History*, p. 293.

16 Schedvin, *Australia and the Great Depression*, pp. 346–7.

17 McLean, 'Unequal Sacrifice', p. 348.

18 Forster, 'Unemployment and the Australian Economic Recovery of the 1930s', pp. 300–1.

19 Schedvin, *Australia and the Great Depression*, p. 340.
20 Ibid., p. 285.
21 McLean, 'Unequal Sacrifice', pp. 348–51.
22 Clement William Semmler, quoted in Lowenstein, *Weevils in the Flour*, p. 293.
23 Quoted in Potts, *The Myth*, p. 146.
24 See Barrett, *We Were There*, p. 26; Charlton, *The Thirty-Niners*, pp. 20–1.
25 James Murray, 21 July 1994, Knott Depression interviews, NBAC, Z562, Box 3/1.
26 Haig-Muir, 'The Economy at War', ch. 5.
27 Bill Ince, quoted in Lowenstein, *Weevils in the Flour*, p. 268.

Chapter 35: An emergency government without an emergency

 1 Bolton, *A Fine Country*, p. 263.
 2 P.A. Howell, 'Playford, Sir Thomas (Tom) (1896–1981)', *ADB*.
 3 McMullin, *The Light on the Hill*, p. 192.
 4 See also Reynolds, *A History of Tasmania*, pp. 243–4.
 5 For the ALP in Victoria, see Strangio, *Neither Power Nor Glory*, pp. 209–29.
 6 Ibid., pp. 217, 219.
 7 John M. Ward, 'Stevens, Sir Bertram Sydney (1889–1973)', *ADB*.
 8 Costar, 'Labor, Politics and Unemployment', pp. 212–35; Evans, *A History of Queensland*, p. 182.
 9 The following discussion of Lyons, unless otherwise stated, draws on Hart, 'J.A. Lyons', pp. 189–268; and Lloyd, 'The Formation', pp. 220–43.
10 'Pioneer's Monument', *Sydney Morning Herald*, 29 November 1932.
11 Quoted in Hart, 'J.A. Lyons', p. 224.
12 Ibid., p. 223.
13 Menzies, *Afternoon Light*, p. 122.
14 Hart, 'J.A. Lyons', pp. 201–2.
15 Hasluck, *The Government and the People*, p. 109.
16 Hazlehurst, *Menzies Observed*, p. 123.
17 Australian Government, *The Commonwealth Grants Commission*, p. 1.
18 'The Lack of Leadership', *Age* (Melbourne), 30 July 1935.
19 Commonwealth of Australia, *Royal Commission Appointed to Inquire into the Monetary and Banking Systems*, pp. 205–6.
20 Gilbert, *The Australian Loan Council*, pp. 207–8.
21 Watts, *The Foundations*, p. 7.
22 Quoted in Hart, 'J.A. Lyons', p. 193.
23 For detail of Stewart's role, see Watts, *The Foundations*, pp. 11–13.
24 For the Trade Diversion Policy, see Cumpston, 'The Australian–Japanese Dispute', pp. 45–55; Tsokhas, 'Business', pp. 44–51; Tsokhas, 'Protection', pp. 78–81; Tsokhas, 'The Wool Industry', pp. 442–61; O'Brien, 'Empire v. National Interests', pp. 569–86; Ross, 'Australian Overseas Trade', pp. 184–204; and Sissons, 'Manchester v Japan', pp. 480–502.
25 Tsokhas, 'Business', pp. 4, 9; and Tsokhas, 'Protection', p. 80.
26 Norman Cowper, quoted in Sissons, 'Manchester v Japan', p. 483.
27 For Lyons' foreign and defence policies, see Andrews, *Isolationism and Appeasement*; Bird, *J.A. Lyons*. Ross, *Armed and Ready*, provides a useful revisionist analysis of the economic constraints on rearmament.
28 See Ross, *Armed and Ready*, pp. 110 ff.

29 The arguments are developed in Ross, *Armed and Ready*, pp. 125–7.
30 Watts, *The Foundations*, p. 18.
31 Quoted in Hart, 'J.A. Lyons', p. 222.
32 Andrews, *Joseph Lyons*, p. 76.
33 Hart, 'J.A. Lyons', p. 222; Bird, *J.A. Lyons*, p. 333.
34 Marsden, *Joseph Lyons*, p. 16.
35 'Melbourne Mass', *Sydney Morning Herald*, 13 April 1939.
36 Bede Nairn, 'Lang, John Thomas (Jack) (1876–1975)', *ADB*.
37 Robertson, *J.H. Scullin*, pp. 435, 450.
38 The best account of Curtin's activities can be found in Day, *John Curtin*, chs 27–29.
39 Ibid., p. 353.
40 McMullin, *The Light on the Hill*, p. 197.

Epilogue: A resilient nation

1 For discussion of the issue of quiescence, see Spenceley, 'Assessing the Responses', passim.

REFERENCES

Adams, Keith, *Crocodile Safari Man: My Tasmanian Childhood in the Great Depression*, Rockhampton: Central University of Queensland Press, 2000.

Ahamed, Liaquat, *Lords of Finance: The Bankers who Broke the World*, New York: Penguin, 2009.

Aldrich, Daniel P. and Meyer, Michelle A., 'Social Capital and Community Resilience', *American Behavioural Scientist*, vol. 59, no. 2, 2014–15, pp. 254–69.

Amos, Keith, *The New Guard Movement 1931–1935*, Melbourne: Melbourne University Press, 1976.

Andrews, E.M., *The Anzac Illusion: Anglo–Australian Relations during World War I*, Melbourne: Cambridge University Press, 1993.

——*Isolationism and Appeasement in Australia: Reactions to the European Crises, 1935–1939*, Canberra: ANU Press, 1970.

Andrews, Kevin, *Joseph Lyons and the Management of Adversity*, Redland Bay, Qld: Connor Court Publishing, 2016.

Anstey, Frank, *Money Power*, Melbourne: Fraser & Jenkinson, 1921.

——*Red Europe*, Glasgow: Socialist Labour Press, 1921.

Armstrong, Mick, 'The Secret History of Fascism in Australia', *Red Flag*, 14 July 2015, <https://redflag.org.au/article/secret-history-fascism-australia>.

Attard, Bernard, 'The Bank of England and the Origins of the Niemeyer Visit, 1921–1930', *Australian Economic History Review*, vol. 32, no. 1, 1992, pp. 66–83.

——'Financial Diplomacy', in Carl Bridge and Bernard Attard (eds), *Between Empire and Nation: Australia's External Relations from Federation to the Second World War*, Melbourne: Australian Scholarly Press, 2000, pp. 111–32.

——'The Limits of Influence: The Political Economy of Australian Commercial Policy after the Ottawa Conference', *Australian Historical Studies*, vol. 29, no. 111, 1998, pp. 325–43.

Australian Bureau of Statistics, *Year Book Australia*, 1929–32, Melbourne: Government Printer.

Australian Government, Commonwealth Grants Commission, *The Commonwealth Grants Commission: The Last 25 Years*, Canberra: Commonwealth of Australia, 2008.

Baird, Julia, *Phosphorescence: On Awe, Wonder and Things that Sustain You When the World Goes Dark*, Sydney: Fourth Estate, 2020.

Barnes, Felicity, 'Bringing Another Empire Alive? The Empire Marketing Board and the Construction of Dominion Identity, 1926–33', *Journal of Imperial and Commonwealth History*, vol. 42, no. 1, pp. 61–85.

Barrett, John, *We Were There: Australian Soldiers of World War II Tell Their Stories*, Melbourne: Viking, 1987.

Bartrop, Paul, *Bolt from the Blue: Australia, Britain and the Chanak Crisis*, Sydney: Halstead Press, 2002.

Batt, Neil, 'Tasmania's Depression Elections', *Labour History*, no. 17, 1969, pp. 111–20.

Beaumont, Joan, *Broken Nation: Australians and the Great War*, Sydney: Allen & Unwin, 2013.

——'Remembering the Resilient', in Carolyn Holbrook and Keir Reeves (ed.), *The Great War: Aftermath and Commemoration*, Sydney: UNSW Press, 2019, pp. 135–53.

——'The Returned Soldier as a Site of Memory: Employment Preference and War Pensions during the Great Depression in Australia', *Australian Historical Studies*, vol. 52, no. 1, 2021, pp. 8–26.

——'Whatever Happened to Patriotic Women, 1914–1918?', *Australian Historical Studies*, vol. 31, no. 115, 2000, pp. 273–86.

Berkes, Fikret and Ross, Helen, 'Community Resilience: Toward an Integrated Approach', *Society & Natural Resources*, vol. 26, no. 1, 2013, pp. 5–20.

Berzins, Baiba, 'Douglas Credit and the A.L.P.', *Labour History*, no. 17, 1969, pp. 148–60.

Billiet, Jaak, Meuleman, Bart and de Witte, Hans, 'The Relationship between Ethnic Threat and Economic Insecurity in Time of Economic Crisis', *Migration Studies*, vol. 2, no. 2, 2014, pp. 135–61.

Bird, David S., *J.A. Lyons—the 'Tame Tasmanian': Appeasement and Rearmament in Australia, 1932–39*, Melbourne: Australian Scholarly Publishing, 2008.

Blackmore, Kate, *The Dark Pocket of Time: War, Medicine and the Australian State, 1914–1935*, Adelaide: Lythrum Press, 2008.

Blaikie, George, *Remember Smith's Weekly? A Biography of an Uninhibited National Australian Newspaper, Born 1 March 1919, Died 28 October 1950*, Adelaide: Rigby, 1975.

Bland, F., 'Unemployment Relief in Australia', *International Labour Review*, vol. 30, no. 1, 1934, reproduced in Louis and Turner, *The Depression of the 1930s*, Sydney: Cassell, 1968, pp. 97–112.

Bland, F.A. and Mills, R.C., 'Financial Reconstruction: An Examination of the Plan Adopted at the Premiers' Conference, 1931', *Economic Record*, vol. 7, no. 2, 1931, pp. 161–76.

Blythe, Ronald, *The Age of Illusion: England in the Twenties and Thirties 1919–1940*, London: Hamish Hamilton, 1963.

Bolton, Geoffrey, *A Fine Country to Starve In*, Perth: UWA Press, 1994, first published 1972.

Bongiorno, Frank, 'Post-war Economies (Australia)', 1914–18 Online, International Encyclopedia of the First World War, <https://encyclopedia.1914-1918-online.net/article/post-war_economies_australia>.

——'Search for a Solution, 1923–29', in Alison Bashford and Stuart Macintyre (eds), *The Cambridge History of Australia*, vol. 2, *The Commonwealth of Australia*, Cambridge: Cambridge University Press, 2013, pp. 64–87.

——*The Sex Lives of Australians: A History*, Melbourne: Black Inc., 2012.

Bordo, Michael D., Goldin, Claudia and White, Eugene N. (eds), *The Defining Moment: The Great Depression and the American Economy in the Twentieth Century*, Chicago: University of Chicago Press, 1998.

Botterill, Linda and Cockfield, Geoff, 'From "Unstable" to "Stable" Minority Government: Reflections on the Role of the Nationals in Federal Coalition Governments', *Australian Journal of Politics and History*, vol. 61, no. 1, 2015, pp. 53–66.

Bottoms, T., 'The Battle of Parramatta Park, Cairns, North Qld, 1932', <www.researchgate.net/publication/301786686_The_Battle_of_Parramatta_Park_Cairns_North_Qld_1932>.

——*Cairns: City of the South Pacific: A History 1770–1995*, Cairns: Bunu Bunu Press, 2015.

REFERENCES

Bowden, Bradley, 'The Rise and Decline of Australian Unionism: A History of Industrial Labour from the 1820s to 2010', *Labour History*, no. 100, 2011, pp. 51–82.

Boyce, Robert, *The Great Interwar Crisis and the Collapse of Globalization*, London: Palgrave Macmillan, 2009.

Brady, Edwin J., *Australia Unlimited*, Melbourne: George Robertson, nd (1918?).

Brett, Judith, *Australian Liberals and the Moral Middle Class: From Alfred Deakin to John Howard*, Cambridge: Cambridge University Press, 2003.

Brockett, Richard, 'Douglas Social Credit in Queensland, 1929–1939', BA(Hons) thesis, University of Queensland, 1993.

Broek, Diane van den, 'Partners in Protest: The Case of the 1929 Timber Workers' Strike', *Labour and Industry*, vol. 7, no. 2, 1996, pp. 145–63.

——'Trouble on the Bay: Glebe's Community Response to the 1929 Timber Strike', *Leichhardt Historical Journal*, no. 19, 1975, pp. 3–8, 33–5.

Broome, Richard, *Aboriginal Australians: A History since 1788,* 4th edn, Sydney: Allen & Unwin, 2010.

——'"No One Thinks of Us": The Framlingham Aboriginal Community in the Great Depression', in P. Bastien and R. Bell (eds.), *Through Depression and War: The United States and Australia*, Sydney: Australian and American Fulbright Commission & Australian and New Zealand American Studies Association, 2002.

Broomhill, Ray, *Unemployed Workers: A Social History of the Great Depression in Adelaide*, Brisbane: Queensland University Press, 1978.

——'Unemployment and the Great Depression in Adelaide', Labour History South Australia, 13 May 2018, <http://communitywebs.org/labourhistory/wp-content/uploads/2018/05/Ray-Broomhill-13-May-2018.pdf>.

Bush, Janine, 'Crisis of Moral Authority: The Ladies Benevolent Societies in the Victorian Welfare Field, 1920–1939', PhD thesis, Australian National University, 2002.

Butlin, M.W. and Boyce, P.M., 'Monetary Policy in Depression and Recovery', Working Papers in Economic History, no. 44, Canberra: Australian National University, 1985.

Cain, Frank, *Jack Lang and the Great Depression*, Melbourne: Australian Scholarly Publishing, 2005.

Cain, Neville, 'Australian Economic Advice in 1930: Liberal and Radical Alternatives', Working Papers in Economic History, no. 78, Canberra: Australian National University, 1987.

—— 'The Australian Economists and Controversy over Depression Policy, 1930—Early 1931', Working Papers in Economic History, no. 79, Canberra: Australian National University, 1987.

Campbell, Eric, *The New Road*, Sydney: Briton Publications, 1934.

——*The Rallying Point: My Story of the New Guard*, Melbourne: Melbourne University Press, 1965.

Cannon, Michael, *The Human Face of the Great Depression*, Mornington: Today's Australia Publishing Company, 1996.

Carmichael, Gordon A., 'So Many Children: Colonial and Post-colonial Demographic Patterns', in Kay Saunders and Raymond Evans, *Gender Relations in Australia: Domination and Negotiation*, Sydney: Harcourt Brace Jovanovich, 1992, pp. 103–43.

Carroll, J.J. (Digger), *My Ninety Years*, Ganmain, NSW: self-published, 1983.

Carter, Zachary, *The Price of Peace: Money, Democracy, and the Life of John Maynard Keynes*, New York: Random House, 2020.

Castle, R.G. and Hagan, J.S., 'Dependence and Independence', in Anne Curthoys and Andrew Markus (eds), *Who Are Our Enemies? Racism and the Australian Working Class*, Sydney: Hale & Iremonger, 1978, pp. 158–62.

Cathcart, Michael, *Defending the National Tuckshop: Australia's Secret Army Intrigue of 1931*, Melbourne: McPhee Gribble, 1988.

Charlton, Peter, *The Thirty-Niners*, Melbourne: Macmillan, 1981.

Childers, Thomas and Weiss, Eugene, 'Voters and Violence: Political Violence and the Limits of National Socialist Mobilization', *German Studies Review*, vol. 13, no. 3, 1990, pp. 481–98.

Clarke, Hugh V., *The Broke and the Broken*, Brisbane: Boolarong Publications, 1982.

Cohen, Deborah, *The War Come Home: Disabled Veterans in Britain and Germany, 1914–1939*, Los Angeles: University of California Press, 2001.

Coleman, William, Cornish, Selwyn and Hagger, Alf, *Giblin's Platoon: The Trials and Triumph of the Economist in Australian Public Life*, Canberra: ANU E-press, 2006.

Commonwealth of Australia, *Report of the Royal Commission into the Monetary and Banking Systems at Present in Operation in Australia*, Canberra: Government Printer, 1937.

Conley, Tom, *The Vulnerable Country: Australia and the Global Economy*, Sydney: UNSW Press, 2009.

Conlon, R.M. and Perkins, John, 'Australian Governments and Automotive Manufacturing, 1919–1939', *Australian Journal of Politics and History*, vol. 45, no. 3, 1999, pp. 376–91.

Connor, John S., 'The War Munitions Supply Company of Western Australia and the Popular Movement to Manufacture Artillery Ammunition in the British Empire in the First World War', *Journal of Imperial and Commonwealth History*, vol. 39, no. 5, 2011, pp. 795–813.

Connor, John, Stanley, Peter and Yule, Peter, *The War at Home*, vol. 4, *The Centenary History of Australia and the Great War*, ed. Jeffrey Grey, Melbourne: Oxford University Press, 2015.

Constantine, S., 'Bringing the Empire Alive: The EMB and Imperial Propaganda, 1926–33', in J.M. McKenzie (ed.), *Imperialism and Popular Culture*, Manchester: Manchester University Press, 1986, pp. 192–231.

Cook, Peter, 'Labor and the Premiers' Plan', *Labour History*, no. 17, 1969, pp. 97–110.

——'The Scullin Government 1929–1932', PhD thesis, Australian National University, 1971.

Cooper, D.W., 'The Armidale Electorate in the New South Wales Election of 1932', *Armidale and District Historical Society Journal*, no. 30, 1987, pp. 47–59.

Copland, Douglas, *Australia in the World Crisis 1929–1933*, Cambridge: Cambridge University Press, 1934, 2013 reissue.

——*The Banking System of Australia*, Holt: New York, 1929.

——*Developments in Economic Thought*, Melbourne: Economic Society of Australia and New Zealand, 1950.

——'The Gold Standard and Australian Exchange', *AQ: Australian Quarterly*, vol. 80, no. 5, 2008, pp. 30–4, first published 1931.

Cornish, Selwyn, *The Evolution of Central Banking in Australia*, Sydney: Reserve Bank of Australia, 2010.

Cornish, Selwyn and Coleman, William, 'Making a Land Fit for a Gold Standard: Monetary Policy in Australia, 1920–1925', Canberra: ANU, <https://ideas.repec.org/p/auu/hpaper/027.html>.

Costar, Brian, 'Christianity in Crisis: Queensland Churches during the Great Depression', *Journal of the Royal Historical Society of Queensland*, vol. 13, no. 6, 1988, pp. 201–13.

REFERENCES

—'Controlling the Victims: The Authorities and the Unemployed in Queensland During the Great Depression', *Labour History*, no. 56, 1989, pp. 1–14.

—'The Great Depression: Was Queensland Different?', *Labour History*, no. 26, 1974, pp. 32–48.

—'Labor, Politics and Unemployment: Queensland during the Great Depression', PhD thesis, University of Queensland, 1981.

Cottle, Drew, *Life Can Be Oh So Sweet on the Sunny Side of the Street: A Study of the Rich of Woollahra During the Great Depression 1928–1934*, London: Minerva Press, 1998.

Cottle, Drew and Keys, Angela, 'Anatomy of an "Eviction Riot" in Sydney during the Great Depression', *Journal of Royal Australian Historical Society*, vol. 94, no. 2, 2008, pp. 186–200.

Cotton, James (ed.), *Documents on Australian Foreign Policy, 1920–30, Australia and the World, 1920–1930*, Sydney: Department of Foreign Affairs and Trade, 2019.

—'William Morris Hughes, Empire and Nationalism: The Legacy of the First World War', *Australian Historical Studies*, vol. 46, no. 1, 2015, pp. 100–18.

Cowdell, John, 'The Anglican Church in Western Australia during the Great Depression', *Studies in Western Australian History*, no. 9, 1987, pp. 83–93.

Crafts, Nicholas and Fearon, Peter, 'Lessons from the 1930s Great Depression', *Oxford Review of Economic Policy*, vol. 26, no. 3, 2010, pp. 285–317.

Crisp, L.F., 'The Appointment of Sir Isaac Isaacs as Governor-General of Australia, 1930: J.H. Scullin's Account of the Buckingham Palace Interview', *Historical Studies*, vol. 11, no. 42, 1964, pp. 253–7.

Crotty, Martin, 'The Returned Sailors' and Soldiers' Imperial League of Australia, 1916–46', in Martin Crotty and Marina Larrson (eds), *Anzac Legacies: Australians and the Aftermath of War*, Melbourne: Australian Scholarly Publishing, 2010, pp. 166–86.

—'"What More Do You Want?" Billy Hughes and Gilbert Dyett in Late 1919', *History Australia*, vol. 16, no. 1, 2019, pp. 52–71.

Crotty, Martin and Edele, Mark, 'Total War and Entitlement: Towards a Global History of Veteran Privilege', *Australian Journal of Politics and History*, vol. 59, no. 1, 2013, pp. 15–32.

Crotty, Martin, Diamant, Neil and Edele, Mark, *The Politics of Veteran Benefits in the Twentieth Century: A Comparative History*, Ithaca and London: Cornell University Press, 2020.

Cuffe, Honae, 'The 1936 Trade Diversion Policy: China, the United States and Australia: A Balancing Act in Retrospect, *Australian Policy and History*, <https://aph.org.au/2018/07/the-1936-trade-diversion-policy-china-the-united-states-and-australia-a-balancing-act-in-retrospect>.

Cumpston, I.M., The Australian–Japanese Dispute of the Nineteen-thirties', *Australian Quarterly*, vol. 29, no. 2, 1957, pp. 45–55.

—*Lord Bruce of Melbourne*, Melbourne: Longman Cheshire, 1989.

Cunningham, Matthew, 'Australian Fascism? A Revisionist Analysis of the New Guard', *Politics, Religion & Ideology*, vol. 13, no. 3, 2012, pp. 375–93.

—'The Reactionary and the Radical: A Comparative Analysis of Mass Conservative Mobilisation in Australia and New Zealand during the Great Depression', PhD thesis, Victoria University of Wellington, New Zealand, 2015.

Curson, Peter and McCracken, Kevin, 'An Australian Perspective of the 1918–1919 Influenza Pandemic', *NSW Public Health Bulletin*, vol. 17, pp. 103–7.

Curthoys, Ann and Moore, Clive, 'Working for White People: An Historiographic Essay on Aboriginal and Torres Strait Islander Labour', *Labour History*, no. 69, 1995, pp. 1–29.

Darling, Barbara, 'The Church of England in Melbourne and the Great Depression 1929 to 1935', MA thesis, University of Melbourne, 1982.

Davidson, B.R., 'Agriculture and the Recovery from the Depression', in R.G. Gregory and N.G. Butlin (eds), *Recovery from the Depression: Australian and the World Economy in the 1930s*, Cambridge: Cambridge University Press, 1988, pp. 273–88.

Day, David, *John Curtin: A Life*, Sydney: HarperCollins, 1999.

Day, Lincoln H., 'Divorce in Australia', *Australian Quarterly*, vol. 35, no. 2, 1963, pp. 57–66.

Deacon, Desley, *Managing Gender: The State, the New Middle Class and Women Workers, 1830–1930*, Oxford: Oxford University Press, 1989.

Denning, Warren, *Caucus Crisis: The Rise and Fall of the Scullin Government*, Sydney: Cumberland Argus, 1937.

Derriman, Philip, *Bodyline: The Day England Declared War on Australia*, Sydney: Collins, 1984.

Devanny, Jean, *Sugar Heaven*, Melbourne: Vulgar Press, 2002, first published 1936.

Dickenson, Jackie, '"God Give Us Men": Attitudes towards Parliamentary Representation in Australia, 1929–1933', *History Australia*, vol. 8, no. 2, pp. 87–105.

Dickey, Brian and Martin, Elaine, *Building Community: A History of the Port Adelaide Central Mission*, Adelaide: Port Adelaide Wesley Centre, 1999.

Dixson, Miram, 'Rothbury', *Labour History*, no. 17, 1969, pp. 14–26.

——'The Timber Strike of 1929', *Historical Studies*, vol. 10, no. 40, 1963, pp. 479–92.

Douglas, Tom, *Scapegoats: Transferring Blame*, London: Routledge, 1995.

Douglass, William A., *From Italy to Ingham: Italians in North Queensland*, Brisbane: University of Queensland Press, 1995.

Drummond, Ian M., *Imperial Economic Policy 1917–1939: Studies in Expansion and Protection*, London: George Allen & Unwin, 1974.

Durack, Mary, *The Rock and the Sand*, London: Constable, 1969.

Dyster, Barrie and Meredith, David, *Australia in the Global Economy: Continuity and Change*, 2nd edn, Melbourne: Cambridge University Press, 2012.

Eather, Wayne and Cottle, Drew, '"As Good as Cash All the Time": Trapping Rabbits in South-Eastern Australia, 1870–1950', *Labour History*, no. 111, 2016, pp. 125–48.

Eckermann, C.V., *Kooniba: The Mission and the Nunga People*, self-published, 2010.

Edele, Mark and Gerwarth, Robert, 'The Limits of Demobilization: Global Perspectives on the Aftermath of the Great War', *Journal of Contemporary History*, vol. 50, no. 1, 2015, pp. 3–14.

Egan, Ted, *Justice All Their Own: The Caledon Bay and Woodah Island Killings 1932–1933*, Melbourne: Melbourne University Press, 1996.

Eichengreen, Barry. 'The Australian Recovery of the 1930s in International Comparative Perspective', in R.G. Gregory and N.G. Butlin, (eds), *Recovery from the Depression: Australia and the World Economy in the 1930s*, Cambridge: Cambridge University Press, 1988, pp. 33–60.

——*Golden Fetters: The Gold Standard and the Great Depression 1919–1939*, Oxford: Oxford University Press, 1992.

Eichengreen, Barry and Portes, Richard, 'Dealing with Debt: The 1930s and the 1980s, NBER Working Paper no. 2867, Cambridge, Mass., 1989, pp. 21–4, <www.nber.org/papers/w2867>.

Eichengreen, Barry and Sachs, J., 'Exchange Rates and the Economic Recovery in the 1930s', *Journal of Economic History*, vol. 45, no. 4, 1985, pp. 925–46.

REFERENCES

Ekins, Ashley, 'Fighting to Exhaustion: Morale, Discipline and Combat Effectiveness in the Armies of 1918', in Ashley Ekins (ed.), *1918 Year of Victory: The End of the Great War and the Shaping of History*, Auckland: Exisle, 2010, pp. 111–29.

Elder, Smith and Co., Limited: The First Hundred Years, Adelaide: Elder, Smith and Co., 1940.

Evans, Raymond, *A History of Queensland*, Cambridge: Cambridge University Press, 2007.

——*The Red Flag Riots: A Study of Intolerance*, Brisbane: University of Queensland Press, 1988.

Evans, Richard, '"A Menace to this Realm": The New Guard and the New South Wales Police, 1931–32', *History Australia*, vol. 5, no. 3, 2008, 76.1–76.20.

——'"Murderous Coppers": Police, Industrial Disputes and the 1929 Rothbury Shootings', *History Australia*, vol. 9, no. 1, 2012 pp. 176–200.

Evatt, Herbert Vere, *The King and His Dominion Governors: A Study of the Reserve Powers of the Crown in Great Britain and the Dominions*, Melbourne: F.W. Cheshire, 1967, first published 1936.

Everett, Guerra, 'Trading under the Laws of Australia', *Trade Information Bulletin*, no. 412, United States Department of Commerce, 1926.

Fahey, Charles and Lack, John, 'The Great Strike of 1917 in Victoria: Looking Fore and Aft, and from Below', *Labour History*, no. 106, 2014, pp. 69–97.

Fathi, Romain, *Our Corner of the Somme: Australia at Villers-Bretonneux*, Cambridge: Cambridge University Press, 2019.

Fielding, Trisha, *Queen City of the North: A History of Townsville*, Townsville: self-published, 2016.

Fishbank, Price V., 'Relief during the Great Depression in Australia and America', *Australian Economic History Review*, vol. 52, no. 3, 2021, pp. 221–49.

Fisher, Chay and Kent, Christopher, 'Two Depressions, One Banking Collapse', Research Discussion Paper RDP 1999-06, Reserve Bank of Australia, <www.rba.gov.au/publications/rdp/1999/1999-06.html>.

Fisher, Nick, 'Lacking the Will to Power? Australian Anti-communists 1917–1935', *Journal of Australian Studies*, vol. 26, no. 72, pp. 221–33.

Fitzgerald, Ross, *A History of Queensland from 1915 to the 1980s*, Brisbane: University of Queensland Press, 1984.

——*'Red Ted': The Life of E.G. Theodore*, Brisbane: University of Queensland Press, 1994.

Fitz-Gibbon, Bryan and Gizycki, Marianne, 'A History of Last-resort Lending and Other Support for Troubled Financial Institutions in Australia', Research Discussion Paper RDP 2001-07, Reserve Bank of Australia, section 8, <www.rba.gov.au/publications/rdp/2001/2001-07>.

Fitzhardinge, L.F., *William Morris Hughes: A Political Biography*, vol. II, *The Little Digger 1914–1952*, London: Angus & Robertson, 1979.

Foley, Meredith Anne, 'The Women's Movement in New South Wales and Victoria, 1918–1938', PhD thesis, University of Sydney, 1985.

Foott, Bethia, *Dismissal of a Premier: The Philip Game Papers*, Sydney: Morgan Publications, 1968.

Forster, C., 'Unemployment and the Australian Economic Recovery of the 1930s', in R.G. Gregory and N.G. Butlin, *Recovery from the Depression: Australia and the World Economy in the 1930s*, Cambridge: Cambridge University Press, 1988, pp. 289–310.

Foster, Robert, 'Contested Destinies: Aboriginal Advocacy in South Australia's Interwar Years', *Aboriginal History*, vol. 42, 2018, pp. 73–95.

Fox, Charlie, *Fighting Back: The Politics of the Unemployed in Victoria in the Great Depression*, Melbourne: Melbourne University Press, 2000.

Fox, L. (ed.), *Depression Down Under*, Sydney: Hale & Iremonger, 1992.

Frances, Raelene, 'Christianity on the Coalfields: A Case Study of Collie in the Great Depression', *Studies in Western Australian History*, no. 9, 1987, pp. 115–26.

——'The History of Female Prostitution in Australia', in Roberta Perkins, Garrett Prestage, Rachel Sharp and Frances Lovejoy, *Sex Work and Sex Workers in Australia*, Sydney: UNSW Press, 1994, pp. 27–52.

——*Selling Sex: A Hidden History of Prostitution*, Sydney: UNSW Press, 2007.

Fraser, Don, *Working for the Dole: Commonwealth Relief during the Great Depression*, Canberra: National Archives of Australia, 2020.

Frith, David, *Bodyline Autopsy: The Full Story of the Most Sensational Test Cricket Series: Australia v England 1932–33*, Sydney: ABC Books, 2002.

Gahan, Peter, 'Did Arbitration Make for Dependent Unionism? Evidence from Historical Case Studies', *Journal of Industrial Relations*, vol. 38, no. 4, 1996, pp. 648–98.

Galbraith, James K., *The Great Crash, 1929*, Boston and New York: Mariner, 2009, first published 1954.

Galenson, Walter and Zellner, Arnold, 'International Comparison of Unemployment Rates', in *The Measurement and Behaviour of Unemployment*, Cambridge, Mass.: National Bureau of Economic Research, 1957, pp. 439–584.

Garton, Stephen, *The Cost of War: Australians Return*, Melbourne: Oxford University Press, 1996.

——'Demobilization and Empire: Empire Nationalism and Soldier Citizenship in Australia after the First World War—in Dominion Context', *Journal of Contemporary History*, vol. 50, no. 1, 2015, pp. 124–43.

Gerwarth, Robert and Horne, John, 'The Great War and Paramilitarism in Europe', *Contemporary European History*, vol. 19, no. 3, 2010, pp. 267–73.

Gibson, Geoffrey C., *Tolley: A Family of Winemakers: A History of Tolley Wines, 1892–1992*, Hope Valley, SA: Tolley Wines, 1994.

Gifford, Peter, 'The Effects of the British Seamen's Strike of 1925 on Fremantle', *The Great Circle*, vol. 14, no. 2, 1992, pp. 73–87.

Gilbert, R.S. *The Australian Loan Council in Federal Fiscal Adjustments, 1890–1965*, Canberra: ANU Press, 1973.

Gill, Alan, *Likely Lads and Lasses: Youth Migration to Australia, 1911–1983*, Sydney: BBM Ltd, 2005.

Gleeson, D.J., 'Catholic Charity during the 1930s Great Depression', *Australasian Catholic Record*, vol. 73, no. 1, 1996, pp. 68–80.

Golder, Hilary and Allen, Judith, 'Prostitution in New South Wales, 1870–1932: Restructuring an Industry', *Refractory Girl*, nos 18–19, 1979–80, pp. 17–25.

Gollan, Robin, *The Coalminers of New South Wales: A History of the Union, 1860–1960*, Melbourne: Melbourne University Press in association with the Australian National University, 1963.

——*Revolutionaries and Reformists: Communism and the Australian Labour Movement, 1920–1955*, Richmond, Surrey: Richmond Publishing, 1975.

Goodall, Heather, *Invasion to Embassy: Land in Aboriginal Politics in New South Wales, 1770–1972*, Sydney: Sydney University Press, 2008.

Graham, B.D., *The Formation of the Australian Country Parties*, Canberra: ANU Press, 1966.

REFERENCES

Gray, Sheilah, *Newcastle in the Great Depression*, Newcastle: Council of the City of Newcastle, 1984.

Gregory, R.G. and Butlin, N.G. (eds), *Recovery from the Depression: Australian and the World Economy in the 1930s*, Cambridge: Cambridge University Press, 1988.

Gregson, Sarah, "'It All Started on the Mines"? The 1934 Kalgoorlie Riots Revisited', *Labour History*, no. 80, 2001, pp. 21–40.

Griggs, Peter D., *Global Industry, Local Innovation: The History of Sugar Cane Production in Australia, 1820–1995*, Bern: Peter Land, 2011.

Grove, F.T., 'Queensland and the Moore Government', *Australian Quarterly*, vol. 4, no. 13, 1932, pp. 81–97.

Reviews of Robert Boyce, *The Great Interwar Crisis and the Collapse of Globalization*, in *H-Diplo Roundtable Review* vol. XII, no. 12, 2011, <https://issforum.org/roundtables/PDF/Roundtable-XII-12.pdf>.

Haebich, Anna, *For Their Own Good: Aborigines and Government in the South West of Western Australia 1900–1940*, Perth: UWA Press, 1992.

Haig-Muir, Marnie, 'The Economy at War', in Joan Beaumont (ed.) *Australia's War 1939–45*, Sydney: Allen & Unwin, 1995, pp. 93–124.

Harper, Marjorie, *Douglas Copland: Scholar, Economist, Diplomat*, Melbourne: Miegunyah Press, 2013.

Hart, Philip R., 'J.A. Lyons: A Political Biography', PhD thesis, Australian National University, 1967.

——'Lyons: Labor minister: Leader of the U.A.P.', *Labour History*, no. 17, 1969, pp. 37–51.

Haskins, Victoria, "'A Better Chance"? Sexual Abuse and the Apprenticeship of Aboriginal Girls under the NSW Aborigines Protection Board', *Aboriginal History*, vol. 28, 2004, pp. 33–58.

——"'& So We Are 'Slave Owners'!" Employers and the NSW Aborigines Protection Board Trust Funds', *Labour History*, no. 88, 2005, pp. 147–64.

Hasluck, Paul, *The Government and the People 1939–1941*, vol. 1, series 4 (Civil), *Australia and the War of 1939–1945*, Canberra: Australian War Memorial, 1952.

Hawkins, John, 'Ted Theodore: The Proto-Keynesian', *Economic Round-up*, no. 1, 2010, pp. 91–110.

Hazlehurst, Cameron, *Menzies Observed*, Sydney: George Allen & Unwin, 1979.

Head, Brian, 'Economic Crisis and Political Legitimacy: The 1931 Federal Election', *Journal of Australian Studies*, vol. 2, no. 3, 1978, pp. 14–29.

Hearn, Mark and Knowles, Harry, *One Big Union: A History of the Australian Workers Union 1886–1994*, Melbourne: Cambridge University Press, 1996.

Henderson, Anne, *Joseph Lyons: The People's Prime Minister*, Sydney: NewSouth, 2011.

Henderson, Lyn, *Little Italy: Italians in Ingham, 1921–1939*, Sydney: Common Ground, 1995.

——'More than Rates, Roads and Rubbish: A History of Local Government in Action in Thuringowa Shire, 1879–1985', PhD thesis, James Cook University, 1992.

Hirst, John, 'Communism and Australia's Historians', *Quadrant*, vol. 34, no. 4, 1990, pp. 26–31.

Hodson, Sally, 'Nyungars and Work: Aboriginal Experiences in the Rural Economy of the Great Southern Region of Western Australia', *Aboriginal History*, vol. 17, no. 1, 1993, pp. 73–92.

Hogan, E.J., *Memoirs of Honorable E.J. Hogan*, Melbourne: Parliamentary Library, nd.

Holbrook, Carolyn, *Anzac: The Unauthorised Biography*, Sydney: NewSouth, 2014.

Holder, R.F., *Bank of New South Wales: A History*, vol. II, *1894–1970*, Sydney: Angus & Robertson, 1970.

Holland, Alison, *Breaking the Silence: Aboriginal Defenders and the Settler State, 1905–1939*, Melbourne: Melbourne University Press, 2019.

Hopgood, Don, 'Lang Labor in South Australia', *Labour History*, no. 17, 1969, pp. 161–73.

Horne, John, 'Demobilizing the Mind: France and the Legacy of the Great War, 1919–1939', George Rudé Society, 2017, <https://h-france.net/rude/vol2/horne2>.

Huelin, Frank, *Keep Moving: An Odyssey*, Sydney: Australasian Book Society, 1973.

Hunt, Harold, *The Story of Rotary in Australia 1921–1971*, Sydney (?): Rotary, 1971.

Hynes, William, Jacks, David S. and O'Rourke, Kevin H., 'Commodity Market Disintegration in the Inter-war Period', *European Review of Economic History*, vol. 16, no. 2, 2012, pp. 119–43.

Inglis, K.S., *Sacred Places: War Memorials in the Australian Landscape*, Melbourne: Melbourne University Press, 2005, first published 1998.

James, Harold, *The End of Globalization: Lessons from the Great Depression*, Cambridge, Mass: Harvard University Press, 2002.

Jessop, David, 'The Colonial Stock Act of 1900: A symptom of the new imperialism?', *Journal of Imperial and Commonwealth History*, vol. 4, no. 2, 1976, pp. 154–63.

Jones, Benjamin T., Bongiorno, Frank and Uhr, John, *Elections Matter: Ten Federal Elections that Shaped Australia*, Melbourne: Monash University Publishing, 2018.

Jorgesen, Erika and Sachs, Jeffrey, 'Default and Renegotiation of Latin American Foreign Bonds in the Interwar Period', NBER Working Paper no. 2636, Cambridge, Mass., 1988, pp. 21–2.

Kaplan, Howard B., 'Toward an Understanding of Resilience: A Critical Review of Definitions and Models', in Meyer D. Glantz and Jeannette L. Johnson (eds), *Resilience and Development: Positive Life Adaptations*, New York: Kluwer Academic Publications, 2002, pp. 17–83.

Kennedy, Sally, 'Segregation for Integration: Women and Work in Factories and Shops in Western Australia during the Great Depression', *Studies in Western Australian History*, no. 5, 1982, pp. 38–47.

Kimber, Julie, 'Poor Laws: A Historiography of Vagrancy in Australia', *History Compass*, vol. 11, no. 8, 2013, pp. 537–50.

Kindleberger, Charles P., *The World in Depression 1929–1939*, London: Allen Lane, 1973.

King, Terry, 'The Tarring and Feathering of J.K. McDougall: "Dirty Tricks" in the 1919 Federal Election', *Labour History*, vol. 45, 1983, pp. 54–67.

Kirk, Neville, '"Australians for Australia": The Right, the Labor Party and Contested Loyalties to Nation and Empire in Australia, 1917 to the early, 1930s', *Labour History*, no. 91, 2006, pp. 95–111.

Kristianson, G.L. *The Politics of Patriotism: The Pressure Group Activities of the Returned Servicemen's League*, Canberra: ANU Press, 1966.

Lack, John (ed.), *Anzac Remembered: Selected Essays of K.S. Inglis*, Melbourne: University of Melbourne, 1998.

——*A History of Footscray*, Melbourne: Hargreen Publishing Company in conjunction with the City of Footscray, 1991.

Lake, Marilyn, *The Limits of Hope: Soldier Settlement in Victoria 1915–38*, Melbourne: Oxford University Press, 1987.

——'The Power of Anzac', in M. McKernan and M. Browne (eds), *Australia: Two Centuries of*

REFERENCES

War and Peace, Canberra: Australian War Memorial in association with Allen & Unwin Australia, 1988, pp. 194–222.

Lamm, Gilda, 'The Role of the Salvation Army in Melbourne during the Depression Years, 1928–1933', Honours essay, University of Melbourne School of History, 1972.

Lang, J.T., *The Great Bust: The Depression of the Thirties*, Sydney: Angus & Robertson, 1962.

——*The Turbulent Years*, Sydney: Alpha Books, 1970.

Lawrence, Jon, 'Forging a Peaceable Kingdom: War, Violence, and Fear of Brutalization in Post–First World War Britain', *Journal of Modern History*, vol. 75, no. 3, 2003, pp. 557–89.

Lee, David, *Stanley Melbourne Bruce: Australian Internationalist*, London: Continuum, 2010.

——'States Rights and Australia's Adoption of the Statute of Westminster, 1931–1942', *History Australia*, vol. 13, no. 2, 2016, pp. 258–74.

Ling, Ted, *Commonwealth Government Records about the Northern Territory*, Canberra: National Archives of Australia, 2011.

Linn, Rob, *Community of Strength: Loxton and its People*, Waikerie, SA: District Council of Loxton Waikerie, 2007.

——*The History of the Adelaide Benevolent and Strangers' Friend Society 1849–2012*, Adelaide: Adelaide Benevolent and Strangers' Friend Society, 2012.

——*Those Turbulent Years: A History of the City of Adelaide, 1929–1979*, Adelaide: Adelaide City Council, 2006.

Lloyd, Clem, 'The Formation and Development of the United Australia Party', PhD thesis, Australian National University, 1964.

——'The Rise and Fall of the United Australia Party', in J.R. Nethercote (ed.), *Liberalism and the Australian Federation*, Sydney: Federation Press, 2001, pp. 134–62.

Lloyd, Clem and Rees, Jacqui, *The Last Shilling: A History of Repatriation in Australia*, Melbourne: Melbourne University Press, 1994.

Lonie, John, 'Non-Labor in South Australia', in Judy Mackinolty (ed.), *The Wasted Years? Australia's Great Depression*, Sydney: George Allen & Unwin, 1981, pp. 146–58.

Loudon, Irvine, 'Puerperal Fever, the Streptococcus, and the Sulphonamides, 1911–1945', *British Medical Journal*, vol. 295, no. 6596, 1987, pp. 485–90.

Louis L.J. and Turner, Ian, *The Depression of the 1930s*, Sydney: Cassell, 1968.

Love, Peter, 'Frank Anstey: From Heroic Persona to Embattled Identity', *Labour History*, no. 87, 2004, pp. 123–45.

——*Labour and the Money Power: Australian Labour Populism, 1890–1950*, Melbourne: Melbourne University Press, 1984.

——'Niemeyer's Australian Diary and Other English Records of his Mission', *Historical Studies*, vol. 20, no. 79, 1982, pp. 267–77.

Loveday, Peter, 'Anti-political Political Thought', in Robert Cooksey (ed.), *The Great Depression in Australia*, Canberra: Australian Society for the Study of Labour History, 1970, pp. 136–47.

Lowenstein, Wendy, *Weevils in the Flour: An Oral Record of the 1930s Depression in Australia*, Melbourne: Hyland House, 1978.

Lyons, Enid, *So We Take Comfort*, London: Heinemann, 1965.

McCalman, Janet, *Journeyings: The Biography of a Middle-Class Generation 1920–1990*, Melbourne: Melbourne University Press, 1993.

——*Sex and Suffering: Women's Health and a Women's Hospital*, Melbourne: Melbourne University Press, 1998.

——*Struggletown: Private and Public Life in Richmond 1906–1965*, Melbourne: Melbourne University Press, 2021, first published 1984.

MacDonald, Don, *Random Recollections 1913–2005*, Townsville: North Queensland Preservation Society, 2013.

McGrath, Ann, '"Black Velvet": Aboriginal Women and Their Relations with White Men in the Northern Territory 1910–40', in Kay Daniels (ed.), *So Much Hard Work: Women and Prostitution in Australian History*, Sydney: Fontana/Collins, c. 1984, pp. 235–97.

——*Born in the Cattle: Aborigines in Cattle Country*, Sydney: Allen & Unwin, 1987.

Macintyre, Stuart, *The Oxford History of Australia*, vol. 4, *1901–1942*, Melbourne: Oxford University Press, 1986.

——*The Reds*, Sydney: Allen & Unwin, 1998.

McKewon, Elaine, *The Scarlet Mile: A Social History of Prostitution in Kalgoorlie 1894–2004*, Perth: UWA Press, 2005.

Mackinolty, Judith, 'Sugar Bag Days: Sydney Workers and the Challenge of the 1930s Depression', MA thesis, Macquarie University, 1972.

——'Woman's Place . . .', in Judy Mackinolty (ed.), *The Wasted Years? Australia's Great Depression*, Sydney: George Allen & Unwin, 1981, pp. 94–110.

McLean, Ian W., 'Unequal Sacrifice: Distributional Aspects of Depression and Recovery in Australia', in R. G. Gregory and N.G. Butlin (eds), *Recovery from the Depression: Australia and the World Economy in the 1930s*, Cambridge: Cambridge University Press, 1988, pp. 335–56.

——*Why Australia Prospered: The Shifting Sources of Economic Growth*, Princeton: Princeton University Press, 2013.

McMullin, Ross, *The Light on the Hill: The Australian Labor Party, 1891–1991*, Melbourne: Oxford University Press, 1992, first published 1991.

Maddock, Rodney and McLean, Ian, *The Australian Economy in the Long Run*, Cambridge: Cambridge University Press, 1987.

Madsen, Jakob, 'Trade Barriers and the Collapse of World Trade During the Great Depression', *Southern Economic Journal*, vol. 67, no. 4, 2001, pp. 848–68.

Magnus, P. and Saskowsky, K., 'Mortality over the Twentieth Century in Australia: Trends and Patterns in Major Causes of Death', Canberra: Australian Institute of Health and Welfare, 2006.

Maguire, John P., *Prologue: A History of the Catholic Church as Seen from Townsville, 1863–1983*, Toowoomba: Church Archives Society, 1990.

Mandle, W.F., *Going it Alone: Australia's Identity in the Twentieth Century*, Melbourne: Penguin, 1980, first published 1978.

Margo, Robert A., 'Employment and Unemployment in the 1930s', *Journal of Economic Perspectives*, vol. 7, no. 2, 1993, pp. 41–59.

Markus, Andrew, *Governing Savages*, Sydney: Allen & Unwin, 1990.

——'Talka Longa Mouth', *Labour History*, no. 35, 1978, pp. 138–57.

Markwell, Donald J., 'Keynes and the Depression in Australia', Research Discussion Paper, 2000-04: Keynes and Australia, Reserve Bank of Australia, <www.rba.gov.au/publications/rdp/2000/pdf/rdp2000-04.pdf>.

Marsden, Susan, *A History of Woodville*, Woodville: Corporation of the City of Woodville, 1977.

——*Joseph Lyons: Guide to Archives of Australia's Prime Ministers*, Canberra: National Archives of Australia, 2002.

Martin, Nick, '"Bucking the Machine": Clarrie Martin and the NSW Socialisation Units, 1929–35', *Labour History*, no. 93, 2007, pp. 177–95.

Matthews, Trevor, 'The All for Australia League', *Labour History*, no. 17, 1969, pp. 136–47.

Maynard, John, *Fight for Liberty and Freedom: The Origins of Aboriginal Activism*, Canberra: Aboriginal Studies Press, 2007.

——'The Rise of the Modern Aboriginal Political Movement, 1924–39', in Joan Beaumont and Alison Cadzow (eds), *Serving Our Country: Indigenous Australians, War, Defence and Citizenship*, Sydney: NewSouth, 2018, pp. 113–34.

Menghetti, Diane, *The Red North: The Popular Front in North Queensland*, Townsville: History Department, James Cook University, 1981.

Menzies, Robert, *Afternoon Light: Some Memoirs of Men and Events*, Melbourne: Cassell, 1967.

Meredith, David, 'Imperial Images: The Empire Marketing Board, 1926–32', *History Today*, vol. 37, 1987, pp. 30–6.

Merrett, David and Ville, Simon, 'Tariffs, Subsidies and Profits: A Re-assessment of Structural Change in Australia 1901–39', *Australian Economic History Review*, vol. 51, no. 1, pp. 46–70.

Millmow, Alex, 'Douglas Copland and the Aftershocks of the Premiers' Plan, 1931–1938', *History of Economics Review*, vol. 53, no. 1, 2011, pp. 25–43.

——'Niemeyer, Scullin and the Australian Economists', *Australian Economic History Review*, vol. 44, no. 2, 2004, pp. 142–60.

——'1929: The Patrician and the Orator', in Benjamin T. Jones, Frank Bongiorno and John Uhr, *Elections Matter: Ten Federal Elections that Shaped Australia*, Melbourne: Monash University Publishing, 2018.

——*The Power of Economic Ideas: The Origins of Keynesian Macroeconomic Management in Interwar Australia 1929–39*, Canberra: ANU Press, 2010.

Moore, Andrew, 'Another Wild Colonial Boy? Francis de Groot and the Harbour Bridge', *Australian Journal of Irish Studies*, vol. 2, 2002, pp. 135–48.

——'Discredited Fascism: The New Guard after 1932', *Australian Journal of Politics and History*, vol. 57, no. 2, 2011, pp. 188–206.

——*Francis de Groot: Irish Fascist, Australian Legend*, Sydney: Federation Press, 2005.

——'The New Guard and the Labour Movement, 1931–35', *Labour History*, no. 89, 2005, pp. 55–72.

——'The Pastoral Workers' Industrial Union, 1930–1937', *Labour History*, no. 49, 1985, pp. 61–74.

——'Red Devils and White Reaction: Jack Fegan and the Workers Defence Corps of the 1930s', *Journal of Australian Studies*, vol. 33, no. 2, 2009, pp. 165–79.

——*The Secret Army and the Premier: Conservative Paramilitary Organisations in New South Wales, 1930–32*, Sydney: New South Wales University Press, 1989.

——'Superintendent Mackay and the Curious Case of the Vanishing Secret Army', *History Australia*, vol. 6, no. 3, 2009, 72.1–72.18.

——'Writing about the Extreme Right in Australia', *Labour History*, no. 89, 2005, pp. 1–15.

Moore, David E., *The Curse of Mungana*, Brisbane: Boolarong Press, 2017.

Morris, Barry, 'From Underemployment to Unemployment: The Changing Role of Aborigines in a Rural Economy', *Mankind*, vol. 13, no. 6, 1983, pp. 499–516.

Morrison, James, 'The 1925 Return to Gold: Keynes and Mr Churchill's Economic Crisis', APSA Toronto Meeting Paper, 2009.

Moseley Report, see Parliament of Western Australia.

Moses, John A. and Davis, George F., *Anzac Day Origins: Canon DJ Garland and Trans–Tasman Commemoration*, Canberra: Barton Books, 2013.

Munday, Bruce, *Those Wild Rabbits: How They Shaped Australia*, Adelaide: Wakefield Press, 2017.

Murray, Robert, *The Confident Years: Australia in the Twenties*, London: Allen Lane, 1978.

Nairn, Bede, *The 'Big Fella': Jack Lang and the Australian Labor Party, 1891–1949*, Melbourne: Melbourne University Press, 1986.

Neale, R.G., 'New States Movements', *Australian Quarterly*, vol. 22, no. 3, 1950, pp. 9–23.

Nelson, Elizabeth, 'Civilian Men and Domestic Violence in the Aftermath of the First World War', *Journal of Australian Studies*, vol. 27, no. 76, 2003, pp. 97–108.

——'Victims of War: The First World War, Returned Soldiers, and Understandings of Domestic Violence in Australia', *Journal of Women's History*, vol. 19, no. 4, 2007, pp. 83–106.

Nicholls, P., 'Australian Protestantism and the Politics of the Great Depression', *Journal of Religious History*, vol. 17, no. 2, 1992, pp. 210–21.

O'Brien, Anne, 'National Shame/National Treasure: Narrating the Homeless Veterans in Australia 1915–1930s', *Australian Historical Studies*, vol. 49, no. 2, 2018, pp. 167–83.

O'Brien, J.B., 'Empire v. National Interests in Australian–British Relations during the 1930s', *Historical Studies*, vol. 22, no. 89, 1987, pp. 569–86.

O'Farrell, Patrick, *The Catholic Church in Australia: A Short History, 1788–1967*, Melbourne: Thomas Nelson, 1968.

Oliver, Bobbie, '"In the Thick of Every Battle for the Cause of Labor": The Voluntary Work of the Labor Women's Organisations in Western Australia, 1900–1970', *Labour History*, no. 81, 2001, pp. 93–108.

——*War and Peace in Western Australia: The Social and Political Impact of the Great War, 1914–26*, Perth: UWA Press, 1995.

Oppenheimer, Melanie, *The Power of Humanity: 100 Years of Australian Red Cross*, Sydney: HarperCollins, 2014.

Pagliano, Muriel J., *Country Women: History of the First Seventy-five Years: The Queensland Country Women's Association*, Brisbane: Merino Lithographics, 1998.

Paisley, Fiona, 'An Echo of Black Slavery: Emancipation, Forced Labour and Australia in 1933', *Australian Historical Studies*, vol. 45, no. 1, 2014, pp. 103–25.

Parliament of Australia, Senate, *Lost Innocents—Righting the Record—Report on Child Migration*, Canberra, 2001.

Parliament of Australia, *Reports of the Sugar Inquiry Committee, 1931*, Canberra: Government Printer, 1931.

——*Sixth Annual Report by the Attorney-General on the Bankruptcy Act 1924–1933*, Canberra: Government Printer, 1934.

Parliament of South Australia, *Report of the Chief Protector of Aboriginals for the Year Ended June 30, 1931*, Adelaide: Government Printer, 1932.

Parliament of Western Australia, *Report of the Royal Commissioner Appointed to Investigate, Report, and Advise upon Matters in Relation to the Condition and Treatment of Aborigines* (Moseley report), Perth: Government Printer, 1935.

Parr, George, 'Letters to Clare', in Judy Mackinolty (ed.), *The Wasted Years? Australia's Great Depression*, Sydney: George Allen & Unwin, 1981, pp. 111–28.

Pear, David A., 'Muscular Christianity: The Rev. R.G. Nichols in Fitzroy, 1925–1942', *Victorian Historical Journal*, vol. 62, nos 1–2, 1991, pp. 3–17.

Pearn, John, *A Scottish Chain*, Brisbane: Amphion Press, 2003.

REFERENCES

Peel, Mark, 'Charity, Casework and the Dramas of Class in Melbourne, 1920–1940: "Feeling Your Position"', *History Australia*, vol. 2, no. 3, 2005, pp. 83.1–83.15.

Pendall, Rolf, Foster, Kathryn A. and Cowell, Margaret, 'Resilience and Regions: Building Understanding of the Metaphor', *Cambridge Journal of Regions, Economy and Society*, vol. 3, no. 1, 2010, pp. 71–84.

Penrose, Beris, 'Medical Experts and Occupational Illness: Weil's Disease in North Queensland', *Labour History*, vol. 75, 1998, pp. 125–43.

Perkins, Diane, 'Crime in the North-West, 1925–1950', Master of Arts thesis, University of Queensland.

Perkins, John and Moore, Andrew, 'Fascism in Interwar Australia', in Stein Ugelik Larsen (ed.), *Fascism Outside Europe: The European Impulse against Domestic Conditions in the Diffusion of Global Fascism*, New York: Columbia University Press, 2001, pp. 269–86.

Peter, Phyllis, 'Social Aspects of the Depression in New South Wales, 1930–1934', PhD thesis, Australian National University, 1964.

Phillips, P.D. and Wood, G.L., 'The Australian Population Problem', in P.D. Phillips and G.L. Wood (eds), *The Peopling of Australia*, Melbourne: Macmillan in association with Melbourne University Press, 1928, pp. 1–47.

Pincus, J.J., 'Australian Budgetary Policies in the 1930s', in R.G. Gregory and N.G. Butlin (eds), *Recovery from the Depression: Australia and the World Economy in the 1930s*, Cambridge: Cambridge University Press, 1988, pp. 173–92.

Polden, Kenneth, 'The Collapse of the Government Savings Bank of New South Wales, 1931', *Australian Economic History Review*, vol. 12, no. 1, 1972, pp. 52–70.

Potts, David, 'A Positive Culture of Poverty Represented in Memories of the 1930s Depression', *Journal of Australian Studies*, vol. 14, no. 26, 1990, pp. 3–14.

——*The Myth of the Great Depression*, Melbourne: Scribe, 2009, first published 2006.

Quartly, Marian and Smart, Judith, *Respectable Radicals: A History of the National Council of Women of Australia, 1896–2006*, Melbourne: Monash University Press, 2015.

Ranald, Patricia, 'Feminism and Class: The United Associations of Women and the Council of Action for Equal Pay in the Depression', in Margaret Bevege, Margaret James and Carmel Shute (eds), *Worth Her Salt: Women at Work in Australia*, Sydney: Hale & Iremonger, 1982, pp. 270–85.

Rathbone, Ron, *A Very Present Help: Caring for Australians since 1813: The History of the Benevolent Society of New South Wales*, Sydney: State Library of New South Wales Press, 1994.

Regnaud, Muriel, *Abergowrie College: The Dream and the Journey, 1933–2008*, Townsville: North Queensland Preservation Society, 2009.

Reid, Richard and Botterill, Linda, 'The Multiple Meanings of "Resilience": An Overview of the Literature', *Australian Journal of Public Administration*, vol. 72, no. 1, pp. 31–40.

Reynolds, Henry, *A History of Tasmania*, Cambridge: Cambridge University Press, 2012.

Richardson, Gary, 'The Collapse of the United States Banking System during the Great Depression, 1923 to 1933: New Archival Evidence', *Australasian Accounting, Business and Finance Journal*, vol. 1, no. 1, 2007, pp. 39–50.

Richardson, Len, *The Bitter Years: Wollongong during the Great Depression*, Sydney: Hale & Iremonger, 1984.

Richmond, K., 'Response to the Threat of Communism: The Sane Democracy League and the People's Union of New South Wales', *Journal of Australian Studies*, vol. 1, no. 1, 1977, pp. 70–83.

Richmond, W.H., 'S.M. Bruce and Australian Economic Policy, 1923–9', *Australian Economic History Review*, vol. 23, no. 2, 1983, pp. 238–57.

Robertson, John, *J.H. Scullin: A Political Biography*, Perth: University of Western Australia Press, 1974.

——'J.H. Scullin as Prime Minister: Seven Critical Decisions', *Labour History*, no. 17, 1969, pp. 27–36.

Robinson, Geoff, 'The All for Australia League in New South Wales', *Australian Historical Studies*, vol. 39, no. 1, 2008, pp. 36–52.

——*When the Labor Party Dreams: Class, Politics and Policy in NSW, 1930–32*, Melbourne: Australian Scholarly Publishing, 2008.

Robinson, Shirleene, *Something Like Slavery? Queensland's Aboriginal Child Workers, 1842–1945*, Melbourne: Australian Scholarly Publishing, 2008.

——'"We Do Not Want One Who Is Too Old": Aboriginal Child Domestic Servants in late 19th and early 20th century Queensland', *Aboriginal History*, vol. 27, 2003, pp. 162–82.

Roe, Michael, *Australia, Britain and Migration, 1915–1940*, Cambridge: Cambridge University Press, 1995.

Romer, Christina D., 'Great Depression', *Encyclopaedia Britannica*, <www.britannica.com/event/Great-Depression/Sources-of-recovery>.

——'What Ended the Great Depression?', *Journal of Economic History*, vol. 52, no. 4, 1992, pp. 757–84.

Rooth, Tim, 'Ottawa and After', in Carl Bridge and Bernard Attard (eds), *Between Empire and Nation: Australia's External Relations from Federation to the Second World War*, Melbourne: Australian Scholarly Publishing, 2000, pp. 133–57.

Ross, Andrew T., *Armed and Ready: The Industrial Development and Defence of Australia, 1900–1945*, Sydney: Turton & Armstrong, 1995.

——'Australian Overseas Trade and National Development Policy 1932–1939: A Story of Colonial Larrikins or Australian Statesmen', *Australian Journal of Politics and History*, vol. 36, no, 2, 1990, pp. 184–204.

Rowley, Charles, *Outcasts in White Australia*, Canberra: ANU Press, 1971.

——*The Remote Aborigines: Aboriginal Policy and Practice*, Canberra: ANU Press, 1971.

Saint-Etienne, Christian, *The Great Depression 1929–1938: Lessons for the 1980s*, Stanford, Cal.: Hoover Institution Press, 1984.

Sales, Peter, 'W.M. Hughes and the Chanak Crisis of 1922', *Australian Journal of Politics and History*, vol. 17, no. 3, 1971, pp. 392–405.

Saunders, Malcolm and Lloyd, Neil, 'Arbitration or Collaboration? The Australasian Society of Engineers in South Australia, 1904–68', *Labour History*, no. 101, 2011, pp. 123–44.

Scates, Bruce and Oppenheimer, Melanie, *The Last Battle: Soldier Settlement in Australia, 1916–1939*, Melbourne: Cambridge University Press, 2016.

Schedvin, C.B., *Australia and the Great Depression*, Sydney: Sydney University Press, 1973, first published 1970.

——'The Long and the Short of Depression Origins', *Labour History*, no. 17, 1969, pp. 1–13.

Schivelbusch, Wolfgang, *The Culture of Defeat: On National Trauma, Mourning and Recovery*, New York: Picador, 2003.

Scott, Ernest, *Australia During the War*, vol. XI, *The Official History of Australia in the War of 1914–1918*, ed. C.E.W. Bean, Brisbane: University of Queensland Press, 1989, first published 1936.

REFERENCES

Scott, Joanne and Saunders, Kay, 'Happy Days are Here Again? A Reply to David Potts', *Journal of Australian Studies*, vol. 17, no. 36, 1993, pp. 10–22.

Scott, Joanne '"A Place in Normal Society"': Unemployed Protest in Queensland in the 1930s', *Labour History*, no. 65, 1993, pp. 136–49.

——'Making Ends Meet: Brisbane Women and Unemployment in the Great Depression', *Queensland Review*, vol. 13, no. 1, 2006, pp. 51–62.

Seal, E. Graham, *Inventing Anzac: The Digger and National Mythology*, Brisbane: University of Queensland Press, 2004.

Sekuless, Peter and Rees, Jacqueline, *Lest We Forget: The History of the Returned Services League 1916–1986*, Sydney: Rigby, 1986.

Self, Robert, *The Neville Chamberlain Diary Letters*, vol. III, *The Heir Apparent, 1928–33*, Aldershot, Hampshire: Ashgate, 2002.

——'Treasury Control and the Empire Marketing Board: The Rise and Fall of Non-tariff Preference in Britain, 1924–1933', *Twentieth Century British History*, vol. 5, no. 2, 1994, pp. 153–82.

Sendziuk, Paul and Forster, Robert, *A History of South Australia*, Cambridge: Cambridge University Press, 2018.

Serle, Geoffrey, *John Monash: A Biography*, Melbourne: Melbourne University Press, 1982.

Shann, E.O.G. and Copland, D.B., *The Crisis in Australian Finance 1929 to 1931: Documents on Budgetary and Economic Policy*, Sydney: Angus & Robertson, 1931.

Sheldon, Peter, 'State-level Basic Wages in Australia during the Depression: Institutions and Politics over Markets', *Australian Economic History Review*, vol. 47, no. 3, 2007, pp. 249–77.

Singley, Blake, '"Skilful Handling and Scientific Treatment": The Charity Organisation of Brisbane during the Great Depression', *Queensland Review*, vol. 17, no. 2, 2010, pp. 89–99.

Sissons, D.C.S., 'Manchester v Japan: The Imperial Background of the Australian Trade Diversion Dispute with Japan, 1936', *Australian Outlook*, vol. 30, no. 3, 1976, pp. 480–502.

Sissons, Robert and Stoddart, Brian, *Cricket and Empire: The 1932–33 Bodyline Tour of Australia*, London: George Allen & Unwin, 1984.

Skerman, A.P., *Repatriation in Australia: A History of Development to 1958*, Melbourne: Repatriation Department, 1961.

Smith, F.B., 'Australian Public Health during the Depression of the 1930s', *Australian Cultural History*, vol. 16, 1997–98, pp. 96–106.

Smith, Keith, *Australian Battlers Remember: The Great Depression*, Sydney: Random, House, 2003.

Snooks, G.D., 'Development in Adversity, 1913–1946', in C.T. Stannage (ed.), *A New History of Western Australia*, Perth: UWA Press, 1981, pp. 96–106.

——'Government Unemployment Relief in the 1930s: Aid or Hindrance to Recovery?', in R.G. Gregory and N.G. Butlin, *Recovery from the Depression: Australian and the World Economy in the 1930s*, Cambridge: Cambridge University Press, 1988, pp. 311–34.

——'Robbing Peter to Pay Paul: Australian Unemployment Relief in the Thirties', Working Papers in Economic History, no. 41, Canberra: Australian National University, 1985.

Spenceley, Geoff, 'Assessing the Responses of the Unemployed to the Depression of the 1930s', *Journal of Australian Studies*, vol. 13, no. 24, 1989, pp. 70–87.

——'The Broadmeadows Camp, 1930: A Microscope of Social Control and Human Rights in the Depression of the 1930s, *Labour History*, no. 67, 1995, pp. 57–73.

——*The Depression Decade: Commentary and Documents*, Melbourne: Nelson, 1981.

——'"The Minister for Starvation": Wilfred Kent Hughes, Fascism and the Unemployment Relief (Administration) Act of 1933', *Labour History*, no. 81, 2001, pp. 135–54.

——'Social Control, the Charity Organisation Society and the Evolution of Unemployment Relief Policy in Melbourne during the Depression of the 1930s, *Historical Studies*, vol. 2, no. 87, 1986, pp. 232–51.

——'The Social History of the Depression of the 1930s on the Basis of Oral Accounts: People's History or Bourgeois Construction?' *Journal of Australian Studies*, vol. 18, no. 41, 1994, pp. 35–49.

Stanley, Peter, *Bad Characters: Sex, Crime, Mutiny, Murder and the Australian Imperial Force*, Sydney: Pier 9, 2010.

Stanton, Sue, 'The Australian Half-Caste Progressive Association', *Journal of Northern Territory History*, vol. 4, 1993, pp. 37–46.

Stolling, Max, *Grandeur and Grit: A History of Glebe*, Sydney: Halstead Press, 2007.

Stone, Gerald, *1932*, Sydney: Pan Macmillan, 2005.

Strangio, Paul, *Neither Power Nor Glory: 100 Years of Political Labor in Victoria, 1856–1956*, Melbourne: Melbourne University Press, 2012.

Stubbings, Leo, *Look What You Started Henry! A History of the Australian Red Cross 1914–1991*, Melbourne: Australian Red Cross Society, 1992.

Sturrock, Morna, 'Gilbert Dyett: Architect of the R.S.L.', MA thesis, Monash University, 1992.

Swain, Shurlee, 'Besmirching our Reputation: Sectarianism and Charity in Geelong', *Victorian Historical Journal*, vol. 63, no. 1, 1992, pp. 51–60.

Taylor, Lynne, 'Food Riots Revisited', *Journal of Social History*, vol. 30, no. 2, 1996, pp. 483–96.

Taylor, Richard, Lewis, Milton and Powles, John, 'The Australian Mortality Decline: All-cause Mortality, 1788–1990', *Australian and New Zealand Journal of Public Health*, vol. 22, no. 1, 1998, pp. 27–36.

Tennant, Kylie, *The Battlers*, Sydney: Angus & Robertson, 1983, first published 1941.

——*Tiburon*, Gawler: Michael Walmer, 2013, first published 1935.

Theobald, Marjorie and Dwyer, Donna, 'An Episode in Feminist Politics: The Married Women (Lecturers and Teachers) Act, 1932–47', *Labour History*, no. 76, 1999, pp. 59–77.

Thirkell, Angela, *Trooper to the Southern Cross*, Melbourne: Sun Books, 1966, first published 1964.

Thomas, Mark, 'Manufacturing and Economic Recovery in Australia, 1932–1937', in R.G. Gregory and N.G. Butlin (eds), *Recovery from the Depression: Australia and the World Economy in the 1930s*, Cambridge: Cambridge University Press, 1988, pp. 246–71.

Throssell, Ric, *My Father's Son*, Melbourne: Heinemann, 1989.

Tkaczuk, Wasily Joseph, 'Communists and the Great Depression in Tasmania, 1930–1935', BA (Hons) thesis, University of Tasmania.

Toose, P.B., *Independent Enquiry into the Repatriation System*, Canberra: Australian Government Publishing Service, 1975.

Tooze, Adam, *The Deluge: The Great War, America and the Remaking of the Global Order, 1916–1931*, New York: Penguin, 2015, first published 2014.

Torpey, Doris, *The Way it Was: A History of the Mallee, 1910–1949*, Red Cliffs, Vic.: Sunnyland Press, 1986.

Tsokhas, Kosmos, 'Anglo-American Economic Entente and Australian Financial Diplomacy', *Diplomacy and Statecraft*, vol. 5, no. 3, 1994, pp. 620–41.

——'Business, Empire and the United Australia Party', *Politics*, vol. 24, no. 2, 1989, pp. 39–52.

REFERENCES

——'"A Pound of Flesh": War Debts and Anglo–Australian Relations, 1919–1932', *Australian Journal of Politics and History*, vol. 38, no. 1, 1992, pp. 12–26.

——'Protection, Imperial Preference, and Australian Conservative Politics, 1923–39', *Journal of Imperial and Commonwealth History*, vol. 20, no. 1, 1992, pp. 65–87.

——'Shifting the Burden: Graziers and Pastoral Workers in the 1930s', *Journal of Australian Studies*, vol. 14, no. 27, 1990, pp. 40–51.

——'Sir Otto Niemeyer, the Bankrupt State and the Federal System', *Australian Journal of Political Science*, vol. 30, 1995, pp. 18–38.

——'W.M. Hughes, the Imperial Wool Purchase and the Pastoral Lobby, 1914–20', *Journal of Imperial and Commonwealth History*, vol. 17, no. 2, 1989, pp. 232–63.

——'The Wool Industry and the 1936 Trade Diversion Dispute between Australia and Japan', *Australian Historical Studies*, vol. 23, no. 93, 1989, pp. 442–61.

Tsoukala, Anastassia, 'Boundary-creating Processes and the Social Construction of Threat', *Alternatives: Global, Local, Political*, vol. 33, no. 2, 2008, pp. 137–52.

Turner, Ian and Sandercock, Leonie, *In Union is Strength: A History of Trade Unions in Australia 1788–1983*, 3rd edn, Melbourne: Nelson, 1983.

Valentine, T.J., 'The Battle of the Plans: A Macroeconometric Model of the Interwar Economy', in R.G. Gregory and N.G. Butlin (eds), *Recovery from the Depression: Australia and the World Economy in the 1930s*, Cambridge: Cambridge University Press, 1988, pp. 152–71.

——'The Depression of the 1930s', in Rodney Maddock and Ian McLean (eds), *The Australian Economy in the Long Run*, Cambridge: Cambridge University Press, 1987, pp. 61–77.

Vamplew, Wray (ed.), *Australians: Historical Statistics*, Sydney: Fairfax, Syme & Weldon Associates, 1987.

Victoria, *Report of the Royal Commission on Migrant Land Settlement*, Melbourne: Government Printer, 1933.

Vodicka, Peter, *Coup d'État!? 6 March 1931—Revolution and Counter-revolution in Victoria's Wimmera and Mallee: A Curious Case of Communism, Reaction and Sectarianism during the Great Depression*, Sydney: self-published, 2019.

Walker, Alan, *Coaltown: A Social Survey of Cessnock*, Melbourne: Melbourne University Press, 1945.

Walmsley, M.O., 'The Battle of Parramatta Park, Sunday 17th June, 1932', *Cairns Historical Society Bulletin*, no. 14, 1968, pp. 1–3.

Walter, James with Moore, Todd, *What Were They Thinking? The Politics of Ideas in Australia*, Sydney: UNSW Press, 2010.

Ward, John Manning, 'The Dismissal', in Heather Radi and Peter Spearritt (eds), *Jack Lang*, Sydney: Hale & Iremonger and *Labour History*, 1977, pp. 160–70.

Watts, Rob, *The Foundations of the National Welfare State*, Sydney: Allen & Unwin, 1987.

Way, Wendy, *A New Idea Each Morning: How Food and Agriculture Came Together in One International Organisation*, Canberra: ANU Press, 2013.

——'F.L. McDougall and Commodity Diplomacy', in Carl Bridge and Bernard Attard (eds), *Between Empire and Nation: Australia's External Relations from Federation to the Second World War*, Melbourne: Australian Scholarly Publishing, 2000, pp. 93–110.

Wegner, Janice H., 'Hinchinbrook: The Hinchinbrook Shire Council, 1879–1979', MA thesis, James Cook University, 1984.

Weller, Patrick (ed.), *Caucus Minutes, 1901–1949: Minutes of Meetings of the Federal Parliamentary Labor Party, 1901–1949*, vol. 2, *1917–1931*, Melbourne: Melbourne University Press, 1975.

White, Kate, *Joseph Lyons*, Melbourne: Black Inc., 1987.

Wickens, C.H., 'Australian Population: Its Nature and Growth', in P.D. Phillips and G.L. Wood (eds), *The Peopling of Australia*, Melbourne: Macmillan in association with Melbourne University Press, 1930, pp. 48–71.

Wilcox, Craig, *For Hearth and Homes: Citizen Soldiering in Australia, 1854–1945*, Sydney: Allen & Unwin, 1998.

Wilks, Steven, *'Now Is the Psychological Moment': Earle Page and the Imagining of Australia*, Canberra: ANU Press, 2020.

Williams, John F., *The Quarantined Culture: Australian Reactions to Modernism, 1913–1939*, Cambridge: Cambridge University Press, 1995.

Windle, Michael, 'Critical Conceptual Measurement Issues in the Study of Resilience', in M.D. Glantz and L.L. Johnson (eds), *Resilience and Development*, Boston, Mass.: Springer, 2002.

Winter, J.M., *Sites of Memory, Sites of Mourning: The Great War in European Cultural History*, Cambridge: Cambridge University Press, 1995.

Wu, Jialu, 'How Severe was the Great Depression? Evidence from the Pittsburgh Region', in John Komlos (ed.), *Stature, Living Standards, and Economic Development: Essays in Anthropometric History*, Chicago: University of Chicago Press, 1994, pp. 129–52.

Yule, Peter, 'Organization of War Economies (Australia)', *1914–18 Online: International Encyclopedia of the First World War*, <https://encyclopedia.1914-1918-online.net/article/organization_of_war_economies_australia>.

INDEX

Page numbers in *italics* refer to figures

INDEX

INDEX

INDEX

INDEX